Fourth Canadian Edition

An Introduction to Language

Fourth Canadian Edition

An Introduction to Language

Victoria Fromkin
University of California, Los Angeles
(Deceased)

Robert Rodman
North Carolina State University, Raleigh

Nina Hyams
University of California, Los Angeles

Kirsten M. Hummel
Laval University

NELSON

NELSON

An Introduction to Language, Fourth Canadian Edition
by Victoria Fromkin, Robert Rodman, Nina Hyams, and Kirsten Hummel

Vice-President, Editorial Director:
Evelyn Veitch

Editor-in-Chief, Higher Education:
Anne Williams

Executive Editor:
Laura Macleod

Marketing Manager:
Amanda Henry

Developmental Editor:
Theresa Fitzgerald

Photo Researcher:
Daniella Glass

Permissions Coordinator:
Daniella Glass

Content Production Manager:
Christine Gilbert

Production Service:
MPS Limited

Copy Editor:
Marcia Gallego

Proofreader:
Dianne Fowlie

Indexer:
Patti Schiendelman

Production Coordinator:
Ferial Suleman

Design Director:
Ken Phipps

Managing Designer:
Franca Amore

Cover Design:
Peter Papayanakis

Cover Image:
© Imagezoo/Jupiter Images

Compositor:
MPS Limited

Library and Archives Canada Cataloguing in Publication

An introduction to language / Victoria Fromkin . . . [et al.]. — 4th Canadian ed.

Includes bibliographical references and index.
ISBN 978-0-17-650119-8

1. Language and languages—Textbooks. 2. Linguistics—Textbooks. I. Fromkin, Victoria

P106.I57 2009   410   C2009-902827-1

ISBN-13: 978-0-17-650119-8
ISBN-10: 0-17-650119-3

Preface

This fourth Canadian edition of *An Introduction to Language* is aimed at providing the same accessible approach to the scientific study of language that characterizes the previous editions of this book. No previous linguistic knowledge is assumed on the part of the reader, and therefore this new edition continues to be suitable for a wide range of academic programs, as well as for the general reader interested in learning more about language.

An Introduction to Language endeavours to provide readers with an up-to-date overview of the principal areas of study that make up the field of linguistics, with a focus on introducing important concepts and the methodological tools of linguistic analysis. As in the previous editions, a Canadian perspective is highlighted: examples and research were selected to reflect Canadian sources and circumstances insofar as possible.

This edition has been modified and updated to reflect ongoing developments in theoretical and applied linguistics. For example, Chapter 3, "Syntax: The Sentence Patterns of Language," now includes a section on X-bar syntax. Similarly, Chapter 8, "Second Language Acquisition," has been updated to include sections on the sociocultural approach and task-based learning/teaching.

Furthermore, chapter material has been reorganized for a more focused presentation of content material. In particular, the previous Chapter 9, "Language Processing: Human and Computer," has been reorganized into two separate units: Chapter 9, "Psycholinguistics: Language Processing," and Chapter 10, "Computational Linguistics: Computer Language Processing."

As in previous editions, a prominent characteristic in this latest edition is the use of cartoons and quotations to highlight concepts and terms introduced in the book. New cartoons and quotations have been added to continue to entertain and inform the reader.

A new feature in this edition is highlighted textboxes placed throughout the book that draw the reader's attention to important concepts and to concrete examples illustrating fundamental notions in the text.

In view of the proliferation of Internet resources in recent years, a section has been added at the end of each chapter indicating websites that readers can consult for supplemental information about various topics covered in each chapter. In addition, the references in the Further Reading sections have been updated.

As in previous editions, each chapter concludes with a summary and a set of exercises; the answers to exercises marked with an asterisk are included in the book's answer key. A complete answer key is available online for instructors. To further assist readers, a glossary of technical terms is provided at the end of the book.

To improve the pedagogical value of this revised textbook, supplementary materials have been developed: an exercise workbook and its answer key are available from Nelson Education Ltd. for instructors' use. In addition, a test bank has been developed for use in conjunction with this edition.

We hope this latest edition will continue to arouse readers' curiosity about language and the many ways it relates to our daily lives.

Acknowledgments

This most recent edition remains indebted to the original authors of the U.S. edition: Victoria Fromkin, Robert Rodman, and Nina Hyams, and to the authors of the first two Canadian editions, Neil Hultin and Harry Logan. I have tried to add improvements to the previous editions, and my task is significantly easier due to the breadth and depth of the contributions of the previous authors.

Sincere gratitude goes to colleagues at Laval University who generously offered advice in their areas of expertise: Claudia Borgonovo, Darlene Lacharité, Susan Parks, and Philippe Prévost. The previous and current editions of this book are vastly improved thanks to their collaboration.

Thanks go as well to graduate students who worked closely with the previous edition: Faramarz Amin-Lari, Maryse Arseneau, Julie Goncharov, Bruno Guedes, Tim Mellin, and Michal Pawica. The Laval University undergraduate students who were introduced to linguistics through previous editions of *An Introduction to Language* deserve special mention as their remarks and reactions served as a guide to improving the latest edition. Thanks are also due to several anonymous reviewers of the previous edition as well as the following reviewers of the draft of this edition, whose constructive comments and detailed suggestions have been tremendously helpful in improving the book: Michael Fox, University of Alberta; Rosario Gomez, University of Guelph; Monica-Alexandrrina Irimia, University of Toronto; and Anna Moro, McMaster University.

I also want to thank Andy Van Drom for his outstanding collaboration on the supplemental exercise workbook and key, and Rosario Gomez at the University of Guelph for producing the test bank.

Acknowledgments are due as well to the editorial team at Nelson Education, whose expertise and patience at all stages in the preparation of this edition were invaluable: Laura Macleod, executive editor; Theresa Fitzgerald, developmental editor; Christine Gilbert, content production manager; Marcia Gallego, copy editor; and Gunjan Chandola, project manager.

Finally, on a personal note, I wish to express my profound gratitude to my parents, Louis and Cleo Hummel, whose unqualified support and encouragement continue to provide solid foundations for all my endeavours. And to my daughters, Louissa and Marlyse, heartfelt thanks for their frequent reminders that my most important job is being their mother.

The responsibility for errors in fact or judgment remains, of course, mine alone.

Kirsten M. Hummel

Table of Contents

PART TWO
Grammatical Aspects of Language

PART THREE

The Psychology and Biology of Language

CHAPTER 9   PSYCHOLINGUISTICS: LANGUAGE PROCESSING   409

CHAPTER 10   COMPUTATIONAL LINGUISTICS: COMPUTER LANGUAGE PROCESSING   430

PART FOUR
Social Aspects of Language

CHAPTER 14   WRITING: THE ABCs OF LANGUAGE   593

PART FIVE
Animal Communication

PART ONE
The Nature of
Human Language

Reflecting on ... Noam Chomsky's ideas on the innateness of the fundamentals of grammar in the human mind, I saw that any innate features of the language capacity must be a set of biological structures, selected in the course of the evolution of the human brain. ...

S.E. Luria, *A Slot Machine, a Broken Test Tube, an Autobiography* (1984)

Language is not an abstract construction of the learned, or of dictionary-makers, but is something arising out of the work, needs, ties, joys, affections, tastes, of long generations of humanity, and has its bases broad and low, close to the ground.

Walt Whitman (1819–1892)

Linguistics shares with other sciences a concern to be objective, systematic, consistent, and explicit in its account of language. Like other sciences, it aims to collect data, test hypotheses, devise models, and construct theories. Its subject matter, however, is unique: at one extreme it overlaps with such "hard" sciences as physics and anatomy; at the other, it involves such traditional "arts" subjects as philosophy and literary criticism. The field of linguistics includes both science and the humanities, and offers a breadth of coverage that, for many aspiring students of the subject, is the primary source of its appeal.

David Crystal, *The Cambridge Encyclopedia of Language* (1997)

CHAPTER 1
What Is Language?

When we study human language, we are approaching what some might call
the "human essence," the distinctive qualities of mind that are, so far as we
know, unique to man.

Noam Chomsky, *Language and Mind* (1972)

CALVIN AND HOBBES © 1993 Watterson. Dist. by UNIVERSAL PRESS SYNDICATE.
Reprinted with permission. All rights reserved.

Whatever else people do when they come together — whether they play, fight,
make love, or make automobiles — they talk. We live in a world of language. We
talk to our friends, our associates, our wives and husbands, our lovers, our
teachers, and our parents and in-laws. We talk to bus drivers and total strangers.
We talk face to face and over the telephone, and everyone responds with more
talk. Television and radio further swell this torrent of words. Hardly a moment of
our waking lives is free from words, and even in our dreams we talk and are talked
to. We also talk when there is no one to answer. Some of us talk aloud in our sleep.
We talk to our pets and sometimes to ourselves.

The possession of language, perhaps more than any other attribute, distinguishes humans from other animals. To understand our humanity, we must understand the nature of language that makes us human. According to the
philosophy expressed in the myths and religions of many peoples, it
is language that is the source of human life and power. To some
people of Africa, a newborn child is a *kuntu* "a thing," not yet a
muntu "a person." Only by the act of learning does the child become
a human being. Thus, according to this tradition, we all become "human"
because we all know at least one language. But what does it mean to "know" a
language?

> It is estimated that
> about 5,000 lan-
> guages are spoken
> in the world.

Linguistic Knowledge

When you know a language, you can speak and be understood by others who know that language. This means you have the capacity to produce sounds that signify certain meanings and to understand or interpret the sounds produced by others. We are, of course, referring to normal-hearing individuals. Deaf people produce and understand sign languages just as hearing persons produce and understand spoken languages.

Everyone knows a language. Five-year-old children are almost as proficient at speaking and understanding as are their parents. Yet the ability to carry out the simplest conversation requires profound knowledge that most speakers are unaware of. This is as true of speakers of Japanese as of English, of Armenian as of Navajo. A speaker of English can produce a sentence having relative clauses without knowing what a relative clause is, as, for example, in this proverb from Dr. Seuss:

> Be who you are and say what you feel because those who mind don't matter
> and those who matter don't mind.

In a parallel fashion, a child can walk without understanding or being able to explain the principles of balance and support or the neurophysiological control mechanisms that permit one to do so. The fact that we may know something unconsciously is not unique to language.

What, then, do speakers of English or Quechua or French or Mohawk or Arabic know?

Knowledge of the Sound System

Knowing a language means knowing what sounds (or signs, in the case of sign languages of the deaf) are in that language and what sounds are not. This unconscious knowledge is revealed by the way speakers of one language pronounce words from another language. If you speak only English, for example, you may substitute an English sound for a non-English sound when pronouncing "foreign" words. Most English speakers pronounce the name *Bach* with a final *k* sound because the sound represented by the letters *ch* in German is no longer an English sound. If you pronounce it as the Germans do, you are using a sound outside the English sound system. Many French Canadians, though otherwise fluent in English, pronounce words such as *this* and *that* as if they were spelled *dis* and *dat*. The English sound represented by the initial letters *th* is not part of the French sound system, and the French "mispronunciation" reveals the speakers' unconscious knowledge of this fact.

Knowing the sound system of a language includes more than knowing the inventory of sounds: sounds may start a word, end a word, or follow each other. The name of a former president of Ghana was *Nkrumah*, pronounced with an initial sound identical with the single sound spelled *ng* in the English word *sing*. While this sound does appear in English medially and finally before *k*, no word in English begins with it. As a result, most speakers of English mispronounce Mr. Nkrumah's name (by

© K. Lemieux

the first century, the Arabic scholars at Basra in the eighth century, and numerous English grammarians of the eighteenth and nineteenth centuries held this view. They wished to prescribe rather than describe the rules of grammar, which gave rise to the writing of **prescriptive grammars**.

With the rise of capitalism, a new middle class emerged who wanted their children to speak the dialect of the "upper" classes. This desire led to the publication of many prescriptive grammars. In 1762, an influential grammar, *A Short Introduction to English Grammar with Critical Notes*, was written by Bishop Robert Lowth. Lowth, influenced by Latin grammar, logic, and personal preference, prescribed a number of new rules for English. Before the publication of his grammar, practically everyone — upper-class, middle-class, and lower-class speakers of English — said *I don't have none, You was wrong about that,* and *Mathilda is fatter than me.* Lowth, however, decided that "two negatives make a positive" and therefore that one should say *I don't have any;* that even when *you* is singular it should be followed by the plural *were;* and that *I* not *me, he* not *him, they* not *them,* and so forth, should follow *than* in comparative constructions. Many of these prescriptive rules were based on Latin grammar, which had already given way to different rules in the languages that developed from Latin. Because Lowth was influential and because the rising new class wanted to speak "properly," many of these new rules were legislated into English grammar, at least for the **prestige dialect**.

The view that dialects that regularly use double negatives are inferior cannot be justified if one looks at the standard dialects of other languages in the world, as the following examples from French and Italian illustrate:

French: Je ne veux parler avec personne.
          I not want speak with no-one.

Italian: Non voglio parlare con nessuno.
           not I-want speak with no-one.

English translation: "I don't want to speak with anyone."

Grammars such as Lowth's — with their appeal to Latin, logic, and writing — are different from the descriptive grammars we have been discussing. Their goal is not to describe the rules people know but to tell them what rules they should know.

In 1908, a grammarian, Thomas R. Lounsbury, wrote that "there seems to have been in every period in the past, as there is now, a distinct apprehension in the minds of very many worthy persons that the English tongue is always in the condition approaching collapse and that arduous efforts must be put forth persistently to save it from destruction."

Today our bookstores are filled with books by language "purists" attempting to do just that. Edwin Newman, for example, in his books *Strictly Speaking* (1974) and *A Civil Tongue* (1976), rails against those who use the word *hopefully* to mean "I hope," as in "Hopefully, it will not rain tomorrow," instead of using it "properly" to mean "with hope." What Newman fails to recognize is that language changes in the course of time and that words change meaning, and the meaning of *hopefully* has been broadened for most English speakers to include both usages. Incidentally, neither "I hope" nor "with hope" captures the useful sense of this sentence adverb (like *incidentally*, incidentally) in making a hopeful prediction (*I say/pray hopefully . . .*). Other "saviours" of the English language blame television, the schools, and even teachers of English for failing to preserve the standard language, and they mount attacks against those college and university professors who suggest that other dialects are viable, living, complete languages. The authors of this textbook would clearly be among those criticized by these new prescriptivists.

There is even a list of banished words that has been produced every year since 1976 by a group at Lake Superior State University in Michigan. Words deserving "banishment" that were chosen from public nominations in 2005 included "blog" for personal journals appearing on the Internet, "carbs" as a shortened form of "carbohydrates," and "improvised explosive device" for "bomb" or "mine." At least these guardians of the English language have a sense of humour, but they as well as the other prescriptivists are bound to fail. Language is vigorous and dynamic and constantly changing. All languages and dialects are expressive, complete, and logical, as much so as they were 200 or 2,000 years ago. If sentences are muddled, it is not because of the language but because of the speakers. Prescriptivists should be concerned more about the thinking of the speakers than about the language they use. Hopefully, this book will convince you of this idea.

We as linguists wish you to know that all languages and dialects are rule governed and that what is grammatical in one language may be ungrammatical in another (equally prestigious) language. While we admit that the grammars and usages of particular groups in society may be dominant for social and political reasons, they are neither superior nor inferior, from a linguistic point of view, to the grammars and usages of less prestigious segments of society.

Having said all this, it is undeniable that the **standard** dialect (defined in Chapter 12) may indeed be a better dialect for someone wishing to obtain a particular job or achieve a position of social prestige. In a society where "linguistic profiling" is used to discriminate against speakers of a minority dialect, it may behoove those speakers to learn the prestige dialect rather than wait for social change. But linguistically, prestige and standard dialects do not have superior grammars.

Finally, all of the preceding remarks apply to *spoken* language. Writing (see Chapter 14), which is not acquired through exposure, but must be taught, follows certain prescriptive rules of grammar, usage, and style that the spoken language does not, and is subject to little if any dialectal variation.

Teaching Grammars and Reference Grammars

> At painful times, when composition is impossible and reading is not enough, grammars and dictionaries are excellent for distraction.
>
> Elizabeth Barrett Browning (1806–1861)

The descriptive grammar of a language attempts to describe everything speakers know about their language. It is different from a **teaching grammar**, which is used to learn another language or dialect. Teaching grammars are those we use in school to fulfil language requirements. They can be helpful to those who do not speak the standard or prestige dialect but find it would be advantageous socially and economically to do so. Teaching grammars state explicitly the rules of the language, list the words and their pronunciations, and aid in learning a new language or dialect. It is often difficult for adults to learn a second language without being instructed, even when living for an extended period in a country where the language is spoken. Teaching grammars assume that the student already knows one language and compare the grammar of the target language with the grammar of the native language. The meaning of a word is given by providing a **gloss** — the parallel word in the student's native language, such as *maison*, "house" in French. It is assumed that the student knows the meaning of the gloss "house" and so the meaning of the word *maison*.

Sounds of the target language that do not occur in the native language are often described by reference to known sounds. Thus, the student might be aided in producing the French sound *u* in the word *tu* by instructions such as "Round your lips while producing the vowel sound in *tea*."

The rules on how to put words together to form grammatical sentences also refer to the learners' knowledge of their native language. Thus, the teaching grammar *Learn Zulu* by Sibusiso Nyembezi (1997) states that "the difference between singular and plural is not at the end of the word but at the beginning of it" and warns that "Zulu does not have the indefinite and definite articles 'a' and 'the.'" Such statements assume that students know the rules of English. Although such grammars might be considered prescriptive in the sense that they attempt to teach the student what is or is not a grammatical construction in the new language, their aim is different from grammars that attempt to change the rules or usage of a language already learned.

Another kind of grammar that might be mentioned here is a **reference grammar**, which tries to be as comprehensive as possible so that it might serve as a reference for those interested in establishing grammatical facts (Crystal, 1997). Examples include several great European grammars of English, especially Otto Jespersen's seven-volume *Modern English Grammar on Historical Principles* (1909–1949) and the monumental English grammar of Randolph Quirk et al., *A Comprehensive Grammar of the English Language* (1985), some 1,779 pages in length.

This book is not primarily concerned with either prescriptive or teaching grammars. The matter is considered in Chapter 12, however, in the discussion of standard and nonstandard dialects.

Language Universals

> In a grammar there are parts which pertain to all languages; these components form what is called the general grammar. In addition to these general (universal) parts, there are those which belong only to one particular language; and these constitute the particular grammars of each language.
>
> Du Marsais (c. 1750)

The way we are using the word *grammar* differs in another way from its most common meaning. In our sense, the grammar includes everything speakers know about their language — the sound system, called **phonology**; the system of meanings, called **semantics**; the rules of word formation, called **morphology**; and the rules of sentence formation, called **syntax**. It also, of course, includes the vocabulary of words — the dictionary or **lexicon**. Some people think that the word *grammar* applies primarily to morphology and claim that Latin has "more grammar" than English because of its many grammatical endings (inflections). Still others think of the grammar of a language as referring solely to the syntactic rules. This latter sense is what students usually mean when they talk about "English grammar."

Our aim is more in keeping with that stated in 1784 by John Fell in his *Essay towards an English Grammar*: "It is certainly the business of a grammarian to find out, and not to make, the laws of a language." This business is just what the linguist attempts — to find out the laws of a language and the laws that pertain to all languages. Those laws that pertain to all human languages, representing the universal properties of language, constitute a **Universal Grammar**.

About 1630, J.H. Alsted, a German philosopher, first used the term *general grammar* as distinct from special grammar. He believed that the function of a general grammar was to reveal those features "which relate to the method and etiology of grammatical concepts. They are common to all languages." Pointing out that "general grammar is the pattern 'norma' of every particular grammar whatsoever," he implored "eminent linguists to employ their insight in this matter" (Salmon, 1969).

Three and a half centuries before Alsted, Robert Kilwardby, Archbishop of Canterbury (c. 1215–1279), held that linguists should be concerned with discovering the nature of language in general. So concerned was Kilwardby with Universal Grammar that he excluded considerations of the characteristics of particular languages, which he believed to be as "irrelevant to a science of grammar as the material of the measuring rod or the physical characteristics of objects were to geometry" (Salmon, 1969). Kilwardby was perhaps too much of a universalist; the particular properties of individual languages are relevant to the discovery of language universals, and they are of interest for their own sake.

Someone attempting to study Latin, Greek, French, or Swahili as a second language may assert, in frustration, that those ancient scholars were so hidden in their ivory towers that they confused reality with idle speculation; yet the more we investigate this question, the more evidence accumulates to support Chomsky's view that there is a Universal Grammar that is part of the human biologically endowed **language faculty**. It may be thought of "as a system of principles which characterizes the class of possible grammars by specifying how particular grammars are organized (what are the components and their relations), how the different rules of these components are constructed, how they interact, and so on" (Chomsky, 1979, p.180).

To discover the nature of this Universal Grammar whose principles characterize all human languages is the major aim of **linguistic theory**. The linguist's goal is to discover the "laws of human language," as the physicist's goal is to discover the "laws of the physical universe." The complexity of language, a product of the human brain, undoubtedly means that this goal will never be fully achieved. But all scientific theories are incomplete; new hypotheses are proposed to account for more data. Theories are continually changing as new discoveries are made. Just as Newtonian physics was enlarged by Einsteinian physics, so the linguistic theory of Universal Grammar develops, and new discoveries, some of which are discussed in this book, shed new light on the nature of human language.

The Development of Grammar

Linguistic theory is concerned not only with describing the knowledge that an adult speaker has of his or her language, but also with explaining how that knowledge is acquired. All normal children acquire (at least one) language in a relatively short period with apparent ease. They do this despite the fact that parents and other caregivers do not provide them with any specific language instruction. Indeed, it is often remarked that children seem to "pick up" language just from hearing it spoken around them. Children are language learners par excellence — whether a child is male or female, from a rich family or a disadvantaged one, whether she grows up on a farm or in the city, attends day care or is home all day — none of these factors fundamentally affect the way language develops. A child can acquire any language he is exposed to with comparable ease — English, Dutch, French, Swahili, Japanese — and even though each of these languages has its own peculiar characteristics, children learn them all in very much the same way. For example, all children start out by using one word at a time. They then combine words into simple sentences. When they first begin to combine words into sentences, certain parts of the sentence may be missing. For example, the English-speaking two-year-old might say *Cathy build house* instead of *Cathy is building the house*. On the other side of the world, a Swahili-speaking child will say *mbuzi kula majani,* which translates as "goat eat grass," and which also lacks many required elements. Children pass through other linguistic stages on their way to adultlike competence, but by about age five children speak a language that is almost indistinguishable from the language of the adults around them.

In just a few short years, without the benefit of explicit guidance and regardless of personal circumstances, the young child — who may be unable to tie her shoes or do even the simplest arithmetic computation — masters the complex grammatical structures of her language and acquires a substantial lexicon. Just how children accomplish this remarkable cognitive achievement is a topic of intense interest to linguists. The child's success, as well as the uniformity of the acquisition process, points to a substantial innate component of language development. Chomsky, following the lead of the early rationalist philosophers, proposed that human beings are born with an innate "blueprint" for language, what we referred to earlier as Universal Grammar. Children are able to acquire language as quickly and effortlessly as they do because they do not have to figure out all the rules of their language, only those that are specific to their particular language. The universal properties — the laws of language — are part of their biological endowment. Linguistic theory aims to uncover those principles that characterize all human languages and to reveal the innate component of language that makes language acquisition possible. In Chapter 7 we will discuss language acquisition in more detail.

Sign Languages: Evidence for Language Universals

It is not the want of organs that [prevents animals from making] ... known their thoughts ... for it is evident that magpies and parrots are able to utter words just like ourselves, and yet they cannot speak as we do, that is, so as to give evidence that they think of what they say. On the other hand, men who, being born deaf and mute ... are destitute of the organs which serve the

others for talking, are in the habit of themselves inventing certain signs by
which they make themselves understood.

René Descartes, *Discourse on Method* (1637/1967)

The **sign languages** of deaf people provide some of the best evidence to support
the notion that humans are born with the ability to acquire language and that these
languages are governed by the same universal properties.

Deaf children, who are unable to hear the sounds of spoken language, do not
acquire spoken languages as hearing children do. However, deaf children of deaf
parents who are exposed to sign language learn it in stages parallel to language
acquisition by hearing children learning oral languages. These sign languages are
human languages that do not utilize sounds to express meanings. Instead, sign
languages are visual–gestural systems that use hand and body gestures as the
forms used to represent words. Sign languages are fully developed languages, and
those who know sign language are capable of creating and comprehending an
unlimited number of new sentences, just like speakers of spoken languages.

Current research on sign languages has been crucial in the attempt to understand the biological underpinnings of human language acquisition and use. Some
understanding of sign languages is therefore essential.

About one in a thousand babies is born deaf or with a severe hearing deficiency.
One major effect is the difficulty deaf people have in learning a spoken language.
It is nearly impossible for those unable to hear language to learn to speak natu-
rally. Normal speech depends to a great extent on constant auditory feedback.
Hence, deaf children will not learn to speak without extensive training in schools
or programs designed especially for them.

Although deaf people can be taught to speak a language intelligibly, they can
never understand speech as well as a hearing person can. Seventy-five percent of
spoken English words cannot be read on the lips with any degree of accuracy. The
ability of many deaf individuals to comprehend spoken language is therefore
remarkable; they combine lip reading with knowledge of the structure of language, the meaning redundancies that language has, and context.

If, however, human language is universal in the sense that all members of the human
species have the ability to learn a language, then it is not surprising that nonspoken languages have developed as a substitute for spoken languages among nonhearing individuals. The more we learn about the human linguistic ability, the clearer it is that
language acquisition and use are dependent not on the ability to produce and hear
sounds but on a much more abstract cognitive ability, biologically determined, that
accounts for the similarities between spoken and sign languages.

American Sign Language (ASL)

The major language used by deaf people in North America is **American Sign
Language** (or **ASL** or AMESLAN). ASL is an independent, fully developed lan-
guage that is an outgrowth of the sign language used in France and brought to the
United States in 1817 by the great educator Thomas Hopkins Gallaudet. Gallaudet

was hired to establish a school for deaf people, and, after studying the language and methods used in the Paris school founded by the Abbé de l'Epée in 1775, he returned to the United States with Laurent Clerc, a young deaf instructor, and established the basis for ASL.

ASL, like all human languages, has its own grammar that includes everything signers know about their language — the system of gestures equivalent to the phonology of a spoken language; the morphological, syntactic, and semantic systems; and a mental lexicon of signs. The term *phonology*, first used to describe the sound systems of language, has here been extended to include the gestural systems of sign languages.

Another sign language used in North America is called Signed English (or Siglish). Essentially, it consists of the replacement of each spoken English word (and grammatical elements such as the -*s* ending for plurals or the -*ed* ending for past tense) by a sign. The syntax and semantics of Signed English are thus approximately the same as those of ordinary English. The result is unnatural in that it is similar to speaking French by translating every English word or ending into its French counterpart. Problems result because there are not always corresponding forms in the two languages.

If there is no sign in ASL, signers utilize another mechanism, the system of **finger spelling**. This method is also used to add new proper nouns or technical vocabulary. Sign interpreters of spoken English often finger-spell such words. A manual alphabet consisting of various finger configurations, hand positions, and movements gives visible symbols for the alphabet and ampersand.

Signs, however, are produced differently than are finger-spelled words. "The sign DECIDE cannot be analyzed as a sequence of distinct, separable configurations of the hand. Like all other lexical signs in ASL, but unlike the individual finger-spelled letters in D-E-C-I-D-E taken separately, the ASL sign DECIDE does have an essential movement, but the hand shape occurs simultaneously with the movement. In appearance, the sign is a continuous whole" (Klima & Bellugi, 1979).

An accomplished signer can sign at a normal rate, even when there is a lot of finger spelling. Television stations sometimes have programs that are interpreted in sign in a corner of the TV screen. If you have ever seen such a program, you may have noted how well the interpreter kept pace with the spoken sentences.

Language arts are not lost to the deaf community. Poetry is composed in sign language, and stage plays such as Richard Brinsley Sheridan's *The Critic* (1779) have been translated into sign language and acted by the National Theatre of the Deaf (NTD).

Deaf children acquire sign language much in the way that hearing children acquire a spoken language. Deaf children often sign themselves to sleep just as hearing children talk themselves to sleep. Deaf children report that they dream in sign language as French-speaking children dream in French and Hopi children dream in Hopi. Deaf children sign to their dolls and stuffed animals. Slips of the hand occur similar to slips of the tongue; finger fumblers amuse signers as tongue twisters amuse speakers. Sign languages resemble spoken languages in all major aspects, showing that there truly are universals of language despite differences in the modality in which the language is performed. This universality is predictable because regardless of the modality in which it is expressed, language is biologically based.

In the Beginning: The Origin of Language

> Nothing, no doubt, would be more interesting than to know from historical documents the exact process by which the first man began to lisp his first words, and thus to be rid for ever of all the theories on the origin of speech.
>
> M. Muller (1871)

One question that has long fascinated people is, how did language first arise? All religions and mythologies contain stories of language origin. Philosophers through the ages have argued the question. Scholarly works have been written on the subject. Prizes have been awarded for the "best answer" to this eternally perplexing

problem. Theories of divine origin, evolutionary development, and language as a human invention have all been suggested.

The difficulties inherent in answering this question are immense. Anthropologists think that the species has existed for at least one million years and perhaps for as long as five or six million years. But the earliest deciphered written records are barely 6,000 years old, dating from the writings of the Sumerians of 4000 B.C.E. These records appear so late in the history of the development of language that they provide no clue to its origin.

For these reasons, scholars in the latter part of the nineteenth century, who were interested only in "hard science," ridiculed, ignored, and even banned discussions of language origin. In 1886, the Linguistic Society of Paris passed a resolution "outlawing" any papers concerned with this subject.

Despite the difficulty of finding scientific evidence, speculations on language origin have provided valuable insights into the nature and development of language, which led Otto Jespersen (1922/1964) to remind us that "linguistic science cannot refrain forever from asking about the whence (and about the whither) of linguistic evolution." A brief look at some of these notions will reveal something of both the difficulty and the value in such speculations.

God's Gift to Humanity?

> And out of the ground the Lord God formed every beast of the field, and every fowl of the air, and brought them unto Adam to see what he would call them; and whatsoever Adam called every living creature, that was the name thereof.
>
> Genesis 2:19

According to Judeo–Christian beliefs, God gave Adam the power to name all things. Similar beliefs are found throughout the world. According to the Egyptians, the creator of speech was the god Thoth. Babylonians believed the language giver was the god Nabu, and the Hindus attributed our unique language ability to a female god: Brahma was the creator of the universe, but language was given to us by his wife, Sarasvati.

Belief in the divine origin of language is closely intertwined with the magical properties that have been associated with language and the spoken word. Children in all cultures utter "magic" words such as *abracadabra* to ward off evil or bring good luck. Despite the childish jingle "Sticks and stones may break my bones, but names will never hurt me," name calling is insulting, cause for legal punishment, and feared. In some cultures, when certain words are used, one is required to counter them by "knocking on wood."

In many religions, only special languages may be used in prayers and rituals. The Hindu priests of the fifth century B.C.E. believed that the original pronunciations of Vedic Sanskrit had to be used. This led to important linguistic study, since their language had already changed greatly since the hymns of the Vedas had been composed. The first linguist known to us is Panini, who, in the fourth century B.C.E., wrote a detailed grammar of Sanskrit in which the phonological rules revealed the earlier pronunciation for use in religious worship.

While myths and customs and superstitions do not tell us very much about language origin, they do tell us about the importance ascribed to language.

There is no way to prove or disprove the divine origin of language, just as one cannot argue scientifically for or against the existence of God.

The First Language

> Imagine the Lord talking French! Aside from a few odd words in Hebrew, I took it completely for granted that God had never spoken anything but the most dignified English.
> Clarence Day, *Life with Father* (1935)

Among the proponents of the divine origin theory, a great interest arose in the language used by God, Adam, and Eve. For millennia, experiments have reportedly been devised to verify particular theories of the first language. In the fifth century B.C.E., the Greek historian Herodotus reported that the Egyptian Pharaoh Psammetichus (664–610 B.C.E.) sought to determine the most primitive "natural" language by experimental methods. The monarch was said to have placed two infants in an isolated mountain hut, to be cared for by a mute servant. The pharaoh believed that without any linguistic input the children would develop their own language and would thus reveal the original human language. The Egyptian waited patiently for the children to become old enough to talk. According to the story, the first word uttered was *bekos*, the word for "bread" in Phrygian, the language spoken in a province of Phrygia in the northwest corner of what is now modern Turkey. This ancient language, which has long since died out, was thought, on the basis of this "experiment," to be the original language.

History is replete with other proposals. In the thirteenth century, the Holy Roman Emperor Frederick II of Hohenstaufen was said to have carried out a similar test, but the children died before they uttered a single word. James IV of Scotland (1473–1513), however, supposedly succeeded in replicating the experiment with the surprising results, according to legend, that the Scottish children "spak very guid Ebrew," providing "scientific evidence" that Hebrew was the language used in the Garden of Eden.

But J.G. Becanus in the sixteenth century argued that German must have been the primeval language, since God would have used the most perfect language. In 1830, Noah Webster asserted that the "proto-language" must have been Chaldee (Aramaic), the language spoken in Jerusalem during the time of Jesus. In 1887, Joseph Elkins maintained that "there is no other language which can be more reasonably assumed to be the speech first used in the world's gray morning than can Chinese."

The belief that all languages originated from a single source — the **monogenetic theory of language origin** — is found not only in the Tower of Babel story in Genesis but also in a similar legend of the Toltecs, early inhabitants of Mexico, and in the myths of other peoples as well.

Clearly, we are no further along in discovering the original language (or languages) than was Psammetichus, given the obscurities of prehistory.

Human Invention or the Cries of Nature?

> Language was born in the courting days of mankind; the first utterances of speech I fancy to myself like something between the nightly love lyrics of puss upon the tiles and the melodious love songs of the nightingale.
>
> Otto Jespersen, *Language: Its Nature, Development, and Origin* (1922/1964)

The Greeks speculated about everything in the universe, including language. The earliest surviving linguistic treatise that deals with the origin and nature of language is Plato's *Cratylus*. A common view among the classical Greeks, expressed by Socrates in this dialogue, was that at some ancient time there was a "legislator" who gave the correct, natural name to everything and that words echoed the essence of their meanings.

Despite all the contrary evidence, the idea that the earliest form of language was imitative, or "echoic," was proposed up to the twentieth century. Called the *bow-wow* theory, it claimed that a dog would be designated by the word *bow-wow* because of the sounds of its bark.

A parallel view states that language at first consisted of emotional ejaculations of pain, fear, surprise, pleasure, anger, and so on. That the earliest manifestations of language were "cries of nature" was proposed by Jean-Jacques Rousseau in the middle of the eighteenth century.

Another hypothesis suggests that language arose out of the rhythmical grunts of people working together. A more charming view was suggested by Jespersen, who proposed that language derived from song as an expressive rather than a communicative need, with love being the greatest stimulus for language development.

Just as with the beliefs in a divine origin of language, these proposals are untestable.

What We Know about Language

There are many things we do not yet know about human languages, their origins, structures, and use. The science of linguistics is concerned with these questions. The investigations of linguists throughout history and the analysis of spoken languages date back at least to 1600 B.C.E. in Mesopotamia. We have learned a great deal since that time. A number of facts pertaining to all languages can now be stated.

1. Wherever humans exist, language exists.
2. There are no "primitive" languages — all languages are equally complex and equally capable of expressing any idea in the universe. The vocabulary of any language can be expanded to include new words for new concepts.
3. All languages change over time.

4. The relationships between the sounds and meanings of spoken languages and between the gestures and meanings of sign language are for the most part arbitrary.

5. All human languages utilize a finite set of discrete sounds (or gestures) that are combined to form meaningful elements or words, which themselves form an infinite set of possible sentences.

6. All grammars contain rules for the formation of words and sentences of a similar kind.

7. Every spoken language includes discrete sound segments such as *p*, *n*, or *a* that can all be defined by a finite set of sound properties or features. Every spoken language has a class of vowels and a class of consonants.

8. Similar grammatical categories (e.g., noun, verb) are found in all languages.

9. There are semantic universals, such as "male" or "female," "animate" or "human," found in every language in the world.

10. Every language has a way of referring to past time, negating, forming questions, issuing commands, and so on.

11. Speakers of all languages are capable of producing and comprehending an infinite set of sentences. Syntactic universals reveal that every language has a way of forming sentences such as the following:

    Linguistics is an interesting subject.
    I know that linguistics is an interesting subject.
    You know that I know that linguistics is an interesting subject.
    Cecilia knows that you know that I know that linguistics is an interesting subject.
    Is it a fact that Cecilia knows that you know that I know that linguistics is an interesting subject?

12. Any normal child, born anywhere in the world, of any racial, geographical, social, or economic heritage, is capable of learning any language to which she is exposed. The differences we find among languages cannot be due to biological reasons.

It seems that Alsted and Du Marsais — like many other universalists from all ages — were not spinning idle thoughts. We all possess "human language."

Summary

We are all intimately familiar with at least one language — our own. Yet few of us ever stop to consider what we know when we know a language. There is no book that contains the English or Russian or Zulu language. The words of a language can be listed in a dictionary, but not all the sentences, and a language consists of sentences as well as words. Speakers use a finite set of rules to produce and understand an infinite set of possible sentences.

These rules constitute the **grammar** of a language, which is learned when you acquire the language and includes the sound system (the **phonology**), the structure of words (the **morphology**), how words may be combined into phrases and sentences (the **syntax**), the ways in which sounds and meanings are related (the **semantics**), and the words or **lexicon**. The sounds and meanings of these words are related in an **arbitrary** fashion. If you had never heard the word *syntax*, you would not, by its sounds, know what it meant. The gestures used by deaf signers are also arbitrarily related to their meanings. Language, then, is a system that relates sounds (or hand and body gestures) to meanings; when you know a language, you know this system.

This knowledge (**linguistic competence**) is different from behaviour (**linguistic performance**). If you woke one morning and decided to stop talking (as the Trappist monks did after they took a "vow of silence"), you would still have knowledge of your language. This ability or competence underlies linguistic behaviour. If you do not know the language, you cannot speak it; but if you know the language, you may choose not to speak it.

Grammars are of different kinds. The **descriptive grammar** of a language represents the unconscious linguistic knowledge or capacity of its speakers. Such a grammar is a model of the **mental grammar** every speaker of the language knows. It does not teach the rules of the language; it describes the rules that are already known. A grammar that attempts to legislate what your grammar should be is called a **prescriptive grammar**. It prescribes; it does not describe, except incidentally. **Teaching grammars** are written to help people learn a foreign language or a dialect of their own language. **Reference grammars** are written to help people find out the grammatical facts of a language.

The more linguists investigate the thousands of languages of the world and describe the ways in which they differ from one another, the more they discover that these differences are limited. There are linguistic universals that pertain to all parts of grammars, the ways in which these parts are related, and the forms of rules. These principles make up **Universal Grammar**, which forms the basis of the specific grammars of all possible human languages and constitutes the innate component of the human **language faculty** that makes normal language development possible.

A basic property of human language is its **creative aspect** — a speaker's ability to combine the basic linguistic units to form an *infinite* set of "well-formed" grammatical sentences, most of which are novel, never before produced or heard.

The fact that deaf children learn **sign language** shows that the ability to hear or produce sounds is not a prerequisite for language learning. All the sign languages in the world, which differ as spoken languages do, are visual–gestural systems that are as fully developed and as structurally complex as spoken languages. The major sign language used in North America is **American Sign Language** (also referred to as **ASL** or AMESLAN).

The idea that language was God's gift to humanity is found in religions throughout the world. The continuing belief in the miraculous powers of language is tied to this notion. The assumption of the divine origin of language stimulated interest in discovering the first primeval language. There are legendary "experiments" in which children were kept in isolation in the belief that their first words would reveal the original language.

Opposing views suggest that language is a human invention. The Greeks believed that an ancient "legislator" gave the true names to all things. Others have suggested that language developed from "cries of nature," "early gestures," **onomatopoeic** words, or even songs to express love.

All of these proposals are untestable. The cooperative efforts of linguists, evolutionary biologists, and neurologists may in time provide some answers to this intriguing question. Because of linguistic research throughout history, we have learned much about Universal Grammar, the properties shared by all languages.

Note

1. The **asterisk** is used before examples that native speakers, for any reason, find unacceptable. This notation will be used throughout the book.

Exercises

1. An English speaker's knowledge includes the sound sequences of the language. When new products are put on the market, the manufacturers have to think up new names for them that conform to the allowable sound patterns. Suppose you were hired by a manufacturer of soap products to name five new products. What names might you come up with? List them.

   We are not interested in the spelling of the words but in how they are pronounced. Therefore, describe in any way you can how the words you list should be pronounced. Suppose, for example, you named one soap powder *Blick*. You could describe the sounds in any of the following ways:

   bl as in *blood*, *i* as in *pit*, *ck* as in *stick*
   bli as in *bliss*, *ck* as in *tick*
   b as in *boy*, *lick* as in *lick*

*2. Consider the following sentences. Put an asterisk (*) before those that do not seem to conform to the rules of your grammar, that are ungrammatical for you. State, if you can, why you think the sentence is ungrammatical.

   a. Robin forced the sheriff go.
   b. Napoleon forced Josephine to go.
   c. The Devil made Faust go.
   d. He passed by a large sum of money.
   e. He came by a large sum of money.
   f. He came a large sum of money by.

g. Did in a corner little Jack Horner sit?
h. Elizabeth is resembled by Charles.
i. Nancy is eager to please.
j. It is easy to frighten Emily.
k. It is eager to love a kitten.
l. That birds can fly amazes.
m. The fact that you are late to class is surprising.
n. Has the nurse slept the baby yet?
o. I was surprised for you to get married.
p. I wonder who and Mary went swimming.
q. Myself bit John.

3. It was pointed out in this chapter that a small set of words in languages may be onomatopoeic — that is, their sounds "imitate" what they refer to. *Ding-dong, tick-tock, bang, zing, swish,* and *plop* are such words in English. Construct a list of ten new words. Test them on at least five friends to see if they are truly "nonarbitrary" as to sound and meaning.

4. Although sounds and meanings of most words in all languages are arbitrarily related, there are some communication systems in which the "signs" unambiguously reveal their "meaning."

    a. Describe (or draw) five different signs that directly show what they mean. Example: a road sign indicating an S curve.
    b. Describe any other communication system that, like language, consists of arbitrary symbols. Example: traffic signals, where red means stop and green means go.

5. Consider these two statements:

    I learned a new word today.
    I learned a new sentence today.

    Do you think the two statements are equally probable? If not, why not?

6. State a "rule of grammar" that you have learned is the "correct" way to say something but that you do not generally use in speaking. For example, you may have heard that *It's me* is incorrect and that the correct form is *It's I.* Nevertheless, you always use *me* in such sentences, your friends do also, and, in fact, *It's I* sounds odd to you.

    Write a short essay presenting arguments against someone who tells you that you are wrong. Discuss how this disagreement demonstrates the difference between descriptive and prescriptive grammars.

7. Think of song titles that are "bad" grammar, but which, if corrected, would lack effect. For example, the 1929 "Fats" Waller classic "Ain't Misbehavin'" is clearly superior to the bland "I am not misbehaving." Try to come up with five or ten such titles.

References

Chomsky, N. (1972). *Language and mind* (Enlarged ed.). New York: Harcourt Brace Jovanovich.

Chomsky, N. (1979). *Language and responsibility.* New York: Pantheon.

Chomsky, N., (1986). *Knowledge of language: Its nature, origin, and use.* New York: Praeger.

Chomsky, N. & Halle, M. (1968). *The sound pattern of English.* New York: Harper & Row.

Crystal, D. (1997). *The Cambridge encyclopedia of language* (2nd ed.). Cambridge, UK: Cambridge University Press.

de Saussure, F. (1969). *Course in general linguistics* (W. Baskin, Trans.). New York: McGraw-Hill. (original work published 1916)

Descartes, R. (1967). Discourse on method. In *The philosophical works of Descartes* (Vol. 1, E.S. Haldane & G.R. Ross, Trans.). Cambridge, UK: Cambridge University Press.

Jespersen, O. (1909–1949). *Modern English grammer on historical principles* (7 vols.). London: Allen & Unwin.

Jespersen, O. (1964). *Language: Its nature, development, and origin.* New York: W.W. Norton. (Original work published 1922).

Klima, E.S., & Bellugi, U. (1979). *The signs of language.* Cambridge, MA: Harvard University Press.

Newman, E. (1974). *Strickly speaking.* New York: Macmillan.

Newman, E. (1976). *A civil tongue.* Indianapolis, IN: Bobbs-Merrill.

Nyembezi, C.L.S. (1997). *Learn Zulu.* Pietemaritzburg, South Africa: Shuter and Shooter.

Quirk, R., Svartvik, L., Leech, G., & Greenbaum, J. (1985). *A comprehensive grammar of the English language.* London: Longman.

Salmon, V. (1969). [Review of *Cartesian Linguistics* by N. Chomsky.] *Journal of Linguistics, 5,* 165–187.

Further Reading

Bolinger, D. (1980). *Language — The loaded weapon: The use and abuse of language today.* London: Longman.

Botha, R, & Knight, C. (2009). *The cradle of language.* Oxford: Oxford University Press.

Chomsky, N. (1975). *Reflections on language.* New York: Pantheon Books.

Crow, T.J. (Ed.). (2004). *The speciation of modern homo sapiens.* Oxford: Oxford University Press.

Crystal, D. (1984). *Who cares about usage?* New York: Penguin.

Crystal, D. (2003). *Cambridge encyclopedia of the English language* (2nd ed.). Cambridge, UK: Cambridge University Press.

Jackendoff, R. (1994). *Patterns in the mind: Language and human nature.* New York: Basic Books.

Jackendoff, R. (1997). *The architecture of the language faculty.* Cambridge, MA: MIT Press.

Klima, E.S., & Bellugi, U. (1979). *The signs of language.* Cambridge, MA: Harvard University Press.

Lane, H. (1984). *When the mind hears: A history of the deaf.* New York: Random House.

Milroy, J., & Milroy, L. (1985). *Authority in language: Investigating language prescription and standardisation.* London: Routledge & Kegan Paul.

Newmeyer, F.J. (1983). *Grammatical theory: Its limits and possibilities.* Chicago: University of Chicago Press.

Pinker, S. (1994). *The language instinct.* New York: William Morrow.

Pinker, S. (1999). *Words and rules: The ingredients of language.* New York: HarperCollins.

Pinker, S. (2007). *The stuff of thought: Language as a window into human nature.* New York: Viking Penquin.

Safire, W. (1980). *On age.* New York: Avon Books.

Stam, J. (1976). *Inquiries into the origin of language: The fate of a question.* New York: Harper & Row.

Sternberg, M.L.A. (1998). *American sign language dictionary.* New York: Harper Collins.

Stokow, W. (1960). *Sign language structure: An outline of the visual communication system of the American deaf.* Silver Springs, MD: Linstok Press.

Valli, C., & Lucas, C. (2001). *Linguistics of American Sign Language: An Introduction* (3rd ed.). Washington, DC: Gallaudet University Press.

Websites

http://www.ethnologue.com Provides examples of some of the world's languages.

http://www.linguistlist.org A website for linguists. Includes linguistic resources.

http://www.cal.org The website for the Center for Applied Linguistics (U.S.). Contains numerous links to language- and linguistics-related information.

http://www.zompist.com/langfaq.html Answers frequently asked questions about linguistics.

http://www.omniglot.com/links/language.html Supplies numerous links to linguistics and language sites.

PART TWO
Grammatical Aspects of Language

The theory of grammar is concerned with the question: What is the nature of a person's knowledge of his language, the knowledge that enables him to make use of language in the normal, creative fashion? A person who knows a language has mastered a system of rules that assigns sound and meaning in a definite way for an infinite class of possible sentences.

N. Chomsky, *Language and Mind* (1972)

CHAPTER 2
Morphology: The Words of Language

A word is dead
When it is said,
Some say.
I say it just
Begins to live
That day.

Emily Dickinson, "A Word" (1955)

Every speaker of every language knows thousands of words, but none know all of the words of their native language. *Webster's Third International Dictionary of the English Language*, for example, has more than 450,000 entries, but it is estimated that the average high school graduate knows about 60,000 words. The university graduate should, we assume, know more words than that, including many in this book. It has been estimated that children of six know as many as 13,000 words. If they produced their first word at the age of two then they have learned 3,250 words a year, an average of nine new words a day.

Words are an important part of linguistic knowledge and constitute a component of our mental grammars. But one can learn thousands of words in a language and still not know the language. Those who have tried to make themselves understood in a foreign country by simply using a dictionary know this to be true. On the other hand, without words we would be unable to convey our thoughts through language.

What is a word? What do you know when you know a word? Suppose you hear someone say *morpheme* and haven't the slightest idea what it means, and you don't know what the "smallest unit of linguistic meaning" is called. Then you don't know the word *morpheme*. A particular string of sounds must be united with a meaning, and a meaning must be united with specific sounds, in order for the sounds or the meaning to be a **word** in our mental dictionaries. Once you learn both the sounds and their related meaning, you know the word. It becomes an entry in your mental **lexicon** (the Greek word for *dictionary*), part of your linguistic knowledge.

Someone who doesn't know English would not know where one word begins or ends in an utterance such as *Thecatsatonthemat*. We separate written words by spaces, but in the spoken language there are no pauses between most words. Without knowledge of the language, one can't tell how many words are in an utterance. A speaker of English has no difficulty in segmenting the stream of sounds into six individual words: *the*, *cat*, *sat*, *on*, *the*, and *mat*. Similarly, a speaker of the Native North American language Potawatomi knows that *kwap-muknanuk* (which means "they see us") is just one word.

The lack of pauses between words in speech has provided humorists and song-writers with much material. During World War II, the chorus of one of the top ten tunes used this fact about speech to amuse us:

Mairzy doats and dozy doats   (Mares eat oats and does eat oats,
And liddle lamzy divey,   And little lambs eat ivy,
A kiddley-divey too,   A kid'll eat ivy too,
Wooden shoe?   Wouldn't you?)

The fact that the same sounds can be interpreted differently, even between languages, gave birth to an entertaining book. The title, *Mots d'heures: Gousses, rames* (see Van Rooten, 1993), was derived from the fact that *Mother Goose Rhymes*, spoken in English, sounds to a French speaker like the French words meaning "Words of the Hours: Root, Branch." The first rhyme in French starts with

Un petit d'un petit
S'etonne aux Halles.

When interpreted as if it were English, it would sound like

Humpty dumpty
Sat on a wall.

This shows that in a particular language the form (sounds or pronunciation) and the meaning of a word are inseparable; they are like two sides of a coin. *Un petit d'un petit* in French means "a little one of a little one," but in English the sounds represent the name *Humpty Dumpty*.

Similarly, in English the sounds of the letters *bear* and *bare* represent four **homophones** (different words with the same sounds but different meanings), as shown in the following sentences:

She can't bear (tolerate) children.
She can't bear (give birth to) children.
Exit, pursued by a bear.
He stood there — bare and beautiful.

Couch, sofa, chesterfield, and *davenport*, though they have the same meaning, are called **synonyms** because they are represented by four different strings of sounds.

Sometimes we think we know a word even though we don't know what it means. It is hard to find an English speaker who hasn't heard the word *antidis-establishmentarianism*, and most will tell you that it is the longest word in the English language. Yet many of these people are unsure about its meaning. According to the way we have defined what it means to "know a word" — pairing a string of sounds with a particular meaning — such individuals do not really know this word.

Information about the longest or shortest word in the language is not part of the linguistic knowledge of a language but general conceptual knowledge *about* a language. Children do not learn such facts the way they learn the sound–meaning correspondences of the words *of* their language. Both children and adults have to be told that *antidisestablishmentarianism* is the longest word in English or discover it through an analysis of a dictionary. Actually, should they wish to research this question, they would find that the longest word in *Webster's Third International Dictionary* is *pneumonoultramicroscopicsilicovolcanoconiosis*, a disease of the lungs. As we shall see in Chapter 7, children learn words such as *elephant, disappear, mother*, and all the other words they know without being taught them explicitly.

Since each word is a sound–meaning unit, each word stored in our mental dictionaries must be listed with its unique phonological representation, which determines its pronunciation, and with its meaning. For literate speakers, the spelling or **orthography** of most of the words we know is also in our lexicons.

Each word listed in your mental dictionary must include other information as well, such as whether it is a noun, a pronoun, a verb, an adjective, an adverb, a preposition, or a conjunction. That is, its **grammatical category** or syntactic category is specified. You may not consciously know that a form such as *love* is listed as both a verb and a noun, but a speaker has such knowledge, as shown by the phrases *I love you* and *You are the love of my life*. If such information were not in your mental dictionary, you would not know how to form grammatical sentences or be able to distinguish grammatical from ungrammatical sentences. The classes of words, the syntactic categories — such as nouns, verbs, adjectives — and the semantic properties of words, which represent their meanings, will be discussed in later chapters.

Dictionaries

> Dictionary, n. A malevolent literary device for cramping the growth of a language and making it hard and inelastic.
>
> Ambrose Bierce, *The Devil's Dictionary* (1911)

The dictionaries that one buys in a bookstore contain some of the information found in our mental dictionaries. But this information appeared only gradually in the development of dictionaries (Landau, 1984; Murray, 1970). Dictionaries grew out of the earlier practice of writing words as translations or "glosses" above especially difficult words in Latin texts and, later, in French ones. Students may still do this as an aid for their own translations or as a way of remembering the meaning of an unusual word in an English text. Words and their glosses might then be listed separately as a "glossary"; from this developed bilingual Latin and English dictionaries. The earliest proper dictionaries in English were alphabetical lists of "hard words" with glosses of their meanings in ordinary words. The first, by Robert Cawdrey, appeared in 1604 with the title *A Table Alphabetical, Containing and Teaching the True*

Writing, and Understanding of Hard Usuall English Words, etc. It listed some 2,500 "hard words" with their explanations in ordinary language. They ranged alphabetically from *Abandon*, "cast away, or yeelde up, to leave, or forsake," to *Zodiack*, "a circle in the heaven, wherein be placed the 12 signes, and in which the Sunne is moved." About twenty years later, H. Cockeram's *English Dictionarie* of 1623 included not only a list of hard words but also a list going the other way, giving an ordinary word its hard-word equivalent — small talk with big words. Thus, for *abound,* one could use "exuperate"; for *youthful babbling*, "juvenile inaniloquence"; for *baked*, "pistated." Later in the seventeenth century, technical dictionaries giving new terms appeared, such as that of Edward Philips (1671), Milton's nephew, who listed technical consultants such as Robert Boyle for chemistry and Izaak Walton for fishing. He also indicated the subject field of each term and gave the language of origin.

It was not until the next century that anyone thought of including in the dictionary *all* words in the language, common words as well as hard words. Nathanael Bailey first included ordinary words in his *Universal Etymological English Dictionary* (1721) as much for his interest in etymology as for completeness. The aim of most early lexicographers, whom Samuel Johnson called "harmless drudges," was to "prescribe" rather than "describe" the words of a language, to be, as in the stated aim of one of Noah Webster's dictionaries, the "supreme authority" of the "correct" pronunciation and meaning of a word. Johnson's great *Dictionary of the English Language*, published in 1755 in two volumes, with its wealth of illustrative quotations, mostly drawn from literary sources, was intended to serve as such a standard, and indeed it did for over a century (Murray, 1970). But Johnson himself soon gave up on the possibility of standardizing the language, seeing it as constantly changing. He stated that he could not construct the language but only "register the language." Moreover, his dictionary was always personal, as seen in his definition of *excise*, "a hateful tax levied upon commodities, and adjudged not by the common judges of property, but wretches hired by those to whom excise is paid." Still a pretty good definition of the GST! By the end of the eighteenth century, pronouncing dictionaries appeared to show not only how words such as *colonel, enough,* or *phthisical* were spelled but also how they were pronounced, and pronunciations became a regular part of dictionaries (e.g., Thomas Sheridan, 1780; John Walker, 1791).

In the United States, Noah Webster attempted to rival Johnson's dictionary in his *American Dictionary of the English Language* in two volumes (1828). Webster was fired with the idea that the United States should have its own form of English, distinct from British usage, and included many new words and senses that had originated or been changed by usage in the United States. He also included a number of new scientific and technical terms among the 70,000 entries. The latest revision of Merriam-Webster is *Webster's Third New International Dictionary of the English Language: Unabridged* (1961), containing some 450,000 entries.

The end of the nineteenth century saw the beginning of the monumental *Oxford English Dictionary: A New English Dictionary on Historical Principles* (often

. referred to as *OED*), called the greatest lexicographic work in English produced to date. The second edition appeared in 1989 in twenty volumes (see Murray et al., 1989) and since then in an electronic version, a second CD-ROM version, and now on the World Wide Web. As Sidney Landau (1984) has said,

> The *OED* not only provides a historical record of the development of the meaning of each word, with illustrative quotations and definitions for each sense, it also shows the changes in spelling, the different forms each word assumed during its history. It gives by far the most complete and authoritative etymologies that existed up until that time, a body of information that is still unchallenged as a whole.

A *Dictionary of Canadianisms on Historical Principles* appeared in Canada's centennial year of 1967. Modelled on the *OED*, it is an indispensable source for the study of Canadian language and its development and for cultural information about Canada's past.

All dictionaries, from the *OED* to the more commonly used "collegiate dictionaries," provide the following information about each word: (1) spelling, (2) the "standard" pronunciation, (3) definitions to represent the word's one or more meanings, and (4) parts of speech — for example, noun, verb, preposition. Other information may be included, such as the etymology or history of the word, whether the word is nonstandard (e.g., *ain't*) or slang, vulgar, or obsolete. Many dictionaries provide quotations from published literature to illustrate the given definitions, as was first done by Johnson.

In recent years, perhaps due to the increasing specialization in science and the arts or the growing fragmentation of the populace, we have seen the proliferation of hundreds of specialty and subspecialty dictionaries. Dictionaries of slang and jargon have been around for many years, as have multilingual dictionaries, but the shelves of bookstores and libraries are now filled with dictionaries written specifically for biologists, engineers, agriculturists, economists, artists, architects, printers, gays and lesbians, transvestites, athletes, tennis players, and almost any group that has its own set of words to describe what its members think and do. These dictionaries partly reflect the information in our mental dictionaries, stored in highly complex ways. Our own mental dictionaries probably include only a small number of the entries in these dictionaries, but each word is in someone's lexicon.

Content Words and Function Words

Languages make an important distinction between two kinds of words — content words and function words. Nouns, verbs, adjectives, and adverbs are the **content words**. These words denote concepts such as objects, actions, attributes, and ideas that we can think about like *children, anarchism, soar,* and *purple.* Content words are sometimes called the **open class** words because we can and regularly do add new words to these classes. A new word, *steganography,* which is the art of hiding information in electronic text, entered English with the Internet revolution. Verbs like *disrespect* and *download* entered the language quite recently, as have nouns like *byte* and *email*.

Different languages may express the same concept using words of different grammatical classes. For example, in Akan, the major language of Ghana, there are only a handful of adjectives. Most concepts that would be expressed with adjectives in English are expressed by verbs in Akan. Instead of saying "The sun is bright today," an Akan speaker will say "The sun brightens today."

There are other classes of words that do not have clear lexical meaning or obvious concepts associated with them, including conjunctions such as *and, or,* and *but*; prepositions such as *in* and *of*; the articles *the, a/an,* and pronouns such as *it* and *he*. These kinds of words are called **function words** because they have a grammatical function. For example, the articles indicate whether a noun is definite or indefinite —*the* boy or *a* boy. The preposition *of* indicates possession as in "the book of yours," but this word indicates many other kinds of relations too.

Function words are sometimes called **closed class** words. It is difficult to think of new conjunctions, prepositions, or pronouns that have recently entered the language. The small set of personal pronouns such as *I, me, mine, he, she,* and so on are part of this class. With the growth of the feminist movement, some proposals have been made for adding a neutral singular pronoun that would be neither masculine nor feminine and that could be used as the general, or **generic**, form. If such a pronoun existed, it might have prevented the department chairperson in a large university from making the incongruous statement: "We will hire the best person for the job regardless of his sex." UCLA psychologist Donald MacKay suggested that we use "e," pronounced like the letter name, for this pronoun with various alternative forms. Others point out that *they* and *their* are already being used as neutral third-person singular forms, as in "Anyone can do it if they try hard enough" or "Everyone can do their best." The use of the various forms of *they* is standard on the BBC (British Broadcasting Corporation) as pronoun replacements for *anyone* and *everyone,* which may be regarded as singular or plural.

The difference between content and function words is illustrated by the following test that circulated recently over the Internet:

Please count the number of F's in the following text:

> FINISHED FILES ARE THE
> RESULT OF YEARS OF SCIENTIFIC
> STUDY COMBINED WITH THE
> EXPERIENCE OF YEARS.

If you are like most people, your answer will be three. That answer is wrong. The correct answer is six. Count again. This time pay attention to the function word *of*.

What this little test illustrates is that the brain treats content and function words differently. Indeed, there is a great deal of psychological and neurological evidence to support this claim. For example, the effect that we just illustrated with the *of* test is much more pronounced in brain-damaged people. Some brain-damaged patients have greater difficulty in using, understanding, or reading function words than they do with content words. Some are unable to read function words like *in* or *which* but can read the lexical content words *inn* and *witch*. Other patients do just the opposite. The two classes of words also seem to function differently in slips of the tongue produced by normal individuals. For example, a speaker may inadvertently switch words, producing "the journal of the editor" instead of "the editor of the journal," but the switching or exchanging of function words has not been observed. There is also evidence for this distinction from language acquisition (discussed in Chapter 7). In the early stages of development, children often omit function words from their speech, for example, "doggie barking." These two classes of words have different functions in language. Content words have semantic content (meaning). Function words play a grammatical role; they connect the content words to the larger grammatical context in ways that will be discussed in Chapter 3.

Morphemes: The Minimal Units of Meaning

> "They gave it me," Humpty Dumpty continued, "for an un-birthday present."
> "I beg your pardon?" Alice said with a puzzled air.
> "I'm not offended," said Humpty Dumpty.
> "I mean, what is an un-birthday present?"
> "A present given when it isn't your birthday, of course."
>
> Lewis Carroll, *Through the Looking-Glass* (1871)

In the dialogue above, Humpty Dumpty is well aware that the prefix *un-* means "not," as is further shown in the following pairs of words:

A	B
desirable	undesirable
likely	unlikely
inspired	uninspired
happy	unhappy
developed	undeveloped
sophisticated	unsophisticated

Webster's Third New International Dictionary lists about 2,700 adjectives beginning with *un-*.

If the most elemental units of meaning, the basic linguistic signs, are assumed to be the words of a language, then it would be a coincidence that *un-* has the same meaning in all the column B words. But this is no coincidence. The words *undesirable, unlikely, uninspired, unhappy*, and the others in column B consist of at least two meaningful units: *un + desirable, un + likely, un + inspired*, and *un + happy*.

Just as *un-* occurs with the same meaning in the words above, so does *phon* in the following words. (You may not know the meanings of some of them, but you will when you finish this book.)

phone	phonology	phoneme
phonetic	phonologist	phonemic
phonetics	phonological	allophone
phonetician	telephone	euphonious
phonic	telephonic	symphony

Phon is a minimal form in that it can't be divided into more elemental structures. *Ph* doesn't mean anything; *pho,* though it is pronounced like *foe,* has no relation in meaning to it; and *on* is not the preposition spelled *o-n.* In all the words in the list, *phon* has the identical meaning, "pertaining to sound."

The internal structure of words is rule governed. Thus, *uneaten, unadmired,* and *ungrammatical* are words in English, but **eatenun, *admiredun,* and **grammaticalun* (to mean "not eaten," "not admired," and "not grammatical") are not, because we form a negative meaning of a word not by suffixing *-un* (i.e., by adding it to the end of the word) but by prefixing it (i.e., by adding it to the beginning).

When Samuel Goldwyn, the pioneer moviemaker, announced "In two words: impossible," he was reflecting the common view that words are the basic meaningful elements in a language. We have already seen that this cannot be so, since some words are formed by combining a number of distinct units of meaning. The traditional term for the most elemental unit of grammatical form is **morpheme**. The word is derived from the Greek word *morphe,* meaning "form." Linguistically speaking, then, Goldwyn should have said "In two morphemes: im-possible."

The study of the internal structure of words, and of the rules by which words are formed, is **morphology**. *Morphology* itself consists of two morphemes, *morph + ology.* The morphemic suffix *-ology* means "science of" or "branch of knowledge concerning." Thus, the meaning of *morphology* is "the science of word forms." Knowing a language implies knowing its morphology. Like most linguistic knowledge, this is generally unconscious knowledge.

A single word may be composed of one or more morphemes:

one morpheme	boy
	desire
two morphemes	boy + ish
	desire + able
three morphemes	boy + ish + ness
	desire + able + ity
four morphemes	gentle + man + li + ness
	un + desire + able + ity
more than four	un + gentle + man + li + ness
	anti + dis + establish + ment + ari + an + ism

Some speakers will have even more morphemes for *antidisestablishmentarianism* than are shown here if they are familiar with some of the roots of the word.

A morpheme may be represented by a single sound, such as the morpheme *a* meaning "without" as in *amoral* or *asexual,* or by a single syllable, such as *child* and *-ish* in *child + ish.* A morpheme may also consist of more than one syllable: two syllables, as in *aardvark, lady, water;* three syllables, as in *Winnipeg* or *crocodile;* or four or more syllables, as in *salamander.* A morpheme — the minimal linguistic sign — is thus a grammatical unit in which there is an arbitrary union of a sound and a meaning that cannot be further analyzed. This may be too simple a definition, but it will serve our purposes for now. Every word in every language is composed of one or more morphemes.

The decomposition of words into morphemes illustrates one of the fundamental properties of human language — **discreteness**. In all languages, discrete linguistic units combine in rule-governed ways to form larger units. Sound units combine to form morphemes, morphemes combine to form words, and words combine to form larger units — phrases and sentences.

Discreteness is one of the properties that distinguish human languages from the communication systems of other species. Our knowledge of these discrete units and the rules for combining them accounts for the creativity of human language. Linguistic creativity refers to a person's ability to produce and understand an infinite range of sentences and words never before heard.

With respect to words, linguistic creativity means that not only can we understand words that we have never heard before, but also we can create new words. In the first case, we can decompose a word into its component parts and if we know the meaning of those parts, we have a good guess at the meaning of the whole. In the second case, we can combine morphemes in novel ways to create new words whose meaning will be apparent to other speakers of the language. If you know that "to write" to a disk or a CD means to put information on it, you automatically understand that a *writable* CD is one that can take information; a *rewritable* CD is one where the original information can be written over; and an *unrewritable* CD is one that does not allow the user to write over the original information. You know the meanings of all these words by virtue of your knowledge of the individual morphemes *write, re-, -able,* and *un-* and the rules for their combination.

Bound and Free Morphemes

Prefixes and Suffixes

Our morphological knowledge has two components: knowledge of the individual morphemes and knowledge of the rules that combine them. One of the things we know about particular morphemes is whether they can stand alone or whether they must be attached to a host morpheme.

Some morphemes, such as *boy, desire, gentle,* and *man,* can constitute words by themselves. These are **free morphemes**. Other morphemes, such as *-ish, -able, -ness, -ly, dis-, trans-,* and *un-,* are never words by themselves but are always parts of words. These **affixes** are **bound morphemes**. We know whether each affix precedes or follows other morphemes. Thus, *un-, pre-* (*premeditate, prejudge*), and *bi-* (*bipolar, bisexual*) are **prefixes**. They occur before other morphemes. Some morphemes occur only as **suffixes**, following other morphemes. English examples of suffix morphemes are *-ing* (e.g., *sleeping, eating, running, climbing*), *-er* (e.g., *singer, performer, reader,* and *quantifier*), *-ist* (e.g., *typist, copyist, pianist, novelist,* and *linguist*), and *-ly* (e.g., *manly, sickly, spectacularly,* and *friendly*) to mention just a few.

Morphemes are the minimal linguistic signs in all languages, and many languages have prefixes and suffixes. But languages may differ in how they deploy their morphemes. A morpheme that is a prefix in one language may be a suffix in another and vice versa. In English, the plural morpheme -s is a suffix (e.g., *boys, machines, diskettes*). On the other hand, in Isthmus Zapotec, a language of Mexico, the plural morpheme *ka-* is a prefix:

zigi	"chin"	kazigi	"chins"
zike	"shoulder"	kazike	"shoulders"
diaga	"ear"	kadiaga	"ears"

Languages may also differ in what meanings they express through affixation. In English a noun can be derived from a verb without adding an affix. For example, we have the verb *dance* as in "I like to dance" and we have the noun *dance* as in "The salsa is a Latin dance." The form is the same in both cases. In Turkish, you derive a noun from a verb with the suffix -*ak*, as in the following examples:

dur	"to stop"	dur + ak	"stopping place"
bat	"to sink"	bat + ak	"sinking place" or "marsh/swamp"

In English, in order to express reciprocal action, we use the phrase *each other*, as in *understand each other, love each other.* In Turkish, one simply adds a morpheme to the verb:

anla	"understand"	anla + s	"understand each other"
sev	"love"	sev + is	"love each other"

The "reciprocal" suffix in these examples is pronounced as *s* after a vowel and as *is* after a consonant. This is similar to the process in English in which we use *a* as the indefinite article morpheme before a noun beginning with a consonant, as in *a dog*, and *an* before a noun beginning with a vowel, as in *an apple*. We will discuss the various pronunciations of morphemes in Chapter 6.

In Piro, an Arawakan language spoken in Peru, a single morpheme, *kaka*, can be added to a verb to express the meaning "cause to":

cokoruha	"to harpoon"	cokoruha + kaka	"cause to harpoon"
salwa	"to visit"	salwa + kaka	"cause to visit"

In Karok, a Native North American language spoken in the Pacific Northwest of the United States, the locative adverbial meaning "in," "on," or "at" is formed by adding -*ak* to a noun:

ikrivaam	"house"	ikrivaamak	"in a house"

It is accidental that both Turkish and Karok have a suffix -*ak*. Despite the similarity in form, the two meanings are different. Similarly, the reciprocal suffix -*s* in Turkish is similar in form to the English plural -*s*. Also in Karok, the suffix -*ara* has the same meaning as the English -*y*, that is, "characterized by":

aptiik	"branch"	aptiikara	"branchy"

These examples illustrate again the arbitrary nature of the linguistic sign.

In Russian, the suffix -*shchik* (pronounced like the beginning of the word *she* followed by *chick*) added to a noun is similar in meaning to the English suffix -*er* in words such as *reader, teacher*, or *rider*, which when added to a verb means "one who —." The Russian suffix, however, is added to nouns and verbs, as shown in the following examples:

atom	"atom"	atomshchik	"atom-warmonger"
baraban	"drum"	barabanshchik	"drummer"
kalambur	"pun"	kalamburshchik	"punner"
beton	"concrete"	betonshchik	"concrete worker"
lom	"scrap"	lomshchik	"salvage collector"

The examples given above from different languages also illustrate "free" morphemes such as *boy* in English, *dur* in Turkish, *salwa* in Piro, and *lom* in Russian.

Infixes

Some languages also have **infixes**, morphemes that are inserted into root morphemes. Bontoc, a language spoken in the Philippines, is such a language:

Nouns/Adjectives		Verbs	
fikas	"strong"	fumikas	"to be strong"
kilad	"red"	kumilad	"to be red"
fusul	"enemy"	fumusul	"to be an enemy"

In this language, the infix -*um*- is inserted after the first consonant of the noun or adjective. Thus, a speaker of Bontoc who learns that *pusi* means "poor" would understand the meaning of *pumusi*, "to be poor," on hearing the word for the first time. Just as an English speaker who learns the verb *blog* would know that *blogger* is "one who *blogs*," a Bontoc speaker who knows that *ngumitad* means "to be dark" would know that the adjective "dark" must be *ngitad*.

English has a very limited set of infixes. A fossil infix in English is the *n* in a few words such as *stand* (cf. *stood*), *think* (*thought*), and *bring* (*brought*). English infixing was a subject of the Linguist List, a discussion group on the Internet, in November 1993 and again in July 1996. The interest in these infixes in English may be due to the fact that one can only infix obscenities as full words inserted in other words, usually into adjectives or adverbs. The most common infix in North America is the word *fuckin* and all the euphemisms for it, such as *friggin, freakin, flippin,* or *fuggin* as in *abso + fuggin + lutely* or *Winni + flippin + peg*. In Britain, a common infix is *bloody*, an obscene term in British English, and its euphemisms, such as *bloomin*. In the movie and stage musical *My Fair Lady, abso + bloomin + lutely* occurs in one of the songs sung by Eliza Doolittle.

Circumfixes

Some languages have **circumfixes**, morphemes that are attached to a root or stem morpheme both initially and finally. These are sometimes called **discontinuous morphemes**. In Chickasaw, a Muskogean language spoken in Oklahoma, the negative is formed by using both the prefix *ik-* and the suffix *-o*. The final vowel of the declarative is deleted before the negative suffix is added.

Declarative		Negative	
chokma	"he is good"	ik + chokm + o	"he isn't good"
lakna	"it is yellow"	ik + lakn + o	"it isn't yellow"
palli	"it is hot"	ik + pall + o	"it isn't hot"
tiwwi	"he opens (it)"	ik + tiww + o	"he doesn't open (it)"

An example of a more familiar "circumfixing" language is German. The past participle of regular verbs is formed by adding the prefix *ge-* and the suffix *-t* to the verb root. Thus, this circumfix added to the verb root *lieb* "love" produces *geliebt* "loved" (or "beloved," when used as an adjective).

Roots and Stems

Morphologically complex words consist of a **root** and one or more affixes. A root is a lexical content morpheme that cannot be analyzed into smaller parts. Some examples of English roots are *paint* in *painter, read* in *reread,* and *ceive* in *conceive*. A root may or may not stand alone as a word (*paint* does; *ceive* doesn't). In languages that have circumfixes, the root is the form around which the circumfix attaches, for example, the Chickasaw root *chokm* in *ikchokmo* ("he isn't good"). In infixing languages the root is the form into which the infix is inserted, for example, *fikas* in the Bontoc word *fumikas* ("to be strong").

Semitic languages like Hebrew and Arabic have a unique morphological system. Nouns and verbs are built on a foundation of three consonants, and one derives related words by varying the pattern of vowels and syllables. For example, the root for "write" in Egyptian Arabic is *ktb* from which the following words (among others) are formed:

katab	"he wrote"
kaatib	"writer"
kitáab	"book"
kútub	"books"

When a root morpheme is combined with an affix, it forms a **stem**, which may or may not be a word (*painter* is both a word and a stem; *-ceive + er* is only a stem). Other affixes can be added to a stem to form a more complex stem, as shown in the following:

root	Chomsky	(proper) noun
stem	Chomsky + ite	noun + suffix
word	Chomsky + ite + s	noun + suffix + suffix
root	believe	verb
stem	believe + able	verb + suffix
word	un + believe + able	prefix + verb + suffix
root	system	noun
stem	system + atic	noun + suffix

stem	un + system + atic	prefix + noun + suffix
stem	un + system + atic + al	prefix + noun + suffix + suffix
word	un + system + atic + al + ly	prefix + noun + suffix + suffix + suffix

As one adds each affix to a stem, a new stem and a new word are formed.

Huckles and Ceives

> It had been a rough day, so when I walked into the party I was very chalant, despite my efforts to appear gruntled and consolate. I was furling my wieldy umbrella ... when I saw her.... She was a descript person.... Her hair was kempt, her clothing shevelled, and she moved in a gainly way.
>
> Jack Winter, "How I Met My Wife," *The New Yorker* (July 25, 1944)

A morpheme was defined as the basic element of meaning, a phonological form that is arbitrarily united with a particular meaning and that cannot be analyzed into simpler elements. This definition has presented problems for linguistic analysis for many years, although it holds for most of the morphemes in a language. Consider words such as *cranberry, huckleberry,* and *boysenberry.* The *berry* part is no problem, but *huckle* and *boysen* occur only with *berry*, as did *cran-* until *cranapple* juice came on the market, and other morphologically complex words using *cran-* followed. The *boysen-* part of *boysenberry* was named for Boysen, who developed it as a hybrid from the blackberry and the raspberry. But few people are aware of this, and it is a bound stem morpheme that occurs only in this word. *Lukewarm* is another word with two stem morphemes, with *luke* occurring only in this word, because it is not the same morpheme as the name *Luke*.

Bound forms such as *huckle-, boysen-,* and *luke-* require a redefinition of the concept of morpheme. Some morphemes have no meaning in isolation but acquire meaning only in combination with other specific morphemes. Thus, the morpheme *huckle-*, when joined with *berry*, has the meaning of a special kind of berry that is small, round, and purplish-blue; *luke-*, when combined with *warm*, has the meaning "sort of" or "somewhat"; and so on.

Just as there are some morphemes that occur only in a single word (combined with another morpheme), there are other morphemes that occur in many words but seem to lack a constant meaning. What is the meaning of *-ceive* in *receive, perceive, conceive,* and *deceive*, or the *-mit* in *remit, permit, commit, submit, transmit,* and *admit*? Since these forms were morphemes in Latin and French before the words were borrowed in English, they are sometimes known as **etymemes** because of their etymological relevance. The meanings of such morphemes depend on the words in which they occur, on their morphological contexts. The roots may have been meaningful at one time in Latin, but they no longer are in English. In the mental lexicons of many speakers, these words would be monomorphemic, but words that appear to have a transparent structure to some speakers are opaque to others. One child, for instance, was surprised to learn that orange juice is made with oranges. Once these loan words enter the language, they may reveal a pattern by which they can be disassembled and their parts combined with others.

	-duce	-fer	-cur	-tain
re-	reduce	refer	recur	retain
con-	conduce	confer	concur	contain
in-	induce	infer	incur	*intain
de-	deduce	defer	*decur	detain

The starred "words" do not occur in English, but they could; they are at least possible words.

There are other words that seem to be composed of prefix + stem morphemes in which the stems, like the *cran-* or *-ceive,* never occur alone but always with a regular prefix. Thus, we find *inept* but no *ept, inane* but no *ane, incest* but no *cest, inert* but no *ert, disgusted* but no *gusted.*

Similarly, the stems of *upholster, downhearted*, and *outlandish* do not occur by themselves: *holster* and *hearted* (with these meanings) and *landish* are not free morphemes. In addition, *downholster, uphearted*, and *inlandish*, their "opposites," are not found in any English lexicon.

To complicate things a little further, there are words such as *strawberry* in which the *straw* has no relationship to any other kind of *straw, gooseberry*, which is unrelated to *goose*, and *blackberry*, which may be blue or red. While some of these words may have historical origins, there is no present meaningful connection. The *Oxford English Dictionary* entry for the word *strawberry* states that "the reason for the name has been variously conjectured. One explanation refers the first element to Straw . . . a particle of straw or chaff, a mote, describing the appearance of the achenes scattered over the surface of the strawberry." That may be true of the word's origin, but today the *straw* in *strawberry* is not the same morpheme as that found in *strawlike* or *straw-coloured.*

The meaning of a morpheme must be constant. The morpheme *-er* means "one who does" in words such as *singer, painter, lover*, and *worker*, but the same sounds represent the "comparative" morpheme, meaning "more," in *nicer, prettier*, and *taller.* Thus, two morphemes may be pronounced identically but represent two distinct morphemes because of their difference in meaning. The same sounds may occur in another word and not represent any separate morpheme, as is shown by the final syllable in *butcher*; *-er* does not represent any morpheme, since a butcher is not one who butches. (In an earlier form of English, the word *butcher* was *bucker*, "one who dresses bucks." The *-er* in this word was then a separate morpheme.) Similarly, in *water* the *-er* is not a distinct morpheme ending; *butcher* and *water* are single morphemes or **monomorphemic** words. This follows from the concept of the morpheme as a sound–meaning unit.

To summarize, all morphemes are bound or free. Affixes (prefixes, suffixes, and infixes) are bound morphemes. Root morphemes can be bound or free:

	Free	Bound
Root	dog, cat, aardvark, corduroy, run, bottle, hot, separate, phone, museum, school . . . (and thousands more)	huckle(berry), (dis)gruntle, (un)couth, (non)chalance, (per)ceive, (in)ept, (re)mit, (in)cest, (homo)geneous . . . (and fewer than a hundred more)
Affix		(lead)er, re(do), trans(sex)ual, (sad)ly, (tall)ish, a(moral) . . . (and many others)

Note that there are some morpheme types not listed in this chart, such as *-ing* as in *going* or *the* or *and*.

Rules of Word Formation

"I never heard of 'Uglification,' " Alice ventured to say. "What is it?"

The Gryphon lifted up both its paws in surprise. "Never heard of uglifying!" it exclaimed. "You know what to beautify is, I suppose?"

"Yes," said Alice doubtfully: "it means — to make — anything — prettier."

"Well, then," the Gryphon went on, "if you don't know what to uglify is, you are a simpleton."

Lewis Carroll, *Alice's Adventures in Wonderland* (1871)

When the Mock Turtle listed the different branches of arithmetic for Alice as "Ambition, Distraction, Uglification, and Derision," Alice was very confused. She wasn't really a simpleton, since *uglification* was not a common word in English until Lewis Carroll used it.

By using the **morphological rules** of English he created a new word. The rules that he used are as follows:

Adjective + ify	→	Verb	"to make Adjective"
Verb + cation	→	Noun	"the process of making Adjective"

Derivational Morphology

Bound morphemes like *-ify* and *-cation* are called **derivational morphemes**. When they are added to a root morpheme or stem, a new word with a new meaning is derived. The addition of *-ify* to *pure — purify —* means "to make pure" and the addition of *-ation — purification —* means "the process of making pure." If we invent an adjective, *pouzy,* to describe the effect of static electricity on hair, you will immediately understand the sentences "Walking on that carpet really pouzified my hair" and "The best method of pouzification is to rub a balloon on your head." This means that we must have a list of the derivational morphemes in our mental dictionaries as well as the rules that determine how they are added to a root or stem. The form that results from the addition of a derivational morpheme is called a **derived word**.

Chris Cassatt and Gary Brookins, Copyright Tribune Media Services. Reprinted with permission.

The Hierarchical Structure of Words

We saw above that morphemes are added in a fixed order. This order reflects the **hierarchical structure** of the word. A word is not a simple sequence of morphemes. It has an internal structure. For example, the word *unsystematic* is composed of three morphemes, *un-, system,* and *-atic*. The root is *system,* a noun, to which we add the suffix *-atic* resulting in an adjective, *systematic*. To this adjective, we add the prefix *un-*, forming a new adjective, *unsystematic*.

In order to represent the hierarchical organization of words (and sentences) linguists use **tree diagrams**. The tree diagram for *unsystematic* is as follows:

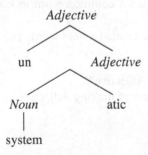

This tree represents the application of two morphological rules:

1. Noun + atic   →   Adjective
2. Un + Adjective   →   Adjective

Rule 1 attaches the derivational suffix *-atic* to the root noun, forming an adjective. Rule 2 takes the adjective formed by rule 1 and attaches the derivational prefix *un-*. The diagram shows that the entire word — *unsystematic* — is an adjective that is composed of an adjective — *systematic* — plus *un*. The adjective is itself composed of a noun — *system* — plus the suffix *atic*.

Like the property of discreteness discussed earlier, hierarchical structure is an essential property of human language. Words (and sentences) have component parts, which relate to each other in specific, rule-governed ways. Although at first glance it may seem that, aside from order, the morphemes *un-* and *-atic* each relate to the root *system* in the same way, this is not the case. The root *system* is "closer" to *-atic* than it is to *un-*, and *un-* is actually connected to the adjective *systematic,* and not directly to *system.* Indeed, **unsystem* is not a word.

Further morphological rules can be applied to the structure given above. For example, English has a derivational suffix *-al,* as in *egotistical, fantastical,* and *astronomical.* In these cases, *-al* is added to an adjective — *egotistic, fantastic, astronomic* — to form a new adjective. The rule for *-al* is as follows:

3. Adjective + al   →   Adjective

Another affix is *-ly,* which is added to adjectives — *happy, lazy, hopeful* — to form adverbs *happily, lazily, hopefully.* Following is the rule for *-ly:*

4. Adjective + ly   →   Adverb

Applying these two rules to the derived form *unsystematic,* we get the following tree for *unsystematically:*

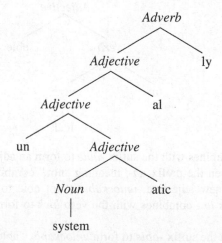

This is a rather complex word. Despite its complexity, it is well formed because it follows the morphological rules of the language. On the other hand, a very simple word can be ungrammatical. Suppose in the above example, we first added *un-* to the root *system.* That would have resulted in a nonword, **unsystem.*

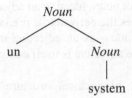

Unsystem is not a possible word because there is no rule of English that allows *un-* to be added to nouns. The large soft-drink company whose ad campaign promoted the *Uncola* successfully flouted this linguistic rule to capture people's attention. Part of our linguistic competence includes the ability to recognize possible vs. impossible words, like **unsystem* and **Uncola*. Possible words are those that conform to the rules of morphology (as well as of phonology; see Chapter 6); impossible words are those that do not.

Tree diagrams are the linguist's hypothesis of how speakers represent the internal structure of the morphologically complex words in their language. In speaking and writing, we string morphemes together sequentially as in *un + system + atic*. As shown by tree diagrams, however, our mental representation of words is much more complex.

The hierarchical organization of words is most clearly shown by structurally ambiguous words, words that have more than one meaning by virtue of having more than one structure. Consider the word *unlockable*. Imagine you are inside a room and you want some privacy. You would be unhappy to find the door is *unlockable* — "not able to be locked." Now imagine you are inside a locked room trying to get out. You would be very relieved to find that the door is *unlockable* — "able to be unlocked." These two meanings correspond to two different structures, as follows:

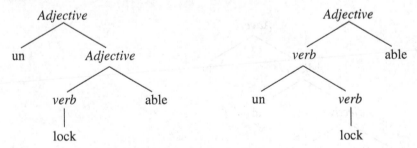

In the first structure the verb *lock* combines with the suffix *-able* to form an adjective *lockable* ("able to be locked"). Then the prefix *un-*, meaning "not," combines with the derived adjective to form a new adjective, *unlockable* ("not able to be locked"). In the second case, the prefix *un-* combines with the verb *lock* to form a derived verb, *unlock*.

Then the derived verb combines with the suffix *-able* to form *unlockable*, "able to be unlocked." An entire class of words in English follows this pattern: *unbuttonable*, *unzippable*, and *unlatchable*, among others. The ambiguity arises because the prefix *un-* can combine with an adjective, as illustrated in rule 2 above, or it can combine with a verb, as in *undo, unstaple, unearth,* and *unloosen.*

If words were only strings of morphemes without any internal organization, we could not explain the ambiguity of words like *unlockable.* These words also illustrate another important point, which is that structure is important to determining meaning. The same three morphemes occur in both versions of *unlockable,* yet there are two distinct meanings. The different meanings arise because of the two different structures.

More about Derivational Morphemes

Derivational morphemes have clear semantic content. In this sense they are like content words, except that they are not words. As we have seen, when a derivational morpheme is added to a root or stem, it adds meaning. The derived word may also be of a different grammatical class than the original word, as shown by suffixes such as *-able* and *-ly.* When a verb is suffixed with *-able,* the result is an adjective, as in *desire + able, adore + able.* When the suffix *-en* is added to an adjective, a verb is derived, as in *dark + en.* One may form a noun from an adjective, as in *sweet + ie.* Other examples are:

Noun to Adjective	Verb to Noun	Adjective to Adverb
boy + ish	acquitt + al	exact + ly
virtu + ous	clear + ance	quiet + ly
Elizabeth + an	accus + ation	
pictur + esque	confer + ence	
affection + ate	sing + er	
health + ful	conform + ist	
alcohol + ic	predict + ion	
life + like	free + dom	

Noun to Verb	Adjective to Noun	Verb to Adjective
moral + ize	tall + ness	read + able
vaccin + ate	specific + ity	creat + ive
brand + ish	feudal + ism	migrat + ory
haste + n	abstract + ion	run + (n)y

Not all derivational morphemes cause a change in grammatical class.

Noun to Noun	Verb to Verb	Adjective to Adjective
friend + ship	un + do	pink + ish
human + ity	re + cover	in + sane

Many prefixes fall into this category:

a + moral   mono + theism
auto + biography   re + print
ex + wife   semi + annual
super + human   sub + minimal

There are also suffixes of this type:

vicar + age   Vancouver + ite
old + ish   fadd + ist
Paul + ine   music + ian
Nova Scotia + n   pun + ster

When a new word enters the lexicon by the application of morphological rules, other complex derivations may be blocked. For example, when *Commun + ist* entered the language, words such as *Commun + ite* (as in *Trotsky + ite*) or *Commun + ian* (as in *grammar + ian*) were not needed and were not formed. Sometimes, however, alternative forms coexist: for example, *Chomskyan* and *Chomskyist* and perhaps even *Chomskyite* (all meaning "follower of Chomsky's views of linguistics"). *Linguist* and *linguistician* are both used, but the possible word *linguite* is not.

Peanuts: © United Feature Syndicate, Inc.

Lexical Gaps

The redundancy of alternative forms such as those mentioned, all of which conform to the regular rules of word formation, may explain some of the **accidental**, or **lexical**, **gaps** in the lexicon. Accidental gaps are well-formed but nonexisting words. The actual words in the language constitute only a subset of the possible words. Speakers of a language may know tens of thousands of words. Dictionaries, as we noted, include hundreds of thousands of words, all of which are known by some speakers of the language. But no dictionary can list all **possible words** since it is possible to add to the vocabulary of a language in many ways. (Some of these will be discussed here and some in Chapter 13 on language change.) There are always gaps in the lexicon — words that are not in the dictionary but that can be added. Some of the gaps are due to the fact that a permissible sound sequence has no meaning attached to it (like *blick,* or *slarm,* or *krobe*). Note that the sequence of sounds must be in keeping with the constraints of the language; **bnick* is not a "gap" because no word in English can begin with a *bn*. We will discuss such constraints in Chapter 6.

Other gaps result when possible combinations of morphemes never come into use. Speakers can distinguish between impossible words such as **unsystem* and **speakly,* and possible, but nonexisting words such as *disobvious, linguisticism,* and *antiquify.* The ability to do this is further evidence that the morphological component of our mental grammar consists of not just a lexicon, a list of existing words, but also of rules that enable us to create and understand new words, and to recognize possible and impossible words.

Rule Productivity

Some morphological rules are **productive**, meaning that they can be used freely to form new words from the list of free and bound morphemes. The suffix *-able* appears to be a morpheme that can be conjoined with any verb to derive an adjective with the meaning of the verb and the meaning of *-able*, which is something like "able to be" as in *accept + able, blam(e) + able, pass + able, change + able, breath + able, adapt + able,* and so on. The meaning of *-able* has also been given as "fit for doing" or "fit for being done." The productivity of this rule is illustrated by the fact that we find *-able* affixed to new verbs such as *downloadable* and *faxable.*

We have already noted that there is a morpheme in English meaning "not" that has the form *un-* and that, when combined with adjectives like *afraid, fit, free, smooth, Canadian,* and *British,* forms the **antonyms**, or negatives, of these adjectives—for example, *unafraid, unfit, un-Canadian.* Note that unlike *-able, un-* does not change the grammatical category of the stem it attaches to.

We also saw that the prefix *un-* can be added to derived adjectives that have been formed by morphological rules:

> un + believe + able
> un + accept + able
> un + speak + able
> un + lock + able

We can also add *un-* to morphologically complex verbs that consist of a verb plus a particle plus *-able* such as:

> pick + up + able
> turn + around + able
> chop + off + able
> talk + about + able

Un- prefixation derives the following words:

> un + pick + up + able
> un + chop + off + able
> un + talk + about + able

Yet *un-* is not fully productive. We find *happy* and *unhappy, cowardly* and *uncowardly,* but not *sad* and **unsad, brave* and **unbrave,* or *obvious* and **unobvious.* The starred forms that follow may be merely accidental gaps in the lexicon. If someone refers to a person as being **unsad* we would know that the person referred to was "not sad," and an **unbrave* person would not be brave. But, as the linguist Sandra Thompson (1975) points out, it may be the case that the "un-Rule" is most productive for adjectives that are themselves derived from verbs, such as *unenlightened, unsimplified, uncharacterized, unauthorized, undistinguished,* and so on.

Morphological rules may be more or less productive. The rule that adds an *-er* to verbs in English to produce a noun meaning "one who performs an action (once or habitually)" appears to be a very productive morphological rule. Most English verbs accept this suffix: *examiner, exam-taker, analyzer, lover, hunter, predictor,* and so forth (*-or* and *-er* have the same pronunciation and are the same morpheme even though they are spelled differently). Now consider the following:

sincerity	from	*sincere*
warmth	from	*warm*
moisten	from	*moist*

The suffix *-ity* is found in many other words in English, like *chastity, scarcity,* and *curiosity;* and *-th* occurs in *health, wealth, depth, width,* and *growth.* We find *-en* in *sadden, ripen, redden, weaken,* and *deepen.* Still, the phrase "*The fiercity of the lion" sounds somewhat strange, as does the sentence "*I'm going to thinnen the sauce." Someone may use the word *coolth,* but, as Thompson points out, when words such as *fiercity, thinnen, fullen,* and *coolth* are used, usually it is either an error or an attempt at humour. It is possible that in such cases a morphological rule that was once productive (as shown by the existence of related pairs like *scarce/scarcity*) is no longer so. Our knowledge of the related pairs, however, may permit us to use these examples in forming new words, by analogy with the existing lexical items. Other derivational morphemes in English are not very productive, such as the suffixes meaning "diminutive," as in the words *pig + let* and *sap + ling.*

In the morphologically complex words that we have seen so far, we can easily predict the meaning based on the meaning of the morphemes that make up the word. *Unhappy* means "not happy" and *acceptable* means "fit to be accepted." However, one cannot always know the meaning of the words derived from free and derivational morphemes by knowing the morphemes themselves. The following *un-* forms have unpredictable meanings:

unloosen	"loosen, let loose"
unrip	"rip, undo by ripping"
undo	"reverse doing"
untread	"go back through in the same steps"
unearth	"dig up"
unfrock	"deprive (a cleric) of ecclesiastic rank"
unnerve	"fluster"

Morphologically complex words whose meanings are not predictable must be listed individually in our mental lexicons. However, the morphological rules must also be in the grammar, revealing the relation between words and providing the means for forming new words.

"Pullet Surprises"

That speakers of a language know the morphemes of that language and the rules for word formation is shown as much by the errors made as by the non-deviant forms produced. Morphemes combine to form words. These words form our internal dictionaries, but given our knowledge of the morphemes of the language and the morphological rules, we can often guess the meaning of a word we do not know. Sometimes our guesses are wrong.

Amsel Greene collected errors made by her students in vocabulary-building classes and published them in a book called *Pullet Surprises* (1969). The title is taken from a sentence written by one of her high school students: "In 1957 Eugene O'Neill won a Pullet Surprise" (note that the Pulitzer Prize is a U.S. award for literacy achievement). What is most interesting about these errors is how much they reveal about the students' knowledge of English morphology. Consider the creativity of these students in the following examples:

Word	Student's Definition
gubernatorial	"to do with peanuts"
bibliography	"holy geography"
polyglot	"more than one glot"
gullible	"to do with sea birds"

The student who used the word *indefatigable* in the sentence

She tried many reducing diets, but remained indefatigable.

clearly recognized morphological structures in the spelling: *in*, meaning "not" as in *ineffective*; *de,* meaning "off" as in *decapitate*; *fat*, as in *fat*; *able*, as in *able*; and combined meaning, "not able to take the fat off." But a still more convincing example is that of E.H. Sturtevant's grandson, who suffered from an earache and was taken to the doctor to have the ear irrigated. When he had a nosebleed, he asked if it had to be "nosigated." The same child apparently saw four planes flying overhead and was told that it was a "formation"; later, upon seeing two planes flying overhead, he claimed that it was a "twomation."

Such misidentifications of morphemes have occurred in the history of the language to produce new words and affixes. Some words ending in *s* or *z* sounds were at times mistaken for the plural forms so that a new singular was formed: for example, the originally singular form *pease* (as in *pease porridge* "pea soup") was taken as a plural (since peas seldom come singularly), and a new singular form, *pea*, was established; so also with *cherry, asset, pry* (from *prize*). Sometimes it went the other way with the fusion of the plural ending with the root to form a new singular, as with *chintz* (and then *chintzy*), originally the plural of *chint*, and *bodice* from *bodies*. Another example is the famous *burger* series, which developed from the German *Hamburger Wurst*, like *Frankfurter Wurst* or *Wiener Wurst* "a sausage (*Wurst*) made in Hamburg, Frankfurt, Vienna." In German, *Hamburger* was made up of the morphemes *Hamburg* (the city) and the suffix *-er*, indicating the place of origin. In English, this was interpreted as *ham* and *burger* "a piece of the previously mentioned food in a roll and served hot," thus *beefburger, cheeseburger, pizzaburger*, and just plain *burger*. Among some speakers — especially older speakers — of Canadian English, this sandwich is known as a *hamburg* and the ground meat used in the roll as *hamburg steak*. The *Nelson Canadian Dictionary* lists both of these along with *hamburgers* and *hamburger steak*, but there can be little doubt that the *-er* forms now dominate, perhaps through the pervasive influence of U.S.–based fast-food restaurant chains.

Additional Word Formation Processes

As we have seen, new words may be added to the vocabulary or lexicon of a language by derivational processes. New words may also enter the language in a variety of other ways.

In computer speech processing, the new words *cepstrum* and *cepstral* were purposely formed by reordering the letters of *spectrum* and *spectral*. Greek roots borrowed in English have also provided a means for adding new words. *Thermos* ("hot") plus *metron* ("measure") give us *thermometer*. From akros ("topmost") and *phobia* ("fear"), we get *acrophobia* "dread of heights."

Latin, like Greek, has also provided prefixes and suffixes that are used productively with both native and non-native roots. The prefix *ex-* comes from Latin:

    ex-husband   ex-wife   ex–sister-in-law

This prefix has been turned into a word, as in *my ex*, referring particularly to an ex-spouse (probably a form of abbreviation or clipping, discussed on page 61).

The suffix *-able/-ible* discussed earlier is also Latin, borrowed via French, and can be attached to almost any English verb:

    writable   readable   answerable   movable

Compounds

New words may be formed by stringing together other words to create **compound** words. There is almost no limit on the kinds of combinations that occur in English, as the following list of compounds shows:

	-Adjective	**-Noun**	**-Verb**
Adjective-	bittersweet	bluenose	highborn
Noun-	headstrong	rainbow	spoonfed
Verb-	carryall	slapshot	sleepwalk

Frigidaire is a compound formed by combining the adjective *frigid* with the noun *air*. Some compounds that have been introduced very recently into English are *carjack*, *mall rat*, *road rage*, and *Palm Pilot*.

When the two words are in the same grammatical category, the compound will be in this category: noun + noun — *girlfriend, baby bonus, paper clip, bush pilot, landlord, rink rat*; adjective + adjective — *icy cold, red hot, worldly wise*. In many cases, when the two words fall into different categories, the class of the second or final word will be the grammatical category of the compound: noun + adjective — *headstrong, userfriendly, watertight, lifelong*; verb + noun — *pickpocket, pinchpenny, daredevil, sawbones*. On the other hand, compounds formed with a preposition are in the category of the nonprepositional part of the compound: *overtake, hanger-on, undertake, sundown, afterbirth, downfall, uplift*.

Although two-word compounds are the most common in English, it would be difficult to state an upper limit: consider *golden handshake, three-time loser, four-dimensional space-time, sergeant-at-arms, mother-of-pearl, man about town, master of ceremonies*, and *daughter-in-law*. Dr. Seuss (1965, p. 51) uses the rules of compounding when he explains "when tweetle beetles battle with paddles in a puddle, they call it a *tweetle beetle puddle battle*."

Spelling does not tell us what sequence of words constitutes a compound; whether a compound is spelled with a space between the two words, with a hyphen, or with no separation at all is idiosyncratic, as shown in *blackbird, goldtail, black-eyed*, and *black spruce*.

Like derived words, compounds have internal structure. This is clear from the ambiguity of a compound like *top + hat + rack*, which can mean "a rack for top

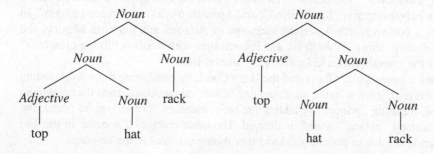

hats" corresponding to the structure in tree diagram (1), or "the highest hat rack," corresponding to the structure in (2).

Meanings of Compounds

The meaning of a compound is not always the sum of the meanings of its parts; a *blackboard* may be green or white. Not everyone who wears a red coat is a *redcoat*. The difference between the sentences *She has a red coat in her closet* and *She has a redcoat in her closet* could be highly significant under certain circumstances.

Other compounds show that underlying the juxtaposition of words different grammatical relations are expressed. A *boathouse* is a house for boats, but a *cathouse* is not a house for cats. A *jumping bean* is a bean that jumps, a *falling star* is a "star" that falls, and a *magnifying glass* is a glass that magnifies, but a *looking glass* is not a glass that looks, nor is an *eating apple* an apple that eats; *laughing gas* does not laugh, and *running shoes* do not run.

In all these examples, the meaning of each compound includes at least to some extent the meanings of the individual parts. However, there are other compounds that do not seem to relate to the meanings of the individual parts at all. A *jack-in-a-box* is a tropical tree, and a *turncoat* is a traitor. A *highbrow* does not necessarily have a high brow, nor does a *bigwig* have a big wig, nor does an *egghead* have an egg-shaped head. A *Bluenose* is a Nova Scotian, and a *Digby chicken* is a smoke-cured herring, not a rooster or hen.

As we pointed out earlier in the discussion of the prefix *un-*, the meanings of many compounds must be learned as if they were individual simple words. Some of the meanings may be figured out. If you have never heard the word *hunchback*, it might be possible to infer the meaning, but if you have never heard the word *flat-foot* it is doubtful you would know it means "detective" or "police officer," even though the origin of the word, once you know the meaning, can be figured out.

The pronunciation of a compound differs from the way we pronounce the sequence of two words forming a noun phrase. In a compound, the first word is usually stressed (pronounced somewhat louder and higher in pitch), and in a noun phrase the second word is stressed. Thus, we stress *red* in *redcoat* but *coat* in *red coat*.

Universality of Compounding

Other languages have rules for conjoining words to form compounds, as seen by French *cure-dent* "toothpick"; German *Panzerkraftwagen* "armoured car"; Russian *cetyrexetaznyi* "four-storied"; and Spanish *tocadiscos* "record player." In Papago, a Native North American language of Arizona and northern Mexico, the word meaning "thing" is *haʔichu*, and it combines with *doakam* "living creatures" to form the compound *haʔichu doakam* "animal life."

In Twi, a language of Ghana and the Ivory Coast, by combining the word meaning "son" or "child," *ɔba*, with the word meaning "chief," *ɔhene*, one derives the compound *ɔheneba*, meaning "prince." By adding the word meaning "house," *ofi*, to *ɔhene*, the word meaning "palace," *ahemfi*, is derived. The other changes that occur in the Twi compounds are due to phonological and morphological rules in the language.

In Thai, the word for "cat" is *mɛɛw*, the word for "watch" (in the sense of "to watch over") is *fâw*, and the word for "house" is *bâan*. The word for "watchcat" (like a watchdog) is the compound *mɛɛwfâwbâan* — literally, "catwatchhouse."

Compounding is therefore a common and frequent process for enlarging the vocabularies of all languages.

Conversion

Often considered a type of derivational process, **conversion** is another means by which words enter a language's lexicon. Conversion refers to the process in which an existing word becomes assigned to another syntactic category. For example, the word *ink*, originally used as a noun, has come to be used as a verb, as in *to ink a contract*. Other category changes are also possible, such as noun from verb (*a call* from *to call*) and verb from adjective (*to total a car* from *a total wreck*, or *to compact* from *a compact car*, as illustrated by the following cartoon).

Fred interpreted the word compact as a verb,
not as an adjective.

McHumor.com by T. McCracken

Blends

Words may be combined to produce **blends**. Blends are similar to compounds, but parts of the words combined are deleted, so they are "less than" compounds. *Smog*, from *smoke* + *fog*; *motel*, from *motor* + *hotel*; *urinalysis*, from *urine* + *analysis*; *breathalyzer*, from *breath* + *analyzer*; and *medicare*, from *medical* + *care* are examples of blends that have attained full lexical status in English. The computer term *bit,* with its pun on the word meaning "a small piece," may be seen as a blend of *b(inary dig)it.* Blending seems to have created new suffixes such as *-alyzer,* as in *eye(a)lyzer; -flation,* as in *gradefla-tion, oilflation,* and *taxflation;* and *-cast,* as in *telecast, newscast,* and *sportscast(er).* The word *cranapple* may be a blend of *cranberry* + *apple. Broasted,* from *broiled* + *roasted,* is a blend that has limited acceptance in the language, as does Lewis Carroll's *chortle,* from *chuckle* + *snort.* Carroll is famous for both the coining and the blending of words. In *Through the Looking-Glass,* he describes the "meanings" of the made-up words in "Jabberwocky" as follows:

> "Brillig" means four o'clock in the afternoon — the time when you begin broiling things for dinner. . . . "Slithy" means "lithe and slimy." . . . You see it's like a portmanteau — there are two meanings packed up into one word.... "Toves" are something like badgers — they're something like lizards — and they're something like corkscrews . . . also they make their nests under sun-dials — also they live on cheese. . . . To "gyre" is to go round and round like a gyroscope. To "gimble" is to make holes like a gimlet. And "the wabe" is the grass-plot round a sun-dial. . . . It's called "wabe" . . . because it goes a long way before it and a long way behind it. . . . "Mimsy" is "flimsy and miserable" (there's another portmanteau . . . for you).

Carroll's "portmanteaus" are what we have called blends, and such words can become part of the regular lexicon. Blending is even done by children; Elijah Peregrine, the grandson of a friend of one of the authors, when less than three years old formed the word *crocogator* by blending *crocodile* and *alligator.*

Back-Formations

Ignorance can sometimes be creative. A new word may enter the language because of an incorrect morphological analysis. For example, *peddle* was derived from *peddler* on the mistaken assumption that *-er* was the "agentive" suffix. Such words are called **back-formations**. The verbs *hawk, stoke, swindle,* and *edit* all came into the language as back-formations — of *hawker, stoker, swindler,* and *editor. Pea* was derived from a sin-gular word, *pease,* by speakers who thought *pease* was plural. Language purists some-times rail against back-formations and cite *enthuse* (from *enthusiasm*) and *ept* (from *inept*) as examples of language corruption; but language is not corrupt (although the speakers who use it may be), and many words have entered the language in this way.

Some word coinage, similar to the kind of wrong morphemic analysis that pro-duces back-formations, is deliberate. The word *bikini* is from the Bikini atoll of the Marshall Islands. Because the first syllable *bi-* in other words, such as *bipolar,* means "two," some clever person, seeing the written word and ignoring differences in pronunciation, called a topless bathing suit a *monokini.* Historically, a number of new words have entered the English lexicon in this way. Based on analogy with pairs such as *act/action, exempt/exemption,* and *revise/revision,* the new words *res-urrect, pre-empt,* and *televise* were formed from the existing words *resurrection, pre-emption,* and *television.*

Abbreviations or Clipping

Abbreviations of longer words or phrases may also become "lexicalized"; *narc* for *narcotics agent, hydro* for *hydro-electric, telly*, the British word for *television, prof* for *professor, piano* for *pianoforte*, and *gym* for *gymnasium* are only a few examples of such "short forms" that are now used as whole words. Other examples are *ad, bike, math, gas, phone, bus*, and *van* (from *advertisement, bicycle, mathematics, gasoline, telephone, omnibus*, and *caravan*). More recently, *dis* and *rad* (from *disrespect* and *radical*) have entered the language, and *dis* has come to be used as a verb meaning "to show disrespect." This process is sometimes called **clipping**.

Word Coinage

Some words are **coined**, or created outright to fit some purpose. Advertising has added many new words in English, such as *Kodak, nylon, Orlon*, and *Dacron*, Specific brand names such as *Xerox, Kleenex, Jell-O, Frigidaire, Brillo*, and *vaseline* are now sometimes used as the generic names for different brands of these types of products. Notice that some of these words were created from existing words: *Kleenex* from the word *clean* and *Jell-O* from *gel*, for example. The language may still use imitation sounds to produce imitative, echoic, or onomatopoeic words such as *bebop, beep(er), bleep, blimp, burp, gack*, and *globbledygook* (Algeo, 1991).

    Eponyms are words derived from proper names and are another of the many creative ways that the vocabulary of a language expands. Thus *Bytown*, the original name of Ottawa, bore the name of Colonel By, the builder of the Rideau Canal, and *Stanfields*, long used as a synonym for underwear, were named after the manufacturers, Stanfields, Ltd., of Truro, Nova Scotia. The Canadian writer Marshall McLuhan, who stated the principle that "the medium is the message," gave his name to *McLuhanism*, referring to his social ideas (e.g., that the effect of the introduction of the mass media is to deaden the critical faculties of individuals); hence also *McLuhanesque, McLuhanite*, and *McLuhanize*.

    Willard R. Espy (1978) compiled a book of 1,500 such words. They include some old favourites:

sandwich	Named for the fourth Earl of Sandwich, who put his food between two slices of bread so that he could eat while he gambled.
gargantuan	Named for Gargantua, the creature with a huge appetite depicted in a novel by Rabelais.
jumbo	After an elephant brought to the United States by P.T. Barnum. ("Jumbo olives" need not be as big as an elephant, however.)

Espy admits to ignorance of the Susan, an unknown servant, from whom we derived the compound *lazy Susan*, or the Betty or Charlotte or Chuck from whom we got *brown betty, charlotte russe*, and *chuckwagon*. He does point out that *denim* was named for the material used for overalls and carpeting, which originally was imported "de Nimes" ("from Nimes") in France, and *argyle* for the kind of socks worn by the chiefs of Argyll of the Campbell clan in Scotland.

Acronyms

Acronyms are words derived from the initials of several words. Such words are pronounced as the spelling indicates: SARAH from *S*earch *a*nd *R*escue *a*nd *H*oming, NAFTA from *N*orth *A*merican *F*ree *T*rade *A*greement, UNESCO from *U*nited *N*ations *E*ducational, *S*cientific, and *C*ultural *O*rganization, and UNICEF from *U*nited *N*ations *I*nternational *C*hildren's *E*mergency *F*und. *Radar* from "*ra*dio *d*etecting *a*nd *r*anging," *laser* from "*l*ight *a*mplification by *s*timulated *e*mission of *r*adiation," and *scuba* from "*s*elf-*c*ontained *u*nderwater *b*reathing *a*pparatus" show the creative efforts of word coiners, as does *snafu*, coined by soldiers in World War II and rendered in polite circles as "*s*ituation *n*ormal, *a*ll *f*ouled *up*." An acronym that has recently been added to the English language and that is used frequently these days is AIDS, from the initials of *A*cquired *I*mmune *D*eficiency *S*yndrome. When the string of letters is not easily pronounced as a word, the acronym is produced by sounding out each letter and consequently may be called an *initialism*, as in CFL for *C*anadian *F*ootball *L*eague, RCMP for *R*oyal *C*anadian *M*ounted *P*olice ("Mounties" or "Horsemen" as they have been called, though their horses have long been retired except for ceremonial occasions), CBC (*C*anadian *B*roadcasting *C*orporation), or UBC (*U*niversity of *B*ritish *C*olumbia), as well as the ubiquitous GST (*G*oods and *S*ervices *T*ax). Another example is CARP for *C*anadian *A*ssociation of *R*etired *P*ersons. When the Reform Party reorganized to form a new party, it was forced to reconsider its first attempt at a name (the *C*onservative *R*eform *A*lliance *P*arty) when its opposition gleefully pointed out the acronym that would result.

Acronyms are being added to the vocabulary daily with the proliferation of computers and the widespread use of the Internet, including MORF (*m*ale *or f*emale), FAQ (*f*requently *a*sked *q*uestions), WYSIWYG (*w*hat *y*ou *s*ee *i*s *w*hat you *g*et), POP (*p*ost *o*ffice *p*rotocol), IMHO (*i*n *m*y *h*umble *o*pinion), and LOL (*l*aughing *o*ut *l*oud, or sometimes *l*ots *o*f *l*ove).

Grammatical Morphemes

"... and even ... the patriotic archbishop of Canterbury found it advisable —"

"Found what?" said the Duck.

"Found it," the Mouse replied rather crossly; "of course you know what 'it' means."

"I know what 'it' means well enough, when I find a thing," said the Duck; "it's generally a frog or a worm. The question is, what did the archbishop find?"

Lewis Carroll, *Alice's Adventures in Wonderland* (1871)

Morphological rules for combining morphemes into words differ from the syntactic rules of a language that determine how words are combined to form sentences. There is, however, an interesting relationship between morphology and syntax. In the discussion of derivational morphology, we saw that certain aspects of morphology have syntactic implications in that nouns can be derived from verbs, verbs from adjectives, adjectives from nouns, and so on. There are other ways in which morphology is dependent on syntax.

When we combine words to form sentences, these sentences are combinations of morphemes, but some of these morphemes, similar to *-ceive* or *-mit*, which were shown to derive a meaning only when combined with other morphemes in a word, derive a meaning only when combined with other morphemes in a sentence. For example, what is the meaning of *it* in the sentence ***It's** hot in July* or in *The archbishop found **it** advisable*? What is the meaning of *to* in *He wanted her **to** go*? *To* has a grammatical meaning as an infinitive marker, and it is a morpheme required by the syntactic, sentence-formation rules of the language. Similarly, *have* in *Cows **have** walked here* is a grammatical marker for the present perfect, and the different forms of *be* in both *The baby **is** crying* and *The baby's diaper **was** changed* function, respectively, as a progressive marker and a passive voice marker.

Inflectional Morphemes

Function words like *to*, *it*, and *be* are free morphemes. Many languages, including English, also contain bound morphemes that, like *to*, are for the most part purely grammatical markers, representing properties such as tense, number, gender, case, and so forth.

Such "bound" **grammatical morphemes** are called **inflectional morphemes**. They never change the syntactic category of the words or morphemes to which they are attached. Consider the forms of the verb in the following sentences:

(a) I sail the ocean blue.
(b) He sails the ocean blue.
(c) John sailed the ocean blue.
(d) John has sailed the ocean blue.
(e) John is sailing the ocean blue.

In sentence (b), the *s* at the end of the verb is an agreement marker; it signifies that the subject of the verb is third person and singular and that the verb is in the present tense. It doesn't add any lexical meaning. The *-ed* and *-ing* endings are morphemes required by the syntactic rules of the language to signal tense or aspect.

English is no longer a highly inflected language. But we do have other inflectional endings. The plurality of many count nouns, for example, is usually marked by a plural suffix attached to the singular

> **Derivational and inflectional morphemes**
> Derivational morphemes normally change the meaning or lexical category of words when added (e.g., *act\action*); inflectional morphemes contribute grammatical information such as plurality (e.g., *kitten\kittens*).

noun, as in *boy/boys* and *cat/cats*. At the present stage of English history, there are a total of eight bound inflectional affixes:

English Inflectional Morphemes		Examples
-s	third person singular present	She wait-**s** at home.
-ed	past tense	She wait-**ed** at home.
-ing	progressive	She is eat-**ing** the doughnut.
-en	past participle	Mary has eat-**en** the doughnuts.
-s	plural	She ate the doughnut-**s**.
-'s	possessive	Disa'**s** hair is short.
-er	comparative	Disa has short-**er** hair than Karin.
-est	superlative	Disa has the short-**est** hair.

Inflectional morphemes in English typically follow derivational morphemes. Thus, to the derivationally complex word *commit + ment*, one can add a plural ending to form *commit + ment + s* but not **commitsment*. However, with compounds such as those previously discussed, the situation is complicated. Thus, for many speakers, the plural of *mother-in-law* is *mothers-in-law*, whereas the possessive form is *mother-in-law's*.

Compared to many languages of the world, English has relatively little inflectional morphology. Some languages are highly inflected. In Swahili, a Bantu language spoken in eastern and central Africa, a verb can be inflected with up to eight morphemes. For example, in *hatutawapikishia* the verb *pik* "to cook" has negative tense, subject agreement, object agreement, indicative mood, and prefixes as well as suffixes:

Ha + tu + ta + wa + pik + i + sh + i + a   "We will not have made him
                                               cook for them"[1]

Even the more familiar European languages have many more inflectional endings than English. In the Romance languages (languages descended from Latin), the verb has different inflectional endings depending on the subject of the sentence. The verb is inflected to agree in person and number with the subject, as illustrated by the Italian verb *parlare*, meaning "to speak":

Io parl**o**	"I speak"	Noi parl**iamo**	"We speak"
Tu parl**i**	"You (singular) speak"	Voi parl**ate**	"You (plural) speak"
Lui/Lei parl**a**	"He/she speaks"	Loro parl**ano**	"They speak"

Some languages can also add content morphemes to the verb. Many North American languages are of this type. For example, in Mohawk the word *wahonwa-tia'tawitsherahetkenhten* means "she made the thing that one puts on one's body ugly for him." In such languages words are equivalent to sentences. As the linguist Mark Baker (2001, p. 655)notes, languages like Mohawk "use a different division of labor from languages like English, with more burden on morphology and less on syntax to express complex relations" (2001, p. 655).

Students often ask for definitions of derivational morphemes as opposed to inflectional morphemes. There is no easy answer. Perhaps the simplest answer is that derivational morphemes are affixes that are not inflectional. Inflectional morphemes signal grammatical relations and are required by the rules of sentence formation. Derivational morphemes, when affixed to roots and stems, change the grammatical word class and/or the basic meaning of the word, which may then be inflected as to number (singular or plural), tense (present, past, future), and so on.

Exceptions and Suppletions

The regular rule that forms plurals from singular nouns does not apply to words such as *child/children, man/men, sheep/sheep, criterion/criteria*. These words are exceptions to the English inflectional rule of plural formation. Similarly, verbs such as *go*, *sing*, or *bring* are exceptions to the regular past-tense rule in English.

When, as children, we are acquiring (or constructing) the grammar, we have to learn specifically that the plural of *man* is *men* and that the past of *go* is *went*. For this reason, we often hear children say *mans* and *goed*; they first learn the regular rules, and, until they learn the exceptions to these rules, they apply them generally to all the nouns and verbs. These children's errors, in fact, support our position that the regular rules exist.

Some of the irregular forms must be listed separately in our mental lexicons, as **suppletive forms**. That is, one cannot use the regular rules of inflectional morphology to add affixes to words that are exceptions. One cannot form the past tense of *bring* by adding *-ed* (**bringed*); one must substitute another word (*brought*) for the inflected form. It is possible that for regular words only the singular forms are listed since we can use the inflectional rules to form plurals. But this cannot be so with exceptions.

When a new word enters the language, it is generally the regular inflectional rules that apply. The plural of *Bic* is *Bics*, not **Bicken*. The exception to this may be a loan word, a word borrowed from a foreign language. For example, the plural of Latin *datum* has always been *data*, never *datums*, although nowadays *data*, the one-time plural, is treated by many as a singular word, like *information*.

The past tense of the verb *hit*, as in the sentence *Yesterday John hit the roof*, and the plural of the noun *sheep*, as in *The sheep are in the meadow*, show that some morphemes seem to have no phonological shape at all. We know that *hit* in the above sentence is *hit* + *past* because of the time adverb *yesterday*, and we know that *sheep* is the phonetic form of *sheep* + *plural* because of the plural verb form *are*. Thousands of years ago, Hindu grammarians suggested that some morphemes have a zero-form: that is, they have no phonological representation. In our view, however, because we would like to hold to the definition of a morpheme as a constant sound–meaning form, the morpheme *hit* is marked as both present and past in the dictionary, and the morpheme *sheep* is marked as both singular and plural; we suggest there are no zero-forms.

Morphology and Syntax

"Curiouser and curiouser!" cried Alice (she was so much surprised, that for the moment she quite forgot how to speak good English).

Lewis Carroll, *Alice's Adventures in Wonderland* (1871)

Some grammatical relations can be expressed either inflectionally (morphologically) or syntactically (as part of the sentence structure). We can see this in the following sentences:

England's queen is Elizabeth II.	The queen of England is Elizabeth II.
He loves books.	He is a lover of books.
The planes that fly are red.	The flying planes are red.
He is hungrier than she.	He is more hungry than she.

Grammatical relations are also signalled morphologically by derivational affixes and compounding. Thus, the second sentence in the above list shows the correspondence of "He loves books" and "He is a lover of books," which uses both the function word *of* and the derivational affix *-er*. Derivation may also be seen in "He is a bibliophile" and compounding in "He is a booklover." Consider also the relations signalled in "the wheels of my car" (function word), "my car's wheels" (inflection), and "my carwheels" (compounding).

Some people form the comparative of *beastly* only by adding *-er*. *Beastlier* is often used interchangeably with *more beastly*. There are speakers who say either. We know the rule that determines when either form of the comparative can be used or when just one can be used, as pointed out by Lewis Carroll in the quotation above.

What one language signals with inflectional affixes another does with word order and another with function words. For example, in English, the sentence *Maxim defends Victor* means something different from *Victor defends Maxim*. The word order is very important. In Russian, all the following sentences mean "Maxim defends Victor": (The letter *č* is pronounced like the *ch* in the word *cheese*; the *j* is pronounced like the *y* in *yet*.)

Maksim zasčisčajet Viktora.
Maksim Viktora zasčisčajet.
Viktora Maksim zasčisčajet.
Viktora zasčisčajet Maksim.
Zasčisčajet Maksim Viktora.
Zasčisčajet Viktora Maksim.

The inflectional suffix *-a* added to the name *Viktor* to derive *Viktora* shows that Victor, not Maxim, is defended.

Like many languages, Russian has **case** markers, which are grammatical morphemes added to nouns to indicate whether the noun is a subject, object, possessor, or some other grammatical rule. Many of the grammatical relations that Russian expresses with case morphology, English expresses with prepositions.

To convey the future meaning of a verb, speakers of English use the function word *will*, as in *John will come Monday*. In French, the verb is inflected for future tense. Notice the difference between "John is coming Monday," *Jean* **vient** *lundi,* and "John will come Monday," *Jean* **viendra** *lundi*. Similarly, where English uses the grammatical markers *have* and *be*, mentioned earlier, other languages use affixing to achieve the same meaning, as illustrated by Indonesian:

dokter mem + eriksa saja	"The doctor examines me."
saja dip + eriksa oleh dokter	"I was examined by the doctor."

In discussing derivational and compounding morphology, we noted that knowing the meaning of the distinct morphemes may not always reveal the meaning of the morphologically complex word. This problem is not true of inflectional morphology. If we know the meaning of the word *linguist*, then we also know the meaning of the plural form *linguists*; if we know the meaning of the verb *analyze*, then we know the meaning of *analyzed* and *analyzes* and *analyzing*. This reveals another difference between derivational and inflectional morphology.

The mental grammar of the language that is internalized by the language learner includes a lexicon listing all the morphemes and the derived words of the language. The morphological rules of the grammar permit speakers to use and understand the morphemes and words in forming and understanding sentences and in forming and understanding new words. Figure 2.1 shows how English morphemes can be classified.

Morphological Analysis: Identifying Morphemes

Speakers of a language are usually able to analyze a word of their language into its component morphemes, since their mental grammars include a mental lexicon of morphemes and the morphological rules for their combination. Of course, there are mistakes while learning, but these are usually quickly remedied. But suppose you didn't know English and were a linguist from the planet Mars wishing to analyze the language. How would you find out what the morphemes of English were? How would you determine whether a word in that language had one or two or more morphemes?

The first thing to do would be to ask native speakers how they would say various words. (It would help, of course, if the speakers knew Martian so that you could ask your questions in Martian. If not, then you would have to do quite a bit of miming and gesturing and acting.) Suppose, then, you collected the following sets or **paradigms** of forms:

Adjective	Meaning
ugly	"very unattractive"
uglier	"more ugly"
ugliest	"most ugly"
pretty	"nice looking"
prettier	"more nice looking"
prettiest	"most nice looking"
tall	"large in height"
taller	"more tall"
tallest	"most tall"

To determine the morphemes in such a list, the first thing a field linguist would do is see if there are any forms that mean the same thing in different words — that is, look for recurring forms. We find them: *ugly* occurs in *ugly, uglier,* and *ugliest,* all three of which words include the meaning "very unattractive." We also find

FIGURE 2.1

Classification of English morphemes

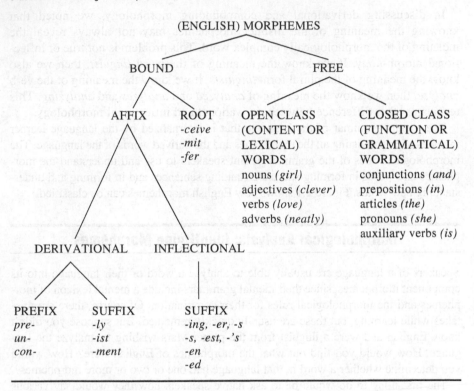

that *-er* occurs in *prettier* and *taller*, adding the meaning "more" to the adjectives to which it is attached. Similarly, *-est* adds the meaning "most." Furthermore, by asking additional questions of our English speaker, we find that *-er* and *-est* do not occur in isolation with the meanings of "more" and "most." We can therefore conclude that the following morphemes occur in English:

ugly	root morpheme	
pretty	root morpheme	
tall	root morpheme	
-er	bound morpheme	"comparative"
-est	bound morpheme	"superlative"

As we proceed further, we find other words that end with *-er* — *singer, lover, writer, teacher,* and many more words — in which the *-er* ending does not mean "comparative" but, when attached to a verb, changes it to a noun that "verbs" — *sings, loves, writes, teaches.* So we conclude that this is a different morpheme even though it is pronounced the same as the comparative. We go on and find words such as *number, bitter butter, member*, and many others in which the *-er* has no separate meaning at all — a number is not one who numbs, and a member does not memb — and therefore these words must be monomorphemic.

Once you have fully described the morphology of English, you might want to go on to describe another language. A language called Paku was invented by a linguist for a former television series called *Land of the Lost*. This was a language used by the monkey people called Pakuni. Suppose you found yourself in this strange land and attempted to determine the morphemes of Paku. You would collect your data from a native Paku speaker and proceed as the Martian did with English. Consider the following data from Paku:

me	"I"	meni	"we"
ye	"you (singular)"	yeni	"you (plural)"
we	"he"	weni	"they (masculine)"
wa	"she"	wani	"they (feminine)"
abuma	"girl"	abumani	"girls"
adusa	"boy"	adusani	"boys"
abu	"child"	abuni	"children"
Paku	"one Paku"	Pakuni	"more than one Paku"

By examining these words, you find that all the plural forms end in *-ni* and that the singular forms do not. You therefore conclude that *-ni* is a separate morpheme meaning "plural," which is attached as a suffix to a noun.

These are simple examples of how one conducts a morphological analysis, but the principles remain the same for more complex languages.

Sign Language Morphology

It appears that sign languages are rich in morphology. Like spoken languages, they have root and affix morphemes, free and bound morphemes, lexical content and grammatical morphemes, derivational and inflectional morphemes, and morphological rules for their combination to form signed words.

Inflection of sign roots also occurs in ASL and all other sign languages, which characteristically modify the movement of the hands and the spatial contours of the area near the body in which the signs are articulated.

Summary

Knowing a language means knowing the words of that language. When you know a word, you know both its **form** (sound) and its **meaning**; these are inseparable parts of the linguistic sign. The relationship between the form and the meaning is **arbitrary**. That is, by hearing the sounds (form), you cannot know the meaning of those sounds without having learned it previously. Each word is stored in our mental **lexicons** with information on its pronunciation (phonological representation), its meaning (semantic properties), and its syntactic class or category specification. For literate speakers, its spelling or **orthography** will also be given.

In spoken language, words are not separated by pauses (or spaces as in written language). One must know the language in order to segment the stream of speech into separate words.

Words are not the most elemental sound–meaning units; some words are structurally complex. The most elemental grammatical units in a language are **morphemes**. A morpheme is the minimal unit of linguistic meaning or grammatical function. Thus, *moralizers* is an English word composed of four morphemes: *moral + ize + er + s*.

The study of word formation and the internal structure of words is called **morphology**. Part of one's linguistic competence includes knowledge of the morphology of the language — the morphemes, words, their pronunciation, their meanings, and how they are combined. Morphemes combine according to the morphological rules of the language. A word consists of one or more morphemes. Lexical content morphemes that cannot be analyzed into smaller parts are called **root** morphemes. When a root morpheme is combined with affix morphemes, it forms a **stem** or word. Other affixes can be added to a stem to form a more complex stem, which may also be a word.

Some morphemes are **bound** in that they must be joined to other morphemes; they are always parts of words and never words by themselves. Other morphemes are **free** in that they need not be attached to other morphemes. *Free, king, serf*, and *bore* are free morphemes; *-dom*, as in *freedom, kingdom, serfdom*, and *boredom*, is a bound morpheme. **Affixes**, that is, **prefixes**, **suffixes**, **infixes**, and **circumfixes**, are bound morphemes. Prefixes occur before, suffixes after, infixes in the middle of, and circumfixes around stems or roots.

Some morphemes, such as *huckle-* in *huckleberry* and *-ceive* in *perceive* or *receive*, have constant phonological form but meanings determined only by the words in which they occur. They are also bound morphemes.

Lexical content, or root, morphemes constitute the major word classes — nouns, verbs, adjectives, and adverbs. These are **open class** items because their classes are easily added to.

Morphemes may be classified as **derivational** or **inflectional**. **Morphological rules** are rules of word formation. Derivational morphemes, when added to a root or stem, may change the syntactic word class and/or the meaning of the word. For example, adding *-ish* to the noun *boy* derives an adjective, and prefixing *un-* to *pleasant* changes the meaning by adding a negative element. Inflectional morphemes are determined by the rules of syntax. They are added to complete words, simple **monomorphemic** words, or complex polymorphemic words (i.e., words with more than one morpheme). Inflectional morphemes never change the syntactic category of the word.

Grammatical morphemes or **function words** constitute a **closed class**; that is, new function words do not enter the language. Function words and bound inflectional morphemes are inserted into sentences according to the syntactic structure. The past-tense morpheme, often written as *-ed*, is added as a suffix to a verb, and the future-tense morpheme, *will*, is inserted in a sentence according to the syntactic rules of English.

Grammars also include ways of increasing the vocabulary, of adding new words and morphemes to the lexicon. Words can be **coined** outright, limited only by the coiner's imagination and the phonetic constraints of English word formation. **Compounds** are also a source of new words. Morphological rules combine two or more morphemes or words to form complex compounds, such as *lamb chop, deep-sea diver*, and *laptop*. Frequently, the meaning of compounds cannot be predicted from the meanings of their individual morphemes.

Conversion accounts for words assigned to new syntactic categories. **Blends** are similar to compounds but usually combine shortened forms of two or more morphemes or words. *Brunch*, a late-morning meal, is a blend of *breakfast + lunch*. **Eponyms** (words taken from proper names, such as *sandwich* from the Earl of Sandwich), **back-formations**, and **abbreviations** also add to the given stock of words. **Acronyms** are words derived from the initials of several words — such as AWOL, which came into the language as the initials for "*a*way *wi*thout *leave*," but the acronym is pronounced as a word. Initialisms are types of acronyms that are pronounced as separate letters (e.g., *MP* for *M*ember of *P*arliament).

While the particular morphemes and the particular morphological rules are language dependent, the same general processes occur in all languages.

Note

1. Swahili examples provided by Kamil Deen.

Exercises

1. Here is how to estimate the number of words in your mental lexicon. Consult any standard dictionary.

   a. Count the number of entries on a typical page. They are usually bold-faced.
   b. Multiply the number of words per page by the number of pages in the dictionary.
   c. Pick four pages in the dictionary at random, say pages 50, 75, 125, and 303. Count the number of words on these pages.
   d. How many of these words do you know?
   e. What percentage of the total words on the four pages do you know?
   f. Multiply the words in the dictionary by the percentage you arrived at in question e. This number will tell you approximately how many English words you know.

2. Divide these words by placing a + between their separate morphemes. (Some of the words may be *monomorphemic* and therefore indivisible.)

Example: replaces re + place + s

a.	retroactive	f.	psychology	k.	mistreatment
b.	befriended	g.	unpalatable	l.	airsickness
c.	televise	h.	holiday	m.	distraction
d.	margin	i.	grandmother	n.	ketchup
e.	endearment	j.	morphemic		

3. Match each expression under A with the one statement under B that characterizes it.

A		B	
a.	noisy crow	1.	compound noun
b.	eat crow	2.	phrase consisting of adjective plus noun
c.	scarecrow	3.	root morpheme plus inflectional affix
d.	the crow	4.	root morpheme plus derivational suffix
e.	crowlike	5.	grammatical morpheme followed by lexical morpheme
f.	crows	6.	idiom

4. Write the one proper description from the list under B for the italicized part of each word in A.

A		B	
a.	terroriz*ed*	1.	free root
b.	un*civil*ized	2.	bound root
c.	terror*ize*	3.	inflectional suffix
d.	*luke*warm	4.	derivational suffix
e.	*im*possible	5.	inflectional prefix
		6.	derivational prefix
		7.	inflectional infix
		8.	derivational infix

*5. A. Consider the following nouns in Zulu and proceed to look for the recurring forms. Note that the ordering of morphemes is not identical across languages. Thus, what is a prefix in one language may be a suffix or an infix in another.

umfazi	"married woman"	abafazi	"married women"
umfani	"boy"	abafani	"boys"
umzali	"parent"	abazali	"parents"
umfundisi	"teacher"	abafundisi	"teachers"
umbazi	"carver"	ababazi	"carvers"
umlimi	"farmer"	abalimi	"farmers"
umdlali	"player"	abadlali	"players"
umfundi	"reader"	abafundi	"readers"

    a. What is the morpheme meaning "singular" in Zulu?

    b. What is the morpheme meaning "plural" in Zulu?

    c. List the Zulu stems (and their meanings) to which the singular and plural morphemes are attached.

B. The following Zulu verbs are derived from noun stems by adding a verbal suffix.

fundisa	"to teach"	funda	"to read"
lima	"to cultivate"	baza	"to carve"

    d. Compare these to the words in section A that are related in meaning — for example, *umfundisi* ("teacher"), *abafundisi* ("teachers"), *fundisa* ("to teach"). What is the derivational suffix morpheme that specifies the category verb?

    e. What is the nominal suffix morpheme (i.e., the suffix that forms nouns)?

    f. State the morphological "noun formation rule" in Zulu.

    g. What is the morpheme meaning "read"?

    h. What is the morpheme meaning "carve"?

6. Examine the following words from Michoacan Aztec.

nokali	"my house"	mopelo	"your dog"
nokalimes	"my houses"	mopelomes	"your dogs"
mokali	"your house"	ipelo	"his dog"
ikali	"his house"	nokwahmili	"my cornfield"
kalimes	"houses"	mokwahmili	"your cornfield"
		ikwahmili	"his cornfield"

    a. The morpheme meaning "house" is

       (1) kal   (2) kali   (3) kalim   (4) ikal   (5) ka

    b. The morpheme meaning "cornfields" is

       (1) kwahmilimes   (2) nokwahmilimes   (3) nokwahmili
       (4) kwahmili   (5) ikwahmilimes

    c. The word meaning "his dogs" is

       (1) pelos   (2) ipelomes   (3) ipelos   (4) mopelo   (5) pelomes

    d. If the word meaning "friend" in this language is *mahkwa,* then the word meaning "my friends" is

       (1) momahkwa   (2) imahkwas   (3) momahkwames
       (4) momahkwaes   (5) nomahkwames

    e. The word meaning "dog" in this language is

       (1) pelo   (2) perro   (3) peli   (4) pel   (5) mopel

7. The following infinitive and past participle verb forms are found in Dutch.

Root	Infinitive	Past Participle	
wandel	wandelen	gewandeld	"walk"
duw	duwen	geduwd	"push"
zag	zagen	gezagd	"saw"
stofzuig	stofzuigen	gestofzuigd	"vacuum-clean"

With reference to the morphological processes of prefixing, suffixing, infixing, and circumfixing discussed in this chapter and the specific morphemes involved,

a.   State the morphological rule for forming an infinitive in Dutch.

b.   State the morphological rule for forming the Dutch past participle form.

*8. Below are some sentences in Swahili.

mtoto	amefika	"The child has arrived."
mtoto	anafika	"The child is arriving."
mtoto	atafika	"The child will arrive."
watoto	wamefika	"The children have arrived."
watoto	wanafika	"The children are arriving."
watoto	watafika	"The children will arrive."
mtu	amelala	"The person has slept."
mtu	analala	"The person is sleeping."
mtu	atalala	"The person will sleep."
watu	wamelala	"The persons have slept."
watu	wanalala	"The persons are sleeping."
watu	watalala	"The persons will sleep."
kisu	kimeanguka	"The knife has fallen."
kisu	kinaanguka	"The knife is falling."
kisu	kitaanguka	"The knife will fall."
visu	vimeanguka	"The knives have fallen."
visu	vinaanguka	"The knives are falling."
visu	vitaanguka	"The knives will fall."
kikapu	kimeanguka	"The basket has fallen."
kikapu	kinaanguka	"The basket is falling."
kikapu	kitaanguka	"The basket will fall."
vikapu	vimeanguka	"The baskets have fallen."
vikapu	vinaanguka	"The baskets are falling."
vikapu	vitaanguka	"The baskets will fall."

One of the characteristics of Swahili (and Bantu languages in general) is the existence of noun classes. There are specific singular and plural prefixes that occur with the nouns in each class. These prefixes are also used for purposes of agreement between the subject–noun and the verb. In the sentences given, two of these classes are included (there are many more in the language).

a. Identify all the morphemes you can detect, and give their meanings.

Example: -toto "child"

m-   noun prefix attached to singular nouns of Class I

a-   prefix attached to verbs when the subject is a singular noun of Class I

Be sure to look for the other noun and verb markers, including tense markers.

b. How is the "verb" constructed? That is, what kinds of morphemes are strung together and in what order?

c. How would you say the following in Swahili?

(1) The child is falling.
(2) The baskets have arrived.
(3) The person will fall.

9. One morphological process not discussed in this chapter is called **reduplication** — the formation of new words through the repetition of part or all of a word — which occurs in a number of languages. The following examples from Samoan exemplify this kind of morphological rule.

manao	"he wishes"	mananao	"they wish"
matua	"he is old"	matutua	"they are old"
malosi	"he is strong"	malolosi	"they are strong"
punou	"he bends"	punonou	"they bend"
atamaki	"he is wise"	atamamaki	"they are wise"
savali	"he travels"	pepese	"they sing"
laga	"he weaves"		

a. What is the Samoan for the following?

(1) they weave
(2) they travel
(3) he sings

b. Formulate a general statement (a morphological rule) that explains how to form a plural verb form from the singular verb form.

10. Below are listed some words followed by incorrect definitions. (All these errors are taken from Amsel Greene's [1969] *Pullet Surprises*.)

Word	Student's Definition
stalemate	"husband or wife no longer interested"
effusive	"able to be merged"

tenet	"a group of ten singers"
dermatology	"a study of derms"
ingenious	"not very smart"
finesse	"a female fish"

For each of these incorrect definitions, give some possible reasons why the students made the guesses they did. Where you can exemplify by reference to other words or morphemes, giving their meanings, do so.

11. Acronyms have become a part of many people's vocabularies. Often these people are unable to explain what the letters in an acronym stand for or even, sometimes, that the word is an acronym at all.

    a. List ten acronyms currently in use in Canadian English and explain the origin of each word. Do not use the ones given in the text.
    b. Invent five new acronyms (listing the words as well as the initials).

12. There are many asymmetries in English in which a root morpheme combined with a prefix constitutes a word but without the prefix is a nonword. A number of these are given in this chapter.

    a. Below is a list of such nonword roots. Add a prefix to each root to form an existing English word.

Words	Nonwords
_____	*descript
_____	*cognito
_____	*beknownst
_____	*peccable
_____	*promptu
_____	*plussed
_____	*domitable
_____	*nomer

    b. There are many more such multimorphemic words for which the root morphemes do not constitute words by themselves. How many can you think of?

13. A. Consider the Inuktitut verbs below. Inuktitut is an Eskimo-Aleut language spoken mainly in Nunavut in Canada, and in some parts of Greenland and Alaska.

    | takuvunga | "I see." |
    | takujumavuq | "He/she/it wants to see." |
    | takusivuq | "He/she/it starts to see." |
    | takuvutit | "You (singular) see." |
    | sanasivunga | "I start to work." |
    | sanajumavutit | "You (singular) want to work." |
    | nirisivutit | "You (singular) start to eat." |

nirijumavunga	"I want to eat."
isumavuq	"He/she thinks."
qaujimavunga	"I know."
iglu	"house"
igluuvuq	"It is a house."
paliisiuvunga	"I am a policeman."
ataatauvutit	"You (singular) are a father."
ilinniaqtittijiuvuq	"He/she is a teacher."

B. Write the Inuktitut morpheme for each of the following English words:

a. I
b. you (singular)
c. he/she/it
d. see
e. work
f. know
g. want to
h. start to
i. be (is/are/am)
j. father

C. Translate each of the following into Inuktitut:

I am a teacher. _____

You eat. _____

I start to think. _____

D. What can you say about the following grammatical features in the Inuktitut words you studied?

gender
tense
indefinite article "*a*"

14. One of the characteristics of Italian is that articles and adjectives have inflectional endings that mark agreement in gender (and number) with the noun they modify. Based on this information, answer the questions that follow the list of Italian phrases.

un uomo	"a man"
un uomo robusto	"a robust man"
un uomo robustissimo	"a very robust man"
una donna robusta	"a robust woman"
un vino rosso	"a red wine"
una faccia	"a face"
un vento secco	"a dry wind"

a. What is the root morpheme meaning "robust"?

b. What is the morpheme meaning "very"?

    c.   What is the Italian for:

       (1) "a robust wine"

       (2) "a very red face"

       (3) "a very dry wine"

15. The following is a list of words from Turkish. In Turkish, articles and morphemes indicating location are affixed to the verb.

deniz	"an ocean"	evden	"from a house"
denize	"to an ocean"	evimden	"from my house"
denizin	"of an ocean"	denizimde	"in my ocean"
eve	"to a house"	elde	"in a hand"

    a.   What is the Turkish morpheme meaning "to"?

    b.   What kind of affixes in Turkish correspond to English prepositions (e.g., prefixes, suffixes, infixes, free morphemes)?

    c.   What would the Turkish word for "from an ocean" be?

    d.   How many morphemes are there in the Turkish word *denizimde?*

16. The following are some verb forms in Chickasaw, a member of the Muskogean family of languages spoken in south-central Oklahoma. Chickasaw is an endangered language. Currently, there are only about 100 speakers of Chickasaw, most of whom are over seventy years old. (The Chickasaw examples are provided by Pamela Munro.)

Sachaaha	"I am tall."
Chaaha	"He/she is tall."
Chichaaha	"You are tall."
Hoochaaha	"They are tall."
Satikahbi	"I am tired."
Chitikahbitok	"You were tired."
Chichchokwa	"You are cold."
Hopobatok	"He was hungry."
Hoohopobatok	"They were hungry."
Sahopoba	"I am hungry."

    a.   What is the root morpheme for the following verbs?

       (1) "to be tall"

       (2) "to be hungry"

    b.   What is the morpheme meaning:

       (1) past tense

       (2) "I"

       (3) "You"

       (4) "He/she"

    c.   If the Chickasaw root for "to be old" is *sipokni,* how would you say:

       (1) "You are old"

       (2) "He was old"

       (3) "They are old"

References

Algeo, J. (Ed.). (1991). *Fifty years among the new words: A dictionary of neologisms, 1941–1991.* Cambridge, UK: Cambridge University Press.

Avis, W. (Ed.). (1967). *Dictionary of Canadianisms on historical principles.* Toronto: W.J. Gage.

Baker, M. (2001). Polysynthetic languages. In R.A. Wilson & F.C. Keil (Eds.), *The MIT Encyclopedia of the Cognitive Sciences* (pp. 654–656). Cambridge, MA: MIT Press.

Chomsky, N. (1972). *Language and mind.* New York: Harcourt Brace Jovanovich.

Espy, W.R. (1978). *O thou improper, thou uncommon noun: An etymology of words that once were names.* New York: Clarkson N. Potter.

Geisel, T.S. (Dr. Seuss). (1965). *Fox in socks.* New York: Random House.

Greene, A. (1969). *Pullet surprises.* Glenview, IL: Scott, Foresman.

Landau, S.I. (1984). *Dictionaries: The art and craft of lexicography.* Cambridge, UK: Cambridge University Press.

Murray, J.A.H. (1970). *The evolution of English lexicography.* The Romanes lecture 1900. College Park, MD: McGrath.

Murray, J.A.H., et al. (Eds.). (1989). *Oxford English dictionary: A new English dictionary on historical principles, founded mainly on the materials collected by the philological society.* 1888–1933 (2nd ed.). Oxford: Oxford University Press.

Sturtevant, E.H. (1947). *An introduction to linguistic science.* New Haven: Yale University Press.

Thompson, S.A. (1975). On the issue of productivity in the lexikon. *Kritikon Litterrarum 4*, 332–349.

Tulloch, S. (Ed.). (1991). *The Oxford dictionary of new words: A popular guide to words in the news.* Oxford: Oxford University Press.

Van Rooten, L. (Ed.). (1993). *Mots d'heures: gousses, rames. The d'Antin manuscript.* London: Grafton.

Further Reading

Anderson, S.R. (1992). *A-morphous morphology.* Cambridge, UK: Cambridge University Press.

Aronoff, M. (1976). *Word formation in generative grammar.* Cambridge, MA: MIT Press.

Aronoff, M., & Fuderman, K. (2004). *What is morphology?* Malden, MA: Blackwell.

Bauer, L. (1983). *English word-formation.* New York: Cambridge University Press.

Bauer, L. (2003). *Introducing linguistic morphology* (2nd ed.). Washington, DC,: Georgetown University Press.

Bauer, L. (2004). *A glossary of morphology.* Edinburgh: Edinburgh University Press.

Booij, G. (2007). *The grammar of words: An introduction to linguistic morphology* (2nd ed.). New York: Oxford University Press.

Hammond, M., & Noonan, M. (Eds.). (1988). *Theoretical morphology: Approaches in modern linguistics.* San Diego: Academic Press.

Jensen, J.T. (1990). *Morphology: Word structure in generative grammar.* Amsterdam/Philadelphia: John Benjamins.

Marchand, H. (1969). *The categories and types of present-day English word-formation* (2nd ed.). Munich: C.H. Beck'sche Verlagsbuchhandlung.

Matthews, P.H. (1976). *Morphology: An introduction to the theory of word structure.* Cambridge, UK: Cambridge University Press.

Scalise, S. (1984). *Generative morphology* (2nd ed.). Dordrecht, The Netherlands: Foris.

Spencer, A. (1991). *Morphological theory: An introduction to word structure in generative grammar.* London: Basil Blackwell.

Winchester, S. (1999). *The professor and the madman.* New York: HarperCollins.

Websites

http://www2.hawaii.edu/~bender/paradox.html A website by Byron Bender, of the University of Hawai'i, on morphological paradoxes.

http://www.facstaff.bucknell.edu/rbeard/ A website by Robert Beard, of Bucknell University, on morphology (Lexeme-Morpheme Base Morphology, or LMBM).

CHAPTER 3
Syntax: The Sentence Patterns of Language

Grammar is what gives sense to language.... Sentences make words yield up their meaning. Sentences actively create sense in language. And the business of the study of sentences is grammar.

David Crystal, British linguist

Like everything metaphysical the harmony between thought and reality is to be found in the grammar of the language.

Ludwig Wittgenstein, *Philosophical Investigations* (1953)

"We get a lot of foreign visitors."

Any speaker of a human language can produce and understand an infinite number of sentences. We can show this quite easily through examples such as the following:

> The long Canadian winter drew to an end.
> The long, cold Canadian winter drew to an end.
> The long, cold, icy Canadian winter drew to an end.
>
> .
> .
> .
>
> The hikers climbed mountains in British Columbia.
> The hikers climbed mountains in British Columbia and Alberta.
> The hikers climbed mountains in British Columbia, Alberta, and Quebec.
>
> .
> .
> .
>
> The cat chased the mouse.
> The cat chased the mouse that ate the cheese.
> The cat chased the mouse that ate the cheese that came from the cow.
> The cat chased the mouse that ate the cheese that came from the cow that grazed in the field.

In each case the speaker could continue creating sentences by adding an adjective, or a noun connected by *and*, or a relative clause. In principle this could go on forever. All languages have mechanisms such as these — modification, coordination, and clause insertion — that make the number of sentences limitless. Obviously, the sentences of a language cannot be stored in a dictionary format in our heads. Sentences are composed of discrete units that are combined by rules. This system of rules explains how speakers can store infinite knowledge in a finite space — our brains.

The part of the grammar that represents a speaker's knowledge of sentences and their structures is called **syntax**. The aim of this chapter is to show you what syntactic structure is and what the rules that determine syntactic structure are like. Most of the examples will be from the syntax of English, but the principles that account for syntactic structures are universal.

Part of what we mean by *structure* is word order. The meaning of a sentence depends largely on the order in which words occur in a sentence. Thus,

> She has what a man wants.

does not have the same meaning as

> She wants what a man has.

Sometimes, however, a change of word order has no effect on meaning.

> The Governor General swore in the new Canadian citizens.
> The Governor General swore the new Canadian citizens in.

The grammars of all languages include **rules of syntax** that reflect speakers' knowledge of these facts.

Grammatical or Ungrammatical?

Grammar, which knows how to control even kings ...
J.B. Moliére, *Les Femmes Savantes* (1672, Act II, sc. vi)

Although the following sequence consists of meaningful words, the entire expression is without meaning because it does not comply with the syntactic rules of the grammar.

Governor swore citizens the General the in new Canadian.

In English and in every language, every sentence is a sequence of words, but not every sequence of words is a sentence. Sequences of words that conform to the rules of syntax are **well formed** or grammatical, and those that violate the syntactic rules are **ill formed** or ungrammatical.

What Grammaticality Is Based On

In Chapter 1 you were asked to indicate strings of words as grammatical or ungrammatical according to your linguistic intuitions. Here is another list of word sequences. Disregarding the sentence meanings, use *your* knowledge of English and place an asterisk in front of the ones that strike you as peculiar or funny in some way.

1. (a) The boy found the ball
   (b) The boy found quickly
   (c) The boy found in the house
   (d) The boy found the ball in the house
2. (e) Disa slept the baby
   (f) Disa slept soundly
3. (g) Zack believes Robert to be a gentleman
   (h) Zack believes to be a gentleman
   (i) Zack tries Robert to be a gentleman
   (j) Zack tries to be a gentleman
   (k) Zack wants to be a gentleman
   (l) Zack wants Robert to be a gentleman
4. (m) Jack and Jill ran up the hill
   (n) Jack and Jill ran up the bill
   (o) Jack and Jill ran the hill up
   (p) Jack and Jill ran the bill up
   (q) Up the hill ran Jack and Jill
   (r) Up the bill ran Jack and Jill

We predict that speakers of English will "star" (b), (c), (e), (h), (i), (o), and (r). If we are right, this shows that grammaticality judgments are neither idiosyncratic nor capricious, but are determined by rules that are shared by the speakers of a language.

The syntactic rules that account for the ability to make these judgments include other constraints in addition to rules of word order. For example:

- The rules specify that *found* must be followed directly by an expression like *the ball* but not by *quickly* or *in the house* as illustrated in (a) through (d).
- The verb *sleep* patterns differently than *find* in that it may be followed solely by a word like *soundly* but not by other kinds of phrases such as *the baby* as shown in (e) and (f).
- Examples (g) through (l) show that *believe* and *try* function in opposite fashion while *want* exhibits yet a third pattern.
- Finally, the word-order rules that constrain phrases such as *run up the hill* differ from those concerning *run up the bill* as seen in (m) through (r).

Sentences are not random strings of words. Some strings of words that we can interpret are not sentences. For example, we can understand example (o) even though we recognize it as ungrammatical. We can fix it up to make it grammatical. To be a sentence, words must conform to specific patterns determined by the syntactic rules of the language.

What Grammaticality Is Not Based On

> *Colorless green ideas sleep furiously.* This is a very interesting sentence, because it shows that syntax can be separated from semantics — that form can be separated from meaning. The sentence doesn't seem to mean anything coherent, but it sounds like an English sentence.
>
> Howard Lasnik, *The Human Language* (1995)

The ability to make grammaticality judgments does not depend on having heard the sentence before. You may never have heard or read the sentence

> Enormous crickets in pink socks danced at the prom.

but your syntactic knowledge tells you that it is grammatical.

Grammaticality judgments do not depend on whether the sentence is meaningful or not, as shown by the following sentences:

> Colourless green ideas sleep furiously.
> A verb crumpled the milk.

Although these sentences do not make much sense, they are syntactically well formed. They sound "funny," but they differ in their "funniness" from the following strings of words:

*Furiously sleep ideas green colourless.
*Milk the crumpled verb a.

You may understand ungrammatical sequences even though you know they are not well formed. Most English speakers could interpret

*The boy quickly in the house the ball found.

although they know that the word order is irregular. On the other hand, grammatical sentences may be uninterpretable if they include nonsense strings, that is, words with no agreed-on meaning, as shown by the first two lines of "Jabberwocky" by Lewis Carroll:

'Twas brillig, and the slithy toves
Did gyre and gimble in the wabe;

Such nonsense poetry is amusing because the sentences comply with syntactic rules and sound like good English. Ungrammatical strings of nonsense words are not entertaining:

*Toves slithy the and brillig 'twas
wabe the in gimble and gyre did.

Grammaticality does not depend on the truth of sentences. If it did, lying would be impossible. Nor does it depend on whether real objects are being discussed, nor on whether something is possible. Untrue sentences can be grammatical, sentences discussing unicorns can be grammatical, and sentences referring to pregnant fathers can be grammatical.

Our unconscious knowledge of the syntactic rules of grammar permits us to make grammaticality judgments. These rules are not the prescriptive rules that are taught in school. Children develop the rules of grammar long before they attend school, as is discussed in Chapter 7.

What Else Do You Know about Syntax?

Syntax, my lad. It has been restored to the highest place in the republic.

John Steinback (American writer, when asked his reaction to John F. Kennedy's inaugural address)

© TUMBLEWEEDS comic (c) 2009 Tom K. Ryan

Syntactic knowledge goes beyond being able to decide which strings are grammatical and which are not. It accounts for the multiple meanings, or **ambiguity**, of expressions like *synthetic buffalo hides* in the Tumbleweeds cartoon, which can mean "buffalo hides that are synthetic," or "hides of synthetic buffalo."

This example illustrates that within a phrase, certain words are grouped together. Sentences have **hierarchical structure** as well as word order. The words in the phrase *synthetic buffalo hides* can be grouped in two ways. When we group like this:

synthetic (buffalo hides)

we get the first meaning. When we group like this:

(synthetic buffalo) hides

we get the second meaning.

The rules of syntax allow both these groupings, which is why the expression is ambiguous. The following diagrams illustrate the two structures:

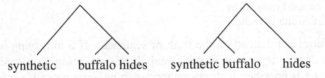

This is similar to the rules of morphology that allow multiple structures for words such as *unlockable,* as we saw in Chapter 2.

Many sentences exhibit such ambiguities, often leading to humorous results. Consider the following two sentences, which appeared in classified ads:

For sale: an antique desk suitable for lady with thick legs and large drawers.

We will oil your sewing machine and adjust tension in your home for $10.00.

In the first ad, the humorous reading comes from the grouping . . . (*for lady with thick legs and large drawers*) as opposed to the intended . . . (*for lady*) (*with thick legs and large drawers*) where the legs and drawers belong to the desk. The second case is similar.

Because these ambiguities are a result of different structures, they are instances of **structural ambiguity**.

Contrast these sentences with

This will make you smart.

The two interpretations of this sentence are due to the two meanings of *smart* — "clever" or "burning sensation." Such lexical or word-meaning ambiguities, as opposed to structural ambiguities, will be discussed in Chapter 4.

Syntactic knowledge also enables us to determine the **grammatical relations** in a sentence, such as **subject** and **direct object**, and how they are to be understood. Consider the following sentences:

1. Mary hired Bill.
2. Bill hired Mary.
3. Bill was hired by Mary.

In (1) *Mary* is the subject and is understood to be the employer who did the hiring. *Bill* is the direct object and is understood to be the employee. In (2) *Bill* is the subject and *Mary* is the direct object, and as we would expect, the meaning changes so that we understand Bill to be Mary's employer. In (3) the grammatical relationships are the same as in (2), but we understand it to have the same meaning as (1), despite the structural differences between (1) and (3).

Syntactic rules reveal the grammatical relations among the words of a sentence and tell us when structural differences result in meaning differences and when they do not. Moreover, the syntactic rules permit speakers to produce and understand a limitless number of sentences never produced or heard before — the creative aspect of language use.

Thus, the syntactic rules in a grammar account for at least:

1. The grammaticality of sentences
2. Word order
3. Hierarchical organization of sentences
4. Grammatical relations such as subject and object
5. Whether different structures have differing meanings or the same meaning
6. The creative aspect of language

A major goal of linguistics is to show clearly and explicitly how syntactic rules account for this knowledge. A theory of grammar must provide a complete characterization of what speakers implicitly know about their language.

Sentence Structure

> I really do not know that anything has ever been more exciting than diagramming sentences.

> Gertrude Stein, "Poetry and Grammar" (1935)

Syntactic rules determine the order of words in a sentence, and how the words are grouped. The words in the sentence

The child found the puppy.

may be grouped into (*the child*) and (*found the puppy*), corresponding to the subject and predicate of the sentence. A further division gives (*the child*) ((*found*)(*the puppy*)), and finally the individual words: ((*the*)(*child*)) ((*found*)((*the*) (*puppy*))). It is easier to see the parts and subparts of the sentence in a **tree diagram**:

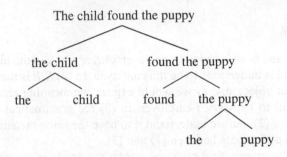

The "tree" is upside down with its "root" being the entire sentence, *The child found the puppy,* and its "leaves" being the individual words, *the, child, found, the, puppy.* The tree conveys the same information as the nested parentheses, but more clearly. The groupings and subgroupings reflect the hierarchical structure of the tree.

The tree diagram shows among other things that the phrase *found the puppy* divides naturally into two branches, one for the verb *found* and the other for the direct object *the puppy.* A different division, say *found the* and *puppy,* is unnatural.

The natural groupings of a sentence are called **constituents**. Various linguistic tests reveal the constituents of a sentence. For example, the set of words that can be used to answer a question is a constituent. So in answer to the question "what did you find?" a speaker might answer, *the puppy,* but not *found the.*

Pronouns can also substitute for natural groups. In answer to the question "where did you find the puppy?" a speaker can say, "I found *him* in the park." There are also words such as *do* that can take the place of the entire expression *found the puppy,* as in "John found the puppy and so *did* Bill," or "John found the puppy and Bill *did* too."

Constituents can also be "relocated" as in the following examples:

> It was *the puppy* the child found.
> *The puppy* was found by the child.

In the first example the constituent *the puppy* is relocated; in the second example both *the puppy* and *the child* are relocated. In all such rearrangements the constituents *the puppy* and *the child* remain intact. *Found the* does not remain intact, because it is not a constituent.

In the sentence *the child found the puppy,* the natural groupings or constituents are the subject *the child,* the predicate *found the puppy,* and the direct object *the puppy.*

Some verbs take a direct object and a prepositional phrase.

The child put the puppy in the garden.

We can use our tests to show that *in the garden* is also a constituent, as follows:

1. Where did the child put the puppy?   *In the garden.*
2. The child put the puppy *there.*
3. *In the garden* is where the child put the puppy.
4. It was *in the garden* that the child put the puppy.

In (1) *in the garden* is an answer to a question. In (2) the word *there* can substitute for the phrase *in the garden.* In (3) and (4) *in the garden* has been relocated.

Our knowledge of the **constituent structure** may be graphically represented as a tree structure. The tree structure for the sentence *The child put the puppy in the garden* is as follows:

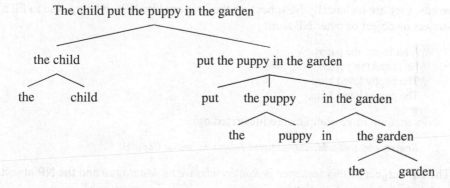

Every sentence in a language is associated with one or more constituent structures. If a sentence has more than one constituent structure, it is ambiguous, and each tree will correspond to one of the possible meanings. Multiple tree structures can account for structural ambiguity, as in the following examples:

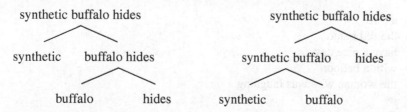

Syntactic Categories

Each grouping in the tree diagram of *The child put the puppy in the garden* is a member of a large family of similar expressions. For example, *the child* belongs to a family that includes *the police officer, your neighbour, this yellow cat, he,* and countless others. We can substitute any member of this family for *the child* without affecting the grammaticality of the sentence, although the meaning of course would change.

> A police officer found the puppy in the garden.
> Your neighbour found the puppy in the garden.
> This yellow cat found the puppy in the garden.

A family of expressions that can substitute for one another without loss of grammaticality is called a **syntactic category**.

The child, a police officer, and so on belong to the syntactic category **noun phrase (NP),** one of several syntactic categories in English and every other language in the world. NPs may function as the subject or as an object in a sentence. They often contain some form of a noun or proper noun, but may consist of a pronoun alone, or even contain a clause or a sentence.

Even though a proper noun like *John* and pronouns such as *he* and *him* are single words, they are technically NPs, because they pattern like NPs in being able to fill a subject or object or other NP slot.

> John found the puppy.
> He found the puppy.
> The puppy loved him.
> The puppy loved John.

NPs that are more complex are illustrated by:

> *Romeo who was a Montague* loved *Juliet who was a Capulet.*

The NP subject of this sentence is *Romeo who was a Montague* and the NP object is *Juliet who was a Capulet.*

Part of the syntactic component of a grammar is the specification of the syntactic categories in the language, since this constitutes part of a speaker's knowledge. That is, speakers of English know that only items (a), (b), (e), (f), (g), and (i) in the following list are noun phrases even if they have never heard the term before.

1. (a) a bird
   (b) the red banjo
   (c) have a nice day
   (d) with a balloon
   (e) the woman who was laughing
   (f) it
   (g) John
   (h) went
   (i) that the earth is round

As we discussed earlier, you can test this claim by inserting each expression into three contexts: for example, "Who discovered _____ ?", "_____ was heard by everyone," and "What I heard was _____." Only those sentences into which NPs can be inserted are grammatical, because only NPs can function as subjects and objects.

There are other syntactic categories. The expression *found the puppy* is a **verb phrase (VP)**. Verb phrases always contain a **verb (V)** and they may contain other categories, such as a noun phrase or **prepositional phrase (PP)**, which is a preposition followed by a noun phrase. In (2) the VPs are those phrases that can complete the sentence "The child _____."

2. (a) saw a clown
   (b) a bird
   (c) slept
   (d) smart
   (e) is smart
   (f) found the cake
   (g) found the cake in the cupboard
   (h) realized that the earth was round

Inserting (a), (c), (e), (f), (g), and (h) will produce grammatical sentences, whereas the insertion of (b) or (d) would result in an ungrammatical string. Thus, in list 2 (a), (c), (e), (f), (g), and (h) are verb phrases.

Other syntactic categories are **sentence (S)**, **adjective phrase (AP)**, **determiner (Det)**, **adjective (Adj)**, **noun (N)**, **preposition (P)**, **adverb (Adv)**, and **auxiliary verb (Aux)**, but this is not a complete list. Some of these syntactic categories have traditionally been called "parts of speech." All languages have such syntactic categories. In fact, categories such as noun, verb, and noun phrase are present in the grammars of all human languages. Speakers know the syntactic categories of their language, even if they do not know the technical terms. Our knowledge of the syntactic classes is revealed when we substitute equivalent phrases, as we just did in examples (1) and (2), and when we use the various syntactic tests just discussed.

In addition to syntactic tests, there is experimental evidence for constituent structure. In these experiments subjects listen to sentences that have clicking noises inserted into them at random points. In some cases the click occurs at a constituent boundary, for example, between the subject NP and the VP. In other sentences, the click is inserted in the middle of a constituent, for example, between a determiner and an NP. The subjects are then asked to report where the click occurred. There were two important results: First, subjects noticed the click and recalled its location best when it occurred at a constituent boundary. Second, clicks that occurred inside the constituent were reported to have occurred between constituents. In other words, subjects displaced the clicks and put them at constituent boundaries. These results show that speakers perceive sentences in chunks corresponding to grammatical constituents. This argues for the psychological reality of constituent structure (Fodor & Bever, 1965).

> Constituent structure reflects the speaker's mental representation of sentences.

Phrase Structure Trees

Who climbs the Grammar-Tree distinctly knows
Where Noun and Verb and Participle grows.

John Dryden, "The Sixth Satyr of Juvenal" (1693)

The following tree diagram provides labels for each of the constituents of the sentence *The child put the puppy in the garden*. These labels show that the entire sentence belongs to the syntactic category of Sentence, that *the child* and *the puppy* are noun phrases, that *put the puppy* is a verb phrase, that *in the garden* is a prepositional phrase, and so on.

A tree diagram with syntactic category information is called a **phrase structure tree**, sometimes called a **constituent structure tree**. This tree shows that a sentence is both a linear string of words and a hierarchical structure with phrases nested in phrases. Phrase structure trees are graphic representations of a speaker's knowledge of the sentence structure in her language.

Three aspects of a speaker's syntactic knowledge are represented in phrase structure trees:

1. The linear order of the words in the sentence
2. The groupings of words into syntactic categories
3. The hierarchical structure of the syntactic categories (e.g., a sentence is composed of a noun phrase followed by a verb phrase, a verb phrase is composed of a verb that may be followed by a noun phrase, and so on)

A phrase structure tree that explicitly reveals these properties can represent every sentence of English and of every human language. Notice, however, that the phrase structure tree above is correct, but redundant. The word *child* is repeated three times in the tree, *puppy* is repeated three times, and so on. We can streamline the tree by writing the words only once at the bottom of the diagram. Only the syntactic categories to which the words belong need to remain at the higher levels.

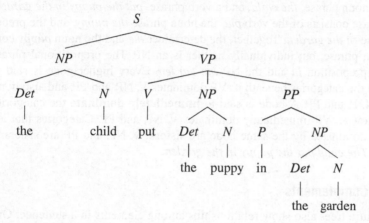

No information is lost in this simplified version. The syntactic category of each word appears immediately above it. In this way, *the* is shown to be a determiner, *child* a noun, and so on. (The category *determiner* includes the **articles** *the* and *a* as well as a number of expressions such as *these, every, five, my, your cousin Mabel's,* and so forth.) In Chapter 2 we discussed the fact that the syntactic category of each word is listed in our mental dictionaries. We now see how this information is used by the syntax of the language. Words occur in trees under labels that correspond to their syntactic category. Nouns are under N, prepositions under P, and so on.

We have not given definitions of these syntactic categories. Traditional definitions usually refer to meaning and are either imprecise or wrong. For example, a noun is often defined as "a person, place, or thing." However, in the sentence *Seeing is believing, seeing* and *believing* are nouns but are neither persons, nor places, nor things. Syntactic categories are better defined in terms of the syntactic rules of the grammar. For example, defining a noun as "the head of an NP," or "a grammatical unit that occurs with a determiner," or "can be relocated in passive sentences" is a more accurate characterization.

The larger syntactic categories, such as verb phrase, are identified as consisting of all the syntactic categories and words below that point, or **node**, in the tree. The VP in the above phrase structure tree consists of syntactic category nodes V, NP, and PP, and the words *put, the, puppy, in, the,* and *garden.* Since *the puppy* can be traced up the tree to the node NP, this constituent is a noun phrase. Since *in the garden* can be traced up the tree to a PP, this constituent is a prepositional phrase. The phrase structure tree reflects the speaker's intuitions about the natural groupings of words in a sentence.

The phrase structure tree also states implicitly what combinations of words are not syntactic categories. For example, since there is no node above the words *put* and *the* to connect them, the two words do not constitute a syntactic category, reflecting our earlier judgments.

The phrase structure tree also shows that some syntactic categories are composed of other syntactic categories. The sentence *The child put the puppy in the garden* consists of a noun phrase, *the child*, and a verb phrase, *put the puppy in the garden*. The verb phrase consists of the verb *put*, the noun phrase *the puppy*, and the prepositional phrase *in the garden*. Together, the determiner *the* and the noun *puppy* constitute a noun phrase, but individually neither is an NP. The prepositional phrase contains the preposition *in* and the NP *the garden*. Every higher node is said to **dominate** all the categories beneath it. VP dominates V, NP, and PP, and also dominates Det, N, P, and PP. A node is said to **immediately dominate** the categories one level below it. VP immediately dominates V, NP, and PP. Categories that are immediately dominated by the same node are **sisters**. V, NP, and PP are sisters in the sentence *The child put the puppy in the garden*.

Heads and Complements

Phrase structure trees also show relationships among elements in a sentence. One kind of relationship is the relationship between the **head** of a phrase and the other members of the phrase. We said earlier that every VP contains a verb. The verb is the head of the VP. The VP may also contain other categories, such as a noun phrase or prepositional phrase. Loosely speaking, the entire phrase refers to whatever the head verb refers to. For example, the verb phrase *put the puppy in the garden* refers to the event of "putting." The other constituents contained in the VP that complete its meaning and are essential to its interpretation are called **complements**. The direct object *the puppy* is a complement, as is the PP *in the garden*. A sentence can also be a complement to a verb, as in the sentence *I thought that the child found the puppy*.

Every phrasal category has a head of its same syntactic type. NPs are headed by nouns, PPs are headed by prepositions, adjective phrases (APs) are headed by adjectives, and so on; and every category can have complements. In the sentence *The road to Banff stretched ahead*, the PP *to Banff* is the complement to the head noun *road*. Other examples of NP complements are shown in the following examples:

> The destruction of Rome
> A picture of Mary
> The question whether euthanasia is ethical

Each of these examples is an NP containing a head noun followed by a PP (*of Rome, of Mary*), or a sentence complement (*whether euthanasia is ethical*). The head–complement relation is universal. All languages have phrases that are headed and that contain complements.

However, the order of the two constituents may differ in different languages. In English, for example, we see that the head comes first, followed by the complement. English is an SVO (subject–verb–object) language; the verb precedes its object in the VP. In the preceding examples, the noun *picture* precedes its PP complement *of Mary, destruction* comes before *of Rome,* and *question* before *whether euthanasia is ethical.* In Japanese, on the other hand, complements precede the head, as shown in the following examples:

Taro-ga	inu-o	mituketa		
Taro	dog	found		(Taro found a dog)
Taro-ga	inu-o	isu-ni	oita	
Taro	dog	chair	put	(Taro put the dog on the chair)

In the first sentence, the direct object *dog* precedes the verb *found.* In the second, both objects *dog* and *chair* precede the verb.

Selection

Whether a verb takes one or more complements depends on the properties of the verb. For example, the verb *find* is a **transitive verb**. A transitive verb requires a noun phrase direct object complement. This additional specification, called **selection**, is included in the lexical entry of each word.

> The boy found the ball.
> *The boy found quickly.
> *The boy found in the house.

The examples where *found* does not have a direct object are not grammatical. Verbs select different kinds of complements, and the complements they select must be present. The verb *put* occurs with both an NP and a PP, and cannot occur with either alone:

> Sam put the milk in the refrigerator.
> *Sam put the milk.
> *Disa put in the refrigerator.
> (But note that the phrasal verb *put in* with the sense of "to install" would be grammatical.)

Sleep is an **intransitive verb**; it cannot take an NP complement. Thus, if a verb fails to select a complement, it must not be present.

> Michael slept.
> *Michael slept a fish.

Complements can be distinguished from *adjuncts*. When an additional, omissible element is added as a modifier, it is considered to be an adjunct. In the following sentences, the italicized PPs are adjuncts — they are not selected by the verb and are not essential for interpretation of the verb's meaning:

Michael slept *last night*.
Michael slept *on the floor*.

Some verbs such as *think* select a sentence as complement. Other verbs such as *tell* select an NP and an S, while *feel* selects an AP or an S:

I think that Sam won the race.
I told Sam that Michael was on his bicycle.
They felt strong as oxen.
They feel that they can win.
*They feel

Other categories besides verbs also select their complements. For example, the noun *belief* selects either a PP or an S, as shown by the following two examples:

the belief in freedom of speech
the belief that freedom of speech is a basic right

The noun *sympathy,* however, selects a PP, but not an S:

their sympathy for the victims
*their sympathy that the victims are so poor

The adjective *tired* selects a PP:

tired of stale sandwiches

Some selectional properties are optional. For example, the nouns *belief* and *sympathy* can also appear without complements, as can the adjective *tired:*

John has many beliefs.
The people showed their sympathy.
The students were tired.

In addition, many verbs such as *eat* are optionally transitive:

John ate a sandwich.
John eats regularly.

The information about whether a complement is optional or obligatory is contained in the lexical entry of particular words.

The well-formedness of a phrase depends on at least two factors: whether the phrase conforms to the phrase structure requirements of the language, and whether the phrase conforms to the selectional requirements of the head.

What Heads the Sentence?

We said earlier that all phrases have heads. One category that we have not yet discussed in this regard is sentence (S). For uniformity's sake, we want all the categories to be headed, but what would the head of S be? To answer this question, let us consider sentences such as the following:

> Sam will kick the ball.
> Sam has kicked the ball.
> Sam is kicking the ball.
> Sam may kick the ball.

Words like *will, have, is,* and *may* are in a class of auxiliary verbs (Aux), which includes *might, would, could, can,* and several others. The auxiliaries other than *be* and *have* are also referred to as **modals**. Auxiliaries are function words, as discussed in Chapter 2. They occur in structures such as the following:

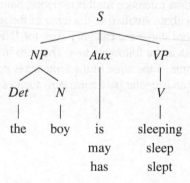

Auxiliary verbs specify a time frame for the sentence, whether the situation described by the sentence will take place, already took place, or is taking place now. A modal such as *may* contains "possibility" as part of its meaning, and says it is possible that the situation will occur at some future time. The category Aux is a natural category to head S. Just as the VP is about the event described by the verb — *eat ice cream* is about "eating" — so a sentence is about a situation or state of affairs that occurs at some point in time.

To express the idea that Aux is the head of S, the symbols **INFL** (= inflection) and **IP** (= inflection phrase) are often used instead of Aux and S, as in the following phrase structure tree:

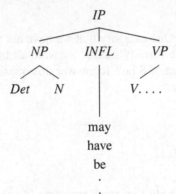

We will continue to use the symbols S and Aux, but you should think of Aux and S as having the same relationship to each other as V and VP, N and NP, and so on.

Not all sentences have auxiliaries. For example, the sentence *Sam kicked the ball* has no modal, *have* or *be*. There is, however, a time reference for this sentence, namely, the past tense of the verb *kicked*. In sentences without auxiliaries, the tense of the sentence is its head. Instead of having a function word under the category Aux (or INFL), we have a tense specification, *present* or *past,* as in the following tree. The verb in the VP must agree with the tense in Aux. For example, if the tense of the sentence is *past* then the verb must have an *-ed* affix (or must be an irregular past-tense verb such as *ate*).

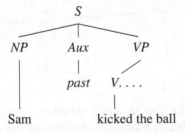

A property of English and many languages is that the head of S may contain only an abstract tense specification and no actual word as is the case for English past tense. But for English future tense, the word *will* occurs as the Aux. The word *do* is a tense-bearing word that is found in negative sentences such as *John did not go* and questions such as *Where did John go?* In these sentences *did* means "past tense."

In addition to specifying the time reference of the sentence, Aux specifies the agreement features of the subject. For example, if the subject is "we," Aux contains the features first-person plural; if the subject is "he" or "she," Aux contains the features third-person singular. Thus, another function of the syntactic rules is to use Aux as a "matchmaker" between the subject and the verb. When the subject and the verb bear the same features, Aux makes a match; when they have incompatible features, Aux cannot make a match and the sentence is ungrammatical. This matchmaker function of syntactic rules is more obvious in languages such as Italian, which have many different agreement morphemes, as discussed in Chapter 2. Consider the Italian sentence for "I go to school."

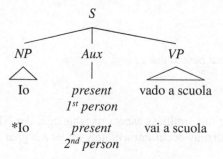

The verb *vado* "go" in the first sentence bears the first-person singular morpheme, *-o,* which matches the agreement feature in Aux, which in turn matches the subject *Io* "I." Hence, the sentence is grammatical. In the second sentence, there is a mismatch between the first-person subject and the second-person features in Aux (and on the verb), and so the sentence is ungrammatical.

The Infinity of Language

> So, naturalists observe, a flea
> Hath smaller fleas that on him prey;
> And these have smaller fleas still to bite 'em,
> And so proceed ad infinitum.
>   Jonathan Swift, "On Poetry, A Rhapsody" (1733)

As we noted earlier, the number of sentences in a language is infinite, because speakers can lengthen any sentence by various means, such as adding an adjective or including sentences within sentences. Even children know how to produce and understand very long sentences, and know how to make them even longer, as illustrated by the children's rhyme about the house that Jack built.

> This is the farmer sowing the corn,
>   that kept the cock that crowed in the morn,
>   that waked the priest all shaven and shorn,
>   that married the man all tattered and torn,
>   that kissed the maiden all forlorn,
>   that milked the cow with the crumpled horn,
>   that tossed the dog,
>   that worried the cat,
>   that killed the rat,
>   that ate the malt,
>   that lay in the house that Jack built.

The child begins the rhyme with *This is the house that Jack built,* continues by lengthening it to *This is the malt that lay in the house that Jack built,* and so on.

You can add any of the following to the beginning of the rhyme and still have a grammatical sentence:

> I think that . . .
> What is the name of the unicorn that noticed that . . .
> Ask someone if . . .
> Do you know whether . . .

Phrase structure trees also capture this limitless aspect of language. An NP may appear immediately under a PP, which may occur immediately under a higher NP, as in *the man with the telescope:*

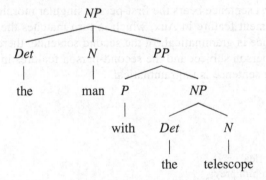

The complex (but comprehensible) noun phrase *the girl with the feather on the ribbon on the brim,* as shown in the following phrase structure tree, illustrates that one can repeat the number of NPs under PPs under NPs without a limit.

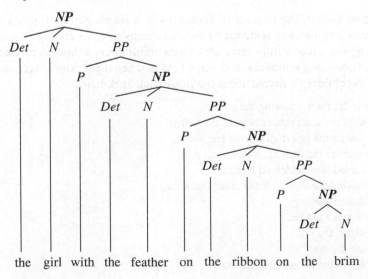

The NP diagrammed above, though cumbersome, violates no rules of syntax and is a grammatical noun phrase. Moreover, it can be made even longer by expanding the final NP — *the brim* — by adding a PP — *of her hat* — to derive the longer phrase — *the girl with the feather on the ribbon on the brim of her hat.*

The repetition of categories within categories is common in all languages. It allows speakers to use the same syntactic categories several times, with different functions, in the same sentence. Our brain capacity is finite, able to store only a finite number of categories and rules for their combination. Yet, these finite means place an infinite set of sentences at our disposal.

This linguistic property also illustrates the difference between competence and performance discussed in Chapter 1. All speakers of English have as part of their linguistic competence — their mental grammars — the ability to put NPs in PPs in NPs ad infinitum. However, as the structures grow longer they become increasingly more difficult to produce and understand. This could be due to short-term memory limitations, muscular fatigue, breathlessness, or any number of performance factors. (We will discuss performance factors more fully in Chapter 9.)

Thus, while such rules give a speaker access to infinitely many sentences, no speaker utters or hears an infinite number in a lifetime, nor is any sentence of infinite length, although in principle there is no upper limit on sentence length. This property of grammars also accounts for the creative aspect of language use, since it permits speakers to produce and understand sentences never spoken before.

Phrase Structure Rules

> Everyone who is master of the language he speaks . . . may form new . . . phrases, provided they coincide with the genius of the language.
>
> Michaelis, *Dissertation* (1769)

A phrase structure tree is a formal device for representing the knowledge that a speaker has of the structure of sentences in his language. When we speak, we are not aware that we are producing sentences with such structures, but controlled experiments show that we use them in speech production and comprehension, as we will see in Chapter 9.

When we look at phrase structure trees that represent the sentences of English, certain patterns emerge. In ordinary sentences, the S always subdivides into NP Aux VP. As we said earlier, NPs always contain nouns; VPs always contain verbs; PPs consist of a preposition followed by a noun phrase, the **prepositional object**; and APs consist of an adjective possibly followed by a complement.

Of all logically possible tree structures, few actually occur, just as not all word combinations constitute grammatical phrases or sentences. For example, a non-occurring tree structure in English is:

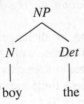

The speaker of a language knows whether any sentence or phrase is a possible or impossible structure in her language. The structure given in the preceding tree is not possible in English.

Just as a speaker cannot have an infinite list of sentences in her head, so she cannot have an infinite set of phrase structure trees in her head. Rather, a speaker's knowledge of the permissible and impermissible structures must exist as a finite set of rules that "generate," or provide a tree for, any sentence in the language. These are **phrase structure rules**. Phrase structure rules specify the structures of a language precisely and concisely. They express the regularities of the language, such as the head complement order, and other relationships.

For example, in English a noun phrase may simply contain a determiner followed by a noun. One of the several allowable NP subtrees looks like this:

The phrase structure rule that makes this explicit is:

NP → Det N

This rule conveys two facts:

1. A noun phrase can contain a determiner followed by a noun.
2. A determiner followed by a noun is a noun phrase.

To the left of the arrow is the category whose components appear on the right side. The right side of the arrow also shows the linear order of these components. Phrase structure rules make explicit speakers' knowledge of the order of words and the grouping of words into syntactic categories.

An NP may also contain a complement, as in the example *a picture of Mary* or *the destruction of Rome*. We can accommodate this fact by revising the rule to include an optional prepositional phrase. The parentheses around the PP indicate that it is optional. Not all NPs in the language have PPs inside them.

NP → Det N (PP)

This revised rule says that an NP can contain a determiner followed by a noun followed by an optional PP.

The phrase structure trees of the previous section show that the following phrase structure rules are also part of the grammar of English.

1. VP → V NP
2. VP → V NP PP

Rule 1 states that a verb phrase can consist of a verb followed by a noun phrase. Rule 2 states that a verb phrase can also consist of a verb followed by a noun phrase followed by a prepositional phrase. These rules are general statements, which do not refer to any specific verb phrase, verb, noun phrase, or prepositional phrase.

Rules 1 and 2 can be summed up in one statement: A verb phrase may be a verb followed by a noun phrase, which may or may not be followed by a prepositional phrase. By putting parentheses around the optional element, we can abbreviate rules 1 and 2 to a single rule:

VP → V NP (PP)

In fact, the NP is also optional, as shown in the following trees:

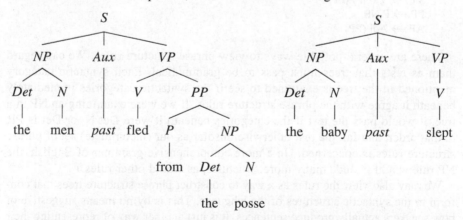

In the first case we have a verb phrase consisting of a verb plus a prepositional phrase, corresponding to the rule VP → V PP. In the second case, the verb phrase consists of a verb alone, corresponding to the rule VP → V. All the facts about the verb phrase we have seen so far are explicit in the single rule:

VP → V (NP) (PP)

This rule states that a verb phrase may consist of a verb followed optionally by a noun phrase and/or a prepositional phrase.

Other rules of English are:

S → NP Aux VP
PP → P NP
AP → Adj (PP)

Growing Trees: The Relationship between Phrase Structure Rules and Phrase Structure Trees

I think that I shall never see
A poem lovely as a tree

Joyce Kilmer, "Trees" (1913)

Phrase structure trees may not be as lovely to look at as the trees Kilmer was thinking of, but if a poem is written in grammatical English, its phrases and sentences can be represented by trees, and those trees can be specified by phrase structure rules.

The rules that we have discussed, repeated here, define some of the phrase structure trees of English.

S → NP Aux VP
NP → Det N (PP)
VP → V (NP) (PP)
PP → P NP
AP → Adj (PP)

There are several possible ways to view phrase structure rules. We can regard them as tests that trees must pass to be grammatical. Each syntactic category mentioned in the tree is examined to see if the syntactic categories immediately beneath it agree with the phrase structure rules. If we were examining an NP in a tree, it would pass the test if the categories beneath it were Det N, or Det N PP, in that order, and fail the test otherwise, insofar as our (incomplete) set of phrase structure rules is concerned. (In a more comprehensive grammar of English, the NP rule would include many more structures, as would other rules.)

We may also view the rules as a way to construct phrase structure trees that conform to the syntactic structures of the language. This is by no means suggestive of how speakers actually produce sentences. It is just another way of representing their knowledge, and it applies equally to speakers and listeners.

In generating or specifying trees, certain conventions are followed. The S occurs at the top of the tree despite being called "the root." Another convention specifies how the rules are applied: First, find a rule with an S on the left side of the arrow, and put the categories on the right side below the S, as shown here:

Once started, continue by matching any syntactic category at the bottom of the partially constructed tree to a category on the left side of a rule, then expand the tree with the categories on the right side. For example, we may expand the tree by applying the NP rule to produce:

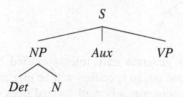

The categories at the bottom are Det, N, and VP, but only VP occurs to the left of an arrow in the set of rules and so needs to be expanded. The VP rule is actually four rules abbreviated by parentheses. They are:

VP → V
VP → V NP
VP → V PP
VP → V NP PP

Any of them may apply next; the order in which the rules appear in the grammar is irrelevant. (Indeed, we might equally have begun by expanding the VP rather than the NP.) Suppose VP → V PP is next. Then the tree has grown to look like this:

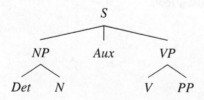

Convention dictates that we continue in this way until none of the categories at the bottom of the tree appears on the left side of any rule. The PP must expand into a P and an NP, and the NP into a Det and an N. We can use a rule as many times as it can apply. In this tree, we used the NP rule twice. After we have applied all the rules that can apply, the tree looks like this:

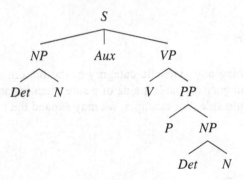

By following these conventions, we can generate only trees specified by the phrase structure rules. By implication, any tree not so specified will be ungrammatical. Whether we choose to use the rules to generate only well-formed trees or use the rules to test the grammaticality of all possible trees is immaterial. Both methods achieve the goal of revealing syntactic knowledge. Most books on language use the rules to generate trees.

Categories such as NP, VP, AP, IP (= S) are **phrasal categories**. The categories N, V, P, Adj, and Adv are **lexical categories**. The categories such as Det and Aux that house function words are **functional categories**. Phrase structure trees always have lexical and functional categories at the bottom since the rules must apply until no phrasal categories remain. The lexical and functional categories are "the parts of speech" in a traditional "grammar" book. You may know some of them by other names. Members of Aux are sometimes called "helping verbs." Members of Det may be called "articles," "demonstrative pronouns," and so on.

The previous tree structure corresponds to a very large number of sentences because there are numerous combinations of nouns, verbs, prepositions, and so on that conform to this structure. Here are just a few:

The boat sailed up the river.
A girl laughed at the monkey.
The sheepdog rolled in the mud.
The lions roared in the jungle.

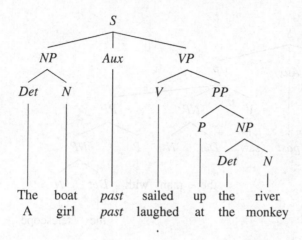

At any point during the construction of a tree, any rule may be used as long as its left-side category occurs somewhere at the bottom of the tree. At the point where we chose the rule VP → V PP, we could equally well have chosen VP → V or VP → V NP PP. This would have resulted in different structures corresponding to sentences such as:

> The boys left. (VP → V)
> The wind swept the kite into the sky. (VP → V NP PP)

Since there is an infinite number of possible sentences in every language, there are limitless numbers of trees, but only a finite set of phrase structure rules that specify the trees allowed by a grammar of the language.

Structural Ambiguities

> The structure of every sentence is a lesson in logic.
>
> John Stuart Mill, inaugural address at St. Andrews (1867)

As mentioned earlier, certain ambiguous sentences have more than one phrase structure tree, each corresponding to a different meaning. The sentence *The boy saw the man with the telescope* is ambiguous. Its two meanings correspond to the following two phrase structure trees.

(1)

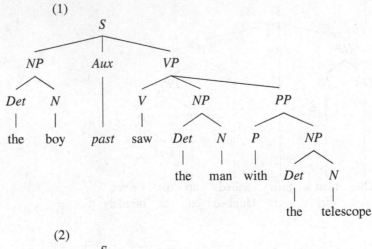

(2)

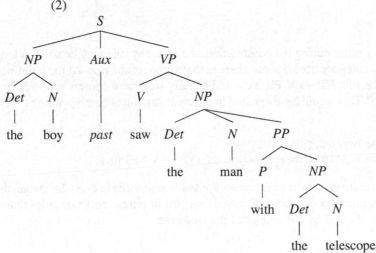

One meaning of this sentence is "the boy used a telescope to see the man." The first phrase structure tree represents this meaning. The key element is the position of the PP directly under the VP. Although the PP is under the VP, it is not a complement because it is not selected by the verb. The verb *see* selects an NP only. In this sentence, the PP has an adverbial function and modifies the verb.

In its other meaning, "the boy saw a man who had a telescope," the PP *with the telescope* occurs under the direct object NP, where it modifies the noun *man*. In this second meaning, the complement of the verb *see* is the entire NP — *the man with the telescope*. In both cases, the PP acts as an adjunct.

The PP in the first structure is generated by the rule:

VP → V NP PP

In the second structure the PP is generated by the rule:

NP → Det N PP

Two interpretations are possible because the rules of syntax permit different structures for the same linear order of words.

Trees That Won't Grow

Just as speakers know which structures and strings of words are permitted by the syntax of their language, they know which are not. The phrase structure rules specify this knowledge implicitly.

Since the rule S → NP Aux VP is the only S rule in our (simplified) grammar of English, the following word sequences and their corresponding structures do not constitute English sentences.

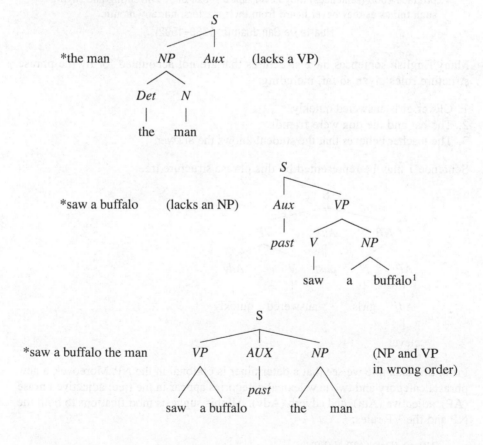

Similarly, *boy the*

```
          NP
        /    \
       N      Det
       |       |
      boy     the
```

cannot be an NP in English because none of the NP rules of English syntax allows a determiner to follow a noun.

More Phrase Structure Rules

> Normal human minds are such that . . . without the help of anybody, they will produce 1000 (sentences) they never heard spoke of . . . inventing and saying such things as they never heard from their masters, nor any mouth.
>
> Huarte De San Juan (c. 1530–1592)

Many English sentences have structures that are not accounted for by the phrase structure rules given so far, including:

1. Clever girls answered quickly.
2. The cat and the dog were friends.
3. The teacher believes that the student knows the answer.

Sentence 1 may be represented by this phrase structure tree:

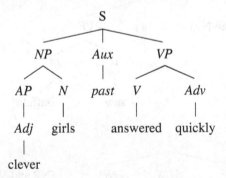

```
                    S
           _____|_____
          |         |         |
         NP        Aux        VP
        /  \        |        /   \
      AP    N      past     V     Adv
      |     |              |       |
     Adj   girls        answered  quickly
      |
    clever
```

From this example we see that a determiner is optional in the NP. Moreover, a new phrasal category and two new lexical categories appear in the tree: adjective phrase (AP), adjective (Adj), and adverb (Adv). All this suggests modifications to both the NP and the VP rules:

$$NP \rightarrow (Det)\ (AP)\ N\ (PP)$$
$$VP \rightarrow V\ (NP)\ (PP)\ (Adv)$$
$$AP \rightarrow Adj\ (PP)^2$$

The addition of an optional adverb to the VP rule allows for four more sentence types:

The wind blew softly.
The wind swept through the trees noisily.
The wind rattled the windows violently.
The wind forced the boat into the water suddenly.

The NP in sentence 2, *The cat and the dog,* is a **coordinate structure.** A coordinate structure results when two constituents of the same category (in this case, two NPs) are joined with a conjunction such as *and* or *or.* The NP has the following structure:

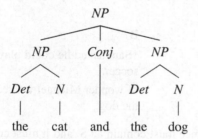

The phrase structure rule that generates this coordinate structure is:

NP → NP conj NP

Sentence 3 is particularly interesting. It includes another sentence within itself. The inside sentence, *the student knows the answer,* is **embedded** in the larger sentence *The teacher believes that the student knows the answer.* What is the structure of such sentences?

Recall that verbs (like other heads) take complements. These complements can be of different categories, for example, a PP or an AP. In sentence 3 the complement to the verb *believe* is a sentence —S. The embedded sentence *that the student knows the answer* bears the same local relationship to the verb that a simple direct object does in a sentence such as *The teacher believes the student.* We know therefore that the embedded sentence is inside the VP with the verb:

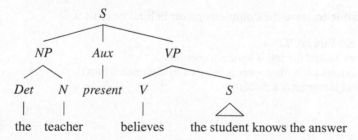

However, the structure is incomplete. It is missing a piece of the sentence, the word *that*. The word *that* belongs to the class of **complementizers**, which also includes words such as *if* and *whether* in sentences like:

> I don't know whether I should talk about this.
> The teacher asked if the students understood the syntax lesson.

A complementizer is an element that turns a sentence into a complement. In English, the word *that* is not always required in embedded sentences. The sentence *I know John is happy* is as grammatical as *I know that John is happy*. In many languages, a sentence can be a complement (that is, it can be embedded in another sentence) only if it is accompanied by a word like *that*. In English the other complementizers *if* and *whether* cannot be omitted, as illustrated by the ungrammaticality of the B sentences:

A	**B**
Sam asked if he could play soccer.	*Sam asked he could play soccer.
I wonder whether Michael walked the dog.	*I wonder Michael walked the dog.

So the structure of the embedded sentence must contain an S, and it must contain a position for a complementizer. But how are these two elements situated with respect to each other? If we do some constituency tests, as we did earlier for NP and VP, we see that the complementizer and the S form a constituent. For example, the question test, the relocation test, and the pronoun test all show that the embedded S and the complementizer act together as a constituent.

> Sam asked if he could play soccer.
> What did Sam ask? If he could play soccer.
> I wonder whether Michael walked the dog.
> Whether Michael walked the dog is always a question.
> The teacher believes that the students know the answer.
> The teacher believes it.
> That the students know the answer is believed by the teacher.
> It is a problem that Sam lost his watch.
> That Sam lost his watch is a problem.

It is not possible to leave the complementizer behind or omit it.

> *What did Sam ask if.
> *Michael walked the dog is always a question.
> *The students know the answer is believed by the teacher (that).
> *Sam lost his watch is a problem.

We now have all the information we need to determine the structure of the embedded sentence. The embedded sentence is a complement to the verb, therefore inside the VP. The complementizer *that* forms a constituent with S, which means there must be a category dominating both *that* and S that is inside the VP. The relevant structure is:

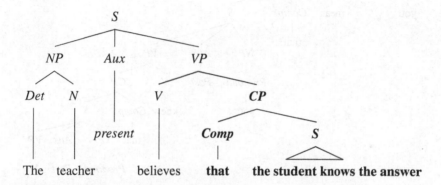

The complementizer (*that, if, whether*) appears under a node Comp, which, like Det and Aux, is a functional category. Comp is the head of a category CP (complementizer phrase). CP is the complement to the verb. The structure is parallel to a simple structure with an NP complement, such as *The teacher believes the student,* except that there is a CP instead of an NP.

We have omitted the internal structure of the embedded S in the preceding tree because it is the same as the internal structure of a root sentence, as described by the phrase structure rule for S. This suggests a rule for the category CP:

CP → Comp S

In addition, we need another VP rule:

VP → V CP

If we combine this with the previous VP rules, we get:

VP → V (NP) (PP) (CP)

We now see how the grammar reflects the knowledge that all speakers have to embed sentences in sentences. Here is an illustrative phrase structure tree:

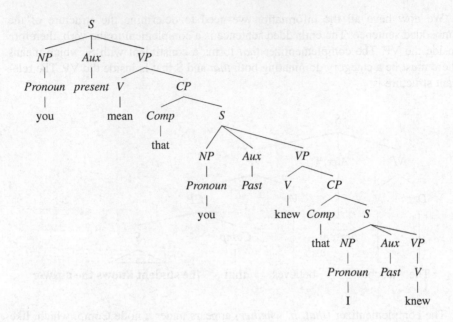

Here are the phrase structure rules we have discussed so far. These are all the phrase structure rules we will present in this chapter.

1. S → NP Aux VP
2. NP → (Det) (AP) N (PP)
3. VP → V (NP) (PP) (Adv) (CP)
4. PP → P NP
5. AP → Adj (PP)
6. CP → Comp S

Here is one tree illustrating some of these rules :

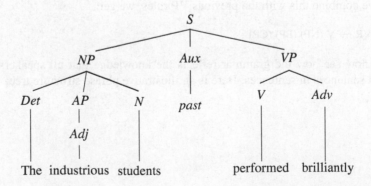

A complete grammar of English would have more rules. However, even this mini-grammar can specify an infinite number of possible sentences because several categories (S, NP, VP) appear on both the left and right sides of several rules. Thus, the rules explain our observations that language is creative and that speakers with their finite brains can still produce and understand an infinite set of sentences.

Many structures of English remain unaccounted for by our mini-grammar. For example, many types of determiners besides the articles *the* and *a* may precede the noun in a noun phrase, such as *each, several, these, many of Bruce Cockburn's,* and so on.

> *Each* boy found several eggs.
> They sang *many of Bruce Cockburn's* songs.

Also, rules 3 and 6 show that a whole sentence (preceded by a complementizer) may be embedded in a VP. There are other forms of embedded sentences such as the following:

> Hilary is waiting *for you to sing.* (Cf. You sing.)
> The host regrets *the president's having left early.* (Cf. The president has left early.)
> The host wants *the president to leave early.* (Cf. The president leaves early.)
> The host believes *the president to be punctual.* (Cf. The president is punctual.)

Although the detailed structure of these different embedded sentences is beyond the scope of this introduction, you should note that an embedded sentence may be an **infinitive**. An infinitive sentence does not have a tense. The embedded sentences *for you to sing, the president to leave early,* and *the president to be punctual* are infinitives. Such verbs as *want* and *believe* among many others can take an infinitive complement. This information, like other selectional properties, belongs to the lexical entry of the selecting verb (the higher verb in the tree).

We noted earlier that Aux is the head of S, and that the tense features of the sentence are in Aux. In sentences without tense, Aux is specified as "infinitive." Whether the sentence is tensed or infinitive has consequences for other aspects of the sentence. For example, reflexive pronouns can be subjects of infinitives but not of embedded tensed sentences:

> Frank believes himself to be a superstar.
> *Frank thinks himself is a superstar.

Also, the subject of an infinitive can be questioned while the subject of a tensed clause cannot:

> Paul believed Melissa to be his wife.
> Who did Paul believe to be his wife?
> Sam thinks that Michael is his cousin.
> *Who does Sam think that is his cousin?

These sentences provide further evidence of the central role that Aux plays in the structure of the sentence, and of its "headlike" properties.

Sentence Relatedness

Most wonderful of all are . . . [sentences], and how they make friends one with another.

O. Henry, (1862–1910), as modified by a syntactician

Sentences may be related in various ways. For example, they may have the same phrase structure, but differ in meaning because they contain different words. We saw this earlier in sets of sentences such as *The boat sailed up the river* and *A girl laughed at the monkey*.

Two sentences with different meanings may contain the same words in the same order, and differ only in structure, like *the boy saw the man with the telescope*. These are cases of structural ambiguity.

Two sentences may differ in structure, possibly with small differences in grammatical morphemes, but with no difference in meaning:

The father wept silently.	The father silently wept.
The astronomer saw a quasar with a telescope.	With a telescope, the astronomer saw a quasar.
Bethany hired Boris.	Boris was hired by Bethany.
I know that you know.	I know you know.

Two sentences may have structural differences that correspond systematically to meaning differences.

The boy is sleeping.	Is the boy sleeping?
The boy can sleep.	Can the boy sleep?
The boy will sleep.	Will the boy sleep?

Earlier we discussed auxiliaries. Auxiliaries are very important in forming certain types of sentences in English, including questions. In questions, the auxiliary appears at the beginning of the sentence. This difference in position is not accounted for by the phrase structure rules we have presented, which specify that in a sentence the NP comes first, followed by Aux, followed by VP.

We could easily add a phrase structure rule to our mini-grammar that would generate the questions above. It would look like the following:

S → Aux NP VP

Although such a rule might do the job of producing the right word order, it would fail to capture the generalization that interrogatives are systematically related (in both form and meaning) to their declarative counterparts. For example, the declarative sentence *Balkar is sleeping* is well formed, as is the question *Is Balkar sleeping?* The declarative sentence *The rock is sleeping* is semantically odd, as is the question *Is the rock sleeping?* A speaker of English will be able to immediately provide the interrogative counterpart to any declarative sentence that we present.

Phrase structure rules account for much syntactic knowledge, but they do not account for the fact that certain sentence types in the language relate systematically to other sentence types.

Since the grammar must account for all of a speaker's syntactic knowledge, we must look beyond phrase structure rules.

Transformational Rules

> Method consists entirely in properly ordering and arranging the things to which we should pay attention.
>
> René Descartes, *Oeuvres*, Vol. X (1596–1650)

A way to capture the relationship between a declarative and a question is to allow the phrase structure rules to generate the structure corresponding to the declarative sentence, and have another formal device, called a **transformational rule**, move the auxiliary in front of the subject.

The rule "Move Aux" is formulated as follows:

> Take the first auxiliary verb following the subject NP and move it to the left of the subject.

For example:

> The boy is sleeping → Is the boy ___ sleeping

The rule takes a basic structure generated by the phrase structure rules and derives a second tree (the dash represents the position from which a constituent has been moved):

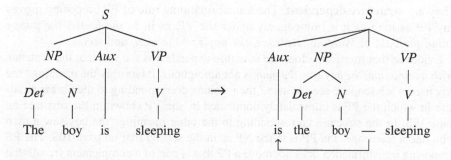

Questions are generated in two steps.

1. The phrase structure rules generate a basic structure.
2. Aux movement applies to produce the derived structure.

The basic structures of sentences, also called **deep structures**, are specified by the phrase structure rules. Variants on those basic sentence structures are derived via transformations. By generating questions in two steps, we are claiming that for speakers there is a relationship between a question and its corresponding statement. Intuitively, we know that such sentences are related. The transformational rule is a formal way of representing this relationship.

The structures that result from the application of transformational rules are called **surface structures**. The phonological rules of the language (pronunciation rules) apply to surface structures. If no transformations apply, then deep structure and surface structure are the same. If transformations apply, then surface structure is the result after all transformations have had their effect. Much syntactic knowledge that is not expressed by phrase structure rules is accounted for by transformations, which can alter phrase structure trees by moving, adding, or deleting elements.

Other sentence types that are transformationally related are:

active sentence / passive sentence

The cat chased the mouse → The mouse was chased by the cat.

there **sentences**

There was a man on the roof → A man was on the roof.

PP preposing

The astronomer saw the quasar with the telescope → With the telescope, the astronomer saw the quasar.

Structure-Dependent Rules

Transformations act on structures without regard to the words that they contain. They are **structure dependent**. The transformational rule of PP preposing moves any PP as long as it is immediately under the VP, as in *In the house, the puppy found the ball*, or *With the telescope, the boy saw the man,* and so on.

Evidence that transformations are structure dependent is the fact that the sentence *With a telescope, the boy saw the man* is not ambiguous. It has only the meaning "the boy used a telescope to see the man," the meaning corresponding to the phrase structure in which the PP is immediately dominated by the VP shown in the first tree on page 108. In the structure corresponding to the other meaning "the boy saw a man who had a telescope" the PP is in the NP as in the second tree on page 108. The PP preposing transformation does not move a PP that is part of a complement (recall that *the man with a telescope* is a complement to the verb *saw*).

Another rule allows *that* to be omitted when it precedes a sentence complement but not in subject position, as illustrated by these pairs:

I know that you know.   I know you know.
That you know bothers me.   *You know bothers me.

This is a further demonstration that rules are structure dependent.

Agreement rules are also structure dependent. In many languages, including English, the verb must agree with the subject. The verb has an "s" added whenever the subject is third-person singular.

The guy seems kind of cute.
The guys seem kind of cute.

Now consider these sentences:

The guy we met at the party next door *seems* kind of cute.
The guys we met at the party next door *seem* kind of cute.

The verb *seem* must agree with the subject, *guy* or *guys*. Even though there are various words between the head noun and the verb, the verb always agrees with the head noun. Moreover, there is no limit to how many words may intervene, as the following sentence illustrates:

The guys (guy) we met at the party next door that lasted until three A.M. and was finally broken up by the cops who were called by the neighbours seem (seems) kind of cute.

The phrase structure tree of such a sentence explains this aspect of linguistic competence:

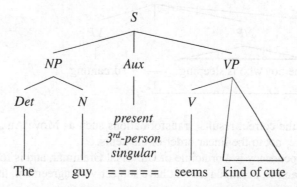

In the tree, "= = = = =" represents the intervening structure, which may, in principle, be indefinitely long and complex. But speakers of English know that agreement depends on sentence structure, not the linear order of words. Agreement is between the subject and the main verb, where the subject is structurally defined as the NP immediately below the S, and the main verb is structurally defined as the verb in the VP. The agreement relation is mediated by Aux, which contains the tense and agreement features that match up the subject and verb. Other material can be ignored as far as the rule of agreement is concerned, although in actual performance, if the distance is too great, the speaker may forget what the head noun was.

A final illustration of structure dependency is found in the declarative-question pairs discussed above. Consider the following sets of sentences:

> The boy who is sleeping was dreaming.
> Was the boy who is sleeping dreaming?
> *Is the boy who sleeping was dreaming?
> The boy who can sleep will dream.
> Will the boy who can sleep dream?
> *Can the boy who sleep will dream?

The ungrammatical sentences show that to form a question, it is the auxiliary of the topmost S, that is, the one following the entire first NP, that moves to the position before the subject, not simply the *first* auxiliary in the sentence. We can see this in the following simplified phrase structure trees.

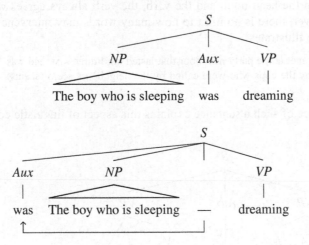

To produce the correct results, transformations such as Move Aux must refer to phrase structure, not to the linear order of elements.

Structure dependency is a principle of Universal Grammar, and is found in all languages. For example, in languages that have subject-verb agreement, the dependency is between the verb and the head noun, and never some other noun such as the closest one, as shown in the following examples from Italian, German, Swahili, and English, respectively (the third-person singular agreement morpheme is in boldface):

> La madre con tanti figli lavora molto.
> Die Mutter mit vielen Kindern arbeitet viel.
> Mama anao watoto wengi.
> The mother with many children works a lot.

Syntactic Dependencies

Sentences are organized according to two basic principles: constituent structure and syntactic dependencies. As we discussed earlier, constituent structure refers to the hierarchical organization of the subparts of a sentence. The second important property is that there are dependencies among elements in the sentence. In other words, the presence of a particular word or morpheme can depend on the presence of some other word or morpheme in a sentence. We have already seen at least two examples of syntactic dependencies. Selection is one kind of dependency. Whether there is a direct object in a sentence depends on whether the verb is transitive or intransitive. More generally, complements depend on the properties of the head of the phrase. Agreement is another kind of dependency. The features in Aux (and on the verb) must match the features of the subject.

Wh *Questions*

> Whom are you? said he, for he had been to night school.
>
> George Ade, *Bang! Bang!: The Steel Box*

The following sentences illustrate another kind of dependency:

1. (a) What will Max chase?
   (b) Where has Pete put his ball?
   (c) Which dog do you think loves bones?

There are some points of interest in these sentences. First, the verb *chase* in sentence (a) is transitive, yet there is no direct object following it. There is a "gap" where the direct object should be. The verb *put* in sentence (b) selects a direct object and a prepositional phrase, yet there is no PP following *his ball*. Finally, we note that the embedded verb *loves* in sentence (c) bears the third-person -*s* morpheme, yet there is no obvious subject to trigger this agreement. Normally these omissions would result in ungrammaticality, as in the examples in (2):

2. (a) *Max will chase _____.
   (b) *Pete has put his ball _____.
   (c) *Do you think _____ loves bones.

The possibility of a gap in the sentence depends on there being a *wh* phrase at the beginning of the sentence. The sentences in (1) are grammatical because the *wh* phrase is acting like the object in (a), the prepositional phrase object in (b), and the embedded subject in (c).

We can capture the relationship between the *wh* phrase and the missing constituent if we assume that in each case the *wh* phrase originated in the position of the gap:

3. (a) Max will chase what?
   (b) Pete has put his ball where?
   (c) You think which dog loves bones?

The *wh* phrase is then moved to the beginning of the sentence by a transformational rule: Move *wh*.

If we allow the phrase structure rules to apply so that *wh* questions are CPs, then the *wh* phrase can move to the empty Comp position at the beginning of the sentence.

Wh questions are generated by the grammar in three steps:

1. The phrase structure rules generate the basic (deep) structure with the *wh* phrase occupying an NP position: direct object in 3(a); prepositional object in 3(b); and subject in 3(c).
2. Move Aux moves the auxiliary to the beginning of the sentence.
3. Move *wh* moves the *wh* phrase to Comp.

The following tree shows the deep structure in the sentence *What will Max chase?*

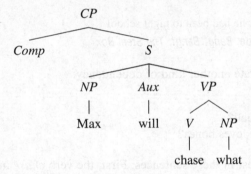

The surface structure representation of this sentence is:[3]

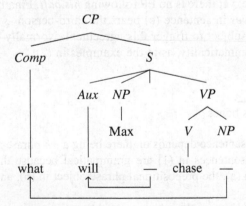

In question 1(c), there is an auxiliary *do*. Unlike the other auxiliaries (e.g., *can, have, be,* etc.), *do* is not part of the deep structure of the question. The deep structure of the question *Which dog do you think loves bones* is "you think which dog loves bones." Like all transformations, the rule of Move Aux is structure dependent and ignores the content of the category. It will move Aux even when Aux contains only a tense feature such as *past*. In this case another transformational rule, called "*do* support," inserts *do* into the structure to carry the tense:

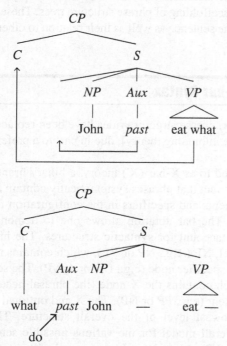

The first tree represents the deep structure to which Move Aux and *wh* movement apply. The second tree shows the output of those transformations and the insertion of *do. Do* combines with past to yield *did*.

Unlike the other rules we have seen, which operate inside a phrase or clause, *wh* movement can move the *wh* phrase outside its own clause. In fact there is no limit to the distance that a *wh* phrase can move, as illustrated by the following sentences. The blank lines indicate the position from which the *wh* phrase has been moved.

Whom did Helen say the MP wanted to hire ____?

Whom did Helen say the MP wanted the senator to try to hire ____?

Whom did Helen say the MP wanted the senator to try to convince the Speaker of the House to get the Prime Minister to hire ____?

"Long-distance" dependencies created by *wh* movement are a fundamental part of human language. They provide further evidence that sentences are not simply strings of words but are supported by a rich scaffolding of phrase structure trees. These trees express the underlying structure of the sentence as well as their relation to other sentences in the language.

X-bar Syntax

In more recent approaches to syntax, phrase structure rules have been replaced by more general constraints (e.g., those in binding theory), due in part to a preference for more economical descriptions.

In the approach originally referred to as X-bar (X') theory, a binary branching pattern is adopted to account for the fact that phrases systematically contain heads (X) and may also contain complements and specifiers in the configuration for all categories, lexical and functional. The bar notation allows one to demonstrate three hierarchical levels needed to account for syntactic structures. The highest hierarchical level is the phrasal level, XP (e.g., NP or VP), which contains the X' node and may or may not contain a specifier node (e.g., Det or AdvP). The second level is the X' level (e.g., V'), which contains the X node (the phrasal head) and may or may not include a complement (e.g., PP or NP). The X and optional complement occur at the third and lowest level of the overall structure. The X' approach therefore provides an overall model for the various possible sentence and phrase structures in a language. The underlying pattern can be illustrated as follows:

```
                    XP
                  /    \
    (specifier)       X'
                     /   \
                   X      (complement)
```

The following tree diagrams are further illustrations of some of these relationships. (Note that this is a simplified version of current views on phrase structure, for pedagogical purposes.)

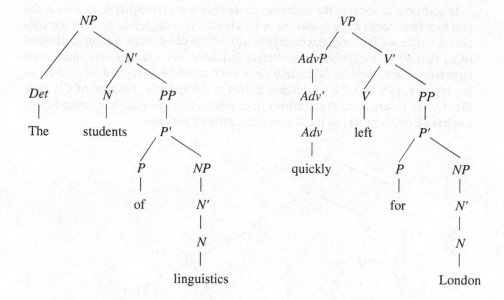

Further, instead of the *S* node, sentences are identified as IP for "inflected phrase" and consist of the NP and I'; I' includes the sentence head, i.e., the tense marker I (for "inflection"), followed by the complement VP node. These relationships are displayed in the following illustration of the phrase marker for the sentence *Canadians read*. The sentence (now IP) therefore also follows the X' schema.

Similar to the approach discussed previously in this chapter in which Aux is obligatory in sentences, the sentence head I (inflection) is obligatory, accounting for the presence of tense (present, past) and agreement in sentences.

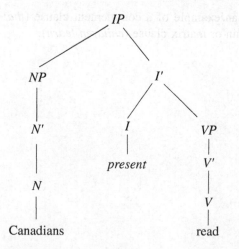

In addition, to account for sentences containing complementizers, as well as the fact that sentences can be questions or statements, it is suggested that IPs are contained within a CP (complementizer phrase), which can contain a complementizer (e.g., *that if*) or a question or statement indicator. For example, the underlying structure of the question *What will John eat?* could be described as in the following tree, in which the *wh-* phrase moves to the specifier position of CP. Note that for the inversion of the auxiliary in questions like this one, it is assumed that the head I (will) moves to the C (complementizer) position.

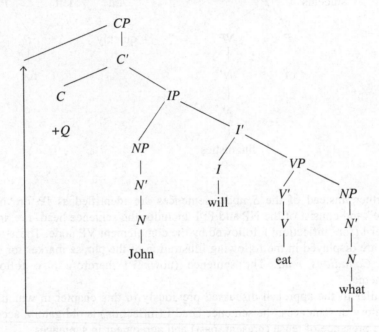

The following is an example of a complement clause (*that snow melts*) contained within the main or matrix clause (*children learn*):

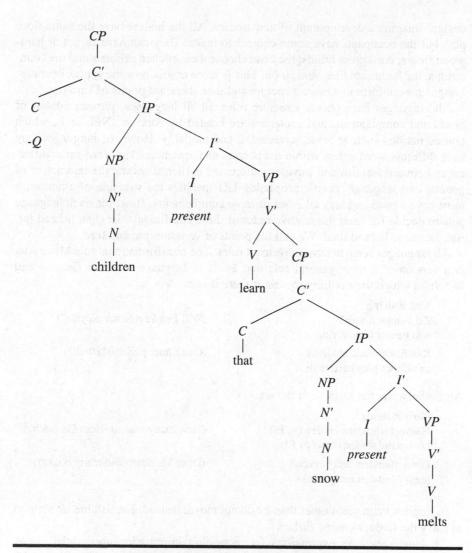

UG Principles and Parameters

Whenever the literary German dives into a sentence, that is the last you are going to see of him till he emerges on the other side of the Atlantic with his Verb in his mouth.

Mark Twain, *A Connecticut Yankee in King Arthur's Court* (1889)

As we emphasize throughout this book, Universal Grammar (UG) provides the basic design for human language. Individual languages are variations on this basic design. Imagine a development of new houses. All the houses have the same floor plan but the occupants have some choices to make. They can have carpet or hard-wood floors, curtains or blinds; they can choose their kitchen cabinets and the countertops, the bathroom tiles, and so on. This is more or less how the syntax operates. Languages conform to a basic structure and then there are points of variation.

All languages have phrase structure rules. In all languages, phrases consist of heads and complements, and sentences are headed by Aux (or INFL or I), which houses notions such as tense, agreement, and modality. However, languages may have different word orders within the phrases and sentences. The word-order differences between English and Japanese, discussed earlier, illustrate the interaction of general and language-specific properties. UG specifies the structure of a phrase. It must have a head and may take one or more complements. However, each language gets to decide for itself the relative order of these constituents: English is head initial, Japanese is head final. We call the points of variation **parameters**.

All languages seem to have movement rules. The transformational rule Move Aux is a version of a more general rule that exists in languages such as German and Dutch, in which the auxiliary moves, if there is one:

Aux Raising

| Zal Femke fiesten? | (Will Femke ride her bicycle?) |
| will Femke bicycle ride | |

| Kan Elmer baskenballen? | (Can Elmer play basketball?) |
| can Elmer play basketball | |

And otherwise, the main verb moves:

Verb Raising

| Hoeveel studenten onderwijst Els? | (How many students does Els teach?) |
| how many students teaches Els | |

| Leest Meindert veel boeken? | (Does Meindert read many books?) |
| reads Meindert many books | |

In English main verbs other than *be* do not move. Instead, English has *do* support to carry the tense, as noted earlier.

All languages have expressions for requesting information about *who, when, where, what, why,* and *how*. Even if the question words do not always begin with "wh," we will refer to such questions as *wh* questions.

In some languages, such as Japanese and Swahili, the *wh* phrase does not move. It remains in its original deep structure position. In Japanese the sentence is marked with a question morpheme, *no:*

| Taro-ga | nani-o | mituketa-no? |
| Taro | what | found ? |

Recall that Japanese word order is SOV, so the *wh* phrase *nani* ("what") is an object and occurs before the verb.

In Swahili the *wh* phrase — *nani* by pure coincidence — also does not move to Comp:

Ulipatia   nani   kitabu
you gave   who   a book

However, in all languages with *wh* movement (that is, movement of the question phrase), the moved element goes to Comp. The "landing site" of the moved phrase is determined by UG. Among the *wh* movement languages, there is some variation. In the Romance languages such as Italian, the *wh* phrase moves as in English, but when the *wh* phrase questions the object of a preposition, the preposition must move together with the *wh* phrase, whereas in English the preposition can be "stranded" behind:

A chi hai dato il libro?
To whom (did) you give the book?

*Chi hai dato il libro a
Who did you give the book to

In some dialects of German, "long-distance" *wh* movement leaves a trail of *wh* phrases in the Comp position of the embedded sentence:[4]

Mit   wem   glaubst   du   mit   wem   Hans   spricht?
With   whom   think   you   with   whom   Hans   talks
(Whom do you think Hans talks to?)

Wen   willst   du   wen   Hans   anruft?
Whom   want   you   whom   Hans   call
(Whom do you want Hans to call?)

In Czech the question phrase "how much" can be moved, leaving behind the NP it modifies:

Jak   velké   Václav   koupil   auto?
how   big   Václav   bought   car
(How big a car did Václav buy?)

Despite these variations, *wh* movement adheres to certain constraints. Although a *wh* phrase such as *what, who, which boy* can be inserted into any NP position, and it is then free in principle to move to Comp, there are specific instances in which *wh* movement is blocked. For example, the rule cannot move a *wh* phrase out of a relative clause such as ". . . the MP who wanted to hire whom" as in 1(b), or a clause beginning with *whether* or *if* as in 2(c) and (d). (Remember that the position from which the *wh* phrases have been moved is indicated with _____.)

1. (a) Emily paid a visit to the MP who wants to hire whom?
   (b) *Whom did Emily pay a visit to the MP who wants to hire _____?

2. (a) Miss Marple asked Sherlock whether Poirot had solved the crime.
   (b) Whom did Miss Marple ask ____ whether Poirot had solved the crime?
   (c) *Who did Miss Marple ask Sherlock whether ____ had solved the crime?
   (d) *What did Miss Marple ask Sherlock whether Poirot had solved ____?

The only difference between the grammatical 2(b) and the ungrammatical 2(c) and (d) is that in the former case the *wh* phrase originates in the higher clause, whereas in the latter cases the *wh* phrase comes from inside the *whether* clause. This illustrates that the constraint against movement depends on structure and not on the length of the sentence.

In fact some sentences can be very short and still not allow *wh* movement:

3. (a) Sam Spade insulted the fat man's henchman.
   (b) Whom did Sam Spade insult?
   (c) Whose henchman did Sam Spade insult?
   (d) *Whose did Sam Spade insult henchman?
4. (a) John ate bologna and cheese.
   (b) John ate bologna with cheese.
   (c) *What did John eat bologna and?
   (d) What did John eat bologna with?

The sentences in 3 show that a *wh* phrase cannot be extracted from inside a possessive NP. In 3(b) it is of course okay to question the whole direct object, and prepose the *wh* word. In 3(c) it is even okay to question a piece of the possessive NP, providing the entire *wh* phrase is moved. But 3(d) shows that it is not permitted to move the *wh* word alone out of the possessive NP.

Sentence 4(a) is a coordinate structure and has approximately the same meaning as 4(b), which is not a coordinate structure. In 4(c) moving a *wh* word out of the coordinate structure results in ungrammaticality, whereas in 4(d), it's okay to move the *wh* word out of the PP. The ungrammaticality of 4(c), then, is related to its structure and not to its meaning.

The constraints on *wh* movement are not specific to English. Such constraints operate in all languages that have *wh* movement. Like the principle of structure dependency and the principles governing the organization of phrases, the constraints on *wh* movement are part of Universal Grammar. These aspects of grammar need not be learned. They are part of what the child brings to the task of acquiring a language.

What children must learn are the language-specific aspects of grammar. Where there are parameters of variation, children must determine what is correct for their language. The Japanese child must determine that the verb comes after the object in the VP, and the English-speaking child acquires the VO order. The Dutch-speaking child acquires a rule that moves the verb, while the English-speaking child must restrict his rule to auxiliaries. Italian, English, and Czech children learn that to form a question the *wh* phrase moves, while Japanese and Swahili children determine that there is no movement. We will have more to say about how children "fix" the parameters of UG in Chapter 7.

Sign Language Syntax

All languages, including English, have rules of syntax similar in kind, if not in detail; sign languages are no exception. Signed languages have phrase structure rules that provide hierarchical structure and order constituents. A signer is as capable as an oral speaker of distinguishing *dog bites man* from *man bites dog* through the order of signing. The basic order of ASL is SVO. Unlike English, however, adjectives follow the head noun in ASL.

ASL has a category Aux, which expresses notions such as tense, agreement, modality, and so on. In Thai, to show that an action is continuous, the auxiliary verb *kamlang* is inserted before the verb. Thus *kin* means "eat" and *kamlang kin* means "is eating." In English a form of *be* is inserted and the main verb is changed to an *-ing* form. In ASL the sign for a verb such as *eat* may be articulated with a sweeping, repetitive movement to achieve the same effect. The sweeping, repetitive motion is a kind of auxiliary.

Many languages, including English, have a transformation that moves a direct object to the beginning of the sentence to draw particular attention to it, as in:

> Many greyhounds, my wife has rescued.

The transformation is called **topicalization** because an object to which attention is drawn generally becomes the topic of the sentence or conversation. (The deep structure underlying this sentence is *my wife has rescued many greyhounds*.)

In ASL a similar reordering of signs accompanied by raising the eyebrows and tilting the head upward accomplishes the same effect. The head motion and facial expressions of a signer function as markers of the special word order, much as intonation does in English, or the attachment of prefixes or suffixes might in other languages.

There are constraints on topicalization similar to those on *wh* movement illustrated in a previous section. In English the following strings are ungrammatical:

> *Henchman, Sam Spade insulted the fat man's.
> *This film, Austin asked Naomi whether she liked.
> *Cheese, John ate bologna and for lunch.

Compare this with the grammatical:

> The fat man's henchman, Sam Spade insulted.
> This film, Austin asked Naomi to see with him.
> Bologna and cheese, John ate for lunch.

Sign languages exhibit similar constraints. An attempt to express in ASL sequences like *Henchman, Sam Spade insulted the fat man's* or the other starred examples would result in an ungrammatical sequence of signs.

ASL has *wh* phrases. The *wh* phrase in ASL may move or it may remain in its deep structure position as in Japanese and Swahili. The ASL equivalents of *who did Bill see yesterday* and *Bill saw who yesterday* are both grammatical. As in topicalization, *wh* questions are accompanied by a nonmanual marker. For questions, this marker is a facial expression with furrowed brows and the head tilted back. Nonmanual markers are an integral part of the grammar of ASL, much like intonation in spoken languages.

ASL and other sign languages show an interaction of universal and language-specific properties, just as spoken languages do. The grammatical rules of sign languages are structure dependent, and movement rules are constrained in various ways, as illustrated above. Other aspects are particular to sign languages, such as the facial gestures, which are part of the grammar of sign languages but not of spoken languages. The fact that the principles and parameters of UG hold in both the spoken and manual modalities shows that the human brain is designed to acquire and use language, not simply speech.

Summary

Speakers of a language recognize the grammatical sentences of their language and know how the words in a sentence must be ordered and grouped to convey a certain meaning. All speakers are capable of producing and understanding an unlimited number of new sentences never before spoken or heard. They also recognize ambiguities, know when different sentences mean the same thing, and correctly perceive the grammatical relations in a sentence such as **subject** and **direct object**. This kind of knowledge comes from their knowledge of the **rules of syntax**.

Sentences have structure that can be represented by **phrase structure trees** containing **syntactic categories**. Phrase structure trees reflect the speaker's mental representation of sentences. Ambiguous sentences may have more than one phrase structure tree.

Phrase structure trees reveal the linear order of words, and the constituency of each syntactic category. There are different kinds of syntactic categories: **phrasal categories**, such as NP and VP, which are decomposed into other syntactic categories; **lexical categories**, such as Noun and Verb; and **functional categories**, such as Det, Aux, and Comp. The internal structure of the phrasal categories is universal. It consists of a **head** and its **complements**. The particular order of elements within the phrase is accounted for by the **phrase structure rules** of each language. The sentence is headed by Aux, which carries such information as tense, agreement, and modality.

A grammar is a formally stated, explicit description of the mental grammar or speaker's linguistic competence. Phrase structure rules characterize the basic phrase structure trees of the language, the **deep structures**.

Some categories that appear on the left side of a phrase structure rule may also occur on the right side. Such rules allow the same syntactic category to appear repeatedly in a phrase structure tree, such as a sentence embedded in another sentence. These rules reflect a speaker's ability to produce an infinite number of sentences.

The lexicon represents the knowledge that speakers have about the vocabulary of their language. This knowledge includes the syntactic category of words and what elements may occur together, expressed as selectional restrictions.

Transformational rules account for relationships between sentences such as declarative and interrogative pairs including *wh* questions. Transformations can move constituents or insert function words such as *do* into a sentence. Much of the meaning of a sentence is interpreted from its deep structure. The output of the transformational rules is the **surface structure** of a sentence, the structure to which the phonological rules of the language apply.

The basic design of language is universal. Universal Grammar specifies that syntactic rules are **structure dependent** and that movement rules may not move phrases out of certain structures such as coordinate structures. These constraints exist in all languages — spoken and signed — and need not be learned. UG also contains **parameters** of variation such as the order of heads and complements, and the variations on movement rules. A child acquiring a language must "fix" the parameters of UG for any particular language.

Notes

1. Nonpertinent parts of the tree are sometimes omitted, in this case the Det and N of the NP, *a buffalo.*

2. As pointed out earlier, any number of adjectives may be strung together. For simplicity our rules will allow only one adjective and would need to be changed to fully account for the English speaker's knowledge.

3. For ease of exposition we have presented Comp with only a single slot to accommodate moved constituents. In fact, Comp may have two positions, one for *wh* and one for the Aux.

4. Other languages such as Romani, the language of Roma, once called gypsies, exhibit similar properties.

Exercises

1. Besides distinguishing grammatical from ungrammatical strings, the rules of syntax account for other kinds of linguistic knowledge, such as

   a. when a sentence is structurally ambiguous. (Cf. *The boy saw the man with a telescope.*)
   b. when two sentences of different structure mean the same thing. (Cf. *The father wept silently* and *The father silently wept.*)
   c. when two sentences of different structure and meaning are nonetheless structurally related, like declarative sentences and their corresponding interrogative form. (Cf. *The boy can sleep* and *Can the boy sleep?*)

In each case, draw on your linguistic knowledge of English to provide an example different from the ones in the chapter, and explain why your example illustrates the point. If you know a language other than English, provide examples in that language, if possible.

2. Consider the following sentences:

   a. I hate war.
   b. You know that I hate war.
   c. He knows that you know that I hate war.
      (1) Write another sentence that includes sentence (c).
      (2) What does this set of sentences reveal about the nature of language?
      (3) How is this characteristic of human language related to the difference between linguistic competence and performance? (*Hint:* Review these concepts in Chapter 1.)

3. Paraphrase each of the following sentences in two ways to show that you understand the ambiguity involved:

   Example: Smoking grass can be nauseating.
   i. Putting grass in a pipe and smoking it can make you sick.
   ii. Fumes from smouldering grass can make you sick.

   a. Dick finally decided on the boat.
   b. The professor's appointment was shocking.
   c. The design has big squares and circles.
   d. That sheepdog is too hairy to eat.
   e. Could this be the invisible man's hair tonic?
   f. The premier is a dirty street fighter.
   g. I cannot recommend him too highly.
   h. Terry loves his wife and so do I.
   i. They said she would go yesterday.
   j. No smoking section available.

*4. Draw two phrase structure trees representing the two meanings of the sentence *The magician touched the child with the wand.* Be sure you indicate which meaning goes with which tree.

5. Write out the phrase structure rules that each of the following rules abbreviate. Give an example sentence illustrating each expansion.

   (*Hint:* Do not mix the rules. That is, VP → V Det N is not one of the rule expansions of the VP rule. There are 16 rules altogether.)

   VP → V (NP) (PP) (Adv)
   NP → (Det) (AP) N (PP)

6. In all languages, sentences can occur within sentences. For example, in exercise 2, sentence (b) contains sentence (a), and sentence (c) contains sentence (b). Put another way, sentence (a) is embedded in sentence (b), and sentence (b) is embedded in sentence (c). Sometimes embedded sentences appear slightly changed from their "normal" form, but you should be able to recognize and underline the embedded sentences in the examples below. Underline the embedded sentences in the non-English sentences, when given, not in the translations. (The first one is done as an example.)

    a.   Yesterday I noticed <u>my accountant repairing the toilet.</u>
    b.   Becky said that Jake would play the piano.
    c.   I deplore the fact that bats have wings.
    d.   That Guinevere loves Lorian is known to all my friends.
    e.   Who promised the teacher that Maxine wouldn't be absent?
    f.   It's ridiculous that he washes his own Rolls-Royce.
    g.   The woman likes for the waiter to bring water when she sits down.
    h.   The person who answers this question will win $100.
    i.   The idea of Romeo marrying a thirteen-year-old is upsetting.
    j.   I gave my hat to the nurse who helped me cut my hair.
    k.   For your children to spend all your royalty payments on recreational drugs is a shame.
    l.   Give this fork to the person I'm getting the pie for.
    m.   khǎw chyâ   wǎa khruu maa. (Thai)
         He   believe that teacher come
         He believes that the teacher is coming.
    n.   Je me demande quand il partira. (French)
         I me ask   when he will leave
         I wonder when he'll leave.
    o.   Jan zei dat Piet dit boek niet heeft gelezen. (Dutch)
         Jan said that Piet this book not has   read
         Jan said that Piet has not read this book.

*7. Following the patterns of the various tree examples in the text, and the rules on page 114, draw phrase structure trees for the following sentences:

    a.   The puppy found the child.
    b.   A frightened passenger landed the crippled airliner.
    c.   The house on the hill collapsed in the wind.
    d.   The ice melted.
    e.   The hot sun melted the ice.
    f.   A fast car with twin cams sped by the children on the grassy lane.
    g.   The old tree swayed in the wind.
    h.   The children put the toy in the box.
    i.   The reporter realized that the MP lied.

   j. Broken ice melts in the sun.
   k. The guitarist practises daily.

8. Use the rules on page 114 to create five phrase structure trees of sentences not given in the chapter of six, seven, eight, nine, and ten words. Use your mental lexicon to fill in the bottom of the tree.

9. Follow the examples in the section on X-bar syntax (p. 124) and draw phrase markers for the following sentences:

   1. The journalist read the announcement.
   2. The cyclists thought that the path ended at the beach.
   3. What should the jury decide?

10. We stated that the rules of syntax specify all and only the grammatical sentences of the language. Why is it important to say "only"? What would be wrong with a grammar that specified as grammatical sentences all of the truly grammatical ones plus a few that were not grammatical?

11. Here is a set of made-up phrase structure rules. The "initial" symbol is still S, and the "terminal symbols" (the ones that do not appear to the left of an arrow) are actual words:

   a. S → A B C
   b. A → *the*
   c. B → *children*
   d. C → *ran*
   e. C → C *and* D
   f. D → *ran and* D
   g. D → *ran*

   A. Give three phrase structure trees that these rules characterize.
   B. How many phrase structure trees could these rules characterize? Explain your answer.

12. Using one or more of the constituency tests (question word substitution, pronoun substitution, and relocation) discussed in the chapter, determine which boldfaced portions in the sentences are constituents. Provide the grammatical category of the constituents.

   a. Martha found **a lovely pillow** for the couch.
   b. The **light in this room** is terrible.
   c. I wonder **if Bonnie has finished packing her books**.
   d. Melissa hated the students **in her class**.
   e. **Pete and Max** are fighting over **the bone**.

13. The two sentences below contain a verbal particle.

a. He ran *up* the bill.
b. He ran the bill *up*.

The verbal particle *up* and the verb *run* depend on each other for the unique meaning of the phrasal verb *run up*. We know this because *run up* has a meaning different from *run in* or *look up*.

Sentences (a) and (b) have the same deep structure:

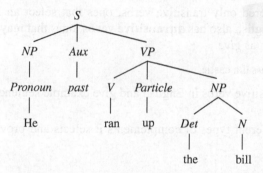

The surface structure of (b), however, illustrates a **discontinuous dependency**. The verb is separated from its particle by the direct object NP.

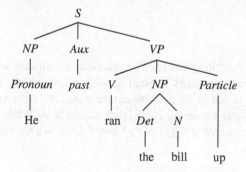

A particle movement transformation derives this surface structure from the deep structure.

A. Explain why the particle movement transformation would not derive **he ran the hill up* from the deep structure of *he ran up the hill*.

B. Many of the transformations encountered in this chapter are *optional*. Whether they apply or not, the ultimate surface structure is grammatical. This is true of the particle movement transformation in most cases, but there is one condition under which the particle movement transformation is obligatory. That is, failure to apply the rule will lead to ungrammatical results. What is that condition? (This exercise may require native English competency.)

*14. In terms of selectional restrictions, explain why the following are ungrammatical.

  a. *The man located.
  b. *Jesus wept the apostles.
  c. *Robert is hopeful of his children.
  d. *Robert is fond that his children love animals.
  e. *The children laughed the man.

15. In the chapter, we considered only transitive verbs, ones that select an NP direct object like *chase*. English also has **ditransitive verbs**, ones that may be followed by two NPs, such as *give*:

> The emperor gave the vassal a castle.

Think of three other ditransitive verbs in English and give example sentences.

16. For each verb, list the different types of complements it selects and provide an example of each type:

  a. want
  b. force
  c. try
  d. believe
  e. say

17. All of the *wh* words exhibit the "long-distance" behaviour illustrated with *who* in the chapter. Invent three sentences beginning with *what, which,* and *where,* in which the *wh* word is not in its deep structure position in the sentence. Give both versions of your sentence. Here is an example with the *wh* word *when: When could Marcy catch a flight out of here?* from *Marcy could catch a flight out of here when?*

18. There are many systematic, structure-dependent relationships among sentences similar to the one discussed in the chapter between declarative and interrogative sentences. Here is another example, based on ditransitive verbs (see exercise **15**):

> The boy wrote the MP a letter.
> The boy wrote a letter to the MP.
> A philanthropist gave the Animal Rights movement $1,000,000.
> A philanthropist gave $1,000,000 to the Animal Rights movement.

  A. Describe the relationship between the first and second members of the pairs of sentences.

B. State why a transformation deriving one of these structures from the other is plausible.

19. State at least three differences between English and the following languages, using just the sentence(s) given. Ignore lexical differences — that is, the different vocabulary. Here is an example:

Thai: dèg   khon   níi   kamlang   kin.
        boy   *classifier*   this   *progressive*   eat
        "This boy is eating."

        măa   tua   nán   kin   khâaw.
        dog   *classifier*   that   eat   rice
        "That dog ate rice."

Three differences are (1) Thai has "classifiers." They have no English equivalent. (2) The words (determiners, actually) "this" and "that" follow the noun in Thai, but precede the noun in English. (3) The "progressive" is expressed by a separate word in Thai. The verb does not change form. In English, the progressive is indicated by the presence of the verb *to be* and the adding of *-ing* to the verb.

a. French

    cet   homme   intelligent   comprendra   la question.
    this   man   intelligent   will understand   the question
    "This intelligent man will understand the question."

    ces   hommes   intelligents   comprendront   les questions.
    these   men   intelligent   will understand   the questions
    "These intelligent men will understand the questions."

b. Japanese

    watashi   ga   sakana   o   tabete   iru.
    I   *subject   fish   *object   eat (ing)   am
              marker*   marker*
    "I am eating fish."

c. Swahili

    mtoto   alivunja   kikombe.
    m-   toto   a-   li-   vunja   ki-   kombe
    *class   child   he   *past* break   *class   cup
    marker*   marker*
    "The child broke the cup."

    watoto   wanavunja   vikombe.
    wa-   toto   wa-   na-   vunja   vi-   kombe
    *class   child   they *present* break *class   cup
    marker*   marker*

"The children break the cups."

d. Korean

kɨ sonyɔn-iee wɨyu-lɨl masi-ass-ta.

kɨ	sonyɔn- iee	wɨyu- lɨl	masi- ass- ta
the boy	*subject marker*	milk *object marker*	drink *past assertion*

"The boy drank milk."

kɨ-nɨn muɔs-il mɔk-ass-nɨnya.

kɨ- nɨn	muɔs- il	mɔk- ass- nɨnya
he *subject marker*	what *object marker*	eat *past question*

"What did he eat?"

e. Tagalog

nakita ni Pedro-ng puno na ang bus.

nakita	ni	Pedro -ng	puno	na	ang	bus.
saw	*article*	Pedro that	full	already	*topic marker*	bus

"Pedro saw that the bus was already full."

20. (advanced) Compare the following French and English sentences:

French	English
Jean boit toujours du vin.	John always drinks some wine.
Jean drinks always some wine	*John drinks always some wine.
Marie lit jamais le journal.	Mary never reads the newspaper.
Marie reads never the newspaper	*Mary reads never the newspaper.
Pierre lave souvent ses chiens.	Peter often washes his dogs.
Pierre washes often his dogs	*Peter washes often his dogs.

A. Based on the above data, what would you hypothesize concerning the position of adverbs in French and English?

B. Now suppose that UG specifies that *in all languages* adverbs of frequency (e.g., *always*, *never*, *often*, *sometimes*) are between the Aux and VP constituents, as in the tree below. What rule would you need to hypothesize to derive the correct surface structure word order for French? (*Hint:* Adverbs are not allowed to move.)

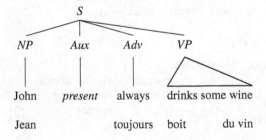

C. Are there any verbs in English that follow the same pattern as the French verbs?

21. In this chapter we proposed that there is a category Aux that is a separate constituent from the subject NP and the VP. One source of evidence that Aux is a separate constituent is that it undergoes movement in questions:

Have you seen John?

Will John come to the party?

Think of at least two other sentence types in English that demonstrate the constituency of Aux.

References

Fodor, J., & Bever, T. (1965). The psychological reality of linguistic segments. *Journal of Verbal Learning and Verbal Behavior, 4,* 414–420.

Lasnik, H. (Consultant). (1995). *The human language, program one.* [Video series]. Alexandria, VA: PBS.

Further Reading

Akmajian, A., Demers, R.A., Farmer, A., & Harnish, R.M. (1995). *Linguistics: An introduction to language and communication* (4th ed.). Cambridge, MA: MIT Press.

Baker, M.C. (2001). *The atoms of language: The mind's hidden rules of grammar.* New York: Basic Books.

Chomsky, N. (1957). *Syntactic structures.* The Hague: Mouton.

Chomsky, N. (1965). *Aspects of the theory of syntax.* Cambridge, MA: MIT Press.

Chomsky, N. (1972). *Language and mind* (Rev. ed.). New York: Harcourt Brace Jovanovich.

Chomsky, N. (1982). *Some concepts and consequences of the theory of government and binding.* Cambridge, MA: MIT Press.

Chomsky, N. (1988). *Language and problems of knowledge: The Managua lectures.* Cambridge, MA: MIT Press.

Emonds, J.E. (2007), *Discovering syntax: Clause structures of English, German and Romance. Studies in Generative Grammar 93.* New York: Mouton de Gruyter.

Gazdar, G., Klein, E., Pullum, G., & Sag, I. (1985). *Generalized phrase structure grammar.* Cambridge, MA: Harvard University Press.

Haegeman, L. (1994). *Introduction to government and binding theory* (2nd ed.). Oxford: Blackwell.

Haegeman, L., & Guéron, J. (1999). *English grammar: A general perspective.* Oxford: Blackwell.

Horrocks, G. (1987). *Generative grammar.* New York: Longman.

Jackendoff, R.S. (1977). *X-bar syntax: A study of phrase structure.* Cambridge, MA: MIT Press.

Jackendoff, R.S. (1994). *Patterns in the mind: Language and human nature.* New York: Basic Books.

Learning a language includes learning the agreed-upon meanings of certain strings of sounds and learning how to combine these meaningful units into larger units that also convey meaning. The relationship between word and meaning is arbitrary and conventional. That is, there is no necessary natural connection between word and meaning (it is arbitrary), but speakers of a language agree upon the meaning of a word (it is conventional). We are not free to change the meanings of these words at will, for if we did we would be unable to communicate with anyone.

As we see from the above quotation, Humpty Dumpty certainly accepted the arbitrariness of the meaning of *glory*, but he was unwilling to accept its conventionality. Alice, on the other hand, is right. You cannot make words mean whatever you want them to mean. Of course, if you wish to redefine the meaning of each word as you use it, you are free to do so, but this would be an artificial and clumsy use of language, and most people would not wait around for very long to talk to you.

Fortunately, there are few Humpty Dumptys. All the speakers of a language share a basic vocabulary — the sounds and meanings of morphemes and words.

Dictionaries are filled with words and their meanings. So is the head of every human being who speaks a language. We are walking dictionaries. We know the meanings of thousands of words. Our knowledge of their meanings permits us to use them to express our thoughts and to understand them when heard, even though we probably seldom stop and ask ourselves "What does *boy* mean?" or "What does *walk* mean?" The meanings of words are part of linguistic knowledge and are therefore part of the grammar. Our mental storehouses of information about words and morphemes are what we have been calling the lexicon.

Semantic Properties

Words and morphemes have meanings. We will talk about the meanings of words, even though words may be composed of several morphemes, as noted in Chapter 2.

Suppose someone said

The hackers stole data from two major banks.

If the word *hacker* exists in your mental dictionary, then you know that it refers to a person who uses programming skills to gain access to computer networks or files. Your knowledge of the meaning of *hacker* tells you that it was not an animal that stole the data, and that the stealing of data was carried out through computer programming skills. In other words, your knowledge of the meaning of *hacker* includes knowing that the individual to whom that word refers is human and is someone who is able to use programming skills to gain unauthorized entry into computer systems. These pieces of information, then, are some of the **semantic properties** of the word upon which speakers of the language agree. The meanings of all nouns, verbs, adjectives, and adverbs — the content words — and even some of the function words such as *with* or *over* can be at least partially specified by such properties.

The same semantic property may be part of the meanings of many different words. "Female" is a semantic property that helps to define

tigress	hen	actress	maiden
doe	mare	debutante	widow
ewe	vixen	girl	woman

The words in the last two columns are also distinguished by the semantic property "human," which is also found in

doctor	dean	professor	athlete	parent	baby	child

The meanings of the last two of these words are also specified as "young." That is, part of the meanings of the words *baby* and *child* is that they are "human" and "young." (We will continue to indicate words by using *italics* and semantic "properties" by using double quotation marks.)

The meanings of words have other properties. The word *father* has the property "male," as do *uncle* and *bachelor*, but *father* also has the property "parent," which distinguishes it from the other two words.

Mare, in addition to "female" and "animal," must also denote a property of "horseness." Words have general semantic properties such as "human" or "parent," as well as more specific properties that give the word its particular meaning.

The same semantic property may occur in words of different categories. "Female" is part of the meaning of the noun *mother*, of the verb *breast-feed*, and of the adjective *pregnant*. "Cause" is a verbal property of *darken, kill,* and *simplify*:

darken	"cause to become dark"
kill	"cause to die"
simplify	"cause to become simple"

Other semantic properties of verbs are shown in the following table:

Semantic Property	Verbs Having It
motion	bring, fall, plod, walk, run ...
contact	hit, kiss, touch ...
creation	build, imagine, make ...
sense	see, hear, feel ...

For the most part, no two words have the same meaning (but see the discussion of synonyms starting on page 151). Additional semantic properties make for finer and finer distinctions in meaning. *Plod* is distinguished from *walk* by the property "slow," and *stalk* is distinguished from *plod* by properties such as "purposeful."

Evidence for Semantic Properties

Semantic properties are not directly observable. Their existence must be inferred from linguistic evidence. One source of such evidence is found in the speech errors, or "slips of the tongue," that we all produce. Consider the following unintentional word substitutions (semantic substitutions) that some speakers have actually spoken.

Intended Utterance	Actual Utterance (Error)
bridge of the nose	bridge of the neck
when my gums bled	when my tongues bled
he came too late	he came too early
Mary was young	Mary was early
the lady with the dachshund	the lady with the Volkswagen
that's a horse of another colour	that's a horse of another race
he has to pay her alimony	he has to pay her rent

These errors and thousands of others that have been collected reveal that the incorrectly substituted words are not random substitutions but share some semantic properties with the intended words. *Nose* and *neck, gums* and *tongues*, are all "body parts" or "parts of the head." *Young, early*, and *late* are related to "time." *Dachshund* and *Volkswagen* are both "German" and "small." The common semantic properties between *colour* and *race* and even between *alimony* and *rent* are rather obvious.

Besides the confusion in semantic properties, these errors show other influences that may indicate how the lexicon is organized in our heads. For example, the similarities in the initial sounds of *nose* and *neck*, and the vowel sounds of *gums* and *tongues* also contribute to the confusion; and the frequent collocation or co-occurrence (words found together) of *horse* and *race* and of *pay* and *rent* influences the mistaken choice of words in the last two examples.

The semantic properties that describe the linguistic meaning of a word should not be confused with other nonlinguistic properties, such as physical properties. Scientists know that water is composed of hydrogen and oxygen, but such knowledge is not part of a word's meaning. We know that water is an essential ingredient of lemonade or a bath. We need not know any of these things, though, to know what the word *water* means and to be able to use and understand this word in a sentence. Scientifically, perhaps, a whale is a kind of mammal, but most people think of it as a kind of fish since it lives in water. In German, it is even called a *Wahlfisch*. Apparently we consider certain features more important than others in identifying entities.

Semantic Properties and the Lexicon

The lexicon is the part of the grammar that contains the knowledge speakers have about individual words and morphemes, including semantic properties. Words that share a semantic property are said to be in a semantic class, such as that of "female" words. Semantic classes may intersect, such as the class of words with the properties "female" and "young." The words *girl* and *filly* would be members of this class. In some cases, the presence of one semantic property can be inferred from the presence or absence of another. For example, words with the property "human" also have the property "animate."

In the lexicon of the Nuu-chah-nulth people, who live on the western coast of Vancouver Island and make their livelihood from fishing, there are at least fifteen distinct words to designate members of the semantic class "salmon" (e.g., *sa cin* "young spring salmon"; *kʷihnin* "old salmon"; *hisit* "sockeye salmon" when in the river or ocean; *ma wił* "freshwater salmon").

One way of expressing these facts about semantic properties is through the use of **semantic features**. Semantic features are a formal or notational device for expressing the presence or absence of semantic properties by pluses and minuses. For example, the lexical entries for words such as *father, girl, woman, mare,* and *stalk* would appear as follows (with other information omitted):

father	**girl**	**woman**	**mare**	**stalk**
+male	+female	+female	+female	+motion
+human	+human	+human	−human	+slow
+parent	+young	−young	−young	+purposeful
...	...	...	+equine	...
			...	

Intersecting classes share the same features; members of the class of words referring to human females are marked "plus" for the features "human" and "female." Some features need not be specifically mentioned. For example, if a word is [+human], then it is automatically [+animate]. This generalization can be expressed as a **redundancy rule**, which is part of the lexicon.

> A word that is [+human] is [+animate].

This rule specifies that [+animate] need not be specified in the lexical entries for *father, girl, professor,* and so on, since it can be inferred from the feature [+human].

Another difference between nouns may be captured by the use of the feature [+/− count]. Nouns that can be enumerated — *one potato, two potatoes* — are called **count nouns**. They can be preceded by the indefinite article *a* in the singular or by the quantifier *many* but not by *much* with plural forms. Nouns such as *rice, water,* and *milk,* which cannot be enumerated or preceded by *a* or *many* but can by *much* or by nothing at all, are called noncount or **mass nouns**:

I have a dog.	*I have a rice.
I have two dogs.	*I have two rice(s).
I have many dogs.	*I have many rice(s).
*I have much dog(s).	I have much rice.
*I like dog.	I like rice.

They may be distinguished in the lexicon by one feature:

dog	potato	rice	water	milk
+count	+count	−count	−count	−count

Count nouns may be either abstract (e.g., *idea*) or concrete (e.g., *girl*), as may mass nouns (e.g., *information* or *soup*). We cannot speak of "a bravery" or "braveries," nor do we generally speak of "two soups," though we do informally use such an expression instead of "two cups of soup." In so doing, we are deliberately treating a mass noun as if it were a count noun. Other mass nouns are more resistant to such use; few speakers of English would talk about "a furniture."

Some semantic redundancy rules involve "negative" properties. For example, if something is "human," then it is not "abstract"; an activity that is "slow" is not "fast." Thus, we can state the following two redundancy rules:

A word that is [+human] is [–abstract].
A word that is [+slow] is [–fast].

Thus, without further specification in the lexicon, *woman* is [–abstract], and the verb *crawl*, which is [+slow], is also [–fast] by the second redundancy rule.

More Semantic Relationships

Consider the following knowledge about words that speakers of English have:

If something *swims*, then it is in a liquid.
If something *splashes* when hit by an object, then it is a liquid.

If you say you saw a bug swimming in a container of *goop*, anyone who understands English would agree that *goop* is surely a liquid — that is, it has the semantic feature [+liquid]. Even without knowing what *goop* refers to, you know you can talk about pouring goop, drinking goop, or plugging a hole where goop is leaking out and forming droplets. The words *pour, drink, leak,* and *droplet* are all used with items relating to the property "liquid."

Similarly, we would know that *sawing goop in half, melting goop*, or *bending goop* are semantically ill-formed expressions because none of these activities applies sensibly to objects that are [+liquid].

In some languages, the fact that certain verbs can occur appropriately with certain nouns is reflected in the verb morphology. For example, in the Native North American language Navajo, there are different verb forms for objects with different semantic properties. The verbal suffix *-léh* is used with words with semantic features [+long] and [+flexible], such as *rope*, whereas the verbal suffix *-túh* is used for words such as *spear*, which is [+long] and [–flexible].

In other languages, nouns occur with **classifiers**, grammatical morphemes that mark their semantic class. In Swahili, for example, nouns that refer to human beings are marked with a prefix *m-* if singular and *wa-* if plural, as in *mtoto* "child" and *watoto* "children." Nouns that refer to human artifacts such as beds, chairs, and cutlery are marked with the classifiers *ki* if singular and *vi* if plural, for example, *kiti* "chair" and *viti* "chairs."

Homonyms and Ambiguity

"Mine is a long and sad tale!" said the Mouse, turning to Alice and sighing.
"It is a long tail, certainly," said Alice, looking with wonder at the Mouse's tail, "but why do you call it sad?"

Lewis Carroll, *Alice's Adventures in Wonderland* (1865)

© Dan Piraro. King Features Syndicate.

Knowing a word means knowing both its sounds (pronunciation) and its meaning. Both are crucial in determining whether two words are the same or different. If two words differ in pronunciation but have the same meaning, such as *chesterfield* and *couch*, they are different words. Likewise, two words with identical pronunciation but significantly different meanings, such as *tale* and *tail*, are also considered different words, as indicated by the difference in spelling. But even if the spelling and pronunciation are identical and the meaning is different, the words are different. *Bat* the flying rodent and *bat* for hitting baseballs are different words because they have different meanings even though they are pronounced and spelled identically.

Words such as the two *bats* or *tale* and *tail* are called **homonyms**. Homonyms are different words that are pronounced the same, but may or may not be spelled the same. The term **homophone** is sometimes used instead of *homonym*. *To, too*, and *two* are also homonyms.

Different words that are spelled the same, whether or not they are pronounced the same, are called **homographs**. Of course, if they are pronounced the same, they are also homonyms. Thus, *pen* the writing instrument and *pen* the cage are both homographs and homonyms. *Lead* the verb and *lead* the metal are homographs but not homophones. *Tail* and *tale* are homonyms but not homographs.

Complete homonymy occurs when both the spelling and the pronunciation are the same but the meaning differs (*pen*, *bat*). Partial homonymy (called **heteronyms**) occurs where words are spelled the same but are pronounced differently. Examples would be *dove* the bird and *dove* the past tense of *dive*, as well as *bass, bow, lead, wind*, and well over a hundred others.

The following diagram illustrates these terms.

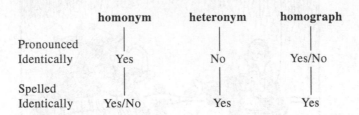

	homonym	heteronym	homograph
Pronounced Identically	Yes	No	Yes/No
Spelled Identically	Yes/No	Yes	Yes

When a word has multiple meanings that are related conceptually or historically, it is said to be **polysemous**. It is difficult to determine whether a word with several different meanings should be treated as one word (polysemous) or as several words that happen to look or sound the same (homonyms). *Bear* is polysemous, with meanings "to tolerate," "to carry," and "to support," among others found in the dictionary. *Bear* is also a homonym. Homonyms generally have separate dictionary entries, often marked with superscripts to indicate differences. One *bear* is the polysemous verb just mentioned. The other *bear* refers to the animal. It, too, is polysemous, with other meanings such as "a falling stock market." *Bare*, which is pronounced the same as *bear*, is a third homophone.

Homonyms and polysemous words can create ambiguities. A word or sentence is **ambiguous** if it can be understood or interpreted in more than one way. The sentence *I'll meet you by the bank* may mean "I'll meet you by the financial institution" or "I'll meet you by the riverside." Sometimes additional context can help to disambiguate the sentence:

I'll meet you by the bank, in front of the automated teller machine.
I'll meet you by the bank. We can go skinny-dipping.

Homonyms are good candidates for humour as well as for confusion.

"How is bread made?"
"I know *that*!" Alice cried eagerly.
"You take some flour —"
"Where do you pick the flower?" the White Queen asked. "In a garden, or in the hedges?"
"Well, it isn't *picked* at all," Alice explained; "it's *ground* —"
"How many acres of ground?" said the White Queen.

Lewis Carroll, *Through the Looking-Glass* (1871)

The humour of this passage is due to the two sets of homonyms: *flower* and *flour* and the two meanings of *ground*. Alice means *ground* as the past tense of *grind*, whereas the White Queen is interpreting *ground* to mean "earth." Another example is the witty couplet by Hilaire Belloc:

> When I am dead, I hope it may be said,
> "His sins were scarlet, but his books were read."

> Hilaire Belloc, from *Complete Verse*, Random House UK Ltd. By permission
> of Peters, Fraser & Dunlop on behalf of the Estate of Hilaire Belloc.

The humour here, of course, depends on the pronunciation of *read* (past tense verb) with its homonym *red* and the linking of both words with *books* and *scarlet*.

A somewhat different instance of homonyms occurs with *have* and *be*. In the following sentences, both are verbs:

(1) Robert *has* a dog named Cecelia.
(2) Dogs *are* intelligent animals.

Both also occur as auxiliaries. In addition, the auxiliary *be* has two homonyms, one that occurs with *-ing* forms and one that indicates the passive voice:

(3) Cecelia *has* seen ten squirrels today.
(4) They *are* running fast.
(5) The women *were* given gifts by their children.

Ambiguity may also result from the use of these homonyms, as in

(6) They are moving sidewalks.

When *are* is understood as a verb (called a **copula** when used in this way), *moving* is a participle modifying *sidewalks*. The overall meaning is something like "those things are sidewalks that move." If *are* is an auxiliary, then the meaning is "those workers are relocating the sidewalks."

Synonyms

> Does he wear a turban, a fez or a hat?
> Does he sleep on a mattress, a bed or a mat, or a Cot,
> The Akond of Swat?
> Can he write a letter concisely clear,
> Without a speck or a smudge or smear or Blot,
> The Akond of Swat?

> Edward Lear, "The Akond of Swat" (1877)

> A synonym is a word you use when you can't spell the other one.
> Baltasar Gracián (1601-1658)

There are not only words that sound the same but have different meanings; there are also words that sound different but have the same or nearly the same meaning. Such words are called **synonyms**. For example, the famous "parrot" sketch in which John Cleese insists that

> This parrot is no more. It has ceased to be. It's expired and gone to meet its maker. This is a late parrot. It's a stiff. Bereft of life, it rests in peace. If you hadn't nailed it to the perch, it would be pushing up the daisies. It's rung down the curtain and joined the choir invisible. This is an ex-parrot.

Monty Python

There are dictionaries of synonyms that contain hundreds of entries, such as

apathetic/phlegmatic/passive/sluggish/indifferent
pedigree/ancestry/genealogy/descent/lineage

It has been said that there are no perfect synonyms — that is, no two words ever have *exactly* the same meaning. Still, the following pairs of sentences have very similar meanings.

(1) He's sitting on the chesterfield. / He's sitting on the sofa. / He's sitting on the couch.
(2) I'll be happy to come. / I'll be glad to come.

Some individuals may always use *chesterfield* or *sofa* instead of *couch*, but if they know the three words they will understand the sentences and interpret them to mean the same thing. The degree of semantic similarity between words depends to a great extent on the number of semantic properties they share. *Chesterfield, sofa*, and *couch* refer to the same type of object and share most, if not all, of their semantic properties. However, there is always some context in which one could appear and not the other. For example, a patient might lie on a psychiatrist's couch rather than on a psychiatrist's chesterfield or sofa, and even in Canada we have *couch potatoes* rather than *chesterfield potatoes*.

A polysemous word may share one of its meanings with another word, a kind of partial synonymy. For example, *mature* and *ripe* are polysemous words that are synonyms when applied to fruit but not when applied to animals. *Deep* and *profound* are another such pair. Both may apply to thought, but only *deep* applies to water.

Sometimes words that are ordinarily opposites can mean the same thing in certain contexts; thus, a *good* scare is the same as a *bad* scare. Similarly, a word with a positive meaning in one form, such as the adjective *perfect*, when used adverbially, undergoes a "weakening" effect, so that *a perfectly good bicycle* is neither perfect nor always good. *Perfectly good* means something more like "adequate."

When synonyms occur in otherwise identical sentences, the sentences will be paraphrases. Sentences are **paraphrases** if they have the same meaning (except possibly for minor differences in emphasis). Consider *She forgot her handbag* and

She forgot her purse. This use of synonyms creates **lexical paraphrase**, just as the use of homonyms may create lexical ambiguity.

Antonyms

As a rule, man is a fool;
When it's hot, he wants it cool;
When it's cool, he wants it hot;
Always wanting what is not.

Anonymous

The meaning of a word may be partially defined by saying what it is not. *Male* means *not female. Dead* means *not alive*. Words that are opposite in meaning are often called **antonyms**. Ironically, the basic property of two words that are antonyms is that they share all but one semantic property. *Beautiful* and *tall* are not antonyms; *beautiful* and *ugly*, or *tall* and *short*, are. The property they do not share is present in the one and absent in the other.

There are several kinds of antonymy. There are **complementary pairs**:

alive/dead   present/absent   awake/asleep

They are complementary in that *not alive = dead, not dead = alive*, and so on.

There are **gradable pairs** of antonyms:

big/small   hot/cold   fast/slow   happy/sad

With gradable pairs, the negative of one word is not synonymous with the other. For example, someone who is *not happy* is not necessarily *sad*. It is also true of gradable antonyms that more of one is less of another. More bigness is less small-ness, wider is less narrow, and taller is less short. Gradable antonyms are often found among sets of words that partition a continuum:

tiny–small–medium–large–huge–gargantuan
euphoric–elated–happy–so-so–sad–gloomy–despondent

Another characteristic of many pairs of gradable antonyms is that one is **marked** and the other **unmarked**. The unmarked member is the one used in questions of degree. We ask, "How *high* is it?" (not "How low is it?") or "How *tall* is she?" We answer "Three hundred metres high" or "Five feet tall" but never "Five feet short," except humorously. *High* and *tall* are the unmarked members of *high/low* and *tall/short*. Notice that the meanings of these adjectives and other similar ones are relative. The words themselves provide no information about absolute size. Because of our knowledge of the language, and of things in the world, this relativity normally causes no confusion. Thus, we know that *a small elephant* is much bigger than *a large mouse*.

Another kind of "opposite" involves pairs such as

give/receive   buy/sell   teacher/pupil

They are called **relational opposites**, and they display symmetry in their meaning. If X *gives* Y to Z, then Z *receives* Y from X. If X is Y's *teacher*, then Y is X's *pupil*. Pairs of words ending in *-er* and *-ee* are usually relational opposites. If Athina is Bill's *employer*, then Bill is Athina's *employee*.

Comparative forms of gradable pairs of adjectives often form relational pairs. Thus, if Sally is *taller* than Alfred, then Alfred is *shorter* than Sally. If a Cadillac is *more expensive* than a Ford, then a Ford is *cheaper* than a Cadillac.

If meanings of words were indissoluble wholes, then there would be no way to make the interpretations that we do. We know that *big* and *red* are not opposites because they have too few semantic properties in common. They are both adjectives, but *big* is of the semantic class involving size, whereas *red* is a colour. On the other hand, *buy* and *sell* are relational opposites because both contain the semantic property "transfer of goods or services," and they differ only in one property, "direction of transfer."

Semantic redundancy rules such as those discussed above can reveal knowledge about antonyms:

A word that is [+married] is [–single].
A word that is [+single] is [–married].

These rules show that any word that bears the semantic property "married," such as *wife*, is understood to lack the semantic property "single"; conversely, any word that bears the semantic property "single," such as *bachelor*, will not have the property "married."

Some words are their own antonyms. These "autoantonyms" are words such as *cleave* "to split apart" or "to cling together" and *dust* "to remove something" or "to spread something," as in dusting furniture or dusting crops. Antonymic pairs that are pronounced the same but spelled differently are similar to autoantonyms: *raise* and *raze* are one such pair.

Formation of Antonyms

In English, there are a number of ways to form antonyms. You can add the prefix *un-*

likely/unlikely   able/unable   fortunate/unfortunate

or you can add *non-*

entity/nonentity   conformist/nonconformist

or you can add *in-*

tolerant/intolerant   discreet/indiscreet   decent/indecent

Other prefixes may also be used to form negative words morphologically: *il-*, as in *illegal; mis-*, as in *misbehave; dis-*, as in *displease.* The suffix *-less*, as in *toothless*, also negates the meaning of a stem morpheme.

These strategies occasionally backfire, however. *Loosen* and *unloosen, flammable* and *inflammable, valuable* and *invaluable,* and a few other "antiantonyms" actually have the same or nearly the same meaning.

Hyponyms

There are words with many semantic properties in common that are neither synonyms nor near synonyms. Speakers of English know that the words *red, white*, and *blue* are "colour" words indicating a class to which they all belong. Similarly, *lion, tiger, leopard*, and *lynx* have the feature [+feline]. Such sets of words are called **hyponyms**. The relationship of hyponymy is between the more general term (the superordinate or hypernym), such as *colour*, and the more specific instances of it, such as *red* or *white*. Thus, *red* is a hyponym of *colour*, and *lion* is a hyponym of *feline*; equivalently, *colour* has the hyponym *red*, and *feline* has the hyponym *lion*.

Words such as *man* and *boy* may be considered as hyponyms of *human*. You can say *A man is a human* but not *A human is a man* (the person might be a woman, a girl, or a boy, which are all co-hyponyms of *man*). Hyponymy is thus a "kind of" relationship. (A man is a *kind* of human; red is a *kind* of colour.)

Sometimes there is no single word in the language that encompasses a set of hyponyms. *Clarinet, guitar, horn, marimba, piano, trumpet,* and *violin* are hyponyms because they are "musical instruments," but there isn't a single word meaning "musical instrument" that has these words as its hyponyms.

Because we know the semantic properties of words, we know when two words are antonyms, synonyms, hyponyms, or homonyms or are unrelated in meaning.

Metonyms and Meronyms

A **metonym** is a word used in place of another word or expression to convey the same meaning. The use of *brass* to refer to military officers and the use of *Ottawa* to indicate the federal government are examples of metonymy. *Crown* is a metonym for the monarchy or for an agent of the monarchy, such as the prosecutor in a criminal trial. Metonyms need not be a single word. *Bay Street* is a metonym referring to the financial industry.

A related term is **meronym**. This is a part-to-whole relationship in which the meronym is "part of" a larger entity. *Leaf, branch*, and *root* are meronyms or parts of *tree*, but unlike metonyms they do not represent "tree."

Retronyms

Day baseball, silent movie, surface mail, and *whole milk* are all expressions that once were redundant. In the past, all baseball games were played in daylight, all movies were silent, air and electronic mail didn't exist, and low-fat and skim milk were not yet available. **Retronym** is the term reserved for these expressions, but strictly speaking it applies not to the individual words themselves but to the combinations.

Proper Names

"My name is Alice . . ."

"It's a stupid name enough!" Humpty Dumpty interrupted impatiently. "What does it mean?"

"Must a name mean something?" Alice asked doubtfully.

"Of course it must," Humpty Dumpty said with a short laugh. "My name means the shape I am — and a good handsome shape it is, too. With a name like yours, you might be any shape, almost."

Lewis Carroll, *Through the Looking-Glass* (1871)

I was Joan Foster, there was no doubt about that; people called me by that name and I had authentic documents to prove it. But I was also Louisa K. Delacourt.

Margaret Atwood, *Lady Oracle* (1976)

"What's in a name?" is a question that has occupied philosophers of language for centuries. Plato was concerned with whether names were "natural"; Humpty Dumpty thinks his name means his shape, and in part it does.

Usually, when we think of names, we think of names of people or places, which are **proper names**. Proper names are different from most words in the language in that they refer to a specific object or entity but usually have little meaning or sense beyond a power of referral. Of course, if a word with sense, such as *lake*, is incorporated into a proper name such as *Lake Louise*, then the proper name has the semantic properties of *lake*. Caution is needed, though, since a restaurant named *Lake Louise* would not have any lakelike meaning.

The meaning of a word such as *dog* or *sincerity* imparts a sense that permits you to recognize specific instances of that class of entities or even to have an abstract vision of what is meant, but you cannot pet *dog* or doubt *sincerity*. You can only pet a specific dog, Fido, or doubt a specific instance of sincerity, such as a political promise. Nothing in the world corresponds to *dog* the way *Paris* refers to the city of Paris.

Within their contexts, proper names refer to unique objects or entities. The entities may be extant, such as those designated by

Margaret Atwood
Hudson Bay
the Stanley Cup

or no longer physically present, such as

Pierre Elliott Trudeau
Socrates
Troy

or even fictional, such as

> Sherlock Holmes
> Anne of Green Gables
> Oz

Proper names are **definite**, which means they refer to a unique object insofar as the speaker and the listener are concerned. If I say

> Mary Smith is coming to dinner.

my spouse understands Mary Smith to refer to our friend Mary Smith, not to one of the dozens of Mary Smiths in the phone book.

Because they are inherently definite, proper names in English are not in general preceded by *the*:

> *the Mary Smith
> *the Alberta

There are exceptions, such as the names of rivers, ships, and erected structures

> the St. Lawrence
> the Jacques Cartier Bridge
> the *Bluenose*
> the Eiffel Tower
> the CN Tower

and there are special cases such as *the Al Hakomakis* to refer to the family of Al Hakomaki. Also, for the sake of clarity or literary effect, it is possible to precede a proper name by an article if the resulting noun phrase is followed by a modifying expression such as a prepositional phrase or a sentence:

> The Paris of the 1920s ...
> The Toronto that everyone loves to hate ...

In some languages, such as Greek and Hungarian, articles normally occur before proper names. Thus, we find in Greek

> O Spiros agapai tin Sophia.

which is literally "The Spiro loves the Sophie," where *O* is the masculine nominative form of the definite article and *tin* the feminine accusative form. This indicates that some of the restrictions we observed are particular to English and may be due to syntactic rather than semantic rules of language.

Proper names cannot usually be pluralized, though they can be plural, such as *the Great Lakes* or *the Pleiades*. There are exceptions, such as *the Al Hakomakis* already mentioned or expressions such as *the linguistics department has three Marys*, meaning three people named Mary, but they are special locutions used in particular circumstances. Because proper names generally refer to unique objects, it is not surprising that they occur mainly in the singular.

For the same reason, proper names cannot in general be preceded by adjectives. Many adjectives have the semantic effect of **narrowing** the field of reference, so that the noun phrase *a red house* is a more specific description than simply *a house*; but what proper names refer to is already completely narrowed down, so modification by adjectives seems peculiar. Again, as in all these cases, extenuating circumstances give rise to exceptions. Language is nothing if not flexible, and we find expressions such as *young John* used to distinguish between two people named John. We also find adjectives applied to emphasize some quality of the object referred to, such as *the wicked Borgias* or *the brilliant Professor Einstein*.

Proper names are found in all languages and are therefore a linguistic universal.

Names may be coined or drawn from the stock of names that the language provides, but once a proper name has been coined it cannot be pluralized or preceded by *the* or any adjective (except in cases like those cited above), and it will be used to refer uniquely, for these rules are among the many rules already in the grammar, and speakers know they apply to all proper names, even new ones.

Phrase and Sentence Meaning

"Then you should say what you mean," the March Hare went on.

"I do," Alice hastily replied, "at least — I mean what I say — that's the same thing, you know."

"Not the same thing a bit!" said the Hatter. "You might just as well say that 'I see what I eat' is the same thing as 'I eat what I see'!"

"You might just as well say," added the March Hare, "that 'I like what I get' is the same thing as 'I get what I like'!"

"You might just as well say," added the Dormouse . . . "that 'I breathe when I sleep' is the same thing as 'I sleep when I breathe'!"

"It *is* the same thing with you," said the Hatter.

Lewis Carroll, *Alice's Adventures in Wonderland* (1865)

Words and morphemes are the smallest meaningful units in language. We have been studying their meaning relationships and semantic properties as lexical semantics. For the most part, however, we communicate in phrases and sentences. The **principle of compositionality** states that the meaning of a phrase or sentence depends on both the meaning of its words and how those words are combined structurally. The sentence *Visiting relatives can be boring* can have two meanings because it has two structures.

Some of the semantic relationships we observed between words are also found between sentences. While words may be synonyms, two sentences may be paraphrases because they contain synonymous words or because of structural differences that do not affect meaning:

They ran the bill up.
They ran up the bill.

Similarly, words may be homonyms, hence ambiguous when spoken; sentences may also be ambiguous because they contain homonyms, as in *I need to buy a pen for Shelby*, or because of their structures, as in the sentence from Chapter 3, *The boy saw the man with the telescope.*

Words have antonyms, and sentences can be negated. Thus, the opposite of *He is alive* is both *He is dead*, using an antonym, and *He is not alive*, using syntactic negation.

Words are used for naming purposes, and sentences can be used that way as well. Both words and sentences can be used to refer to, or point out, objects, and both may have further meaning beyond this referring capability, as we will see in a later section.

The study of how word meanings combine into phrase and sentence meanings, and the meaning relationships among these larger units, is called phrasal or **sentential semantics** to distinguish it from lexical semantics.

Phrasal Meaning

> ... I placed all my words with their interpretations in alphabetical order. And thus in a few days, by the help of a very faithful memory, I got some insight into their language.
>
> Jonathan Swift, *Gulliver's Travels* (1726)

Although it is sometimes believed that learning a language is merely learning the words of that language and what they mean — a myth apparently accepted by Gulliver — there is more to it than that, as you know if you have ever tried to learn a foreign language. We comprehend sentences because we know the meanings of individual words and because we know the rules for combining their meanings.

Noun-Centred Meaning

We know the meanings of *red* and *balloon*. The semantic rule to interpret the combination *red balloon* adds the property "redness" to the properties of *balloon*. The phrase *the red balloon*, because of the presence of the definite article *the*, means "a particular instance of redness and balloonness." A semantic rule for the interpretation of *the* accounts for this.

The phrase *large balloon* would be interpreted by a different semantic rule, because part of the meaning of *large* is that it is a relative concept. *Large balloon* means "large for a balloon." What is large for a balloon may be small for a house and gargantuan for a cockroach, yet we correctly comprehend the meanings of *large balloon*, *large house*, and *large cockroach*.

The semantic rules for adjective-noun combinations are complex. A *good friend* is a kind of friend, just as a *red brick* is a kind of brick. But a *false friend* is not any kind of friend at all. The semantic properties of "friendness" are cancelled out by the adjective *false*. Thus, semantic rules for noun phrases containing *good* and *false* are quite different. A third kind of rule governs adjectives such as *alleged*; the meaning of *alleged murderer* is someone accused of murder, but the semantic rules in this case do not tell us whether an alleged murderer is or is not a murderer.

The examples in the previous three paragraphs, and many examples below, all illustrate the principle of compositionality, and how it is manifested differently, depending on the semantic properties of the individual words, and the syntactic structures in which they occur — in particular, which word is the head of the phrase.

Exemplars of Class of Adjective (Adj)	Truth of "An Adj X is an X" (e.g., A *red ball* is a *ball*.)
good, red, large, etc.	true
false, counterfeit, phony, etc.	false
alleged, purported, putative, etc.	undetermined

There are many more rules involved in the semantics of noun phrases. Because noun phrases may contain prepositional phrases, semantic rules are needed for expressions such as *the house with the white fence*. We have seen how the rules account for *the house* and *the white fence*. The semantic rule for prepositions indicates that two objects stand in a relationship determined by the meaning of the particular preposition. For *with*, that relationship is "accompanies" or "is part of." A preposition such as *on* means a certain spatial relationship, and so on for other prepositions.

The syntactic notion of *head* plays a significant role in semantic rules; in the structure of a phrase, its head determines the phrase's principal meaning. The head of a noun phrase will be the noun, the head of a verb phrase the verb, and so on. Since *brick* is the head of the noun phrase *the red brick*, the meaning of *a red brick* is a kind of brick. On the other hand, *red* is the head of the adjective phrase *brick red*, and the meaning of *brick red* is a certain shade of red.

In noun compounds, the final noun is generally the head; it provides the core meaning and specifies the syntactic class of the compound. So a *doghouse* is a kind of a house, namely one suitable for dogs, whereas a *housedog* is a kind of dog. Similar analyses apply to compounds consisting of mixed categories. The noun-adjective compound *headstrong* is an adjective; the noun-verb compound *spoonfeed* is a verb; the verb-noun compound *pickpocket* is a noun, and so on. Exceptions are compounds like *redneck,* which is a type of person, not a type of neck. These items must be individually stored along with their meaning in the mental lexicon. Their meaning cannot be predicted by rule.

Meanings build on meanings. Noun phrases are combinations of meanings of nouns, adjectives, articles, and even sentences. (The noun phrase *the fact he knew too much* is a combination of *the, fact*, and the sentence *he knew too much*.) In turn, sentences are combinations of noun phrases, verb phrases, and so on. All these combinations make sense because the semantic rules of grammar, like rules of phonology or syntax, operate systematically and predictably to incorporate the meanings of the phrasal components into the meaning of the phrase.

Sense and Reference

> It is natural ... to think of there being connected with a sign ... besides ... the reference of the sign, also what I should like to call the sense of the sign. ...

Gottlob Frege, *On Sense and Reference* (1892)

Just as knowing the meaning of a declarative sentence means knowing how to determine its truth value, knowing the meanings of certain noun phrases means knowing how to discover what objects the noun phrases refer to. For example, in the sentence

The boy put the red brick on the wall.

knowing the meaning of *the red brick* enables us to identify the object being referred to. As with the truth of sentences, we need know only, in principle, how to identify the object; a blindfolded person would comprehend the meaning.

> A word's denotation refers to the object or event it references in the world. A word's connotation refers to the associations (emotional, psychological, etc.) it evokes.

The object "pointed to" in such a noun phrase is called its **referent**, and the noun phrase is said to have **reference**.

For many noun phrases, there is more to meaning than just reference. For example, *the red brick* and *the first brick from the right* may refer to the same object — that is, they may be **coreferential**. Nevertheless, we would be reluctant to say that the two expressions have the same meaning because they have the same reference. There is some additional meaning to these expressions, often termed **sense**. Thus, noun phrases may have sense and reference, which together compose the meaning. Knowing the sense of a noun phrase allows us to identify its referent. Sometimes the term **extension** is used for *reference* and **intension** for *sense*. Another example of sense and reference might be the relations between *the prime minister of Canada, the leader of the Conservative Party*, and *Stephen Harper*. In 2009, these all referred to the same person — they all had the same reference — but the sense of each is different, so that one might know what the prime minister of Canada was but not who it was. Several years ago, the prime minister of Canada and the leader of the Liberal Party was Paul Martin, and earlier the prime minister of Canada was the leader of the Progressive Conservatives, Joe Clark, then Brian Mulroney, and then Kim Campbell. And the prime minister of Great Britain is someone else.

Certain proper names appear to have only reference. Thus, a name such as Kelly Jones points out a certain person, its referent, but seems to have little meaning beyond that. Nonetheless, some proper names do seem to have meaning over and above their ability to refer. Humpty Dumpty suggested that his name means "a good round shape." Certainly, the name *Sue* has the semantic property "female," as evinced by the humour in "A Boy Named Sue," a song sung by Johnny Cash. *The Pacific Ocean* has the semantic properties of "ocean," and even names such as *Fido* and *Bossie* are associated with dogs and cows, respectively.

Sometimes two different proper names have the same referent, such as Superman and Clark Kent, or Dr. Jekyll and Mr. Hyde. It is a hotly debated question in the philosophy of language whether two such expressions have the same meaning or differ in sense.

While some proper nouns appear to have reference but no sense, other noun phrases have sense but no reference. If not, then we would be unable to understand sentences such as

> The present king of France is bald.
> By the year 3000, our descendants will have left Earth.

Speakers of English can understand these sentences even though France now has no king and our descendants of a millennium from now do not exist.

Verb-Centred Meaning

In all languages, the verb plays a central role in sentence structure and meaning. In English, the verb determines the number of objects and limits the semantic properties of both the subject and its objects. For example, *find* requires an animate subject and selects a direct object; *put* selects for both a direct object and a prepositional object that has a locative meaning. In formal, written English, the presence of a verb is essential for a complete sentence. Languages of the world may be classified according to whether the verb occurs initially, medially, or finally in their basic sentences. This is evidence for the centrality of the verb.

Thematic Roles

The noun phrase subject of a sentence and the constituents of the verb phrase are semantically related in various ways to the verb. The relations depend on the meaning of the particular verb. For example, the NP *the boy* in *The boy found a red brick* is called the **agent** or "doer" of the action of finding. The NP *a red brick* is the **theme** and undergoes the action. (The boldfaced words are technical terms of semantic theory.) Part of the meaning of *find* is that its subject is an agent and its direct object is a theme.

The noun phrases within a verb phrase whose head is *put* have the relation of theme and **goal**. In the verb phrase *put the red brick on the wall, the red brick* is the theme, and *on the wall* is the goal. The entire phrase is interpreted to mean that the theme of *put* changes its position to the goal. The subject of *put* is also an agent, so that, in *The boy put the red brick on the wall*, the boy performs the action. The knowledge speakers have about *find* and *put* is revealed in their lexical entries:

> find, V _____ NP (agent, theme)
> put, V _____ NP, PP (agent, theme, goal)

The thematic roles are contained in parentheses. The first one states that the subject is an agent.

This formal representation is one way of stating the selectional restrictions of the verb, and the semantic relationships between the subject and the selected objects.

The semantic relationships we have called theme, agent, and goal are among the **thematic roles** of the verb. Other thematic roles are **location**, where the action occurs; **source**, where the action originates; **instrument**, an object used to accomplish the action; **experiencer**, one receiving sensory input; **causative**, a natural force that brings about a change; and **possessor**, one who owns or has something. (Note that this list is not complete.) These thematic roles may be summed up as follows:

Thematic Role	Description	Example
Agent	the one who performs an action	*Joyce* ran.
Theme	the one or thing that undergoes an action	Mary called *Bill*.
Location	the place where an action occurs	It rains *in Spain*.
Goal	the place to which an action is directed	Put the cat *on the porch*.
Source	the place from which an action originates	He flew from *Winnipeg* to Regina.
Instrument	the means by which an action is performed	Jo cuts hair *with a razor*.
Experiencer	one who perceives something	*Helen* heard Robert playing the piano.
Causative	a natural force that causes a change	*The wind* damaged the roof.
Possessor	one who has something	The tail of *the dog* got caught in the door.

Our knowledge of verbs includes their syntactic category; which objects, if any, they select; and the thematic roles that their NP subject and object(s) have; this knowledge is explicitly represented in the lexicon.

Thematic roles are the same in sentences that are paraphrases. In both these sentences,

> The dog bit the man.
> The man was bitten by the dog.

the dog is the agent, and *the man* is the theme.

Thematic roles may remain the same in sentences that are not paraphrases, as in the following examples:

> The boy opened the door with the key.
> The key opened the door.
> The door opened.

In all three sentences, *the door* is the theme, the thing that gets opened. In the first two sentences, *the key*, despite its different structural positions, retains the thematic role of instrument. The three examples illustrate the fact that English allows many different thematic roles to be the subject of the sentence (S) — that is, the first NP under the S. These sentences have as subjects an agent (*the boy*), an instrument (*the key*), and a theme (*the door*).

The sentences below illustrate other kinds of subjects:

> This hotel forbids dogs.
> It seems that Terrell has lost his strength.

In the first example, *this hotel* has the thematic role of location. In the second, the subject *it* is semantically empty and lacks a thematic role entirely.

Thematic Roles in Other Languages

Contrast English with German. German is much stingier about which thematic roles can be subjects. For example, to express the idea "This hotel forbids dogs," a German speaker would have to say

> In diesem Hotel sind Hunde verboten.

Literally, this means "In this hotel are dogs forbidden." German does not permit the thematic role of location to occur as a subject; it must be expressed as a prepositional phrase. If we translated the English sentence word for word into German, then the results would be ungrammatical in German:

> *Dieses Hotel verbietet Hunde.

Differences such as these between English and German show that learning a foreign language is not a matter of simple word-for-word translation. You must learn the grammar, and that includes learning the syntax and semantics and how the two interact.

In many languages, thematic roles are reflected in the case assumed by the noun. The *case*, or **grammatical case**, of a noun is the particular morphological shape that it takes. English does not have an extensive case system, but the possessive form of a noun, as in *the boy's red brick*, is called the genitive or possessive case.

In languages such as Finnish, the noun assumes a morphological shape according to its thematic role in the sentence. For example, in Finnish *koulu-* is the root meaning "school," and *-sta* is a case ending that means "directional source." Thus, *koulusta* means "from the school." Similarly, *kouluun* (*koulu + un*) means "to the school."

Some of the information carried by grammatical case in languages such as Finnish is borne by prepositions in English. Thus, *from* and *to* often indicate the thematic roles of source and goal. Instrument is marked by *with*; location by prepositions such as *on* and *in*; possessor by *of*; and agent, experiencer, and causative with *by* in passive sentences. The role of theme is generally unaccompanied by a preposition, as its most common syntactic function is direct object. Agent is also unaccompanied by a preposition when it is the structural subject of the sentence. What we are calling thematic roles in this section has sometimes been studied as **case theory**.

In German, case distinctions appear on articles as well as on nouns and adjectives. Thus, in

> Sie liebt den Mann.

"She loves the man," the article *den* is in the accusative case. In the nominative case, it would be *der*. Languages with a rich system of case are often more constraining as to which thematic roles can occur in the subject position. German, as we saw above, is one such language.

The Theta-Criterion

The process of assigning thematic roles is sometimes called **theta assignment**. This term refers to the grammatical activity of spreading information from the verb to its noun phrase and prepositional phrase satellites. In a sentence like *The boy opened the door with the key, open* is represented in the lexicon as follows:

> open, V, _____ NP, PP (agent, theme, instrument)

Theta assignment assigns agent to the subject noun phrase, theme to the direct object, and instrument to the prepositional phrase.

In Chapter 3, we noted that the meaning of a sentence corresponds most closely to its deep structure. This is because theta assignment happens at deep structure. We find the evidence in sentences such as *Who will Bill kiss? Who* is the theme of *kiss,* and *Bill* is the agent, despite their relative positions in the sentence. If we examine the deep structure, *Bill will kiss who,* we see that theta assignment assigns the role of subject to *Bill* and theme to *who,* in accordance with the lexical entry of *kiss*:

> kiss, V, _____ NP (agent, theme)

The transformational rules of *wh* movement and Move Aux produce the surface structure *Who will kiss Bill?* leaving the thematic role relationships intact. In fact, an important constraint on transformations is that they do not affect thematic roles, which are determined in deep structure.

A universal principle has been proposed called the **theta-criterion**, which states in part that a particular thematic role may occur only once in a sentence. Thus sentences like

> *The boy opened the door with the key with a lock-pick.

are semantically anomalous because two noun phrases bear the thematic role of instrument. The theta-criterion is a constraint on theta assignment. It permits one assignment per thematic role. If all objects do not receive a thematic role after theta assignment is completed, the result is anomalous.

In English the thematic role of possessor is indicated two ways syntactically: either as *the boy's red hat* or as *the red hat of the boy*. However, *the boy's red hat of Bill* is semantically anomalous according to the theta-criterion because both *the boy* and *Bill* have the thematic role of possessor.

The semantic relations that exist between verbs and noun phrases are part of every speaker's linguistic competence, and account for much of the meaning in language.

Sentential Meaning

The meaning of a sentence is built, in part, from the meanings of noun phrases and verb phrases — the principle of compositionality again. Adverbs may add to or qualify the meaning. *The boy found the ball yesterday* specifies a time component to the meaning of the boy's finding the ball. Adverbs such as *quickly, fortunately, often*, et cetera would affect the meaning in other ways.

Like noun phrases, sentences have sense, or *intension*, which is usually what we are referring to when we talk about the meaning of a sentence. Some linguists would also say that certain sentences have reference, or *extension*, namely ones that can be true or false. Their extension is *true* if the sentence is true and *false* if the sentence is false.

The "Truth" of Sentences

> All truths are easy to understand once they are discovered; the point is to discover them.
>
> Galileo Galilei (1564–1642)

We have seen how sentence meaning is partially based on the meanings of its words and phrases. Knowing the meaning of a declarative sentence means knowing under what circumstances that sentence would be true. Those "circumstances" are called the **truth conditions** of the sentence.

In the world as we know it, the sentence

The Canadian Constitution was patriated in 1982.

is true, and the sentence

The Canadian Constitution was patriated in 1992.

is false. We know the meanings of both sentences equally well, and knowing their meanings means knowing their truth conditions. We compare their truth conditions with "the real world" or historical facts, and we can thus say which one is true and which one false. The truth or falsehood of these sentences is their *reference*, their *extension*.

We can, however, understand well-formed sentences of our language without knowing their truth values. Knowing the truth conditions is not the same as knowing the actual facts. Rather, the truth conditions permit us to examine the world and learn the actual facts. If we did not know the linguistic meaning — if the sentence were in an unknown language — then we could never determine its truth, even if we had memorized an encyclopedia. We may not know the truth of

> The Mecklenburg Charter was signed in 1770.

but if we know its meaning we know in principle how to discover its truth, even if we do not have the means to do so. For example, consider the sentence

> The moon is made of green cheese.

We knew before space travel that going to the moon would test the truth of the sentence.

Now consider this sentence:

> Rufus believes that the Constitution was patriated in 1992.

This sentence is true if some individual named Rufus does believe the statement, and it is false if he does not. Those are its truth conditions.

It does not matter that a subpart of the sentence is false. An entire sentence may be true even if one or more of its parts are false and vice versa. The sense of a sentence is determined by the semantic rules that permit us to combine its subparts and still know under what conditions it is true or false.

Sentences and Truth Conditions

> If you tell the truth you don't have to remember anything.
>
> Mark Twain (1835–1910)

Linguists distinguish two types of truthful sentences. One set of sentences is linguistically true — that is, a sentence is necessarily true because of the definitions of the words used in the sentence. Thus, *A widow is a person whose husband is no longer alive* is said to be analytically true because the word *widow* implies that we are speaking of a woman (a man is a *widower*). The woman was at one time married (hence had a husband), her husband is no longer living, and, finally, she has not remarried. Should all of these conditions not be met, the sentence will be untrue because of the way speakers of English understand the word *widow*. **Analytic** sentences are thus "true by definition."

The truth of the second type of truthful sentence depends on its agreement with the world as we know it. The truth of a sentence such as *The widow's husband died last year* can be determined only if we know something of last year's events. Our understanding of the truth of such sentences depends on our knowing something of the events and conditions in the world. In this case, we may have to speak with our neighbours or consult the public records. Such sentences are known as **synthetic** and, unlike analytic sentences, require more than linguistic knowledge.

A sentence such as *A unicorn is a single-horned beast* may be considered analytically true because, as the name itself tells us, this creature has but one horn;

so, too, a *triangle*, by its very name, must be a three-sided figure. The difference between a unicorn and a triangle, however, rests in the fact that most people encounter triangles but never a unicorn. Certainly, a sentence such as *Unicorns live in the Winnipeg Zoo* can easily be checked and will confirm that unicorns, along with dragons and fairies, exist only in art or fantasy.

The opposite of analytic sentences is **contradictory** sentences, which are necessarily false because of the meanings of the words themselves. If we were to hear that *A widow's husband was alive and well in Calgary*, then we would conclude that this "widow" was no *widow* at all. Sentences calling attention to the fourth side of a triangle or to *colourless green ideas* are clearly contradictory and necessarily false.

Knowing a language includes knowing the semantic rules for combining meanings and the conditions under which sentences are true or false.

Paraphrase

We can now give a formal definition of *paraphrase:*

> Two sentences are paraphrases if they have the same truth conditions.

This means whenever one is true, the other is true; and when one is false, the other is false, without exception. The following sets of sentences are paraphrases. Despite subtle differences in emphasis, they have the same truth conditions:

> The horse threw the rider.
> The rider was thrown by the horse.

Active-passive pairs like this example are often paraphrases, but not always. When quantifiers are involved — words like *every, each, many, few,* and *several* — an active and its corresponding passive may have different truth conditions; that is, they may not be paraphrases. Consider

> Every person in this room speaks two languages.
> Two languages are spoken by every person in this room.

These two sentences do *not* have the same truth conditions; they are not paraphrases. Suppose there are three people in the room, Tom, Dick, and Harry. Tom speaks English and Russian; Dick speaks French and Italian; and Harry speaks Chinese and Thai. Then the first sentence is true. The second, however, is false because there are no two languages that everyone speaks.

Here are other sets of paraphrases involving more or less the same vocabulary in different syntactic structures:

> It is easy to play sonatas on this piano.
> This piano is easy to play sonatas on.
> On this piano it is easy to play sonatas.
> Sonatas are easy to play on this piano.

Margaret Atwood wrote *The Edible Woman.*
It was Margaret Atwood who wrote *The Edible Woman.*
It was *The Edible Woman* that was written by Margaret Atwood.
The person who wrote *The Edible Woman* was Margaret Atwood.

The students gave money to the beggar.
The students gave the beggar money.

In these three sets, the sentences in each set are related via transformations. Since transformations do not change thematic roles, they tend in many cases to preserve the truth conditions, that is, to preserve meaning.

Paraphrase may also arise with certain semantic concepts such as "ability," "permission," and "obligation." These may be expressed through auxiliary verbs:

He *can* go.
He *may* go.
He *must* go.

They may also be expressed phrasally, without the auxiliaries:

He is *able* to go. / He has *the ability* to go.
He is *permitted* to go. / He has *permission* to go.
He is *obliged* to go. / He has an *obligation* to go.

Finally, it is often possible to substitute a phrase for a word without affecting the sense of the sentence.

Perry saw Nicole.
Perry perceived Nicole using his eyes.

The professor lectured the class.
The professor delivered a lecture to the class.

Entailment

Sometimes knowing the truth of one sentence **entails** or necessarily implies the truth of another sentence. For example, if we know it is true that

Corday assassinated Marat.

then we know it is true that

Marat is dead.

It is logically impossible for the former to be true and the latter false. The sentence *The brick is red* entails *The brick is not white*, *Mortimer is a bachelor* entails *Mortimer is male*, and so on. These **entailments** are part of the semantic rules we have been discussing. Much of what we know about the world comes about from knowing the entailments of true sentences.

Contradiction

Contradiction is negative entailment — that is, where the truth of one sentence necessarily implies the falseness of another sentence. For example,

> Elizabeth II is the queen of Canada.
> Elizabeth II is a man.

If the first sentence is true, then the second is necessarily false. A pair of sentences such as

> Scott is a baby.
> Scott is an adult.

generally involves contradiction — though, of course, it is possible that Scott is an adult but that we object to his behaviour.

Events vs. States

Some sentences describe **events**, such as *John kissed Mary,* or *John ate oysters.* Other sentences describe **states** such as *John knows Mary,* or *John likes oysters.* These differences appear to have syntactic consequences. Eventive sentences sound natural when passivized, when expressed progressively, when used imperatively, and with certain adverbs:

Eventives

Mary was kissed by John.	Oysters were eaten by John.
John is kissing Mary.	John is eating oysters.
Kiss Mary!	Eat oysters!
John deliberately kissed Mary.	John deliberately ate oysters.

The stative sentences seem peculiar, if not ungrammatical or anomalous, when cast in the same form. (The preceding "?" indicates the strangeness.)

Statives

?Mary is known by John.	?Oysters are liked by John.
?John is knowing Mary.	?John is liking oysters.
?Know Mary!	?Like oysters!
?John deliberately knows Mary.	?John deliberately likes oysters.

These examples show yet another way in which syntax and semantics interact.

Pronouns and Coreferentiality

Another example of how syntax and semantics interact has to do with **reflexive pronouns**, such as *herself* and *themselves.* The meaning of a reflexive pronoun always refers back to some antecedent. In *Jane bit herself, herself* refers to Jane.

Syntactically, reflexive pronouns and their antecedents must occur within the same S in the phrase structure tree. Compare the phrase structure tree of *Jane bit herself* with that of **Jane said that herself slept:*

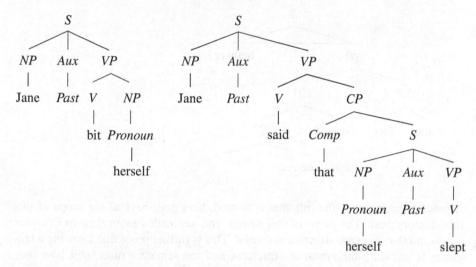

In the first tree *Jane* and *herself* are in the same S, and are understood to be **coreferential**, that is, to refer to the same person. In the second tree, *Jane* and *herself* are in different S-rooted trees and cannot be coreferential. Moreover, syntactic and semantic rules do not allow reflexive pronouns to be subjects so the second tree is ungrammatical. It would be ungrammatical even if the sentence were **Jane said that Bill bit herself*, with *herself* as the direct object, because the only possible referent for *herself* is not in the same S-rooted tree.

Sentence structure also plays a role in determining when a pronoun and a noun phrase in different clauses can be coreferential. For example in

John believes that he is a genius.

the pronoun *he* can be interpreted as John or as some person other than John. However in

He believes that John is a genius.

the coreferential interpretation is impossible. *John* and *he* cannot refer to the same person. It may appear that a pronoun antecedent cannot occur to the left of its noun phrase if the two are to be coreferential, but this is deceiving. It is really a matter of structure. In the sentence

The fact that he is considered a genius bothers John.

he and *John* can be interpreted as coreferential. The critical factor is that the pronoun is in a "lower" S, as this abbreviated phrase structure tree shows:

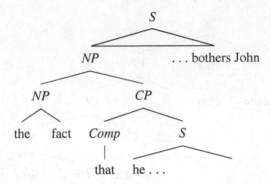

A precise statement of the rule that is at work here goes beyond the scope of this introductory text. The point is that syntax and semantics interrelate in complex ways, and that sentence structure is crucial. This is further proof that knowing a language is knowing the syntactic structures and the semantic rules, and how they interact.

When Rules Are Broken

> For all a rhetorician's rules
> Teach nothing but to name his tools.
> Samuel Butler, *Hudibras* (c. 1663–1678)

The rules of language are not laws of nature. Only by a "miracle" can the laws of nature be broken, but the rules of language are broken every day by everybody. This lawlessness is not human perversity but another way in which language is put to use.

We will examine three ways in which meaning may be obscured or absent: **anomaly**, a violation of semantic rules to create "nonsense"; **metaphor**, or nonliteral meaning; and **idioms**, in which the meaning of an expression may be unrelated to the meaning of its parts.

Anomaly: No Sense and Nonsense

> Don't tell me of a man's being able to talk sense; everyone can talk sense. Can he talk nonsense?
> William Pitt, British Politician (1759–1806)

If in a conversation someone said to you

> My brother is an only child.

you might think that he was making a joke or that he did not know the meanings of the words he was using. You would know that the sentence was strange or **anomalous**, yet it is certainly an English sentence. It conforms to all the grammatical rules of the language. It is strange because it represents a contradiction; the meaning of *brother* includes the fact that the individual referred to is a male human who has at least one sibling.

The sentence

> That bachelor is pregnant.

is anomalous for similar reasons; the word *bachelor* contains the semantic property "male," whereas the word *pregnant* has the semantic property "female." Through a semantic redundancy rule, *pregnant* will also be marked [−male]. The anomaly arises from trying to equate something that is [+male] with something that is [−male].

The semantic properties of words determine what other words they can be combined with. One sentence used by linguists to illustrate this fact is Noam Chomsky's (1957) famous sentence

> Colourless green ideas sleep furiously.

The sentence seems to obey all the syntactic rules of English. The subject is *colourless green ideas*, and the predicate is *sleep furiously*. It has the same syntactic structure as the sentence

> Dark green leaves rustle furiously.

but there is obviously something wrong *semantically* with the sentence. The meaning of *colourless* includes the semantic property "without colour," but it is combined with the adjective *green*, which has the property "green in colour." How can something be both "without colour" and "green in colour" simultaneously? Other such semantic violations also occur in the sentence.

There are other sentences that sound like English sentences but make no sense because they include words that have no meaning; they are **uninterpretable**. We can interpret them only if we dream up some meaning for each "no-sense" word. Lewis Carroll's "Jabberwocky" (from *Through the Looking-Glass*) is probably the most famous poem in which most of the content words have no meaning — they do not exist in the lexicon of the grammar. Still, all the sentences "sound" as if they should be or could be English sentences:

> 'Twas brillig, and the slithy toves
>   Did gyre and gimble in the wabe;
> All mimsy were the borogoves,
>   And the mome raths outgrabe.

. . .
> He took his vorpal sword in hand:
> >   Long time the manxome foe he sought —
> So rested he by the Tumtum tree,
> >   And stood awhile in thought.

Without knowing what *vorpal* means, we nevertheless know that

> He took his vorpal sword in hand.

means the same thing as

> He took his sword, which was vorpal, in hand.
> It was in his hand that he took his vorpal sword.

Knowing the language, and assuming that *vorpal* means the same thing in the three sentences (because the same sounds are used), we can decide that the sense or truth conditions of the three sentences are identical. In other words, we are able to decide that two things mean the same thing even though we do not know what either one means. We decide by assuming that the semantic properties of *vorpal* are the same whenever it is used.

We now see why Alice commented, when she had read "Jabberwocky,"

> "It seems very pretty, but it's *rather* hard to understand!" (You see she didn't like to confess, even to herself, that she couldn't make it out at all.) "Somehow it seems to fill my head with ideas — only I don't exactly know what they are!"

The semantic properties of words show up in other ways in sentence construction. For example, if the meaning of a word includes the semantic property "human" in English, then we can replace it with one sort of pronoun but not another. This semantic feature determines that we call a boy *he* and a table *it*, not vice versa.

According to Mark Twain, Eve had such knowledge in her grammar, for she writes in her diary that

> If this reptile is a man, it ain't an *it*, is it? That wouldn't be grammatical, would it? I think it would be *he*. In that case one would parse it thus: nominative *he*; dative, *him*; possessive, *his'n*.

Semantic violations in poetry may form strange but interesting aesthetic images, as in Dylan Thomas's phrase *a grief ago*. *Ago* is ordinarily used with words specified by some temporal semantic feature:

a week ago		*a table ago
an hour ago	but not	*a dream ago
a month ago		*a mother ago
a century ago		

When Thomas used the word *grief* with *ago*, he was adding a durational feature to *grief* for poetic effect.

In the poetry of e.e. cummings, there are phrases such as

> the six subjunctive crumbs twitch
> a man . . . wearing a round jeer for a hat
> children building this rainman out of snow

Although all of these phrases violate some semantic rules, we can understand them; it is the breaking of the rules that creates the imagery desired. The ability to understand these phrases and at the same time recognize their anomalous or deviant nature demonstrates knowledge of the semantic system and semantic properties of the language.

Metaphor

> Our doubts are traitors.
>
> William Shakespeare

> Walls have ears.
>
> Miguel de Cervantes

> The night has a thousand eyes
> and the day but one.
>
> Francis William Bourdillon

Sometimes the breaking of semantic rules can be used to convey a particular idea. *Walls have ears* is certainly anomalous, but it can be interpreted as meaning "You can be overheard even when you think nobody is listening." In some sense, the sentence is ambiguous, but the literal meaning is so unlikely that listeners stretch their imaginations for another interpretation. That "stretching" is based on semantic properties that are inferred or that provide some kind of resemblance. Such nonliteral interpretations of sentences are called **metaphors**.

The literal meaning of a sentence such as

> My new car is a lemon.

is anomalous. We could, if driven to the wall (another metaphor), provide some literal interpretation that is plausible if given sufficient context. For example, the *new car* may be a miniature toy carved out of a piece of citrus fruit. The more common meaning, however, would be metaphorical and interpreted as referring to a newly purchased automobile that breaks down and requires constant repairs. The imagination stretching in this case may relate to the semantic property "tastes sour" that *lemon* possesses.

Metaphors are not necessarily anomalous when taken literally. The literal meaning of the sentence

> Dr. Jekyll is a butcher.

is that a physician named Jekyll also works as a retailer of meats or a slaughterer of animals used for food. The metaphorical meaning is that the doctor named Jekyll is harmful, possibly murderous, and apt to operate unnecessarily.

Similarly, the sentence

> John is a snake in the grass.

can be interpreted literally to refer to a pet snake named John on the lawn. Metaphorically, the sentence has nothing to do with a scaly, limbless reptile. On the other hand, Emily Dickinson's "narrow fellow in the grass" describes a real snake as human.

To interpret metaphors, we need to understand both the literal meanings and facts about the world. To understand the metaphor

> Time is money.

it is necessary to know that in our society we are often paid according to the number of hours or days worked. In fact, "time," which is an abstract concept, is the subject of multiple metaphors. We "save time," "waste time," "manage time," "push things back in time," "live on borrowed time," and "suffer the ravages of time" as "time marches on."

To recognize that the sentence

> Jack is a pussycat.

has a different meaning from

> Jack is a tiger.

requires knowledge that the metaphorical meaning of each sentence does not depend on the semantic property "feline." Rather, other semantic properties of these two words provide grounds for the metaphor.

Metaphorical use of language is language creativity at its highest. Nevertheless, the basis of metaphorical use is the ordinary linguistic knowledge about words, their semantic properties, and their combining powers that all speakers possess.

In *Metaphors We Live By*, Lakoff and Johnson (2003) show how pervasive the metaphor is in ordinary speech and how it structures thought and experience. For instance, the *Argument is war* metaphor may be seen in sentences such as

> Your claims are indefensible.
> She attacked every weak point in my argument.
> I demolished his argument.

Our attitudes toward arguments might be quite different if the prevailing metaphor were *Argument is dance*.

Idioms

Knowing a language includes knowing the morphemes, simple words, compound words, and their meanings. In addition, it means knowing fixed phrases, consisting of more than one word, with meanings that cannot be inferred from the meanings of the individual words. The usual semantic rules for combining meanings do not apply. Such expressions are called idioms. All languages contain many idiomatic phrases, as in these English examples:

> sell down the river
> haul over the coals
> eat my hat
> let their hair down
> put his foot in his mouth
> throw her weight around
> snap out of it
> cut it out
> hit it off
> get it off
> bite your tongue
> give a piece of your mind

© Dan Piraro. King Features Syndicate.

Idioms are similar in structure to ordinary phrases except that they tend to be frozen in form and do not readily enter into other combinations or allow the word order to change. Thus,

(1) She put her foot in her mouth.

has the same structure as

(2) She put her bracelet in her drawer.

However, whereas

The drawer in which she put her bracelet was hers.
Her bracelet was put in her drawer.

are sentences related to sentence (2),

The mouth in which she put her foot was hers.
Her foot was put in her mouth.

do not have the idiomatic sense of sentence (1).

On the other hand, the words of some idioms can be moved without affecting the idiomatic sense:

The RCMP kept tabs on radicals.
Tabs were kept on radicals by the RCMP.
Radicals were kept tabs on by the RCMP.

Idioms can break the rules on combining semantic properties. The object of *eat* must usually be something with the semantic property "edible," but in

He ate his hat.
Eat your heart out.

this restriction is violated.

Idioms, grammatically as well as semantically, have special characteristics. They must be entered into the lexicon or mental dictionary as single "items," with their meanings specified, and speakers must learn the special restrictions on their use in sentences.

Many idioms may have originated as metaphorical expressions that "took hold" in the language and became frozen in form and meaning.

Pragmatics

The meaning of a word is its use in the language.

Ludwig Wittgenstein (1889–1951)

Pragmatics is concerned with the interpretation of linguistic meaning in context. Two kinds of context are relevant. The first is **linguistic context** — the discourse that precedes the phrase or sentence to be interpreted. Taken by itself, the sentence

> Amazingly, he already loves her.

is essentially uninterpretable. The linguistic meaning is that something male and animate has arrived at a state of loving something female and animate, and the speaker finds something astonishing about it. There are no referents for *he* and *her*, and the reason for *amazingly* is vague. But if the sentence preceding it were *Kevin met Tara yesterday*, its interpretation would be clearer.

> Kevin met Tara yesterday.
> Amazingly, he already loves her.

The discourse suggests the second kind of context — **situational**, or knowledge of the world. To interpret the sentences fully, the listener must know the real-world references of Kevin and Tara. Moreover, the interpretation of *amazingly* is made clear by the general belief that a person ordinarily needs more than a day to complete the act — the completion indicated by *already* — of falling in love.

Even innocent-sounding sentences, such as

> Aaron believes he is a genius.

are ambiguous, for it is unclear in the absence of situational context whether *he* is coreferential with *Aaron* or refers to some other person.

Situational context includes speaker, hearer, and any third parties present, along with their beliefs and their beliefs about what the others believe. It includes what has been previously uttered, the physical environment, the topic of conversation, the time of day, and other circumstances surrounding the participants in the discourse. Almost any imaginable extralinguistic factor may, under appropriate circumstances, influence how language is interpreted.

Pragmatics is also about language use. It tells us that calling someone a *son of a bitch* is not a zoological opinion but an insult. It tells us that when a street person asks *Do you have any spare change?* it is not a fiduciary inquiry but a request for money. It tells us that, when a justice of the peace says, in the appropriate setting, *I now pronounce you husband and wife*, an act of marrying was performed.

Linguistic Context: Discourse

> Put your discourse into some frame, and start not so wildly from my affair.
> William Shakespeare, *Hamlet* (c. 1599–1601)

Linguistic knowledge accounts for speakers' ability to combine phonemes into morphemes, morphemes into words, and words into sentences. Knowing a language also permits combining sentences to express complex thoughts and ideas. These larger linguistic units are called **discourse**.

The study of discourse, or **discourse analysis**, is concerned with how speakers combine sentences into broader speech units. Discourse analysis involves questions of style, appropriateness, cohesiveness, rhetorical force, topic/subtopic structure, differences between written and spoken discourse, as well as grammatical properties.

Our immediate concern in the following discussion is merely to point to a few aspects of discourse that bear on the interpretation of linguistic meaning.

Pronouns

Pronouns may be used in place of noun phrases or may be used to refer to an entity presumably known to the discourse participants. When that presumption fails, miscommunication may result.

Pronominalization occurs both in sentences and across the sentences of a discourse. Within a sentence, the structure limits the choice of pronoun. We saw previously that the occurrence of reflexive pronouns depends on syntactic structure, which also determines whether a pronoun and a noun phrase can be interpreted as coreferential.

In a discourse, prior linguistic context plays a primary role in pronoun interpretation. Consider the following discourse:

> It seems that the man loves the woman.
> Many people think he loves her.

In the most "natural" interpretation, *her* is "the woman" referred to in the first sentence, whomever she happens to be. But it is also possible for *her* to refer to a different person, a person identified contextually, say with a gesture. In such a case, *her* would be spoken with added emphasis:

> Many people think he loves *her*!

Similarly, *he* would be taken as coreferential with *the man*, but that interpretation is not necessarily the case. Intonation and emphasis would provide clues on how the pronoun is to be taken.

As far as syntactic rules are concerned, pronouns are noun phrases and may occur almost anywhere that a noun phrase may occur. Semantic rules of varying complexity establish whether a pronoun and some other noun phrase in the discourse can be interpreted as coreferential. A minimum condition of coreferentiality is that the pronoun and its antecedent have the same semantic feature values for the semantic properties of number and gender. In an attempt to avoid gender-specific language, this condition is often disregarded by the use of the plural *they* in sentences such as *Anyone may come if they like.*

When semantic rules and contextual interpretation determine that a pronoun is coreferential with a noun phrase, we say that the pronoun is **bound** to that noun phrase antecedent. If *her* in the previous example refers to "the woman," then it would be a bound pronoun. When a pronoun refers to some object not explicitly mentioned in the discourse, it is said to be **free** or **unbound**. The reference of a free pronoun must ultimately be determined by the situational context. First- and second- person nonreflexive pronouns (I, we, you) are bound to the speaker and hearer respectively. Reflexive pronouns, sometimes called anaphors, are always bound. They require an antecedent in the sentence.

In the preceding example, semantic rules permit *her* either to be bound to *the woman* or to be a free pronoun, referring to some person not explicitly mentioned. The ultimate interpretation is context dependent.

Anaphora

Referring to the discourse in the previous section, it would not, strictly speaking, be ungrammatical if it went this way:

> It seems that the man loves the woman.
> Many people think the man loves the woman.

However, most people would find such a discourse stilted and would prefer to use the pronouns *he* and *her: Many people think he loves her*. Often the use of pronouns is a stylistic decision, and stylistics is a part of pragmatics.

The process of replacing a longer expression by a pronoun or another kind of "pro-form" is called **anaphora**. Some examples of anaphora in English are

> Jan saw *the boy with the telescope.*
> Dan also saw <u>him</u> (= *the boy with the telescope*). (pronoun)

Technically, what we call *pronouns* are "pro-noun phrases" in that they are *anaphors* that replace entire noun phrases. Pro-forms may substitute for categorical expressions other than noun phrases, for example:

> *Emily hugged* Cassidy, as <u>did</u> (= hugged Cassidy) Zachary. (pro-verb phrase)
> *I am sick, which* (= *I am sick* or *my being sick) depresses me.* (pro-sentence)

In the first sentence *did* replaces the verb phrase *hugged Cassidy*. In the second *which* replaces the entire sentence *I am sick*.

Missing Parts

The process of anaphora replaces whole phrases with pro-forms. Sometimes in discourse, or even within sentences, entire phrases may be omitted and not replaced by a pro-form but still understood because of context. Such utterances taken in isolation appear to violate the rules of syntax, as in the sentence *My uncle has too*, but in the following discourse it is perfectly acceptable:

> First speaker: My aunt has been dieting strenuously.
> Second speaker: My uncle has too.

The second speaker can be understood to mean "My uncle has been dieting strenuously." The missing part of the verb phrase is understood from previous discourse.

Entire sentences may be "filled in" this way:

First speaker: My aunt has been dieting strenuously, and she has lost a good
                   deal of weight.
Second speaker: My mother has too.

The second speaker can be understood to have meant "My mother has been dieting strenuously, and she has lost a good deal of weight." Rules of discourse provide not only the missing parts of the verb phrase but also the entire second sentence meaning.

A process called **gapping** occurs when a repeated verb is omitted in similar contexts. Thus, in the following example, Bill is understood to have *washed* the cherries:

Jill washed the grapes and Bill the cherries.

In a similar process, called **sluicing**, what follows a *wh* word in an embedded sentence is omitted but understood:

Your ex-husband is dancing with someone, but I don't know whom.
My cat ate something, and I wish I knew what.
She said she was coming over, but she didn't say when.

Missing from the end of the first sentence is *he is dancing with*, missing from the second sentence is *she ate*, and missing from the third sentence is *she was coming over.*

The Articles the *and* a

There are discourse rules that apply regularly, such as those that determine the occurrence of the articles *the* and *a*. The article *the* is used to indicate that the referent of a noun phrase is agreed upon by speaker and listener. If someone says

I saw the dog.

then it is assumed that a certain dog is being discussed. No such assumption accompanies

I saw a dog.

Peanuts: © United Feature Syndicate, Inc.

which is more of a description of what was seen than a reference to a particular animal. Nevertheless, there are occasions when the indefinite article may have a specific reference, as seen in the following responses to the statement "I am looking for a dog":

> I hope you find one. (indefinite nonspecific)
> I hope you find it. (indefinite specific)

Often a discourse will begin with the use of indefinite articles, and, once everyone agrees on the referents, definite articles start to appear. A short example illustrates this transition:

> I saw *a* boy and *a* girl holding hands and kissing.
> Oh, it sounds lovely.
> Yes, *the* boy was quite tall and handsome, and he seemed to like *the* girl a lot.

These examples show that some rules of discourse are similar to grammatical rules in that a violation produces unacceptable results. If the final sentence of this discourse were

> Yes, a boy was quite tall and handsome, and he seemed to like a girl a lot.

most speakers would find it unacceptable.

The presence or absence of *the* may make a large difference in the meaning of a sentence. Compare these two sentences:

> The terrorists are in control of the government.
> The terrorists are in *the* control of the government.

In the first, the terrorists are in charge; in the second, the government is in charge of the terrorists.

The article *a* may be interpreted, or used, specifically or nonspecifically. When used specifically, there is one reference; when used nonspecifically, multiple references are possible. Consider the sentence *Robert wants to marry a university professor.* It has two possible meanings. In the first, Robert wants to marry Helen, and Helen is a university professor. This is the specific use of the article *a*. In the second meaning, Robert doesn't have a particular person in mind to marry, but he is confining his search for a mate to university professors. This is the nonspecific use of the article.

Statistics Canada is very good at producing ambiguities of specificity. It often proclaims such facts as "A woman gives birth in Canada every two minutes." Of course context — pragmatics — prevents communication from going awry in most of these cases.

Situational Context

Depending on inflection, [the French] *ah bon* can express shock, disbelief, indifference, irritation, or joy.

Peter Mayle, *Toujours Provence* (1994)

Much discourse is telegraphic in nature. Verb phrases are not specifically mentioned, entire clauses are left out, direct objects disappear, pronouns abound. Yet people still understand one another, partly because rules of grammar and rules of discourse combine with contextual knowledge to fill in gaps and make the discourse cohere. Much of the contextual knowledge is knowledge of who is speaking, who is listening, what objects are being discussed, and general facts about the world we live in, called **situational context**.

Often what we say is not literally what we mean. When we ask at the dinner table if someone can "pass the salt," we are not querying his ability to do so; if someone says "You're standing on my foot," she is not making idle conversation. She is asking you to stand somewhere else. We say "It's cold in here" to mean "Shut the window," "Turn up the heat," "Let's leave," or a dozen other things that depend on the real-world situation at the time of speaking.

In the following sections, we will look briefly (and incompletely) at a few of the ways that real-world context influences and interacts with meaning.

Maxims of Conversation

Though this be madness, yet there is method in't.

William Shakespeare, *Hamlet* (c. 1599–1601)

Speakers recognize when a series of sentences hangs together or when it is disjointed. The discourse below, which gave rise to Polonius's remark quoted at the head of this section, does not seem quite right — it is not coherent.

POLONIUS: What do you read, my lord?

HAMLET: Words, words, words.

POLONIUS: What is the matter, my lord?

HAMLET: Between who?

POLONIUS: I mean, the matter that you read, my lord.

HAMLET: Slanders, sir: for the satirical rogue says here that old men have grey beards, that their faces are wrinkled, their eyes purging thick amber and plum-tree gum, and that they have a plentiful lack of wit, together with most weak hams: all of which, sir, though I most powerfully and potently believe, yet I hold it not honesty to have it thus set down; for yourself, sir, should grow old as I am, if like a crab you could go backward.

Hamlet, who is feigning insanity, refuses to answer Polonius's questions "in good faith." He has violated certain conversational conventions or **maxims of conversation** first discussed by H. Paul Grice in a series of lectures at Harvard University in 1967–1968. One such maxim — the **maxim of quantity** — states that a speaker's contribution to the discourse should be as informative as is required — neither more nor less. Hamlet has violated this maxim. In answering "Words, words, words" to the question of what is being read, he is providing too little information. His final remark goes to the other extreme in providing more information than required.

He also violates the **maxim of relevance**, when he "misinterprets" the question about the reading matter as a matter between two individuals.

The "run-on" nature of Hamlet's final remark, a violation of the **maxim of manner**, is another source of incoherence. This effect is increased in the final sentence by the somewhat bizarre choice of phrasing to compare growing younger with walking backward, a violation of the **maxim of quality**, which requires sincerity and truthfulness.

The four conversational maxims, parts of the broad **cooperative principle**, may be summarized as follows:

Name of Maxim	Description of Maxim
Quantity	Say neither more nor less than the discourse requires.
Relevance	Be relevant.
Manner	Be brief and orderly; avoid ambiguity and obscurity.
Quality	Do not lie; do not make unsupported claims.

Unless, like Hamlet, we are being deliberately uncooperative, we adhere to these maxims as well as to other conversational principles such as **turn-taking** (i.e., knowing when it is our time to speak and when to listen). And we assume that others will adhere to them as well.

Bereft of context, if one man says (truthfully) to another *I have never slept with your wife*, that would be grounds for provocation because the topic of conversation should be unnecessary, a violation of the maxim of quantity.

Asking an able-bodied person at the dinner table *Can you pass the salt?*, if answered literally, would force the responder into stating the obvious, a violation of the maxim of quantity. To avoid this, the person asked seeks a reason for the question and deduces that the asker would like to have the salt.

The maxim of relevance explains how saying *It's cold in here* to a person standing by an open window might be interpreted as a request to close it, else why make the remark to that particular person in the first place?

Conversational conventions such as these allow the various sentence meanings to be sensibly combined into discourse meaning and integrated with context, much as rules of sentence grammar allow word meanings to be sensibly (and grammatically) combined into sentence meaning.

Speech Acts

We can use language to do things: make promises, lay bets, issue warnings, christen boats, place names in nomination, offer congratulations, or swear testimony. The theory of **speech acts** describes how this is done.

By saying *I warn you that there is a sheepdog in the closet*, we not only say something but also *warn* someone. Verbs such as *bet, promise, warn*, and so on are **performative verbs**. Using them in a sentence does something extra to the statement.

There are hundreds of performative verbs in every language. The following sentences illustrate their usage:

> I *bet* you five dollars the Renegades win.
> I *challenge* you to a match.
> I *dare* you to step over this line.
> I *fine* you $100 for speeding.
> I *move* that we adjourn.
> I *nominate* Denise for mayor.
> I *promise* to improve.
> I *resign*!

In all these sentences, the speaker is the subject (i.e., the sentences are in the "first person") who, by uttering the sentence, is accomplishing some additional action, such as daring, nominating, or resigning. Also, all these sentences are affirmative, declarative, and in the present tense. They are typical **performative sentences**.

An informal test to see whether a sentence contains a performative verb is to begin it with the words *I hereby. . . .* Only performative sentences sound right when begun this way. Compare *I hereby apologize to you* with the somewhat strange *I hereby know you*. The first is generally taken as an act of apologizing. In all the examples given, insertion of *hereby* would be acceptable.

Actually, every utterance is some kind of speech act. Even when there is no explicit performative verb, as in *It is raining*, we recognize an implicit performance of *stating*. On the other hand, *Is it raining?* is a performance of *questioning*, just as *Leave!* is a performance of *ordering*. In all these instances, we could use, if we chose, an actual performative verb: *I state that it is raining; I ask if it is raining; I order you to leave.*

In studying speech acts, we are acutely aware of the importance of the *context of the utterance*. In some circumstances, *There is a sheepdog in the closet* is a warning, but the same sentence may be a promise or even a mere statement of fact, depending on circumstances. We call this purpose — a warning, a promise, a threat, or whatever — the **illocutionary force** of a speech act. The way a sentence is taken — its effect — is its *perlocutionary force*. Thus, *There is a sheepdog in the closet* might be intended as a warning but taken as a simple statement of fact.

Speech act theory aims to tell us when we appear to ask questions but are really giving orders or when we say one thing with special (sarcastic) intonation and mean the opposite. Thus, at a dinner table, the question *Can you pass the salt?* means the order *Pass the salt!* It is not a request for information, and *Yes* is an inappropriate response.

Because the illocutionary force of a speech act depends on the context of the utterance, speech act theory is a part of pragmatics.

Presuppositions

> You mentioned your name as if I should recognize it, but beyond the obvious facts that you are a bachelor, a solicitor, a Freemason, and an asthmatic, I know nothing whatever about you.

Sir Arthur Conan Doyle, "The Norwood Builder," *The Memoirs of Sherlock Holmes* (1894)

Speakers often make implicit assumptions about the real world, and the sense of an utterance may depend on those assumptions. The **presuppositions** of an utterance are facts whose truth is required for the utterance to be appropriate. Consider the following sentences:

(1) Have you stopped hugging your sheepdog?
(2) Who bought the badminton set?
(3) John doesn't write poems anymore.
(4) The present king of France is bald.
(5) Would you like another beer?

In sentence (1), the speaker has *presupposed* that the listener has at some past time hugged his sheepdog. In (2), there is the presupposition that someone has already bought a badminton set, and in (3) it is assumed that John once wrote poetry.

We have already run across the somewhat odd (4), which we decided we could understand even though France does not currently have a king. The use of the definite article *the* usually presupposes an existing referent. When presuppositions are inconsistent with the actual state of the world, the utterance is felt to be strange, unless a fictional setting is agreed upon by the conversants, as in a play.

Sentence (5) presupposes or implies that you have already had at least one beer. Part of the meaning of the word *another* includes this presupposition. The Mad Hatter in *Alice's Adventures in Wonderland* appears not to understand presuppositions:

> "Take some more tea," the March Hare said to Alice, very earnestly.
>
> "I've had nothing yet," Alice replied in an offended tone, "so I can't take more."
>
> "You mean you can't take *less*," said the Hatter. "It's very easy to take *more* than nothing."

The humour in this passage comes from the meaning of the word *more*, which presupposes some earlier amount.

These phenomena may also be described as **implication**. Part of the meaning of *more* implies that there has already been something. The definite article *the*, in these terms, entails or implies the existence of the referent within the current context.

Presuppositions can be used to communicate information indirectly. If someone says *My brother is rich*, we assume that person has a brother, even though that fact is not explicitly stated. Much of the information that is exchanged in a conversation or discourse is of this kind. Often, after a conversation has ended, we will realize that some fact was imparted to us that was not specifically mentioned. That fact is often a presupposition.

The use of language in a courtroom is restricted so that presuppositions cannot influence the court or jury. The famous type of question *Have you stopped beating your wife?* is disallowed in court, because accepting the validity of the question means accepting its presuppositions; the question contains an inevitable conclusion. Unfortunately, questions and comments are not usually as transparent as this above example, and we must be especially alert to underlying presuppositions that may encourage prejudice and bigotry. Presuppositions are so much a part of natural discourse that they become second nature and we do not think of them, any more than we are directly aware of the many other rules and maxims that govern language and its use in context.

Deixis

In all languages, there are many words and expressions whose reference relies entirely on the situational context of the utterance and can be understood only in light of these circumstances. This aspect of pragmatics is called **deixis** (pronounced "dike-sis") or indexicality, both of which derive from classical Greek and Latin, in which they referred to pointing or indicating. First- and second-person pronouns such as

> my   mine   you   your   yours   we   ours   us

are always deictic because they are free pronouns and their reference is entirely dependent on context. You must know who the speaker and listener are in order to interpret them.

Third-person pronouns are deictic if they are *free*. If they are *bound*, then their reference is known from the linguistic context. One peculiar exception is the "pronoun" *it* when used in sentences such as

> It appears as though sheepdogs are the missing link.
> The patriotic hockey coach found it advisable. . . .

In these cases, the *it* does not function as a true pronoun by referring to some entity. Rather, *it* is a grammatical morpheme, a place-holder as it were, required to satisfy the English rules of syntax.

Expressions such as

> this person
> that man

these women
those children

are deictic, for they require situational information in order for the listener to make a referential connection and understand what is meant. The above examples illustrate **person deixis**. They also show that the use of **demonstrative articles** such as *this* and *that* is deictic.

There is also **time deixis** and **place deixis**. The following examples are all deictic expressions of time:

now	then	tomorrow
this time	that time	seven days ago
two weeks from now	last week	next April

In order to understand what specific times such expressions refer to, we need to know when the utterance was said. Clearly, *next week* has a different reference when uttered today rather than a month from today. If you found an advertising leaflet on the street that said "BIG SALE NEXT WEEK" with no date given, you would not know whether the sale had already taken place.

Expressions of place deixis require contextual information about the place of the utterance, as shown by the following examples:

here	there	this place
that place	this ranch	those towers over there
this city	these parks	yonder mountains

Directional terms such as

before/behind   left/right   front/back

are deictic insofar as you need to know which way the speaker is facing. In Japanese, the verb *kuru* "come" can be used only for motion toward the place of utterance. A Japanese speaker cannot call up a friend and ask

May I *kuru* to your house?

as you might, in English, ask "May I come to your house?" The correct verb is *iku* "go" which indicates motion away from the place of utterance. In Japanese, these verbs thus have a deictic aspect to their meaning.

Deixis abounds in language use and marks one of the boundaries of semantics and pragmatics. Deictic expressions such as *I*, *an hour from now*, and *behind me*, have meaning to the extent that they have *sense*. To complete their meaning, to determine their *reference*, it is necessary to know the context.

Summary

Knowing a language means to know how to produce and understand sentences with particular meanings. The study of linguistic meaning is called semantics. **Lexical semantics** is concerned with the meanings of morphemes and words,

phrasal semantics with phrases and sentences. The study of how context affects meaning is called **pragmatics**.

The meanings of morphemes and words are defined in part by their **semantic properties**, whose presence or absence is indicated by **semantic features**. Evidence for semantic properties is found in "slips of the tongue" that people make, which indicates their knowledge of these properties.

When two words are pronounced the same but have different meanings, they are **homonyms** (e.g., *bear* and *bare*). **Heteronyms** are words spelled the same but pronounced differently with different meanings, such as *sow*, a female pig, and *sow*, meaning to scatter seeds, or *I* and *eye*. **Homographs** are words spelled the same, possibly pronounced the same, and having different meanings, such as *trunk* of an elephant and *trunk* for storing clothes. The use of homonyms and heteronyms may result in **ambiguity**, which occurs when an utterance has more than one meaning.

When two words have the same meaning but different sounds, they are **synonyms** (e.g., *sofa* and *couch*). The use of synonyms may result in **lexical paraphrases**, two sentences with the same meaning.

When a word has differing meanings that conceptually and historically related, it is said to be **polysemous**. For example, *good* means "well behaved" in *good child,* and "sound" in *good investment*. Polysemous words may be partially synonymous in that they share one or more of their meanings with other words, such as *ripe* and *mature*.

Two words that are opposite in meaning are **antonyms**. Antonyms have the same semantic properties except for the one that accounts for their oppositeness. There are antonymous pairs that are **complementary** (*alive/dead*), **gradable** (*hot/cold*), and **relational opposites** (*buy/sell, employer/employee*).

Other meaning relations are also described by "-nym" words. **Hyponyms** are words like *red, white,* and *blue,* which share a feature indicating they all belong to the class of colour words. **Metonyms** are "substitute" words, such as *Rome* meaning "The Catholic Church"; and **retronyms** are expressions like *broadcast television* that once were redundant, but that now make necessary distinctions as a result of changes in the world — in this case, the advent of cable television.

Proper names are "shortcut" words used to designate particular objects uniquely, that is, they are **definite**. Proper names cannot ordinarily be preceded by an article or an adjective, or be pluralized, in English.

The **principle of compositionality** states that the meaning of sentences and phrases is determined by the meaning of the individual morphemes and words they contain, together with the syntactic structure of the larger expression. All languages have rules for combining the meanings of parts into the meaning of the whole. For example, *red balloon* has the semantic properties of *balloon* to which the semantic properties of *red* are added, because *balloon* is the head of the phrase. *Brick red* has the semantic properties of *red* modified by those of *brick,* because *red* is the head of that adjective phrase. Such combinations are not always additive. The phrase *counterfeit dollar* does not simply have the semantic properties of *dollar* plus something else.

Words, phrases, and sentences generally have **sense**, which is a part of their meaning. By knowing the sense of an expression, you can determine its **reference**, if any, namely, what it points to in the world. Some meaningful expressions (e.g., *the present King of France*) have sense but no reference; others, such as proper names, often have reference but no sense. Deictic terms have sense, but require context to determine their reference. The sense of a declarative sentence is its **truth conditions**, that aspect of meaning that allows you to determine whether the sentence is true or false. The reference of a declarative sentence, when it has one, is its truth value, either true or false. Two sentences are **paraphrases** if they have the same truth conditions. Words like *you, yesterday,* and *behind* have sense, but their reference is context dependent.

The meaning of a sentence is determined in part by the **thematic roles** of the noun phrases in relation to the verb. These semantic relationships indicate who, to whom, toward what, from which, with what, and so on.

In building larger meanings from smaller meanings, the semantic rules interact with the syntactic rules of the language. For example, if a noun phrase and a nonreflexive pronoun occur within the same S, semantic rules cannot interpret them to be **coreferential**, that is, having the same referent. Thus in *Sara bit her, her* refers to someone other than Sara. Pronoun reference is structure dependent. In *he annoys Darren, he* and *Darren* may not be coreferential, but in *The fact that he can't swim annoys Darren, he* and *Darren* can be coreferential because the pronoun is in a "lower" S.

Often, the truth of one sentence **entails** the truth or falseness another. If the sentence *I managed to kiss my sheepdog* is true, then the sentence *I kissed my sheepdog* is necessarily true by the semantic rules for entailment.

Sentences are **anomalous** when they deviate from certain semantic rules. *The six subjunctive crumbs twitched* and *The stone ran* are anomalous. Other sentences are **uninterpretable** because they contain **nonsense words**, such as *An orkish sluck blecked nokishly.*

Many sentences have both a literal and a nonliteral or **metaphorical** interpretation. *He's out in left field* may be a literal description of a baseball player or a metaphorical description of someone mentally deranged. The use of metaphor is fundamental to the creativity and flexibility of language.

Idioms are phrases that do not adhere to the principle of compositionality, that is, whose meaning is *not* the combination of the meanings of the individual words, (e.g., *put her foot in her mouth*). Idioms often violate co-occurrence restrictions of semantic properties.

The general study of how context affects linguistic interpretation is **pragmatics**. Context may be *linguistic* — what was previously spoken or written — or *knowledge of the world,* what we've called **situational context**.

Discourse consists of several sentences, including exchanges between speakers. Pragmatics is important when interpreting discourse, for example, in determining whether a pronoun in one sentence has the same referent as a noun phrase in another sentence. Pro-forms can replace various constituents such as NPs, VPs, and sentences. In addition, parts of sentences can be omitted, but speakers can interpret what is missing. Linguistic context often reveals the reference of the pro-form or the missing parts. For example, it supplies the "will wash" in *Jan will wash grapes and Jon _____ cherries.*

Well-structured discourse follows certain rules and **maxims**, such as "be relevant," that make the discourse coherent. There are also grammatical rules that affect discourse, such as those that determine when to use the definite article *the*.

Pragmatics includes **speech acts**, **presuppositions**, and **deixis**. Speech act theory is the study of what an utterance does beyond just saying something. The effect of what is done is called the **illocutionary force** of the utterance. For example, use of a **performative verb** like *bequeath* may be an act of bequeathing, which may even have legal status.

Presuppositions are implicit assumptions that accompany certain utterances. *Have you stopped hugging Sue?* carries with it the presupposition that at one time you hugged Sue. Presuppositions are necessary in language for efficiency; otherwise, we would always longwindedly have to state "the obvious."

Deictic terms such as *you, there,* and *now* require knowledge of the circumstances (the person, place, or time) of the utterance to be interpreted referentially.

Exercises

1. For each group of words given below, state what semantic property or properties are shared by the (a) words and the (b) words, and what semantic property or properties differentiate the classes of (a) words and (b) words.

   Example: (a) widow, mother, sister, aunt, seamstress
   (b) widower, father, brother, uncle, tailor
   The (a) and (b) words are "human."
   The (a) words are "female," and the (b) words are "male."

   A. (a) bachelor, man, son, paperboy, pope, chief
      (b) bull, rooster, drake, ram
      The (a) and (b) words are _____
      The (a) words are _____
      The (b) words are _____
   B. (a) table, stone, pencil, cup, house, ship, car
      (b) milk, alcohol, rice, soup, mud
      The (a) and (b) words are _____
      The (a) words are _____
      The (b) words are _____
   C. (a) book, temple, mountain, road, tractor
      (b) idea, love, charity, sincerity, bravery, fear
      The (a) and (b) words are _____
      The (a) words are _____
      The (b) words are _____
   D. (a) pine, elm, ash, weeping willow, sycamore
      (b) rose, dandelion, aster, tulip, daisy

The (a) and (b) words are _____

The (a) words are _____

The (b) words are _____

E. (a) book, letter, encyclopedia, novel, notebook, dictionary

    (b) typewriter, pencil, ballpoint, crayon, quill, charcoal, chalk

The (a) and (b) words are _____

The (a) words are _____

The (b) words are _____

F. (a) walk, run, skip, jump, hop, swim

    (b) fly, skate, ski, ride, cycle, canoe, hang-glide

The (a) and (b) words are _____

The (a) words are _____

The (b) words are _____

G. (a) ask, tell, say, talk, converse

    (b) shout, whisper, mutter, drawl, holler

The (a) and (b) words are _____

The (a) words are _____

The (b) words are _____

H. (a) alleged, counterfeit, false, putative, accused

    (b) red, large, cheerful, pretty, stupid

    (*Hint*: Is an alleged murderer always a murderer?)

The (a) and (b) words are _____

The (a) words are _____

The (b) words are _____

2. Explain the semantic ambiguity of the following sentences by providing two sentences that paraphrase the two meanings. Example: *She can't bear children* can mean either *She can't give birth to children* or *She can't tolerate children*.

    a. He waited by the tower.

    b. Is he really that kind?

    c. The proprietor of the fish store was the sole owner.

    d. The long drill was boring.

    e. When he got the clear title to the land, it was a good deed.

    f. It takes a good ruler to make a straight line.

    g. He saw that gasoline can explode.

3. The following sentences may be either lexically or structurally ambiguous or both. Provide paraphrases showing you comprehend all the meanings.

    Example: I saw him walking by the bank.

    Meaning 1: I saw him, and he was walking by the riverbank.

    Meaning 2: I saw him, and he was walking by the financial institution.

    Meaning 3: I was walking by the riverbank when I saw him.

    Meaning 4: I was walking by the financial institution when I saw him.

a. We laughed at the colourful ball.
b. He was knocked over by the punch.
c. The police were urged to stop drinking by the fifth.
d. I said I would file it on Thursday.
e. I cannot recommend visiting professors too highly.
f. The licence fee for pets owned by senior citizens who have not been altered is $1.50. (actual notice)
g. What looks better on a handsome man than a tux? Nothing! (attributed to Mae West)

*4. There are several kinds of antonymy. Which of the pairs in columns A and B are complementary, gradable, or relational opposites?

A	B
good	bad
expensive	cheap
parent	offspring
beautiful	ugly
false	true
lessor	lessee
pass	fail
hot	cold
legal	illegal
larger	smaller
poor	rich
fast	slow
asleep	awake
husband	wife
rude	polite

5. For each definition write in the first blank the word that has that meaning and in the second (and third if present) a differently spelled homonym that has a different meaning.

Example: "A pair:" t(*wo*) t(*oo*) t(*o*)

a. "Naked": b _____ b _____
b. "Base metal": l _____ l _____
c. "Worships": p _____ p _____ p _____
d. "Eight bits": b _____ b _____ b _____
e. "One of five senses": s _____ s _____ c _____
f. "Several couples": p _____ p _____ p _____
g. "Not pretty": p _____ p _____
h. "Purity of gold unit": k _____ c _____
i. "A horse's coiffure": m _____ m _____ M _____
j. "Sets loose": f _____ f _____ f _____

*6. The following sentences consist of a verb, its noun phrase subject, and various objects. Identify the thematic relation of each noun phrase, indicating whether it is *agent, theme, location, instrument, source, goal, experiencer, causative,* or *possessor.*

a *t* *s* *i*

Example: The boy took the books from the cupboard with a handcart.

   a.   Natalie found a ball in the house.
   b.   The children ran from the playground to the wading pool.
   c.   One of the men unlocked all the doors with a paper clip.
   d.   Joshua melted the ice with a blowtorch.
   e.   The sun melted the ice.
   f.   The ice melted.
   g.   The farmer loaded hay onto the truck.
   h.   The farmer loaded the hay with a pitchfork.
   i.   The hay was loaded on the truck by the farmer.

*7. Some linguists and philosophers distinguish between two kinds of truthful statements: one follows from the definition or meaning of a word; the other simply happens to be true in the world as we know it. Thus, *Kings are monarchs* is true because the word *king* has the semantic property "monarch" as part of its meaning, but *Kings are rich* is circumstantially true. We can imagine a poor king, but a king who is not a monarch is not truly a king. Sentences such as *Kings are monarchs* are said to be analytic, true by virtue of meaning alone. Examine the following sentences to determine which are analytic and which are not.

   a.   Queens are monarchs.
   b.   Queens are female.
   c.   Queens are mothers.
   d.   Dogs are four legged.
   e.   Dogs are animals.
   f.   Cats are felines.
   g.   Dogs are stupid.
   h.   Audrey McLaughlin is Audrey McLaughlin.
   i.   Audrey McLaughlin was the first woman to lead a federal political party in Canada.
   j.   Uncles are male.

8. The opposite of *analytic* (see previous exercise) is *contradictory*. A sentence that is false due to the meaning of its words alone is contradictory. *Kings are female* is an example. Which of the following sentences are contradictory?

   a.   My aunt is a man.
   b.   Witches are wicked.

c. My brother is an only child.
d. The evening star isn't the morning star.
e. The evening star isn't the evening star.
f. Babies are adults.
g. Babies can lift one tonne.
h. Puppies are human.
i. My bachelor friends are all married.
j. My bachelor friends are all lonely.

*9. State for each pronoun in the following sentences whether it is free, bound, or either bound or free. Consider each sentence independently.

> Example: André finds himself in love with her.
> himself — bound; her — free
> Example: André said that he loved her.
> he — bound or free; her — free

a. Louise said to herself in the mirror: "I'm having a bad hair day."
b. The fact that he considers her astute pleases Maria.
c. Whenever I see you, I think of her.
d. Avi discovered that a picture of himself was hanging in the post office, and that fact bugged him, but it pleased her.
e. It seems that she and he will never stop arguing with them.
f. Persons are prohibited from picking flowers from any but their own graves. (on a sign in a cemetery)

10. In sports and games, many expressions are "performative." By shouting *"You're out!"* the first-base umpire performs an act. Think of a half-dozen or so similar examples and explain their use.

11. A criterion of a "performance sentence" is whether you can begin it with *I hereby*. Notice that if you say sentence (a) aloud it sounds like a genuine apology, but to say sentence (b) aloud sounds odd because you cannot perform an act of knowing.

a. I hereby apologize to you.
b. I hereby know you.

Test whether the following sentences are performance sentences by inserting *hereby* and seeing whether they sound "right."

c. I testify that she met the agent.
d. I know that she met the agent.
e. I suppose the Jays will win.
f. He bet her $2500 that the Liberals would win.
g. I dismiss the class.
h. I teach the class.

    i.   We promise to leave early.
    j.   I owe Canada Customs and Revenue Agency $1 000 000.
    k.   I bequeath $1 000 000 to Canada Customs and Revenue Agency.
    l.   I swore I didn't do it.
    m. I swear I didn't do it.

*12. The following sentences make certain presuppositions. What are they? (The first one has been done for you.)

    a.   The police ordered the minors to stop drinking.
        Presupposition: <u>The minors were drinking.</u>
    b.   Please take me out to the ball game again.
    c.   Valerie regretted not receiving a new T-bird for Labour Day.
    d.   That her pet turtle ran away made Emily very sad.
    e.   The administration forgot that the professors support the students.
        (Cf. *The administration believes that the professors support the students*, in which there is no such presupposition.)
    f.   It is strange that Canada entered World War II in 1939.
    g.   Isn't it strange that Canada entered World War II in 1939?
    h.   Disa wants more popcorn.
    i.   Why don't pigs have wings?
    j.   Who arrived in America in 1492?

13. A. Consider the following "facts" and then answer the questions.

    Roses are red, and bralkions are too.
    Jane skied at Whistler and Jacques at Mont Tremblant.
    Casca stabbed Caesar, and so did Cinna.
    Frodo was exhausted, as was Sam.

    a.   What colour are bralkions?
    b.   What did Jacques do at Mont Tremblant?
    c.   What did Cinna do to Caesar?
    d.   What state was Sam in?

  B. Now consider these facts and explain how it is that you are able to determine the truth of each statement in (a) through (e).

    Black Beauty was a stallion.
    Lily is a widow.
    Rick remembered to send Lily a birthday card.
    Rick didn't remember to send Jane a birthday card.
    Flipper is walking.

    a.   Black Beauty was male?
    b.   Lily was never married?
    c.   Rick sent Lily a card?

    d.   Rick sent Jane a card?

    e.   Flipper has legs?

Part A illustrates your ability to interpret meanings when syntactic rules have deleted parts of the sentence. Part B illustrates your knowledge of semantic features and presuppositions.

14. Circle any deictic expressions in the following sentences. (*Hint:* Proper names and noun phrases containing *the* are not considered deictic expressions.)

    a.   I saw her standing there.

    b.   Dogs are animals.

    c.   Yesterday, all my troubles seemed so far away.

    d.   The name of this rock band is The Beatles.

    e.   The Canadian Constitution was patriated in 1982.

    f.   The Canadian Constitution was patriated last year.

    g.   Copper conducts electricity.

    h.   The treasure chest is on the right.

    i.   These are the times that try men's souls.

    j.   There is a tide in the affairs of men which taken at the flood leads on to fortune.

References

Chomsky, N. (1957). *Syntactic structures*. The Hague: Mouton.

Lakoff, G., & Johnson, M. (2003). *Metaphors we live by* (2nd ed.). Chicago: University of Chicago Press.

Further Reading

Austin, J.L. (1962). *How to do things with words*. Cambridge, MA: Harvard University Press.

Blakemore, D. (1992) *Understanding utterances: An introduction to pragmatics*. Malden, MA: Wiley-Blackwell.

Brown, G., & Yule, G. (1983). *Discourse analysis*. Cambridge, UK: Cambridge University Press.

Chierchia, G., & McConnell-Ginet, S. (1990). *Meaning and grammar: An introduction to syntax*. Cambridge, MA: MIT Press.

Davidson, D., & Harman, G. (Eds.). (1972). *Semantics of natural language*. Dordrecht, The Netherlands: Reidel.

Fraser, B. (1995). *An introduction to pragmatics*. Oxford: Blackwell.

Green, G.M. (1989). *Pragmatics and natural language understanding*. Hillsdale, NJ: Lawrence Erlbaum Associates.

Grice, H.P. (1971). Utterer's meaning. In J.R. Searle (Ed.), *The philosophy of language.* Oxford: Oxford University Press.

Grice, H.P. (1975). Logic and conversation. In P. Cole & J. Morgan (Eds.), *Syntax and semantics, 3*, 41–58. New York: Academic Press.

Hawkins, J.A. (1985). *A comparative typology of English and German.* Austin: University of Texas Press.

Horn, L., & Ward, G. (Eds.). (2006). *The handbook of pragmatics.* Wiley-Blackwell. Malden, MA: Wiley-Blackwell.

Hurford, J.R., & Heasley, B. (2007). *Semantics: A coursebook* (2nd ed.). Cambridge, UK: Cambridge University Press.

Jackendoff, R. (1983). *Semantics and cognition.* Cambridge, MA: MIT Press.

Jackendoff, R. (1993). *Patterns in the mind.* New York: HarperCollins.

Katz, J. (1972). *Semantic theory.* New York: Harper & Row.

Lakoff, G. (1987). *Women, fire, and dangerous things: What categories reveal about the mind.* Chicago: University of Chicago Press.

Larson, R., & Segal, G. (1995). *Knowledge of meaning.* Cambridge, MA: MIT Press.

Levinson, S.C. (1983). *Pragmatics.* Cambridge, UK: Cambridge University Press.

Lyons, J. (1977). *Semantics.* Cambridge, UK: Cambridge University Press.

Mey, J.L. (1993). *Pragmatics: An introduction.* Oxford: Blackwell.

Murphy, M.L. (2003). *Semantic relations and the lexicon: Antonymy, synonymy and other paradigms.* Oxford: Oxford University Press.

Palmer, F.R. (1994). *Grammatical roles and relations.* Cambridge, UK: Cambridge University Press.

Parsons, T. (1994). *Events in the semantics of English: A study in subatomic semantics.* Cambridge, MA: MIT Press.

Saeed, J. (2008). *Semantics* (3rd ed.). Boston: Blackwell.

Searle, J.R. (1969). *Speech acts: An essay in the philosophy of language.* Cambridge, UK: Cambridge University Press.

Sperber, D., & Wilson, D. (1986). *Relevance: Communication and cognition.* Oxford: Blackwell.

Tanz, C. (1980). *Studies in the acquisition of deictic terms.* Cambridge, UK: Cambridge University Press.

Websites

http://semanticsarchive.net/ Contains links to semantics-related resources.

http://www.teachit.co.uk/armoore/lang/semantics.htm A UK website containing basic concepts and terminology in semantics.

CHAPTER 5
Phonetics: The Sounds of Language

Phonetics is concerned with describing the speech sounds that occur in the languages of the world. We want to know what these sounds are, how they fall into patterns, and how they change in different circumstances.... The first job of a phonetician is ... to try to find out what people are doing when they are talking and when they are listening to speech.

Peter Ladefoged, *A Course in Phonetics* (2001)

Many people, when asked about language, think first of the written form because they recall most vividly those years in school when, under the guidance of a teacher, they mastered the fundamentals of reading and writing. Few, if any of us, can recall the earlier years in which we mastered the sound system of our mother tongue.

Language may manifest itself in many ways apart from the written system learned in school; it may be encoded electronically or appear in the signing system employed by deaf people. For most people, however, language was first realized through sounds that are created and manipulated by the lungs and thorax and in the oral and nasal passages.

From our first waking moment to the moment we surrender our consciousness, most of us are submerged in the sounds of speech as we talk with family, friends, acquaintances, and strangers, or listen to the talk on radio or television. While we display great skill in producing and interpreting speech sounds, we also consciously know little about those sounds.

We might ask why, if we are able to employ the sounds of our language with such skill, we need to learn any more about them. A first, more philosophical, response might be that, as language is arguably the most defining of all human actions, understanding any aspect of language is part of our continual attempt to understand what it means to be human. Most of us learn our "mother tongue" by first discriminating speech sounds from all the noise that surrounds us and then attempting to replicate those sounds and the patterns we hear in them. The fact that we learn language in this manner has been seen as one cause of constant change in every living language; as children attempt to replicate the sounds of their parents, they do so imperfectly, and this leads to changes, each of which may seem minute in itself but may become significant over time.

But the physical nature of sounds is not only of historical interest. The fact that language most commonly manifests itself in sounds produced by the human vocal apparatus helps to explain many things that we hear in everyday speech. It is not unusual, for example, in informal conversation to hear the word *something* pronounced with an intrusive *p* in it (as in *sumpthing*); this is the result of slight incoordination in moving between the *m* and the *th* sounds. If we are to understand why and how this occurs, we must first understand something about the sounds themselves and the qualities they share. It is the purpose of this chapter to make us more aware of speech sounds, in particular the sounds of English.

Knowledge of a language includes knowledge of the morphemes, words, phrases, and sentences, but it also includes knowing what sounds are in the language and how they may be "strung" together to form meaningful units. Although the sounds of French or Xhosa or Quechua are uninterpretable to someone who does not speak those languages, and although there may be some sounds in one language that are not in another, the sounds of all the languages of the world together constitute a limited set of the sounds that the human vocal tract can produce. This chapter will discuss these speech sounds, how they are produced, and how they may be characterized.

Sound Segments

The study of speech sounds is called **phonetics**. To describe these sounds, it is necessary to know what an individual sound is and how each sound differs from all others.

This is not as easy as it may seem. A speaker of English knows that there are three sounds in the word *cat*, the initial sound represented by the letter *c*, the second sound by *a*, and the final sound by *t*. Yet physically the word is just one continuous sound. You can **segment** the one sound into parts because you know English. The ability to analyze a word into its individual sounds does not depend on knowledge of how the word is spelled. Both *not* and *knot* have three sounds even though the first sound in *knot* is represented by the two letters *kn*. The word *psycho* has six letters that represent only four sounds — *ps, y, ch, o*.

It is difficult, if not impossible, to segment the sounds of a throat being cleared into a sequence of discrete units because these sounds are not the sounds of any morpheme in any human language. This difficulty does not arise because clearing the throat is a single continuous sound; in ordinary speech, we do not normally produce one sound followed by another and finally by a third sound in, for example, the word *cat*. We move our organs of speech continuously and produce a continuous signal.

Although the sounds we produce, hear, and comprehend during speech are continuous, everyone throughout history who has attempted to analyze language has recognized that speech utterances can be segmented into individual units. According to an ancient Hindu myth, the god Indra, in response to an appeal made by the other gods, attempted for the first time to segment speech into its separate elements. After he accomplished this feat, according to the myth, the sounds could be regarded as language. Indra thus may have been the first phonetician.

5-30 © 1978 Jim Unger

"Keep out! Keep out! K-E-E-P O-U-T."

HERMAN © is reprinted with permission from LaughingStock Licensing Inc., Ottawa, Canada.
All Rights Reserved.

Speakers of English can, despite the Herman cartoon, separate *keep out* into two words because they know the language. We do not, however, pause between words even though we sometimes have that illusion. Children learning a language reveal this problem. A two-year-old child going down a flight of stairs, when told to *hold on*, replied *I'm holding don*, not knowing where the break between the words occurred. In the course of history, the errors in deciding where a boundary falls between two words can change the forms of words. At an earlier stage of English, the words *apron* was *napron*. However, the phrase *a napron* was so often misperceived as *an apron* that the word lost its initial *n*.

The lack of breaks between words and individual sounds often makes us think that speakers of foreign languages run their words together, not realizing that we do so also. X-ray motion pictures of someone speaking make this lack of breaks in the speech chain clear. One can see the tongue, jaw, and lips in continuous motion while the "individual sounds" are being produced.

Yet, if you know a language, you have no difficulty segmenting the continuous sounds. In this way, speech is similar to music. A person who has not studied music cannot write the sequence of individual notes combined by a violinist into one changing continuous sound. A trained musician, however, finds it a simple task. Every human speaker, without special training, can segment a speech signal. Just as one cannot analyze a musical passage without musical knowledge, so also linguistic knowledge is required to segment speech into pieces.

Identity of Speech Sounds

It is amazing, given the continuity of speech, that we are able to understand which words are put together to form an utterance. This achievement is even more surprising because no two speakers ever say "the same thing." The speech signal produced when one speaker says *cat* will not be exactly the same as the signal produced by another speaker's *cat* or even the repetition of the word by the same speaker. Yet speakers understand each other because they know the same language.

Our knowledge of a language determines when we judge physically different sounds to be the same; we know which aspects or properties of the signal are linguistically important and which are not. For example, if someone coughs in the middle of saying "How (cough) are you?" a listener will interpret this simply as "How are you?" Men's voices are usually lower in overall pitch than women's, and some people speak more slowly than others, but differences in pitch or tempo are not linguistically significant.

Our linguistic knowledge, our mental grammar, makes it possible to ignore nonlinguistic differences in speech. Furthermore, we are capable of making many sounds that we know intuitively are not speech sounds in our language. Many English speakers can make a clicking sound that writers sometimes represent as *tsk tsk tsk*. But these sounds are not part of the English sound system. They never occur as part of the words of the sentences we produce. It is, in fact, difficult for many English speakers to combine this clicking sound with other sounds. Yet clicks are speech sounds in Xhosa, Zulu, Sotho, and Khoikhoi — languages spoken in southern Africa — just like the *k* or *t* in English. Speakers of those languages have no difficulty producing them as parts of words. The word *Xhosa* begins with one of these clicks. Thus, *tsk* is a speech sound in Xhosa but not in English. The sound represented by the letters *th* in the word *think* is a speech sound in English but not in French. The sound produced with a closed mouth when we are trying to clear a tickle in the throat is not a speech sound in any language, nor is the sound produced when we sneeze.

The science of phonetics attempts to describe all the sounds used in human language — sounds that constitute a subset of the totality of sounds that humans are capable of producing.

The way we use our linguistic knowledge to produce meaningful utterances is complicated. It can be viewed as a chain of events starting with an idea or message in the mind of the speaker and ending with a similar message in the brain of the hearer. The message is put into a form that is dictated by the language we are speaking. It must then be transmitted by nerve signals to the organs of speech articulation, which produce the different physical sounds.

Speech sounds can be described at any stage in this chain of events. The study of the physical properties of the sounds themselves is called **acoustic phonetics**, and the study of the way listeners perceive these sounds is called **auditory phonetics**.

Articulatory phonetics — the study of how the vocal tract produces the sounds of language — is the primary concern of this chapter.

Spelling and Speech

> Beware of heard, a dreadful word
> That looks like beard and sounds like bird.
> And dead: it's said like bed, not bead;
> For goodness' sake, don't call it deed!
> Watch out for meat and great and threat.
> (They rhyme with suite and straight and debt.)
> A moth is not a moth in mother,
> Nor both in bother, broth in brother.
>
> Richard Krogh

Alphabetic spelling represents the pronunciations of words. Frequently, the sounds of the words in a language are unsystematically represented by orthography — that is, by spelling — and it can become confusing to refer to the sounds as they are spelled in English words. Suppose, for example, all Earthlings were destroyed by some horrible catastrophe, and years later Martian astronauts exploring Earth discovered some fragments of English writing that included the following sentence:

Did he bel**ie**ve that C**ae**sar could s**ee** the p**eo**ple s**ei**ze the s**ea**s?

How would a Martian linguist decide that *e, ie, ae, ee, eo, ei*, and *ea* all represent the same sound? To add to the confusion, this sentence might crop up later:

The sill**y** am**oe**ba stole the k**ey** to the machine.

English speakers learn how to pronounce these words when learning to read and write and know that *y, oe, ey*, and *i* also represent the same sound as the boldface letters in the first sentence.

On the other hand, consider:

My f**a**ther w**a**nted m**a**ny **a** village d**a**me badly.

Here the letter **a** represents the several sounds in *father, wanted, many,* and so on.

In any science, the objects of study, when different, must be given different names or symbols, and the science of phonetics is no exception. Each distinct sound must have a distinct symbol to represent it; and each symbol must represent one and only one distinct sound.

The Phonetic Alphabet

> The English have no respect for their language, and will not teach their children to speak it. They cannot spell it because they have nothing to spell it

with but an old foreign alphabet of which only the consonants — and not all of them — have any agreed speech value.

George Bernard Shaw, Preface, *Pygmalion* (1913)

The discrepancy between spelling and sound gave rise to a movement of "spelling reformers" called **orthoepists**. They wanted to revise the alphabet so that one letter would correspond to one sound and one sound to one letter, thus simplifying spelling. This is a **phonetic alphabet**.

George Bernard Shaw followed in the footsteps of three centuries of spelling reformers in England. In typical Shavian manner, he pointed out that we could use the English spelling system to spell *fish* as *ghoti* — the *gh* like the sound in *enough*, the *o* like the sound in *women*, and the *ti* like the sound in *nation*. Shaw was so concerned about English spelling that he included a provision in his will for a new "Proposed English Alphabet" to be administered by a "Public Trustee" who would have the duty of seeking and publishing a more efficient alphabet. This alphabet was to have at least forty letters to enable "the said language to be written without indicating single sounds by groups of letters or by diacritical marks." After Shaw's death in 1950, 450 designs for such an alphabet were submitted from all parts of the globe. Four alphabets were judged to be equally good, and the £500 sterling prize was divided among their designers, who collaborated to produce the alphabet designated in Shaw's will. Shaw also stipulated in his will that his play *Androcles and the Lion* be published in the new alphabet, with "the original Doctor Johnson's lettering opposite the transliteration page by page and a glossary of the two alphabets." This version of the play was published in 1962.

It is easy to understand why spelling reformers believe there is a need for a phonetic alphabet. Different letters may represent a single sound, as is shown in the following instances:

| to | too | two | through | threw | clue | shoe |

A single letter may represent different sounds:

| dame | dad | father | village | many |

A combination of letters may represent a single sound:

shoot	character	Thomas	physics
either	deal	rough	nation
coat	glacial	theatre	plain

Some letters have no sound at all in certain words:

mnemonic	whole	resign	ghost
pterodactyl	write	hole	corps
psychology	sword	debt	gnaw
bough	lamb	island	knot

Some sounds are not represented in the spelling. In many words, the letter *u* represents a *y* sound followed by a *u* sound:

cute (compare c**oo**t)
futile (compare r**u**le)
utility (compare **U**zbek)

One letter may represent two sounds; the final *x* in *Xerox* represents a *k* followed by an *s*.

Whether we support or oppose spelling reform, it is clear that we cannot depend on the spellings of words to describe the sounds of English. The alphabets designed to fulfil Shaw's will were not the first phonetic alphabets. One of the earliest was produced by Robert Robinson in 1617. In Shaw's lifetime, the phonetician Henry Sweet, the prototype for Shaw's own Henry Higgins in the play *Pygmalion* (and in the film version, *My Fair Lady*), produced a phonetic alphabet.

In 1888, the interest in the scientific description of speech sounds led the **International Phonetic Association (IPA)** to develop the **International Phonetic Alphabet (IPA)**, a phonetic alphabet that could be used to symbolize the sounds found in all languages. Since many languages use a Roman alphabet like that used in the English writing system, the IPA used Roman letters as well as invented symbols. These phonetic symbols have a consistent value — unlike ordinary letters, which may or may not represent the same sounds in the same or different languages.

> **IPA**
>
> The International Phonetic Association was founded in 1886 by a group of language teachers in France who wished to promote phonetics, as they found it useful in language teaching.

A phonetic alphabet should include enough symbols to represent the "crucial" linguistic differences. At the same time, it should not, and cannot, include non-crucial differences, since such differences are infinitely varied.

A list of phonetic symbols that can be used to represent speech sounds of English is given in Table 5.1. The symbols omit many details about the sounds and how they are produced in different words and in different places in words. These symbols are meant to be used by people knowing English. These are not all the phonetic symbols needed for English sounds; when we discuss the sounds in more detail later in the chapter we will add appropriate symbols.

The symbol [ə] is called a *schwa*. It will be used in this book only to represent unstressed vowels. There is great variation in the way speakers of English produce this unstressed vowel, but it is phonetically similar to the wedge symbol [ʌ], which will be used only in stressed syllables. It is important to note that the pronunciation of vowels in general can vary slightly depending on surrounding sounds; also, there is a great amount of dialectal variation in how vowels are pronounced. The same is even more true for diphthongs, whose quality varies enormously according to both surrounding sounds and the speaker's particular dialect (MacKay, 1987).

In this regard, speakers of some English dialects pronounce some entire words differently from the way speakers of other dialects do. For example, some speakers pronounce the words *which* and *witch* identically, in which case the initial sound of both words is symbolized by *w* in the chart. Other speakers of English pronounce *bought*

TABLE 5.1
A Phonetic Alphabet for English Pronunciation

Consonants						Vowels			
p	pill	t	till	k	kill	i	beet	ɪ	bit
b	bill	d	dill	g	gill	e	bait	ɛ	bet
m	mill	n	nil	ŋ	ring	u	boot	ʊ	put
f	feel	s	seal	h	heal	o	boat	ɔ	bore
v	veal	z	zeal	l	leaf	æ	bat	ɑ	pot
θ	thigh	č	chill	r	reef	ʌ	but	ə	sofa
ð	thy	ǰ	Jill	j	you	aj	bite	aw	cow
ʃ/š	shrill	ʍ	which	w	witch	ɔj	boy		
ʒ/ž	azure								

and *pot* with the same vowel; and still others pronounce them with the vowel sound in *bore* and *saw*, respectively. Similarly, some speakers — notably, speakers of Canadian English — distinguish the diphthong in *bite* and *bide* as [bʌjt] and [bajd]. Unfortunately, it is not possible in an introductory text to include all the phonetic symbols required to represent each English dialect. We apologize if a vowel sound in your dialect is not included in the table.

Some of the symbols in Table 5.1 are those traditionally used by linguists in North America in place of IPA symbols. Here are some equivalencies:

North America	IPA
š	ʃ
ž	ʒ
č	tʃ
ǰ	dʒ
ʊ	ʊ

We will use [š], [ʃ] and [ž], [ʒ] interchangeably to familiarize readers with both notations, since both are common in books on language and linguistics. We will, however, use [č] and [ǰ] instead of the IPA symbols for the first and last sounds in *church* and *judge,* respectively.

Using these symbols, we can now unambiguously represent the pronunciations of words. For example, words spelled with *ou* may have different pronunciations. To distinguish between the symbols representing sounds and the alphabet letters, we put the phonetic symbols between brackets:

Spelling	Pronunciation
though	[ðo]
thought	[θɑt]
rough	[rʌf]
bough	[baw]
through	[θru]
would	[wʊd]

Only in *rough* do the letters *gh* represent any sound — that is, the sound [f]; *ou* represents six different sounds, and *th* represents two different sounds. The *l* in *would*, like the *gh* in all but one of the words above, is not pronounced at all.

We will continue to use square brackets around the phonetic transcription to distinguish it from ordinary spelling.

Articulatory Phonetics

> The voice is articulated by the lips and the tongue. . . . Man speaks by means of the air which he inhales into his entire body and particularly into the body cavities. When the air is expelled through the empty space it produces a sound, because of the resonances in the skull. The tongue articulates by its strokes; it gathers the air in the throat and pushes it against the palate and the teeth, thereby giving the sound a definite shape. If the tongue would not articulate each time, by means of its strokes, man would not speak clearly and would only be able to produce a few simple sounds.
>
> Hippocrates (460–377 B.C.E.)

The production of any sound involves the movement of air. Most speech sounds are produced by pushing lung air through the opening between the vocal cords, up the throat, and into the mouth or nose, and finally out of the body. The opening between the vocal cords is the **glottis** and is located in the **larynx** (often referred to as the "voice box"). Vibration of the vocal cords results in voiced sounds (see Figure 5.1). The tubular part of the throat above the larynx is the **pharynx.** What sensible people call "the mouth," linguists call the **oral cavity** to distinguish it from the **nasal cavity**, which is the nose and the plumbing that connects it to the throat, plus the sinuses. All of it together is the **vocal tract**. Figure 5.2 should make these descriptions more clear.

FIGURE 5.1

Larynx.

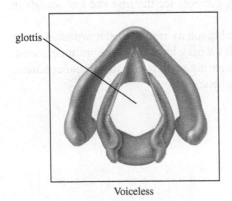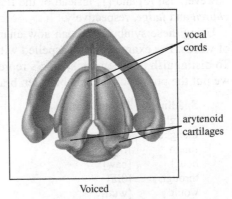

Voiceless   Voiced

FIGURE 5.2

The vocal tract: Places of articulation.

1. bilabial   2. labiodental   3. interdental   4. alveolar   5. (alveo) palatal   6. velar
7. uvular   8. glottal

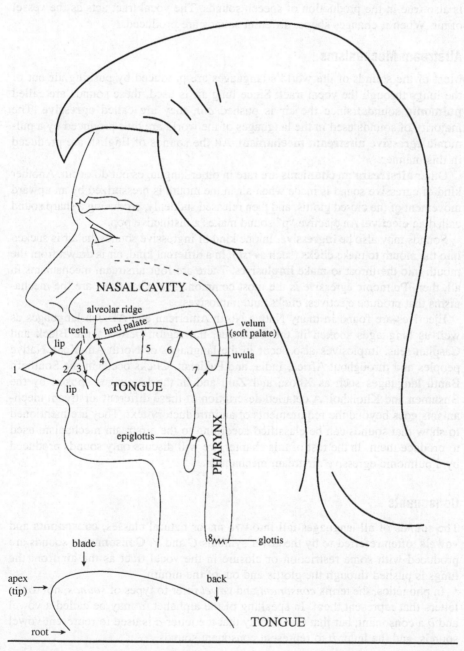

What distinguishes one sound from the other? If you bang a large round drum you will get one sound; if you bang a small round drum you will get a different sound; if you bang a small oblong drum you will get still another sound. The size and shape of the vessel containing the air that is moving makes a difference. This is also true in the production of speech sounds. The vocal tract acts as the vessel of air. When it changes shape, different sounds are produced.

Airstream Mechanisms

Most of the sounds of the world's languages are produced by pushing air out of the lungs through the vocal tract. Since lung air is used, these sounds are called **pulmonic** sounds; since the air is pushed *out*, they are called **egressive**. The majority of sounds used in the languages of the world are thus produced by a pulmonic **egressive airstream mechanism**. All the sounds of English are produced in this manner.

Other **airstream mechanisms** are rare in other languages but do occur. Another kind of egressive sound is made when air in the mouth is pressurized by an upward movement of the closed glottis, and then released suddenly, producing a sharp sound called an **ejective.** An ejective "p" sound makes a distinctive pop.

Sounds may also be **ingressive**. In one kind of ingressive sound, the air is sucked into the mouth to make **clicks** (such as *tsk*). In a different kind, air is drawn from the mouth into the throat to make **implosives**. There are four airstream mechanisms in all, then. Pulmonic egressive is the most common. The other three are the mechanisms that produce ejectives, clicks, and implosives.

Ejectives are found in many Native North American and African languages as well as languages spoken in the Caucasus, the region between the Black and Caspian seas. Implosives also occur in the languages of North American Native peoples and throughout Africa, India, and Pakistan. Clicks occur in the Southern Bantu languages such as Xhosa and Zulu and in the languages spoken by the Bushmen and Khoikhoi. A detailed description of these different airstream mechanisms goes beyond the requirements of an introductory text. They are mentioned to show that sounds can be classified according to the airstream mechanism used to produce them. In the rest of this chapter, we will discuss only sounds produced by a pulmonic egressive airstream mechanism.

Consonants

The sounds of all languages fall into two major natural classes, **consonants** and **vowels**, often referred to by the cover symbols *C* and *V*. **Consonantal** sounds are produced with some restriction or closure in the vocal tract as the air from the lungs is pushed through the glottis and out of the mouth.

In phonetics, the terms *consonant* and *vowel* refer to types of *sounds*, not to the letters that represent them. In speaking of the alphabet, *a* may be called a vowel and *b* a consonant, but that means only that the letter *a* is used to represent vowel sounds, and the letter *b* to represent consonant sounds.

TABLE 5.2

Place of Articulation of English Consonants

Bilabial:	p	b	m
Labiodental:	f	v	
Interdental:	θ	ð	
Alveolar:	t	d	n	s	z	l	r
Palatal:	ʃ/š	ʒ/ž	č	ǰ	j
Velar:	k	g	ŋ	w
Glottal:	h		

Manners of Articulation

We have described a number of classes of consonants according to their places of articulation, yet we are unable to distinguish the sounds in each class from one another. What distinguishes [p] from [b] or [b] from [m]? All are bilabial sounds. What is the difference between [t], [d], and [n], all alveolar sounds?

Speech sounds are also differentiated by the way the airstream is affected as it travels from the lungs up and out through the mouth and nose. It may be blocked or partially blocked; the vocal cords may vibrate or not vibrate. We refer to this as the **manner of articulation**.

Voiced and Voiceless Sounds

If the vocal cords are apart when the airstream is pushed from the lungs, then the air passes freely into the supraglottal cavities (those parts of the vocal tract above the glottis). The sounds produced in this way are **voiceless sounds**; for example, [p], [t], [k], and [s] in the words *seep* [sip], *seat* [sit], and *seek* [sik] are voiceless.

If the vocal cords are together, then the airstream forces its way through and causes them to vibrate. Sounds such as [b], [d], [g], and [z] in words such as *cob* [kɑb], *cod* [kɑd], *cog* [kɑg], and *daze* [dez] are **voiced sounds**. If you put a finger in each ear and say "z-z-z-z-z-," you will feel the vibrations of the vocal cords. If you now say "s-s-s-s-s-," you will not feel these vibrations (although you might hear a hissing sound in your mouth). When you whisper, you are making all the speech sounds voiceless.

The voiced/voiceless distinction is an important one in English. It is this phonetic feature or property that distinguishes between word pairs such as the following:

rope/robe	fate/fade	rack/rag	wreath/wreathe
[rop]/[rob]	[fet]/[fed]	[ræk]/[ræg]	[riθ]/[rið]

The first word of each pair ends with a voiceless sound and the second word with a voiced sound. All other aspects of the sounds of these words are identical; the position of the lips and tongue is the same in each of the paired words.

The voiced/voiceless distinction is also shown in the following pairs; the first word begins with a voiceless sound and the second with a voiced sound:

fine/vine	seal/zeal	choke/joke
[fajn]/[vajn]	[sil]/[zil]	[čok]/[ǰok]

The initial sounds of the first words of the following pairs are also voiceless, and for many speakers of English the second words begin with voiced sounds. (We will discuss other differences between the initial [p] and [b] sounds below; the phonetic transcriptions of many of these words have been simplified to help the reader grasp basic concepts and may include other details in subsequent sections.)

peat/beat	tune/dune	cane/gain
[pit]/[bit]	[tun]/[dun]	[ken]/[gen]

Aspirated and Unaspirated Sounds

In our discussion of the voiceless bilabial stop [p], we did not distinguish the initial sound in the word *pit* from the second sound in the word *spit*. There is, however, a phonetic difference in these two voiceless stops. During the production of voiceless sounds, the glottis is open, and air passes freely through the opening between the vocal cords. When a voiceless sound is followed by a voiced sound such as a vowel, the vocal cords must close in order to permit them to vibrate.

Voiceless sounds fall into two classes depending on the "timing" of the vocal cord closure. In English, when we pronounce the word *pit*, there is a brief period of voicelessness immediately after the *p* sound is released. That is, after the lips come apart, the vocal cords remain open for a very short time. Such sounds are called **aspirated** because an extra puff of air escapes through the open glottis.

When we pronounce the *p* in *spit*, however, the vocal cords start vibrating as soon as the lips are opened. Such sounds are called **unaspirated**. The *t* in *tick* and the *k* in *kin* are also aspirated voiceless stops, while the *t* in *stick* and the *k* in *skin* are unaspirated. If you hold a strip of paper in front of your lips and say *pit*, a puff of air (the aspiration) will push the paper. The paper will not move when you say *spit*.

When a fully voiced [b], or any voiced stop, is produced, the vocal cords vibrate throughout the articulation. In English, voiced stops may not be fully voiced. Figure 5.3 shows in diagrammatic form the timing of the articulators (in this case the lips) in relation to the state of the vocal cords. Notice that, in the production of the voiced [b], the vocal cords are vibrating throughout the closure of the lips and continue to vibrate for the vowel production after the lips are opened. Most English speakers do not voice initial [b] to the full extent. Because we heavily aspirate an initial [p], there is no difficulty in distinguishing these two sounds. In the unaspirated *p* in *spin*, the vocal cords are open during the lip closure and come together and start vibrating as soon as the lips open. In the production of the aspirated *p* in *pin*, the vocal cords remain apart for a brief period after the lip closure is released. These remarks apply to all English stops.

FIGURE 5.3

Timing of articulators and vocal cord vibration for voiced, voiceless unaspirated, and voiceless aspirated stops.

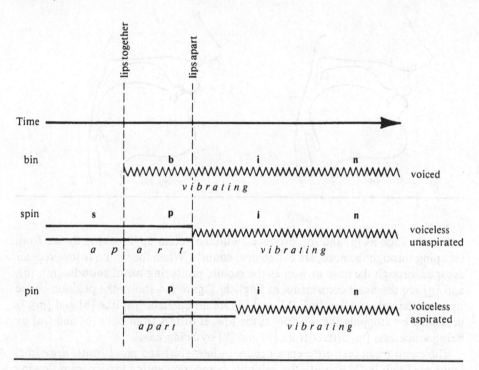

Aspirated stops may be indicated by following the phonetic symbol with a raised [h]:

pate [pʰet]	spate [spet]
tale [tʰel]	stale [stel]
kale [kʰel]	scale [skel]

Nasal and Oral Sounds

The voiced/voiceless distinction differentiates the bilabial [b] from [p], but [m] is also voiced. What, then, distinguishes [m] from [b]? Perhaps the first thing to notice is that when you produce [m], air escapes not only through the mouth (when the lips are opened) but through the nose as well. [m], in other words, is a nasal sound.

In Figure 5.2, the roof of the mouth is divided into the hard palate and the soft palate (or velum). The palate is the hard bony structure we can feel at the front of the mouth. As we move back toward the throat, we encounter the velum, where the flesh becomes soft and movable. Hanging from the end of the velum is the uvula. When the velum is raised all the way to touch the back of the throat, the passage through the nose is cut off, and air can escape only through the mouth.

FIGURE 5.4
Position of lips and velum for [m] (lips together, velum down) and [b] or [p] (lips together, velum up).

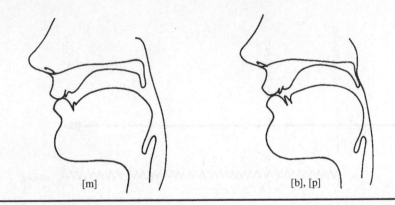

[m]   [b], [p]

Sounds such as [p] and [b], produced with the velum up, blocking the air from escaping through the nose, are called **oral sounds**. When the velum is lowered, air escapes through the nose as well as the mouth, producing **nasal sounds**. [m], [n], and [ŋ] are the nasal consonants of English. Figure 5.4 shows the position of the lips and the velum when [m], [b], and [p] are articulated. [p], like [b] and [m], is produced by stopping the air flow at the lips. It differs from both [b] and [m] by being voiceless; [m] differs from [p] and [b] by being nasal.

The same nasal/oral difference occurs in *beet* [bit] and *meat* [mit], *dear* [dir] and *near* [nir]; in [b] and [d], the velum is raised, preventing the air from flowing through the nose, whereas in [m] and [n] the velum is down, letting the air go through both the nose and the mouth when the closure is released. [m], [n], and [ŋ] are therefore nasal sounds, and [b], [d], and [g] are oral sounds.

These **phonetic features** or properties permit the classification of all speech sounds into four classes: voiced, voiceless, nasal, and oral. One sound may belong to more than one class, as shown in Table 5.3.

We now have three ways of classifying consonants: by voicing, by place of articulation, and oral versus nasal. For example, [p] is a voiceless, bilabial, oral sound; [n] is a voiced, alveolar, nasal sound.

Stops: [p], [b], [m], [t], [d], [n], [k], [g], [ŋ], [č], [ǰ], [ʔ]

We witness ever finer distinctions of speech sounds as we attempt to define how it is that one sound differs from another. We might note that [t] is a voiceless, alveolar, oral sound, but then [s] is also a voiceless, alveolar, oral sound — yet it is quite different. What distinguishes these two sounds?

The airstream, after entering the oral cavity, may be stopped completely, may be partially obstructed, or may flow freely out of the mouth. Sounds that are stopped completely in the oral cavity for a brief period, such as [t], are, not

TABLE 5.3
Classes of Speech Sounds

	Oral	Nasal
Voiced	b d g	m n ŋ
Voiceless	p t k	*

*Nasal consonants in English are usually voiced.
Both voiced and voiceless nasal sounds occur in
other languages.

surprisingly, called **stops**. In the production of the nasal stops [n], [m], and [ŋ], although air flows freely through the nose, it is blocked completely in the mouth; consequently, nasal consonants are stops. The initial and final sounds in the following words are stops in English: *top, bomb, dude, dune, boot, tack, nag, bang*.

Sounds in which there is no stoppage in the oral tract are **continuants**. All the sounds of a language are either stops or continuants (nonstops).

Nonnasal or oral stops are also called **plosives** because the air that is blocked in the mouth "explodes" when the closure is released. This explosion does not occur with nasal stops because the air escapes through the nose.

[p], [b], and [m] are *bilabial stops*, with the airstream stopped at the mouth by the complete closure of the lips.

[t], [d], and [n] are *alveolar stops*; the airstream is stopped by the tongue, which makes a complete closure at the alveolar ridge.

[k], [g], and [ŋ] are *velar stops* with complete closure at the velum.

[č] and [ǰ] are *palatal* (or alveopalatal) *affricates* with complete stop closure. They will be discussed below.

[ʔ] is a *glottal stop*; though there is no stoppage of air in the oral cavity, air is completely stopped at the glottis.

In Quechua, a major language spoken in Bolivia and Peru, one also finds uvular stops that are produced when the back of the tongue is raised and moved backward to form a complete closure with the uvula. The letter *q* in words in this language, as in the name of the language, usually represents a voiceless uvular stop [q]. The voiced uvular stop [G] also occurs in Quechua. Glottal stops are also found in other languages such as Arabic.

Fricatives: [f], [v], [θ], [ð], [s], [z], [š], [ž], [h]

In the production of some sounds, the airstream is not completely stopped but is obstructed from flowing freely. If you put your hand in front of your mouth and produce an [f], [v], [θ], [ð], [s], [z], [š], [ž], or [h] sound, you will feel the air coming out of your mouth. The passage in the mouth through which the air must pass, however, is very narrow, causing friction or turbulence. Such sounds are called **fricatives**.

In the production of the *labiodental fricatives* [f] and [v], the friction is created at the lips and teeth, where a narrow passage permits the air to escape.

In the production of the *interdental fricatives* [θ] and [ð], represented by *th* in *thin* and *then*, the friction occurs at the opening between the tongue and the teeth.

[s] and [z] are *alveolar fricatives* with the friction created at the alveolar ridge.

The *palatal* (or alveopalatal) *fricatives*, [š] and [ž], such as those in *mission* [mɪšən] and *measure* [mɛžər], are produced with friction created as the air passes through the narrow opening behind the alveolar ridge. In English, the voiced palatal fricative never begins words (except words borrowed from the French, such as *genre* or *gendarme*, which some English speakers produce with a French pronunciation). The voiceless palatal sound begins the words *shoe* [šu] and *sure* [šur] and ends the words *rush* [rʌš] and *push* [pʊš].

The [h] occurring at the beginning of words such as *high* and *happy* is classi-fied as a *voiceless glottal fricative*. However, [h] differs from "true" consonants in that there is no obstruction in the oral cavity. It also differs from vowels that are articulated by moving the tongue. When it is both preceded and followed by a vowel, it is often voiced in English, as in *ahead* and *cohabit*.

Most dialects of modern English do not include velar fricatives, although they occurred in an earlier stage of English in words such as *right, knight, enough*, and *through*, where the *gh* occurs in the spelling. If you raise the back of the tongue as if you were about to produce a [g] or [k], but stop just short of touching the velum, you will produce a velar fricative. The *ch* ending in the German pronunciation of the composer's name *Bach* is a velar fricative. Some speakers of modern English sub-stitute a voiceless velar fricative in words such as *bucket* and a voiced velar fricative in words such as *wagon* for the velar stops that occur for other speakers in those words. [x] is the IPA symbol for the voiceless velar fricative and [ɣ] for the voiced velar fricative.

In some languages of the world, such as French, *uvular fricatives* occur as the sound represented by *r* in French words such as *rouge* "red" or *rose* "pink." In Arabic, *pharyngeal fricatives* are produced by pulling the tongue root toward the back wall of the pharynx. It is difficult to pull the tongue back far enough to make a complete pharyngeal stop closure, but both voiced and voiceless pharyngeal fricatives can be produced and can be distinguished from velar fricatives.

All fricatives are continuants; although the airstream is obstructed as it passes through the oral cavity, it is not completely stopped.

Affricates: [č], [ǰ]

Some sounds are produced by a stop closure followed immediately by a slow release of the closure characteristic of a fricative. These sounds are called **affricates**. The sounds that begin and end the words *church* and *judge* are voiceless and voiced affricates, respectively. Phonetically, an affricate is a sequence of a stop plus a frica-tive. Thus, the *ch* in *church* is the same as the sound combination [t] + [š] as shown by observing that in fast speech *white shoes* and *why choose* may be pronounced identically. The voiceless and voiced affricates may be symbolized as [tš] (IPA [t ʃ]) and [dž] (IPA [dʒ]), respectively. In the North American tradition, [č] and [ǰ] are the more commonly used symbols for these sounds and the ones used in this book.

Because the air is stopped completely during the initial articulation of an affricate, these sounds are classified as stops.

Liquids: [l], [r]

In the production of the sounds [l] and [r], there is some obstruction of the airstream in the mouth but not enough to cause any real constriction or friction. These sounds are called **liquids**. If, as described earlier, the tongue is raised to the alveolar ridge but the sides are down so that air can escape laterally over the sides, then a lateral liquid [l] is produced.

As mentioned earlier, the *r* sounds found in various dialects of English as well as in other languages differ somewhat from each other. We are using the symbol [r] for this whole class of sounds. In some languages, the *r* may be a **trill**, produced by the tip of the tongue vibrating against the roof of the mouth. A trilled [r] occurs in Scots English and in many languages, such as Spanish. In addition, uvular trills occur, produced by vibrating the uvula. Some French speakers use uvular trills in the pronunciation of *r*; others use uvular fricatives.

In other dialects and languages, the *r* is produced by a single **tap** or **flap** of the tongue against the alveolar ridge. Some speakers of British English pronounce the *r* in the word *very* with this flap. It sounds like a "very fast" *d*. Most American and Canadian speakers produce a flap instead of a [t] or a [d] in words such as *writer* or *rider, latter* or *ladder*. As a test of whether you use a flap in this position, you might try saying the following sentence to a friend: "The painter left the ladder outside the barn and the paint inside." Then ask, "Where was the latter?" If the answer is "Outside," then you can be pretty sure you use a flap. The IPA symbol for the alveolar tap or flap is [ɾ]. North American linguists often use the uppercase [D] to represent the sound.

In English, [l] and [r] are regularly voiced. When they follow voiceless sounds, as in *please* and *price*, they may be partially devoiced; that is, the voicing doesn't begin until partway through the consonant. Many languages, such as Welsh, have a voiceless *l* as an independent sound, in which case it is actually a fricative; the name *Lloyd* in that language starts with such a voiceless fricative consonant.

Some languages may lack liquids entirely or have only one. The Cantonese dialect of Chinese has the single liquid, [l]. Some English words are difficult for Cantonese speakers to pronounce, and they may substitute an [l] for an [r] when speaking English. The acoustic similarity of these sounds disposes speakers of languages with only one liquid to use that liquid as a substitute when speaking other languages for the sound that their own language lacks. This physical similarity is why they are grouped in one class and why they function as a single class of sounds in certain circumstances.

In English, the only two consonants that occur after an initial [k], [g], [p], or [b] are the liquids [l] and [r]. Thus, we have *crate* [kret], *clock* [klɑk], *plate* [plet], *prate* [pret], *bleak* [blik], *break* [brek], but no word starting with [ps], [bt], [pk], and so on. (Notice that in words such as *psychology* or *pterodactyl* the *p* is not pronounced. Similarly, in *knight* or *knot* the *k* is not pronounced, although at an earlier stage in English it was.)

Glides: [j], [w]

The sounds [j] and [w], the initial sounds of *you* [ju] and *woo* [wu], are produced with little or no obstruction of the airstream in the mouth. When occurring in a word, they must always be either preceded or followed directly by a vowel. In articulating [j] or [w], the tongue moves rapidly in gliding fashion either toward or away from a neighbouring vowel, hence the term **glide**. Glides are transitional sounds that are sometimes called semivowels.

[j] is a *palatal glide*; the blade of the tongue is raised toward the hard palate in a position almost identical to that in producing the vowel sound [i] in the word *beat* [bit]. In pronouncing *you* [ju], the tongue moves rapidly from the [j] to the [u] vowel.

The glide [w] is produced by both raising the back of the tongue toward the velum and simultaneously rounding the lips. It is thus a **labiovelar** glide or a rounded velar glide. In the dialect of English in which speakers have different pronunciations for the words *which* and *witch*, the velar glide in the first word is voiceless [ʍ] (an "upside-down" *w*), and in the second word it is voiced [w]. The position of the tongue and the lips for [w] is similar to that for producing the vowel sound in *lute* [lut], but the [w] is a glide because the tongue moves quickly to the following vowel.

Phonetic Symbols for North American English Consonants

The place and manner properties of speech sounds make it possible to distinguish each consonant sound from all others that occur in American English. Table 5.4 lists the consonants by their phonetic features. The rows stand for manner of articulation and the columns for place of articulation. Symbols for aspirated stops and the glottal stop are not included since this is a minimal list of symbols by which all morphemes and words can be distinguished. Thus, the symbol [p] for the voiceless bilabial stop is sufficient to differentiate the word *peat* [pit] from the voiced bilabial stop symbol [b] in *beat* [bit]. If a more detailed **phonetic transcription** of these words (sometimes referred to as a narrow phonetic transcription) is desired, then the symbol [pʰ] can be used, as in [pʰit].

Examples of words in which these sounds occur are given in Table 5.5.

Vowels

HIGGINS: Tired of listening to sounds?

PICKERING: Yes. It's a fearful strain. I rather fancied myself because I can pronounce twenty-four distinct vowel sounds, but your hundred and thirty beat me. I can't hear a bit of difference between most of them.

HIGGINS: Oh, that comes with practice. You hear no difference at first, but you keep on listening and presently you find they're all as different as A from B.

George Bernard Shaw, *Pygmalion* (1913)

The quality of a vowel is determined by the particular configuration of the vocal tract during its production. Different parts of the tongue may be raised or lowered;

TABLE 5.4

Minimal Set of Phonetic Symbols for North American English Consonants

	Bilabial	Labiodental	Interdental	Alveolar	Palatal	Velar	Glottal
Stop (oral)							
voiceless	p			t		k	
voiced	b			d		g	
Nasal (stop)	m			n		ŋ	
Fricative							
voiceless		f	θ	s	š		h[1]
voiced		v	ð	z	ž		
Affricate							
voiceless					č		
voiced					ǰ		
Glide							
voiceless						ʍ	h[1]
voiced	w[2]				j	w[2]	
Liquid				l r			

1. [h] is sometimes classified as a fricative because of the hissing sound produced by air or noise at the glottis. It is also sometimes classified with the glides because in many languages it combines with other sounds the way that glides do.

2. In this chart [w] is classified as both a bilabial because it is produced with both lips rounded and a velar because the back of the tongue is raised toward the velum.

TABLE 5.5

Examples of Consonants in English Words

	Bilabial	Labiodental	Interdental	Alveolar	Palatal	Velar	Glottal
Stop (oral)							
voiceless	*p*ie			*t*ie		*k*ite	
voiced	*b*uy			*d*ie		*g*uy	
Nasal (stop)	*m*y			*n*ight		si*ng*	
Fricative							
voiceless		*f*ie	*th*igh	*s*ue	mi*ss*ion		*h*igh
voiced		*v*ie	*th*y	*z*oo	mea*s*ure		
Affricate							
voiceless					*ch*ime		
voiced					*j*ive		
Glide							
voiceless	*wh*ich[1]					*wh*ich[1]	
voiced	*w*ipe				*y*ank	*w*ipe	
Liquid				*l*ie, *r*ye			

1. For speakers with a voiceless *w*.

the velum may be raised or lowered; and the lips may be spread or pursed. The passage through which the air travels, however, is never so narrow as to obstruct the free flow of the airstream.

Vowel sounds carry pitch and loudness; you can sing vowels. They may be long or short. Vowels can "stand alone" — they can be produced without any consonants before or after them. You can say the vowels of *beat* [bit], *bit* [bɪt], or *boot* [but], for example, without the initial [b] or the final [t].

There have been many different schemes for describing vowel sounds. They may be described by articulatory features, as in classifying consonants. Many beginning students of phonetics find this method more difficult to apply to vowel articulations than to consonant articulations. In producing a [t], you can feel your tongue touch the alveolar ridge. When you make a [p], you can feel your two lips come together, or you can watch the lips move in a mirror. Because vowels are produced without any articulators touching or even coming close together, it is often difficult to figure out just what is happening. You may not understand at first what is meant by "front," "back," "high," and "low" vowels. These terms do have meaning, though. If you watch an X-ray movie of someone talking, you can see why vowels have traditionally been classified according to three questions.

> The Bella Coola language spoken in British Columbia is reported to have some words without any vowels, a rare phenomenon in the world's languages. These words, however, contain at least one continuant (*ɬ*) enabling their pronunciation: *pɬt* "thick"; *k'xɬc* "I looked."

1. How high is the tongue?
2. What part of the tongue is involved — and is that part up, down, or neutral in the mouth?
3. What is the position of the lips?

Tongue Position

The three diagrams in Figure 5.5 show that the tongue in the production of the **high vowels** in the words *he* [hi] and *who* [hu] is very high in the mouth; in [hi], containing a **front vowel**, it is the blade of the tongue that is raised, and in [hu], containing the **back vowel** [u], it is the back part of the tongue that is raised. (Prolong the vowels of these words and try to feel your tongue rise.)

To produce the vowel sound of *hah* [hɑ], the back of the tongue is lowered, as is the jaw, and the mouth is open. (The reason a doctor examining your throat may ask you to say "ah" is that the tongue is low and easy to see over.) This vowel is therefore a **low**, back **vowel**.

The vowels [ɪ] and [ʊ] in the words *hit* [hɪt] and *put* [pʊt] are similar to those in *he* [hi] and *who* [hu], with slightly lowered tongue positions.

The vowel [æ] in *hat* [hæt] is produced with the front part of the tongue lowered, similar to the low vowel [ɑ] but with the front rather than the back part of the tongue lowered. Say "hack, hah, hack, hah . . ." and you should feel your tongue moving forward and back in the low part of your mouth. (Note that the symbol [a] is used for a slightly different sound in many dialects of English.)

FIGURE 5.5

Position of the tongue in producing the vowels in *he, who,* and *hah.*

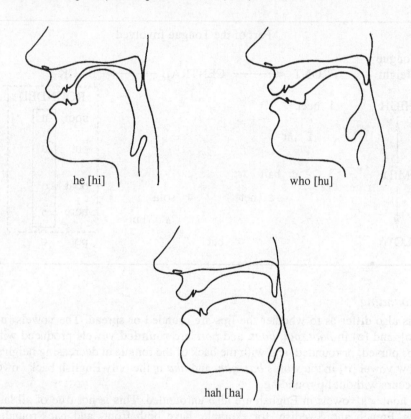

he [hi]

who [hu]

hah [ha]

The vowels [e] and [o] in *bait* [bet] and *boat* [bot] are **mid vowels**, produced by raising the tongue to a position midway between the high and low vowels discussed above. [ɛ] and [ɔ] in the words *bet* [bɛt] and *bore* [bɔr] are also mid vowels, produced with a slightly lower tongue position than [e] and [o]. Note that the sound represented by the letters *ore* in a word like *bore* is sometimes described as a "*rhotic* (meaning 'r-like') *diphthong*"; we will use the [ɔr] symbols for this sound, similar to our use of [ər] for the sound represented by the letters *ir* in words like *bird*, sometimes described as a rhotic vowel.

To produce the vowel [ʌ] in the word *but* [bʌt] or the *schwa* vowel [ə] that occurs in the second syllable of the word *sofa* [sofə] or *Rosa* [rozə], the tongue is neither high nor low, neither front nor back. These are mid, **central vowels**, as shown in Figure 5.6. The vowels on the chart show the part of the tongue from front to back on the horizontal axis that is involved in the articulation of the vowel and the height of the tongue on the vertical axis.

FIGURE 5.6

Classification of North American English vowels.

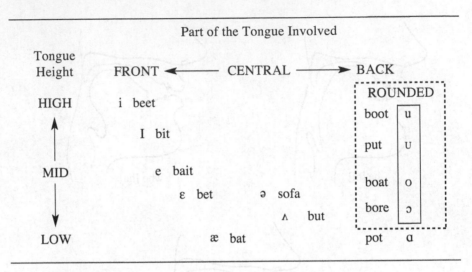

Lip Rounding

Vowels also differ as to whether the lips are rounded or spread. The vowels [u], [ʊ], [o], and [ɔ] in *boot, put, boat,* and *bore* are **rounded vowels** produced with the lips pursed, or rounded, and with the back of the tongue at decreasing heights. The low vowel [ɑ] in the words *bar, bah,* and *aha* is the only English back vowel that occurs without lip rounding.

All nonback vowels in English are also unrounded. This is not true of all languages. French and Swedish, for example, have both front- and back-rounded vowels. In English, a high back-unrounded vowel does not occur, but in Mandarin Chinese, in Japanese, in the Cameroonian language Feʔeʔ, and in many other languages this vowel is part of the phonetic inventory of sounds. There is a Chinese word meaning "four" with an initial [s] followed by a vowel similar to the one in *boot* but with nonrounded spread lips. This Chinese word is distinguished from the word meaning "speed," pronounced like the English word *sue* with a high back-rounded vowel.

Some of these pronunciations may differ from yours. For example, most speakers of Canadian English (and some speakers of American English) pronounce the words *cot* and *caught* identically, while speakers of other dialects will differentiate the two words. There are English dialects in which an *r* sound is not pronounced unless it occurs before a vowel. The inventory of sounds in this book reflects an attempt to provide at least the major symbols that can be used to describe the dialects of North American English. We are aware that this inventory will not necessarily reflect those of speakers of other dialects.

Diphthongs

Many languages, including English, have vowels called **diphthongs** that can also be described as a sequence of two sounds, vowel + glide. The vowels we have studied so far are all simple vowels called **monophthongs**. The vowel sounds in the words *bide* [bajd] and *rye* [raj] are produced with the low **lax vowel** sound [a] followed by the [j] glide. [a] is formed in the central area, between the front [æ] of *bat* and the back [ɑ] of *father*.

The vowels in *bowed* (i.e., "bent") [bawd], *brow* [braw], and *hour* [awr] are produced by some speakers of English with a similar [a] sound followed by the glide [w]. (Some speakers of English produce this diphthong as [æw], with the front low-unrounded vowel instead of the back vowel.) As we shall see in Chapter 12, many Canadians (and some speakers of American dialects) raise the low back vowel [a] to the mid central-unrounded vowel [ʌ] before the glides [j] and [w] in words such as *rice* and *house*, when the diphthong is followed by a voiceless consonant.

The third diphthong that occurs in English is the vowel sound in *boy* [bɔj] and *soil* [sɔjl], which is the vowel that occurs in *bore* (without the [r]) followed by the palatal glide [j], [ɔj]. Some speakers of broad Newfoundland English use the vowel [ʌ] in this diphthong ([ʌj]), thus pronouncing *boy* and *buy* the same.

Note that although Standard English is said to have three diphthong phonemes, as Newfoundland English illustrates, additional diphthongs characterize regional and nonstandard dialects of English as well as dialects of other languages. For instance, the Brooklyn (New York) dialect of English replaces the [ər] of *bird* with the [əi] diphthong. The quality of diphthongs can also vary greatly across individuals, a fact somewhat obscured by the standardized system used to identify diphthongs.

Nasalization of Vowels

Vowels, like consonants, can be produced with a raised velum that prevents the air from escaping through the nose or with a lowered velum that permits air to pass through the nasal passages. When the nasal passages are blocked, *oral* vowels are produced; when the nasal passages are open, nasal (or nasalized) vowels are produced. In English, nasalized vowels occur for the most part before nasal consonants in the same syllable, and oral vowels occur in all other places. In fast colloquial speech, some speakers drop the nasal consonant when it occurs before voiceless stops, as in *hint* or *camp*, leaving just the nasalized vowel, but the words originate with nasal consonants.

The words *bean, bin, bane, Ben, ban, boon, bun, bone, beam, bam, boom, bing, bang*, and *bong* are examples of words that contain nasalized vowels. To show the nasalization of a vowel in a phonetic transcription, a **diacritic** mark [˜] (tilde) is placed over the vowel, as in *bean* [bĩn] and *bone* [bõn]. Because nasalized vowels in English predictably appear before nasal consonants, it is generally unnecessary to show the diacritic unless a more detailed transcription — sometimes referred to as a narrow transcription — is required.

In languages such as French, Polish, and Portuguese, nasalized vowels may occur when no nasal consonant is adjacent. In French, for example, the word meaning

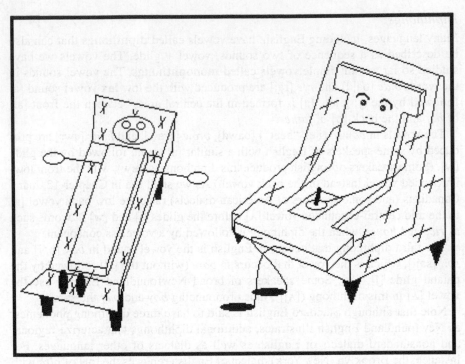

"You know, your problem is that you're just too tense."

Copyright © 1995 Denise P. Meyer.

"year" is *an* [ã], and the word for "sound" is *son* [sõ]. The *n* in the spelling is not pronounced but indicates in these words that the vowels are nasalized.

Tense and Lax Vowels

Figure 5.5 shows that the vowel [i] is produced with a slightly higher tongue position than [ɪ]. This is also true for [e] and [ɛ], [u] and [ʊ], and [o] and [ɔ]. The first vowel in each pair is generally produced with greater tension of the tongue muscles than its counterpart, and they are often a little longer in duration. These vowels can be distinguished from the shorter and less tense vowels by the phonetic features **tense** and **lax** as shown in the following:

Tense (longer)		Lax (shorter)	
i	beat	ɪ	bit
e	bait	ɛ	bet
u	boot	ʊ	put
o	boat	ɔ	bore

Tense vowels are sometimes diphthongized by some speakers of English; in such cases, tense front vowels are followed by a short [j] glide, producing [iʲ] and [eʲ], while tense back vowels conclude with a short [w] glide, [uʷ], and [oʷ]. We will continue to denote these sounds as [i], [e], [u], and [o]. Note that [ɑ] is also classified as a tense vowel.

In some languages, there are vowels and/or consonants that differ phonetically from each other only by duration. That is, neither height of the tongue nor tenseness distinguishes the vowel from its counterpart in pairs of words that contrast in meaning. It is customary to transcribe this difference either by doubling the symbol or by using a diacritic "colon" after the segment — for example, [aa] or [a:], [bb] or [b:]. Long or doubled segments may be referred to as **geminate**. Since English long-tense vowels not only differ in length from their short-lax counterparts but differ qualitatively in tongue height, we use different symbols to distinguish them.

Major Classes

A speech sound may be viewed as a bundle of features such as those we have been examining. Thus, [s] may be described as an alveolar, voiceless, oral fricative. But this and the other classes of sound outlined above also combine to form larger and more general classes that are important in the patterning of sounds in the world's languages, for there are more features that can be ascribed to sounds such as [s].

Noncontinuants and Continuants

Stop sounds are called **noncontinuants** because they are produced with total obstruction of the airstream in the oral cavity and can be distinguished from all other speech sounds. All other consonants, and all vowels, are **continuants** because the stream of air flows continuously out of the mouth. Hence, nasal stops are noncontinuants.

Obstruents and Sonorants

The nonnasal stops, the fricatives, and the affricates form a major class of sounds called **obstruents**. Because the airstream cannot escape through the nose, it is either fully obstructed in its passage through the vocal tract, as in nonnasal stops and affricates, or partially obstructed in the production of fricatives.

Fricatives are continuant obstruents because, although the air is not completely stopped in its passage through the oral cavity, it is obstructed, causing friction.

Nonnasal stops and affricates are noncontinuant obstruents; there is complete blockage of the air during the production of these sounds. The closure of a stop is released abruptly as opposed to the closure of an affricate, which is released gradually, causing friction.

Obstruents are distinguished from the major class of sounds called **sonorants**, which are produced with relatively free airflow through either the mouth or the nose and thus have greater acoustic energy than their obstruent counterparts. Nasal stops are sonorant because, although the air is blocked in the mouth, it continues to resonate and move through the nose. Vowels, the liquids [l] and [r], and the glides [w] and [j] are sonorants because the air resonates without being stopped.

Consonants and Vowels

The sounds of all human languages fall into two major natural classes: consonants and vowels. Consonants include a number of subclasses: stops (including affricates and nasals), fricatives, liquids, and glides. The class of vowels includes oral, nasal, front, central, back, high, mid, and low vowels.

Nasals and liquids, for the reasons given above, are sonorants, yet they resemble the obstruents in that the oral cavity is constricted during their articulation. Obstruents, liquids, and nasals form a natural class of **consonantal** sounds that differ phonetically from the vocalic (or nonconsonantal) class of vowels and glides.

While all consonantal sounds are consonants, not all consonants are consonantal. Glides, in particular, are nonconsonantal consonants. They pattern with the vowels to make up the class of nonconsonantal sounds that are sometimes referred to as **vocalic** sounds.

Here are some other terms used to form classes of consonants. These are not exhaustive (though they may exhaust you while learning them). A full course in phonetics would note further classes that we omit.

Labials: [p], [b], [m], [f], [v]

The class of **labial** consonants includes the class of bilabial sounds — [p], [b], [m] — as well as the labiodentals — [f] and [v]. Labial sounds are those articulated with the involvement of the lips.

Coronals: [d], [t], [n], [s], [z], [š], [ž], [č], [ǰ], [l]

Coronals include the alveolars — [d], [t], [n], [s], [z] — the palatals — [š], [ž] — the affricates — [č], [ǰ] — and the liquid — [l]. (Some articulations of [r] are also coronal.) These are sounds articulated by raising the tongue blade toward the alveolar ridge or the hard palate.

Anteriors: [p], [b], [m], [f], [v], [θ], [ð], [t], [d], [n], [s], [z], [l]

Anterior sounds are consonants produced in the front part of the mouth, that is, from the alveolar area forward. They include the labials, interdentals, and alveolars.

Sibilants: [s], [z], [š], [ž], [č], [ǰ]

Another class of consonantal sounds is characterized by an acoustic, rather than an articulatory, property of its members. The friction created in the production of the fricatives in the words *sit* [sɪt], *zip* [zɪp], *shoe* [šu], and *measure* [mɛžər] and the affricates in the words *chin* [čɪn] and *judge* [ǰʌǰ] causes a "hissing" sound. These sounds are in a class of **sibilants**.

Syllabic Sounds

In the following chapter, we will give a precise definition of *syllable*. Traditionally it has been difficult to provide such a definition, although speakers seem to be able to determine the syllabic structure of a word. From an auditory point of view, syllables have peaks of sonorance (which are also difficult to define). Vowels tend to be the central, or predominant, element in a syllable.

Liquids and nasals can also be syllabic — function as a syllable — as shown by the words *Rachel* [rečl̩], *faker* [fekr̩], *rhythm* [rɪðm̩], and *button* [bʌtn̩]. (The diacritic mark under the [l̩] [r̩] [m̩] and [n̩] shows that these sounds are **syllabic**.) Placing a schwa [ə] before the syllabic liquid or nasal also shows that these are separate syllables. The four words could be written as [rečəl], [fekər], [rɪðəm], and [bʌtən]. We will use this transcription. Similarly, the vowel sound in words like *bird* and *verb* are sometimes written as a syllabic *r*, [br̩d] and [vr̩b]. For consistency we shall transcribe these words using the schwa — [bərd] and [vərb] — the only instances where a schwa represents a stressed vowel.

Prosodic Suprasegmental Features

Speech sounds that are identical in their place or manner features may differ in length (duration), pitch, or loudness. Tense vowels are generally longer than lax vowels, but only by a small amount, perhaps a few milliseconds. (A millisecond is 1/1000 of a second.) However, when a vowel is prolonged to around twice its normal length, it is considered in some languages a different vowel, and it can make a difference between words. In Japanese the word *biru* with a short *i* means "building," but with the *i* prolonged, spelled *bi:ru* or *biiru,* the meaning is "beer." Note again the two ways of denoting a long, or geminate, vowel: add a colon or simply write it twice.

Japanese, and many other languages such as Finnish and Italian, also have long (geminate) consonants that make a difference in words. When a consonant is long, either the closure or obstruction is prolonged. Pronounced with a short k, the word *saki* means "ahead" in Japanese; pronounced with a long k — prolonging the velar closure — the word *sakki* means "before."

English is not a language in which vowel or consonant length can change a word. You might say "stooooooooop!" to emphasize your desire to make someone stop, but the word is not changed. You may also say in English "Whatttttt a dump!" to express your dismay at a hotel room, prolonging the *t*-closure, but the word *what* is not changed.

When we speak, we also change the **pitch** of our voice. The pitch depends on how fast the vocal cords vibrate; the faster they vibrate, the higher the pitch. If the larynx is small, as in women and children, the shorter vocal cords vibrate faster and the pitch is higher, all other things being equal. That is why women and children have higher-pitched voices than men, in general.

In many languages, certain syllables in a word are louder, slightly higher in pitch, and somewhat longer in duration (but not geminate) than other syllables in the word. They are **stressed** syllables. For example, the first syllable of *digest,* the noun meaning "summation of articles," is stressed, while in *digest,* the verb meaning "to absorb food," the second syllable receives greater stress. Stress can be marked in a number of ways: for example, by putting an accent mark over the stressed vowel in the syllable, as in *dígest* versus *digést.*

English is a "stress" language. In general, at least one syllable is stressed in an English word. French is not a stress language. The syllables have approximately the same loudness, length, and pitch. When native English speakers attempt to speak French, they often stress syllables, so that native French speakers hear French with "an English accent." When French speakers speak English, they may fail to put stress where a native English speaker would, and that contributes to what English speakers would call a "French accent."

Length, pitch, and the complex feature stress are **prosodic**, or **suprasegmental**, features. They are features over and above the segmental values such as voicing or place of articulation, thus the "supra" in *suprasegmental*. The term *prosodic* comes from poetry, where it refers to the metrical structure of verse. One of the essential characteristics of poetry is the placement of stress on particular syllables, which defines the versification of the poem.

Tone and Intonation

Speakers of all languages vary the pitch of their voices when they talk; the pitch produced depends on how fast the vocal cords vibrate — the faster they vibrate, the higher the pitch.

The way pitch is used linguistically differs from language to language. In English, it doesn't much matter whether you say *cat* with a high pitch or a low pitch. It will still mean "cat." But if you say [ba] with a high pitch in Nupe (a language spoken in Nigeria), it will mean "to be sour," whereas if you say [ba] with a low pitch, it will mean "to count." Languages that use the pitch of individual vowels or syllables to contrast meanings of words are called **tone languages**.

The majority of the languages in the world are tone languages. There are more than 1,000 tone languages in Africa alone; many languages of Asia, such as Chinese, Thai, and Burmese, are tone languages, as are many Native North American languages.

Thai is a language that has contrasting pitches or **tones**. The same string of segmental sounds represented by [naa] will mean different things if one says the sounds with a low pitch, a mid pitch, a high pitch, a falling pitch from high to low, or a rising pitch from low to high. Thai therefore has five linguistic tones:

[naa]	[___]	low tone	"a nickname"
[naa]	[—]	mid tone	"rice paddy"
[naa]	[‾‾]	high tone	"young maternal uncle or aunt"
[naa]	[⌐\]	falling tone	"face"
[naa]	[_/]	rising tone	"thick"

Diacritics are used to represent distinctive tones in the phonetic transcriptions:

[ˋ]	L	low tone	
[-]	M	mid tone	
[ˊ]	H	high tone	
[ˆ]	HL	falling tone	(high to low)
[ˇ]	LH	rising tone	(low to high)

We can use these diacritics placed above the vowels to represent the tonal contrasts in any language in which the pitch of the vowel is important in conveying meaning, as illustrated by the three contrastive tones in Nupe:

[bá]   "be sour"   [bā]   "cut"   [bà]   "count"
 H   M   L

Akan, sometimes called Twi, the major language of Ghana, has two tones, which are shown in the contrasting two-syllable words:

dù à   [–]   "tail"   dù á   [–]   "tree"
 L L   L H

kɔ̀ tɔ́   [–]   "go buy"   kɔ́ tɔ̀   [–]   "crab"
 L H   H L

In some tone languages, the pitch of each tone is level; in others, the direction of the pitch (whether it glides from high to low or from low to high) is important. Tones that "glide" are called **contour tones**; tones that do not are called **level** or **register tones**. The contour tones of Thai are represented by using a high tone followed by a low tone for a falling glide and a low followed by a high for a rising tone.

In a tone language, it is not the absolute pitch of the syllables that is important but the relations among the pitches of different syllables. After all, some individual speakers have high-pitched voices, others low-pitched, and others medium-pitched. In many tone languages, we find a falling-off of the pitch, a continued downdrifting of the tones.

In the following sentence in Twi, the relative pitch rather than the absolute pitch is important:

"Kofi searches for a little food for his friend's child."

Kòfí   hwèhwɛ́   áduàŋ   kàkrá mà   ǹ' ádàmfò   bá.
 LH   L H   H L   L H L   L H L L   H

7			fí					
6			hwɛ́ á					
5	Kò				krá			
4		hwè						á
3			duàŋ kà					bá
2					mà ǹ'			
1							dàmfò	

The actual pitches of these syllables would be rather different from each other, as shown below (the higher the number, the higher the pitch):

The lowering of the pitch is called **downdrift**. In languages with downdrift — and many tone languages in Africa are downdrift languages — a high tone that occurs after a low tone, or a low tone after a high tone, is lower in pitch than the preceding similarly marked tone. Notice that the first high tone in the sentence is given the pitch value 7. The next high tone (which occurs after an intervening low tone) is 6; that is, it is lower in pitch than the first high tone.

This example shows that in analyzing tones, just as in analyzing segments, all the physical properties need not be considered; only essential features are important in language — in this case, whether the tone is "high" or "low" in relation to the other pitches but not the specific pitch of that tone.

Languages that are not tone languages, such as English, are called **intonation** languages. The pitch contour of the utterance varies, but in an intonation language, as opposed to a tone language, pitch is not used to distinguish words from each other.

Diacritics

In the sections on vowel nasalization, prosodic features, and tone, we presented a number of diacritic marks that can be used to modify the basic phonetic symbols. A [~] over the vowel was used to mark vowel nasalization, the doubling of a symbol or a [:] after the symbol to show length, an acute accent to show stress, and various accent marks to show tones.

Other diacritics provide additional ways of showing phonetic differences between speech sounds.

To differentiate a voiceless lateral liquid such as the sound written *ll* in *Lloyd* as spoken in Welsh, the symbol [̥] is placed under the segmental symbol. Thus, in Welsh the name is pronounced [l̥ɔjd], and in English it is pronounced [lɔjd].

Cover symbols are used when a class of sounds is referred to. A capital C is often used to represent the class of consonants, V for the class of vowels, G for glides, and L for liquids. A syllabic consonant or a syllabic liquid may also be specified as C̩ or L̩. And a rounded consonant, which often occurs before a rounded vowel, can be specified by a superscript small [ʷ].

We can summarize these diacritics and additional symbols as follows:

C = consonant	C: = long C	
V = vowel	V: = long V	V́ = stressed V
	Ṽ = nasalized V	V̥ = voiceless vowel
L = liquid	L̥ = voiceless L	L̩ = syllabic
G = glide	G̥ = voiceless glide	

Tones

V́ = high	V̀ = low	V̄ = mid
V̌ = rising	V̂ = falling	

Phonetic Symbols and Spelling Correspondences

Table 5.6 shows the sound–spelling correspondences for North American English consonants and vowels. Note that all possible spellings are not given; these, however, should provide enough examples to help students pair sounds and English orthography. We have included the symbols for the voiceless aspirated stops to illustrate that what speakers usually consider one sound — for example [p] — may phonetically be two (or more) sounds, [p], [pʰ].

The symbols given in the list are not sufficient to represent the pronunciation of words in all languages. The symbol [x], for example, is needed for the voiceless velar fricative in the German word *Bach*, and [ʁ] is needed for the French voiced uvular fricative. English does not have rounded front vowels, but languages such as French and Swedish do, and English once did. French front rounded vowels can be symbolized as follows:

[y] as in *tu* [ty] "you" (singular) The tongue position is like that for [i], but the lips are rounded.
[ø] as in *bleu* [blø] "blue" The tongue position is like that for [e], but the lips are rounded.
[œ] as in *heure* "hour" The tongue position is like that in [ɛ], but the lips are rounded.

TABLE 5.6
Phonetic Symbol/English Spelling Correspondences

CONSONANTS

Symbol	Examples
p	*s*p*it ti*p* a*pp*le am*p*le*
pʰ	*p*it *p*rick *p*laque a*pp*ear
b	*b*it ta*b* *b*rat *b*u*bb*le
m	*m*itt ta*m* s*m*ack E*mm*y ca*m*p co*mb*
t	s*t*ick pi*t* kiss*ed* wri*t*e
tʰ	*t*ick in*t*end *p*t*erodactyl a*tt*ack
d	*D*ick ca*d* *d*rip love*d* ri*d*e
n	*n*ick ki*n* s*n*ow *mn*emonic *gn*ostic *pn*eumatic *kn*ow
k	s*k*in sti*ck* s*c*at criti*qu*e ex*c*eed
kʰ	*c*url *k*in *ch*aracter *c*ritic me*ch*anic *c*lose
g	*g*irl bur*g* lon*g*er Pittsbur*gh*
ŋ	si*ng* thi*n*k fi*n*ger
f	*f*at *ph*iloso*ph*y *f*lat co*ff*ee ree*f* cou*gh*

(Continued)

TABLE 5.6 *(Continued)*

CONSONANTS, continued

Symbol	Examples
v	*v*at do*v*e gra*v*el
s	*s*ip *s*kip *ps*ychology pa*ss* pat*s* democra*c*y *sc*issors fa*s*ten de*c*eive de*s*cent
z	*z*ip ja*zz* ra*z*or pad*s* kisse*s* *X*erox de*s*ign la*z*y *s*cissor*s* mai*z*e
θ	*th*igh *th*rough wra*th* e*th*er Ma*tth*ew
ð	*th*y *th*eir wea*th*er la*th*e ei*th*er
š	*sh*oe mu*sh* mi*ss*ion na*t*ion fi*sh* gla*c*ial *s*ure
ž	mea*s*ure vi*s*ion a*z*ure ca*s*ual de*c*ision rou*g*e (for those who do not pronounce this word with the final sound of *judge*)
č	*ch*oke ma*tch* fea*t*ure ri*ch* righ*t*eous
ǰ	ju*dge* mi*d*get *G*eorge ma*g*istrate resi*d*ual
l	*l*eaf fee*l* ca*ll* fe*l*t co*ll*ar sing*le*
r	*r*eef fea*r* Pa*r*is singe*r*
j	*y*ou *y*es f*e*ud *u*se
w	*w*itch *sw*im q*u*een
ʍ	*wh*ich *wh*ere *wh*ale (for speakers who pronounce *which* differently from *witch*)
h	*h*at w*h*o w*h*ole re*h*ash
ʔ	bo*tt*le bu*tt*on glo*tt*al (for some speakers)

VOWELS

i	b*ee*t b*ea*t b*e* rec*ei*ve k*ey* bel*ie*ve am*oe*ba p*eo*ple C*ae*sar Vas*e*line ser*e*ne
ɪ	b*i*t cons*i*st *i*njury b*i*n
e	b*a*te b*ai*t r*ay* gr*ea*t *ei*ght g*au*ge r*ei*gn th*ey*
ɛ	b*e*t ser*e*nity s*ay*s g*ue*st d*ea*d s*ai*d
æ	p*a*n *a*ct l*au*gh c*o*mrade
u	b*oo*t l*u*te wh*o* sew*e*r thr*ough* t*o* t*oo* tw*o* m*o*ve L*ou*
ʊ	p*u*t f*oo*t b*u*tcher c*ou*ld
ʌ	c*u*t t*ou*gh am*o*ng *o*ven d*oe*s c*o*ver fl*oo*d
o	c*oa*t g*o* b*eau* gr*ow* th*ough* t*oe* *ow*n *o*ver
ɔ	c*o*re b*o*re m*o*re
ɑ	c*o*t c*au*ght f*a*ther s*a*w mel*o*dic h*o*nour h*o*spital
ə	sof*a* *a*lone symph*o*ny s*u*ppose mel*o*dy tedi*ou*s th*e* *A*merica
aj	b*y* d*ie* d*y*e h*ei*ght *ai*sle ch*oi*r l*i*ar *i*sland s*i*gn
aw, æw	br*ow*n c*ow*ard d*ou*bt
ɔj	b*oy* d*oi*ly f*oi*l

Sign-Language Primes

Just as sign languages have their own morphological, syntactic, and semantic systems, they also have their equivalent of phonetics and phonology. The formal units corresponding to phonetic elements of spoken language are referred to as **primes**. The signs of the language that correspond to morphemes or words can be specified by primes of three classes: hand configuration; the motion of the hand(s) toward or away from the body; and the place of articulation, or the locus, of the sign's movement relative to the body. For example, the sign meaning "arm" is a flat hand, moving to touch the upper arm. It has three prime features: flat hand, motion upward, upper arm.

Figure 5.7 illustrates the hand-configuration primes.

Summary

The science of speech sounds is called **phonetics**. It aims to provide the set of features or properties to describe and distinguish all the sounds in human languages throughout the world.

When we speak, the physical sounds we produce are continuous stretches of sound, which are the physical representations of strings of discrete linguistic **segments**. Knowledge of a language permits one to separate the continuous sound into linguistic units — words, morphemes, and sounds.

The discrepancy between spelling and sounds in English and other languages motivated the development of phonetic alphabets in which one letter corresponds to one sound. The major **phonetic alphabet** in use is that of the **International Phonetic Association (IPA)**, which includes modified Roman letters and **diacritics** by means of which the sounds of all human languages can be represented. To distinguish between the **orthography**, or spelling, of words, and their pronunciations, we write **phonetic transcriptions** between square brackets, as in [fənɛtɪk] for *phonetic*.

All English speech sounds come from the movement of lung air through the vocal tract. The air moves through the **glottis**, or between vocal cords, up the **pharynx**, through the oral (and possibly the nasal) cavity, and out the mouth or nose. Other languages may use different **airstream mechanisms**.

Human speech sounds fall into classes according to their phonetic properties. All speech sounds are either **consonants** or **vowels**, and all consonants are either **obstruents** or **sonorants**. Consonants have some obstruction of the airstream in the vocal tract, and the location of the obstruction defines their **place of articulation**, some of which are **bilabial**, **labiodental**, **alveolar**, **palatal**, **velar**, **uvular**, and **glottal**.

FIGURE 5.7

ASL hand configuration (with descriptive phrases that are used to refer to them). The letters and numbers refer to the signs used for these symbols when words are finger-spelled.

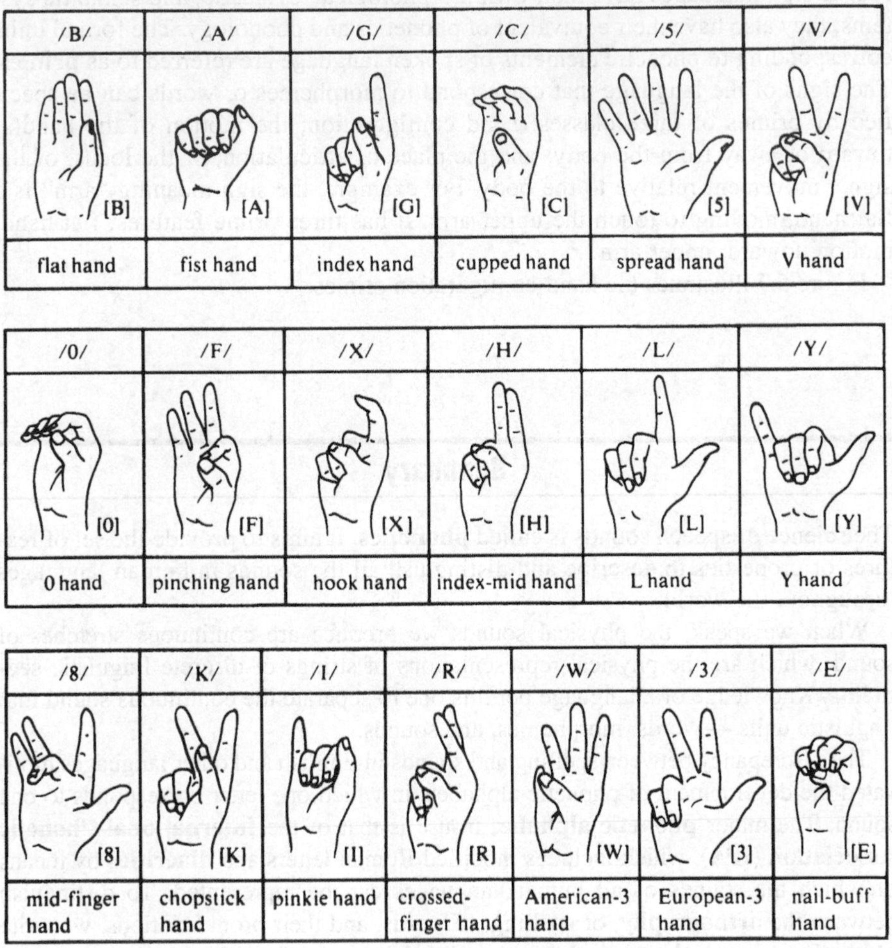

/B/	/A/	/G/	/C/	/5/	/V/
[B]	[A]	[G]	[C]	[5]	[V]
flat hand	fist hand	index hand	cupped hand	spread hand	V hand

/0/	/F/	/X/	/H/	/L/	/Y/
[0]	[F]	[X]	[H]	[L]	[Y]
0 hand	pinching hand	hook hand	index-mid hand	L hand	Y hand

/8/	/K/	/I/	/R/	/W/	/3/	/E/
[8]	[K]	[I]	[R]	[W]	[3]	[E]
mid-finger hand	chopstick hand	pinkie hand	crossed-finger hand	American-3 hand	European-3 hand	nail-buff hand

Reprinted by permission of the publisher from *The signs of language* by Edward Klima and Ursula Bellugi, p. 44, Cambridge, Mass.: Harvard University Press, Copyright © 1979 by the President and Fellows of Harvard College.

Consonants are further classified according to their **manner of articulation**. They may be **voiced** or **voiceless**, **oral** or **nasal**, long or short. They may be **stops**, **fricatives**, **affricates**, **liquids**, or **glides**. During the production of voiced sounds, the vocal cords are together and vibrating, whereas in voiceless sounds they are apart and not vibrating. Voiceless sounds may also be **aspirated** or **unaspirated**. In the production of aspirated sounds, the vocal cords remain apart for a brief time after the stop closure is released, resulting in a puff of air at the time of the release. Consonants may be grouped according to certain features to form larger classes such as **labials**, **coronals**, **anteriors**, and **sibilants**.

Vowels form the nucleus of syllables. They differ according to the position of the tongue and lips: high, mid, or low tongue; front, central, or back of the tongue; **rounded** or unrounded lips. The vowels in English may be **tense** or **lax**. Tense vowels are slightly longer in duration than lax vowels. Vowels may also be **stressed** (longer, higher in pitch, and louder) or unstressed. Vowels, like consonants, may be nasal or oral, though most vowels in all languages are oral.

Length, **pitch**, loudness, and **stress** are **prosodic**, or **suprasegmental**, features. They are imposed over and above the segmental values of the sounds in a syllable.

In many languages, the pitch of the vowel or syllable is linguistically significant. For example, two words may contrast in meaning if one has a high pitch and another a low pitch. Such languages are **tone** languages. There are also **intonation** languages in which the rise and fall of pitch may contrast meanings of sentences. In English the statement *Olga is a teacher* will end with a fall in pitch, but as a question, *Olga is a teacher?* the pitch will rise.

English and other languages use **stress** to distinguish different words, such as *cóntent* and *contént*. In some languages, long vowels and long consonants contrast with their shorter counterparts. Thus *biru* and *biiru (bi:ru), saki* and *sakki* are different words in Japanese. Long sounds are sometimes referred to as **geminates**.

Diacritics to specify such properties as nasalization, length, stress, and tone may be combined with the phonetic symbols for more detailed phonetic transcriptions. A phonetic transcription of *main* would use a tilde diacritic to indicate the nasalization of the vowel: [mẽn].

In sign languages, instead of phonetic features there are three classes of **primes** — hand configuration, the motion of the hand(s) toward or away from the body, and the place of articulation, or the locus, of the sign's movements.

Exercises

---

*1. Write the phonetic symbol for the first sound in each of the following words, according to the way you pronounce it.

Examples: ooze [u]   psycho [s]

a.	judge	e.	pneumonia	i.	civic
b.	Thomas	f.	thought	j.	usual
c.	though	g.	contact		
d.	easy	h.	phone		

*2. Write the phonetic symbol for the *last* sound in each of the following words.

a. fleece   e. watch   i. bleached
b. neigh   f. cow   j. rags
c. long   g. rough
d. health   h. cheese

*3. Write the following words in phonetic transcription according to your pronunciation.

Examples: knot [nɑt]   delightful [dilajtfəl] or [dəlajtfəl]

a. physics   d. coat   g. tease
b. merry   e. yellow   h. heath
c. weather   f. marry   i. (transcribe your name)

*4. Below is a phonetic transcription of one of the verses in the poem "The Walrus and the Carpenter" by Lewis Carroll. The speaker who transcribed it may not have exactly the same pronunciation as you; there are many alternative correct versions. However, there is one major error in each line that is an impossible pronunciation for any North American English speaker. The error may consist of an extra symbol, a missing symbol, or a wrong symbol in the word. Note that the phonetic transcription that is given is a narrow transcription; aspiration is marked, as is the nasalization of vowels. This is to illustrate a detailed transcription. However, none of the errors involves aspiration or nasalization of vowels.

Write the word in which the error occurs in the *correct* phonetic transcription.

Corrected Word

a. ðə tʰájm hæz cʌ̃m   [kʰʌ̃m]
b. ðə wɔlrəs sed
c. tʰu tʰɑlk əv mẽni θĩŋz
d. əv šuz ãnd šɪps
e. æ̃nd silĩŋ wæx
f. əv kʰæbəgəz æ̃nd kʰĩŋz
g. æ̃nd waj ðə si ɪs bɔjlĩŋ hɑt
h. æ̃nd weθər pʰɪgz hæv wĩŋz

5. Write the following transcribed English words using normal English orthography.

a. [huz] _____   f. [šon] _____
b. [græf] _____   g. [čajld] _____
c. [əplaj] _____   h. [west] _____
d. [beð] _____   i. [tawlz] _____
e. [hit] _____   j. [dænts] _____

k. [šɑpt] _____   p. [fez] _____
l. [sʌŋ] _____   q. [nɑləǰ] _____
m. [kæč] _____   r. [fɪfθ] _____
n. [tæks] _____   s. [lɛǰ] _____
o. [plizd] _____   t. [on] _____

6. Write the symbol that corresponds to each of the following phonetic descriptions; then give an English word that contains this sound.

      Example: voiced alveolar stop   [d] *dog*

a. voiceless bilabial unaspirated stop [ ]   f. voiceless affricate [ ]
b. low front vowel [ ]   g. palatal glide [ ]
c. lateral liquid [ ]   h. mid lax front vowel [ ]
d. velar nasal [ ]   i. high back tense vowel [ ]
e. voiced interdental fricative [ ]   j. voiceless aspirated alveolar stop [ ]

7. Give the phonetic symbol and the articulatory description (identify voicing, place, and manner of articulation) for the first and last sounds of each of the following words:

Example:		**symbol**	**description**
	first sound	[č]	voiceless palatal affricate
cheap			
	last sound	[p]	voiceless bilabial stop
	first sound	[ ]	
think			
	last sound	[ ]	
	first sound	[ ]	
tongue			
	last sound	[ ]	
	first sound	[ ]	
fax			
	last sound	[ ]	

*8. In each of the following pairs of words, the boldfaced sounds differ by one or more phonetic properties (features). State both the differences and what properties they have in common.

> Example: phone–phonic   The *o* in *phone* is mid, tense, round.
> The *o* in *phonic* is low, unround.
> Both are back vowels.

a.   **ba**th–**ba**the
b.   **re**duce–**re**duction
c.   **coo**l–**co**ld
d.   wi**f**e–wi**v**es
e.   cat**s**–dog**s**
f.   **im**polite–**in**decent

*9. Write a phonetic transcription of the italicized words in the following stanzas from a poem by Richard Krogh.

> I take it you already *know*
> Of *tough* and *bough* and *cough* and *dough*?
> Some may stumble, but not *you*,
> On *hiccough, thorough, slough* and *through*?
> So now you are ready, perhaps,
> To learn of less familiar traps?
> Beware of *heard*, a dreadful *word*
> That looks like *beard* and sounds like *bird*.
> And *dead*: it's *said* like *bed*, not *bead*;
> For goodness' sake, don't call it *deed*!
> Watch out for *meat* and *great* and *threat*.
> (They rhyme with *suite* and *straight* and *debt*.)
> A *moth* is not a moth in *mother*,
> Nor *both* in *bother*, *broth* in *brother*.

*10. For each group of sounds listed below, state the phonetic feature or features that they all share.

> Example: [p] [b] [m]   Shared features: labial, stop, consonant

a.   [g] [p] [t] [d] [k] [b]
b.   [u] [ʊ] [o] [ɔ]
c.   [i] [ɪ] [e] [ɛ] [æ]
d.   [t] [s] [š] [p] [k] [č] [f] [h]
e.   [v] [z] [ž] [ǰ] [ŋ] [g] [d] [b] [l] [r] [w] [j]
f.   [t] [d] [s] [š] [n] [č] [ǰ]

11. Match the sounds under column A with one or more phonetic properties from column B as illustrated in the first one.

A	B
[u] 5, 8	1. velar
[θ]	2. nasal
[s]	3. coronal
[b]	4. stop
[l]	5. rounded
[t]	6. interdental
[ɑ]	7. voiceless
[m]	8. back
	9. liquid
	10. labial

12. Write the following sentences in regular English spelling.

   a. fənɛtɪks ɪz ðə stʌdi əv spič sawndz
   b. ɑl spokən læŋgwɪǰəz juz sawndz prədust baj ðə ʌpər rɛspərətɔri sɪstəm
   c. ɪn wʌn dajəlɛkt əv ɪŋglɪš kɑt ðə nawn ænd kɔt ðə vərb ar pronawnst ðə sem
   d. sʌm pipəl θɪŋk fənɛtɪks ɪz vɛri ɪntərɛstɪŋ

*13. What phonetic property or feature distinguishes the sets of sounds in column A from those in column B?

A		B	
a.	[i] [ɪ]	a.	[u] [ʊ]
b.	[p] [t] [k] [s] [f]	b.	[b] [d] [g] [z] [v]
c.	[p] [b] [m]	c.	[t] [d] [n] [k] [g] [ŋ]
d.	[i] [ɪ] [u] [ʊ]	d.	[e] [ɛ] [o] [ɔ] [æ] [ɑ]
e.	[f] [v] [s] [z] [š] [ž]	e.	[č] [ǰ]
f.	[i] [ɪ] [e] [ə] [ɛ] [æ]	f.	[u] [ʊ] [o] [ɔ] [ɑ]

References

Ladefoged, P. (2001). *A course in phonetics* (4th ed.). Fort Worth: Harcourt Brace.

MacKay, I.R.A. (1987). *Phonetics: The science of speech production* (2nd ed.). Boston: Little Brown.

Further Reading

Abercrombie, D. (1983). *Elements of general phonetics* (Reprinted). Edinburgh: Edinburgh University Press.

Catford, J.C. (1977). *Fundamental problems in phonetics.* Bloomington: Indiana University Press.

Clark, J., & Yallop, C. (1990). *An introduction to phonetics and phonology.* Oxford: Blackwell.

Crystal, D. (1985). *A dictionary of linguistics and phonetics.* Oxford: Blackwell.

International Phonetic Association. (1989). *Principles of the International Phonetic Association* (Rev. ed.). London: IPA.

Johnson, K. (2003). *Acoustic and auditory phonetics* (2nd ed.) Malden, MA: Wiley-Blackwell.

Ladefoged, P. (2001). *Vowels and consonants: An introduction to the sounds of language.* Oxford: Blackwell.

Ladefoged, P. (2005). *A course in phonetics* (5th ed.). Boston: Wadsworth.

Ladefoged, P., & Maddieson, I. (1996). *The sounds of the world's languages.* Oxford: Blackwell.

Pullum, G.K., & Ladusaw, W.A. (1996). *Phonetic symbol guide* (2nd ed.). Chicago: University of Chicago Press.

Reetz, H., & Jongman, A. (2008). *Phonetics: Transcription, acoustics, and perception.* Malden, MA: Wiley-Blackwell.

Rogers, H. (1991). *Theoretical and practical phonetics.* Toronto: Copp, Clark, Pitman.

Small, L.H. (2004). *Fundamentals of phonetics: A practical guide for students* (2nd ed.). Upper Saddle River, NJ: Allyn & Bacon.

Websites

http://archive.phonetics.ucla.edu The UCLA phonetics lab site. Contains sound files with examples from many languages.

http://www.langsci.ucl.ac.uk/ipa/ The International Phonetics Association website.

http://www.yorku.ca/earmstro/ipa/ A York University website with IPA sound files.

http://faculty.washington.edu/dillon/PhonResources/PhonResources.html Provides numerous links for studying phonetics.

CHAPTER 6
Phonology: The Sound Patterns of Language

Phonology is the study of how we find order within the apparent chaos of speech sounds.

David Crystal, *The Cambridge Encyclopedia of Language* (1997)

From the Arctic Circle to the Cape of Good Hope, people speak to one another. The totality of the sounds they produce constitutes the universal set of human speech sounds. The same relatively small set of phonetic properties or features characterizes all these sounds; the same classes of these sounds are utilized in all spoken languages, and the same kinds of regular patterns of speech sounds occur all over the world. When you learn a language, you learn which speech sounds occur in your language and how they pattern. The study of the ways in which these speech sounds form systems and patterns in human language is **phonology**.

The term *phonology*, like grammar, is used in two ways: as the mental representation of linguistic knowledge and as the description of this knowledge. Thus, the word *phonology* refers either to the representation of the sounds and sound patterns in a speaker's grammar or to the study of the sound patterns in a language or in human language in general.

Phonological knowledge permits a speaker to produce sounds that form meaningful utterances, to recognize a foreign "accent," to make up new words, to add the appropriate phonetic segments to form plurals and past tenses, to produce aspirated and unaspirated voiceless stops in the appropriate context, to know what is or is not a sound in one's language, and to know that different phonetic strings may represent the same morpheme. → *minimal grammatical units of a lang. ex. the, wait, -ed.*

Phonemes: The Phonological Units of Language

In the physical world the naive speaker and hearer actualize and are sensitive to sounds, but what they feel themselves to be pronouncing and hearing are "phonemes."

Edward Sapir, "*The Psychological Reality of Phonemes*" (1933)

Phonological knowledge goes beyond the ability to produce all the phonetically different sounds of a language, but it includes this ability, of course. A speaker of English can produce the sound [θ] and knows that this sound occurs in English, in words such as *thin* [θĩn], *ether* [iθər], and *bath* [bæθ]. English speakers may or may not be able to produce a "click" or a velar fricative, but even if they can they know that such sounds are not part of the phonetic inventory of English. Many speakers are unable to produce such "foreign" sounds.

A speaker of English also knows that [ð], the voiced counterpart of [θ], is a sound of English, occurring in words such as *either* [iðər], *then* [ðɛ̃n], and *bathe* [beð]. French speakers similarly know that [θ] and [ð] are not part of the phonetic inventory of French and often find it difficult to pronounce words such as *this* [ðɪs] and *that* [ðæt], pronouncing them as if they were spelled *dis* and *dat* or *zis* and *zat*.

Sounds That Contrast

Knowing the sounds (the phonetic units) of a language is only a small part of phonological knowledge.

In earlier chapters, we discussed speakers' knowledge of the arbitrary sound–meaning units that compose their vocabulary, the morphemes and words in their mental lexicons. We saw that knowing a word means knowing both its form (its sounds) and its meaning. Most of the words in a language differ in both form and meaning, sometimes by just one sound. The importance of phonology is shown by the fact that one can change one word into another simply by changing one sound.

Consider the forms and meanings of the following English words:

sip	fine	chunk
zip	vine	junk

Each word differs from the other words in both form and meaning. The difference between *sip* and *zip* is "signalled" by the fact that the initial sound of the first word is *s* [s] and the initial sound of the second word is *z* [z]. The forms of the two words — that is, their sounds — are identical except for the initial consonants. [s] and [z] can therefore distinguish or **contrast** words. They are **distinctive** sounds in English. Such distinctive sounds are called **phonemes**.

We see from the contrast between *fine* and *vine* and between *chunk* and *junk* that [f], [v], [č], and [ǰ] must also be phonemes in English for the same reason — because substituting a [v] for [f] or a [č] for [ǰ] produces a different word, a different form with a different meaning.

Minimal Pairs

The "B.C." cartoon on the facing page illustrates the fact that [ɪ] and [i] in the pair *crick* and *creek* and [ʊ] and [o] in the pair *crook* and *croak* are phonemes. The substitution of one for the other makes a different word. The phonological difference

B.C. by permission of Johnny Hart and Creators Syndicate, Inc.

Minimal pairs

Minimal pairs are two words that differ by only one segment found in the same position in each word, for example, *sip* vs. *zip*.

between the two words in each pair is minimal because they are identical in form except for one sound segment that occurs in the same place in the string. For this reason, such pairs of words are referred to as **minimal pairs**. These four words, together with *crake* (a short-billed bird), *crack*, and *crock*, constitute a **minimal set**.

All the words in the set differ by just one sound, and they all differ in meaning. The vowels that contrast these meanings are thus in the class of vowel phonemes in English.

For some speakers, *crick* and *creek* are pronounced identically, another example of regional dialect differences, but most speakers of this dialect still contrast the vowels in *beat* and *bit*, so these high front vowels are contrastive, and therefore phonemes, in their dialect.

The distinct sounds that occur in a minimal pair or a minimal set are phonemes since they contrast meanings. *Sip* and *zip*, *fine* and *vine*, and *chunk* and *junk* are minimal pairs in English; [s], [z], [f], [v], [č], and [ǰ] are phonemes in English.

Seed [sid] and *soup* [sup] are not a minimal pair because they differ in two sounds, the vowels and the final consonants. It is thus not evident which difference in sound makes for the differences in meaning. *Bat* [bæt] and *tad* [tæd] do not constitute a minimal pair because, although only one sound differs in the two words, the [b] occurs initially and the [d] occurs finally. However, [i] and [u] do contrast in the minimal pair *seep* [sip] and *soup* [sup], [d] and [p] contrast in *deed* [did] and *deep* [dip], and [b] and [d] contrast in the following minimal pairs:

bead	[bid]	deed	[did]
bowl	[bol]	dole	[dol]
rube	[rub]	rude	[rud]
lobe	[lob]	load	[lod]

Substituting a [d] for a [b] changes both the phonetic form and its meaning. [b] and [d] also contrast with [g], as is shown by the following:

bill/dill/gill   rib/rid/rig

Therefore, [b], [d], and [g] are all phonemes in English, and *bill, dill*, and *gill* constitute a minimal set. We have many minimal sets in English, so it is relatively easy to determine what the English phonemes are. The words in the following minimal set differ only in their vowels; each vowel thus represents a distinct phoneme:

beat	[bit]	[i]	boot	[but]	[u]
bit	[bɪt]	[ɪ]	but	[bʌt]	[ʌ]
bait	[bet]	[e]	boat	[bot]	[o]
bet	[bɛt]	[ɛ]	bought	[bɔt]	[ɔ] (in many American dialects)
bat	[bæt]	[æ]	bout	[bawt]	[aw]
bite	[bajt]	[aj]	bot	[bɑt]	[ɑ]

Not all these words are part of a minimal pair set for all speakers. Most speakers of Canadian English, for instance, would not distinguish between *bought* and *bot*, pronouncing both [bɑt], even if they knew that a *bot* was the larva of a botfly. The two vowel sounds do not contrast in this dialect, where *cot* and *caught* are the same, though they might contrast in another.

The vowels [ʊ] and [ɔj], which do not appear in the list above, are also phonemes of English. They contrast meanings in other minimal pairs:

[ʊ]	[i]	book	[bʊk]	beak	[bik]
[ɔj]	[aj]	boy	[bɔj]	buy	[baj]

The diphthongs [aj], [aw], and [ɔj] are considered single vowel sounds although each includes a glide because they function like the monophthongal vowels, as further illustrated by the following list that includes all three diphthongs:

bile	[bajl]	bowel	[bawl]	boil	[bɔjl]

In broad Newfoundland English, the two diphthongs [aj] and [ɔj] are not distinguished in any set, and both are pronounced as [aj], so that *boil* and *bile* are pronounced the same. In this dialect, then, there is no phonemic contrast between these two diphthongs.

In some languages, particularly with relatively long words of many syllables, it is not as easy to find minimal sets or even minimal pairs to illustrate the contrasting sounds, the phonemes of these languages. Even in English, which has many **monosyllabic** words (words of one syllable) and hundreds of minimal pairs, there are very few minimal pairs in which the phonemes [θ] and [ð] contrast. In a computer search, only one pair was found in which they contrast initially, one in which they contrast medially, and four in which they contrast finally. All four pairs in which they contrast finally are noun–verb pairs, the result of historical sound change that will be discussed in a later chapter.

[θ]	[ð]
thigh	thy
ether	either
mouth (noun)	mouth (verb)
teeth	teethe
loath	loathe
wreath	wreathe
sheath	sheathe

Some speakers do not exhibit minimal pairs with *ether/either* since they pronounce the latter as [ajðər]. But even if the above pairs did not occur, [θ] and [ð] can be analyzed as distinct phonemes. Each contrasts with other sounds in the language as, for example, *thick* [θɪk]/*sick* [sɪk] and *though* [ðo]/*dough* [do]. Note also that one cannot substitute the voiced and voiceless interdental fricatives in the words in which they do occur without producing nonsense forms; for example, if we substitute the voiced [ð] for the voiceless [θ] in *thick*, we get [ðɪk], which has no meaning, showing that the phonemes that represent its form and its meaning are inseparable. You cannot pronounce the word any way you like, substituting other sounds for the phonemes in the word.

Even when a true minimal pair cannot be found in a language for a given pair of sounds, a near-minimal pair may exist. A near-minimal pair is a pair that would be minimal except for irrelevant differences. For example, the near-minimal pairs for /ð/ and /ž/ exist in English.

> tether [tɛðər] vs. pleasure [plɛžər]
> neither [niðər] vs. seizure [sižər]

In these cases the phonetic environment appears to have little to do with the occurrence of [ð] or [ž]. (Note that true minimal pairs can be found for these sounds in most dialects of English as well, for example, *bathe* vs. *beige*.)

Free Variation

Some words in English are pronounced differently by different speakers. For example, some speakers pronounce the word *economics* with an initial [i] and others with an initial [ɛ]. In this word, [i] and [ɛ] are said to be in **free variation**. However, we cannot substitute [i] and [ɛ] for each other in all words. *Did you beat the drum?* does not mean the same thing as *Did you bet the drum?* An old song of the 1930s was based on the notion of free variation:

> You say [iðər] and I say [ajðər],
> You say [niðər] and I say [najðər],
> [iðər] [ajðər] [niðər] [najðər],
> Let's call the whole thing off.

The difference, however, is often one of dialect, for, as the Irish speaker said when asked which was the correct pronunciation, [iðər] or [ajðər], "It's [neðər]."

Phonemes, Phones, and Allophones

You may be wondering why we have included a second chapter on phonological units. The entire previous chapter discussed these sounds. But as noted earlier in discussing morphology, syntax, and semantics, linguistic knowledge is more complex than it appears to one who knows a language. Since the knowledge is unconscious, we are unaware of many of the complexities.

Phonemes are not physical sounds. They are abstract mental representations of the phonological units of a language, the units used to represent the forms of words in our mental lexicons. These phonemic

> **The psychological reality of phonemes**
>
> There is evidence that speakers mentally store the phonological system of their language in terms of phonemes.

representations of words, together with the phonological rules of the language, determine the phonetic units that represent their pronunciation.

If phonemes are not the actual sounds, what are they? We can illustrate the difference between a phoneme and a phonetic segment, called a **phone**, by referring to the difference between oral and nasalized vowels in English. In Chapter 5, we noted that both oral and nasalized vowels occur *phonetically* in English.

bean	[bĩn]	bead	[bid]
roam	[rõm]	robe	[rob]

Nasalized vowels occur in English syllables only before nasal consonants. If one substituted an oral vowel for the nasal vowels in *bean* and *roam*, the meanings of the two words would not be changed. Try to say these words keeping your velum up until your tongue makes the stop closure of the [n] or your lips come together for the [m]. It will not be easy, because in English we automatically lower the velum when producing vowels before nasals in the same syllable. Now try to pronounce *bead* and *robe* with a nasal vowel. [bĩd] would still be understood as *bead*, although your pronunciation would probably sound very nasal. In other words, nasal and oral vowels *do not contrast*. There is just one set of vowel phonemes in English even though there are two sets of vowel phones: oral vowels and nasal vowels.

There is a general principle or rule in the phonology of English that tells us when nasalized vowels occur — always before nasal consonants, never before oral consonants. The oral vowels in English differ phonemically from one another, whereas the differences between the oral vowels and their nasal counterparts do not. This is because there is no principle or rule to predict when, for example, [i] occurs instead of [e] or [u] or [ɑ] or any of the other vowel phonemes. We must learn that [i] occurs in *beat* and [e] in *bait*. We do not have to learn that the nasalized version of [i] occurs in *beam* [bĩm] or *bean* [bĩn] or that the nasalized [ũ] occurs in *boom* [bũm] or *boon* [bũn]. Rather, we generalize from the occurrences of oral and nasal vowels in English, and we form a mental rule that nasalizes all vowels before nasal consonants.

The rule, or general principle, that predicts when a vowel phoneme will be realized as an oral vowel phone and when the same vowel phoneme will be a nasalized phone is exemplified in the sets of words and nonwords in Table 6.1.

As the words in Table 6.1 illustrate, in English oral vowels occur in final position and before nonnasal consonants; nasalized vowels occur only before nasal

TABLE 6.1

Nasal and Oral Vowels: Words and Nonwords

Words						Nonwords		
bee	[bi]	bead	[bid]	bean	[bĩn]	*[bĩ]	*[bĩd]	*[bin]
lay	[le]	lace	[les]	lame	[lẽm]	*[lẽ]	*[lẽs]	*[lem]
baa	[bæ]	bad	[bæd]	bang	[bæ̃ŋ]	*[bæ̃]	*[bæ̃d]	*[bæŋ]

consonants. More specifically, nasal vowels occur before nasal consonants that follow and are in the same syllable. For most speakers, the [o] vowel in the word *roman* [ro-mə̃n] is not nasalized since it occurs before a syllable break symbolized as -, but the [ə̃] is because the vowel and the [n] are in the same syllable. The "nonwords" show us that nasalized vowels do not occur finally or before nonnasal consonants. Therefore, oral vowels and their nasalized counterparts never contrast.

We can state these generalizations in a more concise way with the following phonological rule: *A vowel or diphthong becomes nasalized before a nasal segment (within the same syllable).*

Most speakers of English are unaware that the vowels in *bead* and *bean* are different sounds; they are aware of phonemes but not of the physical sounds (phones) that they produce and hear.

Since nasalized vowels do occur phonetically but not phonemically, we can conclude that there is no one-to-one correspondence between phonetic segments and phonemes in a language. One phoneme may be realized phonetically (i.e., pronounced) as more than one phone — phonetic segment. A phoneme may also be represented by only one phone.

The different phones that are the realizations of the same phoneme are called the **allophones** of that phoneme. An allophone is therefore a *predictable phonetic variant* of a phoneme. In English, each vowel phoneme has both an oral and a nasalized allophone. The choice of the allophone is not random or haphazard; it is *rule-governed*. No one is explicitly taught these rules.

> An allophone is a predictable phonetic variant of a phoneme.

To distinguish between a phoneme and its allophones (the way the phoneme is pronounced in different contexts), we will use slashes / / to enclose phonemes and continue to use square brackets [ ] for allophones or phones. For example, [i] and [ĩ] are allophones of the phoneme /i/; [ɪ] and [ɪ̃] are allophones of the phoneme /ɪ/, and so on. Thus, we will represent *bead* and *bean* phonemically as /bid/ and /bin/. We refer to these as **phonemic transcriptions** of the two words. The rule for the distribution of oral and nasal vowels in English shows that phonetically these words will be pronounced as [bid] and [bĩn]. The pronunciations of these words are given in **phonetic transcriptions**, between square brackets.

In Chapter 5, we mentioned another example of allophones of a single phoneme. We noted that some speakers of English substitute a glottal stop for the [t] at the end of a word such as *don't* or *can't* or in the middle of a word such as *bottle* or *button*. The substitution of the glottal stop does not change the meanings of any words; [dõnt] and [dõnʔ] do not contrast in meaning, nor do [bɑtəl] or [bɑʔəl]. On the other hand, [ræbəl] and [ræʔəl] do contrast, as the pronunciations of *rabble* and *rattle*, but note that [rætəl] with a [t] or [rærəl] with the flap [ɾ] or [ræʔəl] with a glottal stop are all possible pronunciations of the word *rattle*. The phones [t], [ɾ], and [ʔ] do not contrast; they are all allophones of the phoneme /t/.

The function of phonemes is to contrast meanings. Phonemes in themselves have no meaning, but when combined with other phonemes they constitute the forms by which meanings of words and morphemes are expressed.

Complementary Distribution

Minimal pairs illustrate that some speech sounds are contrastive in a language, and these sounds represent the set of phonemes. We also saw that some sounds are not distinct; they do not contrast meanings. [t] and [ʔ] were cited as examples of sounds that do not contrast. The substitution of one for the other does not create a minimal pair.

Oral and nasal vowels in English are also nondistinct sounds. Unlike the [t], [ʔ], and [ɾ], the allophones of /t/, the oral and nasal allophones of each vowel phoneme never occur in the same phonological context. This was illustrated in Table 6.1. They complement each other and are said to be in **complementary distribution**. This is further shown in Table 6.2.

When oral vowels occur, nasal vowels do not occur, and vice versa. It is in this sense that the phones are said to complement each other or to be in complementary distribution.

The concept of complementary distribution is illustrated by Clark Kent and Superman, who represent in different forms only one person. When Kent is present, Superman is not; when Superman is present, Kent is not. Kent and Superman are therefore in complementary distribution, just as [i] and [ĩ] are in complementary distribution. Of course, there is a difference between their "distribution" and the two allophones of the phoneme /i/ since Kent and Superman can occur in the same environment (e.g., talking to Lois Lane), whereas [i] and [ĩ] never occur in the same environment or under the same conditions. Kent and Superman are thus more similar to the allophones of /t/ — [t] and [ʔ] — which do occur in the same environment. The important point is that the concept of two physical manifestations of a single abstract unit is true of both Kent and Superman and of [i] and [ĩ].

Not all sounds that are in complementary distribution in one dialect of English appear in complementary distribution in another. Unlike most other dialects of Canadian or American English, [ɪ] and [ɛ] are in complementary distribution in some parts of Newfoundland, away from the Avalon Peninsula. [ɪ] occurs everywhere except before [r], where [ɛ] occurs. Thus, *bit* and *bet* are both pronounced as *bit* ([bɪt]), while *beer* and *bear* are pronounced as *bear* ([bɛr]). Both vowels are thus allophones of one phoneme in this dialect (Wells, 1982).

When sounds are in complementary distribution, they do not contrast with each other. The replacement of one sound with the other will not change the meaning of the word, although it might not sound like typical English pronunciation. Given these facts about the patterning of sounds in a language, a phoneme can be defined as a set of phonetically similar sounds that are in complementary distribution. A set

TABLE 6.2
Distribution of Oral and Nasal Vowels in English Syllables

	In Final Position	Before Nasal Consonants	Before Oral Consonants
Oral Vowels	Yes	No	Yes
Nasal Vowels	No	Yes	No

can, of course, consist of only one member. Some phonemes are represented by only one sound, one allophone.

Phonetic Similarity

When there is more than one allophone in the set, the phones must be **phonetically similar** — that is, they must share most of the same phonetic features. This can be illustrated by a particularly salient example. In English, the velar nasal [ŋ] and the glottal fricative [h] are in complementary distribution; [ŋ] does not occur word initially, and [h] does not occur word finally. But they share very few phonetic features; [ŋ] is a voiced velar nasal stop; [h] is a voiceless glottal fricative. Therefore, they are not allophones of the same phoneme; [ŋ] and [h] are allophones of different phonemes.

We mentioned that speakers of a language perceive the different sounds of a single phoneme as being one sound. For example, most speakers of English are unaware that the vowels in *bead* and *bean* are different phones. This is because mentally, speakers produce and hear phonemes, not phones.

Two sounds that are not phonetically similar would not be thus perceived. Furthermore, it would be difficult for children to classify such sounds together as representing one phoneme. The phonetic similarity criterion reflects the ways in which allophones function together and the kinds of generalizations that children make in acquiring the phonological contrasts of the language.

Distinctive Features

We generally are not aware of the phonetic properties or features that distinguish the phonemes of our language. Phonetics provides the means to describe these sounds, showing how they differ; phonology tells us which sounds function as phonemes to contrast the meanings of words.

In order for two phonetic forms to differ and to contrast meanings, there must be some phonetic difference between the substituted sounds. The minimal pairs *seal* [sil] and *zeal* [zil] show that [s] and [z] represent two contrasting phonemes in English. They cannot be allophones of one phoneme since we cannot replace the [s] with the [z] without changing the meaning of the word. Furthermore, they are not in complementary distribution; both occur word initially before the vowel [i]. They therefore are phones that function as allophones of the phonemes /s/ and /z/. From the discussion of phonetics in Chapter 5, we know that the only difference between [s] and [z] is a voicing difference; [s] is voiceless and [z] is voiced. It is this phonetic feature that distinguishes the two words. Voicing thus plays a special role in English (and in many other languages). It also distinguishes *feel* and *veal* [f]/[v] and *cap* and *cab* [p]/[b]. When a feature distinguishes one phoneme from another, it is a **distinctive feature** (or a phonemic feature). When two words are exactly alike phonetically except for one feature, the phonetic feature is **distinctive** since this difference alone accounts for the contrast or difference in meaning.

Feature Values

One can think of voicing and voicelessness as the presence or absence of a single feature, *voiced*. Thus, a single feature can be thought of as having two values, plus (+), which signifies its presence, and minus (–), which signifies its absence. For example, /b/ is [+voiced] and /p/ is [–voiced]. We could have called this feature "voiceless" and specified /b/ as [–voiceless] and /p/ as [+voiceless]. We will, however, refer to these features by their traditional designations.

The presence or absence of nasality can similarly be designated as [+nasal] or [–nasal], with [m] being [+nasal] and [b] or [p] being [–nasal]. A [–nasal] sound is an oral sound.

The phonetic and phonemic symbols are *cover symbols* for a set or bundle of distinctive features, a shorthand method of specifying the phonetic properties of the segment. Phones and phonemes are not indissoluble units; they are similar to molecules, which are composed of atoms. Phones and phonemes are composed of phonetic features. A more explicit description of the phonemes /p/, /b/, and /m/ may thus be given in a **feature matrix**.

	p	b	m
Stop	+	+	+
Labial	+	+	+
Voiced	–	+	+
Nasal	–	–	+

Aspiration is not listed as a feature in the above phonemic specification of these units because it is a **nondistinctive feature** and it is not necessary to include both [p] and [pʰ] as phonemes. In a phonetic transcription, however, the aspiration would be specified where it occurs. This will be discussed below.

A phonetic feature is distinctive when the + value of that feature found in certain words contrasts with the – value of that feature in other words. Each phoneme must be distinguished from all other phonemes in a language by at least one feature value distinction.

Since the phonemes /b/, /d/, and /g/ contrast by virtue of their place of articulation features — *labial*, *alveolar*, and *velar* — these place features are also distinctive in English. Since uvular sounds do not occur in English, the place feature *uvular* is nondistinctive. The distinctive features of the voiced stops in English are shown in the following feature matrix:

> Spelling systems tend to ignore phonetic variation that is nondistinctive (e.g., *p* in English: *pit* [pʰɪt] vs. *spit* [spɪt]).

	b	m	d	n	g	ŋ
Stop	+	+	+	+	+	+
Voiced	+	+	+	+	+	+
Labial	+	+	–	–	–	–
Alveolar	–	–	+	+	–	–
Velar	–	–	–	–	+	+
Nasal	–	+	–	+	–	+

Each of the phonemes in the preceding chart differs from all the other phonemes by at least one distinctive feature.

The following minimal pairs further describe some of the distinctive features in the phonological system of English.

bat	[bæt]	**mat**	[mæt]	The difference between *bat* and *mat* is due only to the difference in nasality between [b] and [m]. [b] and [m] are identical in all features except for the fact that [b] is oral or [–nasal] and [m] is nasal or [+nasal]. Therefore, nasality or [±nasal]* is a distinctive feature of English consonants.
rack	[ræk]	**rock**	[rɑk]	The two words are distinguished only because [æ] is a front vowel and [ɑ] is a back vowel. They are both low, unrounded vowels. Therefore, backness (or [±back]) is a distinctive feature of English vowels.
said	[sɛd]	**zed**	[zɛd]	The difference is due to the voicelessness of the [s] in contrast to the voicing of the [z]. Therefore, voicing ([±voiced]) is a distinctive feature of English consonants.

*The symbol ± before a feature should be read as "plus or minus" that feature, showing that it is a *binary-valued* feature (i.e., a feature that has exactly two possible values).

Predictability of Redundant (Nondistinctive) Features

We saw above that nasality is a distinctive feature of English consonants. Given the arbitrary relationship between form and meaning, there is no way to predict that the word *mean* begins with a nasal bilabial stop [m] and that the word *bean* begins with an oral bilabial stop [b]. You learn this when you learn the words. We also saw that nasality is not a distinctive feature for English vowels; the nasality feature value of the vowels in *bean*, *mean*, *comb*, and *sing* is predictable since they occur before nasal consonants in the same syllable. When a feature value is predictable by rule, it is a **redundant** or **predictable feature**. Thus, nasality is a redundant feature for English vowels but a nonredundant (distinctive or phonemic) feature for English consonants.

This is not the case in all languages. In French, nasality is a distinctive feature for both vowels and consonants: *gars* pronounced [ga] "guy" contrasts with *gant* [gã], which means "glove," and *bal* [bal] "dance" contrasts with *mal* [mal] "evil/pain." In Chapter 5, other examples of French nasalized vowels are presented. Thus, French has both oral and nasal consonant and vowel phonemes; English has oral and nasal consonant phonemes but only oral vowel phonemes. Both languages, however, have oral and nasal consonant and vowel phones.

Like French, the Ghanaian language Akan has both oral and nasal vowel phonemes; in other words, nasalization is a distinctive feature for vowels in Akan, as the following examples illustrate:

[ka]	"bite"	[kã]	"speak"
[fi]	"come from"	[fĩ]	"dirty"

[tu]	"pull"	[tũ]	"hole/den"
[nsa]	"hand"	[nsã]	"liquor"
[či]	"hate"	[čĩ]	"squeeze"
[pam]	"sew"	[pãm]	"confederate"

These examples show that vowel nasalization is not predictable in Akan. As shown by the last minimal pair — [pam]/[pãm] — there is no rule that nasalizes vowels before nasal consonants. We also find word-final oral vowels contrasting with word-final nasalized vowels (after identical initial consonants). The change of form — the substitution of nasalized for oral vowels or vice versa — changes the meaning. Both oral and nasal vowel phonemes must therefore exist in Akan.

Note that two languages may have the same phonetic segments (phones) but two different phonemic systems. Both oral and nasalized vowels exist in English and Akan phonetically; English has no nasalized vowel phonemes, but Akan does. The same phonetic segments function differently in the two languages. Nasalization of vowels in English is redundant and nondistinctive; nasalization of vowels in Akan is nonredundant and distinctive.

Another nondistinctive feature in English is aspiration. In the previous chapter, we pointed out that in English both aspirated and unaspirated voiceless stops occur. The voiceless aspirated stops [pʰ], [tʰ], [kʰ] and the voiceless unaspirated stops [p], [t], [k] are in complementary distribution in English, as shown in the following chart:

Syllable Initial Before a Stressed Vowel			After a Syllable-Initial /s/			*Nonword		
[pʰ]	**[tʰ]**	**[kʰ]**	**[p]**	**[t]**	**[k]**			
pill	*till*	*kill*	*spill*	*still*	*skill*	*[pɪl]	*[tɪl]	*[kɪl]
[pʰɪl]	[tʰɪl]	[kʰɪl]	[spɪl]	[stɪl]	[skɪl]	*[spʰɪl]	*[tʰɪl]	*[skʰɪl]
par	*tar*	*car*	*spar*	*star*	*scar*	*[pɑr]	*[tɑr]	*[kɑr]
[pʰɑr]	[tʰɑr]	[kʰɑr]	[spɑr]	[stɑr]	[skɑr]	*[spʰɑr]	*[stʰɑr]	*[skʰɑr]

Where the unaspirated stops occur, the aspirated do not and vice versa. One can say *spit* with an aspirated [pʰ], as [spʰɪt], and it would be understood as *spit*, but your listeners would probably think you were spitting out your words. Given this distribution, we see that aspiration is a redundant, nondistinctive feature in English; aspiration is predictable, occurring as a feature of voiceless stops when they occur initially in a stressed syllable.

This is the reason speakers of English (if they are not analyzing the sounds as linguists or phoneticians) usually consider the [pʰ] in *pill* and the [p] in *spill* to be the "same" sound, just as they consider the [i] and [ĩ] that represent the phoneme /i/ in *bead* and *bean* to be the "same." They do so because the difference between them, in this case the feature *aspiration*, is *predictable, redundant, nondistinctive,* and *nonphonemic* (all equivalent terms). This distribution of aspirated and unaspirated voiceless stops is a fact about English phonology. There are two *p* sounds (or phones) in English but only one *p* phoneme. (This is also true of /t/ and /k/.)

This illustrates why we referred to the phoneme as an abstract unit. We do not utter phonemes; we produce phones. /p/ is a phoneme in English that is realized phonetically (pronounced) as either [p] or [pʰ]. [p] or [pʰ] are allophones of the phoneme /p/. The notion of abstractness is not unique to phonology. We have many abstract mental concepts. The number 3 is not represented in our cognitive arithmetic system as three physical objects. It represents three of anything — dogs, pencils, continents, jellybeans, linguists, phonemes, dreams, ideas. It is thus even more abstract than the phonemes of a language that are represented by specific physical objects. Children know that 3 can be three of anything; they also know that /p/ can be [p] and [pʰ].

More on Redundancies

The value of some features of a single phoneme is predictable or redundant due to the specification of the other features of that segment. That is, given the presence of certain feature values, one can predict the value of other features in that segment.

In English, all front vowels are predictably nonround. The nonlow back vowels [/u ʊ o ɔ/] are predictably round. Redundant features in phonemic representation need not be specified. Unlike in French, there are no rounded front vowels in English. We can thus say that if a vowel in English is specified as [–back] it is also redundantly, predictably [–round], and the feature value for round is absent from the representation. A "blank" would occupy its place, indicating that the value of that feature is predictable by a phonological rule of the language. Similarly for vowels specified as [–back, –low], which are predictably [–round]. The feature [±low] seems to distinguish [ɑ], which is [+back, +low, –rounded], and [ɔ], which is [+back, –low, +rounded]. Many dialects of English do not distinguish these two sounds phonemically. Some, including Canadian English, have only [ɑ] in words such as *cot* and *caught*, phonemically /kat/, and others have only [ɔ], phonemically /kɔt/.

Similarly, in English all nasal consonant phonemes are predictably voiced. Thus, voicing is nondistinctive for nasal consonants and need not be specified in marking the value of the voicing feature for this set of phonemes. Phonetically in English, the nasal phonemes may be voiceless (indicated by the small ring under the symbol) when they occur after a syllable-initial /s/, as in *snoop*, which phonemically is /snup/ and phonetically may be [sn̥up]. The voicelessness is predictable from the context.

This can be accounted for at the phonemic level by the following:

> **Redundancy Rule: If a phoneme is [+nasal], then it is also [+voiced].**

In Burmese, however, we find the following minimal pairs:

/ma/	[ma]	"health"	/m̥a/	[m̥a]	"order"
/na/	[na]	"pain"	/n̥a/	[n̥a]	"nostril"

The fact that some nasal phonemes are [+voiced] and others [–voiced] must be specified in Burmese; the English redundancy rule does not occur in the grammar of Burmese. We can illustrate this phonological difference between English and Burmese in the following phonemic distinctive feature matrices:

	Burmese:	/m/	/m̥/	English:	/m/
Nasal		+	+		+
Labial		+	+		+
Voicing		+	−		

Note that the value for the voicing feature is left blank for the English phoneme /m/ since the [+] value for this feature is specified by the redundancy rule given above.

As noted earlier, the value of some features in a segment is predictable because of the segments that precede or follow that segment; the phonological context determines the value of the feature rather than the presence of other feature values in that segment. Aspiration cannot be predicted in isolation but only when a voiceless stop occurs in a word, since the presence or absence of the feature depends on where the voiceless stop occurs and what precedes or follows it. It is determined by its *phonological environment*. Similarly, the oral or nasal quality of a vowel depends on its environment. If it is followed by a nasal consonant, then it is predictably [+nasal].

Unpredictability of Phonemic Features

We saw above that the same phones (phonetic segments) can occur in two languages but pattern differently because the phonemic system, the phonology of the languages, is different. English, French, and Akan have oral and nasal vowel phones; in English, oral and nasal vowels are allophones of one phoneme, whereas in French and Akan they represent distinct phonemes.

Aspiration of voiceless stops further illustrates the asymmetry of the phonological systems of different languages. Both aspirated and unaspirated voiceless stops occur in English and Thai (the major language spoken in Thailand), but they function differently in the two languages. Aspiration in English is not a phonemic or distinctive feature, because its presence or absence is predictable. In Thai, however, it is not predictable, as the following examples show:

Voiceless Unaspirated		Voiceless Aspirated	
[paa]	"forest"	[pʰaa]	"to split"
[tam]	"to pound"	[tʰam]	"to do"
[kat]	"to bite"	[kʰat]	"to interrupt"

The voiceless unaspirated and the voiceless aspirated stops in Thai are not in complementary distribution. They occur in the same positions in the minimal pairs above; they contrast and are therefore phonemes in Thai. In both English and Thai, the phones [p], [t], [k], [pʰ], [tʰ], and [kʰ] occur. In English, they represent the phonemes /p/, /t/, and /k/; in Thai, they represent the phonemes /p/, /t/, /k/, /pʰ/,

/tʰ/, and /kʰ/. Aspiration is a distinctive feature in Thai; it is a nondistinctive redundant feature in English.

The phonetic facts alone do not reveal what is distinctive or phonemic.

> The *phonetic representation* of utterances shows what speakers know about the pronunciation of utterances; the *phonemic representation* of utterances shows what the speakers know about the abstract phonological system, the patterning of sounds.

That *pot/pat* and *spot/spat* are transcribed with an identical /p/ reveals the fact that English speakers consider the [pʰ] in *pot* [pʰɑt] and the [p] in *spot* [spɑt] to be phonetic manifestations of the same phoneme /p/. What distinguishes these words for an English speaker is the presence or absence of /s/, not of aspiration.

In learning a language, a child learns which features are distinctive in that language and which are not. One phonetic feature may be distinctive for one class of sounds but predictable or nondistinctive for another class of sounds (e.g., the feature nasality in English).

In Chapter 5, we pointed out that in English the tense vowels /i/, /e/, /u/, and /o/ are also higher (articulated with a higher tongue position) and longer in duration than their lax vowel counterparts /ɪ/, /ɛ/, /ʊ/, and /ɔ/. The distinction between the tense and lax vowels can be shown simply by using the feature tense/lax or [±tense]. Using this specification, the small difference in tongue height between the tense and lax vowels is nondistinctive, as is the length difference. In the low vowels, [æ] and [a] are lax vowels ([–tense]) and [ɑ] is [+tense]. Since [a] and [ɑ] are both [+back], tenseness may also distinguish between them. However, since [a] and [ɑ] do not contrast phonemically, they may be taken as allophones of the phoneme /a/ in contrast to /æ/. The tense vowel phonemes in English would then include /i/, /e/, /u/, /o/, /a/ and the lax vowels /ɪ/, /ɛ/, /ʊ/, /ɔ/, /æ/.

Vowel length is predictable in English: vowels are longest in word-final position (*bee*), longer before voiced sounds than voiceless sounds (*bead* vs. *beat*), and longer before continuants than stops (*beef* vs. *beet*).

In other languages, long and short vowels are identical except for length. Thus, **length** can be a nonpredictable distinctive feature. Vowel length is phonemic in Danish, Finnish, Arabic, and Korean. Consider the following "minimal pairs" in Korean:

il	"day"	i:l	"word"
seda	"to count"	se:da	"strong"
kul	"oyster"	ku:l	"tunnel"

Vowel length is also phonemic in Japanese:

biru	"building"	bi:ru	"beer"
tsuji	"a proper name"	tsu:ji	"moving one's bowels"

When teaching at a university in Japan, one of the authors of this book inadvertently pronounced Ms. Tsuji's name as Tsu:ji-san. (The -*san* is a suffix used to show respect.) The humorous effect of this error on the class of students quickly taught him to understand the phonemic nature of vowel length in Japanese.

Consonant length is also contrastive in Japanese. A consonant may be lengthened by prolonging the closure: a long *t* [t:] or [tt] can be produced by holding the tongue against the alveolar ridge twice as long as for a short *t* [t]. The following minimal pairs illustrate that length is a phonemic feature for Japanese consonants:

šite	"doing"	šitte	"knowing"
saki	"ahead"	sakki	"before"

Luganda, an African language, also contrasts long and short consonants; /kkula/ means "treasure" and /kula/ means "grow up." (In both words, the first vowel is produced with a high pitch and the second with a low pitch.)

The Italian word for "grandfather" is *nonno* /nonno/, contrasting with the word for "ninth," which is *nono* /nono/.

In English, consonants may be pronounced long if they occur across word boundaries. Many English speakers will produce a longer closure of the /t/ in *white tie* than in *why tie?* In such cases, the [t:] is in free variation with a short [t]. Length is not a distinctive feature for English consonants.

The phonemic contrast between long and short consonants and vowels can be symbolized by the colon — /t:/ or /a:/ — or by doubling the segment — /tt/ or /aa/. As discussed in Chapter 5, such long segments are sometimes referred to as geminates. Since phonemic symbols are simply cover symbols for a number of distinctive feature values, it does not matter which symbol one uses. (Note that recent approaches in phonology analyze geminates in terms of *timing slots*, rather than a [±long] feature specification.)

Sometimes the choice of symbol is determined by practicality. Both print-*a* [a] and script-*a* [ɑ] are low back vowels differing in tenseness, [a] being [–tense] and [ɑ] being [+tense]. They do not contrast with each other in context, [a] appearing before glides to form diphthongs and [ɑ] elsewhere. Most North American linguists use one or the other of these characters to represent the phoneme, since they do not contrast phonemically, only phonetically, in most dialects. Since it does not matter which symbol is used, most use print-*a* because it is the character used on typewriters and computer keyboards, so it is conveniently taken as the phonemic symbol for the low back vowel with the phonetic variants [a] and [ɑ].

Natural Classes

Suppose you were writing a grammar of English and wished to include all the generalities that children acquire about the set of phonemes and their allophones. One way of showing what speakers of the language know about the predictable aspects of speech is to include these generalities as **phonological rules** in the phonological component of the grammar. These are not the rules that someone teaches you in school or that you must obey because someone insists on it; they are rules that are known unconsciously and that express the phonological regularities of the language.

In English phonology, such rules determine the conditions under which vowels are nasalized or voiceless stops are aspirated. They are general rules, applying not to a single sound but to classes of sounds. They also apply to all the words in the vocabulary of the language, and they even apply to nonsense words that are not in the language but could enter it (e.g., *sint, peeg*, and *sparg*, which would be /sɪnt/, /pig/, and /sparg/ phonemically and [sĩnt], [pʰig], and [sparg] phonetically).

There are also less general rules found in all languages, and there may be exceptions to these general rules. But what is of greater interest is that, the more we examine the phonologies of the many thousands of languages of the world, the more we find similar phonological rules that apply to the same broad classes of sounds, such as the ones we have mentioned — nasals, voiceless stops, alveolars, labials, and so on.

For example, many languages of the world include the rule that nasalizes vowels before nasal consonants. One need not include a list of the individual sounds to which the rule applies or the sounds that result from its application. This rule, which we discussed earlier in the chapter, can be stated as:

Nasalize a vowel when it precedes a nasal consonant in the same syllable.

This rule will apply to all vowel phonemes when they occur in a context before any segment marked [+nasal] in the same syllable and will add the feature [+nasal] to the feature matrix of the vowels.

Another rule that occurs frequently in the world's languages changes the place of articulation of nasal consonants to the place of articulation of a following consonant. Thus, an /n/ will become an [m] before a /p/ or /b/ and will become a velar [ŋ] before a /k/ or /g/. When two sequential segments agree in their place of articulation, they are called **homorganic consonants**, *homorganic* meaning "same place." This homorganic nasal rule occurs in Akan as well as in English and many other languages and will be further discussed later in this chapter.

Many languages have rules that refer to [+voiced] and [–voiced] sounds. Note that the aspiration rule in English applies to the class of voiceless stops. As in the vowel nasality rule, we did not list the individual segments in the rule since it applies to all the voiceless stops /p/, /t/, and /k/, as well as /č/, which may be analyzed as the voiceless stop /t/ plus the palatal fricative /š/.

That such similar rules apply to the same classes of sounds across languages is not surprising since such rules often have phonetic explanations and these classes of sounds are defined by phonetic features. For this reason, such classes are called **natural classes** of speech sounds.

A natural class is a group of sounds that share one or more distinctive features.

Children find it easier to learn a rule (or construct it) that applies to a natural class of sounds; they do not have to remember the individual sounds, simply the features that these sounds share.

This fact about phonological rules and natural classes illustrates why individual phonemic segments are better regarded as combinations or complexes of features than as indissoluble whole segments. If such segments are not specified as feature matrices, then the similarities among /p/, /t/, and /k/ or /m/, /n/, and /ŋ/ would not be revealed. It should be just as easy for a child to learn a rule such as

(a) **Nasalize vowels before /p/, /i/, or /z/.**

as to learn a rule such as

(b) **Nasalize vowels before /m/, /n/, or /ŋ/.**

Rule (a) has no phonetic explanation, whereas rule (b) does. It is easier to lower the velum to produce a nasalized vowel in anticipation of a following nasal consonant than to prevent the velum from lowering before the consonant closure.

A natural class is a set of phonemes that can be defined by fewer features than any of its individual members. The class that includes the phonemes /p, t, k, b, d, g, m, n, ŋ, č, ǰ/ can be defined by specifying one feature, [–continuant]. The phoneme /p/ requires three feature specifications (bilabial, voiceless, stop) to distinguish it uniquely, as do the other phonemes in this set.

A class of sounds that can be defined by fewer features than another class of sounds is clearly more general. Thus, the class of [–continuant] sounds is in some sense more natural than the class that includes all the noncontinuants except /p/. The only way to refer to such a class is to list all the segments in that class. Try to do this with feature notation; you will see why such a class is far from natural.

This does not mean that no language has a rule that applies to a single sound or even to a class of stops excluding /p/. One does find complex rules in languages, including rules that apply to an individual member of a class, but rules pertaining to natural classes occur more frequently than other types of rules, and an explanation is provided for this fact by reference to phonetic properties.

A phonological segment may be a member of a number of classes; for example, /s/ is a member of the class that can be designated as [+consonantal], or of the class [+alveolar], or of the class [+coronal], or of the class [+continuant, –voice], and so on.

The major classes of sounds discussed in Chapter 5 also define natural classes to which the phonological rules of all languages may refer. They can also be specified by + and – feature values:

[+CONSONANTAL] = consonants
[–CONSONANTAL] = vowels

[+SONORANT] = nasals, liquids, glides, vowels
[–SONORANT] = stops and fricatives (OBSTRUENTS)

[+SYLLABIC] = vowels, some liquids and nasals
[–SYLLABIC] = consonants, glides, some liquids and nasals

All speech sounds can thus be specified as shown in Table 6.3.

TABLE 6.3
Feature Specification of Major Natural Classes of Sounds

Features	Obstruents O	Nasals N	Liquids L	Glides G	Vowels V
Consonantal	+	+	+	−	−
Sonorant	−	+	+	+	+
Syllabic	−	+ / −	+ / −	−	+
Nasal	−	+	−	−	+/−

Feature Specifications for North American English Consonants and Vowels

Using the phonetic properties or features provided in Chapter 5 and the additional features in this chapter, we can provide feature matrices for all the phonemes in English using the + or − value for each feature. One can then easily identify the members of each class of phonemes by selecting all the segments marked + or − for a single feature. Thus, the class of high vowels, /i, ɪ, u, ʊ/, are marked [+high] in the vowel feature chart of Table 6.4; the class of stops, /p, b, m, t, d, n, k, g, ŋ, č, ǰ/, are the phonemes marked [−continuant] on the consonant chart in Table 6.5.

The feature [±mid] is not required to distinguish each vowel. The vowels marked [+mid] are already distinguished from high and low vowels by being specified as [−high], [−low]. The stressed central vowels [a] and [ʌ] are sometimes specified as back vowels; if this were done, then the feature [±front] would not be necessary. We have included the features [mid] and [central] to show more clearly the phonetic quality of the vowel phonemes. Table 6.4 also distinguishes between the phones [a], [ɑ], and [ɔ], where they are phonetically but not phonemically distinct. Canadian English would include them as allophones of /a/.

TABLE 6.4
Specification of Phonemic Features of North American Stressed Vowels

Features	i	ɪ	e	ɛ	æ	u	ʊ	o	ɔ	a	ɑ	ʌ
High	+	+	−	−	−	+	+	−	−	−	−	−
Mid	−	−	+	+	−	−	−	+	+	−	−	+
Low	−	−	−	−	+	−	−	−	−	+	+	−
Back	−	−	−	−	−	+	+	+	+	+	+	+
Central	−	−	−	−	−	−	−	−	−	+	−	+
Rounded	−	−	−	−	−	+	+	+	+	−	−	−
Tense	+	−	+	−	−	+	−	+	−	−	+	−

TABLE 6.5
Phonemic Features of North American Consonants

Features	p	b	m	t	d	n	k	g	ŋ	f	v	θ	ð	s	z	š	ž	č	ǰ	l	r	j	w	h
Consonantal	+	+	+	+	+	+	+	+	+	+	+	+	+	+	+	+	+	+	+	+	+	−	−	−
Sonorant	−	−	+	−	−	+	−	−	+	−	−	−	−	−	−	−	−	−	−	+	+	+	+	−
Syllabic	−	−	−/+	−	−	−/+	−	−	−	−	−	−	−	−	−	−	−	−	−	−/+	−/+	−	−	−
Nasal	−	−	+	−	−	+	−	−	+	−	−	−	−	−	−	−	−	−	−	−	−	−	−	−
Voiced	−	+	+	−	+	+	−	+	+	−	+	−	+	−	+	−	+	−	+	+	+	+	+	−
Continuant	−	−	−	−	−	−	−	−	−	+	+	+	+	+	+	+	+	−	−	+	+	+	+	+
Labial	+	+	+	−	−	−	−	−	−	+	+	−	−	−	−	−	−	−	−	−	−	−	+	−
Alveolar	−	−	−	+	+	+	−	−	−	−	−	−	−	+	+	−	−	−	−	+	+	−	−	−
Palatal	−	−	−	−	−	−	−	−	−	−	−	−	−	−	−	+	+	+	+	−	−	+	−	−
Velar	−	−	−	−	−	−	+	+	+	−	−	−	−	−	−	−	−	−	−	−	−	−	+	−
Coronal	−	−	−	+	+	+	−	−	−	−	−	+	+	+	+	+	+	+	+	+	+	−	−	−
Sibilant	−	−	−	−	−	−	−	−	−	−	−	−	−	+	+	+	+	+	+	−	−	−	−	−
Lateral	−	−	−	−	−	−	−	−	−	−	−	−	−	−	−	−	−	−	−	+	−	−	−	−
Anterior	+	+	+	+	+	+	−	−	−	+	+	+	+	+	+	−	−	−	−	+	+	−	−	−

Note: The [+voicing] feature value is redundant for English nasals, liquids, and glides (except for /h/) and could have been left blank for this reason. The feature specifications for [±coronal] and [±sibilant] are also redundant. These redundant, predictable feature specifications are provided simply to illustrate the segments in these natural classes. Note that we have not included the allophones [pʰ, tʰ, kʰ], since the aspiration is predictable at the beginning of syllables and these phones are not distinct phonemes in English. Note also that the precise features continue to be a matter of some debate, but these features are suitable for our purposes.

The Rules of Phonology

No rule is so general which admits not some exception.
        Robert Burton, *The Anatomy of Melancholy* (1621)

But that to come
Shall all be done by the rule.
        William Shakespeare, *Antony and Cleopatra* (1623)

Throughout this chapter we have emphasized that the relationship between the phonemic representation of words and the phonetic representations that reflect the pronunciation of these words is *rule governed*. The phonological rules relate the phonemic representations to the phonetic representations and are part of a speaker's knowledge of the language.

The phonemic representations are minimally specified because some of the features or feature values are predictable. The *underspecification* reflects the redundancy in the phonology, which is also part of a speaker's knowledge of the sound system. The grammars linguists write aim at revealing this knowledge, so it is necessary to exclude predictable features; if predictable features were included, linguists would miss the goal of accurately representing what speakers know.

The phonemic representation, then, should include only the nonpredictable distinctive features of the string of phonemes that represent the words. The phonetic representation derived by applying these rules includes all the linguistically relevant phonetic aspects of the sounds. It does not include all the physical properties of the sounds of an utterance, because the physical signal may vary in many ways that have little to do with the phonological system. The absolute pitch of the sounds, the rate of speech, or its loudness are not linguistically significant. The phonetic transcription is therefore also an abstraction from the physical signal; it includes the nonvariant phonetic aspects of the utterances, those features that remain relatively the same from speaker to speaker and from one time to another.

Although the specific rules of phonology differ from language to language, the kinds of rules, what they do, and the natural classes they refer to are the same cross-linguistically.

Assimilation Rules

We have seen that nasalization of vowels in English is nonphonemic because it is predictable by rule. The vowel nasalization rule is an **assimilation rule**, or a rule that makes neighbouring segments more similar by copying or spreading a phonetic property from one segment to another. For the most part, assimilation rules stem from articulatory or physiological processes. There is a tendency when we speak to increase the **ease of articulation** — that is, to make it easier to move the articulators. We noted above that it is easier to lower the velum while a vowel is being pronounced before a nasal stop closure than to wait for the articulators to come together. We can state the vowel nasalization rule as

> **Nasalize vowels when they occur before nasal consonants (within the same syllable).**

This rule specifies the class of sounds affected by the rule:

> **vowels**

It states what phonetic change will occur by applying the rule:

> **Change phonemic oral vowels to phonetic nasal vowels.**

And it specifies when the rule applies, the context or phonemic environment:

> **before nasal consonants within the same syllable**

All three kinds of information — class of phonemes affected, phonetic change, phonological environment — must be included in the statement of a phonological rule, or it would not explicitly state the regularities that constitute speakers' unconscious phonological knowledge.

Phonologists often use a shorthand notation to write rules, similar to the way scientists and mathematicians use symbols. Every physicist knows that $E = mc^2$ means "Energy equals mass times the square of the velocity of light." We can also use such notations to state the nasalization rule as

> **V → [+nasal]/_____[+nasal](C) \$**

The arrow abbreviates "becomes." The segment to the left of the arrow becomes, or takes on, any feature on the right of the arrow in the specified environment.

It means that a vowel becomes nasalized or takes on the feature [+nasal]. The environment follows the "slash" and in this case indicates that the vowel to be nasalized must be followed by a nasal consonant (the [+nasal] part); and optionally by any consonant (the (C) part); and then the syllable must end, indicated by the \$. (We'll discuss syllables in more detail below.) For example, the condition is met in the word *dam* because the vowel precedes a nasal consonant at the end of the syllable (and word); the condition is also met in the word *damp* because the vowel precedes a nasal consonant and another consonant, whose presence or absence doesn't affect nasalization. The condition is not met in a word like *dab*, because *b* is not [+nasal]; nor is it met by *dozen* (insofar as the *o* is concerned) because the nasal is in a different syllable. The parentheses surrounding the (C) denote *optionality*: the segment may or may not be present. If the optional (C) were not there, the rule could not apply in words like *damp* or *dent* because the nasal consonant is not followed by \$ but by another segment. (Technically, our rule is not quite complete. It doesn't take words like *dumps* into account where two consonants come between the nasal and the syllable boundary \$.)

What occurs on the left side of the arrow fulfils the first requirement for a rule: it specifies the class of sounds affected by the rule. What occurs on the right side of the arrow specifies the change that occurs, thus fulfilling the second requirement of a phonological rule.

To fulfil the third requirement of a rule — the phonological environment or context where the rule will apply — we use the underscore_____ to denote the position of the segment to be changed relative to the conditioning environment. Then the conditioning environment is symbolized.

In this case the segment to be changed precedes a nasal consonant, and possibly another consonant, and is in the same syllable. That's what _____ [+nasal] (C) $ means.

In summary:

> → means "becomes" or "is changed to"
>
> / means "in the environment of"
>
> _____ is placed before or after the segments that condition the change
>
> ( ) enclose optional segments, whose presence or absence are irrelevant to the rule
>
> $ indicates a syllable boundary

The nasalization rule stated formally using symbols can be read in words:

> A vowel becomes nasalized in the environment before a nasal segment, possibly followed by a consonant, in the same syllable.

Rule statements should be as simple and elegant as possible. This principle, known as *Occam's razor*, applies not just in phonology but also in all science. The simpler the rule, the more general the explanation.

Any rule written in formal notation can also be stated in words. The use of notation is, as stated above, a shorthand way of presenting the information. It also often reveals the function of the rule more explicitly. It is easy to see in the formal statement that this is an assimilation rule since the change to [+nasal] occurs before [+nasal] segments.

Assimilation rules in languages reflect what phoneticians often call **coarticulation** — the spreading of phonetic features either in anticipation of sounds or in the perseveration (the "hanging on") of articulatory processes. This tendency may become regularized as rules of the language.

The following example illustrates how the English vowel nasalization rule applies to the phonemic representation of words and shows the assimilatory nature of the rule — that is, the feature value of the vowel in the phonemic representation changes from [–nasal] to [+nasal] in the phonetic representation:

	"Bob"			"Bomb"		
Phonemic representation	/b	a	b/	/b	a	m/
Nasality: phonemic feature value	–	–	–	–	–	+
Apply nasal rule		NA*			↓	
Nasality: phonetic feature value	–	–	–	–	+	+
Phonetic representation	[b	ɑ	b]	[b	ã	m]

*NA = "not applicable."

Another example of an assimilation rule in English happens when the voiced /z/ of the regular plural suffix is changed to [s] after a voiceless sound; similarly, the voiced /d/ of the regular past tense suffix is changed to [t] after a voiceless sound. We can describe both of these changes with the following rule:

Notation: [+voiced] → [–voiced] /[–voiced] ____

Words: A voiced segment becomes voiceless when the preceding segment is voiceless. (Application of this rule is restricted to the plural and past-tense morphemes; we will discuss the intersection between phonology and morphology in a later section in this chapter.)

There are many other examples of assimilation rules in English and other languages. There is an optional ("free variation") rule in English that, particularly in fast speech, devoices the nasals and liquids in words such as *snow* /sno/ [sn̥o], *slow* /slo/ [sl̥o], *smart* /smart/ [sm̥art], *probe* /prob/ [pʰr̥ob], and so on. The feature [–voiced] of the /s/ or /p/ carries over onto the following segment. Because voiceless nasals and liquids do not occur phonemically — do not contrast with voiced sonorants — the vocal cords need not react quickly. The devoicing will not change the meanings of the words; [slɑt] and [sl̥ɑt] both mean "slot."

Vowels may also become devoiced or voiceless in a voiceless environment. In Japanese, high vowels are devoiced when preceded and followed by voiceless obstruents; in words such as *sukiyaki*, the /u/ becomes [u̥]. This assimilation rule can be stated as follows:

$$\begin{bmatrix} -\text{consonantal} \\ +\text{syllabic} \end{bmatrix} \rightarrow [-\text{voiced}]/ \begin{bmatrix} -\text{sonorant} \\ -\text{voiced} \end{bmatrix} \underline{\quad\quad} \begin{bmatrix} -\text{sonorant} \\ -\text{voiced} \end{bmatrix}$$

This rule states that any Japanese vowel (a segment that is nonconsonantal and syllabic) becomes devoiced ([–voiced]) in the environment of, or when it occurs (/) between, voiceless obstruents. The rule applies most often to high vowels but may apply to other vowels as well. Notice that the dash occurs not immediately after the slash or at the end of the rule but between the segment matrices represented as [–sonorant, –voiced].

This rule includes the three kinds of information required:

1. The class of sounds affected: vowels
2. The phonetic change: devoicing
3. The phonemic environment: between two voiceless obstruents

The rule does not specify the class of segments to the left of the arrow as [+voiced] because phonemically all vowels in Japanese are voiced. It therefore simply has to include the change on the right side of the arrow.

We can illustrate the application of this rule in Japanese as we did with the vowel nasalization rule in English:

	"sukiyaki"							
Phonemic representation	/s	u	k	i	j	a	k	i/
Voicing: phonemic feature value	−	+	−	+	+	+	−	+
Apply devoicing rule		↓						
Voicing: phonetic feature value	−	−	−	+	+	+	−	+
Phonetic representation	[s	u̥	k	i	j	a	k	i]

Feature-Changing Rules

The English vowel nasalization and devoicing rules and the Japanese devoicing rule change feature specifications. That is, in English the [−nasal] value of phonemic vowels is changed to [+nasal] phonetically through an assimilation process when the vowels occur before nasals. Vowels in Japanese are phonemically voiced, and the rule changes vowels that occur in the specified environment into phonetically voiceless segments.

The rules we have discussed are phonetically plausible, as are other assimilation rules, and can be explained by natural phonetic processes. This fact does not mean that all these rules have to occur in all languages. In fact, if they always occurred, then they would not have to be learned at all; they would apply automatically and universally and therefore would not have to be included in the grammar of any particular language. They are not, however, universal.

There is a nasal assimilation rule in Akan that nasalizes voiced stops when they follow nasal consonants:

/ɔ bá/   [ɔbá]   "he comes"   /ɔ m̀ bá/   [ɔmmá]   "he doesn't come"
he come   *he not come*

The /b/ of the verb "come" becomes an [m] when it follows the negative morpheme /m/. (The diacritics are tone marks.)

This assimilation rule also has a phonetic explanation; the velum is lowered to produce the nasal consonant and remains down during the following stop. Although it is a phonetically "natural" assimilation rule, it does not occur in the grammar of English; the word *amber*, for example, shows an [m] followed by a [b]. It is not pronounced "ammer."

Assimilation rules such as the ones we have discussed in English, Japanese, and Akan often have the function of changing the value of phonemic features. They are **feature-changing** or **feature-spreading rules**. Although nasality is nondistinctive for vowels in English, it is a distinctive feature for consonants, and the nasalization rule therefore changes a feature value.

The Akan rule is a feature-changing rule that states that [m] is an allophone of /b/ as well as an allophone of /m/. The more general point that this example illustrates is the following:

> **There is no one-to-one relationship between phonemes and their allophones**.

This fact can be illustrated in another way:

Akan Phonemes   /b/   /m/

Akan Phones   [b]   [m]

We will provide more examples of this one-to-many or many-to-one mapping between phonemes and allophones below.

Dissimilation Rules

It is understandable why assimilation rules are found in so many languages. As pointed out, they permit greater ease of articulation. It might seem strange, then, to learn that one also finds **dissimilation rules** in languages, rules in which a segment becomes *less* similar to another segment rather than more similar. But such rules do exist. They also have a "natural" explanation, often from the point of view of the hearer rather than the speaker. That is, in listening to speech, if sounds are too similar, we may miss the contrast.

Also, it may be easier to articulate dissimilar sounds. The difficulty of tongue twisters like "the sixth sheik's sixth sheep is sick" is based on the repeated similarity of sounds. If one were to make some sounds less similar, as in "the fifth sheik's fourth sheep is sick," it would be easier to say.

An example of easing pronunciation through dissimilation is found in some varieties of English, where there is a fricative dissimilation rule. This rule applies to sequences /fθ/ and /sθ/, changing them to [ft] and [st]. Here the fricative /θ/ becomes dissimilar to the preceding fricative by becoming a stop. For example, the words *fifth* and *sixth* come to be pronounced as if they were spelled *fift* and *sikst*.

The liquids /l/ and /r/ are sometimes interchanged to create dissimilarity. For example, English adopted the French word *marbre* meaning "marble" and in doing so dissimilated the second /r/ to an /l/.

A classic example of dissimilation occurred in Latin, and the results of this process show up in modern-day English. There was a derivational suffix *-alis* in Latin that was added to nouns to form adjectives. When the suffix was added to a noun that contained the liquid /l/, the suffix was changed to *-aris* — that is, the liquid /l/ was changed to the liquid /r/. These words came into English as adjectives ending in *-al* or, in their dissimilated forms, in *-ar,* as shown in the following examples:

-al	-ar
anecdot-al	angul-ar
annu-al	annul-ar
ment-al	column-ar
pen-al	perpendicul-ar
spiritu-al	simil-ar
ven-al	vel-ar

All the *-ar* adjectives contain an /l/, and as *columnar* illustrates, the /l/ need not be the consonant directly preceding the dissimilated segment.

Although dissimilation rules are somewhat rare, they do occur, as shown by the examples above. The African language Kikuyu also has a dissimilation rule in which a prefix added to a verb begins with a velar fricative if the verb begins with a stop but with a velar stop if the verb begins with a continuant.

Feature Addition Rules

Some phonological rules are neither assimilation nor dissimilation rules. The aspiration rule in English, which aspirates a voiceless stop at the beginning of a syllable, simply adds a nondistinctive feature. As we did in the nasalization rule earlier, we can use the symbol $ to represent a syllable boundary. Generally, aspiration occurs only if the following vowel is stressed. The /p/ in *pit* and *repeat* is aspirated, but the /p/ in *inspect* or *compass* is usually unaspirated (although if aspirated it will not change meaning since aspiration is nonphonemic). Using the feature [+stress] to indicate a stressed syllable, (C) to represent an optional consonant, V́ to symbolize stressed vowels, and $ to represent the syllable boundary, the aspiration rule may be stated as follows:

$$\begin{bmatrix} -\text{continuant} \\ -\text{voiced} \end{bmatrix} \rightarrow [+\text{aspirated}] \,/\, \$ \,\underline{\quad}\, (C) \begin{bmatrix} -\text{consonantal} \\ +\text{stress} \end{bmatrix}$$

Voiceless stops ([−continuant, −voiced]) become aspirated when they occur syllable initially before stressed vowels (/$___ (C) V́).

Aspiration is neither present nor absent in any phonemic feature matrices in English. Assimilation rules do not add new features but change phonemic feature values, whereas the aspiration rule adds a new feature not present in phonemic matrices.

Remember that /p/ and /b/ (and all such symbols) are simply cover symbols that do not reveal the phonemic distinctions. In the phonemic and phonetic feature matrices, these differences are made explicit, as shown in the following phonemic matrices:

	/p/	/b/	
Consonantal	+	+	
Continuant	–	–	
Labial	+	+	
Voiced	–	+	← distinctive difference

The nondistinctive feature "aspiration" is not included in these phonemic representations because aspiration is predictable.

Segment Deletion and Insertion Rules

In addition to assimilation and dissimilation (feature-changing) and feature-addition rules, phonological rules can delete or add entire phonemic segments. In French, for example, as demonstrated by Sanford Schane (1968), word-final consonants are deleted when the following word begins with an obstruent, a liquid, or a nasal consonant, but they are retained when the following word begins with a vowel or a glide, as illustrated in Table 6.6.

TABLE 6.6
Distribution of Word-Final Consonants in French

Before an obstruent:	/pətit tablo/	[pəti tablo]	"small picture"
	/noz tablo/	[no tablo]	"our pictures"
Before a liquid:	/pətit livr/	[pəti livr]	"small book"
	/noz livr/	[no livr]	"our books"
Before a nasal:	/pətit navet/	[pəti navɛ]	"small turnip"
	/noz navets/	[no navɛ]	"our turnips"
Before a vowel:	/pətit ami/	[pətit ami]	"small friend"
	/noz amis/	[noz ami]	"our friends"
Before a glide:	/pətit wazo/	[pətit wazo]	"small bird"
	/noz wazo/	[noz wazo]	"our birds"

Sanford Schane, *French Phonology and Morphology*, MIT Press, 1968. © Sanford Schane, 1968. By permission of the MIT Press.

Table 6.6 represents a general rule in French applying to all word-final consonants. We distinguished these five classes of sounds by the features *consonantal, sonorant, syllabic,* and *nasal* in Table 6.3. We noted that obstruents, liquids, and nasal consonants are [+consonantal] and vowels and glides are [–consonantal]. We can now see why such "natural classes" are important. Using the symbol Ø to represent deletion and # to signify "word boundary," we can state the French rule simply as

[+consonantal] → Ø/ _____ ## [+consonantal]

This rule can be "translated" into words as

A consonantal segment (obstruent, liquid, or nasal) is deleted or becomes null (→Ø) in the environment (/) at the end of a word (_____ #) that is followed by a word beginning with an obstruent, liquid, or nasal (# [+consonantal]).

or simply as

Delete a consonant before a word beginning with any consonant that is not a glide.

In Schane's complete analysis, many words that are pronounced with a final consonant actually have a vowel as their word-final segment in phonemic representation. The vowel prevents the rule of word-final consonant deletion from applying. The vowel itself is deleted by another, later rule. Given this rule in the grammar of French, *petit* would be phonemically /pətit/. It need not be additionally represented as /pəti/, because the rule determines the phonetic shape of the word.

In some cases, different phonetic forms of the same morpheme may be derived by segment deletion rules, as in the following examples:

A		**B**	
sign	[sajn]	signature	[sɪgnəčər]
design	[dəzajn]	designation	[dɛzɪgnešən]
paradigm	[pʰærədajm]	paradigmatic	[pʰærədɪgmærək]

In none of the words in column A is there a phonetic [g], but in each corresponding word in column B a [g] occurs. Our knowledge of English phonology accounts for these phonetic differences. The "[g]–no [g]" alternation is regular, and we apply it to words that we have never heard before. Suppose someone says

He was a salignant [səlɪgnənt] man.

Even if you do not know what the word means, you might ask (perhaps to hide your ignorance)

Why, did he salign [səlajn] somebody?

It is highly doubtful that a speaker of English would pronounce the verb form with the *-ant* dropped as [səlɪgn], because the phonological rules of English would delete the /g/ when it occurred in this context. This rule might be stated as

Delete a /g/ when it occurs before a final nasal consonant.

The /g/ may be deleted under other circumstances as well, as indicated by its absence in *signing* and *signer*. The rule is even more general, as evidenced by the pairs *gnostic* [nostɪk] and *agnostic* [ægnɑstɪk] and the words *cognition, recogni-tion, agnosia*, and others, all of which contain the same morpheme related to knowledge. The rule can be stated as

> **Delete a /g/ when it occurs word initially before a nasal consonant or before a word-final nasal.**

Given this rule, the phonemic representation of the stems in *sign/signature, design/designation, resign/resignation, repugn/repugnant, phlegm/phlegmatic, par-adigm/paradigmatic, diaphragm/diaphragmatic, gnosis, agnosia, agnostic*, and *recognition* will include a phonemic /g/ that will be deleted by the regular rule if a suffix is not added. By stating the class of sounds that follow the /g/ (nasal conso-nants) rather than any specific nasal consonant, the rule deletes the /g/ before both /m/ and /n/.

The phonological rules that delete whole segments, add segments and features, and change features also account for the various phonetic forms of some mor-phemes. This point can be further illustrated by the following words:

A			B		
bomb	/bamb/	[bãm]	bombardier	/bambədir/	[bãmbədir]
iamb	/ajæmb/	[ajæ̃m]	iambic	/ajæmbɪk/	[ajæ̃mbək]
crumb	/krʌmb/	[kʰrʌ̃m]	crumble	/krʌmbl̩/	[kʰrʌ̃mbəl]

A speaker of English knows when to pronounce a /b/ and when not to. The rela-tionship between the pronunciation of the column A words and their column B counterparts is regular and can be accounted for by the following rule:

> **Delete a word-final /b/ when it occurs after an /m/.**

Notice that the underlying phonemic representation of the A and B stems is the same.

The rules that delete the segments are general phonological rules, but their application to phonemic representations results in deriving different phonetic forms of the same morpheme.

Deletion rules also show up as optional rules in fast speech or casual speech in English. They result, for example, in the common contractions changing *he is* [hi ɪz] to *he's* [hiz] or *I will* [aj wɪl] to *I'll* [ajl]. In ordinary speech, most of us also "delete" the unstressed vowels that are shown in bold type in words such as the fol-lowing:

> mystery   general   mem**o**ry   funeral   vig**o**rous   Barb**a**ra

These words in casual speech sound as if they were written

> mystry   genral   memry   funral   vigrous   Barbra

Phonological rules, therefore, can be either optional or obligatory.

Phonological rules may also insert consonants or vowels, which is called **epenthesis.** In some cases, epenthesis occurs to "fix up" nonpermitted sequences.

In English morphemes, nasal/nonnasal **consonant clusters** must be homorganic, both labial, both alveolar, or both velar. We find /m/ before /p/ and /b/ as in *ample* and *amble*; /n/ before /t/ and /d/ in *gentle* and *gender*; and /ŋ/ before /k/ and /g/ in *ankle* and *angle*. (You may not realize that the nasal in the last two words has a velar articulation because the spelling can obscure this fact. If you pronounce these words carefully, you will see that the back of your tongue touches the velum in the articulation of both the *n* and the *k*.) /m/ before /t, d, k, g/ does not occur morpheme internally, nor does /n/ before /p, b, k, g/ or /ŋ/ before /p, b, t, d/. Because of this sequential constraint, many speakers pronounce the name *Fromkin* with an epenthetic [p], as if it were written *Frompkin*.

The same process of epenthesis occurred in the history of English. The earlier form of the word *empty* had no *p*. Similarly, a /d/ was inserted in the word *ganra* to give us the modern *gander* and a /d/ at the end of *soun* to produce *sound*.

In the history of Spanish, many words that now start with an *e* followed by an [s] followed by another consonant came from Latin words that were not vowel initial. For example, the Spanish word *escribir* "to write" was *scribere* in Latin (the *sc* representing /sk/), and the Spanish word for "school," *escuela*, comes from the Latin word *schola* through epenthesis. Similarly, the French *étoile* derived from the Latin *stella*.

Two epenthesis rules insert schwa before the English regular plural and regular past-tense endings when they occur in certain environments. The rule for the plural suffix is stated below, where null becomes schwa (Ø → ə) is the part of the rule that actually performs the insertion.

$$\emptyset \rightarrow \text{ə} \; / \; [\text{+ sibilant}] \; \underline{\quad} \; [\text{+ sibilant}]$$

The rule for the past-tense suffix differs only in the phonological environment:

$$\emptyset \rightarrow \text{ə} \; / \; [\text{+ alveolar, + stop}] \; \underline{\quad} [\text{+ alveolar, + stop}]$$

There is a plausible explanation for insertion of a [ə] in the plural forms of nouns ending with sibilants and in the past-tense forms of verbs ending with alveolar stops. If we added a [z] to *squeeze* we would get [skwizz], which would be hard for English speakers to distinguish from [skwiz]; similarly, if we added [d] to *load,* it would be [lodd] phonetically in the past and [lod] in the present, which would also be difficult to perceive, because in English we do not contrast long and short consonants.

Movement (Metathesis) Rules

Phonological rules may also move phonemes from one place in the string to another. Such rules are called **metathesis** rules. They are less common, but they do exist. In some dialects of English, for example, the word *ask* is pronounced [æks], but the word *asking* is pronounced [æskĩn] or [æskĩŋ]. In these dialects, a metathesis rule "switches" the /s/ and /k/ in certain contexts. In Old English, the verb was *aksian*, with the /k/ preceding the /s/. A historical metathesis rule switched these two consonants, producing *ask* in most dialects of English. Children's speech shows many cases of metathesis (which are later corrected as the child approaches the adult grammar): *aminal* [æmənəl] for *animal* and *pusketti* [pʰəskɛti] for *spaghetti* are common children's pronunciations.

In Hebrew, there is a metathesis rule that reverses a pronoun-final consonant with the first consonant of the following verb if the verb starts with a sibilant. These reversals are in "reflexive" verb forms, as shown in the following examples:

Nonsibilant-Initial Verbs		**Sibilant-Initial Verbs**	
kabel	"to accept"	tsadek	"to justify"
lehit-kabel	"to be accepted"	lehits-tadek	"to apologize"
		(*not* *lehit-tsadek)	
pater	"to fire"	šameš	"to use for"
lehit-pater	"to resign"	lehiš-tameš	"to use"
		(*not* *lehit-šameš)	
bayeš	"to shame"	sader	"to arrange"
lehit-bayeš	"to be shamed"	lehis-tader	"to arrange oneself"
		(*not* *lehit-sader)	

We see, then, that phonological rules have a number of different functions, among which are the following:

1. **Change feature values** (vowel nasalization rule in English).
2. **Add new features** (aspiration in English).
3. **Delete segments** (final consonant deletion in French).
4. **Add segments** (vowel insertion in Spanish).
5. **Reorder segments** (metathesis rule in Hebrew).

These rules, when applied to the phonemic representations of words and phrases, result in phonetic forms that differ from the phonemic forms. If such differences were unpredictable, we would find it difficult to explain how we can understand what we hear or how we produce utterances that represent the meanings we wish to convey. The more we look at languages, however, the more we see that many aspects of the phonetic forms of utterances that appear at first to be irregular and unpredictable are actually rule governed. We learn, or construct, these rules when we are learning the language as children. The rules form an important part of the sound patterns that we acquire.

From One to Many and from Many to One

The discussion on how phonemic representations of utterances are realized phonetically included an example from the African Ghanaian language Akan to show that the relationship between a phoneme and its allophonic realization may be complex. The same phone may be an allophone of two or more phonemes, as [m] was shown to be an allophone of both /b/ and /m/ in Akan.

We can also illustrate this complex mapping relationship in English. Consider the boldfaced vowels in the following pairs of words:

	A		**B**	
/i/	compete	[i]	competition	[ə]
/ɪ/	medicinal	[ɪ]	medicine	[ə]
/e/	maintain	[e]	maintenance	[ə]
/ɛ/	telegraph	[ɛ]	telegraphy	[ə]
/æ/	analysis	[æ]	analytic	[ə]
/a/	solid	[ɑ]	solidity	[ə]
/o/	phone	[o]	phonetic	[ə]
/u/	Talmudic	[u]	Talmud	[ə]

In column A, all the boldfaced vowels are stressed vowels with a variety of different vowel phones; in column B, all the boldfaced unstressed vowels are pronounced [ə]. How can one explain the fact that the same root morphemes that occur in both words of the pairs have different pronunciations?

In Chapter 2, we defined a morpheme as a sound–meaning unit. Changing either would make a different morpheme. It doesn't seem plausible (nor is it necessary) for speakers of English to represent these root morphemes with distinct phonemic forms if there is some general rule that relates the stressed vowels in column A to the unstressed schwa vowel [ə] in column B.

Speakers of English know (unconsciously of course) that one can derive one word from another by the addition of derivational morphemes. This is illustrated above by adding *-ition* and *-ance* to verb roots to form nouns or *-al* and *-ic* to nouns to form adjectives. In English, the syllable that is stressed depends to a great extent on the phonemic structure of the word, the number of syllables, and so on. In a number of cases, the addition of derivational suffixes changes the stress pattern of the word, and the vowel that was stressed in the root morpheme becomes unstressed in the derived form. (The stress rules are rather complex and will not be detailed in this introductory text.) When a vowel is unstressed in English, it is pronounced as [ə], which is a **reduced vowel**.

All the root morphemes of column A are represented phonemically by their value when stressed. A simple rule predicts that their vowels are changed to [ə] when unstressed. We can conclude, then, that [ə] is an allophone of all English vowel phonemes. The rule to derive the schwa can be stated simply as

Change a vowel to a [ə] when it is unstressed.

This rule is oversimplified, because when an unstressed vowel occurs as the final segment of some words it retains its full vowel quality, as shown in words such as *confetti, motto,* and *democracy.* In some dialects, all unstressed vowels, including final vowels, are reduced. A comprehensive rule would be more complex to state.

The rule that "reduces" unstressed vowels to schwas is another example of a rule that changes feature values.

In a phonological description of a language that we do not know, it is not always possible to determine from the phonetic transcription what the phonemic representation is. However, given the phonemic representation and the phonological rules, we can always derive the correct phonetic transcription. Of course, in our internal mental grammars, this derivation is no problem, because the words occur in their phonemic forms in our lexicons and we know the rules of the language.

Another example will illustrate this aspect of phonology. In English, /t/ and /d/ are both phonemes, as is illustrated by the minimal pairs *tie/die* and *bat/bad*. When /t/ or /d/ occurs between a stressed and an unstressed vowel, they both become a flap [ɾ]. For many speakers of English, *writer* and *rider* are pronounced identically as [rajɾər], yet these speakers know that *writer* has a phonemic /t/ because of *write* /rajt/, whereas *rider* has a phonemic /d/ because of *ride* /rajd/. Canadians almost always distinguish between *writer* and *rider* on the basis of the diphthong. The "flap rule" may be stated informally:

> **An alveolar stop becomes a voiced flap when preceded by a stressed vowel and followed by an unstressed vowel.**

The application of this rule is illustrated as follows:

Phonemic representation	write	writer	ride	rider
	/rajt/	/rajt + ər/	/rajd/	/rajd + ər/
Apply rule	NA*	ɾ	NA	ɾ
Phonetic representation	[rajt]	[rʌjɾər]	[rajd]	[rajɾər]

*NA = "not applicable."

The underlying distinction between /t/ and /d/ in *writer* and *rider* is evident in the way they are treated in many varieties of Canadian English, in which the allophone of /aj/ before [t] is [ʌj] and that before [d] is [aj]. When the medial stop became the flap [ɾ], the diphthong [ʌj] remained, thus contrasting *writer* as [rʌjɾər] as opposed to *rider* as [rajɾər]. Now the contrast between the consonant phonemes /t/ and /d/ is indicated by the distinction between the vowel allophones, a paradox first pointed out by Joos (1942) and labelled "Canadian raising" by Chambers (1973). For further discussion of this feature of Canadian English, see Chapter 12.

We are omitting other phonetic details that are also determined by phonological rules, such as the fact that in *ride* the vowel is slightly longer than in *write* because it is followed by a voiced [d], which is a phonetic rule in many languages. We are using the example only to illustrate the fact that two distinct phonemes may be realized phonetically by the same phone.

Such cases show that we cannot arrive at a phonological analysis by simply inspecting the phonetic representation of utterances. If we just looked for minimal pairs as the only evidence for phonology, we would have to conclude that [ɾ] is a phoneme in English because it contrasts phonetically with other phonetic units:

riper [rʌjpər], *rhymer* [rãjmər], *riser* [rajzər], and so forth. Grammars are much more complex than this pairing shows. The fact that *write* and *ride* change their phonetic forms when suffixes are added shows that there is an intricate mapping between phonemic representations of words and phonetic pronunciations.

Notice that in the cases of the "schwa rule" and the "flap rule" the allophones derived from the different phonemes by rule are different in features from all other phonemes in the language. That is, there is no [ɾ] phoneme, but there is a [ɾ] phone. This was also true of aspirated voiceless stops and nasalized vowels. The set of phones is larger than the set of phonemes.

The English "flap rule" also illustrates an important phonological process called **neutralization**; the voicing contrast between /t/ and /d/ is neutralized in the specified environment. That is, /t/ never contrasts with /d/ in the environment between a stressed and an unstressed vowel.

Similar rules showing there is no one-to-one relation between phonemes and phones are found in other languages. In both Russian and German, when voiced obstruents occur at the end of a word or syllable, they become voiceless. Both voiced and voiceless obstruents do occur in German as phonemes, as is shown by the following minimal pair:

> *Tier*   [ti:r]   "animal"   *dir*   [di:r]   "to you"

At the end of a word, however, only [t] occurs; the words meaning "bundle," *Bund* /bʊnd/, and "colourful," *bunt* /bʊnt/, are phonetically identical and pronounced [bũnt] with a final [t].

The German devoicing rule, like the vowel reduction rule in English and the homorganic nasal rule, changes the specifications of features. In German, the phonemic representation of the final stop in *Bund* is /d/, specified as [+voiced]; it is changed by rule to [−voiced] to derive the phonetic [t] in word-final position.

This rule in German further illustrates that we cannot decide what the phonemic representation of a word is, given only the phonetic form; [bũnt] can be derived from either /bund/ or /bunt/. The phonemic representations and the rules of the language together determine the phonetic forms.

The Function of Phonological Rules

The function of the phonological rules in a grammar is to provide the phonetic information necessary for the pronunciation of utterances. We can illustrate this point in the following way:

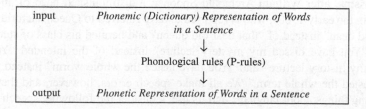

input	*Phonemic (Dictionary) Representation of Words in a Sentence*
	↓
	Phonological rules (P-rules)
	↓
output	*Phonetic Representation of Words in a Sentence*

The input to the P-rules is the phonemic representation; the P-rules apply to or operate on the phonemic strings and produce as output the phonetic representation.

The application of rules in this way is called a **derivation**. We have given a number of examples of derivations, which show how phonemically oral vowels become nasalized, how phonemically unaspirated voiceless stops become aspirated, how contrastive voiced and voiceless alveolar stops in English merge to become flaps, and how German voiced obstruents are devoiced. A derivation is thus an explicit way of showing both the effects of a phonological rule and the function of phonological rules (P-rules) in a grammar.

All the examples of derivations we have considered so far show the applications of just one phonological rule. It must be the case, however, that more than one rule may apply to a word. For example, the word *tempest* is phonemically /tɛmpɛst/ (as shown by the pronunciation of *tempestuous* [tʰɛmpʰɛsčuəs]) but phonetically [tʰɛ̃mpəst]. Three rules apply to it: the aspiration rule, the vowel nasalization rule, and the schwa rule. We can derive the phonetic form from the phonemic representation as follows:

Underlying phonemic representation	/ t ɛ m p ɛ s t /
Aspiration rule	tʰ
Nasalization rule	ɛ̃
Schwa rule	ə
Surface phonetic representation	[tʰ ɛ̃ m p ə s t]

We are using phonetic symbols instead of matrices in which the feature values are changed. These derivatives are equivalent, however, as long as we understand that a phonetic symbol is a *cover term* representing a matrix with all distinctive features marked either + or − (unless, of course, the feature is nondistinctive, such as the nasality value for phonemic vowels in English).

Slips of the Tongue: Evidence for Phonological Rules

Slips of the tongue or **speech errors** in which we deviate in some way from the intended utterance show phonological rules in action. Some of these slips are called **spoonerisms**, after William Archibald Spooner, a distinguished head of an Oxford college in the early 1900s, who is reported to have referred to Queen Victoria as "that queer old dean" instead of "that dear old queen" and berated his class of students by saying "You have hissed my mystery lecture" instead of the intended "You have missed my history lecture" and "You have tasted the whole worm" instead of "You have wasted the whole term." We all make speech errors, however, and they tell us interesting things about language and its use. Consider the following speech errors:

Intended Utterance	**Actual Utterance**
(1) gone to seed	god to seen
[gãn tə sid]	[gɑd tə sĩn]
(2) stick in the mud	smuck in the tid
[stɪk ĩn ðə mʌd]	[smʌk ĩn ðə tʰɪd]
(3) speech production	preach seduction
[spič pʰrədʌkšə̃n]	[pʰrič sədʌkšə̃n]

In the first example, the final consonants of the first and third words were reversed. Notice that the reversal of the consonants also changed the nasality of the vowels. The vowel [ã] in the intended utterance is replaced by [ɑː]; in the actual utterance, the nasalization was "lost," because the vowel no longer occurred before a nasal consonant. The vowel in the third word, which was the nonnasal [i] in the intended utterance, became [ĩ] in the error, because it was followed by /n/. The nasalization rule applied.

In the other two errors, we see the application of the aspiration rule. In the intended *stick*, the /t/ would have been realized as unaspirated because it is not syllable initial; when it was switched with the /m/ in *mud*, it was pronounced as the aspirated [tʰ], because it occurred initially. The third example also illustrates the application of the aspiration rule in action.

The Pronunciation of Morphemes

We noted that a single morpheme may have different pronunciations — that is, different phonetic forms — in different contexts. Thus, *write* /rajt/ is pronounced [rajt] but is pronounced [rʌjɾər] in some dialects of Canadian English and [rajɾər] in most other North American dialects when the suffix -*er* is added.

We also saw that in French a morpheme such as /noz/, meaning "our," is pronounced [no] before words beginning with [+consonantal] sounds and as [noz] before word-initial [–consonantal] sounds.

Furthermore, in English, underlying phonemic vowels "reduce" to schwa [ə] when they are unstressed. The particular phonetic forms of some morphemes are determined by regular phonological rules that refer only to the phonemic context, as is true of the alternative vowel forms of the following sets:

m[ɛ]l[ə]dy	h[a]rm[ə]ny	s[ɪ]mph[ə]ny
m[ə]l[o]dious	h[a]rm[o]nious	s[ɪ]mph[o]nious
m[ə]l[a]dic	h[a]rm[ɑ]nic	s[ɪ]mph[ɑ]nic

The vowel rules that determine these pronunciations are rather complicated and beyond the scope of this text. The examples are presented simply to show that the morphemes in "melody," "harmony," and "symphony" vary phonetically in these words.

Another example of a morpheme in English with different phonetic forms is the plural morpheme that was briefly discussed previously in this chapter. In column

KNOW YOUR OBJETS D'ART

BUST OF PLATO

BUST OF PLAY-DOH

A, all the nouns end in voiced nonsibilant sounds, and to form their plurals you add the voiced [z]. All the words in column B end in voiceless nonsibilant sounds, and you add a voiceless [s]. The words in column C end in both voiced and voiceless sibilants, which form their plurals with the insertion of a schwa followed by [z]. This is another example of an epenthesis rule. The nouns in column D are irregular, and the plural forms must be memorized:

A	B	C	D
cab	cap	bus	child
cad	cat	bush	ox
bag	back	buzz	mouse
love	cuff	garage	sheep
lathe	faith	match	criterion
cam		badge	
can			
bang			
call			
bar			
spa			
boy			
add [z]	**add [s]**	**add [əz]**	

Children do not have to learn the plural rule by memorizing the individual sounds that require the [z] or [s] or [əz] plural ending, because these sounds form natural classes. A grammar that included lists of these sounds would not reveal the regularities in the language or what a speaker knows about the regular plural formation rule.

The regular plural rule does not work for a word such as *child*, which in the plural is *children*, or for *ox*, which becomes *oxen*, or for *sheep*, which is unchanged phonologically in the plural. *Child, ox*, and *sheep* are exceptions to the regular rule. We learn these exceptional plurals when learning the language, often after we have constructed or discovered the regular rule, which occurs at a very early age. The late Harry Hoijer, a well-known anthropological linguist, used to play a game with his two-year-old daughter. He would say a noun, and she would give him the plural form if he said the singular and the singular if she heard the plural. One day he said *ox* [ɑks], and she responded [ɑk], apparently not knowing the word and thinking that the [s] at the end must be the plural suffix. Children also often "regularize" exceptional forms, saying *mouses* and *sheeps*.

If the grammar represented each unexceptional or regular word in its singular and plural forms — for example, *cat* /kæt/, *cats* /kæts/; *cap* /kæp/, *caps* /kæps/; and so on — it would imply that the plurals of *cat* and *cap* were as irregular as the plurals of *child* and *ox*. Of course, they are not. If a new toy appeared on the market called a *glick* /glɪk/, a young child who wanted two of them would ask for two *glicks* /glɪks/ and not two *glicken*, even if the child had never heard the word *glicks*. The child knows the regular rule to form plurals. An experiment conducted by the linguist Jean Berko Gleason showed that very young children can apply this rule to words they have never heard. A grammar that describes such knowledge (the internalized mental grammar) must then include the general rule.

This rule, which determines the phonetic representation or pronunciation of the plural morpheme, is somewhat different from some of the other phonological rules we have discussed. The "aspiration rule" in English applies to a word whenever the phonological description is met; it is not the case, for example, that a /t/ is aspirated only if it is part of a particular morpheme or only in nouns or adjectives. The "flap rule," which changes the phonetic forms of the morphemes *write* and *ride* when a suffix is added, is also completely automatic, depending solely on the phonological environment. The plural rule, however, applies only to the inflectional plural morpheme. To see that it is not "purely" phonological in nature, consider the following words:

race	[res]	ray	[re]	ray + pl.	[rez]	*[res]
sauce	[sɑs]	saw	[sɑ]	saw + pl.	[sɑz]	*[sɑs]
rice	[rajs]	rye	[raj]	rye + pl.	[rajz]	*[rajs]

The examples show that the [z] in the plural is not determined by the phonological context, because in an identical context an [s] occurs. It applies only to certain morphemes.

Morphophonemics

The rule that determines the phonetic form of the plural morpheme is a **morphophonemic rule**, because its application is determined by both the morphology and the phonology. When a morpheme has alternative phonetic forms, these forms are called **allomorphs** by some linguists. [z], [s], and [əz] would be allomorphs of the regular plural morpheme and would be determined by rule.

To show how such a rule may be applied, assume that the regular, productive, plural morpheme has the phonological form /z/, with the meaning "plural." The regular "plural rule" can be stated in a simple way:

(a)   Insert a [ə] before the plural ending when a regular noun ends in a sibilant — /s/, /z/, /š/, /ž/, /č/, or /ǰ/ giving [əz].

(b)   Change the voiced /z/ to voiceless [s] when it is preceded by a voiceless sound.

If neither (a) nor (b) applies, then /z/ will be realized as [z]; no segments will be added, and no features will be changed.

	bus + pl.	*butt* + pl.	*bug* + pl.
Phonemic Representation	/bʌs + z/ ↓	/bʌt + z/	/bʌg + z/
apply rule (a)	ə	NA*↓	NA
apply rule (b)	NA	s	NA
Phonetic Representation	[bʌsəz]	[bʌts]	[bʌgz]

*NA = "not applicable."

The plural formation rule will derive the phonetic forms of plurals for all regular nouns (remember, this plural is /z/).

As we have formulated these rules, (a) must be applied before (b). If we applied the two parts of the rule in reverse order, then we would derive incorrect phonetic forms:

Phonemic Representation	/bʌs + z/ ↓
apply rule (b)	↓ s
apply rule (a)	ə
Phonetic Representation	*[bʌsəs]

An examination of the rule for the formation of the past tense of verbs in English shows some interesting parallels with the plural formation of nouns.

A	B	C	D
grab	reap	state	be
hug	peak	raid	run
seethe	unearth		sing
love	huff		have
buzz	kiss		go
rouge	wish		hit
judge	pitch		
fan			
ram			
long			
kill			
care			
tie			
bow			
hoe			
add [d]	**add [t]**	**add [əd]**	

The productive regular past-tense morpheme in English is /d/ phonemically but [d] (column A), [t] (column B), or [əd] (column C) phonetically, again depending on the final phoneme of the verb to which it is attached. D-column verbs are exceptions.

The following rules describe these variations in the pronunciation of the regular past-tense morpheme.

1. Insert a [ə] before the past-tense morpheme when a regular verb ends in an alveolar stop — /t d/ — giving [əd].
2. Change the past-tense morpheme to a voiceless [t] when a voiceless sound precedes it.

The past-tense morpheme has the basic form /d/, pronounced [d], if no rules apply.

Like the rules for the regular English plural, the rules for the regular past tense are morphophonological, because they apply to the past-tense morpheme specifically, not to all morphemes in English.

The English negative prefix *in*- which, like *un*-, means "not," has three allomorphs:

Allomorph	Environment	Examples
[ɪn]	before vowels	inexcusable, inattentive
	before alveolars	intolerable, indefinable, innovation, insurmountable
[ɪm]	before labials	impossible, imbalance, immaterial
[ɪŋ]	before velars	incomplete, inglorious

The pronunciation of this morpheme is often revealed by the spelling as *im-* when it is prefixed to morphemes beginning with *p*, *b*, or *m*. Because we have no letter "ŋ" in our alphabet, the velar [ŋ] is written as *n* in words like *incomplete*. You may not realize that you pronounce the *n* in *inconceivable, inglorious, incongruous,* and other such words as [ŋ] because this rule is as unconscious as other rules in your grammar. It is the job of linguists and phoneticians to bring such rules to consciousness or to reveal them as part of the grammar. If you say these words in normal tempo without pausing after the *in-*, you should feel the back of your tongue rise to touch the velum.

The rule that accounts for the pronunciation of the *in-* prefix is called the **homorganic nasal rule** because the nasal consonant is produced at the same place of articulation as the following consonant:

> **Change the place of articulation of a nasal consonant so that it agrees with (i.e., is the same as) the place feature of articulation of a following consonant.**

With this rule we can give the *in-* negative prefix morpheme the basic representation /ɪn/. Before vowels and before morphemes beginning with *t* or *d*, the homorganic nasal rule has no effect on the basic form. (Note that another rule nasalizes the vowel so that its pronunciation is [ĩ].) The rule changes the alveolar feature of *n* to labial before a morpheme beginning with a labial consonant *p*, *b*, or *m* to agree with the place of articulation, as in *i**m**possible* and *i**m**modest*. Similarly, this feature-changing rule changes alveolar to velar, so the *n* in /ɪn/ is pronounced as the velar nasal [ŋ] before morphemes that begin with the velar consonants *k* or *g* in words like *incoherent*.

We see, then, that one morpheme may have different phonetic forms or allomorphs. We have also seen that more than one morpheme may occur in the language with the same meaning but in different forms — such as *in-*, *un-*, and *not* (all meaning "not"). It is not possible to predict which of these forms will occur, so they are separate, synonymous morphemes. It is only when the phonetic form is predictable by general rule that we find different phonetic forms of a single morpheme.

Allomorphy in Other Languages

English is not the only language that has morphemes that are pronounced differently in different phonological environments. Allomorphy exists in most languages and can be described by rules similar to the ones we have written for English. For example, the negative morpheme in the West African language Akan also has three nasal allomorphs: [m] before /p/, [n] before /t/, and [ŋ] before /k/, as is shown in the following cases:

mɪ pɛ	"I like"	mɪ mpɛ	"I don't like"
mɪ tɪ	"I speak"	mɪ ntɪ	"I don't speak"
mɪ kɔ	"I go"	mɪ ŋkɔ	"I don't go"

The rule that describes this case of allomorphy is the same as the one for the English *in-* prefix:

Change the place of articulation of a nasal consonant so that it agrees with the place feature value of a following consonant.

In other words, nasal consonants agree in place of articulation with a following consonant.

The Native American language Ojibwa offers a different example of allomorphy. The following data come from a discussion of Ojibwa by Jonathan Kaye (1981).* Examine the words and see if you can discover the allomorphy pattern before reading further. (The diacritic symbol ː that appears after *i, a,* and *e* indicates a longer version of the vowel. It has no bearing on the point of this particular example. Also, ignore the deletion of the final, short vowel in the second column of the Ojibwa words.)

anokkiː	"she works"	nitanokkiː	"I work"
aːkkosi	"she is sick"	nitaːkkos	"I am sick"
maːcaː	"she leaves"	nimaːcaː	"I leave"
takoššin	"she arrives"	nitakoššin	"I arrive"
ayeːkkosi	"she is tired"	kitayeːkkos	"you are tired"
ineːntam	"she thinks"	kitineːntam	"you think"
pakiso	"she swims"	kipakis	"you swim"
wiːsini	"she eats"	kiwiːsin	"you eat"

Both the prefix that means "I" and the prefix that means "you" have two allomorphs. These prefixes end in the consonant [t] when they are added to stems that begin in vowels, as in [nit+anokkiː], where the stem is [anokkiː], and [kit+ayeːkkos], where the stem is [ayeːkkosi]. But the [t] does not appear when the prefixes are added to stems that begin in consonants, as in [ni+maːcaː], where the stem is [maːcaː], and [ki+pakis], where the stem is [pakis]. If we assume that the two prefixes are basically /nit/ and /kit/, then we can write a rule that deletes the final consonant of the prefixes in this environment:

Delete a consonant before another consonant.

Descriptions of Ojibwa report that this rule is morphophonemic (i.e., applies only to particular morphemes). Can you see several examples in the data that suggest that this is the case?

---

*Jonathan Kaye. 1981. Chapter 8 in C. Baker and John McCarthy, Eds. *The Logical Problem of Language Acquisition.* Cambridge, MA: MIT Press. Reprinted by permission of MIT Press.

Prosodic Phonology

Syllable Structure

Words are composed of one or more syllables. A **syllable** is a phonological unit that is composed of one or more phonemes. Every syllable has a **nucleus**, usually a vowel (but it may be a syllabic liquid or nasal). The nucleus may be preceded by one or more phonemes, called the syllable **onset**, and followed by one or more segments, called the syllable **coda**. At an early age, children learn that certain words rhyme. In rhyming words, the nucleus and the coda of the final syllable are identical, as in the following jingle:

> Jack and **J**i**ll**
> Went up the h**ill**
> To fetch a pail of water.
> Jack fell d**own**
> And broke his cr**own**
> And Jill came tumbling after.

For this reason, the nucleus + coda constitute the subsyllabic unit called a **rime**. A syllable thus has a hierarchical structure. Using the Greek letter *sigma* (σ) as the symbol for the phonological unit *syllable*, we can show the hierarchical structure of the monosyllabic word *splints*:

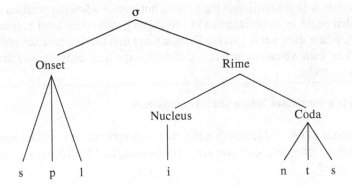

Word Stress

In English and many other languages, one or more of the syllables in each content word (words other than function words like *to, the, a, of,* and so on) are stressed. A stressed syllable, which can be marked by an acute accent (ˊ), is perceived as more prominent than unstressed syllables in the following examples:

pérvert	(noun)	as in	My neighbour is a pervert.
pervért	(verb)	as in	Don't pervert the idea.
súbject	(noun)	as in	Let's change the subject.
subjéct	(verb)	as in	He'll subject us to criticism.

These minimal pairs show that stress is contrastive in English; it distinguishes between nouns and verbs.

In some words, more than one vowel is stressed, but if so then one of these stressed vowels receives greater stress than the others. We have indicated the most highly stressed vowel by an acute accent over the vowel (we say this vowel receives the **accent**, or *primary* **stress**, or *main* stress); the other stressed vowels are indicated by marking a grave accent (`) over the vowels (these vowels receive secondary stress):

rèsignátion	lìnguístics	sỳstemátic
fùndaméntal	ìntrodúctory	rèvolútion

Generally, speakers of a language know which syllable receives primary stress or accent, which receives secondary stress, and which syllables are not stressed at all; it is part of their knowledge of the language.

The stress pattern of a word may differ from dialect to dialect. For example, in most varieties of North American English, the word *láboratòry* has two stressed syllables; in one dialect of British English, it receives only one stress [ləbɔ́rətri]. Because the vowel qualities in English are closely related to whether they are stressed or not, the British vowels differ from the North American vowels in this word; in fact, in the British version, the fourth vowel "drops out" completely because it is not stressed.

Just as stressed syllables in poetry reveal the metrical structure of the verse, so too phonological stress patterns relate to the metrical structure of a language.

There are a number of ways used to represent stress. Above we have used acúte accent marks for primary stress and gràve accent marks for secondary stress. We can also specify which syllable in the word is stressed by marking the syllable **s** if strongly stressed, **w** if weakly stressed, and leaving it unmarked if unstressed:

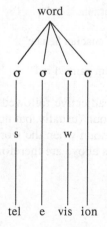
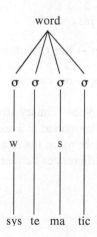

Stress is also sometimes shown by placing a 1 over the primary stressed syllable, placing a 2 over the secondary stressed syllable, and leaving the unstressed vowels unmarked:

2   1   2   1   1   2
fundamental   introductory   secondary

Stress is a property of a syllable rather than a segment, so it is a prosodic or suprasegmental feature.

To produce a stressed syllable, one may change the pitch (usually by raising it), make the syllable louder, or make it longer. We often use all three of these phonetic means to stress a syllable.

Sentence and Phrase Stress

When words are combined into phrases and sentences, one of the syllables receives greater stress than all others. That is, just as there is only one primary stress in a word spoken in isolation (e.g., in a list), so too only one of the vowels in a phrase (or sentence) receives primary stress or accent; all the other stressed vowels are "reduced" to secondary stress. A syllable that receives the main stress when the word is not in a phrase may have only secondary stress in a phrase:

1 1 1 2 tight + rope → tightrope	("a rope for acrobatics")
1 1 2 1 tight + rope → tight rope	("a rope drawn taut")
1 1 1 2 hot + dog → hotdog	("frankfurter")
1 1 2 1 hot + dog → hot dog	("an overheated dog")
1 1 1 2 red + coat → Redcoat	("a British soldier")
1 1 2 1 red + coat → red coat	("a coat that is red")
1 1 1 2 red + chamber → Red Chamber	("the Canadian Senate")
1 1 2 1 red + chamber → red chamber	("a room painted red")

In English, we place primary stress on an adjective followed by a noun when the two words are combined in a compound noun (usually, but not always, written as one word), but we place the stress on the noun when the words are not joined in this way. The differences between the pairs above are therefore predictable:

Compound Noun	Adjective + Noun
tightrope	tight rope
hotdog	hot dog
Redcoat	red coat
Red Chamber	red chamber

These pairs show that stress may be predictable from the morphology and syntax. The phonology interacts with the other components of the grammar. The stress differences between the noun and the verb pairs (*subject* as noun or verb) discussed in the previous section are also predictable from the *syntactic* word category.

Intonation

B.C. by permission of Johnny Hart and Creators Syndicate, Inc.

In Chapter 5, we discussed the use of pitch as a phonetic feature in reference to tone languages and intonation languages. In this chapter, we have discussed the use of phonetic features to distinguish meaning. We can now see that pitch can be a phonemic feature in languages such as Chinese, Thai, and Akan. Such relative pitches are referred to phonologically as **contrasting tones**. We also pointed out that there are languages that are not tone languages, such as English. Pitch may still play an important role in these languages. It is the **pitch contour** or **intonation** of the phrase or sentence that is important.

In English, intonation contours may reflect syntactic or semantic differences. If we say *John is going* with a falling pitch at the end, it is a statement; but if the pitch rises at the end, it is interpreted as a question.

Similarly, *What's in the tea, honey?* may, depending on intonation, be a query to someone called "honey" regarding the contents of the tea (falling intonation on *honey*), or may be a query regarding whether the tea contains honey (rising intonation on *honey*).

A sentence that is ambiguous in writing may be unambiguous when spoken due to differences in the pitch contour, as we saw in the previous paragraph. Here is a somewhat more subtle example. Written, sentence 1 is unclear as to whether Tristram intended for Isolde to read and follow directions, or merely to follow him:

1.   Tristram left directions for Isolde to follow.

Spoken, if Tristram wanted Isolde to follow him, the sentence would be pronounced with a rise in pitch on the first syllable of *follow,* followed by a fall in pitch, as indicated (oversimplistically) in sentence 2.

2.   Tristram left directions for Isolde to follow.

In this pronunciation of the sentence, the primary stress is on the word *follow.*

If the meaning is to read and follow a set of directions, the highest pitch comes on the second syllable of *directions,* as illustrated, also oversimplistically, in sentence 3.

3.   Tristram left directions for Isolde to follow .

The primary stress in this pronunciation is on the word *directions.*

The way we have indicated pitch ignores much detail. Before the big rise in pitch the voice does not remain on the same monotone low pitch. These pitch diagrams merely indicate when there is a special change in pitch.

Pitch plays an important role in both tone languages and intonation languages, but in different ways, depending on the phonological system of the respective languages.

Sequential Constraints

Suppose you were given four cards, each of which had a different phoneme of English printed on it:

If you were asked to arrange these cards to form all the "possible" words that

| k | b | l | I |

these four phonemes could form, you might order them as follows:

```
b   l   ɪ   k
k   l   ɪ   b
b   ɪ   l   k
k   ɪ   l   b
```

These arrangements are the only permissible ones for these phonemes in English. */lbkɪ/, */ɪlbk/, */bkɪl/, and */ɪlkb/ are not possible words in the language. Although /blɪk/ and /klɪb/ are not existing words (you will not find them in a dictionary), if you heard someone say

"I just bought a beautiful new *blick*."

you might ask "What's a 'blick'?" If you heard someone say

"I just bought a beautiful new *bkli*."

you would probably reply "What did you say?"

Your knowledge of English "tells" you that certain strings of phonemes are permissible and that others are not. After a consonant such as /b/, /g/, /k/, or /p/, another stop consonant is not permitted by the rules of the grammar. If a word begins with an /l/ or an /r/, every speaker "knows" that the next segment must be a vowel. That is why */lbɪk/ does not sound like an English word. It violates the restrictions on the sequencing of phonemes.

Other such constraints exist in English. If the initial sounds of *chill* or *Jill* begin a word, then the next sound must be a vowel. /čat/ or /čon/ or /čæk/ are possible words in English, as are /ǰæl/ or /ǰot/ or /ǰalɪk/, but */člit/ and */ǰpurz/ are not. No more than three sequential consonants can occur at the beginning of a word, and these three are restricted to /s/ + /p, t, k/ + /l, r, w, j/. There are even restrictions if this condition is met. For example, /stl/ is not a permitted sequence, so *stlick* is not a possible word in English, but *strick* is.

Other languages have different sequential restrictions. In Polish, *zl* is a permissible combination, as in *zloty*, a unit of currency. Croatian permits words like the name *Mladen*. Japanese has severe constraints on what may begin a syllable; most combinations of consonants (e.g., /br/, /spl/) are not permitted.

The constraints on sequences of segments are called **phonotactic constraints** or simply the phonotactics of the language. Phonotactic constraints have as their basis the syllable, rather than the word. That is, only the clusters that can begin a syllable can begin a word, and only a cluster that can end a syllable can end a word.

Medially in a multisyllabic word, the clusters consist of syllable-final + syllable-initial sequences. Words such as *instruct* /ɪnstrʌkt/, with the medial cluster /nstr/, or *explicit* /ɛksplɪsɪt/, with the medial cluster /kspl/, can be divided into well-formed syllables /ɪn $ strʌkt/ and /ɛk $ splɪs $ ɪt/ (using $ to symbolize a syllable boundary). We, as speakers of English, know that "constluct" is not a possible word because the second syllable starts with a nonpermissible sequence /stl/ or /tl/. Syllables, then, are important phonological units.

In the language Asante Twi, a word may end only in a vowel or a nasal consonant. /pik/ is not a possible Twi word, because it breaks the sequential rules of the language, and /mba/ ("not come" in Twi) is not a possible word in English for similar reasons, although it is a word in Twi.

All languages have constraints on the permitted sequences of phonemes, though different languages have different constraints. Just as spoken language has sequences of sounds that are not permitted in the language, so, too, sign languages have forbidden combinations of features. They differ from one sign language to another, just as the constraints on sounds and sound sequences differ from one spoken language to another. A permissible sign in a Chinese sign language may not be a permissible sign in ASL and vice versa. Children learn these constraints when they learn the spoken or signed language, just as they learn what the phonemes are and how they are related to phonetic segments.

Lexical Gaps

Although *bot* [bɑt] and *crake* [krek] are not words for some speakers, and [bʊt] (to rhyme with *put*), *creck* [krɛk], *cruke* [kruk], *cruk* [krʌk], and *crike* [krajk] are not now words in English, they are "possible words." That is, they are strings of sounds, all of which represent phonemes, in sequences that are permissible in English in that they obey the phonotactic constraints of the language. We might say that they are **nonsense words** (permissible forms with no meanings) or possible words.

Advertisers constantly use possible but nonoccurring words for the names of new products. We would hardly expect a new product to come on the market with the name [xik], because [x] (the voiceless velar fricative) is not a phoneme in English. Nor would a new soap be called *Zhleet* [žlit], because in English the voiced palatal fricative [ž] cannot occur initially before a liquid. Possible but nonoccurring words such as *Bic* [bɪk], before it was coined as a brand name, are **accidental gaps** in the vocabulary. An accidental gap is a form that conforms to all the phonological rules of the language but has no meaning. An occurring word is a combination of both a permitted form and a meaning.

Phonological Analysis: Discovering Phonemes

No one has to teach us, as children, how to discover the phonemes of our language. We do it unconsciously and at an early age know what they are. Before reading this book, or learning anything about phonology, you knew an *l* sound was part of the English sound system, a phoneme in English, because it contrasts words such as *leaf* and *reef*. But you probably did not know that the *l* in *leaf* and the one in *feel* are two different sounds. There is only one /l/ phoneme in English but more than one *l* phone. The /l/ that occurs before back vowels and at the end of words is produced not only as a lateral but also with the back of the tongue raised toward the velum, and it is therefore a *velarized l*. (Without more training in phonetics, you may not hear the difference; try to sense the difference in your tongue position when you say *leaf, lint, lay*, and *let* as opposed to *lude, load, lot, deal, dill, dell*, and *doll*.)

The linguist from Mars, referred to in Chapter 2, who is trying to write a grammar of English, would have to decide whether the two *l* sounds observed in English words represent separate phonemes or are allophones of a single phoneme. How can this be done? How would any phonologist determine what the phonological system of a language is?

To do a phonemic analysis, we must transcribe the words to be analyzed in great phonetic detail since we don't know in advance which phonetic features are distinctive and which are not.

Consider the following Finnish words:

1.	[kudot] "failures"	5.	[madon] "of a worm"
2.	[kate] "cover"	6.	[maton] "of a rug"
3.	[katot] "roofs"	7.	[ratas] "wheel"
4.	[kade] "envious"	8.	[radon] "of a track"

Given these words, do the voiceless/voiced alveolar stops [t] and [d] represent different phonemes, or are they allophones of the same phone?

Here are a few hints as to how a phonologist might proceed:

(1) Check to see if there are any minimal pairs.

(2) 2 and 4 are minimal pairs: [kate] "cover" and [kade] "envious"; 5 and 6 are minimal pairs: [madon] "of a worm" and [maton] "of a rug."

(3) [t] and [d] in Finnish thus represent the distinct phonemes /t/ and /d/.

That was an easy problem. Now consider the data from Greek, concentrating on the following sounds:

[x] voiceless velar fricative
[k] voiceless velar stop
[c] voiceless palatal stop
[ç] voiceless palatal fricative

1.	[kano] "do"	9.	[çeri] "hand"
2.	[xano] "lose"	10.	[kori] "daughter"
3.	[çino] "pour"	11.	[xori] "dances"
4.	[cino] "move"	12.	[xrima] "money"
5.	[kali] "charms"	13.	[krima] "shame"
6.	[xali] "plight"	14.	[xufta] "handful"
7.	[çeli] "eel"	15.	[kufeta] "bonbons"
8.	[ceri] "candle"	16.	[oçi] "no"

To determine the status of [x], [k], [c], and [ç], you should answer the following questions.

(1) Are there any minimal pairs in which these sounds contrast?

(2) Are any noncontrastive sounds in complementary distribution?

(3) If noncontrasting phones are found, what are the phonemes and their allophones?

(4) What are the phonological rules by which the allophones can be derived?

The answers to these four questions follow:

(1) By analyzing the data, we find that [k] and [x] contrast in a number of minimal pairs, for example, in [kano] and [xano]. [k] and [x] are therefore distinctive. [ç] and [c] also contrast in [çino] and [cino] and are therefore distinctive. But what about the velar fricative [x] and the palatal fricative [ç]? And the velar stop [k] and the palatal stop [c]?

We can find no minimal pairs that would conclusively show that these represent separate phonemes.

(2) We now proceed to answer the second question: Are these noncontrasting phones in complementary distribution?

One way to see if sounds are in complementary distribution is to list each phone with the environment in which it is found:

Phone	Environment
[k]	before [a], [o], [u], [r]
[x]	before [a], [o], [u], [r]
[c]	before [i], [e]
[ç]	before [i], [e]

We see that [k] and [x] are not in complementary distribution; they both occur before back vowels. Nor are [c] and [ç] in complementary distribution. They both occur before front vowels. But the stops [k] and [c] are in complementary distribution; [k] occurs before back vowels and [r] and never before front vowels. [c] occurs only before front vowels and never before back vowels or [r]. Similarly, [x] and [ç] are in complementary distribution for the same reason. We therefore conclude that [k] and [c] are allophones of one phoneme and that the fricatives [x] and [ç] are allophones of one phoneme. The pairs of allophones also fulfil the criterion of *phonetic similarity*. The first two are [–anterior] stops; the second two are [–anterior] fricatives. (This similarity discourages us from pairing [k] with [f] and [c] with [x], which are less similar to each other.)

(3) Which of the phone pairs are more basic, and hence the ones whose features would define the phonemes? When two allophones can be derived from one phoneme, one selects as the underlying segment the allophone that makes the rules and the phonemic feature matrix as simple as possible. For example, deriving English unaspirated and aspirated voiceless stops from an underlying /p/ makes aspiration redundant and unnecessary as a feature value. If /pʰ/ were the phoneme, then the features would be more complex.

For the velar and palatal stops and fricatives in Greek, the rules appear to be equal in simplicity. However, in addition to adhering to the simplicity criterion, phonologists attempt to state rules that have natural phonetic explanations. Often these rules turn out to be the simplest solutions. In many languages, velar sounds become palatal before front vowels. This is an assimilation rule; palatal sounds are produced toward the front of the mouth, as are front vowels. Thus, we select /k/ as a phoneme with the allophones [k] and [c], and /x/ as a phoneme with the allophones [x] and [ç].

(4) We can now state the rule by which the palatals can be derived from the velars:

Palatalize velar consonants before front vowels.

Using feature notation, we can state the rule as

[+velar] → [+palatal] /___ [−back]

Since only consonants are marked for the feature [velar] and only vowels for the feature [back], it is not necessary to include the feature [consonantal] or [syllabic] in the rule or any other features that are not required to define the segments to which the rule applies, the change that occurs, or the segments in the environment in which the rule applies. The simplicity criterion constrains us to state the rule as simply as we can.

The flowchart in Figure 6.1 may help you visualize this process.

FIGURE 6.1

Phonological analysis flowchart

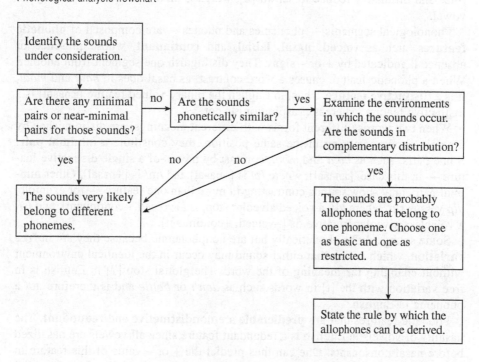

Summary

Part of one's knowledge of a language is knowledge of the **phonology** or sound system of that language — the inventory of **phones**, the phonetic segments that occur in the language, and the ways in which they pattern. It is this patterning that determines the inventory of **phonemes** — the segments that differentiate words.

Phonetic segments are enclosed in square brackets, [ ], and phonemes are enclosed between slashes, / /. When phones occur in **complementary distribution**, they are **allophones** — predictable phonetic variants — of phonemes.

For example, in English aspirated voiceless stops, such as the initial sounds in the words *pill, till,* and *kill,* are in complementary distribution (never occur in the same phonological environment) as the unaspirated voiceless stops following the *s* /s/ in *spill, still,* and *skill*; thus, the aspirated *p, t,* and *k* ([p^h], [t^h], [k^h]) and the unaspirated [p], [t], and [k] are allophones of the phonemes /p/, /t/, and /k/, respectively. On the other hand, phones that occur in the same environment and that differentiate words, such as the [b] and [m] in *boat* [bot] and *moat* [mot], represent two distinct phonemes, /b/ and /m/.

Some phones may be allophones of more than one phoneme. There is no one-to-one correspondence between the phonemes of a language and their allophones. In English, for example, stressed vowels become unstressed according to regular rules and ultimately reduce to schwa [ə], which is an allophone of each English vowel.

Phonological segments — phonemes and phones — are composed of **phonetic features** such as **voiced, nasal, labial,** and **continuant,** whose presence or absence is indicated by + or − signs. They distinguish one segment from another. When a phonetic feature causes a word contrast, as nasal does in *boat* and *moat,* it is a **distinctive feature.** Thus, in English the binary-valued feature [±nasal] is a distinctive feature, whereas [±aspiration] is not.

When two words (different forms with different meanings) are distinguished by a single phone occurring in the same position, they constitute a **minimal pair.** Some pairs, such as *boat* and *moat,* contrast by means of a single distinctive feature — in this case, [±nasal], where /b/ is [−nasal] and /m/ is [+nasal]. Other minimal pairs may show sounds contrasting in more than one feature — for example, *dip* versus *sip,* where /d/, a voiced alveolar stop, is [+voiced, −continuant], and /s/, a voiceless alveolar fricative, is [−voiced, +continuant].

Some sounds differ phonetically but are nonphonemic because they are in **free variation,** which means that either sound may occur in the identical environment without changing the meaning of the word. The glottal stop [ʔ] in English is in free variation with the [t] in words such as *don't* or *bottle* and is therefore not a phoneme in English.

Phonetic features that are **predictable** are **nondistinctive** and **redundant.** The nasality of vowels in English is a redundant feature since all vowels are nasalized before nasal consonants. One can thus predict the + or − value of this feature in vowels. A feature may therefore be distinctive in one class of sounds and nondistinctive in another. Nasality is distinctive for English consonants and nondistinctive predictable for English vowels.

Phonetic features that are nondistinctive in one language may be distinctive in another. Aspiration is distinctive in Thai and nondistinctive in English; both aspirated voiceless stops and unaspirated voiceless stops are phonemes in Thai.

The phonology of a language also includes constraints on the sequences of phonemes in the language, as exemplified by the fact that in English two stop consonants may not occur together at the beginning of a word; similarly, the final sound of the word *sing,* the velar nasal, never occurs word initially. These sequential constraints determine what are *possible* but nonoccurring words in a language and what phonetic strings are "impossible" or "illegal." For example, *blick* [blɪk] is not now an English word, but it could become one, whereas *kbli* [kbli] or *ngos* [ŋos] could not. These possible but nonoccurring words constitute **accidental gaps**.

Words in some languages may also be phonemically distinguished by **prosodic** or **suprasegmental features**, such as **pitch**, **stress**, and segment duration or **length**. Languages in which syllables or words are contrasted by pitch are called **tone** languages. **Intonation** languages may use pitch variations to distinguish meanings of phrases and sentences.

In English, words and phrases may be differentiated by stress, as in the contrast between the noun *pérvert*, in which the first syllable is stressed, and the verb *pervért*, in which the final syllable is stressed. In the compound noun *hótdog* versus the adjective + noun phrase *hot dóg*, the former is stressed on *hot*, the latter on *dog*.

Vowel **length** and consonant **length** may be phonemic features. Both are contrastive in Japanese, Finnish, Italian, and many other languages.

The relationship between the **phonemic representation** of words and sentences and the phonetic representation (the pronunciation of these words and sentences) is determined by general **phonological rules**.

Phonological rules in a grammar apply to phonemic strings and alter them in various ways to derive their phonetic pronunciation:

1. They may be **assimilation rules** that change feature values of segments, thus spreading phonetic properties. The rule that nasalizes vowels in English before nasal consonants is such a rule.
2. They may be **dissimilation rules** that change feature values to make two phonemes in a string more dissimilar, as in the Latin liquid rule.
3. They may *add* **nondistinctive features** that are predictable from the context. The rule that aspirates voiceless stops at the beginning of words and syllables in English is such a rule.
4. They may *insert* segments that are not present in the phonemic string. Insertion is also called **epenthesis**. The rule in Spanish that inserts an [e] before word-initial /s/ consonant clusters is an example of an addition or insertion rule.
5. They may *delete* phonemic segments in certain contexts. Contraction rules in English are **deletion** rules.
6. They may *transpose* or move segments in a string. These **metathesis** rules occur in many languages, including Hebrew. The rule in certain North American dialects that changes an /sk/ to [ks] in final position is also a metathesis rule.

Phonological rules often refer to entire classes of sounds rather than to individual sounds. These are **natural classes**, characterized by the phonetic features that pertain to all the members of each class, such as voiced sounds, or, using +'s and −'s, the class specified as [+voiced]. A natural class can be defined by fewer features than are required to distinguish a member of that class. Natural classes reflect the ways in which we articulate sounds or, in some cases, the acoustic characteristics of sounds. Such classes, therefore, do not have to be learned in the same way as groups of sounds that are not phonetically similar. Natural classes provide explanations for the occurrence of many phonological rules.

In the writing of rules, linguists use formal notations, which often reveal linguistic generalizations of phonological processes.

A morpheme may have different phonetic representations, which are determined by the **morphophonemic** and phonological rules of the language. Thus, the regular plural morpheme is phonetically [z] or [s] or [əz], depending on the final phoneme of the noun to which it is attached.

There is a methodology that linguists (or students of linguistics) can use to discover the phonemes of a language, such as looking for minimal pairs and for sounds that are in complementary distribution. The feature matrix of the allophone of a phoneme that results in the simplest statement of the phonological rules is selected as the underlying phoneme from which all the phonetic allophones are derived.

The phonological and morphophonemic rules in a language show that the phonemic shape of words or phrases is not identical to their phonetic form. The phonemes are not the actual phonetic sounds but are abstract mental constructs that are realized as sounds by the operation of rules such as those described in this chapter. No one is taught these rules, yet everyone knows them subconsciously.

Exercises

All the data in languages other than English are given in phonetic transcription without square brackets unless otherwise stated. The phonetic transcriptions of English words are given within square brackets.

1. The following sets of minimal pairs show that English /p/ and /b/ contrast in initial, medial, and final positions.

Initial	Medial	Final
pit/bit	rapid/rabid	cap/cab

   Find similar sets of minimal pairs for each pair of consonants given:

a. /k/–/g/	d. /b/–/v/	g. /s/–/š/
b. /m/–/n/	e. /b/–/m/	h. /č/–/ǰ/
c. /l/–/r/	f. /p/–/f/	i. /s/–/z/

2. Cree (Plains Cree) is an Aboriginal Canadian language of the Algonquian family.

   Consider the distribution of [p] and [b] in Cree in the following words.

The colon (:) following a vowel indicates a long vowel; however, vowel length should not affect your solution to the problem.

pahki	"partly"
ni:sosa:p	"twelve"
ta:nispi:	"when"
paskwa:w	"prairie"
asaba:p	"thread"
wa:bame:w	"he sees him"
na:be:w	"man"
a:bihta:w	"half"
nibimohta:n	"I walk"
si:si:bak	"ducks"

Are [p] and [b] allophones of one or two phonemes?

a. Do they occur in any minimal pairs?
b. Are they in complementary distribution?
c. In what environments does each occur?
d. If you conclude that they are allophones of one phoneme, state the rule that can derive the phonetic allophonic forms.

* **3.** Consider the distribution of [r] and [l] in Korean in the following words:

rupi	"ruby"	mul	"water"
kiri	"road"	pal	"big"
saram	"person"	səul	"Seoul"
irɯmi*	"name"	ilkop	"seven"
ratio	"radio"	ipalsa	"barber"

Are [r] and [l] allophones of one or two phonemes?

a. Do they occur in any minimal pairs?
b. Are they in complementary distribution?
c. In what environments does each occur?
d. If you conclude that they are allophones of one phoneme, state the rule that can derive the phonetic allophonic forms.

4. Here are some additional data from Korean:

son	"hand"	šihap	"game"
sɔm	"sack"	šilsu	"mistake"
sosəl	"novel"	šipsam	"thirteen"
sɛk	"colour"	šinho	"signal"
us	"upper"	maši	"delicious"

Are [s] and [š] allophones of the same phoneme or is each an allophone of a separate phoneme?

*[ɯ] is a high back unrounded vowel. It does not affect your analysis in this problem.

There are no minimal pairs that will help to answer this question. Determine, instead, whether they are in complementary distribution. If they are, state their distribution. If they are not in complementary distribution, state the contrasting environments.

*5. In Southern Kongo, a Bantu language spoken in Angola, the nonpalatal segments [t, s, z] are in complementary distribution with their palatal counterparts [č, š, ž], as shown in the following words:

tobola	"to bore a hole"	čina	"to cut"
tanu	"five"	čiba	"banana"
kesoka	"to be cut"	nkoši	"lion"
kasu	"emaciation"	nselele	"termite"
kunezulu	"heaven"	ažimola	"alms"
nzwetu	"our"	lolonži	"to wash house"
zevo	"then"	zenga	"to cut"
žima	"to stretch"		

a. State the distribution of each pair of segments given below. (Assume that the nonoccurrence of [t] before [e] is an accidental gap.)

Example: [t]–[č]: [t] occurs before the back vowels [o, a, u]; [č] occurs before [i].

[s]–[š]

[z]–[ž]

b. Using the criteria of simplicity and naturalness discussed in the chapter, state which phones should be used as the basic phoneme for each pair of nonpalatal and palatal segments in Southern Kongo.

c. Using the rules stated in the chapter as examples (phonological rules for Southern Kongo were not given), state in your own words the *one* phonological rule that will derive all the phonetic segments from the phonemes. Do not state a separate rule for each phoneme; state only a general rule for all three phonemes you listed in b. Try to give a formal statement of your rule.

6. As discussed in this chapter, different vowels occur in certain diphthongs in some dialects of English, in particular, in Canadian English. The following words have different vowels, as is shown by the phonetic transcriptions.

A		B		C	
bite	[bʌjt]	bide	[bajd]	die	[daj]
rice	[rʌjs]	rise	[rajz]	by	[baj]
ripe	[rʌjp]	bribe	[brajb]	sigh	[saj]
wife	[wʌjf]	wives	[wajvz]	rye	[raj]
dike	[dʌjk]	dime	[dãjm]	guy	[gaj]
		nine	[nãjn]		

rile	[rajl]
dire	[dajr]
writhe	[rajð]

a. How may the classes of sounds that end the words in columns A and B be characterized? That is, what feature specifies all the final segments in A and all the final segments in B?

b. How do the words in column C differ from those in columns A and B?

c. Are [ʌj] and [aj] in complementary distribution? Give your reasons.

d. If [ʌj] and [aj] are allophones of one phoneme, should they be derived from /ʌj/ or /aj/? Why?

e. Give the phonetic representations of the following words as they would be spoken in the dialect described here:
   life _____ lives _____ lie _____
   file _____ bike _____ lice _____

f. Formulate a rule that will relate the phonemic representations to the phonetic representations of the words given above.

7. Pairs such as *top* and *chop, dunk* and *junk*, and *so* and *show* reveal that /t/ and /č/, /d/ and /ǰ/, and /s/ and /š/ are distinct phonemes in English. Although it is difficult to find a minimal pair to distinguish /z/ and /ž/, they occur in similar if not identical environments, such as *razor* and *azure*. Consider the same pairs of nonpalatalized and palatalized consonants in the following data. (The palatal forms are optional forms that often occur in casual speech.)

Nonpalatalized		Palatalized	
[hɪt mi]	"hit me"	[hɪč ju]	"hit you"
[lid hĩm]	"lead him"	[liǰ ju]	"lead you"
[pʰæs ʌs]	"pass us"	[pʰæš ju]	"pass you"
[luz ðẽm]	"lose them"	[luž ju]	"lose you"

State the rule that specifies when /t/, /d/, /s/, and /z/ become palatalized as [č], [ǰ], [š], and [ž]. Use feature notations to reveal generalizations.

8. Here are some words in Japanese. [č] is the voiceless palatal affricate that occurs in the English word *church*. [ts] is an alveolar affricate that does not occur in English as a single sound but is pronounced as the final sound(s) in *cats*. Japanese words (except for certain loan words) never contain the phonetic sequences *[ti] or *[tu].

tatami	"mat"	tomodači	"friend"	uči	"house"
tegami	"letter"	totemo	"very"	otoko	"male"
čiči	"father"	tsukue	"desk"	tetsudau	"help"
šita	"under"	ato	"later"	matsu	"wait"
natsu	"summer"	tsutsumu	"wrap"	čizu	"map"
kata	"person"	tatemono	"building"	te	"hand"

Consider [č] and [ts] to be a single phone.

a. Based on these data, are [t], [č], and [ts] in complementary distribution?
b. State the distribution, first in words, then using features, of these phones.
c. Give a phonemic analysis of these data insofar as [t], [č], and [ts] are concerned. That is, identify the phonemes and the allophones.
d. Give the phonemic representation of the phonetically transcribed Japanese words given below. Assume phonemic and phonetic representations are the same except for [t], [č], and [ts].

tatami _____	tsukue _____	tsutsumu _____
tomodači _____	tetsudau _____	čizu _____
uči _____	šita _____	kata _____
tɛgami _____	ato _____	koto _____
totemo _____	matsu _____	tatemono _____
otoko _____	deguši _____	te _____
hiči _____	natsu _____	tsuri _____

*9. Consider the following English verbs. Those in column A have stress on the next-to-last syllable (called the *penultimate syllable* or *penult*), whereas the verbs in columns B and C have the last syllable stressed.

A	B	C
astónish	collápse	amáze
éxit	exíst	impróve
imágine	resént	equáte
cáncel	revólt	careén
elícit	adópt	recáll
práctise	insíst	atóne

a. Transcribe the words under columns A, B, and C phonemically. (Use a schwa for the unstressed vowels even if they can be derived from different phonemic vowels. This should make it easier for you.)

Examples: *astonish* /əstanɪš/   *collapse* /kəlæps/   *aflame* /əflem/

b. Consider the phonemic structure of the stressed syllables in these verbs. What is the difference between the final syllables of the verbs in columns A and B? Formulate a rule that predicts where stress occurs in the verbs in columns A and B.
c. In the verbs in column C, stress also occurs on the final syllable. What must you add to the rule to account for this fact? (*Hint:* For the forms in columns A and B, consider the final consonants; for the forms in column C, consider the vowels.)

10. Below are listed the phonetic transcriptions of ten "words." Some are English words, some are not words now but are possible words or nonsense words, and others are definitely "foreign" (they violate English sequential constraints).

Write the English words in regular spelling. Mark the other words "possible" or "foreign." For each word you mark as "foreign," state your reason.

Word	Possible	"Foreign"	Reason
Example:			
[θrot]	throat		
[slig]	X		
[lsig]		X	No English word can begin with a liquid followed by an obstruent.

a.	[pʰril]	e.	[gnostɪk]	i.	[ŋar]
b.	[skrič]	f.	[jūnəkɔrn]	j.	[æpəpʰlɛksi]
c.	[know]	g.	[fruit]		
d.	[maj]	h.	[blaft]		

*11. The following words are found in Paku, a language spoken by the Pakuni in the NBC television series *Land of the Lost*. (The language was created by V. Fromkin.) V́ = [+stress]

(i)	ótu	"evil" (N)		(viii)	mpósa	"hairless"
(ii)	túsa	"evil" (Adj)		(ix)	ámpo	"hairless one"
(iii)	etógo	"cactus" (sg)		(x)	āmpőni	"hairless ones"
(iv)	etogőni	"cactus" (pl)		(xi)	ámi	"mother"
(v)	Páku	"Paku" (sg)		(xii)	āmîni	"mothers"
(vi)	Pakűni	"Paku" (pl)		(xiii)	áda	"father"
(vii)	épo	"hair"		(xiv)	adắni	"fathers"

a. Is stress predictable? If so, what is the rule?

b. Is nasalization a distinctive feature for vowels? Give the reasons for your answer.

*12. Consider these phonetic forms of Hebrew words:

[v]–[b]		[f]–[p]	
bika	"lamented"	litef	"stroked"
mugbal	"limited"	sefer	"book"
šavar	"broke" (masc.)	sataf	"washed"
šavra	"broke" (fem.)	para	"cow"
ʔikev	"delayed"	mitpaxat	"handkerchief"
bara	"created"	haʔalpim	"the Alps"

Assume that these words and their phonetic sequences are representative of what may occur in Hebrew. In your answers below, consider classes of sounds rather than individual sounds.

a. Are [b] and [v] allophones of one phoneme? Are they in complementary distribution? In what phonetic environments do they occur? Can you formulate a phonological rule stating their distribution?

b. Does the same rule, or lack of a rule, that describes the distribution of [b] and [v] apply to [p] and [f]? If not, why not?

c. Here is a word with one phone missing. A blank appears in place of the missing sound: hid____ik. Check the one correct statement.

(1) [b] but not [v] could occur in the empty slot.
(2) [v] but not [b] could occur in the empty slot.
(3) Either [b] or [v] could occur in the empty slot.
(4) Neither [b] nor [v] could occur in the empty slot.

d. Which one of the following statements is correct about the incomplete word ____ana?

(1) [f] but not [p] could occur in the empty slot.
(2) [p] but not [f] could occur in the empty slot.
(3) Either [p] or [f] could fill the blank.
(4) Neither [p] nor [f] could fill the blank.

e. Now consider the following possible words (in phonetic transcription):

laval   surva   labal   palar   falu   razif

If these words actually occurred in Hebrew, would they

(1) force you to revise the conclusions about the distribution of labial stops and fricatives you reached on the basis of the first group of words given above?
(2) support your original conclusions?
(3) neither support nor disprove your original conclusions?

*13. In the African language Maninka, the suffix -*li* has more than one pronunciation (like the -*ed* past-tense ending on English verbs, as in *reaped* [t], *robbed* [d], and *raided* [əd]). This suffix is similar to the derivational suffix -*ing*, which, when added to the verb *cook*, makes it a noun, as in "Her cooking was great," or the suffix -*ion*, which also derives a noun from a verb, as in *create* + *ion*, permitting "the creation of the word."

Consider these data from Maninka:

bugo	"hit"	bugoli	"hitting"
dila	"repair"	dilali	"repairing"
don	"come in"	donni	"coming in"
dumu	"eat"	dumuni	"eating"
gwen	"chase"	gwenni	"chasing"

a. What are the two forms of the "ing" morpheme?
b. Can you predict which phonetic form will occur? If so, state the rule.
c. What are the -*ing* forms for the following verbs?

da   "lie down"

      men   "hear"
      famu   "understand"
      sunogo   "sleep"

*14. Consider the following phonetic data from the Bantu language Luganda. (The data have been somewhat altered to make the problem easier.) In each line, the same root or stem morpheme occurs in both columns A and B, but it has one prefix in column A, meaning "a" or "an," and another prefix in column B, meaning "little."

A		B	
ẽnato	"a canoe"	akaato	"little canoe"
ẽnapo	"a house"	akaapo	"little house"
ẽnobi	"an animal"	akaoobi	"little animal"
ẽmpipi	"a kidney"	akapipi	"little kidney"
ẽŋkoosa	"a feather"	akakoosa	"little feather"
ẽmmããmmo	"a peg"	akabããmmo	"little peg"
ẽŋŋõõmme	"a horn"	akagõõmme	"little horn"
ẽnnĩmiro	"a garden"	akadĩmiro	"little garden"
ẽnugẽni	"a stranger"	akatabi	"little branch"

In answering the following questions, base your answers on only these forms. Assume that all the words in the language follow the regularities shown here.

    You may need to use scratch paper to work out your analysis before writing your answers. (*Hint:* The phonemic representation of the morpheme meaning "little" is /aka/.)

a.   Are nasal vowels in Luganda phonemic? Are they predictable?

b.   Is the phonemic representation of the morpheme meaning "garden" /dimiro/?

c.   What is the phonemic representation of the morpheme meaning "canoe"?

d.   Are [p] and [b] allophones of one phoneme?

e.   If /am/ represents a bound prefix morpheme in Luganda, can you conclude that [ãmdãno] is a possible phonetic form for a word in this language starting with this prefix?

f.   Is there a phonological homorganic nasal rule in Luganda?

g.   If the phonetic representation of the word meaning "little boy" is [aka poobe], give the phonemic and phonetic representations for "a boy."

h.   Which of the following forms is the *phonemic* representation for the prefix meaning "a" or "an"?

      (1) /en/   (2) /ẽn/   (3) /ẽm/   (4) /em/   (5) /eŋ/

i.   What is the *phonetic* representation of the word meaning "a branch"?

j.   What is the *phonemic* representation of the word meaning "little stranger"?

k.   State the three phonological rules revealed by the Luganda data.

References

Crystal, D. (1997). *The Cambridge encyclopedia of language* (2nd ed.). Cambridge, UK: Cambridge University Press.

Chambers, J.K. (1973). Canadian raising. *Canadian Journal of Linguistics, 18*, 113–315.

Joos, M. (1942). A phonological dilemma in Canadian English. *Language, 18*, 141–144.

Kaye, J. (1981). Comments. In C. Baker & J. McCarthy (Eds.), *The logical problem of language acquisition* (pp. 249–256). Cambridge, MA: MIT Press.

Sapir, E. (1933/1949). The psychological reality of phonemes. In D. Mandelbaum (Ed.), *Selected writings of Edward Sapir* (pp. 46–60). Berkeley and Los Angeles; University of California Press. (First published in French translation in *Journal de Psychologie, 30*, 247–265).

Schane, S. (1968). *French phonology and morphology.* Cambridge, MA: MIT Press.

Wells, J.C. (1982). *Accents of English* (Vol. 3). Cambridge, UK: Cambridge University Press.

Further Reading

Anderson, S.R. (1974). *The organization of phonology.* New York: Academic Press.

Anderson, S.R. (1985). *Phonology in the twentieth century: Theories of rules and theories of representations.* Chicago: University of Chicago Press.

Carr, P. (1993). *Phonology.* London: Macmillan.

Chomsky, N., & Halle, M. (1968). *The sound pattern of English.* New York: Harper & Row.

Clark, J., & Yallop, C. (1990). *An introduction to phonetics and phonology.* Oxford: Blackwell.

Clements, G.N., & Keyser, S.J. (1983). *CV phonology: A generative theory of the syllable.* Cambridge, MA: MIT Press.

de Lacy, P. (2007). *The Cambridge handbook of phonology.* New York: Cambridge University Press.

Dell, F. (1980). *Generative phonology.* London: Cambridge University Press.

Goldsmith, J.A. (1990). *Autosegmental and metrical phonology: A new synthesis.* Oxford: Blackwell.

Goldsmith, J. (Ed.). (1995). *The handbook of phonological theory.* Cambridge, MA: Blackwell.

Hale, M., & Reiss, C. (2008). *The phonological enterprise.* Oxford: Oxford University Press.

Hayes, B. (2008). *Introductory phonology.* Malden, MA: Wiley-Blackwell.

Hogg, R., & McCully, C.B. (1987). *Metrical phonology: A coursebook.* Cambridge, UK: Cambridge University Press.

Hyman, L.M. (1975). *Phonology: Theory and analysis.* New York: Holt, Rinehart & Winston.

Kenstowicz, M.J. (1995). *Phonology in generative grammar.* Oxford: Blackwell.

MacKay, I.R.A. (1987). *Phonetics: The science of speech production.* Toronto: Allyn & Bacon.

Odden, D. (2005). *Introducing phonology*. Cambridge, UK: Cambridge University Press.

van der Hulst, H., & Smith, N. (Eds). (1982). *The structure of phonological representations: Part 1*. Dordrecht, The Netherlands: Foris Publications.

Websites

http://www.linguistics.ucsb.edu/projects/featuresoftware/index.php A website created by the Department of Linguistics at the University of California, Santa Barbara, containing links and information on segmental phonology.

http://camba.ucsd.edu/blog/phonoloblog A blogsite for phonologists.

PART THREE
The Psychology and Biology of Language

The field of psycholinguistics, or the psychology of language, is concerned with discovering the psychological processes that make it possible for humans to acquire and use language.

Jean Berko Gleason and Nan Bernstein Ratner, *Psycholinguistics* (1998)

CHAPTER 7
First Language Acquisition

The acquisition of language "is doubtless the greatest intellectual feat any one of us is ever required to perform."

Leonard Bloomfield, *Language* (1933)

Language is a complex, specialized skill, which develops in the child spontaneously, without conscious effort or formal instruction, is deployed without awareness of its underlying logic, is qualitatively the same in every individual, and is distinct from more general abilities to process information or behave intelligently.

S. Pinker, *The Language Instinct* (1994)

The language each person acquires is a rich and complex construction hopelessly underdetermined by the fragmentary evidence available [to the child]. Nevertheless, individuals in a speech community have developed essentially the same language. This fact can be explained only on the assumption that these individuals employ highly restrictive principles that guide the construction of grammar.

N. Chomsky, *Reflections on Language* (1975)

Every aspect of language is extremely complex; yet very young children — before the age of five — already know most of the intricate system we have been calling the grammar of a language. Before they can add 2 + 2, children are conjoining sentences, asking questions, selecting appropriate pronouns, negating sentences, forming relative clauses, and using the syntactic, phonological, morphological, and semantic rules of the grammar.

A normal human being can go through life without learning to read or write, as do millions of people in the world today. Nevertheless, these millions can express, understand, and discuss complex and abstract ideas as effectively as literate speakers can. Learning to speak and understand a language and learning to read and write are different. Similarly, millions of humans never learn algebra or chemistry or how to use a computer. They must be taught these skills or systems, but they do not have to be taught to walk or to talk. In fact, "We are designed to walk. . . . That we are taught to walk is impossible. And pretty much the same is true of language. Nobody is taught language. In fact you can't prevent the child from learning it" (Chomsky, 1994).

The study of the nature of human language itself has revealed a great deal about language acquisition, about what the child does and does not do when learning or acquiring a language:

1. Children do not learn a language by storing all the words and all the sentences in some giant mental dictionary. The list of words is finite, but no dictionary can hold all the sentences, which are infinite in number.
2. Children learn to construct sentences, most of which they have never produced before.
3. Children learn to understand sentences they have never heard before. They cannot do so by matching the "heard utterance" with some stored sentence.
4. Children must therefore construct the "rules" that permit them to use language creatively.
5. No one teaches them these rules. Their parents are no more aware of the phonological, syntactic, and semantic rules than are the children.

Even if you remember your early years, you will not remember anyone telling you to form a sentence by adding a verb phrase to a noun phrase or to add [s] or [z] to form plurals. Children, then, seem to act like efficient linguists equipped with a perfect theory of language, and they use this theory to construct the grammar of the language they hear.

In the preceding chapters you saw something of the richness and complexity of human language. How do children acquire such an intricate system so quickly and effortlessly? Even more difficult, the child must figure out the rules of language from very "noisy" data. She hears sentence fragments, false starts, speech errors, and interruptions. No one tells the child "this is a grammatical utterance and this is not." Yet, somehow she is able to "recreate" the grammar of the language of her speech community based on the language she hears around her. How does the child accomplish this phenomenal task?

Theories of Child Language Acquisition

There have been various proposals concerning the psychological mechanisms involved in acquiring a language. Early theories of language acquisition were heavily influenced by behaviourism, a school of psychology prevalent in the 1950s. As the names implies, behaviourism focused on people's behaviours, which are directly observable, rather than on the mental systems underlying these behaviours. Language was viewed as a kind of verbal behaviour, and it was proposed that children learn language through imitation, reinforcement, analogy, and similar processes.

Do Children Learn through Imitation?

> CHILD: My teacher holded the baby rabbits and we patted them.
> ADULT: Did you say your teacher held the baby rabbits?
> CHILD: Yes.
> ADULT: What did you say she did?
> CHILD: She holded the baby rabbits and we patted them.
> ADULT: Did you say she held them tightly?
> CHILD: No, she holded them loosely.

(Cazden, 1972, p. 92)

There are those who think that children merely imitate what they hear. **Imitation** is involved to some extent, of course, but the sentences produced by children show that they are not simply imitating adult speech. Children do not hear words like *holded* or *tooths* or sentences such as *cat stand up table* or many of the other utterances they produce between the ages of two and three, such as the following:[1]

> A my pencil.
> Two foot.
> What the boy hit?
> Other one pants.
> Mommy get it my ladder.
> Cowboy did fighting me.

Even when children are deliberately trying to imitate what they hear, they are unable to produce sentences that they would not spontaneously produce.

> ADULT: He's going out.   CHILD: He go out.
> ADULT: That's an old-time train.   CHILD: Old-time train.
> ADULT: Adam, say what I say: CHILD: Where I can put them?
>   Where can I put them?

Imitation cannot account for another important phenomenon: children who are unable to speak for neurological or physiological reasons learn the language spoken to them and understand what is said. When they overcome their speech impairment, they immediately use the language for speaking.

Do Children Learn through Reinforcement?

> CHILD: Nobody don't like me.
> MOTHER: No, say "Nobody likes me."
> CHILD: Nobody don't like me.
>   (*dialogue repeated eight times*)
> MOTHER: Now, listen carefully, say *"Nobody likes me."*
> CHILD: Oh, nobody don't likes me.

Another view of language acquisition suggests that children learn to produce grammatical sentences because they are positively reinforced when they say something right and negatively reinforced when they say something wrong. This view assumes that children are being constantly corrected when they use "bad grammar" and rewarded when they use "good grammar." Brown and his colleagues report from their studies that reinforcement seldom occurs, and when it does it is usually incorrect pronunciation or incorrect reporting of facts that is corrected. They report, for example, that the ungrammatical sentence *Her curl my hair* was not corrected because Eve's mother was in fact curling Eve's hair. However, when the syntactically correct sentence *Walt Disney comes on on Tuesday* was produced, Eve's mother corrected Eve because the program on television was shown on Wednesday. They conclude that it is "truth value rather than syntactic well-formedness that chiefly governs explicit verbal reinforcement by parents — which renders mildly paradoxical the fact that the usual product of such a training schedule is an adult whose speech is highly grammatical but not notably truthful" (Brown, 1973, p.330).

Even if syntactic correction occurred more often, it would not explain how or what children learn from such adult responses or how children discover and construct the correct rules.

In fact, attempts to correct a child's language seem to be doomed to failure. Children do not know what they are doing wrong and are unable to make corrections even when they are pointed out, as shown by the example above and by the following one:

> CHILD: Want other one spoon, Daddy.
> FATHER: You mean, you want *"the other spoon."*
> CHILD: Yes, I want other one spoon, please, Daddy.
> FATHER: Can you say "the other spoon?"
> CHILD: Other . . . one . . . spoon.
> FATHER: Say . . . "other."
> CHILD: Other.
> FATHER: Spoon.
> CHILD: Spoon.
> FATHER: Other . . . spoon.
> CHILD: Other . . . spoon. Now give me other one spoon?

Such conversations between parents and children do not occur often. The above conversation was between a linguist studying child language and his child. Mothers and fathers are usually delighted that their young children are talking at all and consider every utterance to be a gem. The "mistakes" children make are cute and repeated endlessly to anyone who will listen.

Do Children Learn through Analogy?

It has also been suggested that children learn how to put words together to form phrases and sentences by **analogy**, by hearing a sentence and using it as a sample to form other sentences. But this doesn't work, as Lila Gleitman (1994) points out:

So suppose the child has heard the sentence "I painted a red barn." So now, by analogy, the child can say "I painted a blue barn." That's exactly the kind of theory that we want. You hear a sample and you extend it to all of the new cases by similarity. . . . In addition to "I painted a red barn" you might also hear the sentence "I painted a barn red." So it looks as if you take those last two words and switch them around in their order. . . . So now you want to extend this to the case of seeing, because you want to look at barns instead of painting them. So you have heard, "I saw a red barn." Now you try (by analogy) a . . . new sentence — "I saw a barn red." Something's gone wrong. This is an analogy, but the analogy didn't work. It's not a sentence of English.

The problem we face here of trying to explain how children learn what is or is not a sentence in their language through the use of analogy arises constantly.

Consider another example. The child hears the following pair of sentences:

The boy was sleeping. Was the boy sleeping?

Based on pairs of sentences like this, he formulates a rule for forming questions, "move the auxiliary to the position preceding the subject." He then acquires the more complex relative clause construction:

The boy who is sleeping is dreaming about a new car.

He now wants to form a question. What does he do? If he forms a question on analogy to the simple yes-no question, he will move the first auxiliary *is* as follows:

*Is the boy who sleeping is dreaming about a new car?

Studies of spontaneous speech, as well as experiments, show that children never make mistakes of this sort. As discussed in Chapter 3, sentences have structure, and the rules of grammar, such as the rule that moves the auxiliary, are sensitive to structure and not to linear order. Children seem to know about the structure dependency of rules at a very early age.

In recent decades, a computer model of language representation and acquisition called **connectionism** has been proposed that relies in part on behaviourist learning principles such as analogy and reinforcement. In the connectionist model no grammatical rules are stored anywhere. Linguistic knowledge, such as knowledge of the past tense, is represented by a set of neuronlike connections between different phonological forms, for example, between *play* and *played, dance* and *danced, drink* and *drank,* and so on. Repeated exposure to particular verb pairs in the input reinforces the connection between them, mimicking rule-like behaviour. Based on similarities between words, the model can produce a past-tense form that it was not previously exposed to. On analogy to *dance-danced,* it will convert *prance* to *pranced;* on analogy to *drink-drank* it will convert *sink* to *sank.*

As a model of language acquisition, connectionism faces some serious challenges. The model relies on specific properties of the input data. However, investigation of the input that actual children receive shows that it is not consistent with the assumptions of this model. Past-tense learning cannot be based on phonological form alone but must also be sensitive to information in the lexicon. For example, the past tense of a verb derived from a noun is always regular even if an irregular form exists. When a fly ball is caught in a baseball game, we say the batter *flied out* not *flew out*. Similarly, when an irregular plural is part of a larger noun, it may be regularized. When we see several images of Walt Disney's famous rodent we describe them as Mickey Mouses, not Mickey Mice.

Do Children Learn through Structured Input?

Yet another suggestion is that children are able to learn language because adults speak to them in a special "simplified" language sometimes called **child-directed speech (CDS)**, **motherese**, or *parentese* (or, more informally, **baby talk**). This theory of acquisition places a lot of emphasis on the role of the environment in facilitating language acquisition.

In our culture adults do typically talk to young children in a special way. We tend to speak more slowly and more clearly, we exaggerate our intonation, and sentences are generally grammatical. However, CDS is not syntactically simpler. It contains a range of sentence types, including syntactically complex sentences such as questions: *Do you want your juice now?* Embedded sentences: *Mommy thinks you should sleep now.* Imperatives: *Pat the dog gently!* Negatives with tag questions: *We don't want to hurt him, do we?* Indeed, it is fortunate that CDS is not syntactically restricted. If it were, children might not have sufficient information to extract the rules of their language.

Although infants prefer to listen to CDS than normal adult speech, controlled studies show that CDS does not significantly affect the child's language development. In many cultures adults do not use a special register with children, and there are even communities in which adults hardly talk to babies at all. Children acquire language in much the same way, irrespective of these varying circumstances. Finally, adults seem to be the followers rather than the leaders in this enterprise. The child does not develop because he is exposed to ever more adultlike language. Rather, the adult adjusts his language to the child's increasing linguistic sophistication.

The exaggerated intonation and other properties of CDS may be useful for getting a child's attention and holding it, but it is not a driving force behind language development.

Imitation, reinforcement, and analogy cannot account for language development because they are based on the (implicit or explicit) assumption that what the child acquires is a set of sentences or forms rather than a set of grammatical rules. Theories that assume that acquisition depends on a specially structured input also place too much emphasis on the environment rather than on the grammar-making abilities of the child. These proposals do not explain the creativity that children show in acquiring language, why they go through stages, or why they make some kinds of "errors" but not others.

The Biological Foundations of Language Acquisition

Language learning is not really something that the child does; it is something that happens to the child placed in an appropriate environment, much as the child's body grows and matures in a predetermined way when provided with appropriate nutrition and environmental stimulation.

Noam Chomsky, *Language and the Problem of Knowledge* (1988)

Language acquisition is a creative process. Children are not given explicit information about the rules, by either instruction or correction. They must somehow extract the rules of the grammar from the language they hear around them, and their linguistic environment does not need to be special in any way for them to do this. Observations of children acquiring different languages under different cultural and social circumstances reveal that the developmental stages are similar, possibly universal. Even deaf children of deaf signing parents go through stages in their signing development that parallel those of children acquiring spoken languages. These factors lead many linguists to believe that children are equipped with an innate template or blueprint for language — Universal Grammar (UG) — and this blueprint aids the child in the task of constructing a grammar for her language. This is referred to as the **innateness hypothesis**.

The Innateness Hypothesis

How comes it that human beings, whose contacts with the world are brief and personal and limited, are able to know as much as they do know?

Bertrand Russell, *Human Knowledge: Its Scope and Limits* (1948)

A major question concerning the *logical problem of language acquisition* was posed by Noam Chomsky: What accounts for the ease, rapidity and uniformity of language acquisition in the face of impoverished data?

The acquisition of language seems to be easy for children. They don't need to be taught the complex rules of language. On the other hand, it is far from easy for a student of linguistics trying to solve a syntax problem in another language, so it can't be that the task itself is easy.

Acquisition is rapid: only two years elapse from the time children produce their first word at around the age of one until the major part of the grammar is acquired at around three. Acquisition is uniform across children and languages; children learning the thousands of languages with all their surface differences go through the

"WHAT'S THE BIG SURPRISE? ALL THE LATEST THEORIES OF LINGUISTICS SAY WE'RE BORN WITH THE INNATE CAPACITY FOR GENERATING SENTENCES."

Copyright © S. Harris.

same stages of phonological, morphological, and syntactic rule acquisition. Although children hear many utterances, the language that is heard is incomplete, noisy, and unstructured. The utterances include slips of the tongue, false starts, ungrammatical and incomplete sentences, and no information as to which utterances heard are well formed and which are not. Yet children seem to learn, or mysteriously know, aspects of the grammar for which they receive no information. This is what is meant by **impoverished data** or the poverty of the stimulus. For example, children at an early age learn to form questions such as the following:

Statement	Question
Jill is going up the hill.	Is Jill going up the hill?
Jack and Jill are going up the hill.	Are Jack and Jill going up the hill?

That doesn't seem to be too hard a rule to learn: move the auxiliary verb to the beginning of the sentence. But this rule doesn't always work:

Statement	Question
Jill, who is my sister, is going up the hill.	*Is Jill, who ___ my sister is, going up the hill?
	Is Jill, who is my sister, ___ going up the hill?

It is not the first auxiliary verb but the auxiliary verb of the main clause that must be moved.

The rules that children construct are **structure dependent**. That is, children use syntactic rules that depend on more than their knowledge of words. They also rely on their knowledge of syntactic structures, which are not overtly marked in the sentences they hear. This is more dramatically shown in the rules for *wh* question formation.

Statement	Question
<u>Jack</u> went up the hill.	<u>Who</u> went up the hill?
<u>Jack and Jill</u> went up the hill.	<u>Who</u> went up the hill?
Jack and Jill went <u>to school</u>.	Jack and Jill went <u>where</u>?
Jack and <u>Jill</u> went <u>home</u>.	Jack and <u>who</u> went home?
Jill ate <u>bagels and lox</u>.	Jill ate <u>what</u>?
Jill ate cookies and <u>ice cream</u>.	Jill ate cookies and <u>what</u>?

To ask a question, the child learns to replace the noun phrase (NP) *Jack, Jill, ice cream*, or *school*, or the coordinate NPs *Jack and Jill* or *bagels and lox*, with the appropriate *wh* question word, *who, what*, or *where*.

It seems as if the *wh* phrase can replace any NP subject or object, but in coordinate structures the *wh* word must stay in the original NP. It can't be moved, as the following sentences show:

> *Who did Jack and _____ go up the hill?
> *What did Jill eat bagels and _____?

These sentences are starred because they are ungrammatical, yet the following are acceptable:

Statement	Question
Jill ate bagels with lox.	What did Jill eat bagels with _____?
Jack went up the hill with Jill.	Who did Jack go up the hill with _____?

What accounts for the difference between the "and" questions that are ungrammatical and the "with" questions that are well formed? *Bagels and lox* is a coordinate NP — that is, two NPs conjoined with *and* (NP *and* NP). But *bagels with lox* is not a coordinate NP but an NP composed of an NP followed by a prepositional phrase (NP + PP), as shown by the following diagrams:

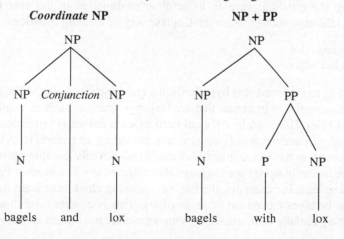

In English and all other languages that have been investigated, there seems to be a **coordinate structure constraint** that prohibits the movement of a *wh* phrase out of a **coordinate structure**. Children make lots of mistakes in their early sentences, but as mentioned earlier they do not produce sentences that could not be sentences in some human language (e.g., the starred sentences above). No one has told them these sentences are not permitted. No one corrects them since they never utter them.

How do children know that *wh* phrases are frozen inside a coordinate structure? According to the innateness hypothesis, children come "prewired" with knowledge of Universal Grammar, including structure dependency and the coordinate structure constraint, among many other principles.

Of course the child must also learn many aspects of grammar from the specific linguistic environment. For example, English-speaking children learn that the subject comes first and that the verb precedes the object inside the VP. More technically, English is an SVO language. Japanese children acquire an SOV language. They learn that the object precedes the verb. Japanese children also learn that to form a yes-no question, the morpheme *-ka* is suffixed to a verb stem. In Japanese, sentence constituents are not rearranged. English-speaking children must learn that yes-no questions are formed by moving constituents. In yes-no questions the auxiliary moves from its original position to the beginning of the sentence, as follows:

> You will come home → Will you ____ come home?

English-speaking children must also learn that in *wh* questions the *wh* phrase moves as follows (with the additional complexity of inserting *do*):

> You like who → Who do you like ____?

In Mandarin Chinese, as in many other Asian languages, speakers form questions by leaving the question word in its original position, as in the example below; Chinese children obviously learn the Chinese way of forming questions:

> Ni xihuan shei
> You like who

According to the innateness hypothesis, the child extracts from the linguistic environment those rules of grammar that are language specific, such as word order and movement rules. However, he does not need to learn universal principles like structure dependency and the coordinate structure constraint, or general rules of sentence formation such as the fact that heads of categories can take complements. They are part of the innate blueprint for language that children use to construct the grammar of their language. For example, the English-speaking child must learn that forming a question involves movement of an auxiliary. This rule takes time to acquire and children may initially form questions with uninverted auxiliaries as follows:

> Where Mommy is going?
> What you can do?

Nevertheless, children never make the mistake of moving the wrong auxiliary in a complex sentence or a *wh* phrase out of a coordinate structure.

The innateness hypothesis provides an answer to the question posed by Chomsky mentioned at the outset of this section: What accounts for the ease, rapidity, and uniformity of language acquisition in the face of impoverished data? The answer is that children acquire a complex grammar quickly and easily without any particular help beyond exposure to the language because they do not start from scratch. UG helps them to extract the rules of their language and to avoid many grammatical errors. Because the child constructs his grammar according to an innate blueprint, all children proceed through similar developmental stages, as will be discussed in a later section.

The innateness hypothesis predicts that all languages will conform to the principles of UG. We are still far from understanding the full nature of the principles of UG. Research on more and more languages provides a way to test principles, such as the coordinate structure constraint, that have been posited to be part of our genetic prewiring. If we investigate some language in which posited UG principles are violated, then we will have to correct our theory and substitute other principles. But there seems to be little doubt that human languages conform to abstract universal principles, and that the human brain is specially equipped for acquisition of human language grammars.

The Critical Period Hypothesis

It has been suggested that there is a **critical period** for language acquisition or at least for language acquisition without special teaching and without the need for special learning. During this period, language learning proceeds easily, swiftly, and without external intervention. After this period, acquisition of the grammar is difficult and, for some individuals, never fully achieved.

The notion of a critical period is true of many species and seems to pertain to species-specific, biologically triggered behaviour. Ducklings, for example, during the period from nine to twenty-one hours after hatching, will follow the first moving object they see, whether or not it looks like a duck. Such behaviour is not the result of conscious decision or external teaching or intensive practice. Its emergence unfolds in a maturationally determined order universal across the species.

In a seminal contribution to the study of the biological basis of language, Eric Lenneberg (1967) first proposed that the ability to learn a native language develops within a fixed period, from birth to puberty.

There have been a number of cases of children reared in environments of extreme social isolation who constitute "experiments in nature" for testing the critical period hypothesis. Such reported cases go back at least to the eighteenth century. In 1758, Carl Linnaeus first included *Homo ferus* (wild or feral human) as a subdivision of *Homo sapiens*. According to Linnaeus, a defining characteristic of *Homo ferus* was lack of speech or observable language of any kind. All the cases in the literature support his view.

The most dramatic cases of children raised in isolation are those described as "wild" or "feral" children, who have reportedly been reared with wild animals or have lived alone in the wilderness. In 1920, two feral children, Amala and Kamala, were found in India, supposedly having been reared with wolves. A celebrated case, documented in François Truffaut's film *The Wild Child*, is that of Victor, "the wild boy of Aveyron," who was found in 1798. It was ascertained that he had been left in the woods when a very young child and had somehow survived.

There are other cases of children whose isolation resulted from deliberate efforts to keep them from normal social intercourse. As recently as 1970, a child, called Genie in the scientific reports, was discovered confined to a small room under conditions of physical restraint and had received only minimal human contact between the ages of eighteen months and almost fourteen years (Curtiss, 1977). None of these children, regardless of the cause of isolation, was able to speak or knew any language at the time of reintroduction to society.

This linguistic inability could simply be because they received no linguistic input, showing that the innate neurological ability of the human brain to acquire language must be triggered by language. In the documented cases of Victor and Genie, however, they were unable to acquire language after exposure and even with deliberate and painstaking linguistic teaching.

Genie did begin to acquire some language, but while she was able to learn a large vocabulary, including colours, shapes, objects, natural categories, and abstract as well as concrete terms, her syntax and morphology never fully developed. Susan Curtiss (1977), who worked with Genie for a number of years after she was found, reports that Genie's utterances were, for the most part, "the stringing together of content words, often with rich and clear meaning but with little grammatical structure." Many of the utterances produced by Genie at the age of fifteen and older, a number of years after her emergence from isolation, were like those of children in the telegraphic stage and like those of aphasia patients:

Man motorcycle have.
Genie full stomach.
Genie bad cold live father house.
Want Curtiss play piano.
Open door key.

Genie's utterances lacked auxiliary verbs, the third-person singular agreement marker, the past-tense marker, and most pronouns. Genie did not invert subjects and verbs to form questions. She started learning language after the critical period and was never able to acquire fully the morphological and syntactic rules of English, a fact that supports the hypothesis.

The case of Chelsea, which came to light in the 1980s, also supports the critical period hypothesis. She was born deaf and was wrongly diagnosed as retarded. Her devoted and caring family never believed this to be true. They knew she was deaf, but in the small town where they lived there were no schools for the deaf so she did not attend school. When she was thirty-one, a neurologist finally diagnosed her deafness, and she was fitted with hearing aids. She received extensive language therapy and was able to acquire a large vocabulary but, like Genie, has not been able to develop a grammar.

More than 90 percent of children who are born deaf or become deaf before they have acquired language are born to hearing parents. These children have also provided information about the critical period of language acquisition. Because most of their parents do not know sign language at the time of their birth, many of these children receive delayed language exposure. A number of studies have investigated the acquisition of American Sign Language (ASL) among deaf signers exposed to the language at different ages. A study by Elissa Newport (1990) revealed that early learners who received ASL input from birth up to six years of age did much better in the production and comprehension of morphologically complex signs than did learners who were not exposed to ASL until after the age of twelve. There was little difference, however, in the vocabularies or the word-order constraints (which are very regular in ASL).

Genie, other such isolated children, and deaf children show that children cannot fully acquire any language to which they are exposed unless they are within the critical period, a biologically determined window of opportunity during which time the brain is prepared to develop language. The human brain is primed to develop language in specific areas of the left hemisphere, but the normal process of brain specialization depends on early and systematic experience with language.

Beyond the critical period, the human brain appears to be unable to acquire the grammatical aspects of language, even with substantial linguistic training. However, it seems that it is possible to acquire words and various conversational skills after this point. In human first language acquisition, the critical period appears to affect specific aspects of language. The critical period hypothesis will be further discussed in the next chapter, Second Language Acquisition.

Stages in Language Acquisition

> ...for I was no longer a speechless infant; but a speaking boy. This I remember; and have since observed how I learned to speak. It was not that my elders taught me words ... in any set method; but I ... did myself ... practice the sounds in my memory.... And thus by constantly hearing words, as they occurred in various sentences ... I thereby gave utterance to my will.
>
> St. Augustine, *Confessions* (c. 400 C.E., trans. F.J. Sheed, 1944)

Children do not wake up one morning with a fully formed grammar in their heads or with the rules of social and communicative intercourse. Linguistic competence develops by stages, and, it is suggested, each successive stage more closely approximates the grammar of the adult language. Observations of children in different language areas of the world reveal that these stages are similar and possibly universal.

Some stages last for a short time; others remain longer. Some stages may overlap for a short period, but the transition between stages is often sudden.

Given the universal aspects of all human languages, signed and spoken, it is not surprising that deaf children of deaf signing parents parallel the stages of spoken language acquisition in their signing development.

The earliest studies of child language acquisition come from diaries kept by parents. More recent studies include the use of tape recordings, videotapes, and controlled experiments. Spontaneous utterances of children are recorded, and various elicitation techniques have been developed so that the child's production and comprehension can be scientifically studied. Researchers have also invented ingenious techniques for investigating the linguistic abilities of infants, who are not yet speaking.

The studies show that child language is not just a degenerate form of adult language. At each stage of development the child's language conforms to a set of rules, a grammar. Although child grammars and adult grammars differ in certain respects, they also share many formal properties. Like adults, children have grammatical categories such as NP and VP, rules for building phrase structures and for moving constituents, as well as phonological rules, morphological rules, and semantic rules, and they adhere to universal principles such as structure dependency.

As we will illustrate, children's early utterances may not completely resemble comparable adult sentences. This is because the words and sentences the child produces conform to the phonology, morphology, and syntax that he has developed to that point. This may be why children do not respond to correction. *Nobody don't like me* and *want 'nother one spoon, daddy* may contain errors from the perspective of the adult grammar, but they are not errors from the child's point of view. They reflect his current grammar. Indeed, the so-called errors that children make provide us with a window into their grammar.

The Perception and Production of Speech Sounds

> An infant crying in the night:
> An infant crying for the light:
> And with no language but a cry.
>
> Alfred Lord Tennyson, "In Memoriam A.H.H." (1850)

The old idea that the neonate is born with a mind that is like a blank slate is belied by a wealth of evidence that infants are highly sensitive to some subtle distinctions in their environment and not to others. That is, the mind appears to be attuned at birth to receive certain kinds of information.

Experiments have shown that infants will increase their sucking rate when stimuli (visual or auditory) presented to them are varied, but will decrease the sucking rate when the same stimuli are presented repeatedly. Infants will respond to visual depth and distance distinctions, to differences between rigid and flexible physical properties of objects, and to human faces rather than to other visual stimuli.

Similarly, newborns respond to phonetic contrasts found in human languages even when these differences are not phonemic in the language spoken in the baby's home. A baby hearing a human voice over a loudspeaker saying [pa] [pa] [pa] will slowly decrease her rate of sucking. If the sound changes to [ba] or even [pʰa], the sucking rate increases dramatically. Controlled experiments show that adults find it difficult to differentiate between the allophones of one phoneme, but for infants it comes naturally. Japanese infants can distinguish between [r] and [l] while their parents cannot; babies can hear the difference between aspirated and unaspirated stops even if students in an introductory linguistics course cannot. Babies can discriminate between sounds that are phonemic in other languages and nonexistent in the language of their parents. For example, in Hindi, there is a phonemic contrast between a retroflex [ʈ] and the alveolar [t]. To English-speaking adults, these sound the same; to their infants, they do not.

Babies will not react, however, to distinctions that never correspond to phonemic contrasts in any human language, such as sounds spoken more or less loudly or sounds that lie between two phonemes. Furthermore, a vowel that we perceive as [i] or [u] or [a] is a different physical sound when produced by a male, female, or child, but babies ignore the nonlinguistic aspects of the speech signal just as we do. An [i] is an [i] is an [i] to an infant even if the physical sound is different. They do not increase their sucking rate when, after hearing many [i]s spoken by a male, they then hear an [i] spoken by a female. Yet, computational linguists still have difficulty programming computers to recognize these different signals as the "same."

An infant could not have learned to perceive linguistically relevant distinctions and ignore others, such as sex of the speaker. Infants appear to be born with the ability to perceive just those sounds that are phonemic in some language. They can perceive voicing contrasts such as [pa] versus [ba], contrasts in place of articulation such as [da] versus [ga], and contrasts in manner of articulation such as [ra] versus [la], or [ra] versus [wa], among many others. This partially accounts for the fact that children can learn any human language to which they are exposed. Infants have the sensory and motor abilities to produce and perceive speech sounds. During the first years of life the infant's job is to uncover the sounds of this language. From around six months, they begin to lose the ability to discriminate between sounds that are not phonemic in their own language. Their linguistic environment moulds their initial perceptions. Japanese infants can no longer hear the difference between [r] and [l], which do not contrast in Japanese, whereas babies in English-speaking homes retain this perception. They have begun to learn the sounds of the language of their parents. Before that, they appear to know the sounds of human language in general.

Babbling

The shaping by the linguistic environment that we see in perception also occurs in the speech the infant is producing. At around six months, the infant begins to babble. The sounds produced in this period include many that do not occur in the language of the household. However, **babbling** is not linguistic chaos. The twelve most frequent consonants in the world's languages make up 95 percent of the consonants infants use in their babbling. There are linguistic constraints even during this very early stage. The early babbles consist mainly of repeated consonant-vowel sequences, like *mama, gaga,* and *dada.* Later babbles are more varied.

Gradually, the child's babbles come to include only those sounds and sound combinations that occur in the target language. Babbles begin to sound like words though they may not have any specific meaning attached to them. At this point adults can distinguish the babbles of an English-babbling infant from those of an infant babbling in Cantonese or Arabic. During the first year of life the infant's perceptions and productions are being fine-tuned to the language(s) of the surroundings.

Deaf infants produce babbling sounds that are different from those of hearing children. Babbling is related to auditory input and is linguistic in nature. Studies of vocal babbling of hearing children and manual babbling of deaf children support the view that babbling is a linguistic ability related to the kind of language input the child receives. These studies show that four- to seven-month-old hearing infants exposed to spoken language produce a restricted set of phonetic forms. At the same age, deaf children exposed to sign language produce a restricted set of signs. In each case the forms are drawn from the set of possible sounds or possible gestures found in spoken and signed languages.

Babbling illustrates the readiness of the human mind to respond to linguistic cues from a very early stage. During the babbling stage, the intonation contours produced by hearing infants begin to resemble the intonation contours of sentences spoken by adults. The semantically different intonation contours are among the first linguistic contrasts that children perceive and produce. During this same period, the vocalizations produced by deaf babies are random and nonrepetitive. Similarly, the manual gestures produced by hearing babies differ greatly from those produced by deaf infants exposed to sign language. The hearing babies move their fingers and clench their fists randomly with little or no repetition of gestures. The deaf infants, however, use more than a dozen different hand motions repetitively, all of which are elements of American Sign Language, or the other sign languages used in deaf communities of other countries.

The generally accepted view is that humans are born with a predisposition to discover the units that serve to express linguistic meanings, and that at a genetically specified stage in neural development, the infant will begin to produce these units — sounds or gestures — depending on the language input the baby receives. This suggests that babbling is the earliest stage in language acquisition, in opposition to the earlier view that babbling was prelinguistic and merely neuromuscular in origin.

First Words

> From this golden egg a man, Prajapati, was born. . . . A year having passed, he wanted to speak. He said *bhur* and the earth was created. He said *bhuvar* and the space of the air was created. He said *suvar* and the sky was created. That is why a child wants to speak after a year. . . . When Prajapati spoke for the first time, he uttered one or two syllables. That is why a child utters one or two syllables when he speaks for the first time.
>
> Hindu myth

Baby's first words

© Mike Baldwin. www.CartoonStock.com

Some time after one year, children begin to use the same string of sounds repeatedly to mean the same thing. By that time, they have learned that sounds are related to meanings, and they are producing their first "words."

Children have been found to utter **protowords**, defined as a sequence of sounds that has a relatively consistent meaning, but which is not necessarily based on an adult word. For instance, the child who says *dodo* to name her favourite blanket can be said to be using a protoword. Recognizable words also begin to appear, such as "mo" for "more." Most children seem to go through the "one word = one sentence" stage. These one-word "sentences" are called **holophrastic** sentences (from *holo* "complete" or "undivided" plus *phrase* "phrase" or "sentence") because these one-word utterances seem to convey a more complex message.

At this stage, the child uses only one word to express concepts or predictions that will later be expressed by complex phrases and sentences.

Many studies have shown that children in the holophrastic stage can perceive or comprehend many more phonological contrasts than they can produce themselves. Therefore, even at this stage, it is not possible to determine the extent of the grammar of the child simply by observing speech production.

One child, "Louise," illustrates how much the young child has learned even before the age of two years. Some of Louise's common one-word utterances between the ages of sixteen and twenty months were:

[kæ]	cat		[wa]	walk
[æp]	apple		[we]	wait
[daw]	down		[mʌ]	milk
[wawa]	water		[tænku]	thank you
[pa]	Grandpa		[dajpə]	diaper
[mama]	Momma		[tæt]	that
[piz]	please		[no]	no
[tiz]	cheese			

According to some child-language researchers, the words in the holophrastic stage serve three major functions: they are linked with a child's own actions or desire for action (as when Louise would say *down* to express her wish to be lifted down), used to convey emotion (Louise's *no*), or serve a naming function (Louise's *cat*, *cheese*, *Momma*, etc.). At this stage, the child uses only one word to express concepts or predictions that will later be expressed by complex phrases and sentences.

The Development of Grammar

Children are neurologically prepared to acquire all aspects of grammar, from phonetics to pragmatics. This section presents evidence and illustrations of the breadth of UG, and the innateness of the several components of grammar discussed in preceding chapters.

The Acquisition of Phonology

In terms of her phonology, Louise is like most children at this stage. Her first words are generally monosyllabic with a CV (consonant-vowel) form. The vowel part may be a diphthong, depending on the language being acquired. Her phonemic or phonetic inventory — at this stage they are equivalent — is much smaller than is found in the adult language. Linguist Roman Jakobson (1971) suggested that children first acquire the small set of sounds common to all languages of the world, no matter what language they hear, and in later stages a child acquires the less common sounds of her own language. For example, most languages have the sounds [p] and

© Baby Blues Partnership. Reprinted with special permission of King Features Syndicate.

[s], but [θ] is a rare sound. Louise's sound system was as Jakobson's theory predicted. Her phonological inventory at an early stage included the consonants [p, m, d, k], which are frequently occurring sounds in the world's languages.

In general, the order of acquisition of classes of sounds goes by manner of articulation: nasals are acquired first, then glides, stops, liquids, fricatives, and affricates. Natural classes characterized by place of articulation features also appear in children's utterances according to an ordered series: labials, velars, alveolars, and palatals. It is not surprising that *mama* is an early word for many children.

In early language, children may not distinguish between voiced and voiceless consonants, although they can perceive the difference. When they first begin to contrast one set — that is, when they learn that /p/ and /b/ are distinct phonemes — they also begin to distinguish between /t/ and /d/, /s/ and /z/, and to perceive all the other contrasts between voiced and voiceless consonants. The generalizations refer, as we would expect, to natural classes of speech sounds.

Controlled experiments show that children at this stage can perceive or comprehend many more phonological contrasts than they can produce. For example, a child who appears to pronounce *wing* and *ring* identically can pick out the correct picture when shown pictures of both. Furthermore, acoustic analyses of children's utterances show that the child's pronunciations of *wing* and *ring* are physically different sounds, although they may seem the same to the adult ear.

A child's first words show many such substitutions of one feature for another or of one phoneme for another. For example, the word *rabbit* is pronounced as *wabbit* in the speech of many children, with the liquid [r] being replaced by the glide [w]. The child's errors in pronunciation are thus not random but rule governed. Typical phonological rules (or processes) found in children's early utterances include:

1. Substituting one sound for another, for example:
    a stop to replace a fricative: sing → [tɪŋ]
    fronting, or moving forward of a sound's place
      of articulation   key → [ti]
    gliding, when a glide replaces a liquid   drip → [dwɪp]
    denasalization, when a nasal is replaced
      by a nonnasal   Sam → [sæb]
2. Assimilations, when sounds come to resemble other sounds,
    as in cases of consonant harmony   duck → [gʌk]
3. Syllable simplification, for example:
    consonant cluster simplification   please → [piz]
    unstressed syllable or sound deletion   telephone → [tɛfo]
    final consonant deletion   cat → [kæ]
    reduplication of a syllable   water → [wawa]

The changes children make are for the most part simplifications of the adult pronunciation. They make articulation easier until the child achieves greater articulatory control.

Of the many phonological rules that children create, no one child will necessarily use all rules. Early phonological rules generally reflect natural phonological processes that also occur in adult language. For example, various adult languages have a rule of syllable-final consonant devoicing (German does, English does not). Children do not create bizarre or whimsical rules. Their rules conform to the possibilities made available by UG.

The Acquisition of Word Meaning

> Suddenly I felt a misty consciousness as of something forgotten — a thrill of returning thought; and somehow the mystery of language was revealed to me. . . . Everything had a name, and each name gave birth to a new thought.
>
> Helen Keller, *The Story of My Life* (1954)

The child's early vocabulary provides insights into how children use words and construct word meanings. The ways in which Louise used early words is of interest. The utterance [daw] was originally used to mean "get me down," when she was in her crib or highchair, but later it was used to direct her mother to "get down" to her level as well. Also, Louise used the word *cat* not only for the family pet, but also for dogs, monkeys, and even fish, as her mother discovered during a trip to a pet shop. Thus, a child may extend the meaning of a word from a particular referent to encompass a larger class.

When children first begin to use words, the stimulus may have to be visible, but soon this is no longer necessary, and pictures of objects can also elicit words. Words having social functions appear in children's early vocabularies, as the appearance of words used for "thank you" and "please" indicate in Louise's utterances. Even in the early holophrastic stage, Louise was using words to convey a variety of ideas, feelings, and social custom.

Most people do not see the acquisition of the meanings of words as posing a great problem. The intuitive view is that children look at an object, the mother or father says a word, and the child connects the sounds with the particular object. However, this is not as easy a task as one might think:

> A child who observes a cat sitting on a mat also observes . . . a mat supporting a cat, a mat under a cat, a floor supporting a mat and a cat, and so on. If the adult now says "The cat is on the mat" even while pointing to the cat on the mat, how is the child to choose among these interpretations of the situation? (Gleitman & Wanner, 1982, p. 10)

Even if the adult simply says *cat*, and the child by accident associates the word with the animal on the mat, the child may interpret *cat* as *Cat*, the name of a particular animal or of an entire species.

In other words, to learn a word for a class of objects such as "cat" or "dog," children have to figure out exactly what the word refers to. Upon hearing the word *dog* in the presence of a dog, how does the child know that "dog" can refer to any four-legged, hairy, barking creature? Should it include poodles, tiny Yorkshire terriers, bulldogs, and Great Danes, all of which look rather different from one another? What about cows, lambs, and other four-legged mammals? Why are they not "dogs"? The important and very difficult question is: What are the relevant features that define the class of objects we call *dog* and how does a child acquire knowledge of them? Even if a child succeeds in associating a word with an object, nobody provides explicit information about how to extend the use of that word to other objects to which that word refers.

It is not surprising, therefore, that children often overextend a word's meaning, as Louise did with the word *cat*. A child may learn a word such as *papa* or *daddy*, which she first uses only for her own father, and then extend its meaning to apply to all men, just as she may use the word *cat* to mean any four-legged creature. After the child has acquired her first seventy-five to one hundred words, the overextended meanings start to narrow until they correspond to those of the other speakers of the language. How this occurs is still not entirely understood.

The mystery surrounding the acquisition of word meanings has intrigued philosophers and psychologists as well as linguists. We know that all children view the world in a similar fashion and apply the same general principles to help them determine a word's meaning. For example, overextensions are usually based on physical attributes such as size, shape, and texture. *Ball* may refer to all round things, *bunny* to all furry things, and so on. However, children will not make overextensions based on colour. In experiments, children will group objects by shape and give them a name, but they will not assign a name to a group of red objects.

If an experimenter points to an object and uses a nonsense word like *blick* to a child, saying *that's a blick,* the child will interpret the word to refer to the whole object, not one of its parts or attributes. Given the poverty of stimulus for word learning, principles like the "form over colour principle" and the "whole object principle" help the child organize experience in ways that facilitate word learning. Without such principles, it is doubtful that children could learn words as quickly as they do. Children learn approximately fourteen words a day for the first six years of their lives. That averages to about 5,000 words per year. How many students know 10,000 words of a foreign language after two years of study?

Furthermore, as children are learning the meaning of words, they are also developing the syntax of the language and the syntactic categories. Syntax can help the child acquire meaning. A child will interpret a word like *blicking* to be a verb if the word is used while the investigator points to a picture of a person or thing performing an action, and will interpret the word *blick* to be a noun if used in the expression *a blick* or *the blick* while looking at the same picture. For example, suppose a child is shown a picture of some funny animal jumping up and down and hears either *See the blicking* or *See the blick.* Later, when asked to show "blicking," the child will jump up and down, but if asked to show a blick, will point to the funny animal. This process is called **syntactic bootstrapping**. Children use their knowledge of syntax to learn the syntactic category of the word: if the word is a verb it has a meaning referring to an action, if the word is a noun it refers to an object of some kind.

The Acquisition of Morphology

Children's errors in morphology reveal that the child has acquired the regular rules of the grammar and overgeneralizes them. This **overgeneralization** of constructed rules is shown when children treat irregular verbs and nouns as if they were regular. We have probably all heard children say *bringed, goed,* and *singed* or *foots, mouses, sheeps,* and *childs.*

These mistakes tell us more about how children learn language than about the correct forms they use. The child cannot be imitating; children use such forms even when their parents never utter such "bad English." In fact, children may say *brought* or *broke* before they begin to use the incorrect forms.

Three phases in the acquisition of an irregular form can be identified:

Phase 1	Phase 2	Phase 3
broke	breaked	broke
brought	bringed	brought

In phase 1 the child uses the correct term such as *brought* or *broke.* At this point the child's grammar does not relate the form *brought* to *bring,* or *broke* to *break.* The words are treated as separate lexical entries. Phase 2 is crucial. This is when the child constructs a rule for forming the past tense and attaches the regular past-tense morpheme to all verbs — *play, hug, help,* as well as *break* and *bring.* Children look for general patterns, for systematic occurrences. What they do not know at phase 2 is that there are exceptions to the rule. Now their language is more regular than the adult language. During phase 3 the child learns that there are exceptions to the rule, and then once again uses *brought* and *broke,* with the difference being that these irregular forms will be related to the root forms.

The child's morphological rules emerge quite early. In 1958, Jean Berko conducted a study that has now become a classic in our understanding of child language acquisition. She worked with preschool children and with children in grades one through three. She showed each child a drawing of a nonsense animal such as the funny creature below and gave the "animal" a nonsense name. She would then say to the child, pointing to the picture, "This is a *wug.*"

Then she would show the child a picture of two of the animals and say, "Now here is another one. There are two of them. There are two _____?"

The child's "task" was to give the plural form, *wugs* [wʌgz]. Another little make-believe animal was called a *bik,* and when the child was shown two *biks* he or she again was to say the plural form [bɪks]. Berko found that the children applied the regular plural-formation rule to words never heard before. Because the children had never seen a *wug* or a *bik* and had not heard these "words," their ability to add a [z] when the animal's name ended with a voiced sound and an [s] when there was a final voiceless consonant showed that the children were using rules based on an understanding of natural classes of phonological segments and not simply imitating words they had previously heard.

More recently, studies of children acquiring languages with more inflectional morphology than English reveal that they learn agreement and case morphology at a very early age. For example, Italian verbs must be inflected for number and person to agree with the subject. This is similar to the English agreement rule "add *s* to the verb" for third-person, singular subjects — *He giggles a lot* but *We giggle a lot* — except that in Italian there are more verb forms that must be acquired. Italian-speaking children between the ages of 1;10 (one year, ten months) and 2;4 correctly inflect the verb, as the following utterances of Italian children show (Hyams, 1986).

Tu legg**i** il libro	"You (2nd-person singular) read the book."
Io vad**o** fuori	"I go (1st-p. sg.) outside."
Dorm**e** miao dorme	"Sleeps (3rd-p. sg.) cat sleeps."
Legg**iamo** il libro	"(We) read (1st-p. plural) the book."

Children acquiring other richly inflected languages such as Spanish, German, Catalan, and Swahili quickly acquire agreement morphology. It is rare for them to make agreement errors just as it is rare for an English-speaking child to say "I goes."

In these languages there is also gender and number agreement between the head noun and the article and adjectives inside the noun phrase. Children as young as two years old respect these agreement requirements, as shown by the following Italian examples.

E mia gonn**a**.	"(It) is my (feminine singular) skirt."
Questo mi**o** bimbo.	"This my (masculine singular) baby."
Guarda **la** mela piccolin**a**.	"Look at the little (fem. sg.) apple."
Guarda **il** topo piccolin**o**.	"Look at the little (masc. sg.) mouse."

Many languages have case morphology where nouns have different forms depending on their grammatical function: subject, object, possessor, and so on. Studies show that children acquiring Russian and German, two languages with extensive case systems, acquire case morphology at a very early age.

Children also show knowledge of the derivational rules of their language and use these rules to create novel words. In English, for example, we can derive verbs from nouns. From the noun *microwave* we now have a verb *to microwave;* from the noun *e(lectronic) mail* we derived the verb *to e-mail.* Children acquire this derivational rule early and use it often since there are lots of gaps in their verb vocabulary.

Child Utterance	**Adult Translation**
You have to scale it.	"You have to weigh it."
I broomed it up.	"I swept it up."
He's keying the door.	"He's opening the door (with a key).

These novel forms provide further evidence that language acquisition is a creative process and that children's utterances reflect their internal grammars, which include both derivational and inflectional rules.

The Acquisition of Syntax

The Two-Word Stage

<table>
<tr><td>

Word spurt

Some children, but not all, appear to go through a period of rapid word learning, a "word spurt", during which they produce one to two new words daily (around eighteen months of age, but timing varies from child to child).

</td><td>

Before they are two years old, children learn a large number of words. According to some estimates, children add a new word to their mental dictionaries every two hours. Then, about the time of their second birthday, something new and exciting occurs. Children begin to put two words together. At first, these utterances appear to be strings of two of the child's earlier holophrastic utterances, each word with its own single-pitch contour. Soon they begin to form actual two-word sentences with clear syntactic and semantic relations. The intonation contour of the two words extends over the whole utterance rather than being separated by a pause between the two words. The following "sentences" illustrate the kinds of patterns that are found in children's utterances at this stage:

</td></tr>
</table>

allgone sock	hi Mommy
byebye boat	allgone sticky
more wet	beepbeep bang
it ball	Katherine sock
dirty sock	here pretty

During the **two-word stage**, there are no syntactic or morphological markers — that is, no inflections for number, person, tense, and so on. Pronouns are rare, although many children use *me* to refer to themselves, and some children use other pronouns as well. Lois Bloom (1972) has noted that, in noun + noun sentences such as *Mommy sock*, the two words can express a number of different grammatical relations that will later be expressed by other syntactic devices. Bloom's conclusions were reached by observing the situations in which the two-word sentence was uttered. Thus, for example, *Mommy sock* can be used to show a subject + object relation in the situation when the mother is putting the sock on the child or a possessive relation when the child is pointing to Mommy's sock. Two nouns can also be used to show a subject–locative relation, as in *sweater chair* to mean "The sweater is on the chair," or to show conjunction, to mean "sweater and chair."

From Telegraph to Infinity

There does not seem to be any "three-word" sentence stage. When a child starts stringing more than two words together, the utterances may be two, three, four, or five words or longer. Since the age at which children start to produce words and put words together may vary, chronological age is not a good measure of a child's language development. A child's **mean length of utterances (MLU)** rather than chronological age is thus used in the study of language development. MLU is the average length of the utterances the child is producing at a particular moment. MLU is usually measured in morphemes rather than words, so a child's words like *goed*, *cows*, and *sleeping* are each two morphemes long. Children with similar MLUs are likely to have similar grammars even though they are at different ages.

A child's first utterances longer than two words have a special characteristic. The small function words (or grammatical morphemes) such as *to, the, can, is*, and so on are missing; only the words that carry the main message — the content words — occur. Children often sound as if they are reading a telegram message, which is why such utterances are sometimes called **telegraphic speech**:

> Cat stand up table.
> What that?
> He play little tune.
> Andrew want that.
> Cathy build house.
> No sit there.

Louise's early sentences also appear telegraphic. (The items in parentheses are missing from her sentences.)

Age in Months

25 months	[mo bænæn]	"(I want) more banana."
26 months	[aj du ɪt]	"I('ll) do it."
	[a dʌn]	"(It's) all done."
27 months	[aj gɛt ɪt]	"I('ll) get it."
	[ta kaju]	"(I) saw Caillou."
	[mami tom]	"Mommy's comb."

It takes many months before children use grammatical morphemes and auxiliary verbs consistently, which is defined to mean "in 90 percent of the contexts in which they are required." For example, the auxiliary *is* is required when the subject of the sentence is third-person singular and the verb has the progressive affix *–ing*, as in *Mommy___ working at computer.*

In an early study of children's morphological development, Roger Brown and his colleagues examined the spontaneous utterances of three English-speaking children — Adam, Eve, and Sarah — over a period of years, noting their use of grammatical morphemes. They found that different morphemes reach the 90 percent criterion level at different times (see Figure 7.1) and that the sequence was the same for all three children (see Table 7.1). The progressive morpheme *-ing*, as in *Me playing*, was found to be among the earliest inflectional morphemes to be used consistently. The prepositions *in* and *on* were next, and then the regular plural ending, as in "two cats" /tu kæts/. The third-person singular marker (as in *Mommy reads*) and the possessive morpheme (as in *baby's toy*), which have the same

TABLE 7.1
Roger Brown Study: Order of Acquisition for Fourteen Grammatical Morphemes

1. present progressive   (talk*ing*, play*ing*)
2./3. prepositions   (*in*, *on*)
4. plural   (toy*s*, block*s*)
5. irregular past tense   (*came, went*)
6. possessive   (baby'*s* toy)
7. uncontractible copular   (This *is* your toy.)
8. articles   (*the* doggie)
9. regular past tense   (play*ed*, climb*ed*)
10. third-person present tense regular   (Mommy read*s*.)
11. third-person present tense irregular   (Baby *has* a new toy.)
12. uncontractible auxiliary   (She *was* playing; *did* you see her?)
13. contractible copula   (She'*s* sleeping; you *are* tired)
14. contractible auxiliary   (Baby'*s* going outside to play.)

Reprinted and adapted by permission of the publisher from *A first language: The early stages* by Roger Brown, p. 55, Cambridge, Mass.: Harvard University Press, Copyright © 1973 by the President and Fellows of Harvard College.

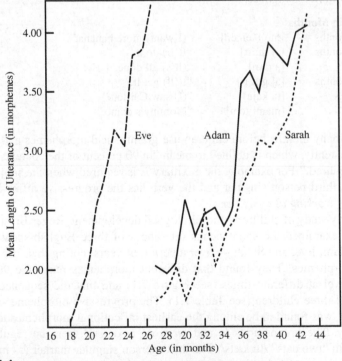

FIGURE 7.1 *Mean length of utterance and chronological age of three children.*
(Reprinted and adapted by permission of the publisher from *A first language: The early stages* by Roger Brown, p. 274, Cambridge, Mass.: Harvard University Press. Copyright © 1973 by the President and Fellows of Harvard College.)

phonological shape as the plural /s/, reached the 90 percent criterion six months to one year after the plural was acquired. This showed that the acquisition of these morphemes depends on the syntax, not the phonology. Eventually all the other inflections became stable features, and the children's utterances sounded like those spoken by adults.

Though the children's utterances are described as telegraphic, the child does not deliberately leave out function words as would an adult sending a telegram. The sentences reflect the child's grammar at that particular stage of language development. Although these sentences may lack certain morphemes, they nevertheless appear to have hierarchical constituent structures and syntactic rules similar to those in the adult grammar. For example, children almost never violate the word-order rules of their language. In languages with relatively fixed word-order such as English, children use SVO order from the earliest stage. In languages with freer word order such as Russian, children typically use several (though not all) of the permissible orders.

In languages with freer word order, like Turkish and Russian, grammatical relations such as subject and object are generally marked by inflectional morphology, such as case markers. Children acquiring these languages quickly learn the morphological case markers. For example, two-year-old Russian-speaking children mark subjects with nominative case, objects with accusative case, and indirect objects with dative case, with very few errors. Most errors arise with words that have an idiosyncratic or irregular case ending. This is reminiscent of the overgeneralization errors that children make with irregular verb morphology in English. Children take longer to acquire aspects of grammar that are not predictable by rule.

As we noted earlier, children acquiring Italian and other languages that mark subject agreement on the verb use correct agreement as soon as they produce multiword utterances. We repeat two of the examples here.

Tu leggi il libro.	"You read (2nd-p. sg.) the book."
Gira il pallone.	"Turns (3rd-p. sg.) the balloon."
	(The balloon turns.)

Various languages have been investigated and they all reveal that children rarely make subject-verb agreement errors.

Children have other agreement rules as well, such as the article-noun-adjective agreement found in Italian. There is nothing intrinsically masculine or feminine about the nouns that are marked for such grammatical gender. Children produce the correct forms based on the syntactic classification of these nouns and the agreement rules of the language.

The correct use of word order, case marking, and agreement rules shows that even though children may often omit function morphemes, they are aware of constituent structure and syntactic rules. Their utterances are not simply words randomly strung together. From a very early stage onward, children have a grasp of the principles of phrase and sentence formation, and of the kinds of structure dependencies mentioned in Chapter 3, as revealed by these constituent structure trees:

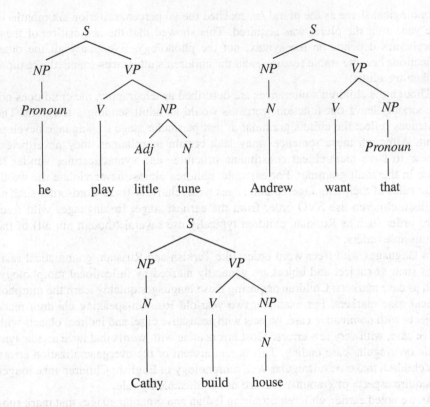

Sometime between the ages of 2;6 and 3;6 there is a virtual language explosion. At this point it is difficult to identify distinct stages because the child is undergoing so much development so rapidly. By the age of 3;0 most children are consistent in their use of function morphemes. Moreover, they have begun to produce and understand complex structures including coordinated sentences and embedded sentences of various kinds.

> He was stuck and I got him out.
> I want this doll because she's big.
> I know what to do.
> I like to play with something else.
> I think she's sick.
> Look at the train Ursula bought.
> I gon' make it like a rocket to blast off with.
> It's too early for us to eat.

The Acquisition of Pragmatics

In addition to acquiring the rules of grammar, children must learn the appropriate use of language in context, or pragmatics.

Context is needed to determine the reference of pronouns. As also discussed in Chapter 4, a sentence like "Amazingly, he loves her" is uninterpretable unless both speaker and hearer understand who the pronouns *he* and *her* refer to. If the sentence were preceded by "I saw Zev and Maya kissing in the park," then it would be clear to the listener whom the pronouns refer to. Children are not always sensitive to the needs of their interlocutors and they may fail to establish the referents for pronouns. It is not unusual for a three- or four-year-old (or even older children) to use pronouns "out of the blue," like the child who cries to his mother "He hit me" when mom has no idea who did the deed.

The speaker and listener form part of the context of an utterance. The meaning of *I* and *you* depends on who's talking and who's listening, and this changes from situation to situation. Younger children (around age two) have difficulty with the "shifting reference" of these pronouns. A typical error that children make at this age is to refer to themselves as "you," for example, saying "You want to take a walk" when meaning "I want to take a walk."

Children also show a lack of pragmatic awareness by the way they sometimes use articles. As with pronouns, the interpretation of articles depends on context. The definite article (*the*) as in "the boy" can be used felicitously only when it is clear to speaker and hearer what boy is being discussed. In a discourse the indefinite article (*a/an*) must be used for the first mention of a new referent; the definite article (or pronoun) may be used in subsequent mentions, as illustrated below:

> A boy walked into the class.
> He was in the wrong room.
> The teacher directed the boy to the right classroom.

Children do not always respect the pragmatic rules for articles. In experimental studies, three-year-olds are just as likely to use the definite article as the indefinite article for introducing a new referent. In other words, the child tends to assume that his listener knows whom he is talking about without having established this in a linguistically appropriate way.

It may take a child several months or years to master those aspects of pragmatics that involve establishing the reference for function words such as determiners and pronouns. Other aspects of pragmatics are acquired very early. Children in the holophrastic stage use their one-word utterances with different illocutionary force. The utterance "up" spoken by a child at sixteen months might be a simple statement such as "The teddy is up on the shelf," or a request "Pick me up."

The Development of Auxiliaries: A Case Study

We have seen in this chapter that language acquisition involves development in various components — the lexicon, phonology, morphology, and syntax, as well as pragmatics. These different modules interact in complex ways to chart an overall course of language development.

As an example, let us take the case of the English auxiliaries. As noted earlier, children in the telegraphic stage do not typically use auxiliaries such as *can, will,* or *do,* and they often omit *be* and *have* from their utterances. Several syntactic constructions in English depend on the presence of an auxiliary, the most central of which are questions and negative sentences. To negate a main verb requires the auxiliary *do* or a modal as in the following examples:

> I don't like this movie.
> I won't see this movie.

An adult does not say "I not read this book."

Similarly, as discussed in Chapter 3, English yes-no and *wh* questions are formed by moving an auxiliary to precede the subject, as in the following examples:

> Can I leave now?
> Where should John put the book?

Although the two-year-old does not have productive control of auxiliaries, she is able to form negative sentences and questions. During the telegraphic stage the child produces questions of the following sort:

Yes-No Questions	*Wh* **Questions**
I ride train?	What cowboy doing?
Mommy eggnog?	Where milk go?
Have some?	Where kitty?

These utterances have a rising intonation pattern typical of questions in English, but since there are no auxiliaries, there can be no auxiliary movement. In *wh* questions there is also no auxiliary but there is generally a *wh* phrase that has moved to the beginning of the sentence. English-speaking children do not produce sentences such as "Cowboy doing what?" in which the *wh* phrase remains in its deep structure position.

The two-year-old has an insufficient lexicon. The lack of auxiliaries means that she cannot use a particular syntactic device associated with question formation in English — auxiliary movement. However, she has the pragmatic knowledge of how to make a request or ask for information, and she has the appropriate prosody, which depends on knowledge of phonology and the syntactic structure of the question. She also knows the grammatical rule that requires a *wh* phrase to be in the Comp position. Many components of language must be in place to form an adult-like question.

In languages that do not require auxiliaries to form a question, children appear more adultlike. For example, in Dutch and Italian, it is the main verb that moves. Since many main verbs are acquired before auxiliaries, Dutch and Italian children in the telegraphic stage produce questions that follow the adult rule:[2]

Dutch

En wat doen ze daar?	And what do they there	(And what are they doing there?)
Wordt mama boos?	Becomes mama angry	(Is mommy angry?)
Weet je n kerk?	Know you a church	(Do you know a church?)
Valt ie hier om?	Falls in here	(Does it fall here?)

Italian

Cosa fanno questi bambini?[3]	What do these children	(What are these babies doing?)
Chando vene a mama?	When comes the mommy	(When is Mommy coming?)
Vola cici?	Flies birdie	(Is the birdie flying?)
Veni teno?	Comes train	(Is the train coming?)

The Dutch and Italian children show us there is nothing intrinsically difficult about syntactic movement rules. The delay that English-speaking children show in producing adultlike questions is mainly because auxiliaries are acquired later than main verbs and English is idiosyncratic in forming questions by moving only auxiliaries.

The lack of auxiliaries during the telegraphic stage also affects the formation of negative sentences. An English-speaking child's negative sentences look like the following:

> He no bite you.
> Wayne not eating it.
> Kathryn not go over there.
> You no bring choo-choo train.
> That no fish school.

Because of the absence of auxiliaries, these utterances do not look very adultlike. However, children at this stage understand the pragmatic force of negation. The child who says "no!" when asked to take a nap knows exactly what he means.

As children acquire the auxiliaries, they generally use them correctly, that is, the auxiliary usually appears before the subject, but not always.

Yes-No Questions

Does the kitty stand up?
Can I have a piece of paper?
Will you help me?
We can go now?

Wh Questions

Which way they should go?
What can we ride in?
What will we eat?

The introduction of auxiliaries into the child's grammar also affects negative sentences. We now find correctly negated auxiliaries, though *be* is still missing in many cases.

Paul can't have one.
Donna won't let go.
I don't want cover on it.
I am not a doctor.
It's not cold.
Paul not tired.
I not crying.

The child always places the negation in the correct position in relation to the auxiliary or *be*. Main verbs follow negation and *be* precedes negation. Children virtually never produce errors such as "Mommy dances not" or "I not am going."

In languages such as French and German, which are like Italian and Dutch in having a rule that moves inflected verbs, the verb shows up before the negative marker. French and German children respect this rule.

French

Veux pas lolo	"want not water"	(I don't want water)
Marche pas	"walks not"	(She doesn't walk)
Ça tourne pas	"that turns not"	(that doesn't turn)

German

Macht nich aua	"makes not ouch"	(It doesn't hurt.)
Brauche nich lala	"need not pacifier"	(I don't need a pacifier.)
Schmeckt auch nich	"tastes also not"	(It doesn't taste good either.)
Ich mach das nich	"I do that not"	(I don't/won't do that.)

Whether they are acquiring Dutch, German, Italian, French, or any other language, all children pass through a "telegraphic" stage, which is but one of many stages that a child goes through on the way to adult linguistic competence. Each of these stages corresponds to a system of rules that the child has internalized — a grammar — and includes a lexicon and pragmatic rules. Although the child's language may not look exactly like the adult language, it is rule governed and not a haphazard approximation of the adult language.

Though the stages of language development are universal, they are shaped by the grammar of the particular adult language the child is acquiring. German-, French-, Italian-, and English-speaking children all go through a telegraphic stage in which they do not use auxiliaries, but they form negative sentences and questions in different ways because the rules of question and negative formation are different in the respective adult languages. This tells us something essential about language acquisition: Children are sensitive to the rules of the adult language at the earliest stages of development. Just as their phonology is quickly fine-tuned to the adult language, so is their syntactic system.

The ability of children to form complex rules and construct grammars of the languages used around them in a relatively short time is indeed phenomenal. The similarity of the language acquisition stages across diverse peoples and languages shows that children are equipped with special abilities to know what generalizations to look for and what to ignore, and how to discover the regularities of language.

Children develop language the way they develop the ability to sit up, stand, crawl, or walk. They are not taught to do these things, but all normal children begin to do them at around the same age. Learning to walk or learning language is different from learning to read or to ride a bicycle. Many people never learn to read because they are not taught to do so, and there are large groups of people in many parts of the world that have no *written* language. However, they all have language.

Setting Parameters

There are aspects of syntax that children acquire very quickly, even while they are still in the telegraphic stage. Most of these early developments correspond to what we earlier referred to as the parameters of UG. One such parameter that we discussed in Chapter 3, the head parameter, determines whether the head of a phrase comes before or after its complements, for example, whether the order of the VP is VO as in English or OV as in Japanese. Children produce the correct word order of their language in their earliest multiword utterances, and they understand word order even when they are in the one-word stage of production. According to the parameter model of UG, the child does not actually have to formulate a word order rule. Rather, he must choose between two already specified values: head first or head last? He determines the correct value based on the language he hears around him. The English-speaking child can quickly figure out that the head comes before its complements; a Japanese-speaking child can equally well determine that his language is head final.

Other parameters of UG involve the verb movement rules. In some languages the verb can move out of the VP to higher positions in the phrase structure tree. We saw this in the Dutch and Italian questions discussed in the last section. In other languages, such as English, verbs do not move (only auxiliaries do). The verb movement parameters provide the child with an option: my language does/does not allow verb movement. As we saw, Dutch- and Italian-speaking children quickly set the verb movement parameters to the "does allow" value, and so they form questions by moving the verb. English-speaking children never make the mistake of moving the verb — even when they don't yet have auxiliaries. In both cases, the children have set the parameter at the correct value for their language. Even after English-speaking children acquire the auxiliaries and the Aux movement rule, they never overgeneralize this movement to include verbs. This supports the hypothesis that the parameter is set early in development and cannot be undone. In this case as well, the child does not have to formulate a rule of verb movement; she does not have to learn when the verb moves and where it moves to. This is all given by UG. She simply has to decide whether verb movement is possible in her language.

The parameters of UG limit the grammatical options to a small well-defined set — is my language head first or head last, does my language have verb movement, and so on. Parameters greatly reduce the acquisition burden on the child and contribute to explaining the ease and rapidity of language acquisition.

The Acquisition of Sign Languages

Given the universal aspects of **sign languages** and spoken languages, it is not surprising that deaf children of deaf signing parents parallel the stages of spoken language acquisition. They babble, then progress to single signs similar to the single words in the holophrastic stage, and then begin to combine signs. There is also a telegraphic stage in which the grammatical signs are omitted. Grammatical or function signs appear at about the same age for deaf children as function words in spoken languages do for hearing children.

Deaf children's acquisition of the negative morphemes in American Sign Language (ASL) shows much the same pattern as in spoken language (Bellugi & Klima, 1976). NO and NEG (a headshake) are frequently used signs in adult ASL, with different restrictions on their use. Children acquiring ASL use them interchangeably in initial position of a signed sentence, in the same way that hearing children start negative sentences with *no*, but not in the ways in which negative signs are used in adult ASL. We see that the acquisition of ASL cannot be simple imitation any more than spoken language is acquired simply by imitation.

Sometimes the parallels between the acquisition of signed and spoken languages are surprising. Some of the grammatical morphemes in ASL are semantically transparent or **iconic**, that is, they look like what they mean. For example, the sign for the pronoun "I" involves the speaker pointing to his chest. The sign for the pronoun "you" is a point to the chest of the addressee. As we discussed earlier, at around age two children acquiring spoken languages often reverse the pronouns "I" and "you." Interestingly, at this same age signing children make this same error. They will point to themselves when they mean "you" and point to the addressee when they mean "I." Children acquiring ASL make this error despite the transparency or iconicity of these particular signs. This is because signing children (like signing adults) treat these pronouns as linguistic symbols and not simply as pointing gestures. As part of the language, the shifting reference of these pronouns presents the same problem for signing children that it does for speaking children.

Hearing children of deaf parents acquire both sign language and spoken language when exposed to both, although studies have shown that the child's first signs emerge a few months before the first spoken words. It is interesting that deaf children appear to begin producing signs earlier than hearing children begin producing spoken words. It has been suggested that this timing may be because control of hand muscles develops earlier than control of oral and laryngeal muscles.

Studies show that Canadian bilingual children who acquire Langue des signes Québécoise (LSQ, i.e., Quebec Sign Language) and French develop the two languages exactly as bilingual children acquiring two spoken languages (Petitto et al., 2001). The LSQ–French bilinguals reached linguistic milestones in each of their languages in parallel with Canadian children acquiring French and English. They produced their first words, as well as their first word combinations, at the same time in each language. In reaching these milestones neither group showed any delay as compared to monolingual children.

Deaf children of hearing parents who are not exposed to manual sign language from birth suffer a great handicap in acquiring language, yet language-learning ability seems to be so strong in humans that even they begin to develop their own manual gestures to express their thoughts and desires. A study of six such children revealed that they not only developed individual signs but also joined pairs and formed sentences (up to thirteen "words") with definite syntactic order and systematic constraints.

This fact, of course, should not be surprising; sign languages are as grammatical and systematic as spoken languages. We saw in Chapter 1 that the signs are conventional or arbitrary and not imitative. Furthermore, because all languages change over time, just as there are many different spoken languages, so too there are many different sign languages, all of which (spoken and sign) reveal the same linguistic universals. As mentioned in Chapter 1, deaf children often sign themselves to sleep and they report that they dream in sign language. Much that applies to the acquisition of spoken languages also applies to the acquisition of signed languages.

Summary

When children acquire a language, they acquire the grammar of that language — the phonological, morphological, syntactic, and semantic rules. They also acquire the pragmatic rules of the language as well as a lexicon. Children are not taught language. Rather, they extract the rules (and much of the lexicon) from the language around them.

A number of learning mechanisms have been suggested to explain the acquisition process. **Imitations** of adult speech, reinforcement, and **analogy** have all been proposed. None of these possible learning mechanisms account for the fact that children creatively form new sentences according to the rules of their language, or for the fact that children make certain kinds of errors but not others. Empirical studies of **child-directed speech** (CDS) show that grammar development does not depend on structured input. **Connectionist models** of acquisition also depend on the child having specially structured input.

The ease and rapidity of children's language acquisition and the uniformity of the stages of development for all children and all languages, despite the **poverty**

of the stimulus they receive, suggest that the language faculty is innate and that the infant comes to the complex task already endowed with a Universal Grammar. UG is not a grammar like the grammar of English or Arabic, but represents the principles to which all human languages conform. Language acquisition is a creative process. Children create grammars based on the linguistic input and are guided by UG.

A **critical period** has been proposed, i.e., a biological period during which humans are predisposed to acquire a language.

Language development proceeds in stages. These stages are universal. During the first year of life, children develop the sounds of their language. They begin by producing and perceiving many sounds that do not exist in their language input. Gradually, their productions and perceptions are fine-tuned to the environment. Children's late **babbling** has all the phonological characteristics of the input language. Deaf children exposed at birth to sign languages also produce manual babbling, showing that babbling is a universal first stage in language acquisition that is dependent on the linguistic input received.

At the end of the first year, children utter their first words. During the second year, they learn many more words and they develop much of the phonological system of the language. Children's first utterances are one-word "sentences" (the **holophrastic** stage). After a few months, the child puts two or more words together, the **two-word stage**. These early sentences are not random combinations of words: the words have definite patterns and express both syntactic and semantic relationships.

During the **telegraphic stage**, the child produces longer sentences that often lack function or grammatical morphemes. The child's early grammar still lacks many of the rules of the adult grammar, but is not qualitatively different from it. Children at this stage have correct word order and rules for agreement and case, which show their knowledge of structure.

Children make various kinds of errors. For example, they will **overgeneralize** morphology. This shows that they are acquiring rules. They also need to learn rules that are particular to their specific language, and there may be errors related to this learning. There are other kinds of errors that children never make, errors that would involve violating principles of Universal Grammar.

Deaf children exposed to **sign language** show the same stages of language acquisition as do hearing children exposed to spoken languages.

The universality of the language acquisition process, of the stages of development, and of the relatively short period in which the child constructs a complex grammatical system without overt teaching suggest that the human species is innately endowed with special language acquisition abilities, and that language is biologically and genetically part of the human neurological system.

All normal children everywhere learn language. This ability is not dependent on race, social class, geography, or even intelligence (within a normal range). This ability is uniquely human.

Notes

1. The following examples, as well as some others in the chapter, were taken from CHILDES (Child Language Data Exchange System), a computerized database of the spontaneous speech of children as they acquire many different languages.

2. In the child language examples from languages other than English, we have included a word-by-word translation and in parentheses the intended meaning of the utterance.

3. Italian data from J. Schaeffer (1990), *The syntax of the subject in child language: Italian compared to Dutch.* Unpublished master's thesis, State University of Utrecht.

Exercises

1. "Baby talk" is a term used to label the word forms that many adults use when speaking to children. Examples in English are *choo-choo* for "train" and *bow-wow* for "dog." Baby talk seems to exist in every language and culture. At least two things seem to be universal about baby talk: the words that have baby talk forms fall into certain semantic categories (e.g., food and animals), and the words are phonetically simpler than the adult forms (e.g., *tummy* /tʌmi/ for "stomach" /stʌmək/). List all the baby talk words you can think of in your native language; then (1) separate them into semantic categories, and (2) try to state general rules for the kinds of phonological reductions or simplifications that occur.

2. With the permission of his parents, play with a child between two and four years of age for about thirty minutes. Keep a list of all words and/or "sentences" that are used inappropriately. Describe what the child's meanings for these words probably are. Describe the syntactic or morphological errors (including omissions). If the child produces multiword sentences, write a grammar that could account for the data you have collected.

3. Chomsky has been quoted as saying,

   > It's about as likely that an ape will prove to have a language ability as that there is an island somewhere with a species of flightless birds waiting for human beings to teach them to fly.

   In the light of evidence presented in this chapter, comment on Chomsky's remark. Do you agree or disagree, or do you think the evidence is inconclusive?

*4. Roger Brown and his co-workers at Harvard University (see Brown, 1973) studied the language development of three children, referred to in the literature as Adam, Eve, and Sarah. The following are samples of their utterances during the "two-word stage."

see boy	push it
see sock	move it
pretty boat	mommy sleep
pretty fan	bye-bye melon
more taxi	bye-bye hot
more melon	

A. Assume that the above utterances are grammatical sentences in the children's grammars.

   (1) Write a mini-grammar that would account for these sentences. One rule might apply to more than one sentence.

   Example: One rule might be VP → V N.

   (2) Draw phrase structure trees for each utterance.

   Example:

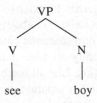

B. One observation made by Brown was that many of the sentences and phrases produced by the children were ungrammatical from the point of view of the adult grammar. The research group concluded, based on utterances such as those below, that a rule in the children's grammar for a noun phrase (NP) was

NP → M N (where M = any modifier)

a coat	my stool	poor man
a celery	that knee	little top
a Becky	more coffee	dirty knee
a hands	more nut	that Adam
my mummy	two tinker-toy	big boot

   (3) Mark with an asterisk any of the above NPs that are ungrammatical in the adult grammar of English. Use a question mark for any that could be grammatical in adult speech under certain circumstances, and define those circumstances.

(4) State the "violation" for each starred item. For example, if one of the utterances were *Lotsa book,* you might say "The modifier *lotsa* must be followed by a plural noun."

*5. In the holophrastic (one-word) stage of child language acquisition, the child's phonological system differs in systematic ways from that in the adult grammar. The inventory of sounds and the phonemic contrasts are smaller, and there are greater constraints on phonotactics. (See Chapter 6 for a discussion on these aspects of phonology.)

A. For each of the following words produced by a child, state what the substitution is.

Example: spook (adult) [spuk], (child) [pʰuk]

Substitution: initial cluster [sp] reduced to single consonant; /p/ becomes aspirated, showing that child has acquired aspiration rule.

1.	don't	[dot]		7.	bath	[bæt]
2.	skip	[kʰɪp]		8.	chop	[tʰap]
3.	shoe	[su]		9.	kitty	[kʰɪdi]
4.	that	[dæt]		10.	light	[wajt]
5.	play	[pʰe]		11.	dolly	[dawi]
6.	thump	[dʌp]		12.	grow	[go]

B. State some general rules that account for the children's deviation from adult pronunciations.

6. Children learn demonstrative words such as *this, that, these,* and *those*; temporal terms such as *now, then,* and *tomorrow*; and spatial terms such as *here, there, right,* and *behind* relatively late. What do all these words have in common? Why might that factor delay their acquisition?

7. We saw in this chapter how children overgeneralize rules such as the plural rule, producing forms such as *mans* and *mouses.* What might a child learning English use instead of the adult words given below?

a.	children	f.	sang
b.	went	g.	geese
c.	better	h.	worst
d.	best	i.	knives
e.	brought	j.	worse

8. The following words are from the lexicons of two children ages 1;6 and 2;0. Compare the pronunciation of the words to adult pronunciation (Kehoe & Gammon, 2001, pp. 393–432).

Child 1 (1;6)					Child 2 (2;0)			
soap	[doup]	bib	[bɛ]		light	[wajt]	bead	[biː]
feet	[bit]	slide	[daɪ]		sock	[sʌk]	pig	[pɛk]
sock	[kɑk]	dog	[dɑ]		geese	[gis]	cheese	[tis]
goose	[gos]	cheese	[čis]		fish	[fɪs]	biz	[bɪs]
dish	[dɪč]	shoes	[dus]		sheep	[šip]	bib	[bɪp]

A.   What happens to final consonants in the language of these two children? Formulate the rule(s) in words. Do all final consonants behave the same way? If not, which consonants undergo the rule(s)? Is this a natural class?

B.   On the basis of these data, are there any pairs of words that allow you to identify any of the phonemes in the grammars of these children? What are they? Explain how you were able to determine your answer.

References

Bellugi, U., & Klima, E.S. (1976). The roots of language in the sign talk of the deaf. *Psychology Today, 6,* 60–64.

Berko, J. (1958). The child's learning of English morphology. *Word, 14,* 150–177.

Berko Gleason, J., & Bernstein Ratner, N. (1998). *Psycholinguistics* (2nd ed.). Austin, Tx: Harcourt Brace Jovanovich.

Bloom, L.M. (1972). *Language development: Form and function in emerging grammar.* Cambridge, MA: MIT Press.

Bloomfield, L. (1933). *Language.* New York: Henry Holt.

Brown, R.O. (1973). *A first language: The early stages.* Cambridge, MA: Harvard University Press.

Cazden, C. (1972). *Child language and education.* New York: Holt, Rinehart and Winston.

Chomsky, N. (1975). *Reflections on language.* New York: Pantheon.

Chomsky, N. (1988). *Language and the problem of knowledge*: The Managua Lectures. Cambridge, MA: MIT Press.

Chomsky, N. (1994). *The human language series: Program 2.* By G. Searchinger. New York: Equinox Films/Ways of Knowing, Inc.

Curtiss, S. (1977). *Genie: A linguistic study of a modern-day "wild child."* New York: Academic Press.

Gleitman, L. (1994). *The human language series: Program 2.* By Gene Searchinger. New York: Equinox Films/Ways of Knowing, Inc.

Gleitman, L.R., & Wanner, E. (1982). *Language acquisition: The state of the art.* Cambridge, UK: Cambridge University Press.

Hyams, N. (1986). *Language acquisition and the theory of parameters.* Dordrecht, The Netherlands: Reidel.

Jakobson, R. (1971). *Studies on child language and aphasia.* The Hague: Mouton.

Kehoe, M., & Stoel Gammon, C. (2001). The development of syllable structure in English-speaking children with particular reference to rhymes. *Journal of Child Language, 28*(2), 393–432.

Keller, H. (1954). *The story of my life.* Garden City, NY: Doubleday.

Lenneberg, E. (1967). *The biological foundations of language.* New York: Wiley.

MacWhinney, B., & Snow, C. (1985). The child language data exchange system. *Journal of Child Language, 12,* 271–296.

Newport, E. (1990). Maturational constraints on language learning. *Cognitive Science, 14,* 11–28.

Petitto, L., Katerelos, M., Levy, B., Guana, K., Tetreault, K., & Ferraro, V. (2001). Bilingual signed and spoken language acquisition from birth: Implications for the mechanisms underlying early bilingual language acquisition. *Journal of Child Language, 28,* 453–496.

Pinker, S. (1994). *The language instinct.* New York: HarperCollins.

Russell, B. (1948). *Human knowledge: Its scope and limits.* New York: Simon and Schuster.

Further Reading

Atkinson, M. (1992). *Children's syntax: An introduction to principles and parameters theory.* Oxford: Blackwell.

Bowerman, M. (1973). *Early syntactic development.* Cambridge, MA: MIT Press.

Cairns, H. (1996). *The acquisition of language.* Austin, TX: PRO-ED.

Clark, E. (1995). *The lexicon in acquisition.* Cambridge, MA: Cambridge University Press.

Clark, H.H., & Clark, E.V. (1977). *Psychology and language.* New York: Harcourt Brace Jovanovich.

Crain, S., & Lillo-Martin, D. (1999). *An introduction to linguistic theory and language acquisition.* Oxford: Blackwell.

de Villiers, P.A., & de Villiers, J.G. (1978). *Language acquisition.* Cambridge, MA: Harvard University Press.

Feldman, H., Goldin-Meadow, S., & Gleitman, L. (1978). Beyond Herodotus: The creation of language by linguistically deprived deaf children. In A. Lock (Ed.), *Action, symbol, and gesture: The emergence of language* (pp. 351–413). New York: Academic Press.

Fischer, S.D., & Siple, P. (1990). *Theoretical issues in sign language research: Vol. 1. Linguistics.* Chicago: University of Chicago Press.

Gillen, J. (2003). *The language of children.* New York: Routledge.

Gleitman, L. (1991). Language. In H. Gleitman (Ed.), *Psychology* (3rd. ed.). New York: Norton.

Goldin-Meadow, S. (2003). *The resilience of language: What gesture creation in deaf children can tell us about how all children learn language.* Oxford, UK: Psychology Press.

Goldin-Meadow, S., & Mylander, C. (1990). Beyond the input given: The child's role in the acquisition of language. *Language, 66*(2), 323–355.

Golinkoff, R., & Hirsh-Pasek, K. (1996). *The origins of grammar.* Cambridge, MA: MIT Press.

Hoff, E. (2008) *Language development* (4th ed.). Belmont, CA: Wadsworth.

Ingram, D. (1989). *First language acquisition: Method, description, and explanation.* New York: Cambridge University Press.

Jusczyk, P.W. (1997). *The discovery of spoken language.* Cambridge, MA: MIT Press.

Klima, E.S., & Bellugi, U. (1979). *The signs of language.* Cambridge, MA: Harvard University Press.

Landau, B., & Gleitman, L.R. (1985). *Language and experience: Evidence from the blind child.* Cambridge, MA: Harvard University Press.

Lust, B.C. (2006). *Child language: Acquisition and growth.* Cambridge, MA: Cambridge University Press.

Lust, B.C., & Foley, C. (2003). *First language acquisition: The essential readings.* Oxford, UK: Blackwell.

Petitto, L. (1987). On the autonomy of language and gesture: Evidence from the acquisition of personal pronouns in American Sign Language. *Cognition, 27*(1), 1–52.

Websites

http://childes.psy.cmu.edu CHILDES: Child Language Data Exchange System.

http://www.bu.edu/linguistics/APPLIED/BUCLD/ The Boston University annual conference on language development website.

https://www.msu.edu/~casby/langdevidcomp/ A collection of short videos showing children and their language development, compiled by Michael Casby.

http://www.pbs.org/wgbh/nova/transcripts/2112gchild.html A PBS website with a transcript discussing the "Genie" case.

CHAPTER 8
Second Language Acquisition

A different language is a different vision of life.

Federico Fellini (1920–1993)

Learn a new language and get a new soul.
You are a person as many times as the languages you know.

Czech proverbs

Second language acquisition (SLA), or second language learning (SLL), is generally considered to include any language learning that begins once the first language (L1) has been basically acquired. In some contexts it is important to make a distinction between *second* language learning (learning a language that is spoken in the learner's environment) and *foreign* language learning (learning a language that is generally not used in the learner's surroundings). However, we will follow general usage patterns and use the phrase "second language" (L2) to refer to what is common to both learning contexts. Also, while our focus is on the acquisition of a second language once the first language has been acquired, we will discuss the simultaneous acquisition of two languages in the final chapter section on bilingualism.

There are a number of intriguing questions that arise in the domain of second language acquisition. Some of these questions include:

- Is L2 acquisition like L1 acquisition?
- Does the L1 help or get in the way of L2 learning?
- Is there a single theoretical model to account for all aspects of L2 acquisition?
- Are there any patterns in L2 grammatical development?
- Is there a method that will successfully teach an L2?
- Can adults learn an L2 successfully?
- Are some people better or faster at L2 acquisition than others? If so, why?
- Do children who learn two languages simultaneously suffer adverse effects?

First Language Acquisition vs. Second Language Acquisition

Learning one's native language as a child and learning a second language once the first language is well established share a number of similarities. In both cases a new linguistic system is being acquired. A new repertoire of sounds, sound patterns, words, phrases, syntactic structures, and knowledge of how to appropriately use these new sounds, words, and structures must be acquired. In both cases, some degree of repetition and practising of structures appears to take place. Similarly, acquisition proceeds in a gradual, systematic fashion; language is not acquired instantaneously. Also, learners appear to build upon previous learning in both situations. However, a closer look reveals a number of important differences that characterize the two situations.

Perhaps the most striking difference is that of **ultimate attainment**. Learning a second language after the first language is well established is not as universally successful as first language acquisition. Essentially all children of normal intelligence acquire their mother tongue with remarkable accuracy and within a relatively short timeframe. In contrast, the later second language learner seems to take longer to attain basic fluency. In addition, even when their learning situations are similar, L2 learners often do not reach similar levels of L2 proficiency.

In addition to the issue of ultimate attainment, there are a number of other important differences that distinguish second language acquisition from first language acquisition. These differences may or may not play a role in explaining why learners achieve various outcomes.

One obvious difference between child acquisition and later acquisition by adolescents or adults is age and the biological and physiological differences that accompany age differences. For instance, there are age-related differences associated with brain development. One of these age-related differences is degree of cognitive development. Very young children learn their mother tongue during a very early stage of cognitive development, while older L2 learners are cognitively more mature and therefore may adopt a different approach to learning.

Furthermore, for the very young L1 acquirer, language is an intrinsic component of the child's overall cognitive and social development; for instance, children tend to acquire the principle of object permanence and the vocabulary to mark it at approximately the same time. In later L2 acquisition, concepts have already been acquired and tagged by L1 labels.

In L1 acquisition, language is a tool for the satisfaction of immediate basic needs. On the other hand, in L2 acquisition the learner already has an established language to draw upon in order to carry out daily activities and satisfy basic needs. In addition, the older learner can draw from a wider experience, and more sophisticated concepts are available. Adolescents and adults also have greater **metalinguistic awareness**, that is, conscious awareness about language, than young children; they also have more world knowledge and literacy skills.

Significant affective differences also characterize L1 vs. L2 acquisition. Affective factors that might play a particularly important role in L2 acquisition include issues such as strength of motivation and attitudes toward language learning as well as toward target-language speakers. Personality characteristics such as degree of self-esteem and self-confidence or whether or not a person has a tendency for risk taking may also play more of a role in L2 learning.

For adolescent and adult learners of a second language, there is the potential factor of feelings of alienation from one's native language and culture. Acquiring a new mode of speech requires at least some degree of adaptation to a new linguistic system; adopting new speech patterns and producing new speech sounds might lead learners to experience feelings of insecurity.

There are also important differences in the area of social expectations. While it is generally the case that young children are allowed to produce utterances in their mother tongue at their own pace, the adult L2 learner in a language classroom or in an L2 environment is often the object of subtle and not so subtle external (and internal) pressures to communicate beyond his current ability level.

Another obvious difference is that in the case of the L2 learner, one language has already been acquired. This entails that transfer or interference across the two languages is a factor. The term **transfer**, or more specifically "positive transfer," refers to the use of words or structures similar to those of the native language in the L2, while "negative transfer," or the more commonly used term **interference**, refers to the use of L1 words or structures where they do not apply in the L2. Thus already knowing one language may constitute an advantage or a disadvantage at various stages in the L2 learning process.

In addition, the sequence in which learners acquire different linguistic skills tends to vary widely across L1 and L2 acquisition contexts. In the case of young children learning the mother tongue, the order proceeds from listening to speaking, with reading and writing skills appearing much later when schooling begins. On the other hand, for the later L2 learner, there is often a different sequencing in the acquisition of skills: adults, who tend to be more visual and literacy minded, often begin with reading.

There are also other important situational differences: the L1 is acquired without deliberate instruction while the L2 is very often learned in an instructional setting with a structured presentation of linguistic material. In addition, the classroom setting can vary depending on the teaching method, the instructor's approach, and the choice of materials, among other variables.

Other differences include the fact that there is at least some exposure to CDS (child-directed speech, see Chapter 7) when acquiring the native language, which has been argued as providing at least some degree of adaptation of language to the young child's developmental level. This is often not the case for older L2 learners, although studies have found some interlocutors do modify their speech to L2 learners.

And finally, another potentially important factor that differentiates L1 from L2 acquisition is simply the sheer amount of time available that is devoted to L1 as opposed to L2 exposure. Young children are generally raised in an environment in which they are surrounded by constant exposure to their native language, while this is often not the case for the L2 learner who may spend most of her time communicating through the first language, rather than the L2.

Aislin, Montreal Gazette.

Trends and Theoretical Approaches in Second Language Acquisition

Behaviourism and the Contrastive Analysis Approach

> Individuals tend to transfer the forms and meanings . . . of their native language and culture to the foreign language and culture. . . .
>
> Robert Lado, *Linguistics across Cultures* (1957)

During the early and middle decades of the twentieth century, the predominant view in psychology was that of **behaviourism**. As discussed briefly in Chapter 7, this theory viewed learning as largely dependent on environmental factors.

Psychologist B.F. Skinner applied the theory of behaviourism to learning language by articulating the view that L1 learning is a process highly dependent on the establishment of a set of habits by means of associations between stimuli and responses linked through repeated practice, reinforcement, and conditioning.

The behaviourist approach to learning in the 1950s tended to emphasize the similarities between acquiring one's native language and learning a second language except for the important difference that the L2 learner already possesses a language. The prevailing mode of thought in psychology influenced the view that like L1 acquisition, L2 learning is a learned behaviour, heavily dependent on environmental factors. According to behaviourist views, L2 learning takes place in the same way as any other kind of learning — it involves procedures such as imitation, repetition, and reinforcement, which enable learners to develop "habits" of the L2.

This view of language as a set of automatic habits, along with a **structuralist approach** to linguistics during this same time period that emphasized language as a set of forms or structures, led to development of the **contrastive analysis (CA) approach** to L2 learning. The CA approach placed a major emphasis on the detrimental role that interference from the L1 plays in L2 learning. What was termed the **contrastive analysis hypothesis (CAH)** was the prediction that a contrastive analysis of structural differences between two languages would allow one to identify areas of contrast and therefore predict where there would be difficulty and errors on the part of the L2 learner.

A major goal of CA was to guide the preparation of language teaching materials. In the foreword to *Linguistics across Cultures (*Lado, 1957), a book that epitomizes the CA approach applied to language teaching, the objectives of this approach are clearly outlined:

> Before any questions of how to teach a foreign language must come the much more important preliminary work of finding the special problems arising out of any effort to develop a new set of language habits against a background of different native language habits. . . .
>
> Learning a second language, therefore, constitutes a very different task from learning the first language. The basic problems arise not out of any essential difficulty in the features of the new language themselves but primarily out of the special "set" created by the first language habits.

The CAH predicts positive transfer for structures that are similar in the two languages. For example, for the English L1 speaker learning French, the subject-verb-object (SVO) word sequence that patterns similarly across the two languages should be easily acquired:

"The boy sees the girl." = "*Le garçon voit la fille.*"

On the other hand, negative transfer, or interference, would be predicted for structures that differ between the two languages. For example, when a noun object is replaced with a pronoun as in "The boy saw her," the French sentence requires the pronoun to precede the verb as in *"Le garçon la voit."* In the CA view, the English L1 speaker, hindered by the native language habit, would be predicted to follow the pattern of the L1: *"*Le garçon voit elle."*

The CA approach led to a number of predictions in the language classroom and in the preparation of pedagogical material for use in the classroom:

1. Language learning involves establishing a new set of habits.
2. The major source of errors in L2 is the L1.
3. One can account for errors by considering L1/L2 differences.
4. The greater the differences, the more errors.
5. Learning an L2 means learning the differences.
6. Difficulty and ease in learning are determined by differences and similarities between the two languages.

Applied to the language classroom, an adherence to the CA view that L1 habits needed to be broken and replaced by L2 habits led to the adoption of the mechanical language drills and sentence and dialogue memorization that characterize the audiolingual method in L2 teaching (see "Language Teaching Approaches," page 374).

Randal Whitman (1970) suggested that four procedures could be applied in carrying out a CA to prepare language teaching materials:

1. *Description*: The two languages are explicitly described using the tools of formal grammar.
2. *Selection*: The specific linguistic structures or rules to be examined are selected.
3. *Contrast*: The two linguistic systems are contrasted with respect to the selected structures.
4. *Prediction*: A prediction of difficulty is made based on the preceding three procedures and with reference to a hierarchy of difficulty.

The **hierarchy of difficulty** mentioned in Whitman's procedures allowed predictions for language contrasts that would cause greater or lesser learning difficulty; areas of least difference were assumed to be the easiest to acquire.

However, the actual application of the hierarchy of difficulty method revealed a number of problems: What was one to do with partial correspondences that could not be slotted easily into one category, as in the example of English speakers learning the French *r* sound, which is often articulated as a uvular fricative in French, but as a retroflex liquid in English? Should it be considered a totally new element or an adaptation of an existing sound? There is a great deal of subjectivity involved in determining what constitutes "similar" or "different" items. Another weakness was the failure to recognize that it is often the subtle differences that cause the most problems for language learners, not simply differences alone. Linguistic difference and psychological difficulty are not the same.

Later research produced evidence that contradicted the major claims of the CAH. For instance, it turned out that in neither child nor adult L2 performance do the majority of the grammatical errors reflect the learner's L1. Many errors were found to be due to overgeneralizing from L2 structures. A second problem for the CAH was that L2 learners were found to make many errors in areas of grammar that are comparable in both the L1 and L2. On the other hand, learners were also found not to make errors that would have been predicted. For instance, the CAH would predict that placement of unstressed object pronouns should be equally difficult for English native speakers learning French as an L2 and French speakers learning English:

"I like them."   *"Je les aime."*

But while English speakers may make the error *"*J'aime les*" early on in their learning, in contrast, French speakers don't appear to have a tendency to make the equivalent error in English: *"I them like," which the CAH would predict. This contrast in performance is difficult to reconcile with the CAH view that differences equal difficulty; therefore it appears that the CAH does not consistently and accurately predict areas of difficulty.

Ultimately, the many discrepancies between the CAH's predictions and actual learner performance led to its substantial moderation. While the original "strong" version stated that CA can predict difficulty and errors, a more moderate version stated that CA can help explain some of these errors, in particular those due to transfer from the L1.

Cognitivism and the Error Analysis Approach

> A learner's errors . . . are significant in [that] they provide to the researcher evidence of how language is learned or acquired, what strategies or procedures the learner is employing in the discovery of the language.
>
> Pit Corder, "The Significance of Learners' Errors" (1967)

In contrast to the strong claims about the similarities between L1 and L2 acquisition in the behaviourist approach, cognitive theorists argue that there are many areas of difference between L1 and L2 acquisition. L2 learning is a complex process that involves the environmental input of the classroom (or other context of learning), some imitation, rote memory, and cognitive learning strategies.

The study of actual learner errors showed that while many errors were caused by transfer from the L1, many other errors could not be traced back to L1 influence. Thus the results of error analyses were used to refute behaviourist views of L2 learning that were dominant at the time.

The study of learner errors revealed that learners were actively trying out solutions based on what they were learning about the new target language. Studying learner errors also revealed that learners appeared to go through acquisition stages, as types of errors varied according to learners' level of development.

The study of errors is carried out by means of **error analysis (EA)** and is closely associated with the work of Pit Corder, who published a number of influential articles in the 1960s and 1970s in which he made a case for examining errors as a way of investigating L2 learning processes. Since it is difficult to directly observe language *comprehension*, the focus in error analysis research is on the occurrence of overt errors in the oral and written *production* of language.

While the CA approach stressed the importance of avoiding errors, Corder pointed out that errors could be significant in a number of ways: they provided the instructor with information about how much the learner had learned; they provided the researcher with evidence of how language was learned; and they served as devices by which the learner discovered the rules of the target language. Similar to the close link discussed earlier between CA research and its classroom application, researchers involved in carrying out error analyses in the 1970s were also very interested in applying the results of EA research to the language classroom.

An important step in EA is the attempt to explain why errors have been made, that is, establishing the source of errors (see Figure 8.1). EA researchers were interested in examining all types of errors, regardless of whether they were due to L1 interference, the predominant issue of interest in contrastive analysis research. Two basic sources of errors were identified: interlingual, due to interference from the L1, or intralingual (within one language), due to overgeneralizing of target language rules. Intralingual errors can be considered developmental since they reflect the learner's active development of the L2 system. Just as children acquiring their L1 make certain errors, L2 learners similarly produce faulty versions of the L2 target language that cannot be explained by interference from their L1.

Additional, although less common, sources of errors include the sociolinguistic communication context, cognitive strategies, and classroom-induced errors. For example, a classroom-induced error might include a student's overuse of tag questions in inappropriate contexts ("I'm going home, aren't I?") due to an overemphasis of that structure in the language classroom.

Some errors appear to become integral parts of the language learner's system. Errors that remain rooted in the learner's language are usually referred to as fossilized errors or **fossilizations.**

Dulay and Burt (1974) carried out a series of studies of the errors made by Spanish learners of English in order to determine which errors were interlingual and which were intralingual. They found that the majority of errors were not due to interference from the L1. This finding gave significant support to the error analysis view that recognizes the importance of intralingual sources of errors. Other studies have similarly found that adult L2 learners are more likely than child L2 learners to make interlingual errors, and even then, no more than 30 percent of their errors are interlingual in origin.

Thus, by the late 1960s, similar to the emerging portrait of the L1 learner in this period, the L2 learner came to be viewed as creatively participating in the emergence of the new linguistic system. Errors were viewed as valuable indications of

FIGURE 8.1
Sources of errors.

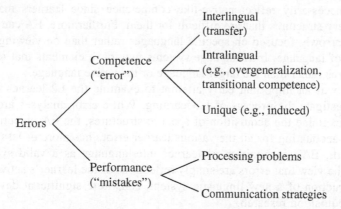

Adapted from *The study of second language acquisition*, by R. Ellis, 1994, Oxford: Oxford University Press, p. 58, fig. 2.2. Adapted with permission.

the current state of learners' hypotheses about the new language. The learner's L2 became worthy of interest in and of itself.

As a reflection of the new importance attributed to the L2 learner's developing system, a number of terms were introduced: "interlanguage," "approximative system," and "idiosyncratic dialect." The most widely used of these is the term **interlanguage,** coined by Selinker (1972). *Interlanguage* refers to the intermediary status of learner language, situated somewhere between the L1 and the target language.

It soon became obvious, however, that there are a number of problems associated with determining the source of a given learner error. For one, a distinction needs to be made between "errors" that reflect the current state of the interlanguage knowledge of the L2 learner, and "mistakes" that are simply temporary lapses that all learners and native speakers make from time to time. This distinction is not always easy to make.

Also, it is not always possible to determine whether a specific error is interlingual or intralingual, or perhaps even due to a contribution from both sources. For instance, it might be relatively easy to conclude that when a French L1 learner of English says: "I wait since two hours," the error is due to interference from the L1 equivalent *"J'attends depuis deux heures."* On the other hand, when an English L1 learner of French says *"Je suis fini"* instead of *"J'ai fini,"* is the error due to interference from the L1 equivalent "I am finished," or might it be due to some overgeneralizing from the French structures of the pattern: *"Je suis allé"* ("I went"), *"Je suis parti"* ("I left"), or perhaps even due to both processes?

Other limitations to the EA approach include the fact that production data are overemphasized; comprehension is just as important. Also, it is important to know what learners do correctly as well as where they make errors. In addition, EA essentially ignores the learner's avoidance of certain linguistic structures: the absence of error doesn't necessarily reflect native-like competence since learners may be avoiding the very structures that are difficult for them. Furthermore, EA can keep attention too narrowly focused on specific languages rather than on viewing universal aspects of language. Interlanguage systems may have elements that reflect universal features rather than the target language or the native language.

In sum, EA was an important early attempt to examine the L2 learner's language and investigate the process of L2 learning. While error analyses are still carried out to examine the acquisition of specific structures, the EA objective of systematically accounting for all the various learner errors has more or less been abandoned. Still, EA's recognition of learner interlanguage as a valid system, together with the view that errors are simply reflections of the learner's active and creative construction of a new linguistic system, constitute significant developments in L2 acquisition research.

The Monitor Model (the Input Hypothesis)

> Learning, conscious knowledge, serves only as an editor, or Monitor.
>
> Steven Krashen, *The Input Hypothesis* (1985)

In the late 1970s and throughout the 1980s, Steven Krashen (e.g., 1977, 1985) developed and articulated what he meant to serve as a general theoretical model of L2 acquisition, based in part on innate principles of language acquisition. His proposed **monitor model** included a set of five hypotheses concerning L2 acquisition. As this model has been the object of intense debate, we will briefly outline each hypothesis and point out critical remarks that have been made in its regard.

1. *Acquisition-learning hypothesis:* The first hypothesis, the acquisition-learning hypothesis, concerns a crucial and controversial distinction Krashen made between what he considered to be very different processes: *acquisition* vs. *learning*. Krashen argued that there are two distinct ways of developing L2 competence: (1) "acquisition," consisting of subconsciously acquired language knowledge typically occurring when the learner's attention is focused on meaning rather than form; and (2) "learning," referring to the learner's conscious knowledge of the rules and patterns of a language, as occurs when studying grammar in the typical language classroom.

    Krashen outlined a strong claim with regard to these two processes: he argued that what is learned cannot become acquired knowledge. In other words, what is consciously learned, such as the grammatical rules learned in a classroom situation, cannot be transformed into the underlying linguistic competence that ultimately allows the language learner to produce fluent utterances in the target language. This strong claim has become known as the "noninterface position."

However, a number of criticisms have been levelled at this hypothesis. Primarily, it has been pointed out that Krashen has not provided a clearly defined distinction between acquisition and learning and the hypothesis is therefore untestable. Critics have also pointed out that it is counterintuitive to affirm that what is learned about the target language is never incorporated into the learner's underlying knowledge that allows him to communicate in that language.

2. *Monitor hypothesis:* With the monitor hypothesis, Krashen proposed that a language editor or **monitor** goes into effect under specific circumstances, allowing the language user to monitor her utterances. The monitor, the result of what is consciously "learned" in the classroom, is under conscious control of the learner and allows her to correct utterances that have been produced by the "acquired" system. The monitor goes into action under specific conditions: there must be a sufficient amount of time; the language task must be focused on the form of utterances, such as a grammar test; and the learner must "know the rule" that is being applied to utterances.

   However, there is no empirical evidence to support the existence of an independent editor or monitor in the learner, and the conditions under which Krashen proposes it would operate are questionable. For instance, by "rules" does Krashen mean the prescriptive rules of some teaching methods and materials, or each learner's own particular understanding of L2 rules?

3. *Natural order hypothesis:* The natural order hypothesis states that the rules of a language are acquired in a predictable order and is based on evidence accumulated from morpheme studies that examined the order in which certain morphemes were acquired in diverse populations of L2 learners. In these studies, it was generally found that despite different L1 backgrounds, L2 learners tended to acquire morphemes in a similar order. For example, the plural ending *-s*, as in "horses," has been found to be acquired before the third-person singular suffix *-s,* as in "she sings."

   Critics pointed out that there are problems with the evidence from the morpheme studies: most of these were cross-sectional in design and not longitudinal. Rather than following the acquisition of morphemes across time, many studies measured accuracy order. That is, if subjects correctly used a given morpheme at least 90 percent of the time it was required, they were considered to have acquired that item. However, accuracy in production is not necessarily the same as an order of acquisition. In addition, subsequent studies revealed that contrary to initial claims from such studies, L1 transfer remains an important factor in L2 learning.

4. *Comprehensible input hypothesis:* The comprehensible input hypothesis was a central component of Krashen's model, as seen by the fact that more recent versions of the model have been called the *input hypothesis.* Krashen argued that the crucial aspect to acquiring the L2 and not simply "learning" is

exposure to **comprehensible input**. He proposed an equation that represents this quantity, $i + 1$, to represent input that is slightly beyond the learner's present state of language fluency. He also argued that speaking is the result of acquisition, not its cause. The argument was that if enough input was understood, the necessary grammar would be automatically provided.

However, critics argued that the definition of comprehensible input is circular and it is therefore impossible to test or falsify. Krashen asserts that acquisition will occur if enough comprehensible input is provided, and comprehensible input is claimed to have been provided if acquisition does indeed occur. But the hypothesis fails to provide a precise way to determine the "slightly beyond" $i + 1$ input level. Other critics point out that the role of the learner's output is ignored. For instance, Swain (1985), a Canadian researcher who has drawn attention to learner output, points to evidence that the learner's own utterances play a role in contributing to the development of the target language system.

5. *Affective filter hypothesis:* A final component is the affective filter hypothesis. This hypothesis proposes that affective factors, such as degree of anxiety or stress, pose a potential barrier to acquisition.

While there is merit to acknowledging the role affective factors might play in L2 learning, factors often ignored in other theoretical approaches, there is little specific information to allow empirical testing of the filter. In addition, the same result would be predicted for both indifferent learners and highly motivated learners: since the filter blocks access to comprehensible input only under affective conditions that hinder learning, it would predict that both unstressed, highly motivated learners and unstressed, indifferent learners would be equally unaffected by the filter and enjoy optimal comprehensible input conditions, a counterintuitive prediction.

In sum, the monitor model seemed to make good intuitive sense on a superficial level. It appeared to offer a global, encompassing theoretical model of L2 acquisition. However, on closer examination, it became clear that it was impossible to test the model in a scientifically rigorous manner. As we have seen, there are aspects of the model that lead to counterintuitive predictions, and the model is self-contradictory in some respects. Still, despite these flaws, the model continues to draw attention and debate, and its influence is still felt in applied L2 research and language classrooms.

Universal Grammar (UG)

> Claims for UG operation in L2 acquisition are simply claims that interlanguage grammars will fall within a limited range, that the "hypothesis space" is specified by UG.
>
> Lydia White, "On the Nature of Interlanguage Representation" (2003)

As has been discussed previously in this book, linguists have proposed that L1 acquisition is constrained by Universal Grammar (UG), i.e., specific innate principles and properties that place limitations on possible grammars. Since UG is considered to be part of our genetic endowment, it offers an explanation for the rapid success in acquiring our first language.

L2 acquisition studies carried out in the UG framework focus on finding evidence for UG rather than on attempting to characterize the L2 learning process.

There are two major reasons for the interest in determining whether UG plays a role in L2 acquisition. The first reason is to learn whether all language learning (L1, L2, L3 . . .) is supported by the same language faculty. The second reason concerns the issue of whether UG remains available to the L2 learner, given evidence that L2 learning beyond early childhood is generally much slower and more difficult than L1 acquisition. This latter fact has led some researchers to suggest UG is available only during a short period of time.

Studies in the UG framework have therefore largely focused on the question of whether UG remains accessible in L2 acquisition and, if so, to what extent. A central issue is to identify the nature of the L2 grammar at the different stages of development, including the initial and the endstate stages. As stated in the citation from White quoted at the beginning of this section, "claims for UG operation in L2 acquisition are simply claims that interlanguage grammars will fall within a limited range, that the 'hypothesis space' is specified by UG" (2003, p. 38). UG theory itself does not attempt to make claims about how or why the interlanguage grammar develops in a particular fashion, since it focuses on issues of representation and not development.

Various hypotheses have been proposed as to whether learners have no access, full (direct) access, or indirect or partial access to UG (see Figure 8.2).

1. *No access hypothesis*: UG is not involved in L2 acquisition; rather, learners must depend on general problem-solving skills.
2. *Full access hypothesis*: UG is directly accessible in L2 acquisition.
3. *Indirect access hypothesis*: UG is not directly involved in L2 acquisition but can be indirectly accessed through the L1.
4. *Partial access hypothesis*: Some UG aspects remain available to the L2 while other aspects do not.

Thus the main question from the UG point of view has been whether interlanguage representations show evidence of being constrained by principles of UG. The question UG researchers ask is, are interlanguage grammars restricted in the same way as the grammars of native speakers? Researchers in this framework point out that it isn't necessary for L2 learners to reveal an interlanguage grammar that is identical to the target language, only that the interlanguage is a possible grammar, but still constrained by principles of UG.

FIGURE 8.2
Four hypotheses about access to UG.

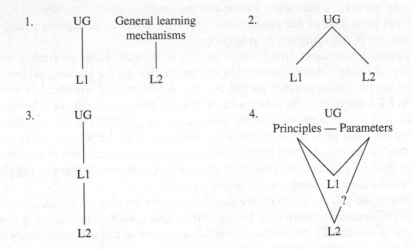

R. Mitchell and F. Myles, *Second Language Learning Theories* 1/e. (Edward Arnold, 1998). Text © 1998. Reproduced by the permission of Edward Arnold.

More recent UG studies changed the focus from the broad UG-access question to more narrow ones that consider the specific grammatical properties that characterize the learner's interlanguage and the degree to which such properties diverge from the target language. A particular focus has been to examine whether or not L2 learners are able to reset their parameters from the L1 values to the L2 values.

The UG-based studies have yielded various results, some of which have been interpreted as supporting the notion that UG remains accessible, others suggesting that no clear support for full or partial access is evident.

For instance, evidence has been found suggesting that adult L2 learners continue to have access to UG. In this regard, some studies report that Japanese adult learners of English are able to acquire the English "head-first" value of the head parameter, even though Japanese is a "head-last" language. As mentioned in Chapter 7, the head parameter determines whether the head of a phrase comes before or after its complements. For example, in English, a "head-first" language, the order in the VP is VO (verb object). In Japanese, on the other hand, the order in the VP is OV (object verb). Similarly, while prepositions precede their complements in English ("in Canada"), prepositions like *ni* are phrase final in Japanese (*Nihon ni* = literally, "Japan in"). Since Japanese adult learners of English appear to easily acquire the English setting for the head parameter, this finding has been interpreted as suggesting that parameters can be reset, and UG remains available to the adult L2 learner.

Another study involved a different parameter, the null-subject parameter, which refers to the fact that some languages allow null (that is, no) subjects in certain contexts. For example, Spanish is considered to be a null-subject language (+ null subject) that permits subject pronouns to be deleted in sentences such as "*Hablo inglés*" ("I speak English"). In a study that looked at Spanish and French speakers learning English, White (1986) found that the Spanish speakers were much more likely to accept ungrammatical null-subject sentences in English (for example, "Should go," "Came Suzanne," etc.) than were French speakers, whose L1 is considered not to accept null subjects (a – null subject language). This finding can be interpreted as an indication that Spanish speakers transfer their L1 setting for the null-subject parameter into English and therefore provides support for indirect access to UG.

On the other hand, another proposal is that interlanguage grammars are fundamentally different from those in L1 acquisition because UG is no longer available to (adult) L2 learners. This would suggest that the interlanguage is not following UG constraints.

UG has had a great deal of influence in the study of second language acquisition. However, it does not claim to be a theory of second language acquisition; its aim is to provide a detailed characterization of linguistic competence. Social and psychological variables that might affect the L2 learning process are not considered within its domain of study and therefore are not examined.

Cognitive Approach

Information-Processing Model

> In general, the fundamental notion of the information-processing approach to psychological inquiry is that complex behaviour builds on simple processes.
>
> McLaughlin and Heredia, "Information-Processing Approaches" (1996)

The **information-processing model** or **approach** falls within a more general **cognitive approach** to language learning that was originally articulated within the discipline of cognitive psychology. In a cognitive approach the focus is on the learner's internal cognitive processes involved in the learning of the second language. There are a number of cognitive-based models applied to second language acquisition, but we will describe only one of the most prominent of these, the information-processing model.

Researchers working in an information-processing approach generally accept that second language learning relies on general cognitive mechanisms (see Table 8.1). Language learning is viewed as skill learning. Two key notions in this framework are **automatization** and **restructuring**. Various subskills in the L2 learning task, such as learning to articulate new sounds, are thought to become automatized through repetition and practice. In addition, learning is restructured as learners become more efficient in organizing their developing system. Thus, during the early stages of learning L2 structures, learners are thought to be mostly dependent on **controlled processing**, which requires a substantial amount of attentional control on the part of the learner. As the learner continues to practise structures, these become automatized. Automatized learning, or automatic processing, requires less attention and occurs more rapidly. In this way, learners are seen as gradually gaining increasing control over their learning as they progress from time-consuming controlled processing to the more rapid, automatic processing. Since attentional capacity is limited, the increasing reliance on automatic processing frees up more attention, which becomes available to deal with more complex aspects of the language learning process, such as focusing on comprehending the message.

The information-processing view of language learning as the acquisition of a complex skill has allowed a focus on cognitive processes such as the role of memory and attention in the language learning process. Techniques derived from psychology, including word recognition tasks, phonological and short-term memory tasks, as well as others, have shed light on the relationship between cognitive processes and language performance and achievement.

In this regard, results of experiments using lexical decision tasks (e.g., Van Hell & Dijkstra, 2002) in which bilinguals are asked to decide whether a given item is a real word or not indicate that words presented in the bilingual's stronger language activate information in the weaker language at the same time: information in both languages is activated automatically and cannot be "turned off." For instance, under a variety of conditions, a French–English bilingual exposed to the item *pain* is likely to process the French meaning of "bread" as well as the English meaning of "discomfort."

Other studies point toward a relationship between aspects of memory and language learning. For instance, some research suggests that phonological working memory, a short-term mental space for holding speech-based information in memory, may play an important role in the early stages of L2 vocabulary learning

TABLE 8.1
Some Characteristics of the Information-Processing Approach

1. Humans are viewed as autonomous and active.
2. The mind is a general-purpose symbol-processing system.
3. Complex behaviour is composed of simpler processes.
4. Component processes can be isolated and studied independently of other processes.
5. Processes take time; therefore, predictions about reaction time can be made.
6. The mind is a limited-capacity processor.

From "Information-processing approaches to research on second language acquisition and use," by B. McLaughlin and R. Heredia, 1996, in Richie and Bhatia (Eds.), *Handbook of second language acquisition*, New York: Academic Press, Table 1, p. 214. Reprinted with permission by Elsevier Limited.

in children (French, 2004; Service & Kohonen, 1995), and has been found to be linked with L2 proficiency in intermediate-level adult learners (Hummel, 2009).

Sociocultural Approach

The **sociocultural approach**, or sociocultural theory (SCT), is gaining increasing attention in second language acquisition (see, for example, Lantolf, 2000; Lantolf & Poehner, 2008; Lantolf & Thorne, 2006). Canadian researchers (e.g., Swain, 2000; Swain & Lapkin, 2002) have applied a sociocultural approach to immersion instructional contexts.

The social nature of language learning is emphasized in this perspective. Sociocultural theory is largely based on the work of Russian psychologist Lev Vygotsky, who viewed language and thought as intimately connected and social interaction as the basis for cognitive development in children. In describing the learning processes of children, Vygotsky defined the notion of the zone of proximal development (ZPD), a concept referring to the difference between what a learner can do with or without external assistance. According to Vygotsky (1978, p. 86), the ZPD is "the distance between the actual developmental level as determined by independent problem solving and the level of potential development as determined through problem solving under adult guidance, or in collaboration with more capable peers." Based on this view, education, including second language education, is best conducted when learners receive experiences within their own ZPD. The notion of ZPD is related to the concept of "scaffolding," the idea that shared activity assists the learner in internalizing knowledge (e.g., Wood, Bruner, & Ross, 1976). Activity theory is also part of a sociocultural approach; in this view, human activity is multifaceted and affected by factors such as context as well as an individual's goals and sociocultural background, leading to diverse outcomes. An emphasis is therefore given to the view that learners bring their own objectives and personal histories to the learning process. A sociocultural approach also highlights the notion of "private speech" as an instrument permitting the learner to develop control over new knowledge (e.g., Ohta, 2001).

The Development of Second Language Grammar

In some important respects, L2 acquisition resembles L1 acquisition. Like children learning their mother tongue, L2 learners go through stages, and although at any particular stage their language may not be native-like, it is rule governed, not haphazard. This section will give examples from phonological, morphological, and syntactic L2 development to illustrate certain systematic patterns.

Phonological Development

Phonology is undoubtedly the aspect of second language learning that most visibly (or audibly!) reveals the influence of the speaker's native language. This transfer effect applies both to the sounds (or segments) of the language and to suprasegmental patterns, or the larger units such as syllables and intonation patterns in the L2.

One hypothesis that has been called upon to explain L2 development, including phonological development, is Eckman's (1977) **markedness differential hypothesis**, based on what is referred to as a theory of **markedness**. In this theory, what is "unmarked" is considered to be what is more commonly found or more usual in the world's languages, while what is "marked" refers to forms that are less common or less usual among the world's languages. According to Eckman's hypothesis, speakers of languages that have a more marked structure than that which occurs in the target language will have less difficulty acquiring the equivalent unmarked target language feature. In contrast, the speaker of a language that has only the unmarked feature will experience more difficulty in acquiring the marked equivalent of that feature in the target language.

This can be illustrated by looking at the issue of voicing contrast, that is, whether sounds are voiced or not in certain positions in a word. A hierarchy of markedness has been proposed in which voicing contrasts in initial word position are considered "least marked" (or most common), while voicing contrasts in final word position are considered "most marked." It is predicted that a language that possesses a "marked" contrast will also maintain a contrast for positions that are less marked.

For instance, English speakers who have a voicing contrast in word-final position (as in word pairs such as *lap* and *lab*) will have little difficulty mastering German pronunciation of words that have no voicing contrast in word-final position where final stops are voiceless. To illustrate, English speakers should easily master pronunciation of the German words *rat* ("advice") and *rad* ("wheel"), which are pronounced identically with a voiceless final [t]. On the other hand, Germans learning English would be expected to have more difficulty learning to make the English voicing contrast in words like *lap* [læp]) and *lab* [læb], since German is considered less marked in terms of voicing contrasts, and the German speaker has to learn a more marked contrast.

On the other hand, if one considers the voicing contrast [š] and [ž] with regard to speakers of English and French, French has the [ž] phoneme in all three possible word positions, at the beginning, middle, and end (*je, agent, image*), while English has this phoneme only in middle and word final positions (*vision, garage*). This means that English speakers learning French must learn to make a new voicing contrast at the beginning of words, while French learners of English have to learn not to make that contrast. It appears that English speakers do not have any particular difficulty learning this new word-initial contrast. Therefore, as predicted by the markedness differential hypothesis, learning the more marked word-final contrasts (as in the example of German speakers learning English) has indeed been found to be more difficult than learning less marked word-initial contrasts (as in the example of English speakers learning French). In cases such as these concerning phonological development, the concept of markedness has been useful in explaining differences in L2 learning patterns.

Morphological Development

A number of research studies were carried out largely during the 1970s in order to determine whether L2 learners acquire morphemes in an invariant order. These studies were largely inspired by Brown's (1973) study (see Chapter 7), which reported that children learning their mother tongue acquire morphemes in a similar sequence.

   The L2 morpheme studies were often cross-sectional in design, in which language samples were gathered from a large number of L2 learners at one point in time. Learners' use of certain morphemes was evaluated as accurate or not from speech samples, often produced from "structured conversation" tools, in which pictures were used to elicit the production of sentences, and an accuracy order was determined. The underlying assumption in these studies was that a morpheme accuracy order was a reflection of acquisition order.

   Many of these cross-sectional studies suggested that grammatical morphemes were indeed acquired in a similar sequence, regardless of age or mother tongue of the L2 learner. Based on studies of children from different L1 backgrounds (Chinese, Spanish), Krashen (1977) proposed the following acquisition sequence of groups of morphemes:

> Group 1: present progressive *-ing* (as in *boy running*)
>   plural *-s* (as in *two books*)
>   copula "to be" (as in *he is big*)
>
> Group 2: auxiliary "to be" (as in *he is running*)
>   articles "the" and "a"
>
> Group 3: irregular past forms (as in *she went*)
>
> Group 4: regular past *-ed* (as in *she climbed*)
>   third-person singular *-s* (as in *she runs*)
>   possessive *-s* (as in *man's hat*)

Studies with adult learners from different L1 backgrounds revealed a similar accuracy order.

   However, additional studies, in particular longitudinal studies that followed the acquisition order of morphemes across time, failed to reveal a similar sequence. For instance, one study (Hakuta, 1974), which followed a five-year-old Japanese girl learning English over several months, revealed that articles (*the, a, an*) and the plural morpheme appeared much later than in the sequence outlined by Krashen. The Hakuta study suggested their later acquisition might be due to influence from the L1, Japanese.

   In sum, while L2 learners appear to follow similar sequences in learning grammatical morphemes, there is evidence that the mother tongue may also influence acquisition order.

   Over the years, interest in determining morpheme acquisition orders waned, as some researchers disputed the validity of extrapolating from accuracy orders to acquisition orders. Researchers also realized that there were important shortcomings associated with focusing too narrowly on disparate, isolated grammatical units in the attempt to characterize the acquisition process.

Syntactic Development

Studies that have looked at the acquisition of syntactic structures, such as negation, also appear to reveal similar developmental orders across L2 learners. L2 learners of English appear to begin by placing the negation particle ("no" or "not") at the beginning of an utterance. Next, learners tend to move the negative particle inside the utterance (for example, "I no can go"). A third step involves attaching the negative particle to modal verbs, although the modals might not be properly analyzed, such as "I can't did it." In the final stage, the English negation rule is acquired and the learner properly attaches the negative particle to auxiliaries (for example, "They didn't know it."). A similar, although not identical, sequence has been found with L2 learners of German. Note that this pattern of development is similar to what is reported in L1 acquisition of English negation. Table 8.2 summarizes the full sequence.

Syntactic development has also been explored in a large-scale project carried out on the L2 learning of German (Clahsen, Meisel, & Pienemann, 1983). This project, carried out by researchers working with immigrant workers in Germany, suggested developmental stages occur due to processing constraints. In other words, since learners cannot handle or process all aspects of the target language immediately, they must proceed one step at a time within their limits of their cognitive capacity.

In this model, during the first stage, the learner begins by using a general (or "canonical") word order strategy for all utterances, namely SVO (subject, verb, object), as in the following L2 speaker's sentence:

> *Die Kinder (S) spielen (V) mim Ball (O).*
> (The children play with the ball.)

TABLE 8.2

General Stages in Second Language English Negation

Stage	Description	Example
1	External negation (e.g., "no" or "not" is placed at the beginning of the utterance).	No you are playing here.
2	Internal negation (i.e., the negator — "no," "not," or "don't" — is placed between the subject and the main verb).	Mariana not coming today.
3	Negative attachment to modal verbs.	I can't play that one.
4	Negative attachment to auxiliary verb as in target language rule.	She didn't believe me. He didn't said it.

Reproduced by permission of Oxford University Press from *OAL: Study of Second Language Acquisition* © Oxford University Press 1994.

Next, in stage 2, the L2 German learner manages to place the adverb at the beginning of the utterance, a psychologically salient position, without inverting the subject and verb:

> *Da Kinder spielen.* (should be: *Da spielen Kinder.*)
> (There children play.)

In stage 3, verb separation, the learner is able to move the verb to the end of the sentence when it is preceded by an auxiliary (*muss* in this sentence):

> *Alle Kinder muss die Pause machen.*
> (All children must the break take.)

In stage 4, inversion of subject and verb is possible after adverbs (*hat sie*, instead of *sie hat*). Sentence-internal changes, such as subject-verb inversion, are considered more complex than the previous stage 3 verb-separation change in which an element is moved to the end of a sentence:

> *Dann hat sie wieder die Knoch gebringt.*
> (Then has she again the bone "bringed.")

In a final stage, the learner is able to move the verb to the end of subordinate or embedded clauses, considered to be the most complex syntactic manipulation:

> *Er sagte, dass er nach Hause kommt.*
> (He said, that he was home coming.)

This pattern of development leaves room for variation according to mother tongue. For instance, the stage 1 SVO order may differ for learners whose native language does not follow a SVO order. In addition, some learners may take longer at some stages than other learners. Indeed, some learners may never advance through all the stages. Predictions based on this model have been made for languages other than German and evidence was found for the predicted stages in the acquisition of English as a second language among migrant workers in Australia.

This model and its proposed development sequence are not without critics. Some have argued that while the model appears to make accurate predictions for German, its heavy reliance on word order may make it less relevant for languages that depend less on word order manipulations.

In sum, studies such as the two outlined here on the acquisition of negation in English and the acquisition of word order in German suggest that learners follow similar stages in acquiring syntactic rules in their second language. However, many more studies need to be carried out on learners from various language backgrounds acquiring languages that are typologically different in order to fully verify and document patterns in L2 syntactic development.

Language Teaching Approaches

Along with the evolution in theoretical views about language acquisition across the years, as well as the development of models based on L2 development data, language teaching approaches have similarly experienced numerous changes as applied linguists and teachers attempted to build upon the new theories and models proposed in linguistics and psychology. What may have been considered a classroom priority in one approach has at times become relegated to taboo status in another approach.

Grammar Translation Approach

In previous centuries, from the mid 1800s through the mid 1900s, much of formal language teaching was directed toward the teaching of the classical languages of Latin and Greek to enable students and scholars to learn to read classical literature. The approach that was most often adopted to teach these languages came to be known as the **grammar translation approach**, since the primary focus was on teaching grammatical rules and practising these through written translation exercises. Vocabulary was learned through memorization of lists of translation equivalents. No effort was made to avoid the L1 in the grammar translation classroom. Language learning through the memorization of rules and vocabulary was also thought to develop mental discipline. The high regard for the formal skills taught in this approach led to its continued use and acceptance in the teaching of languages other than classical languages, such as French and German. Ultimately, its shortcomings became apparent when learners whose goals included oral communication skills found little help in an approach based so heavily on written exercises.

Aspects of the grammar translation approach are still found in use today, particularly in language programs in countries where English and other languages are taught as foreign languages.

The Direct Method

In the late 1800s, a new approach to language teaching appeared on the scene. The **direct method** was largely developed by Charles Berlitz, who started the chain of language schools that were named after him. In the direct method, emphasis was given to speaking and listening skills (see Table 8.3). Explicit grammar instruction was avoided, and students were encouraged to learn through the repetition of sentences and dialogues. The native speakers who were employed as the language instructors in Berlitz schools discouraged any use of students' L1 in the classroom.

The direct method became widely used as the Berlitz private schools spread throughout North America and the rest of the world. This method was less successful in public education where it was less easily used with large classroom sizes and teachers with diverse training backgrounds. Eventually, however, aspects of the direct method reappeared in the audiolingual method.

TABLE 8.3
Key Components of the Direct Method

1. Classroom instruction was conducted exclusively in the target language.
2. Only everyday vocabulary and sentences were taught.
3. Oral communication skills were built up in a carefully graded progression organized around question-and-answer exchanges between teachers and students in small, intensive classes.
4. Grammar was taught inductively.
5. New teaching points were introduced orally.
6. Concrete vocabulary was taught through demonstration, objects, and pictures; abstract vocabulary was taught by association of ideas.
7. Both speech and listening comprehension were taught.
8. Correct pronunciation and grammar were emphasized.

From *Approaches and methods in language teaching* (pp. 9–10), by J.C. Richards and T.S. Rogers, 1986, Cambridge MA: Cambridge University Press. Reprinted with permission.

Audiolingual Method

The direct method failed to take hold throughout public education in North America in the early part of the 1900s, and attention returned to giving priority to the reading and writing skills associated with the grammar translation approach.

However, when World War II broke out, North America was faced with the need to provide language instruction on a large scale for members of the military. The emphasis was on rapid, efficient training that would result in successful oral communication skills. In the United States, this resulted in what was referred to as the "army method," which drew on aspects of the direct method. In the 1950s, as the success of the army method led to its adaptation for use in schools, it became known as the **audiolingual method** (**ALM**).

Popular throughout the 1950s, 1960s, and even into the 1970s, the audiolingual method was grounded in behaviourist views in psychology and the structuralist views in linguistics that characterized that period. Behaviourists viewed language learning as habit formation, and the ALM reflected this belief in the heavy reliance on pattern practice drills and repetitions in language labs. Structuralists' views were reflected in the description and selection of specific linguistic structures that provided the basis of drills and practice routines.

In the audiolingual method, little attention was given to the teaching of specific grammar rules; rather, it was thought that students would acquire grammar through intensive exposure to correct L2 sentence patterns. Similarly, little attention was given to meaning and content. Language labs were heavily used to serve the method's emphasis on oral skills and accurate pronunciation. The audiolingual method was extremely popular for decades, and even today some of its mainstays, such as drills and memorizations, are in use in many language classrooms.

The ALM had such a profound impact on language teaching that it took many years until some of the more obvious shortcomings, such as the heavy dependence on repetitive drills used outside of a communicative context, came to be generally acknowledged.

Humanistic and Communicative Language Teaching Approaches

The shift in perceptions that accompanied Chomsky's views in generative linguistics in which the creative potential of language became highlighted, as well as the shift away from behaviourism and toward cognitive views in psychology, led to a new openness to more learner-centred approaches in language instruction. The new appreciation given to the L2 learner's active role in developing the new language system allowed for new views to surface in language teaching.

The 1970s heralded the appearance of more "humanistic" approaches to language learning that highlighted the important role played by relationships among individuals. For instance, the **community language learning approach** emphasized interpersonal relationships and involved a "counsellor" who directed language instruction in small group settings.

Suggestopedia was characterized by the promotion of a relaxed state of mind arrived at through exposure to classical music and the target language in a comfortable environment. Despite claims that suggestopedia led to highly successful language learning, other researchers pointed out that there were serious flaws in the experimental studies on which those claims were made.

From the 1970s through to the present time, many classrooms have come to be characterized by approaches known as **communicative language teaching** (**CLT**), in which there is an emphasis on the acquisition of overall **communicative competence** (Hymes, 1971). The term "communicative competence" was originally coined to broaden Chomsky's notion of linguistic competence by referring to learners' knowledge of how to use a language in pragmatically and socially appropriate ways. Canadian researchers Canale and Swain (1980) further defined the notion by proposing four specific components: grammatical, discourse, sociolinguistic, and strategic. This detailing of the components of communicative competence has drawn attention to the multiple abilities involved in acquiring effective communication skills in a second language. In communicative language teaching, learners are encouraged to use language to fulfil authentic communicative tasks, such as requesting information and exchanging ideas. Both fluency and accuracy are important goals, but neither is to be sacrificed at the expense of the other, although critics have pointed out that strong versions of this approach promote fluency to the detriment of accuracy. The rigid drills and rote memorization that characterized previous methods are absent from this approach. Rather, learners are viewed as active participants who use language for a meaningful purpose. Instructors are present to guide and direct language learning, and not to control it (see Table 8.4).

Reflective of a communicative approach is the *natural approach*, which was based on Krashen's monitor model (see Table 8.5 on page 376). In this method,

TABLE 8.4
Audiolingual Method vs. Communicative Language Teaching

Audiolingual	Communicative Language Teaching
1. Attends to structure and form more than meaning.	1. Meaning is paramount.
2. Demands memorization of structure-based dialogs.	2. Dialogs, if used, center around communicative functions and are not normally memorized.
3. Language items are not necessarily contextualized.	3. Contextualization is a basic premise.
4. Language learning is learning structures, sounds, or words.	4. Language learning is learning to communicate.
5. Mastery, or "over-learning" is sought.	5. Effective communication is sought.
6. Drilling is a central technique.	6. Drilling may occur, but peripherally.
7. Native-speaker-like pronunciation is sought.	7. Comprehensible pronunciation is sought.
8. Grammatical explanation is avoided.	8. Any device which helps the learners is accepted — varying according to their age, interest, etc.
9. Communicative activities only come after a long process of rigid drills and exercises.	9. Attempts to communicate may be encouraged from the very beginning.
10. The use of the student's native language is forbidden.	10. Judicious use of native language is accepted where feasible.
11. Translation is forbidden at early levels.	11. Translation may be used where students need or benefit from it.
12. Reading and writing are deferred till speech is mastered.	12. Reading and writing can start from the first day, if desired.
13. The target linguistic system will be learned through the overt teaching of the patterns of the system.	13. The target linguistic system will be learned best through the process of struggling to communicate.
14. Linguistic competence is the desired goal.	14. Communicative competence is the desired goal (i.e., the ability to use the linguistic system effectively and appropriately).
15. Varieties of language are recognized but not emphasized.	15. Linguistic variation is a central concept in materials and methodology.
16. The sequence of units is determined solely by principles of linguistic complexity.	16. Sequencing is determined by any consideration of content, function, or meaning which maintains interest.

(Continued)

TABLE 8.4 *(Continued)*

Audiolingual	Communicative Language Teaching
17. The teacher controls the learners and prevents them from doing anything that conflicts with the theory.	17. Teachers help learners in any way that motivates them to work with the language.
18. "Language is habit" so errors must be prevented at all costs.	18. Language is created by the individual often through trial and error.
19. Accuracy, in terms of formal correctness, is a primary goal.	19. Fluency and acceptable language is the primary goal: accuracy is judged not in the abstract but in context.
20. Students are expected to interact with the language system, embodied in machines or controlled materials.	20. Students are expected to interact with other people, either in the flesh, through pair and group work, or in their writings.
21. The teacher is expected to specify the language that students are to use.	21. The teacher cannot know exactly what language the students will use.
22. Intrinsic motivation will spring from an interest in the structure of the language.	22. Intrinsic motivation will spring from an interest in what is being communicated by the language.

Reproduced by permission of Oxford University Press from *The Functional-Notional Approach* © Oxford University Press 1983.

TABLE 8.5
Classroom Implications of Monitor Model (Natural Approach)

1. Maximize students' exposure to natural communication.
2. Incorporate a silent phase in your program.
3. Use concrete referents to make input comprehensible.
4. Devise techniques to relax students and protect their egos.
5. Include time for formal grammar for adults.
6. Learn motivations of your students and incorporate this into the lessons.
7. Create an atmosphere in which students are not embarrassed by their errors.
8. Use socially useful phrases in dialogues.
9. Certain structures should be learned first. The plural, for example, will probably be acquired before the possessive in English.
10. Do not refer to the L1 when teaching the L2.

From *Language Two*, H. Dulay, M. Burt, and S. Krashen, 1982, New York: Oxford University Press. Reprinted with permission.

students are exposed to large amounts of comprehensible input and are not encouraged to speak until they are ready to do so. Older learners, that is, adults, are provided with grammar lessons, but only because they think they need it (Krashen & Terrell, 1983). The later versions of the natural approach put particular emphasis on exposure to input through reading.

Since explicit grammar instruction was largely left out of early communicative language teaching approaches, teachers soon realized that students still needed some means by which they could become aware of the grammatical patterns of a language. Therefore, an issue that emerged from CLT to gain substantial attention has been known as **form-focused instruction** (**FFI**), defined as "any pedagogical effort which is used to draw the learners' attention to language form either implicitly or explicitly" (Spada, 1997, p. 73). Two additional notions within FFI are "focus on forms" and "focus on form." *Focus on forms* generally refers to deliberate, explicit grammar instruction. On the other hand, *focus on form* has been defined as "an occasional shift of attention to linguistic code features — by the teacher and/or one of more students — triggered by perceived problems with comprehension or production" (Long & Robinson, 1998, p. 23). Some studies have shown that as long as form-focused instruction occurs in a communicative, meaningful context, it can have a positive effect.

Task-Based Language Learning/Teaching

Increased attention in second language pedagogy has been given to what is referred to as "task-based language learning" (TBLL) or "tasked-based language teaching" (TBLT). This approach is closely related to sociocultural theory and is predominantly learner-centred. Sociocultural theory and TBLT both emphasize meaningful discourse and meaningful activities or tasks as preferred ways to develop language. In a task-based classroom, meaning is given priority over form, but attention to form can also be accommodated as necessary. A task-based view sees communication as the goal of L2 learning. In this learner-centred pedagogy, learners participate in the construction of activities necessary to carry out a task, for example, going through the communicative steps necessary to buy an airline ticket, with successful completion of the task as the primary objective.

Immersion, Core, and Heritage Language Instruction Programs

A number of innovative language teaching formats have been developed in school systems in the past half-century. Canada has been particularly active in this regard. Due to historical factors, as well as the contributions from two major linguistic heritages, English and French, along with the input from many Aboriginal language communities and immigrant groups, many opportunities have been created in Canada to foster language-learning formats that have been studied and emulated across the globe.

Immersion education refers to the use of the second (or "target" language) as the language of instruction for school subjects. Canadian research and literature on immersion education, which is sometimes even referred to as the "Canadian model," has been a valuable source of information for nations in other parts of the world. The first recorded immersion experience on a wide scale was carried out in a suburb of Montreal (St. Lambert) in 1965 when schools began offering total or partial immersion courses in French to children in the English-speaking communities following strong support on the part of parents.

Since then, immersion classes have sprung up across Canada with large numbers of children enrolling in French immersion classes throughout the country. Statistics indicate that in 2006–2007, over 125,000 students were enrolled in French immersion classes in the province of Ontario. Large enrolments are found in other provinces as well (see Table 8.6). Some Quebec schools also provide various degrees of English immersion classes, sometimes referred to as "bilingual" programs.

Immersion education is actually a term that encompasses many different types and degrees of second-language exposure and instruction. Immersion can be full (all instruction is carried out in the target language until later grades, when instruction is given in both languages) or partial (some courses are taught in the target language, some in students' L1). Immersion can also begin at various times: early (kindergarten or grade 1 or 2), middle (usually grade 4), or late (grade 6 or 7). A large number of immersion-format programs exist across Canada, and immersion instruction is not restricted to the elementary or secondary school system. Immersion programs exist for university students, civil servants in the federal government, and many other groups.

Another instruction format for teaching languages is what is referred to as "core" language instruction. **Core instruction** generally refers to the typical language class in which specific language instruction is given. For instance, many students across Canada learn French as a second language as a classroom subject.

There has been a significant amount of research in Canada and elsewhere that has evaluated the success of immersion instruction. Much of this research suggests that children in immersion programs generally achieve higher levels of L2 proficiency than students enrolled in core or traditional language classrooms. Furthermore, both L1 skills and academic achievement results of immersion students have been found to be equivalent to those found in nonimmersion students.

Other language education programs in Canada include **heritage language programs** in which children from Aboriginal or ethnic minority language communities receive language instruction in their ancestral language in order to help teach or maintain that language. Heritage language programs in Canada exist for languages such as Cree, Ojibwe, Inuktitut, Italian, Chinese, and Ukrainian, to name just a few. In one study (Wright & Taylor, 1995) of Inuit children enrolled in either Inuktitut (heritage language) or L2 (French or English) classes in Northern Quebec, it was found that only the children in the Inuktitut classes experienced significant increases in personal self-esteem over the school year.

TABLE 8.6

Total Second Language Instruction and Immersion Enrolments in Majority-Language School Systems in Canada

	Total Majority-Language School Population	All Second Language Instruction (Includes Immersion)		French Immersion	
		Enrolment	Percentage	Enrolment	Percent-age
Alberta 2006–2007	596,785	170,706	29	32,459	5.4
British Columbia 2006–2007	584,000	250,577	43	39,510	6.8
Manitoba 2006–2007	176,847	85,462	48	17,871	10.1
New Brunswick					
Students in English-language system taking French second language courses					
2006–2007	79,660			21,285	26.7
Students in French-language system taking English second language courses					
2006–2007 n.a. 2002–03e	36,639	27,581	75.3		
Newfoundland and Labrador 2006–2007	74,082	44,639	60	7,222	9.7
Northwest Territories 2006–2007	9,165	2,889	32	630	6.9
Nova Scotia 2006–2007	134,537	72,976	54	14,625	10.9
Nunavut 2006–2007	8,675	271	3	n.a	
Ontario 2006–2007	2,013,657	1,005,627	50	125,453	6.2
Prince Edward Island 2006–2007	20,858	12,975	6	4,108	2

(Continued)

Legend:

e = Estimates from Statistics Canada   n.a. = Data not available

TABLE 8.6 *(Continued)*

	Total Majority-Language School Population	All Second Language Instruction (Includes Immersion)		French Immersion	
		Enrolment	Percentage	Enrolment	Percentage
Quebec *Students in French-language system taking English second language courses*					
2006–2007 n.a.					
2002–03e	912,540	531,631	58.3		
Saskatchewan **2006–2007**	162,198	65,291	40	8,858	5.5
Yukon **2006–2007**	5,007	2,617	52	463	9.2
Total for Canada ——					
Students in English-language system taking French second language courses					
2006–2007	3,984,924	1,853,438	47	314,680	7.9
Students in French-language system taking English second language courses (Quebec and NB)					
2006–2007 n.a.					
2002–03e	949,180	559,213	58.9		

Notes:
Second language figures include enrolments for the majority-language system (French in Quebec and English elsewhere) except for New Brunswick, where second language data are provided for both the English-language and French-language school systems. For all second language enrolment totals, the French immersion enrolments are included and are given separately as well.

Sources: Adapted from Statistics Canada, Centre for Education Statistics and the Department of Canadian Heritage. Immersion and Second Language Instruction Enrolments in Majority-Language School Systems in Canada. *Official Language Annual Report 2002–2003,* 2005 Canadian Parents for French, "Enrolment by Grade and by Province and Territory 2006–2007." http://www.cpf.ca/eng/pdf/resources/reports/enrolment/06-07_stat

Individual Differences in Second Language Acquisition

As mentioned at the beginning of this chapter, an important difference between learning one's mother tongue and learning a second language once the L1 has been learned is the enormous variation among individuals in learning rate and ultimate success in second language learning. One reasonable question to ask in this regard is, what role is played by the differences that characterize the individual learner? Some possible individual differences (ID) include age, attitude, motivation, intelligence, aptitude, cognitive or learning style, personality, and learning strategies. Studying the effects that such differences have on L2 learning success has led to a number of intriguing findings.

Age: Notion of a Critical/Sensitive Period

> The accent of one's birthplace remains in the mind and in the heart as in one's speech.
>
> François de La Rochefoucauld (1613–1680)

For the most part, when L2 learning begins past early childhood, only in rare cases do learners attain a degree of fluency such that they become indistinguishable from native speakers of that language. The most evident lapses from native speaker ability appear to be in the area of pronunciation. Studies tend to reveal subtle pronunciation differences even in highly fluent late L2 learners.

These noticeable attainment differences due to age of acquisition have been largely attributed to the notion of a **critical** or **sensitive period** in language learning, a hypothesized period of time during which learning must occur in order for native-like competence to be the result. As was discussed in Chapter 7 on first language acquisition, Lenneberg (1967) provided the first major articulation of the **critical period hypothesis**. There is considerable evidence in L2 learning that intensive exposure prior to an early age, which researchers have set as early as six years old for some aspects of language learning, is necessary in order to reach native-like mastery of the target language. It has also been proposed that different linguistic aspects (e.g., pronunciation, morphological-syntactic, and lexical aspects of the target language) may be affected by different age limits, with pronunciation having the earliest cut-off age.

One must also keep in mind the general consensus that there is no categorical critical period deadline being proposed. The evidence strongly suggests that there is at least some individual variation in the timing of the critical period limits, and the decline in abilities after the period is gradual and not sudden. It is also important to stress that the critical period hypothesis does not suggest that "later" or "older" learners are unable to achieve success in learning a second language. What it more specifically claims is that *native-like* fluency is beyond the reach of most language learners who begin their learning past a given age.

A number of explanations have been proposed as to what might cause a critical period for language acquisition, but there is as yet no consensus among researchers to support one cause as the single best explanation. Such explanations include references to neurological changes in the brain, the role of cognitive factors, and age-related socioaffective factors in learning.

However, other researchers deny that such a critical period in L2 learning actually exists. They explain results from such studies as being due to other factors, such as less exposure to the target language in the case of later learners compared with the substantial amount received by early learners. Some researchers ask whether adults are underestimated. A few studies reveal that adults can make L2 phonetic contrast discriminations when these are quite distinct from the L1, when the test procedures are very sensitive, or when training is available. Some studies have indicated that later learners are able to perform in the L2 to the degree that native speaker judges are unable to differentiate their language skills from those of L1 speakers. In some cases, later learners have been evaluated as having native-like ability, although these cases remain the exception and not the general rule.

Some of the critical variables that need to be taken into account when examining the issue of the effect of age on native-like acquisition of an L2 are the "age of onset," that is, the age at which an individual begins L2 learning; and "length of residence," which refers to the length of time an individual has been living in the L2 environment. It is of course also very important to specify which aspect of linguistic performance is the object of attention. Very different results might be found depending on whether the L2 learner's pronunciation, syntax, or vocabulary knowledge is being investigated. Other important variables that may impact age of acquisition studies include the L1 and L2 of the subject population, level of educational background, and socioeconomic status.

One early study (Snow & Hoefnagel-Höhle, 1978) that examined evidence for the notion of a critical period for language acquisition was carried out on the acquisition of Dutch by native English speakers living in Holland. The 96 English-speaking subjects included children (8–10 years), adolescents (12–15 years), and adults. They were tested on pronunciation, morphology, imitation tasks, and translation at various time intervals: after three months, after six months, and after nine to ten months of residence in the Netherlands. The overall results revealed that the adolescents and adults outperformed the children after three months, but the children caught up and surpassed the others on several of the tests after ten months. Therefore, it appears that older learners have an initial advantage, but that over time the younger learners' L2 skills match or surpass those of the older learners.

Another early study (Oyama, 1976) examined whether age has an effect on ability to acquire native-like pronunciation. This study included sixty Italian immigrants to the United States, who arrived between the ages of six and twenty years old, and whose length of residence in the United States varied from five to eighteen years. Their pronunciation was evaluated when they were asked to carry out two different activities: read a story and tell an anecdote. Oyama found that the immigrants who arrived in the United States at the youngest ages (between six and ten years old) tended to receive evaluations that resembled those given to native speakers. Those who arrived after the age of twelve tended to be rated as having an accent. The length of time of residence in the United States was not found to have an effect on detection of an accent or not. These results have been corroborated in a number of subsequent studies, using native speakers of other languages and in different geographical contexts. These results give additional support for an age effect for mastery of L2 pronunciation.

Some studies have examined whether there is a critical period effect for other areas of linguistic performance. For instance, Mark Patkowski (1980) examined whether there is any evidence for a sensitive period for the acquisition of syntax. He formulated the hypothesis that complete mastery of L2 syntax can be attained only if learning begins before age fifteen. The subjects in this study were sixty-seven immigrants to the United States who had begun their learning at various ages and who had lived in the United States for various lengths of times, with a minimum of five years. Subjects were evaluated on syntactic proficiency tests carried out by recording transcripts from oral interviews (fifteen to thirty-five minutes long) from which five-minute samples, recorded in writing, were taken. The evaluators were three ESL teachers, and their task was to rate the samples on a scale of 0 to 5 (5 considered as equivalent to that of a native speaker). The results revealed a significant effect for age of arrival (around age fifteen) for L2 grammatical proficiency, with early arrival speakers showing more native-like performance than the late arrival speakers (see Figure 8.3).

Johnson and Newport (1989) carried out a study that found that the ability to distinguish L2 grammatical and ungrammatical sentences appeared to be affected by age of onset. Forty-six Chinese and Korean speakers who had begun to study English at different ages were the subjects in this study. All were students or teachers at an American university and all had been in the United States for at least three years. Subjects carried out a grammaticality judgment task, containing twelve morphological and syntactic rules (tense, pluralization, verb agreement, word order, question formation, article use, and pronoun use). They were asked to listen to recorded sentences and indicate whether or not each sentence was grammatical (half the sentences were ungrammatical). Again, the results revealed that age of arrival in the United States was a significant predictor of success on the test. There was a strong relation between early exposure (three to fifteen years of age) and performance in the L2. In all cases, the older the subject was on arrival, the poorer his performance on the grammaticality judgment test (see Figure 8.4). The authors concluded that the decline appears to begin well before fifteen years, but learning capacity decreases gradually.

On the other hand, a few studies provide evidence that under certain conditions, some individuals who have begun their language learning after early childhood are able to pass as native speakers. For instance, one study (Bongaerts, van Summeren, Planken, & Schils, 1997) found that five of the eleven native speakers of Dutch in their study who began learning English at age twelve were able to pass as native speakers of English on the basis of tape recordings of their speech. Reasons proposed to explain these exceptional results on the part of some L2 learners include their very high motivation, ongoing access to large amounts of L2 input, and intensive training in the perception and production of L2 speech sounds. Table 8.7 summarizes the results from the studies discussed in this section.

A number of general conclusions can be drawn from the research on the critical period in second language learning. First, it appears that older learners (beyond early childhood) initially learn the lexicon and grammar faster than younger

FIGURE 8.3

Bar charts showing population frequencies for pre- and post-puberty learners on syntactic rating.

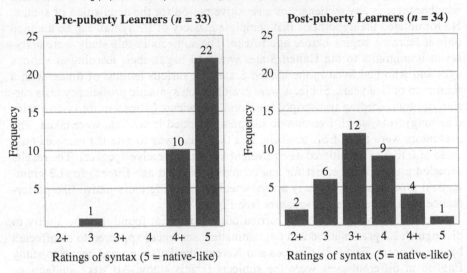

Patkowski, M.S. The sensitive period for the acquisition of syntax in a second language. *Language Learning, 30*, 1980. Figure 1, p. 455. Reprinted by permission of Blackwell Publishing.

FIGURE 8.4

The relationship between age of arrival in the United States and total score correct on the test of English grammar.

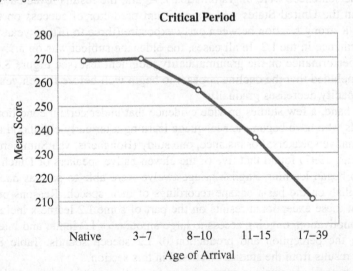

Reprinted from *Cognitive Psychology, 21*(1), 1989, pp. 60–99, Johnson & Newport: "Critical period effects in second language learning: the influence of maturational state on acquisition of ESL," p. 79. Copyright 1989, with permission from Elsevier.

TABLE 8.7
Summary Table for Critical Period Studies

Researchers	Linguistic Aspect	Conclusions
Snow & Hoefnagel-Höhle, 1978	Pronunciation, morphology, translation skill	Initial advantage for adolescents and adults was equalled or surpassed by children after 10 months
Oyama, 1976	Pronunciation	Age of arrival (6 to 10 years) linked with native-like pronunciation
Patkowski, 1980	Syntax	Earlier age of arrival (15 or below) associated with native-like syntax
Johnson & Newport, 1989	Grammaticality judgments	Earlier age of arrival associated with higher L2 performance
Bongaerts et al., 1997	Pronunciation	Post-childhood learners (age 12+) able to pass as native speakers

learners, but their initial advantage is not generally maintained over longer periods of time. Second, sensitive periods seem to exist for different aspects of linguistic competence (e.g., pronunciation, grammar). Third, there is strong evidence that L2 onset after six or seven years of age is related to decreased native-like mastery of pronunciation and perhaps some aspects of grammar. Finally, in some very specific circumstances, late L2 learners (post-childhood) have been able to pass as native speakers.

Attitude and Motivation

It is commonplace to hear remarks made about the importance of having a good attitude in order to be a good language learner. Similarly, motivation is commonly thought to play a major role in any learning situation, including learning another language. Of course it makes sense that a learner with a good attitude and a strong motivation toward learning an L2 would have more success than an otherwise similar learner with a poor attitude and low motivation. But in order to verify this statement of common wisdom, it is necessary to carry out empirical testing. A considerable number of studies have set out to investigate the role of *affective* variables, such as attitudes and motivation, in language learning.

Some important initial distinctions can be made between attitude and motivation. Attitude refers to an individual's evaluation or appreciation of an entity or situation. That appreciation can vary in terms of polarity from extremely negative to extremely positive. On the other hand, motivation refers to a relationship between an individual and a goal or objective that can be measured in terms of intensity. Motivation can vary on a scale ranging from its total absence to its maximal presence.

With regard to the attitudes that might affect language learning, one can differentiate among possible types: (1) attitudes toward a community and the people who speak the L2; (2) attitudes toward learning the L2; (3) attitudes toward languages and language learning in general.

As for motivation, an important distinction can be made between **intrinsic motivation** (when behaviours are carried out for one's own personal satisfaction) and **extrinsic motivation** (when behaviours are carried out for rewards coming from outside the self).

Two Canadian researchers who have played a major role in examining attitudes and motivation in L2 learning are Robert Gardner and Wallace Lambert of McGill University (e.g., Gardner & Lambert, 1972). They drew attention to two main orientations that they suggested have an influence on motivation in language learning: **instrumental motivation**, characterizing situations in which language is largely learned as a tool to reach other goals, and **integrative motivation**, in which the language learner desires to identify with the L2 community. An example of instrumental motivation is that of individuals learning either English or French in order to better qualify as functional bilinguals for employment with the Canadian federal government. An example of integrative motivation is that of minority language speakers of French or English learning the other official language in order to more fully feel a part of their local community.

Gardner and Lambert suggested that both types of motivation played an important role in L2 learning, but they considered that integrative motivation would be particularly effective in sustaining a language learner's motivation over time. Although early studies in both the United States and Canada supported this suggestion, further studies in other contexts, such as in the Philippines, revealed that instrumental motivation played an even greater role than integrative motivation for learners in that setting. The original suggestion was therefore revised to reflect this finding that an instrumental motivation is particularly effective in settings where there is a sense of urgency involved in learning the target language.

More recent discussions tend to make the distinction that instrumental and integrative are types of "orientations," or reasons for being motivated, rather than "motivations" in and of themselves. It has also been pointed out that both types of orientations can be present in a single individual, and other orientations such as "a desire to travel" and "a desire to make friends" are possible.

Gardner offered a specific definition of **motivation** in his socioeducational model of second language acquisition. He defined *motivation* as *effort + desire to achieve a goal + attitudes toward learning the language*. He also developed a tool to measure motivation, the Attitude/Motivation Test Battery (AMTB; see Table 8.8), which has been widely used and adapted for use in various language learning contexts. The excerpt illustrated in Table 8.8 is developed from a version for English native speaking students learning French in Canada.

Applications of the AMTB in various contexts have generally revealed that motivation and attitudes do appear to be important factors in second language acquisition. It has also been generally established that the effects of motivation

TABLE 8.8
Attitude/Motivation Test Battery [Sample AMTB Questions]

1. French Canadians are a very sociable, warm-hearted, and creative people.

| strongly
disagree | moderately
disagree | slightly
disagree | neutral | slightly
agree | moderately
agree | strongly
agree |

2. I would like to know more French Canadians.

| strongly
disagree | moderately
disagree | slightly
disagree | neutral | slightly
agree | moderately
agree | strongly
agree |

3. If I were visiting a foreign country I would like to be able to speak the language of the people.

| strongly
disagree | moderately
disagree | slightly
disagree | neutral | slightly
agree | moderately
agree | strongly
agree |

4. I plan to learn as much French as possible.

| strongly
disagree | moderately
disagree | slightly
disagree | neutral | slightly
agree | moderately
agree | strongly
agree |

5. I think that learning French is dull.

| strongly
disagree | moderately
disagree | slightly
disagree | neutral | slightly
agree | moderately
agree | strongly
agree |

6. Studying French can be important to me because it will allow me to be more at ease with fellow Canadians who speak French.

| strongly
disagree | moderately
disagree | slightly
disagree | neutral | slightly
agree | moderately
agree | strongly
agree |

7. Studying French can be important to me because I think it will someday be useful in getting a good job.

| strongly
disagree | moderately
disagree | slightly
disagree | neutral | slightly
agree | moderately
agree | strongly
agree |

Multiple Choice:

1. I actively think about what I have learned in my French class:
   a) very frequently
   b) hardly ever
   c) once in awhile

2. If my teacher wanted someone to do an extra French assignment, I would:
   a) definitely not volunteer.
   b) definitely volunteer.
   c) only do it if the teacher asked me directly.

3. After I get my French assignments back, I:
   a) always rewrite them, correcting my mistakes.
   b) just throw them in my desk and forget them.
   c) look them over, but don't bother correcting mistakes.

(Continued)

TABLE 8.8 *(Continued)*

4. During French class, I would like:
   a) to have a combination of French and English spoken.
   b) to have as much French as possible spoken.
   c) to have only French spoken.

5. If I had the opportunity to speak French outside of school, I would:
   a) never speak it.
   b) speak French most of the time, using English only if really necessary.
   c) speak it occasionally, using English whenever possible.

Adapted from *Social psychology and second language learning: The role of attitudes and motivation*, by R.C. Gardner, 1985, London: Edward Arnold, appendix.

and attitudes appear to be separate from the effects of aptitude. Research has revealed that both integrative and instrumental orientations may be effective and that other types of orientations are possible as well. Finally, a number of studies reveal that level and type of motivation are strongly influenced by the social context of learning. Social contexts vary from informal to formal learning environments and refer as well to whether the target language is the language spoken in the wider community or not.

Some researchers have argued that rather than motivation playing a causal role in language learning success, it may be the case that it is success in the language classroom that actually feeds motivation. While the debate is far from being definitively resolved, most studies corroborate findings that motivation plays a significant role in L2 success. However, it is highly likely that success in language learning, in turn, also contributes to the strength of a learner's motivation.

Intelligence

Another individual difference factor that has received some attention in L2 acquisition is intelligence. Intelligence is sometimes defined as a general factor underlying the ability to master and use academic skills; it represents the underlying ability to learn (not the actual knowledge), which is supposedly measured by intelligence (IQ) tests. Unsurprisingly, the validity of IQ tests is hotly debated, since it is argued that IQ tests basically measure the same types of skills that are valued in academic settings.

A few studies have nevertheless attempted to evaluate the role that intelligence may play in L2 learning. Genesee (1976) administered standard IQ tests to English-speaking children in grades 4, 7, and 11 in Quebec who were enrolled in two types of language programs, an immersion program and an L2 subject program. His results showed that IQ was strongly related to the development of academic L2 French language skills (reading, grammar, and vocabulary) for students in both programs, but it was unrelated to ratings of oral skills.

In this regard, a distinction between two separate types of language skills has been made (Cummins, 1979): (1) **cognitive/academic language proficiency (CALP)**, or *context-reduced communication*, and (2) **basic interpersonal communicative skills (BICS)**, or *context-embedded communication*. This distinction suggests that it is the cognitive/academic (context-reduced) skills that Genesee found related to IQ, while basic interpersonal communicative (context-embedded) skills appeared to have no direct relation.

Another study found that the best predictor of L2 learning was general reasoning skills when using a symbolic system (such as numbers and words), while other language learning skills such as phonemic encoding (remembering the sounds of a specific language) and memory were more independent of IQ test results.

Apart from the relationship found between academic-based language skills and IQ scores, intelligence appears to have little effect on general second language learning ability, just as it seems to have little to do with learning one's first language.

Aptitude

Do some people have a particular aptitude for learning languages? This is a question that is often posed, and anyone who has taught or sat in a typical language classroom might be inclined to answer "yes." Determining whether a specific talent for language learning exists requires a clear definition and appropriate tests to measure such a talent.

Carroll (1981), a psychologist, defined aptitude and devised a multiple-skill test (described below) to measure this concept. He argued that aptitude is separate from general IQ and achievement and that it must be shown to be separate from motivation. Furthermore, aptitude should be considered as a relatively stable factor, perhaps even innate. Carroll considered aptitude as something to be viewed not as a prerequisite for L2 acquisition, but as a capacity that enhances the rate and ease of learning. In other words, aptitude allows some individuals to learn faster and more easily.

The Modern Language Aptitude Test (MLAT) (Carroll & Sapon, 1959) measures four aptitude factors:
1. Phonemic coding ability (the ability to code foreign sounds in a way that they can be remembered later). This ability is related to the ability to spell and to associate graphic symbols and speech sounds.
2. Grammatical sensitivity (the ability to recognize the grammatical functions of words in sentences). This would include, for example, being able to identify the word in sentence b that plays a role similar to that of the underlined word in sentence a:
   a. He spoke <u>very</u> well of you.
   b. Suddenly the music became *quite* loud.

3. Inductive language-learning ability (the ability to identify linguistic patterns of correspondence and relationships involving form and meaning).
4. Rote learning ability (the ability to make and remember associations between sounds and meanings). For example, remembering that *hon* means "cold" in a new language.

More recent approaches to the study of aptitude in language learning have made different distinctions among aptitude components. Skehan (1998), for instance, proposed three main components: auditory skill, linguistic analysis skill, and memory.

Although interest in aptitude studies declined with the loss of interest in behaviourist claims about language learning, in more recent years there has been a renewed interest in the notion of language-learning aptitude. In general, a fairly strong relationship between language aptitude and L2 learning has been found across various studies. It has even been suggested (Gardner & MacIntyre, 1992, p. 215) that "research makes it clear that in the long run, language aptitude is probably the single best predictor of achievement in a second language."

Cognitive or Learning Style

Cognitive style has been defined as "a predisposition to process information in a characteristic manner," while **learning style** has been defined as "a typical preference for approaching learning in general" (Dornyei & Skehan, 2003, p. 602). It is thought that cognitive or learning style are to some extent related to personality but are not exclusively the result of an innate predisposition.

The L2 cognitive style studies have largely focused on the distinction made between the constructs of **field independence** (FI) and **field dependence** (FD). A cognitive style of field independence is one characterized by an analytic approach to processing information, while a field-dependent style is thought to process information in a more holistic manner. Other traits associated with each style include, for the field-independent individual, a predisposition to dissect information into smaller components, and a more independent approach to problem solving. On the other hand, field-dependent individuals tend to treat structures as whole units, and are sociable, preferring collaborative efforts. Each style is thought to have its advantages for language learning. For instance, an FI style should be useful in the analysis of grammatical structures, while an FD style should promote learning in a communicative interactive context.

The test that has been traditionally used to measure cognitive style is the Group Embedded Figures Test. This test requires individuals to find outlined forms embedded in a more complex visual pattern. A strong performance on the test is interpreted as reflecting a highly field-independent cognitive style. On the other hand, a poor performance is not thought to necessarily indicate a field-dependent style, but simply an absence of field independence. While the test is relatively easy to use, it has been strongly criticized as lacking validity, since it is so heavily dependent on visual interpretation. In addition, despite the claims that each type of cognitive style carries with it certain learning advantages, the positive correlations between language learning and style are nearly always favourable to the FI style. A few studies have found significant relationships between L2 proficiency and measures of FI, but others have failed to find any clear relationship.

Some research has also been carried out on the associated concept of "learning style." While "cognitive style" refers specifically to mental processing, other learning styles that have been proposed include the sensory domain (auditory, visual, kinaesthetic, and tactile preferences), an intuitive vs. concrete approach, and impulsive vs. reflective predispositions, among others. For example, some research suggests individuals differ in the degree to which they prefer auditory vs. visual processing of language stimuli. To date, however, relatively few studies have specifically investigated the role of such styles in language learning, and the extent of their real contribution to language learning has yet to be determined.

Personality

Another possible source of individual differences is the personality that each learner brings to the language-learning task. Included in the area of personality are traits such as self-esteem, inhibition, risk taking, anxiety, empathy, and extroversion/introversion. Much of the problem in studying personality variables has to do with finding accurate and valid tests to measure personality traits. Some psychological tests are successful in distinguishing personality extremes, but they are much less accurate in identifying personality types.

Nevertheless, there have been a number of second-language studies that have investigated personality variables. For instance, one study (Strong, 1983) examined children's social styles and found that more extroverted children, as indicated by measurements of talkativeness and responsiveness, were also more proficient in L2 oral communication skills. On the other hand, another study (Carrell, Prince, & Astika, 1996) found that children who were rated as more introverted tended to have more success in L2 vocabulary learning.

In terms of the extroversion/introversion distinction, it is possible that some aspects of language learning, such as oral production skills, may be more affected by aspects of extroversion, while others, such as reading and writing skills that are closely related to academic learning, may be more affected by aspects of introversion. However, these proposed relationships need to be further investigated by research studies in various contexts and with diverse subject populations.

Learning Strategies

Another area in the domain of individual difference factors that has much intuitive appeal to language researchers, teachers, and learners, is that of **language learning strategies**. The notion that learners actively contribute to their learning process is an attractive one, especially since this suggests that learners can be taught to use strategies.

Definitions of what constitutes a language-learning strategy have varied somewhat from one researcher to another, but one generally accepted definition is "special thoughts or behaviours that individuals use to help them comprehend, learn, or retain new material" (O'Malley & Chamot, 1990, p. 1). In addition, various different classifications of learning strategies have been proposed, such as that between **metacognitive, cognitive**, and **socioaffective** types (see Table 8.9 for a strategy classification list). Metacognitive strategies are higher-order skills that involve planning, monitoring, or evaluating the success of a learning task. Cognitive strategies involve direct operations on incoming information so as to increase learning. Socioaffective strategies involve interactions with others or exercising control over affective aspects that hinder learning.

Strategy studies tend to reveal that the most successful language learners use a variety of types of strategies. On the other hand, training in strategy use has led to mixed results. There continues to be much interest in examining the ways in which individuals actively participate in the language-learning process, but determination of what precisely constitutes a learning strategy and clearly articulated theories linking strategies to L2 acquisition are still lacking.

Bilingualism

Bilingualism, far from being exceptional, . . . affects the majority of the world's population.

William F. Mackey, *Bilingualism as a World Problem* (1967)

Bilingual Acquisition

I didn't know at first that there were two languages in Canada. I just thought that there was one way to speak to my father and another to talk to my mother.

Louis St. Laurent (1948), Prime Minister of Canada from 1948 to 1957

While this chapter has generally focused on the issue of acquiring a second language once the first language has already been acquired, there are many children who are simultaneously exposed to two (or more) languages during their early language learning years. In fact, it is estimated that approximately half of the people in the world are native speakers of more than one language. In many parts of the world, especially Africa and Asia, bilingualism (and even multilingualism) is the norm. In contrast, many Western countries (though by no means all of them) view themselves as monolingual, even though they may be home to speakers of many languages. In the United States and many European countries, bilingualism is often viewed as a transitory phenomenon associated with immigration.

TABLE 8.9
Learning Strategies Classification

Generic Strategy Classification	Representative Strategies	Definitions
Metacognitive strategies	Selective attention	Focusing on special aspects of learning tasks, as in planning to listen for key words or phrases
	Planning	Planning for the organization of either written or spoken discourse
	Monitoring	Reviewing attention to a task, comprehension of information that should be remembered, or production while it is occurring
	Evaluation	Checking comprehension after completion of a receptive language activity, or evaluating language production after it has taken place
Cognitive strategies	Rehearsal	Repeating the names of items or objects to be remembered
	Organization	Grouping and classifying words, terminology, or concepts according to their semantic or syntactic attributes
	Inferencing	Using information in text to guess meanings of new linguistic items, predict outcomes, or complete missing parts
	Summarizing	Intermittently synthesizing what one has heard to ensure the information has been retained
	Deducing	Applying rules to the understanding of language
	Imagery	Using visual images (either generated or actual) to understand and remember new verbal information
	Transfer	Using known linguistic information to facilitate a new learning task
	Elaboration	Linking ideas contained in new information, or integrating new ideas with known information

(Continued)

TABLE 8.9 *(Continued)*

Generic Strategy Classification	Representative Strategies	Definitions
Social/affective strategies	Cooperation	Working with peers to solve a problem, pool information, check notes, or get feedback on a learning activity
	Questioning for clarification	Eliciting from a teacher or peer additional explanation, rephrasing, or examples
	Self-talk	Using mental redirection of thinking to assure oneself that a learning activity will be successful or to reduce anxiety about a task

O'Malley, M., and A. Chamot. *Learning Strategies in Second Language Acquisition.* Cambridge, MA: Cambridge University Press, 1990. Table 2.1, p. 46. © Cambridge University Press, 1990. Reprinted with the permission of Cambridge University Press.

In Canada, French–English bilingualism is officially recognized and promoted, although the degree of implementation of official policy varies from province to province. Across Canada, however, there are numerous families who, deliberately or not, go about raising their children in two or more languages.

The psychological community was interested in the phenomenon of **bilingual acquisition** beginning early in the twentieth century, and a number of studies were carried out in the attempt to verify whether children exposed to two languages were handicapped by what was generally considered at the time to constitute a heavy cognitive burden for young children. Studies carried out in the early and mid part of the 1900s that received much attention at the time revealed that bilingual children performed less well than monolingual children when tested on various mental and verbal ability tests. However, these results were ultimately discredited as researchers came to recognize some serious methodological flaws in these studies. For instance, in some cases the researchers had contrasted not only bilingual vs. monolingual acquirers, but also children of different socioeconomic backgrounds. Since this latter variable is often associated with testing differences, due to decreased academic and other opportunities outside the classroom, it was not surprising that the bilingual group, comprising mainly children from poorer backgrounds, failed to match the performance of the monolingual children from more privileged socioeconomic backgrounds. In other cases, children without full proficiency in their L2 were tested for mental ability through questions posed in the L2.

When researchers carried out additional, better designed, and better controlled studies, interesting results emerged indicating that bilingual children actually performed significantly better than monolingual children on certain types of mental

"Gina is by lingal . . . that means she can say the same thing twice, but you can only understand it once."

reasoning and metalinguistic tests that reveal degree of linguistic awareness. For instance, one Canadian study (Peal & Lambert, 1962) revealed that bilingual children tested higher than comparable monolingual children on verbal and nonverbal intelligence tests. These results were replicated in a number of different social and cultural settings. One hypothesis that has been recently formulated to explain this superior performance on the part of bilingual children is that they have had to develop the ability to selectively suppress one language when using the other and that this attentional control has given them an advantage that can be used in other cognitive domains. For instance, the metalinguistic superiority found in young bilingual children who are able to differentiate words from the concepts they represent might be one manifestation of this cognitive benefit.

A recent suggestion in this regard is that this same attentional control that the bilingual child learns to exercise when choosing one language or the other offers cognitive benefits throughout the lifespan. Psychologist Ellen Bialystok of York

University and her colleagues (2004) have found that older bilinguals appear to possess cognitive protection from certain age-induced learning deficits. This study suggests the attentional control exercised by bilinguals throughout their lives is instrumental in offering protection from some of the negative effects associated with aging. Although more evidence is needed before this intriguing suggestion can be confirmed, it is an indication that bilingualism might entail even more cognitive advantages that have yet to be discovered.

One caveat with respect to bilingual acquisition that is important to highlight is that positive effects may not occur in situations in which one of the languages of the children is not given adequate support, such that acquiring a second language takes place at the expense of basic skill in the first language. This might occur in a situation in which there are few opportunities to use and develop the first language. This situation has been labelled **subtractive bilingualism** as opposed to **additive bilingualism** in which both languages are well supported and maintained (Lambert, 1977). It has been proposed (Cummins, 1976) that a threshold level of attained skill in both languages is necessary in order to allow positive cognitive and educational effects to occur.

It is interesting to point out that despite the large number of studies that reveal no cognitive deficits associated with children acquiring two languages simultaneously, along with the fact that bilingual language acquisition is the norm in many societies, the myth remains deeply entrenched even among some professional educators that exposure to two languages may be detrimental to children's cognitive development.

One System or Two?

One of the theoretical questions that has captured interest on the part of researchers is whether children acquiring two or more languages simultaneously begin with a stage in which their languages are represented in a single fused system, the **unitary system hypothesis,** or whether these children maintain separate representations for each language, the **separate systems hypothesis**. Research showing that children mix elements from both languages in their utterances, as in the example: "Me, I like *dessiner*" ("I like to draw"; French equivalent: *"Moi, j'aime dessiner"*) in which a bilingual French–English child adopts words and grammatical structures from both languages, has been interpreted as support for a unitary view.

However, the unitary system interpretation for mixed language utterances has been called into question. For instance, Genesee (1989) pointed out that in order to uphold the unitary view, it is necessary to establish that bilingual children mix elements from both languages indiscriminately. Yet, this appears not to be the case as children tend to mix their languages in predictable ways. A number of studies suggest that even very young children, before the age of two, make language choices that are sensitive to the context, suggesting that they are able to differentiate languages from a very early age. Other explanations have been suggested for bilingual children's language mixing. One suggestion is simply that children

Canale, M., & Swain, M. (1980). Theoretical bases of communicative approaches to second language teaching and testing. *Applied Linguistics, 1,* 1–47.

Carrell, P.L., Prince, M.S., & Astika, G.G. (1996). Personality types and language learning in an EFL context. *Language Learning, 46*(1), 75–99.

Carroll, J.B. (1981). Twenty-five years of research on foreign language aptitude. In K. Diller (Ed.), *Individual differences and universals in language learning aptitude* (pp. 83–118). Rowley, MA: Newbury House.

Carroll, J.B., & Sapon, S. (1959). *Modern language aptitude test.* New York: The Psychological Corporation.

Clahsen, H., Meisel, J.M., & Pienemann, M. (1983). *Deutsch als zweitspracher: der sprachenerverb auslandischer arbeiter.* Tubingen: Gunter Narr.

Corder, S.P. (1967). The significance of learners' errors. *International Review of Applied Linguistics, 5,* 161–170.

Cummins, J. (1976). The influence of bilingualism on cognitive growth: A synthesis of research findings and explanatory hypotheses. *Working Papers on Bilingualism, 9,* 1–43.

Cummins, J. (1979). Cognitive/academic language proficiency, linguistic interdependence, the optimal age question and some other matters. *Working Papers on Bilingualism, 19,* 197–205.

Dornyei, Z., & Skehan, P. (2003). Individual differences in second language learning. In C. Doughty & M. Long (Eds.), *The handbook of second language acquisition* (pp. 589–630). Malden, MA: Blackwell.

Dulay, H., & Burt, M. (1974). Errors and strategies in child second language acquisition. *TESOL Quarterly, 8,* 129–136.

Dulay, H., Burt, M., & Krashen, S. (1982). *Language two.* New York: Oxford University Press.

Eckman, F. (1977). Markedness and the contrastive analysis hypothesis. *Language Learning, 27,* 315–330.

Ellis, R. (1994). *The study of second language acquisition.* Oxford: Oxford University Press.

Finocchiaro, M., & Brumfit, C. (1983). *The functional-notional approach: From theory to practice.* New York: Oxford University Press.

French, L. (2004). *Phonological working memory and L2 acquisition: A developmental study of Quebec Francophone children learning English.* (Doctoral dissertation, Université Laval, 2003). *Dissertation Abstracts International, 65*(2-A), 487.

Gardner, R.C. (1985). *Social psychology and second language learning: The role of attitudes and motivation.* London: Edward Arnold.

Gardner, R.C., & Lambert, W. (1972). *Attitudes and motivation in second language learning.* Rowley, MA: Newbury House.

Gardner, R.C., & MacIntyre, P.D. (1992). A student's contributions to second language learning: Part I: Cognitive variables, *Language Teaching, 25*(1), 211–220.

Genesee, F. (1976). The role of intelligence in second language learning. *Language Learning, 26,* 267–280.

Genesee, F. (1989). Early bilingual language development: One language or two? *Journal of Child Language, 16,* 161–179.

Hakuta, K. (1974). A preliminary report on the development of grammatical morphemes in a Japanese girl learning English as a second language. *Working Papers on Bilingualism, 3,* 18–43.

Hummel, K.M. (2009). Aptitude, phonological memory, and second language proficiency in nonnovice adult learners. *Applied Psycholinguistics, 30,* 225–249.

Hymes, D. (1971). *On communicative competence*. Philadelphia: University of Pennsylvania Press.

Johnson, J., & Newport, E. (1989). Critical period effects in second language learning: The influence of maturational state on acquisition of ESL. *Cognitive Psychology, 21,* 60–99.

Krashen, S. (1977). The monitor model for adult second language performance. In M. Burt, H. Dulay, & M. Finocchiaro (Eds.), *Viewpoints on English as a second language* (pp. 152–161). New York: Regents.

Krashen, S. (1985). *The input hypothesis*. London: Longman.

Krashen, S., & Terrell, T.D. (1983). *The natural approach: Language acquisition in the classroom*. Oxford: Pergamon Press.

Kroll, J., & de Groot, A. (1997). Lexical and conceptual memory in the bilingual. In A. de Groot & J. Kroll (Eds.), *Tutorials in bilingualism* (pp. 169–199). Mahwah, NJ: Erlbaum.

Kroll, J.F., & Stewart, E. (1994). Category interference in translation and picture naming: Evidence for asymmetric connections between bilingual memory representations. *Journal of Memory and Language, 33,* 149–174.

Lado, R. (1957). *Linguistics across cultures*. Ann Arbor: University of Michigan.

Lambert, W. (1977). The effects of bilingualism on the individual: Cognitive and socio-cultural consequences. In P. Hornby (Ed.), *Bilingualism: Psychological, social and educational implications* (pp. 15–28). New York: Academic Press.

Lantolf, J. (Ed.). (2000). *Sociocultural theory and second language learning*. Oxford: Oxford University Press.

Lantolf, J.P., & Poehner, M.E. (Eds.). (2008). *Sociocultural theory and the teaching of second languages*. Oakville, CT: Equinox.

Lantolf, J.P., & Thorne, S.L. (2006). *Sociocultural theory and the genesis of second language development*. Oxford: Oxford University Press.

Lenneberg, E. (1967). *The biological foundations of language*. New York: Harcourt Brace Jovanovich.

Long, M.H., & Robinson, P. (1998). Focus on form: Theory, research, and practice. In C. Doughty & J. Williams (Eds.), *Focus on form in classroom second language acquisition* (pp. 15–41). Cambridge, MA: Cambridge University Press.

Mackey, W.F. (1967). *Bilingualism as a world problem*. Montreal: Harvest Home.

McLaughlin, B., & Heredia, R. (1996). Information-processing approaches to research on second language acquisition and use. In W.C. Ritchie & T. Bhatia (Eds.), *Handbook of second language acquisition* (pp. 213–228). New York: Academic Press.

Mitchell, R., & Myles, F. (1998). *Second language learning theories*. New York: Edward Arnold.

Ohta, A.S. (2001). *Second language acquisition processes in the classroom: Learning Japanese*. Mahwah, NJ: Lawrence Erlbaum Associates.

O'Malley, J.M., & Chamot, A. (1990). *Learning strategies in second language acquisition*. Cambridge, MA: Cambridge University Press.

Oyama, S. (1976). A sensitive period in the acquisition of a non-native phonological system. *Journal of Psycholinguistic Research, 5,* 261–285.

Paradis, M. (1997). The cognitive neuropsychology of bilingualism. In A.B. de Groot & J.F. Kroll (Eds.), *Tutorials in bilingualism* (pp. 331–354). Mahwah, NJ: Erlbaum.

Patkowski, M.S. (1980). The sensitive period for the acquisition of syntax in a second language. *Language Learning, 30,* 449–472.

Peal, E., & Lambert, W. (1962). The relation of bilingualism to intelligence. *Psychological Monographs, 76,* 1–23.

Richards, J.C., & Rodgers, T.S. (1986). *Approaches and methods in language teaching.* Cambridge, MA: Cambridge University Press.

Selinker, L. (1972). Interlanguage. *International Review of Applied Linguistics, 10,* 201–231.

Service, E., & Kohonen, V. (1995). Is the relation between phonological memory and foreign-language learning accounted for by vocabulary acquisition? *Applied Psycholinguistics, 16,* 155–172.

Skehan, P. (1998). *A cognitive approach to language learning.* Oxford: Oxford University Press.

Snow, C., & Hoefnagel-Höhle, M. (1978). Critical period for language acquisition: Evidence from second language learning. *Child Development, 48,* 1114–1128.

Spada, N. (1997). Form-focussed instruction and second language acquisition: A review of classroom and laboratory research. *Language Teaching, 30,* 73–87.

Strong, M. (1983). Social styles and the second language acquisition of Spanish-speaking kindergartners. *TESOL Quarterly, 17*(2), 241–258.

Swain, M. (1985). Communicative competence: Some roles of comprehensible input and comprehensible output in its development. In S. Gass & C. Madden (Eds.), *Input in second language acquisition* (pp. 235–253). Rowley, MA: Newbury House.

Swain, M. (2000). The output hypothesis and beyond: Mediating acquisition through collaborative dialogue. In J.P. Lantolf (Ed.), *Sociocultural theory and second language learning* (pp. 97–114). Oxford: Oxford University Press.

Swain, M., & Lapkin, S. (2002). Talking it through: Two French immersion learners' responses to reformulation. *International Journal of Educational Research, 37,* 285–304.

Van Hell, J.G., & Dijkstra, A.F.J. (2002). Foreign language knowledge can influence native language performance in exclusively native contexts. *Psychonomic Bulletin and Review, 9*(4), 780–789.

Vygotsky, L. (1978). *Mind in Society: The development of higher psychological processes.* Cambridge, MA: Harvard University Press.

Weinreich, U. (1970). *Languages in contact* (Rev. ed). The Hague: Mouton.

White, L. (1986). Implications of parametric variation for adult second language acquisition: An investigation of the pro-drop parameter. In V.J. Cook (Ed.), *Experimental approaches to second language acquisition* (pp. 55–72). Oxford: Pergamon Press.

White, L. (2003). On the nature of interlanguage representation: Universal grammar in the second language. In C. Doughty & M. Long (Eds.), *The handbook of second language acquisition* (pp. 19–42). Malden, MA: Blackwell.

Whitman, R. (1970). Contrastive analysis: Problems and procedures. *Language Learning, 20,* 191–197.

Wood, D., Bruner, J., & Ross, G. (1976). The role of tutoring in problem-solving. *Journal of Child Psychology and Psychiatry and Allied Disorders, 17,* 89–100.

Wright, S.C., & Taylor, D.M. (1995). Identity and the language of the classroom: Investigating the impact of heritage versus second language instruction on personal and collective self-esteem. *Educational Psychology, 87,* 241–252.

Further Reading

Archibald, J., & Libben, G. (1995). *Research perspectives on second language acquisition.* Toronto: Copp Clark.

Brown, H.D., & Gonzo, S.T. (Eds.). (1995). *Readings on second language acquisition.* Englewood Cliffs, NJ: Prentice Hall Regents.

Cook, V. (1993). *Linguistics and second language acquisition.* London: Macmillan.

DeKeyser, R.M. (2007). *Practice in a second language.* Cambridge/New York: Cambridge University Press.

Dornyei, Z. (2005). *The psychology of the language learner.* Mahwah, NJ: Lawrence Erlbaum.

Doughty, C., & Long, M. (Eds.). (2003). *The handbook of second language acquisition.* Malden, MA: Blackwell.

Ellis, R. (1994). *The study of second language acquisition.* Oxford: Oxford University Press.

Gass, S.M., & Selinker, L. (1994). *Second language acquisition.* Hillsdale, NJ: Lawrence Erlbaum Associates.

Grosjean, F. (2008). *Studying bilinguals.* Oxford: Oxford University Press.

Hakuta, K. (1986). *The mirror of language.* New York: Basic Books.

Hamers, J., & Blanc, M. (2000). *Bilinguality and bilingualism* (2nd ed.). Cambridge, MA: Cambridge University Press.

Larsen-Freeman, D., & Long, M.H. (1991). *An introduction to second language acquisition research.* New York: Longman.

McLaughlin, B. (1987). *Theories of second language learning.* New York: Edward Arnold.

Mitchell, R., & Myles, F. (1998). *Second language learning theories.* New York: Edward Arnold.

Robinson, P. (Ed.). (2002). *Individual differences and instructed language learning.* Philadelphia: John Benjamins.

Romaine, S. (1989). *Bilingualism* (2nd ed.). Oxford: Blackwell.

Skehan, P. (1998). *A cognitive approach to language learning.* Oxford: Oxford University Press.

Websites

http://www.caslt.org/ The Canadian Association of Second Language Teachers website.

http://www.aclacaal.org/index.htm The Canadian Association of Applied Linguists website.

http://www.cal.org The website for the Center for Applied Linguistics in the United States.

http://www.actfl.org The website for the American Council for the Teaching of Foreign Languages, a U.S.-based foreign language teachers association.

http://www.cilt.org.uk The UK Centre for Information on Language Teaching and Research website.

CHAPTER 9
Psycholinguistics: Language Processing

No doubt a reasonable model of language use will incorporate, as a basic component, the generative grammar that expresses the speaker–hearer's knowledge of the language; but this generative grammar does not, in itself, prescribe the character or functioning of a perceptual model or a model of speech production.

Noam Chomsky, *Aspects of the Theory of Syntax* (1965)

The Human Mind at Work: Human Language Processing

Psycholinguistics is the area of linguistics that is concerned with linguistic performance — how we use our linguistic competence, our knowledge of language, in speech (or sign) production and comprehension. The human brain is able not only to acquire and store the mental grammar but also to access that linguistic storehouse to speak and understand what is spoken.

How we process knowledge depends to a great extent on the nature of that knowledge. If, for example, language were not "open ended," if it consisted of a finite store of fixed phrases and sentences, then speaking might simply consist of finding a sentence that expresses a thought we wish to convey with its phonological representation and producing it; comprehension could be the reverse — matching the sounds to a stored string that has been entered with its meaning. We know this is not possible because of the creativity of language. In Chapter 7, we saw that children do not learn language by imitating and storing sentences but by constructing a grammar. When we speak, we access our grammar to find the words, construct novel sentences, and produce the sounds that express the message we wish to convey. When we listen to someone speak and understand what is being said, we also access the grammar to process the utterances in order to assign a meaning to the sounds we hear.

Speaking and comprehending speech can be viewed as a speech chain linking the speaker's brain with the listener's brain, as shown in Figure 9.1. The grammar relates sounds and meanings and contains the units and rules of the language that make speech production and comprehension possible.

However, other psychological processes are used to produce and understand utterances. There are mechanisms that enable us to break the continuous stream of speech sounds into linguistic units such as phonemes, syllables, and words in order to

FIGURE 9.1

The speech chain.
A spoken utterance starts as a message in the brain/mind of the speaker. It is put into linguistic form and interpreted as articulation commands, emerging as an acoustic signal. The signal is processed by the ear of the listener and sent to the brain/mind, where it is interpreted.

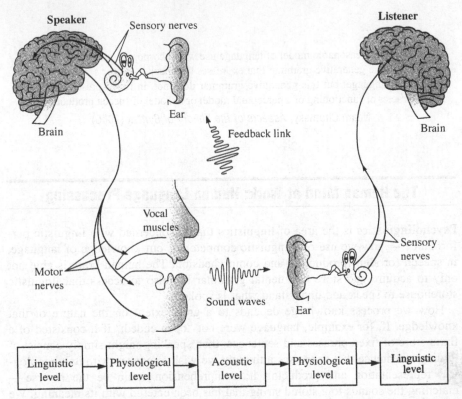

From Gleason. *Psycholinguistics,* 1E © 1993. Wadsworth, a part of Cengage Learning, Inc. Reproduced by permission. www.cengage.com/permissions.

comprehend, and to compose sounds into words in order to produce meaningful speech. Other mechanisms determine how we pull words from the mental lexicon, and still others explain how we construct a phrase structure representation of the words we retrieve.

We usually have no difficulty understanding or producing sentences in our language. We do it without effort or conscious awareness of the processes involved. However, we have all had the experience of making a speech error, of having a word on the "tip of our tongue," or of misunderstanding a perfectly grammatical sentence, such as sentence (1):

(1) The horse raced past the barn fell.

Conversely, there are ungrammatical sentences that are easily understandable such as sentence (2). This inconsistency between grammaticality and interpretability tells us that language processing involves more than grammar.

(2)   *The baby seems sleeping.

A theory of linguistic performance tries to detail the psychological mechanisms that work with the grammar to permit language production and comprehension.

Comprehension

> "I quite agree with you," said the Duchess; "and the moral of that is — 'Be what you would seem to be' — or, if you'd like it put more simply — 'Never imagine yourself not to be otherwise than what it might appear to others that what you were or might have been was not otherwise than what you had been would have appeared to them to be otherwise.' "
> "I think I should understand that better," Alice said very politely, "if I had it written down: but I can't quite follow it as you say it."
>
> Lewis Carroll, *Alice's Adventures in Wonderland* (1865)

The difficulty Alice has in understanding this sentence is not surprising. What is surprising is that we usually do understand long and complex sentences with multiple embedded relative clauses and many conjoined phrases and modifiers. Even young children can do this automatically and without conscious effort. Once in a while, of course, one stops and asks for clarification, as Christopher Robin does in listening to a story about Winnie-the-Pooh:

> Once upon a time, a very long time ago now, about last Friday, Winnie-the-Pooh lived in a forest all by himself under the name of Sanders.
>
> (*"What does 'under the name' mean?" asked Christopher Robin.*
> *"It means he had the name over the door in gold letters, and lived under it."*) . . .
> (Milne, 1926)

If Christopher Robin took the time to think about the meaning of the phrase "under the name of Sanders," then he might realize that it is an ambiguous sentence. In normal conversations, nonlinguistic considerations such as word frequency or what we expect to hear or what we are thinking can influence which meaning of an ambiguous sentence we come up with. One aim of psycholinguistic research is to clarify the processes by which speakers match one or more meanings to the strings of sounds they hear.

The Speech Signal

We are not conscious of the complex processes we use to understand speech. One of the first questions concerns the problem of segmentation of the **acoustic signal**. To understand how this is done, some knowledge of the signal itself is helpful.

In Chapter 5, we described speech sounds according to the ways in which they are produced — the position of the tongue, the lips, and the velum; the state of the vocal cords; the airstream mechanisms; whether the articulators obstruct the free flow of air; and so on. All of these articulatory characteristics are reflected in the physical characteristics of the sounds produced.

Speech sounds can also be described in physical or acoustic terms. Physically, a sound is produced whenever there is a disturbance in the position of air molecules. The question asked by ancient philosophers as to whether a sound is produced if a tree falls in the middle of the forest with no one to hear it has been answered by the science of acoustics. Objectively, a sound is produced; subjectively, there is no sound. In fact, there are sounds we cannot hear because our ears are not sensitive to all changes in air pressure (which result from the movement of air molecules). Acoustic phonetics is concerned only with speech sounds, all of which can be heard by the normal human ear.

When we push air out of the lungs through the glottis, the vocal cords vibrate; this vibration in turn produces pulses of air, which escape through the mouth (and sometimes the nose). These pulses are actually small variations in the air pressure, due to the wavelike motion of the air molecules.

The sounds we produce can be described in terms of how fast the variations of the air pressure occur, which determines the **fundamental frequency** of the sounds and is perceived by the hearer as pitch. We can also describe the magnitude or **intensity** of the variations, which determines the loudness of the sound. The quality of the speech sound — whether it is an [i] or an [ɑ] or whatever — is determined by the kind of vibrations, or **wave form**, which is determined by the shape of the vocal tract when the air is flowing through it. This shape modulates the fundamental frequency into a spectrum of frequencies of greater or lesser intensity, and the particular combination of "greater or lesser" is heard as a particular sound.

An important tool in acoustic research is a computer program that decomposes the speech signal into its frequency components. When you speak into a microphone plugged into the back of the computer (or when a tape recording is played through the computer), an image of the speech sound is displayed. The patterns produced are called **spectrograms**, or, more vividly, **voiceprints**. A spectrogram of the words *heed, head, had*, and *who'd* is shown in Figure 9.2.

Time in milliseconds moves horizontally from left to right; vertically, the graph represents pitch (or, more technically, frequency). The intensity of each frequency component is indicated by the degree of darkness: the more intense, the darker. Notice that for each vowel there are a number of dark bands that differ in their placement according to their frequency. They represent the strongest harmonics (the overtones) produced by the shape of the vocal tract and are called the **formants** of the vowels. (A harmonic is a special frequency that is a multiple [2, 3, etc.] of the fundamental frequency.) Because the tongue is in a different position for each vowel, the formant frequencies, or overtone pitches, differ for each vowel. It is the different frequencies of these formants that account for the different vowel qualities you hear. The pitch of the entire utterance (intonation contour) is shown

FIGURE 9.2

A spectrogram of the words *heed, head, had,* and *who'd*, as spoken with a British accent by Peter Ladefoged, February 16, 1973.

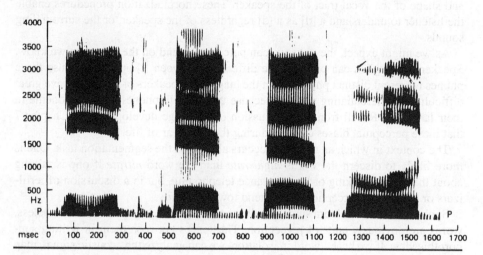

by the voicing bar marked *P* on the spectrogram. When the striations are far apart, the vocal cords are vibrating slowly, and the pitch is low; when the striations are close together, the vocal cords are vibrating rapidly, and the pitch is high.

By studying spectrograms of all speech sounds and many different utterances, acoustic phoneticians have learned a great deal about the basic acoustic components that reflect the articulatory features of speech sounds.

Speech Perception and Comprehension

Speech is a continuous signal. In natural speech, sounds overlap and influence each other, and yet the listener has the impression that he is hearing discrete units such as words, syllables, and phonemes. A central problem of speech perception is to explain how the listener carves up the continuous speech signal into meaningful units. This is referred to as the "segmentation problem."

Another question is, how does the listener manage to recognize particular speech sounds when they occur in different contexts and when they are spoken by different people? For example, how can a speaker tell that a [d] spoken by a man with a very deep voice is the same unit of sound as the [d] spoken in the high-pitched voice of a little child? Acoustically, they are very distinct. In addition, a [d] that occurs before the vowel [i] is somewhat different acoustically than a [d] that occurs before the vowel [u]. How does a listener know that two physically distinct instances of a sound are the same? This is referred to as the "invariance problem."

To address these complex problems, we must first try to understand the perceptual units involved in speech comprehension. Experiments show that perceptual units occur on different levels; we can segment the speech signal into strings of phonemes, syllables, morphemes, words, and phrases. There are also experimental results that show that the listener can calibrate her perceptions to control for differences in size and shape of the vocal tract of the speaker. These normalization procedures enable the listener to understand a [d] as a [d] regardless of the speaker, or the surrounding sounds.

As we might expect, the units we can perceive depend on the language we know. Speakers of English can perceive the difference between [l] and [r] because these phones represent distinct phonemes in the language. Speakers of Japanese have great difficulty in differentiating the two because they are allophones of one phoneme in their language. Recall from our discussion of language development in Chapter 7 that these perceptual biases develop during the first year of life.

The context in which an utterance occurs also helps the segmentation task. One is more likely to discern the words *night rate* than the word *nitrate* if one is talking about the cost of parking or long-distance telephoning, but in a discussion of fertilizers or chemistry, perception would tend toward *nitrate*.

Spoken words are seldom surrounded by boundaries such as pauses. Nevertheless, words are obviously units of perception. The spaces between them in writing support this view. If we hear a word in isolation, we can analyze the acoustic signal, map it onto the phonemic representation, and find its meaning in the mental lexicon. When not in isolation, the perception of words is more difficult.

To see how complex speech processing is, suppose you heard someone say

A sniggle blick is procking a slar.

and were able to perceive the sounds as

/əsnɪgəlblɪkɪzprakɪŋəslar/

You would still be unable to assign a meaning to the sounds, because the meaning of a sentence depends on the meanings of its words, and the only English lexical items in the string are the morphemes *a*, *is*, and *-ing*. The sentence lacks any English content words. (You would, however, accept it as a grammatically formed sentence in English because it conforms to the rules of English syntax.)

You can know that the sentence has no meaning only if you attempt (unconsciously or consciously) to search your mental lexicon for the phonological strings you decide are possible words. This process is called **lexical access**. In effect, it is word recognition. Finding that there are no entries for *sniggle, blick, prock*, or *slar*, you can conclude that the sentence includes *nonsense* strings.

If instead you heard someone say *The cat chased the rat*, through a lexical lookup process you would conclude that an event concerning a cat, a rat, and the activity of chasing had occurred. You could know this by segmenting the words in the continuous speech signal, analyzing them into their phonological word units, and matching these units with similar strings stored in your lexicon, which also includes the meanings attached to these phonological representations. This still would not enable you to tell who chased whom, since that is determined by syntactic processing. Processing speech to get at the meaning of what is said requires syntactic analysis as well as knowledge of *lexical semantics*.

Stress and intonation provide some clues to syntactic structure. We know, for example, that the different meanings of the sentences *He lives in the white house* and *He lives in the White House* can be signalled by differences in their stress patterns. Such prosodic aspects of speech also help to segment the speech signal into words and phrases. Syllables at the end of a phrase are longer in duration than at the beginning. Intonation contours mark boundaries of clauses. Relative loudness, pitch, and duration of syllables thus provide information in the comprehension process.

Speech comprehension is very fast and automatic. We understand an utterance as we hear it or read it. We don't wait for a pause and then say "Hold on. I have to analyze the speech sounds, look the words up in my dictionary, and **parse** (provide a syntactic analysis of) your utterance." But how do we understand a sentence?

Comprehension involves the ability to segment the continuous speech signal into phonemes, morphemes, words, phrases, and sentences; to construct a mental model of the discourse of which the sentence is a part; and to do all that more or less in parallel.

Comprehension Models and Experimental Studies

> I have experimented and experimented until now I know that ... [water] never does run uphill, except in the dark. I know it does in the dark, because the pool never goes dry; which it would, of course, if the water didn't come back in the night. It is best to prove things by experiment; then you know; whereas if you depend on guessing and supposing and conjecturing, you will never get educated.
>
> Mark Twain, *Eve's Diary* (1906)

> In this laboratory the only one who is always right is the cat.
>
> Motto in laboratory of Arturo Rosenblueth (1906–1970)

The psychological stages and processes that a listener goes through in comprehending the meaning of an utterance are very complex. When we listen to a sentence we receive information sequentially (word-by-word from left to right). The listener attempts to construct a linguistic representation *on-line,* i.e., as the words are spoken. He does not wait until the end of the sentence when all the information is available. Because of the sequential nature of the spoken (and written) language, there is a certain amount of guesswork involved in on-line comprehension. Alternative models of speech processing have been proposed in the attempt to clarify the stages involved. Some psycholinguists suggest that speech perception and comprehension involve both **top-down** and **bottom-up** processing.

Top-down processes proceed from semantic and syntactic information to the sensory input. Using such higher-level information, it is suggested, we can predict what is to follow in the signal. For example, upon hearing the determiner *the,* the speaker projects an NP and expects that the next word will be a noun, as in *the girl.* In this instance, the speaker would be using knowledge of phrase structure.

Bottom-up processes move step by step from the incoming acoustic signal to semantic interpretation, building each part of the structure on the basis of the sensory data alone. According to this model, the speaker waits until hearing *the* and *girl* and then constructs an NP, and then waits for the next word, and so on.

Evidence for at least partial top-down processing is provided in a number of experiments. For example, subjects make fewer identification errors of words when the words occur in sentences than when they are presented in isolation. This suggests that subjects use knowledge of syntactic structures in addition to the acoustic input signal. This is true even when the stimuli are presented in the presence of noise. Subjects also do better if the words occur in grammatically meaningful sentences as opposed to grammatically anomalous sentences; identification of words in ungrammatical sentences produced the most errors. This supports the idea that subjects are not responding simply to the input word by word.

Top-down processing is also supported by the fact that when subjects hear recorded sentences in which some part of the signal is removed and a cough substituted, they "hear" the sentence without a missing phoneme and, in fact, are unable to say which phonemic segment the cough replaced. Context plays a major role in determining which sounds the subjects replace. Thus, "[cough] eel" is heard as *wheel, heel, peel,* or *meal* depending on whether the sentence in which the distorted word occurs refers to an axle, shoe, orange, or food, respectively. We have also seen that context plays a role in word segmentation. The phonetic string [w a j t š u z] would be heard as *white shoes* rather than *why choose* in a shoe store.

Lexical Access and Word Recognition

There has been a great deal of research by psycholinguists on *lexical access* or *word recognition*, the process by which we obtain information about the meaning and syntactic category of a word from our mental lexicon. A number of experimental techniques have been used in studies of lexical access.

One technique asks subjects to decide whether a string of sounds (or letters if printed stimuli are used) is or is not a word. They must respond by pressing a button if the stimulus is an actual word. In these **lexical decision** experiments, **response time** or **reaction time** measurements (often referred to as RTs) are taken. The assumption is that the longer it takes to respond to a particular task, the more processing is involved. Using such measurements, it has been found that lexical access depends to some extent on word *frequency* — that is, RT is faster to words that occur more frequently in speech and writing. This is evidence that comprehension performance involves both linguistic and nonlinguistic factors. Another finding is that ambiguous sentences take longer to process than unambiguous sentences. It appears that even if subjects are not aware of the multiple meanings of an ambiguous sentence, both meanings are evoked and interfere with each other. This is true of sentences that are lexically ambiguous (with words that have more than one meaning) and of sentences that are syntactically ambiguous.

Reaction time is also measured in experiments using a **priming** technique. It has been found, for example, that if subjects hear a word such as *nurse* their response to *doctor* will be faster than to a semantically unrelated word such as *flower*. This may be due to the fact that semantically related words are located in the same part of the lexicon, and once the "path" to that section has been taken it is easier to travel that way a second time. It may also be due to the fact that other words are triggered when we "look up" a semantically related word.

An interesting finding in such experiments is that a lexically ambiguous word can be primed by a word referring to either meaning, even if the context of the ambiguous word disambiguates it. For example, either *harbour* or *wine* will prime the word *port* (result in faster response time) in the sentence

> The ship is in port.

This suggests that, in listening to speech, all the meanings represented by a phonological form will be triggered. This argues for at least some bottom-up processing, since both words are accessed even when the preceding sentence disambiguates the ambiguous word.

Although the listener initially retrieves all meanings of the ambiguous word, she very quickly uses the disambiguating information in the sentence to discard the meanings that are not appropriate to the sentence. At this point she is using top-down information.

Another experimental technique, called the **naming task**, asks the subject to read aloud a printed word. Subjects read real words faster than nonwords and irregularly spelled words such as *dough* and *enough* as fast as regularly spelled words such as *doe* and *stuff* and even faster than regularly spelled nonwords such as *cluff*. This shows that the subjects first go to the lexicon to see if the word is there, access the phonological representation, and produce the word. They can use spelling-to-pronunciation rules only if they cannot find the string of letters listed.

In naming, frequency also has an effect. That is, frequent words are read more quickly than infrequent ones.

> A Stroop test is an experimental task that illustrates automatic processing of verbal information: a person is asked to report colour names (red, green, etc.) out loud in either a consistent (same colour name, same ink colour) or an inconsistent (ink colour differs from colour name) condition. Subjects generally take significantly more time in the inconsistent condition, indicating how difficult it is to selectively ignore verbal information.

Working Memory

Memory, and working memory in particular, is thought to play a major role in language comprehension. In a widely accepted framework developed by psychologist Alan Baddeley and his colleagues (e.g., Baddeley, 1986; Baddeley & Hitch, 1974), working memory is considered to be a limited-capacity system involved in temporarily storing and manipulating information needed in the execution of complex cognitive tasks, such as the comprehension of verbal material. Working memory is considered to consist of several components: a central executive, an attention control system responsible for integrating information from different working memory subsystems and long-term memory; a phonological loop, responsible for the temporary maintenance of acoustic- or speech-based material;

FIGURE 9.3
Working memory.

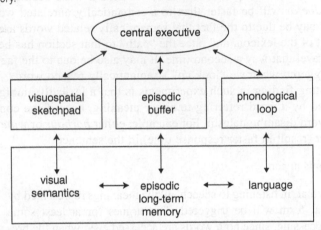

"The Episodic Buffer: A new component of working memory?"by A.D. Baddeley, 2000, *Trends in Cognitive Sciences*, 4, p. 421. Copyright 2000 by Elsevier Science Ltd.

a visuospatial sketchpad, which handles visual images; and an episodic memory subsystem (see Figure 9.3). While the central executive is thought to play a crucial role in comprehension, the phonological loop, considered to represent phonological memory, supports long-term learning of new sound patterns, as when children develop their first language or in adult learning of vocabulary in a second language.

Syntactic Processing

British Left Waffles on Falkland Islands
Enraged Cow Injures Farmer with Ax
Killer Sentenced to Die for Second Time in 10 Years
Stolen Painting Found by Tree

There has been more psycholinguistic research dealing with lexical access than with syntactic processing, possibly because the available experimental techniques can be more easily directed toward this question. In recent years, an increasing number of studies have concentrated on sentence processing.

In addition to recognizing words, the listener must figure out the syntactic and semantic relations among the words and phrases in a sentence, what we earlier referred to as "parsing." The parsing of a sentence is largely determined by the rules of the grammar, but it is also strongly influenced by the sequential nature of language.

The listener actively builds a phrase structure representation of the sentence as she hears it. She must therefore decide for each "incoming" word what its grammatical category is and how it attaches to the tree that is being constructed. Many sentences present "temporary" ambiguities. Some sentences contain a word or words that belong to more than one syntactic category. For example, the string *The warehouse fires*. . . . could continue in one of two ways:

(1) . . . were set by an arsonist.
(2) . . . employees over sixty.

Fires is part of a compound noun in sentence (1) and a verb in sentence (2). Experimental studies of such sentences show that both meanings and categories are activated when the subject encounters the ambiguous word, similar to what was found in the priming experiments. The ambiguity is quickly resolved based on syntactic and semantic context, and on the frequency of the two uses of the word. So quick and seamless are the disambiguations that newspaper headlines such as those at the head of this section are scarcely noticeable except to linguists who collect them.

Another important type of temporary ambiguity concerns sentences in which the phrase structure rules allow two possible attachments of a constituent, as illustrated by the following example:

> After the child visited the doctor prescribed a course of injections.

Experiments that track eye movements of people when they read such sentences show that there are attachment preferences that operate independently of the context. When the mental syntactic processor, or parser, receives the word *doctor,* it attaches it as a direct object of the verb *visit.* For this reason subjects experience a strange perceptual effect when they encounter the verb *prescribed.* They must backtrack and attach *the doctor* as subject of the embedded clause. Sentences that induce this effect are called "garden-path sentences." The sentence presented at the beginning of this chapter, *the horse raced past the barn fell* is also a garden path sentence. People will naturally interpret *raced* as the main verb, when in fact the main verb is *fell.*

These attachment preferences are due to the special procedures that the mental parser uses to construct trees. Two of these procedures are the **minimal attachment principle** and the **late closure principle**. Minimal attachment says "Create the simplest structure consistent with the grammar of the language." In the string *the horse raced past the barn*, the simpler structure is the one in which *the horse* is the subject and *raced* the main verb; the complex subject is "the horse (that was) raced past the barn." In the string *after the child visited the doctor . . . ,* the simplest structure is one in which *the child* is attached as the direct object of *visit.* This attachment becomes problematic when the mental parser subsequently encounters the verb *prescribed.*

Late closure says "Attach incoming material to the phrase that is currently being processed." Late closure is exemplified in the following sentence:

> Jamie said he will leave this morning.

Listeners prefer to interpret *this morning* as modifying the embedded verb *leave* rather than the root verb *said.* By the time the processor gets to *this morning*, it is already parsing the embedded S so it will attach the adverb phrase to the lowest verb, namely *leave.*

The comprehension of sentences depends on syntactic processing that uses the grammar and special parsing procedures to construct trees. Garden-path sentences suggest that the mental parser always pursues a single parse. Although this parse must sometimes be undone, a single parse strategy imposes less of a burden on the processor than attempting to conduct several parses in parallel.

There is also evidence that information about complement structure becomes available when the verb is encountered and that this information is used to aid the parsing process.

Another striking example of processing difficulty is a rewording of a Mother Goose poem. In its original form we have:

> This is the dog, that worried the cat, that killed the rat, that ate the malt, that lay in the house that Jack built.

No problem understanding that? Now try this paraphrase:

> This is the malt that the rat that the cat that the dog worried killed ate.

Although the confusing "sentence" follows the rules of relative clause formation — you have no difficulty with *the cat that the dog worried killed the rat* — it seems that once is enough, and when you apply the same process twice, getting *the rat that the cat that the dog worried killed ate the malt,* it becomes difficult to process. (Put a comma after *killed* to see if that helps you.) If we apply the process three times, all the commas in *War and Peace* will not enable you to process it.

The difficulty with this kind of sentence is related to memory constraints. In processing the sentence you have to keep *the malt* in mind all the way until *ate,* but while doing that you have to keep *the rat* in mind all the way until *killed,* and while doing that . . . it's a form of structure juggling that is difficult to perform. Though we have the competence to create such sentences, just as we have the competence to make a sentence with 10,000 words in it, performance limitations prevent creation of such monsters.

There are a number of other techniques used experimentally in the study of speech perception and comprehension. In a **shadowing task**, subjects are asked to repeat what they hear as rapidly as possible. A few exceptionally good shadowers can follow what is being said only about a syllable behind (300 milliseconds). Most of us, however, shadow with a delay of about a second (500 to 800 milliseconds). This is still quite fast. Shadowers often correct speech errors or mispronunciations unconsciously and even add inflectional endings if they are absent. Even when they are told that the speech they are to shadow includes errors and that they should repeat the errors, they are unable to do so. Lexical corrections are more likely to occur when the target word is predictable from what has been said previously. These shadowing experiments show that speech perception involves more than simply processing the incoming signal.

The ability to understand and comprehend what is said to us is a complex psychological process involving the internal grammar, parsing procedures such as minimal attachment and late closure, frequency factors, memory, and both linguistic and nonlinguistic context.

Speech Production

> And has the reader never asked himself what kind of a mental fact is his intention of saying a thing before he has said it? . . . How much of it consists of definite sensorial images, either of words or of things? Hardly anything! Linger, and the words and things come to mind. . . . The intention welcomes them.
>
> William James (1890)

As we saw, the speech chain starts with a speaker who, through some complicated set of neuromuscular processes, produces an acoustic signal that represents a thought, idea, or message to be conveyed to a listener, who must then decode the signal to arrive at a similar message. It is more difficult to devise experiments that provide information on how the speaker proceeds than to do so from the listener's side of the process. The best information has come from observing and analyzing spontaneous speech.

Planning Units

We might suppose that the thoughts of the speaker are simply translated into words one after the other through a semantic mapping process. Grammatical morphemes would be added as demanded by the syntactic rules of the language. The phonetic representation of each word in turn would then be mapped onto the neuromuscular commands to the articulators to produce the acoustic signal representing it.

We know, however, that this supposition is not a true picture of speech production. Although, when we speak, the sounds we produce and the words we use are linearly ordered, speech errors show that the prearticulation stages involve units larger than the single phonemic segment or even the word, as illustrated by the "U.S. Acres" cartoon. Phrases and even whole sentences are constructed prior to the production of a single sound. Errors show that features, segments, and words can be anticipated — that is, produced earlier than intended or reversed (as in typical **spoonerisms**) — so the later words or phrases in which they occur must already be conceptualized. This point is illustrated in the following examples of

"U.S. Acres" copyright © Paws. All rights reserved.

speech errors (the intended utterance to the left of the arrow, the actual utterance, including the error, to the right of the arrow):

(1) The **h**iring of minority **f**aculty. → The **f**iring of minority faculty.
     (The intended *h* is replaced by the *f* of *faculty*, which occurs later in the intended utterance.)
(2) **a**d h**o**c → **o**dd h**a**ck
     (The vowels /æ/ of the first word and /a/ of the second are exchanged or reversed.)
(3) **b**ig and **f**at → **p**ig and **v**at
     (The values of a single feature are switched: [+voiced] becomes [−voiced] in *big* and [−voiced] becomes [+voiced] in *fat*.)
(4) There are many ministers in our church. → There are many churches in our minister.
     (The stem morphemes *minister* and *church* are exchanged; the grammatical plural morpheme remains in its intended place in the phrase structure.)
(5) Seymour sliced the salami with a knife. → Seymour sliced a knife with the salami.
     (The two entire noun phrases — article + noun — are exchanged.)

In these errors, the intonation contour (primary stressed syllables and variations in pitch) remained the same as in the intended utterances, even when the words were disordered. In the intended utterance of (5), the highest pitch would be on *knife*. In the disordered sentence, the highest pitch occurred on the second syllable of *salami*. The pitch rise and increased loudness are thus determined by the syntactic structure of the sentence and are independent of the individual words. Thus syntactic structures are also units in linguistic performance.

Errors like those cited above are constrained in interesting ways. Phonological errors involving segments or features, as in (1), (2), and (3), primarily occur in content words, not in grammatical morphemes, again showing the distinction between these lexical classes. In addition, while words and lexical morphemes may be interchanged, grammatical morphemes and free or bound inflectional affixes may not be. As example (4) illustrates, the inflectional endings are "stranded," left behind, and subsequently attached, in proper phonological form, to the moved lexical morpheme.

Such errors show that speech production involves different kinds of units — features, segments, morphemes, words, phrases, the very units that exist in the grammar. They also show that, when we speak, words are structured into larger syntactic phrases that are stored in a kind of buffer memory before segments or features or words are disordered. This storage must occur prior to the articulatory stage. Thus, we do not select one word from our mental dictionaries and say it, then select another word and say it. We organize an entire phrase and in many cases an entire sentence.

The constraints on which units can be exchanged or moved also suggest that grammatical morphemes are added at a stage after the lexical morphemes are selected. This provides one of the motivations for a two-lexicon grammatical model, one containing lexical and derivational morphemes, and the other, grammatical morphemes.

Lexical Selection

> Humpty Dumpty's theory, of two meanings packed into one word like a portmanteau, seems to me the right explanation for all. For instance, take the two words "fuming" and "furious." Make up your mind that you will say both words but leave it unsettled which you will say first. Now open your mouth and speak. If . . . you have that rarest of gifts, a perfectly balanced mind, you will say "frumious."
>
> Lewis Carroll, "Preface," *The Hunting of the Snark* (1876)

In Chapter 4, word substitution errors were used to illustrate the semantic properties of words. Such substitutions are seldom random; they show that in speaking, in our attempts to express our thoughts through words in the lexicon, we may make an incorrect lexical selection based on partial similarity or relatedness of meanings.

Blends, in which we produce part of one word and part of another, further illustrate the lexical selection process in speech production; we may select two or more words to express our thoughts and, instead of deciding between them, produce them as "portmanteaus," as Humpty Dumpty calls them. Such blends are illustrated in the following errors:

(1) splinters/blisters → splisters
(2) edited/annotated → editated
(3) a swinging/hip chick → a swip chick
(4) frown/scowl → frowl

Application and Misapplication of Rules

> If you obey all the rules, you miss all the fun.
> Katharine Hepburn (1907–2003)

Spontaneous errors show that the rules of morphology and syntax, discussed in earlier chapters as part of competence, may also be applied (or misapplied) when we speak. It is hard to see this process in normal error-free speech; however, when someone says *groupment* instead of *grouping, ambigual* instead of *ambiguous*, or *bloodent* instead of *bloody*, it shows that regular rules are applied to morphemes to form possible but nonexistent words.

Inflectional rules also surface. The professor who said *We swimmed in the pool* knows that the past tense of *swim* is *swam* but mistakenly applied the regular rule to an irregular form.

Morphophonemic rules appear to be performance rules as well as rules of competence. Consider the *a/an* alternation rule in English. Errors such as *an istem* for the intended *a system* or *a burly bird* for the intended *an early bird* show that, when segmental disordering changes a noun beginning with a consonant to a noun beginning with a vowel, or vice versa, the indefinite article is also changed so that it conforms to the grammatical rule.

Such utterances also reveal that in speech production internal "editing" or monitoring attempts to prevent errors. When an error slips by the editor, such as the disordering of phonemes, the editor prevents a compounding of errors. Thus, when the /b/ of *bird* was anticipated and added to the beginning of *early*, the result was not **an burly bird*. The editor applied (or reapplied) the *a/an* rule to produce *a burly bird*.

An examination of such data also tells us something about the stages in the production of an utterance. Disordering of phonemes must occur before the indefinite article is given its phonological form, or the morphological rule must reapply after the initial error has occurred. An error such as *bin beg* for the intended *Big Ben* shows that phonemes are disordered before phonetic allophones are determined. That is, the intended *Big Ben* phonetically is [bɪg bɛ̃n] with an oral [ɪ] before the [g] and a nasal [ɛ̃] before the [n]. In the utterance that was produced, however, the [ĩ] is nasalized because it now occurs before the disordered [n], whereas the [ɛ] is oral before the disordered [g]. If the disordering occurred after the phonemes had been replaced by phonetic allophones, then the result would have been the phonetic utterance [bɪn bɛ̃g].

Nonlinguistic Influences

The discussion of speech comprehension suggested that nonlinguistic factors are involved in and sometimes interfere with linguistic processing. They also affect speech production. The individual who said *He made hairlines* instead of *He made headlines* was referring to a barber. The facts that the two compound nouns start with the same sound, are composed of two syllables, have the same stress pattern, and contain identical second morphemes undoubtedly played a role in producing the error, but the relationship between *hairlines* and *barbers* may also have been a contributing factor.

Other errors show that thoughts unrelated structurally to the intended utterance may have an influence on what is said. One speaker said "I've never heard of classes *on April 9*" instead of the intended *on Good Friday*. Good Friday fell on April 9 that year. The two phrases are not similar phonologically or morphologically, yet the nonlinguistic association seems to have influenced what was said. This influence is a further example of the distinction between linguistic competence and performance.

Both normal conversational data and experimentally elicited data provide the psycholinguist with evidence in the construction of models of both speech production and comprehension, the beginning and end points of the speech chain of communication.

Summary

Psycholinguistics is concerned with **linguistic performance** or processing, the use of linguistic knowledge (competence) in speech production and comprehension.

Comprehension, the process of understanding an utterance, requires the ability to access the mental lexicon to match the words in the utterance to their meanings. Comprehension starts with the perception of the **acoustic speech signal**. The speech signal can be described in terms of the **fundamental frequency**, perceived as **pitch**; the **intensity**, perceived as loudness; and the quality, perceived as differences in speech sounds, such as an [i] from an [a]. The speech wave can be displayed visually as a **spectrogram**, sometimes called a **voiceprint**. In a spectrogram, vowels exhibit dark bands where frequency intensity is greatest. These are called **formants** and result from the emphasis of certain *harmonics* of the fundamental frequency, as determined by the shape of the vocal tract. Each vowel has a unique formant pattern.

The speech signal is a continuous stream of sounds. Listeners have the ability to segment the stream into linguistic units and to recognize acoustically distinct sounds as the same linguistic unit.

The perception of the speech signal is necessary but not sufficient for the comprehension of speech. To get the full meaning of an utterance, we must **parse** the string into syntactic structures, since meaning depends on word order and constituent structure in addition to the meaning of words. Some psycholinguists believe we use both **top-down** and **bottom-up** processes during comprehension. Top-down processing uses semantic and syntactic information in addition to the incoming acoustic signal; bottom-up processes use only information contained in the sensory input.

Psycholinguistic experimental studies are aimed at uncovering the units, stages, and processes involved in linguistic performance. A number of experimental techniques have proved to be very helpful. In a **lexical decision** task, subjects are asked to respond to spoken or written stimuli by pressing a button if they consider the stimulus to be a word. In **naming tasks**, subjects read from printed stimuli. The measurement of **response times**, **RTs**, in naming and other lexical decision tasks shows that it takes longer to comprehend ambiguous utterances versus unambiguous ones, ungrammatical utterances compared to grammatical sentences, and nonsense forms as opposed to real words.

A word may **prime** another word if the words are related in some way such as semantically, phonetically, or even through similar spelling. The priming effect is shown by experiments in which a word such as *nurse* is spoken in a sentence, and it is found that words related to *nurse* such as *doctor* have lower RTs in lexical decision tasks. If an ambiguous word like *mouse* is used in an unambiguous context such as *the mouse ran up the clock,* words related to both meanings of mouse are primed, for example, *cat* and *computer.*

Eye-tracking techniques can determine the points of a sentence at which readers have difficulty and have to backtrack to an earlier point of the sentence. These experiments provide strong evidence that the parser has preferences in how it constructs trees and that it pursues a single parse consistent with the grammatical options, which may give rise to garden-path effects.

Another technique is **shadowing**, in which subjects repeat as fast as possible what is being said to them. Subjects often correct errors in the stimulus sentence, suggesting that they use linguistic knowledge rather than simply echo the sounds they hear. Other experiments reveal the processes involved in accessing the mental grammar and the influence of nonlinguistic factors in comprehension.

Working memory is thought to play a major role in language comprehension. The phonological loop is considered to be crucial in early stages of first and second language acquisition.

The units and stages in speech production have been studied by analyzing spontaneously produced speech errors. Anticipation errors, in which a sound is produced earlier than in the intended utterance, and **spoonerisms**, in which sounds or words are exchanged or reversed, show that we do not produce one sound or one word or even one phrase at a time. Rather, we construct and store larger units with their syntactic structures specified.

Word substitutions and blends show that words are connected to other words phonologically and semantically. The production of ungrammatical utterances also shows that morphological, inflectional, and syntactic rules may be wrongly applied or fail to apply when we speak, but at the same time show that such rules are actually involved in speech production.

Exercises

1. Speech errors, commonly referred to as "slips of the tongue" or "bloopers," illustrate a difference between linguistic competence and performance, since our very recognition of them as errors shows that we have knowledge of well-formed sentences. Furthermore, errors provide information about the grammar. The utterances listed below were actually produced deviations from the speakers' intended utterances. They are part of the University of California at Los Angeles corpus of over 15,000 speech errors, plus a few from Dr. Spooner.

   a. For each speech error, state what kind of linguistic unit or rule is involved — that is, phonological, morphological, syntactic, lexical, or semantic.
   b. State, to the best of your ability, the nature of the error or the mechanisms that produced it.

   (Note: The intended utterance is to the left of the arrow, the actual utterance to the right.)

   Example: ad hoc → odd hack
   　　　　　a. phonological vowel segment　　　b. reversal or exchange of segments

Example: she gave it away → she gived it away

a. inflectional morphology

b. incorrect application of regular past-tense rule to exceptional verb

Example: When will you leave? → When you will leave?

a. syntactic rule

b. failure to "move the auxiliary" to form a question

(1) brake fluid → blake fruid

(2) Drink is the curse of the working classes. → Work is the curse of the drinking classes. (Spooner)

(3) We have many ministers in our church. → . . . many churches in our minister.

(4) untactful → distactful

(5) an eating marathon → a meeting arathon

(6) executive committee → executor committee

(7) lady with the dachshund → lady with the Volkswagen

(8) stick in the mud → smuck in the tid

(9) He broke the crystal on my watch. → He broke the whistle on my crotch.

(10) a phonological rule → a phonological fool

(11) pitch and stress → piss and stretch

(12) big and fat → pig and vat

(13) speech production → preach seduction

(14) He's a New Yorker. → He's a New Yorkan.

(15) I'd forgotten about that. → I'd forgot abouten that.

*2. The use of spectrograms or "voiceprints" for speaker identification is based on the fact that no two speakers have the same speech characteristics. List some of the differences you have noticed in the speech of several individuals. Can you think of any reasons such differences exist?

3. Using a bilingual dictionary of a language you do not know, attempt to translate the following English sentences by looking up each word.

The children will eat the fish.
Send the professor a letter from your new school.
The fish will be eaten by the children.
Who is the person hugging that dog?
The spirit is willing, but the flesh is weak.

A. Using your own knowledge, or someone else's, give a *grammatically correct* translation of each sentence. What difficulties are brought to light by comparing the two translations? Briefly mention five of them.

B. Have a person who knows the target language translate the grammatical translation back into English. What problems do you observe? Are they related to any of the difficulties you mentioned in part A?

References

Baddeley, A.D. (1986). *Working memory*. Oxford: Oxford University Press.

Baddeley, A.D., & Hitch, G. (1974). Working memory. In G. Bower (Ed.), *The psychology of learning and motivation* (Vol. 8, pp. 47–90). New York: Academic Press.

Chomsky, N. (1965). *Aspects of the theory of syntax*. Cambridge, MA: MIT Press.

Dahl, H. (1979). *Word frequencies of spoken American English*. Essex, CT: Verbatim.

Further Reading

Allen, J. (1987). *Natural language understanding*. Menlo Park, CA: Benjamin/Cummings.

Berwick, R.C., & Weinberg, A.S. (1984). *The grammatical basis of linguistic performance: Language use and acquisition*. Cambridge, MA: MIT Press.

Carlson, G.N., & Tanenhaus, M.K. (Eds.). (1989). *Linguistic structure in language processing*. Dordrecht, The Netherlands: Kluwer Academic Publishers.

Caron, J. (1992). *An introduction to psycholinguistics* (T. Pownall, Trans.). Toronto: University of Toronto Press.

Carroll, D.W. (1994). *Psychology of language*. Pacific Grove, CA: Brooks/Cole.

Clark, H., & Clark, E. (1977). *Psychology and language: An introduction to psycholinguistics*. New York: Harcourt Brace Jovanovich.

Cutler, A. (2005). *Twenty-First century psycholinguistics: Four cornerstones*. Mahwah, NJ: Erlbaum.

Field, J. (2004). *Psycholinguistics: The key concepts*. London and New York: Routledge.

Fodor, J.A., Garrett, M., & Bever, T.G. (1986). *The psychology of language*. New York: McGraw-Hill.

Foss, D., & Hakes, D. (1978). *Psycholinguistics*. Englewood Cliffs, NJ: Prentice-Hall.

Fromkin, V.A. (Ed.). (1980). *Errors in linguistic performance*. New York: Academic Press.

Garman, M. (1990). *Psycholinguistics*. Cambridge, UK: Cambridge University Press.

Garnham, A. (1985). *Psycholinguistics: Central topics*. London and New York: Methuen.

Garrett, M.F. (1988). Processes in language production. In F.J. Newmeyer (Ed.), *The Cambridge Linguistic Survey,* (vol. 3, pp. 69–96). Cambridge, UK: Cambridge University Press.

Gaskell, G. (Ed.)(2007). *The Oxford handbook of psycholinguistics*. Oxford: Oxford University Press.

Gleason, J.B., & Ratner, N.B. (Eds.). (1993). *Psycholinguistics*. Orlando, FL: Harcourt Brace.

Harley, T.A. (2008). *The psychology of language: From data to theory*. (3rd ed.). New York: Psychology Press.

Johnson, M. (1989). Parsing as deduction: The use of knowledge in language. *Journal of Psycholinguistic Research, 18*(1), 105–128.

Jurafsky, D., & Martin, J.H. (2000). *Speech and language processing.* Upper Saddle River, NJ: Prentice-Hall.

Ladefoged, P. (1996). *Elements of acoustic phonetics* (2nd ed.). Chicago: University of Chicago Press.

Lea, W.A. (1980). *Trends in speech recognition.* Englewood Cliffs, NJ: Prentice-Hall.

Levelt, W.J.M. (1993). *Speaking: From intention to articulation.* Cambridge, MA: MIT Press.

Marcus, M.P. (1980). *A theory of syntactic recognition for natural language.* Cambridge, MA: MIT Press.

Stabler, E.P., Jr. (1992). *The logical approach to syntax: Foundations, specifications, and implementations of theories of government and binding.* Cambridge, MA: MIT Press, Bradford Books.

Winograd, T. (1972). *Understanding natural language.* New York: Academic Press.

Winograd, T. (1983). *Language as a cognitive process.* Reading, MA: Addison-Wesley.

Websites

http://www.mpi.nl/ The website of the Max Planck Institute for Psycholinguistics.

http://www.language-experiments.org/ A website with access to psycholinguistic experiments.

http://www.essex.ac.uk/psychology/experiments/lexical.html A University of Essex website illustrating a lexical decision task.

CHAPTER 10
Computational Linguistics: Computer Language Processing

Man is still the most extraordinary computer of all.
John F. Kennedy (1917–1963)

Computers are useless. They can only give you answers.
Pablo Picasso (1881–1973)

© Dan Piraro. King Features Syndicate

Throughout history, only human beings have had the capability to process language. Today, it is common for computers to process language. **Computational linguistics** is a subfield of linguistics and computer science that is concerned with the interactions of human language and computers. Computational linguisitics includes the analysis of written texts and spoken discourse, the translation of text and speech from one language into another, the use of human (not computer) languages for communication between people and computers, and computer modelling and testing of linguistic theories.

Text and Speech Analysis

[The professor had written] all the words of their language in their several moods, tenses, and declensions [on tiny blocks of wood, and had] emptied the whole vocabulary into his frame, and made the strictest computation of the general proportion there is in books between the numbers of particles, nouns, and verbs, and other parts of speech.

Jonathan Swift, *Gulliver's Travels* (1726)

Frequency Analysis, Concordances, and Collocations

Jonathan Swift prophesied one way computers would be put to work in linguistics — in the statistical analysis of language. Computers can be programmed to reveal properties of language, such as the distribution of sounds, allowable word orders, permitted combinations of morphemes, relative frequencies of words and morphemes (i.e., their "general proportion"), and so on for any textual or spoken input or **corpus**.

A frequency analysis of one million words of written American English (Kučera & Francis, 1967) reveals the ten most frequently occurring words: *the, of, and, to, a, in, that, is, was,* and *he.* These "little" words accounted for about 25 percent of the words in the corpus, with *the* leading the pack at 7 percent. A similar analysis of *spoken* American English produced somewhat different results (Dahl, 1979). The "winners" were *I, and, the, to, that, you, it, of, a,* and *know,* accounting for nearly 30 percent. This is but one of the differences between spoken and written language demonstrated by corpus analysis. All English prepositions except *to* occur more frequently in written than in spoken English, and not surprisingly, profane and taboo words (see Chapter 12) were far more numerous in spoken than written language.

A **concordance** takes frequency analysis one step further by specifying the location within the text of each word, and its surrounding context. A concordance of the previous paragraph would not only show that the word *words* occurred five times, but would indicate in which line of the paragraph it appeared, and provide its context. If one chose a "window" of three words on either side for context, the concordance would look like this for *words:*

of one million   **words**   of written American
most frequently occurring   **words:** *the, of, and,*

he. These "little" **words**   accounted for about
percent of the **words,** in the corpus
profane and taboo **words**   (see Chapter 12)

A concordance, as you can see, might be of limited usefulness because of its "raw" nature. A way to refine a concordance is through **collocation analysis**. A collocation is the occurrence of two or more words within a short space of each other in a corpus. The point is to find evidence that the presence of one word in the text affects the occurrence of other words. Such an analysis must be statistical and involve large samples to show significant results. In the above concordance of *words,* there is not enough data to be significant. If we performed a concordance on this entire book, patterns would emerge that would show that *words* and *written, words* and *taboo,* and *words* and *of* are more likely to occur close together than, say, *words* and *million.*

Such analyses can be conducted on existing texts (such as the works of Shakespeare or the Koran) or on any corpus of utterances gathered from spoken or written sources. Authorship attribution is one motivation for these studies. By analyzing the various books of the Bible, for instance, it is possible to get a sense of who wrote what passages. In a notable study of *The Federalist Papers*, the authorship of a disputed paper was attributed to James Madison rather than to Alexander Hamilton. This was accomplished by comparing the statistical analyses of the paper in question with those of known works by the two writers.

A concordance of sounds by computer may reveal patterns in poetry that would be nearly impossible for a human to detect. An analysis of the *Iliad* showed that many of the lines with an unusual number of etas (/i/) related to youth and lovemaking; the line with the most alphas (/a/) was interpreted as being an imitation of stamping feet, the marching of armies. The use of computers permits literary scholars to study poetic and prosaic features such as assonance, alliteration, metre, and rhythm. Today, computers can do the tedious mechanical work that once had to be done painstakingly with paper and pencil.

Information Retrieval and Summarization

Hired
Tired
Fired

A career summary, source obscure

Many people use the search features of the Internet to find information. Typically, one enters a keyword, or perhaps several, and magically the computer returns the location of websites that contain information relating to that keyword. This process is an example of **information retrieval**. It may be as trivial as finding websites that contain the keyword exactly as it is entered, but usually some linguistic analysis is applied. Websites are returned, and even ranked, according to the frequency of occurrence of the keyword, different morphological forms of the keyword, synonyms of the keyword, and concepts semantically related to the keyword. For example, the keyword *bird* might retrieve information based on *bird, birds, to bird, bird feeders, water birds, avian, sparrow, feathers, flight,* and so on.

In general, information retrieval is the use of computers to locate and display data gleaned from possibly very large databases. The input to an information retrieval system consists of words, statements, or questions that the computer analyzes linguistically; it then uses the results to sift through the database for pertinent information. Nowadays, highly refined and complex information retrieval systems identify useful patterns or relationships in corpuses or other computer repositories using highly complex linguistic and statistical analyses. The term **data mining** is used currently for the highly evolved information retrieval systems.

A keyword as general as *bird* may return far more information than could be read in a year if a large database such as an encyclopedia is queried. Much of the data would repeat itself, and some information would outweigh other information. Through **summarization** programs, computers can eliminate redundancy and identify the most salient features of a body of information. World leaders, corporate executives, and even university professors — all of whom may wish to digest large volumes of textual material such as reports, newspapers, and scholarly articles — can benefit from summarization processes providing the material is available in computer-readable form, which is increasingly the case in the first few years of the twenty-first century.

A typical scenario would be to use information retrieval to access, say, a hundred articles about birds. The articles may average 5,000 words. Summarization programs, which can be set to reduce an article by a certain amount, say 1/10 or 1/100, are applied. The human reads the final output. Thus 500,000 words can be reduced to 5,000 or 10,000 words containing the most pertinent information, which may then be read in ten or twenty minutes. It is reported that former U.S. President Bill Clinton, a fast reader, could absorb the contents of relevant articles from upward of 100 news sources from around the world with the help of aides using computer summarizations.

Summarization programs range from the simplistic "print the first sentence of every paragraph," to complex programs that analyze the document semantically to identify the important points, often using "concept vectors." A concept vector is a list of meaningful keywords whose presence in a paragraph is a measure of the paragraph's significance, and therefore an indication of whether the content of that paragraph should be included in a summarization. The summary document contains concepts from as many of the key paragraphs as possible, subject to length constraints.

Spell Checkers

> Take care that you never spell a word wrong. . . . It produces great praise to a lady to spell well.
>
> Thomas Jefferson (1743–1826)

Spell checkers, and perhaps in the future, pronunciation checkers, are an application of computational linguistics that vary in sophistication from mindless, brute force lookups in a dictionary to enough intelligence to flag *your* when it should be *you're,* or *bear* when *bare* is intended. One often finds spell checkers as front ends to information retrieval systems, checking the keywords to prevent misspellings from misleading the search. However, as the following poem reveals, spell checkers cannot replace careful editing:

> I have a spelling checker
> It came with my PC
> It plane lee marks four my revue
> miss steaks aye can knot see
>
> A checker is a bless sing
> It freeze yew lodes of thyme
> It helps me right awl stiles to read
> And aides me when eye rime
>
> To rite with care is quite a feet
> Of witch won should bee proud
> And wee mussed dew the best wee can
> Sew flaws are knot aloud

Found on the Internet, source obscure

Machine Translation

> Egad, I think the interpreter is the hardest to be understood of the two!
>
> R.B. Sheridan, *The Critic* (1779)
>
> There exist extremely simple sentences in English — and . . . for any other natural language — which would be uniquely . . . and unambiguously translated into any other language by anyone with a sufficient knowledge of the two languages involved, though I know of no program that would enable a machine to come up with this unique rendering.
>
> Yeshua Bar-Hillel (1915–1975)

The first use of computers for natural language processing began in the 1940s with the attempt to develop **automatic machine translation**. During World War II, U.S. scientists without the assistance of computers deciphered coded Japanese military communications and proved their skill in coping with difficult language problems. The idea of using deciphering techniques to translate from one language into another was expressed in a letter written to Norbert Wiener by Warren Weaver, a pioneer in the field of computational linguistics: "When I look at any article in Russian, I say:

'This is really written in English, but it has been coded in some strange symbols. I will now proceed to decode' " (Locke & Boothe, 1955).

The aim in automatic translation is to "feed" into the computer a written passage in the **source language** (the input) and to receive a grammatical passage of equivalent meaning in the **target language** (the output). In the early days of machine translation, it was believed that this task could be accomplished by entering into the memory of a computer a dictionary of a source language and a dictionary with the corresponding morphemes and words of a target language. The translating program consisted of matching the morphemes of the input sentence with those of the target language. Unfortunately, what often happened was a process called by early machine translators "language in, garbage out." A classic example of such "translation" was *invisible idiot* for *out of sight, out of mind*.

Translation is more than word-for-word replacement. Often there is no equivalent word in the target language, and the order of words may differ, as in translating from a subject–verb–object (SVO) language such as English to a subject–object–verb (SOV) language such as Japanese. There is also difficulty in translating idioms, metaphors, jargon, and so on.

These problems are dealt with by human translators because they know the grammars of the two languages and draw on general knowledge of the subject matter and the world to arrive at the intended meaning. Machine translation is often impeded by lexical and syntactic ambiguities, structural disparities between the two languages, morphological complexities, and other cross-linguistic differences. It is often difficult to get good translations even when humans do the translating, as is illustrated by some of the "mistranslations" printed on signs in non–English-speaking countries as "aids" to tourists:

> Utmost of chicken with smashed pot (restaurant in Greece)
> Nervous meatballs (restaurant in Bulgaria)
> The nuns harbour all diseases and have no respect for religion (Swiss nunnery hospital)
> All the water has been passed by the manager (German hotel)
> Certified midwife: entrance sideways (Jerusalem)

Similar problems are evident in this brief excerpt from the translation of an interview of the entertainer Madonna in the Hungarian newspaper *Blikk:*

BLIKK: Madonna, let's cut toward the hunt: Are you a bold hussy-woman that feasts on men who are tops?

MADONNA: Yes, yes, this is certainly something that brings to the surface my longings. In America it is not considered to be mentally ill when a woman advances on her prey in a discotheque setting with hardy cocktails present.

Such "translations" represent the difficulties of just finding the "equivalent" words, but word choice is not the only problem in automatic translation. There are challenges in morphology and syntax as well.

We have been implicitly discussing the translation of written texts. In the realm of the machine translation of speech, both speech recognition (speech-to-text) and speech production (text-to-speech) need to be taken into account. Figure 10.1 illustrates the steps involved in the machine translation of speech.

Computers That Talk and Listen

The first generations of computers had received their inputs through glorified typewriter keyboards, and had replied through high-speed printers and visual displays. Hal could do this when necessary, but most of his communication with his shipmates was by means of the spoken word. Poole and Bowman could talk to Hal as if he were a human being, and he would reply in the perfect idiomatic English he had learned during the fleeting weeks of his electronic childhood.

Arthur C. Clarke, *2001: A Space Odyssey* (1968)

The ideal computer is multilingual; it should "speak" computer languages such as C, FORTRAN, and Java as well as languages such as English and Japanese. For many purposes, it would be helpful if we could communicate with computers as we communicate with other humans, through our native language, but the computers portrayed in films and on television as capable of speaking and understanding human language do not yet exist.

The translation processes of Figure 10.1 summarize the areas of computational linguistics concerned with human–machine communication. Speech-to-text on the one end, and text-to-speech on the other end, are the chief concern of **computational phonetics and phonology**. The tasks of machine understanding and of language generation, whether for purposes of translation into a target language or as part of the human–machine communication process, encompasses **computational morphology**, **computational syntax**, **computational semantics**, and **computational pragmatics**, all of which are discussed below.

Computational Phonetics and Phonology

Computational phonetics and phonology has two concerns. The first is with programming computers to analyze the speech signal into its component phones and phonemes. The second is to send the proper signals to an electronic speaker so that it enunciates the phones of the language and combines them into morphemes and words. The first of these is **speech recognition**; the second is **speech synthesis**.

FIGURE 10.1

Logic flow of machine translation of speech.

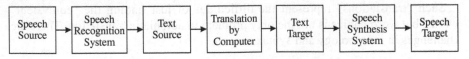

Speech Recognition

> When Frederic was a little lad he proved so brave and daring,
> His father thought he'd 'prentice him to some career seafaring.
> I was, alas! his nurs'rymaid, and so it fell to my lot
> To take and bind the promising boy apprentice to a *pilot* —
> A life not bad for a hardy lad, though surely not a high lot,
> Though I'm a nurse, you might do worse than make your boy a pilot.
> I was a stupid nurs'rymaid, on breakers always steering,
> And I did not catch the word aright, through being hard of hearing;
> Mistaking my instructions, which within my brain did gyrate
> I took and bound this promising boy apprentice to a *pirate.*

Gilbert and Sullivan, *The Pirates of Penzance* (1877)

When you listen to someone speak a foreign language, you notice that it is continuous except for breath pauses, and that it is difficult to segment the speech into sounds and words. It's all run together. The computer faces this situation when it tries to do speech recognition.

Early speech recognizers did not even attempt to "hear" individual sounds. Programmers stored the acoustic patterns of words in the memory of the computer and programmed it to look for those patterns in the speech signal. The computer had a fixed, small vocabulary. Moreover, it best recognized the speech of the same person who provided the original word patterns. It would have trouble "understanding" a different speaker, and if a word outside the vocabulary was uttered, the computer was clueless. If the words were run together, recognition accuracy also fell, and if the words were not fully pronounced, say *saskawan* for Saskatchewan, failure generally ensued. Coarticulation effects also muddied the waters. The computer might have [hɪz] as its representation of the word *his,* but in the sequence *his soap,* pronounced [hɪssop] the *his* is pronounced [hɪs] with a voiceless [s]. As well, the vocabulary best consisted of words that were not too similar phonetically, avoiding confusion between words like *pilot* and *pirate,* which might, as with the young lad in the song, have grave consequences.

Today, many interactive phone systems have a speech recognition component. They will invite you to "press 1 or say 'yes'; press 2 or say 'no,'" or something similar. These systems have very small vocabularies and so can search the speech signal for anything resembling a keyword's prestored acoustic patterns and generally get it right.

The more sophisticated speech recognizers that can be purchased for use on a personal computer have much larger vocabularies, upward of 25,000 words. To be highly accurate they must be trained to the voice of a specific person, and they must be able to detect individual phones in the speech signal. The training consists of the user making multiple utterances known in advance to the computer, which extracts the acoustic patterns of each phone typical of that user. Later the computer uses those patterns to aid in the recognition process.

Because no two utterances are ever identical, and because there is generally noise (nonspeech sounds) in the signal, the matching process that underlies speech recognition is statistical. On the phonetic level, the computations may say [b] with 30 percent confidence, [p] with 35 percent confidence, and [pʰ] with 35 percent confidence. Other factors may be used to help the decision. For example, if the computer is confident that the preceding sound is [s], then [p] is the likely candidate, and the first two phonemes of the word are /sp/. The system takes advantage of its (i.e., the programmer's) knowledge of sequential constraints (see Chapter 6). If, on the other hand, the sound occurs at the beginning of the word, it must be [pʰ] or [b] and further information is needed to determine whether it is the phoneme /p/ or /b/. If the following sounds are [ek] then /b/ is the one, since *bake* is a word but *pake is not. If the computer is unable to decide, it may offer a list of choices such as *pack* or *back* and ask the person using the system to decide.

Even these modern systems are brittle. They break when circumstances become unfavourable. If the user speaks rapidly with lots of coarticulation (*whatcha* for *what are you*), and there is a lot of background noise, recognition accuracy plummets. People do better. If someone mumbles, you can generally make out what they are saying because you have context to help you. In a noisy setting such as a party, you are able to converse with your dance partner despite the background noise because your brain has the ability to filter out irrelevant sounds. This effect is so striking it is given a name: the cocktail-party effect. Computers are not nearly as capable of coping with noise as people, though research directed at the problem is beginning to show positive results.

Speech Synthesis

> Machines which, with more or less success, imitate human speech, are the most difficult to construct, so many are the agencies engaged in uttering even a single word — so many are the inflections and variations of tone and articulation, that the mechanician finds his ingenuity taxed to the utmost to imitate them.
>
> *Scientific American* (January 14, 1871)

> Speak clearly, if you speak at all; carve every word before you let it fall.
>
> Oliver Wendell Holmes, Sr. (1809–1894)

Early efforts toward building "talking machines" were concerned with machines that could produce sounds that imitated human speech. In 1779, Christian Gottlieb Kratzenstein won a prize for building such a machine. It was "an instrument constructed like the vox humana pipes of an organ which . . . accurately express the sounds of the vowels." In building this machine he also answered a question posed by the Imperial Academy of St. Petersburg: "What is the nature and character of the sounds of the vowels *a, e, i, o, u* [that make them] different from one another?" Kratzenstein constructed a set of "acoustic resonators" similar to the

shapes of the mouth when these vowels are articulated and set them resonating by a vibrating reed that produced pulses of air similar to those coming from the lungs through the vibrating vocal cords.

Twelve years later, Wolfgang von Kempelen of Vienna constructed a more elaborate machine with bellows to produce a stream of air to simulate the lungs, and with other mechanical devices to simulate the different parts of the vocal tract. Von Kempelen's machine so impressed the young Alexander Graham Bell, who saw a replica of the machine in Edinburgh, that he, with his brother Melville, attempted to construct a "talking head," making a cast from a human skull. They used various materials to form the velum, palate, teeth, lips, tongue, cheeks, and so on, and installed a metal larynx with vocal cords made by stretching a slotted piece of rubber. They used a keyboard control system to manipulate all the parts with an intricate set of levers. This ingenious machine produced vowel sounds, some nasal sounds, and even a few short combinations of sounds.

With the advances in the acoustic theory of speech production, and the technological developments in electronics, machine production of speech sounds has made great progress. We no longer have to build physical models of the speech-producing mechanism; we can now imitate the process by producing the physical signals electronically.

Research on speech has shown that all speech sounds can be reduced to a small number of acoustic components. One way to produce synthetic speech is to mix these important parts together in the proper proportions, depending on the speech sounds to be imitated. It is rather like following a recipe for making soup, which might read: "Take two quarts of water, add one onion, three carrots, a potato, a teaspoon of salt, a pinch of pepper, and stir it all together."

This method of producing synthetic speech would include a "recipe" that might read:

1. Start with a tone at the same frequency as vibrating vocal cords (higher if a woman's or child's voice is being synthesized, lower for a man's).

2. Emphasize the harmonics corresponding to the formants required for a particular vowel quality.
3. Add hissing or buzzing for fricatives.
4. Add nasal resonances for nasal sounds.
5. Temporarily cut off sound to produce stops and affricates.
6. and so on. . . .

All these "ingredients" are blended electronically, using computers to produce highly intelligible, more or less natural-sounding speech.

Most synthetic speech still has a machinelike quality or "accent," due to small inaccuracies in simulation, and because suprasegmental factors such as changing intonation and stress patterns are not yet fully understood. If not correct, such factors may be more confusing than mispronounced phonemes. Currently, the chief area of research in speech synthesis is concerned precisely with discovering and programming the rules of rhythm and timing that native speakers apply.

Still, speech synthesizers today are no harder to understand than a person speaking a dialect slightly different from one's own, and when the context is sufficiently narrow, as in a synthetic voice reading a telephone number, there are no problems.

A speech synthesizer has two components. One is the electronic device we have been describing that converts a phonetic symbol to an electronic representation that, when played through a speaker, resembles human speech. The other component is a text-to-speech system that translates the input text into a phonetic representation. This task is like the several exercises at the end of Chapter 5 where we asked you for a phonetic transcription of written words.

The difficulties of text-to-speech are legion. We will mention two. The first is the heteronym problem: words spelled alike but pronounced differently (see Chapter 4 for a fuller discussion).

Read may be pronounced like *red* in *She has read the book,* but like *reed* in *She will read the book.* How does the text-to-speech system know which is which? Make no mistake about the answer. The machine must have structural knowledge of the sentence to make the correct choice, just as humans do. Unstructured, linear knowledge will not suffice. For example, we might program the text-to-speech system to pronounce *read* as *red* when the previous word is a form of *have.* But this fails in a number of ways. First, the *have* governs the pronunciation at a distance, both from the left and the right, as in *Has the girl with the flaxen hair read the book?* and *Oh, the girl read the book, has she!* It's the underlying structure that needs to be known, namely that *has* is an auxiliary verb for the main verb *to read.* If we try the ploy of pronouncing *read* as *red* whenever *have* is "in the vicinity," we run into sentences like *The teacher said to have the girl read the book by tomorrow,* where this version of *read* gets the *reed* pronunciation. Even worse for the linear analysis are sentences like *It's the girl that you must have read the book,* where the words *have read* occur next to each other. Of course you know that this occurrence of *read* is of the *reed* type, because you know English and therefore know English syntactic structures. Only through structural knowledge can the heteronym problem be approached effectively. More discussion of this takes place in the section on computational syntax later in this chapter.

The second difficulty is inconsistent spelling, well illustrated by the first two lines of a longer poem:

> I take it you already know
> Of *tough* and *bough* and *cough* and *dough*

Each of the *ough* words is phonetically different, but it is difficult to find rules that dictate when *gh* should be [f] and when it is silent. Modern computers have sufficient storage capacity to store every word in the language, its alternative spellings, and its likely pronunciations. This list may include acronyms, abbreviations, foreign words, proper names, numbers including fractions, and special symbols such as #, whose pronunciation is "pound sign." Such a list is helpful — it is like memorizing rather than figuring out the pronunciations — and encompasses a large percentage of items, including the *ough* words. However, the list can never be complete. New words, new word forms, proper names, abbreviations, and acronyms are constantly being added to the language and cannot be anticipated. The text-to-speech system requires letter-to-phone conversion rules for items not in its dictionary. The challenges here are similar to those faced when learning to read, which are considerable and, when it comes to the pronunciation of proper names, which may be of foreign origin, are utterly daunting.

Speech synthesis has important applications. It benefits visually impaired persons in the form of "reading machines," now commercially available. Mute patients with laryngectomies or other medical conditions that prevent normal speech can use synthesizers to express themselves. For example, researchers at North Carolina State University developed a communication system for an individual with so severe a form of multiple sclerosis that he could utter no sound and was totally paralyzed except for nodding his head. Using a head movement for "yes" and its absence as "no," this individual could select words displayed on a computer screen and assemble sentences to express his thoughts, which were then spoken by a synthesizer.

Most of us these days hear synthesized speech when we call our bank and an "automated bank clerk" tells us our bank balance, or when a telephone information "operator" gives us a requested phone number. Most airlines offer up-to-the-minute arrival and departure information via automatic processing using a synthetic voice. Many information services are automated and deliver timely information, such as stock prices, over the telephone via synthesized speech. Although some people find the speech unpleasant, and even unnerving, it makes information that is accurate and current available to millions of people over the telephone.

Computational Morphology

If we wish our computers to speak and understand grammatical English, we must teach them morphology (see Chapter 2). We can't have machines going around saying, "*The cat is sit on the mat," or "*My five horse be in the barn." Similarly, if computers are to understand English they need to know that *sitting* contains two morphemes, *sit+ing*, whereas *spring* is one morpheme, and *earring* is two but they are *ear+ring*, not *earr+ing*.

The processing of word structures by computers is computational morphology. The computer needs to understand the structure of words both to understand the words and to use the words in a grammatically correct way. To process words the computer is programmed to look for roots and affixes. In some cases this is straightforward. *Books* is easily broken into *book+s, walking* into *walk+ing, fondness* into *fond+ness,* and *unhappy* into *un+happy.* These cases, and many like them, are the easy ones, because the spelling is well behaved, and the morphological processes are general. Other words are more difficult, such as *profundity = profound+ity, galactic = galaxy+ic,* and *democracy = democrat+y.*

One approach is to place all the morphological forms of all the words in the language in the computer's dictionary. Although today's computers can handle such a high computational load — many millions of forms — there would still be problems because of the generality of the processes. As soon as a new word enters the language, as *fax* did some years ago, a whole family of words is possible: *faxes, fax's, faxing, faxed, refax,* and *faxable;* and many others are not possible: **faxify, *exfax, *disfax,* and so on. The dictionary would be continually out of date.

Moreover, not all forms are predictable. Although *uglify* is not a dictionary word, if you hear it you know, and the computer should know, that it means "to make ugly." Likewise, compounding is a general process, and it would be impossible to predict all possible compounds of English. When *skybox* was coined from *sky+box,* no computer could have had it in its dictionary.

The computer needs to have the ability to break words correctly into their component morphemes, and to understand each morpheme and its effect on the word's meaning, and where the word can be placed in a sentence. Computational morphology, then, is a host of interwoven rules, exceptions, and word/morpheme forms, all with the purpose of comprehending the internal structure of words.

Always, difficult problems remain. If the computer sees *resent,* how does it know if it's the monomorphemic *resent* (with a /z/), or *re + sent*? A broader context is needed, and that is the topic of the next section.

Computational Syntax

In the beginning, there was ELIZA.

PATIENT:	Men are all alike.
ELIZA:	In what way?
PATIENT:	They're always bugging me about something or other.
ELIZA:	Can you think of a specific example?
PATIENT:	Well, my boyfriend made me come here.
ELIZA:	Your boyfriend made you come here?
PATIENT:	He says I'm depressed much of the time.
ELIZA:	I am sorry to hear you are depressed.

ELIZA is a computer program designed to simulate a nondirective psychiatrist talking to a patient. ELIZA has a collection of prepared phrases stored in memory such as "In what way?" or "Tell me more" that help keep the conversation going when it doesn't "understand" the patient. When ELIZA recognizes certain syntactic patterns, however, it turns them around to make a sensible response, as when it echoes "Your boyfriend made you come here?" ELIZA was programmed with a small bit of syntactic knowledge, which allowed it to make grammatical utterances based on the patient's statements, but no semantic knowledge at all. If a patient says "My sniggle is untherible," ELIZA would respond with "How long has your sniggle been untherible?" ELIZA was designed by MIT scientist Joseph Weizenbaum in the 1960s. Though its syntactic sophistication is low by today's standards, ELIZA is one of the earliest attempts at human–machine communication that took the syntax of English into account.

Twenty-five years after ELIZA, computer scientists at Duke University and North Carolina State University programmed the "Circuit Fix-It Shop," a system designed to help a technician repair a faulty circuit. Unlike ELIZA, which accepted only typed input and produced printed output, the Circuit Fix-It Shop accepted speech input and spoke its responses. It had its own syntax and was capable both of understanding and speaking syntactically complex utterances, as the following excerpt from a repair session shows:

COMPUTER:	This is the circuit fix-it shop. How may I help you?
TECHNICIAN:	I need to fix the RS111 circuit.
COMPUTER:	I am familiar with that circuit. The LED is supposed to be displaying alternately blinking one and seven.
TECHNICIAN:	Where is the LED?
COMPUTER:	In the middle right of the blue region is the LED.
TECHNICIAN:	No light.
COMPUTER:	What is the switch at when the LED is off?
TECHNICIAN:	The switch is down.
COMPUTER:	You put up the switch.

Once the computer has understood the technician's utterance, it uses rules of semantics and syntax, together with a lexicon of words and morphemes, to formulate a grammatical, sensible response, which its synthesizer program then speaks. The rules in many cases are similar to the phrase structure rules seen in Chapter 3, such as form a noun phrase from an article followed by a noun. It also has semantic rules that tell it to use *the* with the word *switch* since its "world knowledge" tells it that there is only one switch in that particular circuit.

To understand a sentence, you must know its syntactic structure. If you didn't know the structure of *dogs that chase cats chase birds,* you wouldn't know whether dogs or cats chase birds. Similarly, machines that understand language must also determine syntactic structure. A **parser** is a computer program that attempts to replicate what we have been calling the "mental parser." Like the mental parser, the parser in a computer uses a grammar to assign a phrase structure to a string of words. Parsers may use a phrase structure grammar and lexicon similar to those discussed in Chapter 3.

For example, a parser may use a grammar containing the following rules: S → NP VP, NP → Det N, and so forth. Suppose the machine is asked to parse *The child found the kittens.* A top-down parser proceeds by first consulting the grammar rules and then examining the input string to see if the first word could begin an S. If the input string begins with a Det, as in the example, the search is successful, and the parser continues by looking for an N, and then a VP. If the input string happened to be *child found the kittens,* the parser would be unable to assign it a structure because it doesn't begin with a determiner, which is required by this grammar to begin an S.

A bottom-up parser takes the opposite tack. It looks first at the input string and finds a Det (*the*) followed by an N (*child*). The rules tell it that this phrase is an NP. It would continue to process *found, the,* and *kittens* to construct a VP, and would finally combine the NP and VP to make an S.

Parsers may run into difficulties with words that belong to several syntactic categories. In a sentence like *The little orange rabbit hopped,* the parser might mistakenly assume *orange* is a noun. Later, when the error is apparent, the parser *backtracks* to the decision point, and retries with *orange* as an adjective. Such a strategy works on confusing but grammatical sentences like *The old man the boats,* and *The Russian women loved died.*

Another way to handle situations that may require backtracking is to make every parse that the grammar allows in parallel. Only parses that finish are accepted as valid. In such a strategy, the two parses of *The Russian women loved died* would have *Russian* as an adjective, and Russian as a noun. The first parse would get as far as *The Russian women loved* but then fail since *died* cannot occur in that position of a verb phrase. The parser must not allow ungrammatical sentences such as **The young women loved died.* The second parse, when it sees the two nouns *Russian women* together, deduces a relative clause (with a missing *that*) and is able to assign the category of noun phrase to *The Russian women loved.* The sentence is completed with the verb *died,* and that parse is successful. A **backtracking** parser would accomplish the same end by serially processing each possibility, succeeding on one, failing on the other.

In general, humans are far more capable of understanding sentences than computers. But there are some interesting cases where computers outperform humans. For example, try to figure out what the sentence *Buffalo buffalo buffalo buffalo* means. (*Hint:* One occurrence of *buffalo* is a verb meaning "to fool.") Most people have trouble determining its sentence structure, and are thus unable to understand it. A parser, with four simple rules and a lexicon in which *buffalo* has three entries (noun, verb, and adjective) will easily parse this sentence as follows:

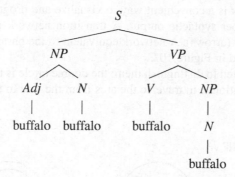

It means "Bison from the city of Buffalo deceive bison."

To produce a sentence it is also necessary to follow the syntactic rules of the grammar. This may be done simplistically. For example, a computer program to generate insults in the style of Shakespeare takes three columns of words, where the first column is a list of simple adjectives, the second a list of hyphenated adjectives, and the third a list of nouns. For example:

Simple Adjectives	Hyphenated Adjectives	Nouns
bawdy	beetle-headed	baggage
churlish	clay-brained	bladder
goatish	fly-bitten	codpiece
lumpish	milk-livered	hedge-pig
mewling	pox-marked	lout
rank	rump-fed	miscreant
villainous	toad-spotted	varlet

The program chooses a word from each column at random, to produce an adjective phrase insult. Instantaneous insults guaranteed, you goatish, pox-marked bladder, you lumpish, milk-livered hedge-pig.

In less simplistic language generation, the computer is given the meaning of what is to be said, which may be the output part of a translation system, or simply the computer's turn to give information, as in the Circuit Fix-It Shop.

The generation system first assigns lexical items to the ideas and concepts to be expressed. These, then, must be fit into phrases and sentences that comply with the syntax of the output language. As in parsing, there are two approaches: top down and bottom up. In the top-down approach, the system begins with the highest-level categories such as S(entence). Lower levels are filled in progressively, beginning with noun phrases and verb phrases, and descending to determiners, nouns, verbs, and other sentence parts, always conforming to the syntactic rules. The bottom-up approach begins with the lexical items needed to express the desired meaning and proceeds to combine them to form the higher-level categories.

A **transition network** is a convenient way to visualize and program the use of a grammar to ensure proper syntactic output. A transition network is a complex of **nodes** (circles) and **arcs** (arrows). A network equivalent to the phrase structure rule S → NP VP is illustrated in Figure 10.2.

The nodes are numbered to distinguish them; the double circle is the "final" node. The object of the generation is to traverse the arcs from the first to the final node.

FIGURE 10.2

Transition network for S —> NP VP.

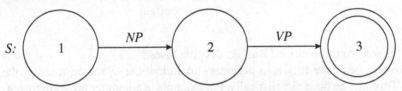

The generator would start at node 1 and realize that a noun phrase is necessary to begin the output. The appropriate concept is assigned to that noun phrase. Other transition networks, in particular, one for NP, determine the structure of the noun phrase. For example, one part of a transition network for a noun phrase would state that an NP may be a pronoun, corresponding to the phrase structure rule NP → Pronoun. It would look like Figure 10.3.

FIGURE 10.3

Transition network for NP —> Pronoun.

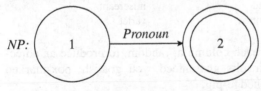

To satisfy the NP *arc* in the S network, the *entire NP network* is traversed. In this case, the NP is to be a pronoun, as determined by the concept needed. The NP arc is then traversed in the S network, and the system is at node 2. To finish, an appropriate verb phrase must be constructed according to the concept to be communicated. That concept is made to comply with the structure of the VP, which is also expressed as a transition network. To get past the VP arc in the S network, the entire VP network is traversed. Figure 10.4 shows one part of the VP complex of transition networks, corresponding to VP → V NP:

Once the VP network is completed, the VP arc in the S network is traversed to the final node, and the system sends the sentence out to be spoken or printed.

The final sentence of the Circuit Fix-It Shop dialogue is *you put up the switch*. The concept is a command to the user (*you*) to move the switch to the up position.

FIGURE 10.4

Transition network for VP —> V NP.

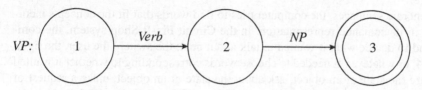

It chooses the verb *put up* to represent this concept, and the noun phrase *the switch* to represent the switch that the computer knows the user is already familiar with. The syntax begins in the S network, moves to the NP network that is finished, and produces the subject of the sentence, the pronoun *you*. The NP arc is traversed to node 2 in the S network. Now the syntax requires a VP. The scene of action moves to the VP network. The first arc is traversed and gives the verb *put up*. An NP network is again required so that the VP can finish up. This network (not shown) indicates that an NP may be a determiner followed by a noun, in this case, *the* and *switch*. When that network is finished, the NP arc in the VP network is traversed, the VP network is finished, the VP arc in the S network is traversed, the S network is finished, and the final output is the sentence *you put up the switch*.

Since a reference to any network may occur in any other network, or even in the same network itself (thus capturing the recursive property of the syntax), a relatively small number of networks can generate the large number of sentences that may be needed by a natural language system. The networks must be designed so that they characterize only grammatical, never ungrammatical, utterances.

Computational Semantics

The question of how to represent meaning is one that has been debated for thousands of years, and it continues to engender much research in linguistics, philosophy, psychology, cognitive science, and computer science. In Chapter 4 we discussed many of the semantic concepts that a natural language system would incorporate into its operation. For simplicity's sake, we consider computational semantics to be the representation of the meaning of words and morphemes in the computer, as well as the meanings derived from their combinations.

Computational semantics has two chief concerns. One is to produce a semantic representation in the computer of language input; the other is to take a semantic representation and produce natural language output that conveys the meaning. These two concerns dovetail in a machine translation system. Ideally — and systems today are *not* ideal — the computer takes input from the source language, creates a semantic representation of its meaning, and from that semantic representation produces output in the target language. Meaning (ideally) remains constant across the entire process. In a dialogue system such as the Circuit Fix-It Shop, the computer must create a semantic representation of the user's input, act on it thus producing another semantic representation, and output it to the user in ordinary language.

To generate sentences, the computer tries to find words that fit the concepts incorporated in its semantic representation. In the Circuit Fix-It Shop system, the computer had to decide what it wanted to talk about next: the switch, the user, the light, wire 134, or whatever. It needed to choose words corresponding to whether it wanted to declare the state of an object, ask about the state of an object, make a request of the user, tell the user what to do next, and so forth. If the query involved the user, the pronoun *you* would be chosen; if the state of the switch were the chief concern, the words *the switch,* or *a switch above the blue light,* would be chosen. When the components of meaning are assembled, the syntactic rules that we have seen already are called upon to produce grammatical output.

To achieve **speech understanding** the computer tries to find concepts in its semantic representation capabilities that fit the words and structures of the input. When the technician says *I need to fix the RS111 circuit,* the system recognizes that *I* means the user, that *need* represents something that the user lacks and the computer must provide. It further knows that if fixing is what is needed, it has to provide information about the workings of something. It recognizes *the RS111 circuit* as a circuit with certain properties that are contained in certain of its files. It infers that the workings of that particular circuit will be central to the ensuing dialogue.

A computer can represent concepts in numerous ways, none of them perfect or preferable over others. All methods share one commonality: a lexicon of words and morphemes that it is prepared to speak or understand. Such a lexicon would contain morphological, syntactic, and semantic information, as discussed in Chapters 2, 3, and 4. Exactly how that information is structured depends on the particular applications it is to be suited for.

On a higher level, the relationships between words are conveniently represented in networks similar (but different in objective) to the transition networks we saw previously. The nodes represent words, and the arcs represent thematic relations (see Chapter 4) between the words. *You put up the switch,* then, might have the representation in Figure 10.5.

This means that the user (*you*) is the agent, or doer, and *put up* is what is to be done, and it is to be done to the THEME, which is *the switch.*

FIGURE 10.5

Semantic network for *You put up the switch.*

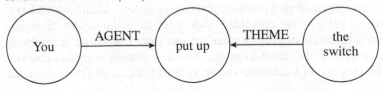

Some systems draw on formal logic for semantic representations. *You put up the switch* would be represented in a function/argument form:

PUT UP(YOU, THE SWITCH)

where PUT UP is a "two-place predicate" in the jargon of logicians, and the arguments are YOU and THE SWITCH. The lexicon indicates the appropriate relationships between the arguments of the predicate PUT UP.

Two well-known natural language processing systems from the 1970s used this logical approach of semantic representation. One, named SHRDLU by its developer Terry Winograd, demonstrated a number of abilities, such as being able to interpret questions, draw inferences, learn new words, and even explain its actions. It operated in the context of a "blocks world," consisting of a table, blocks of various shapes, sizes, and colours, and a robot arm for moving the blocks. Using simple sentences, one could ask questions about the blocks and give commands to have blocks moved from one location to another.

The second system, LUNAR, developed by William Woods, was capable of answering questions phrased in simple English about the lunar rock samples brought back from the Moon by the astronauts. LUNAR translated English questions into a logical representation, which it then used to query a database of information about the lunar samples.

Computational Pragmatics

Pragmatics, as discussed in Chapter 4, is the interaction of the "real world" with the language system. In the Circuit Fix-It Shop the computer knows that there is only one switch, that there is no other switch in (its) the universe, and that the determiner *the* is correct for this item. If the human mentioned *a wire,* however, the computer would ask *which wire* because it knows that there are several wires in the circuit. This is simple, computational pragmatics in action.

When a sentence is structurally ambiguous, such as *He sells synthetic buffalo hides,* the parser will compute each structure. Semantic processing may eliminate some of the structures if they are anomalous, but often some ambiguity remains. For example, the structurally ambiguous sentence *Sean found a book on the Cabot Trail* is semantically acceptable in both its meanings. To decide which meaning is intended, situational knowledge is needed. If Sean is in the library researching history, the "book *about* the Cabot Trail" meaning is most likely; if Sean is on a two-week hike to Nova Scotia, the "book *upon* the Cabot Trail" meaning is more plausible.

Many natural language processing systems have a knowledge base of contextual and world knowledge. The semantic processing routines can refer to the knowledge base in cases of ambiguity. For example, the syntactic component of the Circuit Fix-It Shop will have two structures for *The LED is in the middle of the blue region at the top*. The sentence is ambiguous. Both meanings are semantically well formed and conceivable. However, the Circuit Fix-It Shop's knowledge base "knows" that the LED is in the middle of the blue region, and the blue region is at the top of the work area, rather than that the LED is in the middle, top of the blue region. It uses pragmatic knowledge, knowledge of the world, to disambiguate the sentence.

To conclude this section we return to the subject of machine translation. All the computational *X*'s (phonology, morphology, syntax, etc.) bear on the ability of computers to translate from a source language to a target language. The greater recognition of the role of syntax, and the application of the linguistic principles of semantics and pragmatics that have evolved over the past fifty years, have made it possible to use computers to translate simple texts — ones in a constrained context such as a mathematical proof — grammatically and accurately between well-studied languages such as English and Russian. More complex texts require human intervention if the translation is to be grammatical and semantically faithful. The use of computers to aid the human translator can improve efficiency by a factor of ten or more, but the day when travellers can whip out a "pocket translator," hold it up to the mouth of a native speaker, and receive a translation in their own language is as yet beyond the horizon.

Computer Models of Grammars

I am never content until I have constructed a . . . model of the subject I am studying. If I succeed in making one, I understand; otherwise I do not.

William Thomson (Lord Kelvin), *Molecular Dynamics and the Wave Theory of Light* (1884)

A theory has only the alternative of being right or wrong. A model has a third possibility: it may be right, but irrelevant.

Manfred Eigen, *The Physicist's Conception of Nature* (1973)

The grammars used by computers for parsing may not be the same as the grammars linguists construct for human languages, which are models of linguistic competence, nor are they similar, for the most part, to models of linguistic performance. Computers are different from people, and they achieve similar ends differently. Just as an efficient flying machine is not a replica of any bird, so too efficient grammars for computers do not resemble human language grammars in every detail.

Computers are often used to model physical or biological systems, which allows researchers to study those systems safely and sometimes even cheaply. For example, the performance of a new aircraft can be simulated and the test pilot informed as to safe limits in advance of actual flight.

Computers can also be programmed to model the grammar of a language. An accurate grammar — one that is a true model of a speaker's mental grammar — should be able to generate *all* and *only* the sentences of the language. Failure to generate a grammatical sentence indicates the presence of an error in the grammar, because the human mental grammar has the capacity to generate all possible grammatical sentences — an infinite set. In addition, if the grammar produces a string that speakers consider to be ungrammatical, that also indicates a defect in the grammar; although in actual speech performance we often produce ungrammatical strings — such as sentence fragments, slips of the tongue, word substitutions, and blends — we judge them to be ill formed if we notice them. Our grammars cannot generate these strings.

One computer model of a grammar was developed in the 1960s by the computer scientist Joyce Friedman to test a generative grammar of English written by syntacticians at UCLA. More recently, computational linguists have been developing computer programs to generate the sentences of a language and to simulate human parsing of these sentences using the rules included in various current linguistic theories. The computational models developed by Ed Stabler, Robert Berwick, Amy Weinberg, and Mark Johnson, among other computational linguists, show that it is possible, in principle, to use a transformational grammar, for example, in speech and comprehension, but it is still controversial whether human language processing works in this way. That is, even if we can get a computer program to produce sentences as output and to parse sentences fed into the machine as input, we still need psycholinguistic evidence that this is the way the human mind stores and processes language.

It is because linguistic competence and performance are so complex that computers are being used as a tool in the attempt to understand human language and its use. We have emphasized some of the differences between the way humans process language and the way computers process language. For example, humans appear to do speech recognition, parsing, semantic interpretation, and contextual disambiguation more or less simultaneously and smoothly while comprehending speech. Computers, on the other hand, usually have different components, loosely connected, and perform these functions individually.

One reason for this is that, typically, computers have only a single, powerful processor capable of performing one task at a time. Currently, computers are being designed with multiple processors, albeit less powerful ones, that are interconnected. The power of these computers lies both in the individual processors and in the connections. Such computers are capable of **parallel processing**: carrying out several tasks simultaneously.

With a parallel architecture, computational linguists may be better able to program machine understanding in ways that blend all the stages of processing together, from speech recognition to contextual interpretation, and hence approach more closely the way humans process language.

Summary

Computational linguistics is the study of how computers can process language. Computers aid scholars in analyzing literature and language, translate between languages, and communicate in natural language with human users.

To analyze a **corpus**, or body of data, a computer can do a frequency analysis of words, compute a **concordance**, which locates words in the corpus and gives their immediate context, and compute a **collocation**, which measures how the occurrence of one word affects the probability of the occurrence of other words. Computers are also useful for **information retrieval** based on keywords, automatic **summarization**, and **spell checking**.

Soon after their invention, computers were used to try to translate from one language to another. This is a difficult, complex task, and the results are often humorous as the computer struggles to translate text (or speech) from the **source language** into the **target language**, without loss of meaning or grammaticality.

Whether translating from one language to another, or communicating with a human being, computers must be capable of **speech recognition**, processing the speech signal into phonemes, morphemes, and words. They also must be able to speak its output. **Speech synthesis** is a two-step process in which text is first converted to phones, and the phones are simulated electronically to produce speech.

To recognize speech is not to understand speech, and to speak a text does not necessarily mean that the computer knows what it is saying. To understand or generate speech, the computer must process phonemes, morphemes, words, phrases, and sentences, and it must be aware of the meanings of these units (except for phonemes). The computational linguistics of speech understanding and speech generation has the subfields of **computational phonology**, **computational morphology**, **computational syntax**, **computational semantics**, and **computational pragmatics**.

Computational phonology relates phonemes to the acoustic signal of speech. It is statistical in nature because the acoustic signal of a phoneme varies from person to person, and may be degraded by noise. Computational morphology deals with the structure of words, so it tells the computer that the meaning of *bird* applies as well to *birds*, which has in addition the meaning of plural. Computational syntax is concerned with the syntactic categories of words, and with the larger syntactic units of phrases and sentences. It is further concerned with analyzing a sentence into these components for speech understanding, or assembling these components into larger units for speech generation. A formal device called a **transition network** may be used to model the actions of syntactic processing.

Computational semantics is concerned with representing meaning inside the computer, or semantic representation. To communicate with a person, the computer creates a semantic representation of what the person says to it, and another semantic representation of what it wants to say back. In a machine translation environment, the computer produces a semantic representation of the source language input and outputs that meaning in the target language.

Semantic representations may be based on logical expressions involving predicates and arguments, on **semantic networks**, or on other formal devices to represent meaning.

Computational pragmatics may influence the understanding or the response of the computer by taking into account knowledge that the computer system has about the real world, for example, that there is a unique element in the environment, so the determiner *the* can be used appropriately to refer to it.

Computers may be programmed to model a grammar of a human language and thus rapidly and thoroughly test that grammar. Modern computer architectures include **parallel processing** machines that can be programmed to process language more as humans do insofar as carrying out many linguistic tasks simultaneously.

Exercises

1. Suppose you were given a manuscript of a play and were told that it is by either Christopher Marlowe or William Shakespeare (both born in 1564). Suppose further that this work, and all of the works of Marlowe and Shakespeare, were in a computer. Describe how you would use the computer to help determine the true authorship of the mysterious play.

2. Speech synthesis is useful because it allows computers to convey information without requiring people to be sighted. Think of five other uses for speech synthesis in our society.

3. Some advantages of speech recognition are similar to those of speech synthesis. A computer that understands speech does not require a person to use hands or eyes in order to convey information to the computer. Think of five other possible uses for speech recognition in our society.

4. Consider the following ambiguous sentences. Explain the ambiguity, give the most likely interpretation, and state what a computer would have to know to achieve that interpretation.

   > Example: A cheesecake was on the table. It was delicious and was soon eaten.
   > Ambiguity: "It" can refer to the cheesecake or the table.
   > Likely: "It" refers to the cheesecake.
   > Knowledge: Tables aren't usually eaten.

   a. John gave the boys five dollars. One of them was counterfeit.
   b. The police were asked to stop drinking in public places.
   c. John went to the bank to get some cash.
   d. He saw Lake Louise flying to Toronto.
   e. Do you know the time? (*Hint:* This is a pragmatic ambiguity.)
   f. Concerned with spreading violence, the premier called a press conference.

*5. Here is a transition network for the noun phrase (NP) rule given in Chapter 3.

NP → (Det) (AP)* N (PP)

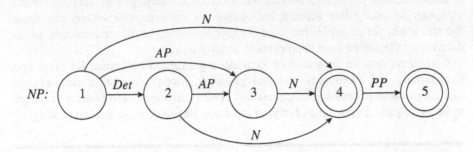

Using this as a model, draw a transition network for the verb phrase rules
VP→V (NP) (PP)
(*Hint:* Recall from Chapter 3 that the above rule abbreviates four rules.)

*6. Here are some sentences along with a possible representation in predicate
logic notation.

(i)   Birds fly. FLY (BIRDS)
(ii) The student understands the question. UNDERSTAND (THE
      STUDENT, THE QUESTION)
(iii) Penguins do not fly. NOT (FLY [PENGUINS])
(iv) The wind is in the willows. IN (THE WIND, THE WILLOWS)
(v)   Kathy loves her cat. LOVE (KATHY, [POSSESSIVE (KATHY, CAT)])

A. Based on the examples in the text, and those in part B of this exercise,
    give a possible semantic network representation for each of these
    examples.
B. Here are five more sentences and a possible semantic network represen-
    tation for each. Give a representation of each using the predicate logic
    notation. (*Hint:* Review Chapter 4 for the meanings of *agent, theme,*
    goal, and so on.)

(i)   Seals swim swiftly.

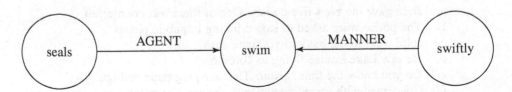

(ii) The student doesn't understand the question.

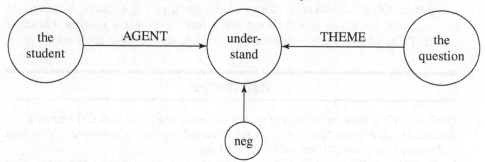

(iii) The pen is on the table.

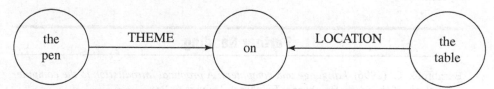

(iv) My dog eats bones.

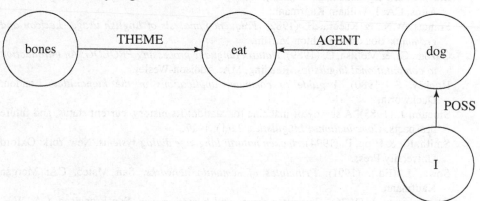

(v) Emily gives money to charity. (*Hint: Give* is a three-place predicate.)

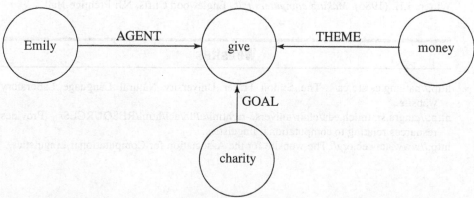

7. Let's play "torment the computer." Imagine a fairly good morphological parser. Give it *kindness*, it returns *kind + ness*; give it *upchuck*, it returns *up + chuck*; but if you give it *catsup* and it returns *cat + s + up*, you will scold it. Think of five more words that are likely to lead to false analyses.

References

Dhal, H. (1979). *Word frequencies of spoken American English*. Essex, CT: Verbatim.

Kučera, H., & Francis, W.N. (1967). *Computational analysis of present-day American English*. Providence, RI: Brown University Press.

Locke, W.N., & Boothe, A.D. (Eds.). (1955). *Machine translation of languages*. New York: Wiley.

Further Reading

Barnbrook, G. (1996). *Language and computers: A practical introduction to the computer analysis of language*. Edinburgh: Edinburgh University Press.

Barr, A., & Feigenbaum, E.A. (Eds.). (1981). *The handbook of artificial intelligence*. Los Altos, CA: I. William Kaufmann.

Francis, W.N., & Kučera, H. (1982). *Frequency analysis of English usage: Lexicon and grammar*. Boston: Houghton Mifflin.

Gazdar, G., & Mellish, C. (1989). *Natural language processing PROLOG: An introduction to computational linguistics*. Reading, MA: Addison-Wesley.

Hockey, S. (1980). *A guide to computer applications in the humanities*. London: Duckworth.

Slocum, J. (1985). A survey of machine translation: Its history, current status, and future prospects. *Computational Linguistics, 11*(1), 1–17.

Smith, R., & Hipp, R. (1994). *Spoken natural language dialog systems*. New York: Oxford University Press.

Sowa, J. (Ed.). (1991). *Principles of semantic networks*. San Mateo, CA: Morgan Kaufmann.

Weizenbaum, J. (1976). *Computer power and human reason*. San Francisco, CA: W.H. Freeman.

Witten, I.H. (1986). *Making computers talk*. Englewood Cliffs, NJ: Prentice-Hall.

Websites

http://natlang.cs.sfu.ca/ The Simon Fraser University Natural Language Laboratory website.

http://tangra.si.umich.edu/clair/universe-rk/html/u/db/acl/html/RESOURCES/ Provides resources relating to computational linguistics.

http://www.aclweb.org/ The website for the Association for Computational Linguistics.

CHAPTER 11
Neurolinguistics: Language and the Brain

The nervous systems of all animals have a number of basic functions in common, most notably the control of movement and the analysis of sensation. What distinguishes the human brain is the variety of more specialized activities it is capable of learning. The preeminent example is language.

Norman Geschwind (1979)

[The brain is] the messenger of the understanding [and the organ whereby] in an especial manner we acquire wisdom and knowledge.

Hippocratic Treatise on the Sacred Disease (C. 377 B.C.E.)

The attempts to understand the complexities of human cognitive abilities and especially the acquisition and use of language are as old and as continuous as history. Three long-standing problems of science include the nature of the brain, the nature of human language, and the relationship between the two. The view that the brain is the source of human language and cognition goes back more than 2,000 years. Assyrian and Babylonian cuneiform tablets mention disorders of intelligence that may develop "when man's brain holds fire." Egyptian doctors in 1700 B.C.E. noted in their papyrus records that "the breath of an outside god" had entered their patients, who had become "silent in sadness." The philosophers of ancient Greece also speculated about the brain–mind relationship, but neither Plato nor Aristotle recognized the brain's crucial function in cognition or language. Aristotle's wisdom failed him when he suggested that the brain is a cold sponge whose function is to cool the blood. But others writing in the same period showed greater insight; as cited above, the Hippocratic treatises from about 377 B.C.E. define the brain as "the messenger of the understanding [and the organ whereby] in an especial manner we acquire wisdom and knowledge."

A major approach in the study of the brain–mind relationship has been through an investigation of language. Research on the brain in humans and in nonhuman primates, anatomically, psychologically, and behaviourally, is, for similar reasons, helping to answer the questions concerning the neurological basis for language. The study concerned with the biological and neural foundations of language is called **neurolinguistics**.

The Human Brain

The functional asymmetry of the human brain is unequivocal, and so is its anatomical asymmetry. The structural differences between the left and the right hemispheres are visible not only under the microscope but to the naked eye. The most striking asymmetries occur in language-related cortices. It is tempting to assume that such anatomical differences are an index of the neurobiological underpinnings of language.

Antonio and Hanna Damasio,
Lesion Analysis in Neuropsychology (1989)

The Brain is wider than the sky.
Emily Dickinson (1830–1886)

We have learned a great deal about the brain — the most complicated organ of the body — in the past two millennia. It lies under the skull and consists of approximately ten billion nerve cells (neurons) and billions of fibres that interconnect them. The neurons or grey matter form the **cortex**, the surface of the brain, under which is white matter, which consists primarily of connecting fibres. The cortex is the decision-making organ of the body. It receives messages from all the sensory organs, and it initiates all voluntary actions. It is "the seat of all which is exclusively human in the mind" and the storehouse of "memory." Somewhere in this grey matter, the grammar that represents our knowledge of language resides.

The brain is divided into two parts (called **cerebral hemispheres**), one on the right and one on the left. These hemispheres are connected like conjoined twins right down the middle by the **corpus callosum**. This "freeway" between the two brain halves consists of two million fibres connecting the cells of the left and right hemispheres, as shown in Figure 11.1.

In general, the left hemisphere controls the movements of the right side of the body, and the right hemisphere controls the movements of the left side. If you point with your right hand, then it is the left hemisphere that has directed your action. This is referred to as **contralateral** brain function.

The Modularity of the Brain

Since the middle of the nineteenth century, there has been a basic assumption that it is possible to find a direct relation between language and the brain and a continuous effort to discover direct centres where language capacities (competence and performance) may be localized.

In the early nineteenth century, Franz Joseph Gall put forth the theory of **localization** — that is, that different human abilities and behaviours were traceable to specific parts of the brain. Some of Gall's views are amusing when looked at from our present state of knowledge. For example, Gall suggested that the frontal lobes

FIGURE 11.1

3-D reconstruction of the normal living human brain. The images were obtained from magnetic resonance data using the Brainvox technique. Left panel = view from the top. Right panel = view from the front following virtual coronal section at the level of the dashed line.

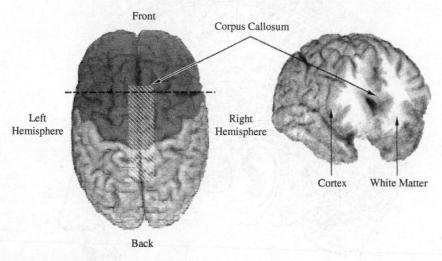

Courtesy Hanna Damasio

of the brain are the locations of language because when he was young he had noticed that the most articulate and intelligent of his fellow students had protruding eyes, which he believed reflected overdeveloped brain material. He also put forth a pseudoscientific theory called "organology" that later came to be known as **phrenology**, the practice of determining personality traits, intellectual capacities, and other matters by examination of the "bumps" on the skull. A disciple of Gall, Johann Spurzheim, constructed elaborate maps and skull models, such as the one shown in Figure 11.2, in which language is located directly under the eye.

Although phrenology has long been discarded as a scientific theory, Gall's view that the brain is not a uniform mass and that linguistic capacities are functions of localized brain areas has largely been upheld. Gall was in fact a pioneer and a courageous scientist in arguing against the prevailing view that the brain is an unstructured organ. He argued instead in favour of **modularity**, with the brain divided into distinct anatomical faculties (referred to as cortical organs) that are directly responsible for specific cognitive functions, including language.

Language was the first distinct cognitive module to be supported by scientific evidence. In 1864, **Paul Broca** specifically related language to the left side of the brain. At a meeting in Paris, he stated that we speak with the left hemisphere on the basis of his finding that damage to the front part of the left hemisphere (now called **Broca's area**) resulted in loss of speech, whereas damage to the right side

FIGURE 11.2
Phrenology skull model.

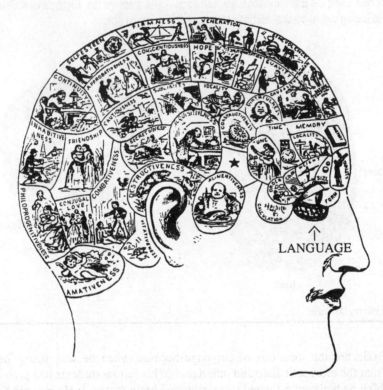

LANGUAGE

Courtesy Hanna Damasio

did not.[1] Language, then, is said to be **lateralized,** a term used to refer to any cognitive function that is primarily localized to one side of the brain or the other.

Today, patients with such damage or lesions in Broca's area are said to have **Broca's aphasia. Aphasia** is the neurological term used to refer to language disorders that follow brain lesions caused by strokes, tumours, wounds, and other traumas. The speech output of many of Broca's aphasia patients is characterized by laboured speech, word-finding pauses, disturbed word order, and difficulties with function words, such as *to* and *if.* Auditory comprehension of colloquial conversation gives the impression of being generally good, although controlled testing reveals a loss of comprehension of complex or ambiguous sentences.

In 1874, **Carl Wernicke** described another variety of aphasia shown by patients with lesions in the back portion of the left hemisphere. Unlike Broca's patients, Wernicke's spoke fluently, with good intonation and pronunciation but with numerous instances of lexical errors (word substitutions), often producing jargon and nonsense words. They also had difficulty in comprehending speech.

The area of the brain that when damaged seems to lead to these symptoms is now, not surprisingly, known as **Wernicke's area**, and the patients are said to suffer from **Wernicke's aphasia**. Figure 11.3, a view of the left side of the brain, shows the location of Broca's and Wernicke's areas.

We no longer have to depend on surgical investigations of the brain or wait until patients die to determine where their brain lesions are. Technologies such as magnetic resonance imaging (MRI) make it possible to see where the sites of lesions are in the living brain. In addition, positron emission tomography (PET) scans have revolutionized the study of the brain, making it possible to detect changes in brain activities and relate these changes to focal brain damage and cognitive tasks. PET permits experimenters to look into a living normal brain and see which areas are affected when different stimuli are involved, since degrees of metabolic activity can be viewed and one can see which areas of the brain are more active than others. MRI and PET studies reaffirm the lateralization of language.

For example, Jaeger et al. (1996), researchers at the State University of New York, Buffalo, conducted an experiment in which they used PET scans to locate and measure cortical activity when subjects were asked to produce the past-tense forms of regular, irregular, and made-up verbs. They summed up their results by noting, "We find very different amounts and areas of cortical activation in the regular and irregular tasks. . . ." All "cortical activation," though in different parts of the brain

FIGURE 11.3

Lateral (external) view of the left hemisphere of the human brain. Note the position of Broca's and Wernicke's areas — two key areas of the cortex related to language processing.

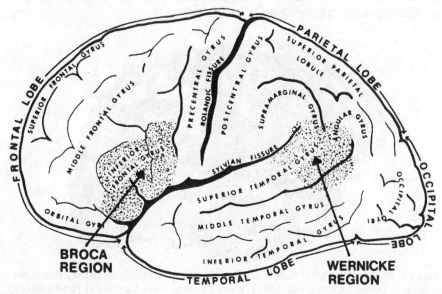

Courtesy Hanna Damasio

depending on the type of verb, was in the left hemisphere. These experiments support both the modular nature of the grammar and the left lateralization of language.

Figures 11.4 and 11.5 show the MRI scans of the brains of a Broca's aphasic patient and a Wernicke's aphasic patient. The black areas show the sites of lesions. Each diagram represents a slice of the left side of the brain.

There is now a consensus that the so-called higher mental functions are highly lateralized. Research shows that though the nervous system is generally symmetrical — that is, what exists on the left exists on the right and vice versa — the two sides of the brain form an exception.

Evidence from Childhood Brain Lesions

> It only takes one hemisphere to have a mind.
>
> A.W. Wigan (1844)

The study of children with prenatal, perinatal, or childhood brain lesions suggests that although lateralization of language to the left hemisphere is a process that begins very early in life, language may be less lateralized initially, with the right hemisphere also playing some role.

Studies of **hemiplegic** children, those with lesions in one side of the brain, show differential cognitive abilities. Those with left-damaged hemispheres show greater deficiency in language acquisition and performance, with the greatest impairments in their ability to form words and sentences, whereas children with right-hemisphere lesions tend to acquire language as do normal children.

FIGURE 11.4

3-D reconstruction of the brain of a living patient with Broca's aphasia. Note the area of damage in the left frontal region (dark grey), which was caused by a stroke.

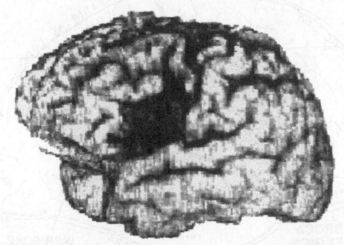

Figure 2.19, Figure 3.17, p. 107 from *Lesion Analysis in Neuropsychology* by Hanna Damasio and Antonio R. Damasio, Copyright © 1989 by Oxford University Press, Inc. Used by permission of Oxford University Press, Inc. Used by permissionof Oxford University Press, Inc.

FIGURE 11.5

3-D reconstruction of the brain of a living patient with Wernicke's aphasia. Note the area of damage in the left posterior temporal and lower parietal region (dark grey), which was caused by a stroke.

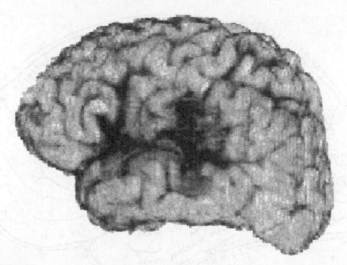

Figure 2.19, Figure 3.17, p. 107, from *Lesion Analysis in Neuropsychology* by Hanna Damasio and Antonio R. Damasio, Copyright © 1989 by Oxford University Press, Inc. Used by permission of Oxford University Press, Inc.

There have also been studies of children with one hemisphere removed (called hemidecorticates) either within the first year of life or later in childhood. Although the IQ scores and cognitive skills proved to be equivalent no matter which hemisphere was removed, children whose left hemisphere was removed outperformed in visual and spatial abilities those with the right hemisphere removed. In language, the right hemidecorticates (those with removal of the right hemisphere) surpassed the left hemidecorticates. Both hemispheres appear to be equivalent in the ability to acquire the meanings and referential structures of common words, but the ability to acquire the complex syntactic rules for sentence formation was impaired in left but not in right hemidecorticates.

It appears that even from birth the human brain is predisposed to specialize for language in the left hemisphere since language does not develop normally in children with left-hemisphere lesions.

Split Brains

"**Split-brain**" patients also provide important evidence for language lateralization and for understanding brain functions. Individuals suffering from serious epilepsy may be treated by cutting the corpus callosum, the membrane connecting the two hemispheres. When this pathway is split, there is no communication between the "two brains." The corpus callosum is shown in Figure 11.6.

FIGURE 11.6

Internal view of the left hemisphere of the human brain. Note the position of the corpus callosum, which joins the structures of the left and right hemispheres across the midline.

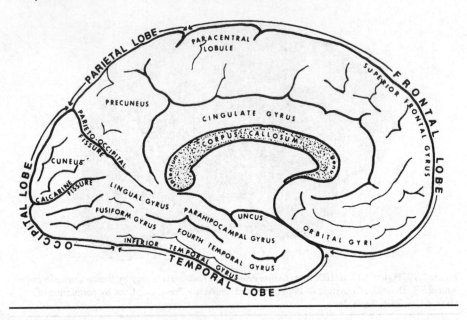

As Michael Gazzaniga (1970) has observed,

> With ... [the corpus callosum] intact, the two halves of the body have no secrets from one another. With it sectioned, the two halves become two different conscious mental spheres, each with its own experience base and control system for behavioural operations.... Unbelievable as this may seem, this is the flavor of a long series of experimental studies first carried out in the cat and monkey.

When the brain is split surgically, certain information from the left side of the body is received only by the right side of the brain and vice versa (because of the crisscross contralateral phenomenon discussed earlier). Suppose, for example, a monkey is trained to respond with its hands to a certain visual stimulus, such as a flashing light. If the brain is split after the training period, and the stimulus is shown only to the left visual field (the right brain), the monkey will perform only with the left hand. Such experiments show the independence of the two sides of the brain.

Studies of split-brain patients show that, as in the monkey brain, the two human hemispheres are distinct. Moreover, tests have shown that messages sent to the two sides of the brain result in different responses, depending on which hemisphere receives the message. If an apple is put in the left hand of a split-brain human whose vision is cut off, the person can use it appropriately but cannot name it. The right brain

"ROGER DOESN'T USE THE LEFT SIDE OF THE BRAIN OR THE RIGHT SIDE. HE JUST USES THE MIDDLE."

senses the apple and distinguishes it from other objects, but the information cannot be relayed to the left brain for naming. By contrast, if a banana is placed in the right hand, the subject is immediately able to name it as well as describe it (see Figure 11.7).

Various experiments of this sort have been performed, all providing information on the different capabilities of the "two halves." The right brain does better than the left in pattern-matching tasks, in recognizing faces, and in spatial orientation. The left hemisphere is superior for language, for rhythmic perception, for temporal-order judgments, and for mathematical thinking. According to Gazzaniga (1970), "the right hemisphere as well as the left hemisphere can emote and while the left can tell you why, the right cannot."

FIGURE 11.7

Sensory information is received in the *contralateral* (opposite) side of the brain from the side of the body from which it is sent. In a split-brain patient, the information in the right hemisphere cannot get across to the left hemisphere; for this reason, this patient cannot produce the word *apple*.

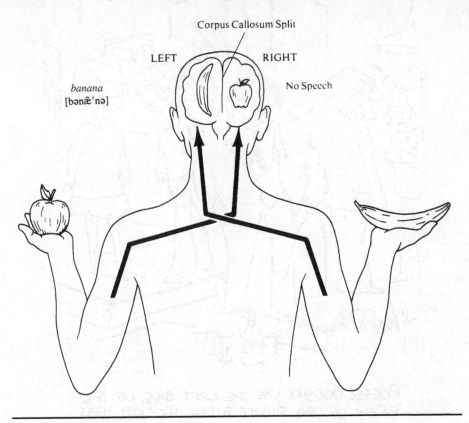

Studies of human split-brain patients have shown that when the interhemispheric visual connections are severed, visual information from the right and left visual fields becomes confined to the left and right hemispheres, respectively. Because of the crucial endowment of the left hemisphere for language, written material delivered to the right hemisphere cannot be read if the brain is split, because the information cannot be transferred to the left hemisphere.

A picture that is flashed to the right visual field of a split-brain patient (and is therefore processed by the left hemisphere) can be named. However, when the picture is flashed in the left visual field and lands in the right hemisphere, it cannot be named.

More Experimental Evidence

Another experimental technique that has been used with normal subjects, called **dichotic listening**, uses auditory signals. Subjects hear two different sound signals simultaneously through earphones. For example, a subject may hear *boy* in one ear and *girl* in the other, or *crocodile* in one ear and *alligator* in the other, or the subject may hear a horn tooting in one ear and rushing water in the other. When asked to state what they heard in each ear, subjects are more frequently correct in reporting linguistic stimuli (words, nonsense syllables, and so on) delivered to the right ear, but they are more frequently correct in reporting nonverbal stimuli (musical chords, environmental sounds, and so on) delivered to the left ear. That is, if subjects hear *boy* in the right ear and *girl* in the left ear, they are more likely to report the word heard in the right ear correctly. If they hear coughing in the right ear and laughing in the left, they are more apt to report the laughing stimulus correctly.

The same acoustic signal may be processed in one hemisphere or the other depending on whether the subjects perceive it as part of their language system or not. Thai speakers show a right-ear advantage (left hemisphere) in distinguishing between syllables that contrast in tone (pitch contours); Thai is a tone language in which syllables pronounced with different pitch are words with different meanings. English subjects do not show the right-ear advantage when they hear the same stimuli, because English is not a tone language.

Both hemispheres receive signals from both ears, but the "crossed" contralateral stimuli (right to left and vice versa) outweigh the "same side" **ipsilateral** stimuli because they are more intense and arrive more quickly. Their pathways are anatomically thicker and are not delayed by the need to cross the corpus callosum. The accuracy with which subjects report what they heard is evidence that the left hemisphere is superior for linguistic processing, and the right hemisphere is superior for nonverbal information.

These experiments are important not only because they show that language is lateralized, but also because they show that the left hemisphere is not superior for processing all sounds, only for those that are linguistic. That is, the left side of the brain is specialized for language, not sounds.

Other experimental techniques are also being used to map the brain and to investigate the independence of different aspects of language and the extent of the independence of language from other cognitive systems. Even before the advances in imaging technology of the 1970s, researchers were taping electrodes to different areas of the skull and investigating the electrical activity of the brain. In such experiments, the electrical signals emitted from the brain in response to different kinds of stimuli (called **event-related brain potentials**, or **ERPs**) are measured. For example, electrical differences may result when the subject hears speech sounds vs. nonspeech sounds. One study showed electrical potential differences in timing and area of response when subjects heard sentences that were meaningless, such as

*The man admired Don's headache of the landscape.

(where the asterisk shows that there is something unacceptable about the sentence), as opposed to meaningful sentences such as

The man admired Don's sketch of the landscape.

These experiments show that neuronal activity in different locations varies with different stimuli and different tasks and again reveal a left hemisphere specialization for grammar.

Additional evidence is provided by the patterns of neuronal activity in people reading different kinds of writing. Japanese has two writing systems. One system, *kana,* is based on the sound system of the language; each symbol corresponds to a syllable. The other system, *kanji,* is ideographic; each symbol corresponds to a word. *Kanji* is not based on the sounds of the language. Japanese people with left-hemisphere damage are impaired in their ability to read *kana,* while people with right-hemisphere damage are impaired in their ability to read *kanji.* In addition, experiments with normal Japanese speakers that isolate the two hemispheres show that the right-hemisphere is better than the left hemisphere at reading *kanji.*

> At least one study has found structural brain differences (greater grey matter density in the left hemisphere) in bilinguals, with the most striking differences in early bilinguals.

The results of these studies, using different techniques and diverse subjects, both normal and brain damaged, are converging to provide the information we seek on the relationship between the brain and various language and nonlanguage cognitive systems.

More Evidence for Modularity

> The human mind is not an unstructured entity but consists of components which can be distinguished by their functional properties.
>
> Neil Smith and Ianthi-Maria Tsimpli, *The Mind of a Savant* (1995)

Although neurolinguistics is still in its infancy, our understanding has progressed a great deal since a day in September 1848 when a foreman of a road construction gang named Phineas Gage became a famous figure in medical history. He achieved his "immortality" when an iron rod over a metre long was blown through his head. Despite the gaping tunnel in his brain, Gage maintained the ability to speak and understand and retained whatever intellectual abilities he had prior to the injury, although he suffered major changes in his personality (he became "cranky" and "inconsiderate"), in his sexual behaviour, and in his ability to control his emotions or make plans. Both Gage and science benefited from this explosion. Gage gained monetarily by becoming a one-man touring circus; he travelled all over the country charging money to those curious enough to see him and the iron rod. Nevertheless, he died penniless in an institution twelve years after the accident. Science benefited because brain researchers questioned why his intelligence remained intact.

No autopsy was performed when Gage died in 1861. Dr. John Harlowe, the doctor first called after Gage's accident, convinced Gage's sister that his body should be exhumed and his skull preserved for science. This was done, and the skull and the iron bar have been kept in the Harvard Medical School since that time. Approximately 130 years after the exhumation, Dr. Hanna Damasio and her colleagues at the University of Iowa School of Medicine, using the most advanced neuro-imaging techniques and a computer program called Brainvox, were able to reconstruct Gage's brain showing the area through which the bar had travelled. They were able to show unequivocally that the damage was neither to the motor area nor to the language area of the brain but to the prefrontal cortex (Damasio et al., 1994). Dr. Antonio Damasio and his colleagues have further shown that patients with damage to this area show the same kind of personality changes as did Gage (Damasio, 1994).

That damage to some parts of the brain results in language loss whereas damage to other parts of the brain shows intact language with other kinds of deficits supports Gall's view of a structured brain with separate faculties.

Aphasia

The interest in aphasia goes back long before Broca. In the New Testament, St. Luke reports that Zacharias could not speak but could write, showing the early recognition of the autonomy of different aspects of linguistic knowledge. And in 30 B.C.E., Roman writer Valerius Maximus described an Athenian who was unable to remember his "letters" after being hit on the head with a stone. Pliny, who lived from 23 to 79 C.E., refers to the same Athenian, noting that "with the stroke of a stone, he fell presently to forget his letters only, and could read no more; otherwise his memory served him well enough." Recognition of the loss of specific parts of language with the retention of other aspects of linguistic competence or performance and other cognitive abilities has important implications for our understanding of the neural basis for language and cognition and will be discussed further below.

It is primarily in the past fifty years that controlled scientific studies of aphasia have been conducted, providing unequivocal evidence that language is predominantly and most frequently a left-hemisphere function. In the great majority of cases, lesions on the left hemisphere result in aphasia, but injuries to the right do not (although such lesions result in deficits in facial recognition, pattern recognition, and other cognitive deficits). If both hemispheres were equally involved with language, this would not be the case. For some people — about a third of all left-handers — there is still lateralization, yet it is the right side that is specialized for language. In other words, the special functions are switched, but asymmetry still exists.

The language impairments suffered by aphasics are not due to any general cognitive or intellectual impairments. Nor are they due to loss of motor or sensory controls of the nerves and muscles of the speech organs or hearing apparatus. Aphasics can produce sounds and hear sounds. Whatever loss they suffer has to do only with the production or comprehension of language (or specific parts of the grammar).

This is dramatically shown by the fact that deaf signers with damage to the left hemisphere show aphasia for sign language similar to the language breakdown in hearing aphasics. Researchers at the Salk Institute found that patients with lesions in Broca's area show language deficits similar to those found in hearing patients — severe dysfluent, agrammatic sign production (Poizner, Klima, & Bellugi, 1987). While deaf aphasic patients show marked sign language deficits, they have no difficulty in processing nonlanguage visuospatial relationships, just as hearing aphasics have no problem with processing nonlinguistic auditory stimuli. Thus, it is not hearing or speech that is lateralized but language.

As shown by the different symptoms of Broca's and Wernicke's aphasias, many aphasias do not show total language loss. Rather, different aspects of language are impaired. Broca's aphasics are often referred to as **agrammatic** because of their particular problems with syntax, as the following sample of the speech of an agrammatic patient with damage to Broca's area illustrates. The patient, asked what brought him back to the hospital, answered:

> Yes — ah — Monday ah — Dad — and Dad — ah — Hospital — and ah — Wednesday — Wednesday — nine o'clock and ah Thursday — ten o'clock ah doctors — two — two — ah doctors and — ah — teeth — yah. And a doctor — ah girl — and gums, and I. (Goodglass, 1973)

As this patient illustrates, agrammatic aphasics produce nongrammatical utterances, frequently omitting words such as articles, prepositions, auxiliary verbs, and bound inflectional affixes. They also have difficulty in interpreting sentences correctly when comprehension depends on syntactic structure. Thus, they have a problem with determining "who did what to whom" in passive sentences such as

> The cat was chased by the dog.

where either the subject or the object of the sentence can logically be doing the chasing, since in real life cats and dogs can chase each other. But they have less difficulty with

> The car was chased by the dog.

where the meaning of the sentence agrees with their nonlinguistic knowledge. They know that cars do not under normal circumstances chase dogs and thus use that knowledge to interpret the sentence, whereas in the first sentence the interpretation depends on a knowledge of the English passive construction. Normal speakers will have no difficulty because they use the syntax for comprehension.

Wernicke's aphasics, on the other hand, often produce fluent but unintelligible speech, and they have serious comprehension problems and difficulty in choosing words. One patient replied to a question about his health with

> I felt worse because I can no longer keep in mind from the mind of the minds to keep me from mind and up to the ear which can be to find among ourselves.

Some aphasics have difficulty naming objects presented to them, which shows a lexical defect. Others produce semantically anomalous jargon, such as the patient who described a fork as "a need for a schedule"; another, when asked about his poor vision, said "My wires don't hire right." While some of these aphasics substitute words that bear no semantic relationship to the correct word, such as calling a chair an *engine*, others substitute words that, like normal speech errors, are related semantically, substituting, for example, *table* for *chair* or *boy* for *girl*.

Another kind of aphasia called **jargon aphasia** results in the substitution of one sound for another. Patients with Wernicke's aphasia often produce such jargon. Thus, *table* might be pronounced as *sable*. The substituted segments often share most of the distinctive features of the intended phonemes. An extreme variety of phonemic jargon results in the production of nonsense forms — nonoccurring but possible words. One patient, a physician prior to his aphasia, when asked if he was a doctor, replied:

> Me? Yes, sir. I'm a male demaploze on my own. I still know my tubaboys
> what for I have that's gone hell and some of them go.

The kind of selective impairment found in aphasics provides information on the organization of grammar. If we find that damage to different parts of the brain leads to impairment of different components of the grammar, this supports the hypothesis that the mental grammar is not a homogenous system but, rather, consists of distinct modules as is proposed in various linguistic models.

Patients who produce long strings of "jargon" that sound like well-formed grammatical language but which are uninterpretable show that knowledge of the sound sequences by which we represent words in our mental dictionaries can be disassociated from their meanings. That is, we may look at a picture, know what it is, but be unable to produce the string of sounds that relates to the concept.

The substitution of semantically related words provides evidence as to the organization of our mental dictionaries. The aphasics' errors are similar to word substitution errors of normal individuals in that the substituted words are not just randomly selected but are similar to the intended words either in their sounds or in their meanings.

Similar observations pertain to reading. Some of the most interesting examples of such substitutions are produced by aphasic patients who become dyslexic after brain damage. Their condition is called **acquired dyslexia** because prior to the brain lesion they were normal readers (unlike developmental dyslexics, who have difficulty learning to read). One group of these patients, when reading aloud words printed on cards, produced the kinds of substitution shown in the following examples (Newcombe & Marshall, 1984):

Stimulus	Response 1	Response 2
act	*play*	*play*
applaud	*laugh*	*cheers*
example	*answer*	*sum*
heal	*pain*	*medicine*
south	*west*	*east*

Note that these patients did not always substitute the same words in two different testing periods. In fact, at times they would read the correct word, showing that the problem was in performance (accessing the correct phonological form in the lexicon), not in competence, since they could sometimes get to the right word and produce it.

The substitution of phonologically similar words — *pool* for *tool* or *crucial* for *crucible* — also provides information on the organization of the lexicon. Words in the lexicon seem to be connected to other words through both sound and meaning.

The difference between word classes is revealed in aphasia cases by the omission of grammatical morphemes in the speech of Broca's aphasics and in some cases of acquired dyslexia. Patient G.R., cited above, who produced semantically similar word substitutions, was unable to read grammatical morphemes at all; when presented with words such as *which* or *would*, he just says "No" or "I hate those little words"; but he can read, though with many semantic mistakes, homophones of these words, as shown in the following reading errors:

Stimulus	Response	Stimulus	Response
witch	*witch*	which	*no!*
bean	*soup*	been	*no!*
hour	*time*	our	*no!*
eye	*eyes*	I	*no!*
hymn	*bible*	him	*no!*
wood	*wood*	would	*no!*

These errors suggest that the mental dictionary is divided into sublexicons, one consisting of major lexical content words and the other of grammatical morphemes. Furthermore, it suggests that these two classes of words are processed in different areas or by different neural mechanisms, further supporting the view that the brain is structured in a complex, modular fashion. One can think of the grammar as a mental module in the brain with submodular parts.

Most of us have experienced word-finding difficulties in speaking if not in reading, as Alice does when she says

> "And now, who am I? I will remember, if I can. I'm determined to do it!" But
> being determined didn't help her much, and all she could say, after a great
> deal of puzzling, was "L, I know it begins with L."

This **tip-of-the-tongue** (**TOT**, as it is often referred to) **phenomenon** is not uncommon. But if you can never find the word you want, you can imagine how serious a problem aphasics have. Aphasics with such problems are said to suffer from **anomia**.

Distinct Categories of Conceptual Knowledge

Dramatic evidence for a differentiated and structured brain is provided by studies of both normal individuals and patients with lesions in other than Broca's and Wernicke's areas. Some patients have difficulty speaking a person's name, others have problems with naming animals, and still others cannot name tools. The patients in each group have brain lesions in separate and distinct regions of the left temporal lobe. Through use of MRI techniques, the exact shape and location of the brain lesions of these patients were located. No overlap in the lesion sites in the three groups was found. In a follow-up study of normal subjects in a PET word-retrieval experiment, researchers found differential activation of just those sites damaged in the lesion patients when the normal subjects were asked to name persons, animals, or tools (Damasio et al., 1996).

Further evidence for the separation of cognitive systems is provided by the neurological and behavioural findings that following brain damage some patients lose the ability to recognize sounds or colours or familiar faces while retaining all other perceptual abilities. A patient may not be able to recognize his wife when she walks into the room until she starts to talk; then he will know who she is. This suggests the differentiation of visual and auditory processing.

The Autonomy of Language

In addition to brain-damaged individuals who have acquired and lost language, there are cases of children (without brain lesions) who have difficulties acquiring language or are much slower than the average child. These children show no other cognitive deficits; they are not autistic or retarded and have no perceptual problems. They are said to be suffering from a **specific language impairment** (**SLI**). It is only their linguistic ability that is affected, and often only specific aspects of the grammar are impaired.

Children with SLI show that language may be impaired while general intelligence remains intact. But can language develop normally with general intelligence impaired? If such individuals can be found, it argues strongly for the view that language does not derive from some general cognitive ability.

The question as to whether the language faculty from birth is domain specific — is in our genes — or whether it is derivative of more general intelligence is controversial and receives much attention and debate among linguists, psychologists, and neuropsychologists. There is a growing body of evidence to support the view that the human animal is biologically equipped from birth with an autonomous language faculty that itself is highly specific and does not derive from general human intellectual ability.

Asymmetry of Abilities

The psychological literature documents numerous cases of intellectually handicapped individuals, referred to as **savants**, who, despite their disabilities in certain spheres, show remarkable talents in others. The classic cases include individuals who are superb musicians, or artists, or draftspeople but lack the simple abilities required to take care of themselves. Some of the most famous savants are human calculators who can perform complex arithmetic processes at phenomenal speed or calendrical calculators who can tell you almost instantaneously on which day of the week falls any date in the past or next century.

Until recently, most savants have been reported to be linguistically handicapped. They may be good mimics who, like parrots, can repeat speech but show meagre creative language ability.

While such cases argue for domain-specific abilities and suggest that certain talents do not require general intelligence, they do not decisively respond to the suggestion that language is one ability that is derivative of general cognitive abilities.

Nevertheless, the literature reports cases of language savants who have acquired the highly complex grammar of their language (as well as other languages in some cases) without parallel nonlinguistic abilities of equal complexity. Further investigation of these cases will contribute to the debate about the autonomy of the language faculty.

Laura

Laura was a severely retarded young woman, with a nonverbal IQ of 41–44. She lacked almost all number concepts, including basic counting principles, could draw at a preschool level, and had a processing auditory memory span limited to three units. Yet, when at the age of sixteen she was asked to name some fruits she responded with *pears, apples*, and *pomegranates*. In this period she produced syntactically complex sentences, such as *He was saying that I lost my battery-powered watch that I loved; I just loved that watch* or *Last year at school when I first went there, three tickets were gave out by a police last year.*

Laura could not add 2 + 2. She was not sure of when "last year" was or whether it was before or after "last week" or "an hour ago," nor did she know how many tickets were "gave out" or whether 3 was larger or smaller than 2. Nevertheless, Laura produced sentences with multiple embeddings. She was able to conjoin verb phrases, produce passives, and inflect verbs for number and person to agree with the grammatical subject. She was able to form past tenses in accord with adverbs. However, she was not able to read or write or tell time. She did not know who the president of the United States was or what country she lived in, and she did not know her own age. Her drawings of humans resembled potatoes with stick arms and legs. Yet in a sentence-imitation task, she both detected and corrected syntactic and morphological errors (Yamada, 1990).

Laura is but one of many examples of children who display well-developed grammatical abilities, less-developed abilities to associate linguistic expressions with the objects they refer to, and severe deficits in nonlinguistic cognitive development.

In addition, any notion that linguistic ability results simply from communicative abilities or develops to serve communication functions is also negated by studies of children with fully developed structural linguistic knowledge, but with an almost total absence of pragmatic or communicative skills. The acquisition and use of language seem to depend on cognitive skills different from the ability to communicate in a social setting.

Christopher

Another dramatic case, that of a twenty-nine-year-old linguistic savant named Christopher, has been reported. Christopher has a nonverbal IQ of between 60 and 70 and is institutionalized because he is unable to take care of himself; he finds the tasks of buttoning a shirt, cutting his fingernails, or vacuuming the carpet too difficult. According to the detailed investigation of Christopher, his "linguistic competence in his first language is as rich and as sophisticated as that of any native speaker." Furthermore, when given written texts in some fifteen to twenty languages, he translates them immediately into English. The languages include Germanic languages such as Danish, Dutch, and German; Romance languages such as French, Italian, Portuguese, and Spanish; as well as Polish, Finnish, Greek, Hindi, Turkish, and Welsh. He learned these languages either from speakers who used them in his presence or from grammar books. Christopher is reported to love to study and learn languages. The investigators of this interesting man conclude that his linguistic ability is independent of his general conceptual or intellectual ability (Smith & Tsimpli, 1995).

The cases of Laura and Christopher argue against the view that linguistic ability derives from more general cognitive "intelligence," since in these cases language developed in spite of other intellectual deficits.

Genetic Evidence for Language Autonomy

Studies of genetic disorders also reveal that one cognitive domain can develop normally simultaneous with abnormal development in other domains. Children with Turner's syndrome (a chromosomal anomaly) reveal normal or advanced language simultaneous with serious nonlinguistic cognitive deficits. Similarly, studies of language development in children with Williams syndrome reveal a unique behavioural profile in which there appears to be a selective preservation of linguistic functions in the face of severe general cognitive deficits or moderate retardation. In addition, developmental dyslexia and at least some types of SLI also appear to have a genetic basis.

Epidemiological studies show that specific language impairment runs in families. A large multigenerational family, half of whom are language impaired, has been studied in detail (Gopnik, 1994). All the people in the study are adult native speakers of English. The impaired members of this family have a very specific grammatical problem. They do not reliably indicate the tense of the verb. They routinely produce sentences such as the following:

> She remembered when she hurts herself the other day.
> He did it then he fall.
> The boy climb up the tree and frightened the bird away.

These results point to SLI as a heritable disorder.

Studies also show that monozygotic (identical) twins are more likely to both suffer from SLI than dizygotic (fraternal) twins.

Thus, evidence from aphasia, specific language impairments, and other genetic disorders, along with the asymmetry of abilities as revealed in linguistic savants, supports the view of the language faculty (and more specifically, grammar) as an autonomous, genetically determined, brain (mind) module.

Summary

The attempt to understand what makes human language acquisition and use possible has led to research on the brain–mind–language relationship. **Neurolinguistics** studies the brain mechanisms and anatomical structures underlying language representation and use.

The brain is the most complicated organ of the body, controlling motor and sensory activities and thought processes. Research conducted for more than a century reveals that different parts of the brain control different bodily functions. The nerve cells that form the surface of the brain are called the **cortex**, which serves as the intellectual decision maker, receiving messages from the sensory organs and initiating all voluntary actions. The brain of each higher animal is divided into two parts called the **cerebral hemispheres**, which are connected by the **corpus callosum**, a pathway that permits the left and right hemispheres to communicate with each other.

Although each hemisphere appears to be a mirror image of the other, the left hemisphere controls the right hand, leg, visual field, and so on, and the right brain controls the left side of the body; this is referred to as **contralateral** control of function. Despite this general symmetry of the human body, there is much evidence that the left and right hemispheres are specialized for different functions. Evidence from **aphasia** — language dysfunction as a result of brain injuries — and from surgical removal of parts of the brain, electrical stimulation studies, emission tomography results, dichotic listening, and experiments measuring brain electrical activity shows a lack of symmetry of function of the two hemispheres. These results are further supported by studies of **split-brain** patients, who, for medical reasons, have had the corpus callosum severed. In the past, studies of the brain and language depended on surgery or autopsy. Today new technologies such as magnetic resonance imaging (MRI) and positron emission tomography (PET) make it possible to see the sites of lesions in the living brain, to detect changes in brain activities, and to relate these changes to focal brain damage and cognitive tasks.

For normal right-handers and many left-handers, the left side of the brain appears to be specialized for language. This **lateralization** of functions is genetically and neurologically conditioned. Lateralization refers to any cognitive functions that are primarily localized to one side of the brain or the other.

In addition to aphasia, other evidence supports the lateralization of language. Children with early brain lesions in the left hemisphere, resulting in the surgical removal of parts or the whole of the left brain, show specific linguistic deficits with other cognitive abilities remaining intact. If the right brain is damaged, however, language is not disordered, but other cognitive disorders may result.

Aphasia studies show impairment of different parts of the grammar. Patients with **Broca's aphasia** exhibit impaired syntax and speech problems, whereas **Wernicke's aphasia** patients are fluent speakers who produce semantically empty utterances and have difficulty in comprehension. **Anomia** is a form of aphasia in which the patient has word-finding difficulties. **Jargon aphasia** patients may substitute words unrelated semantically to their intended messages; others produce phonemic substitution errors, sometimes resulting in nonsense forms, making their utterances uninterpretable.

The **modularity** of the language faculty — its independence from other cognitive systems with which it interacts — is supported by brain-damage studies and studies of children with a **specific language impairment** (**SLI**) who are normal in all other respects. The ability to acquire language seems to be genetically determined, as shown by the cases of linguistic **savants** — individuals who are fluent in language and deficient in general intelligence. Given such individuals, linguistic ability does not seem to be derived from some general cognitive ability.

Note

1. Broca also held extremely racist and sexist views based on incorrect measurements of the brains of men and women and different races. His correlation of brain size with intelligence is thoroughly demolished by Stephen Jay Gould in *The Mismeasure of Man* (New York: W.W. Norton, 1981).

Exercises

---

1. A. Some aphasic patients, when asked to read a list of words, substitute other words for those printed. In many cases, there are similarities between the printed words and the substituted words. The data given below are from actual aphasic patients. In each case, state what the two words have in common and how they differ.

Printed Word	Word Spoken by Aphasic
a. liberty	freedom
canary	parrot
abroad	overseas
large	long
short	small
tall	long

b.	decide	decision
	conceal	concealment
	portray	portrait
	bathe	bath
	speak	discussion
	remember	memory

B. What do the words in groups a and b reveal about how words are likely to be stored in the brain?

2. The following sentences, spoken by aphasic patients, were collected and ana-lyzed by Dr. Harry Whitaker of the University of Maryland. In each case, state how the sentence deviates from normal nonaphasic language.

   a. There is under a horse a new sidesaddle.
   b. In girls we see many happy days.
   c. I'll challenge a new bike.
   d. I surprise no new glamour.
   e. Is there three chairs in this room?
   f. Mike and Peter is happy.
   g. Bill and John likes hotdogs.
   h. Proliferate is a complete time about a word that is correct.
   i. Went came in better than it did before.

*3. A young patient at the Division of Neuropsychology of the Radcliffe Infirmary, Oxford, England, following a head injury, appears to have lost the spelling-to-pronunciation and phonetic-to-spelling rules that most of us can use to read and write new words or nonsense strings. He is also unable to get to the phonemic representations of words in his lexicon. Consider the fol-lowing examples of his reading pronunciation and his writing from dictation.

Reading	**Pronunciation**	**Writing from Dictation**
fame	/fæmi/	FAM
café	/sæfi/	KAFA
time	/tajmi/	TIM
note	/noti/ or /nɔti/	NOT
praise	/pra-aj-si/	PRAZ
treat	/tri-æt/	TRET
goes	/go-ɛs/	GOZ
float	/flɔ-æt/	FLOT

His reading and writing errors are not random but rule-governed. See if you can figure out the rules he uses to relate standard (spelling) orthography to his pronunciation and spelling.

4. What are the arguments and evidence that have been put forth to support the notion that there are two separate parts of the brain?

5. In this chapter, dichotic listening tests in which subjects hear different kinds of stimuli in each ear were discussed. These tests showed that there were fewer errors made in reporting linguistic stimuli such as the syllables *pa, ta, ka* when heard through an earphone on the right ear; other nonlinguistic sounds such as a police car siren were processed with fewer mistakes if heard by the left ear. This is due to the contralateral control of the brain. There is also a technique that permits visual stimuli to be received either by the right visual field, that is, the right eye alone (going directly to the left hemisphere) or the left visual field (going directly to the right hemisphere). What might some visual stimuli be that could be used in an experiment to further test the lateralization of language?

*6. The following utterances were made either by Broca's aphasics or Wernicke's aphasics. Indicate which is which by writing a "B" or "W" next to the utterance.

    a.   Goodnight and in the pansy I can't say but into a flipdoor you can see it

    b.   Well . . . sunset . . . uh . . . horses nine, no, uh, two, tails want swish

    c.   Oh, . . . if I could I would, and a sick old man disflined a sinter, minter.

    d.   Words . . . words . . . words . . . two, four, six, eight, . . . blaze am he.

References

Damasio, A. (1994). *Descarte's error: Emotion, reason, and the human brain.* New York: G.P. Putnam.

Damasio, H., & Damasio, A. (1989). *Lesion analysis in neuropsychology.* New York: Oxford University Press.

Damasio, H., Grabowski, T., Frank, R., Galaburda, A.M., & Damasio, A.R. (1994). The return of Phineas Gage: The skull of a famous patient yields clues about the brain. *Science, 264,* 1102–1105.

Damasio, H., Grabowski, T., Tranel, D., Hichwa, R.D., & Damasio, A.R. (1996). A neural basis for lexical retrieval. *Nature, 380,* 499–505.

Gazzaniga, M.S. (1970). *The bisected brain.* New York: Appleton-Century-Crofts.

Geschwind, N. (1979). Specializations of the human brain. *Scientific American, 206,* 180–199.

Goodglass, H. (1973). Studies on the grammar of aphasics. In H. Goodglass & S. Blumstein (Eds.), *Psycholinguistics and aphasia* (pp. 183–215). Baltimore: Johns Hopkins University Press.

Gopnik, M. (1994). Impairments of tense in a familial language disorder. *Journal of Neurolinguistics, 8*(2), 109–133.

Jaeger, J.J., Lockwood, A.H., Kemmerer, D.L., Van Valin, R.D., Murphy, B.W., & Khlak, H.G. (1996). A positron emission tomographic study of regular and irregular verb morphology in English. *Language*, *72*(3), 451–497.

Newcombe, F., & Marshall, J. (1984). Varieties of acquired dyslexia: A linguistic approach. *Seminars in Neurology, 4*(2), 181–195.

Poizner, H., Klima, E.S., & Bellugi, U. (1987). *What the hands reveal about the brain.* Cambridge, MA: MIT Press.

Smith, N., & Tsimpli, I.M. (1995). *The mind of a savant.* Oxford: Blackwell.

Yamada, J. (1990). *Laura: A case for the modularity of language.* Cambridge, MA: MIT Press, a Bradford Book.

Further Reading

Ahlsen, E. (2006). *Introduction to neurolinguistics.* Philadelphia: John Benjamins.

Blumstein, S. (1973). *A phonological investigation of aphasic speech.* Janua Linguarum Series 153. The Hague: Mouton.

Caplan, D. (1987). *Neurolinguistics and linguistic aphasiology.* Cambridge, UK: Cambridge University Press.

Caplan, D. (1996). *Language: Structure, processing, and disorders.* Cambridge, MA: MIT Press.

Coltheart, M., Patterson, K., & Marshall, J.C. (Eds.). (1980). *Deep dyslexia.* London: Routledge and Kegan Paul.

Dabrowska, E. (2004). *Language, mind, and brain.* Edinburgh: Edinburgh University Press.

Damasio, H. (1981). Cerebral localization of the aphasias. In M. Taylor Sarno (Ed.), *Acquired aphasia* (pp. 27–65). New York: Academic Press.

Gardner, H. (1978). What we know (and don't know) about the two halves of the brain. *Harvard Magazine, 80,* 24–27.

Grodzinsky, Y. (1990). *Theoretical perspectives on language deficits.* Cambridge, MA: MIT Press.

Ingram, J.C.L. (2007). *Neurolinguistics: An introduction to spoken language processing and its disorders.* Cambridge, UK: Cambridge University Press.

Jackendoff, R. (2003). *Foundations of language: Brain, meaning, grammar, evolution.* Oxford: Oxford University Press.

Lesser, R. (1978). *Linguistic investigation of aphasia.* New York: Elsevier.

Lieberman, P. (1984). *The biology and evolution of language.* Cambridge, MA: Harvard University Press.

Patterson, K.E., Marshall, J.C., & Coltheart, M. (Eds.). (1986). *Surface dyslexia.* Hillsdale, NJ: Erlbaum.

Pinker, S. (1994). *The language instinct.* New York: William Morrow.

Segalowitz, S. (1983). *Two sides of the brain.* Englewood Cliffs, NJ: Prentice Hall.

Springer, S.P., & Deutsch, G. (1981). *Left brain, right brain.* San Francisco: W.H. Freeman.

Websites

http://mediabyran.kib.ki.se/projects/cns/atlas/overview.html A website with visual images of the brain.

http://www.crlmb.ca/ The website of the McGill University Centre for Research on Language, Mind, and Brain.

Changes in the grammar do not take place all at once within the speech community. They take place gradually, often originating in one region and slowly spreading to others and often taking place throughout the lives of several generations of speakers.

A change that occurs in one region and fails to spread to other regions of the language community gives rise to dialect differences. When enough such differences give the language spoken in a particular region (e.g., the city of Boston, Massachusetts, or the province of Newfoundland) its own "flavour," that version of the language is referred to as a **regional dialect**.

Accents

Regional phonological or phonetic distinctions are often referred to as different **accents**. A person is said to have a Boston accent, a Newfoundland or a "down East" accent, a Brooklyn accent, an Ottawa Valley twang, and so on. Thus, *accent* refers to the characteristics of speech that convey information about the speaker's dialect, which may reveal in what country or what part of the country the speaker grew up or — in the case of a **social dialect** — to which sociolinguistic group the speaker belongs. People in the United States often refer to someone as having a British accent or an Australian accent; in Britain, people may refer to an American accent, even when speaking of a Canadian.

The term *accent* is also used to refer to the speech of someone who speaks a language nonnatively; for example, a Quebecker speaking English may be thought to have a "French accent" by English speakers. In this sense of the word, *accent* refers to phonological differences of "interference" from a different language spoken elsewhere. A native speaker of Parisian French hearing the same speaker, on the other hand, might recognize the regional dialect and conclude that this is not merely a "French accent" but also a "Quebec French accent." Unlike regional dialectal accents, foreign accents do not reflect differences in the language of the community where the language was acquired.

Dialects of North American English

The educated Southerner has no use for an r except at the beginning of a word.

Mark Twain, *Life on the Mississippi* (1883)

The quantity of consonants in the English language in constant. If omitted in one place, they turn up in another. When a Bostonian "pahks" his "cah," the lost r's migrate southwest, causing a Texan to "warsh" his car and invest in "erl" wells.

Author unknown

The regional dialects of American and Canadian English alike find their roots in the speech of the British colonists who settled North America in the sixteenth through the eighteenth centuries, so it comes as no surprise to discover that they are alike in many respects, so much so that we may speak of Canadian and American English as part of a larger "North American English."

Evidently Aboriginal languages have contributed substantially to Canadian English, as is clear from a number of lexical items (e.g., moose, skunk, totem), as well as geographical names (e.g., Saskatchewan, Quebec).

Colonists to the New World brought with them a variety of English dialects, ranging from the Irish and West Country dialects of the Newfoundlanders in the oldest English colony (1583) to the East Anglian speech of the Puritans in New England. As a result, regional dialect differences were apparent even among the settlers of the first American colonies. In addition to the dialects of the fishing settlements of the Newfoundland coast, three major dialect areas can be discerned in the Thirteen Colonies before the outbreak of the American Revolution: a Northern dialect spoken in New England and around the Hudson River, a Midland dialect spoken in Pennsylvania and parts of New York State, and a Southern dialect. These dialects differed from each other — and from the English spoken in England — in systematic ways, for some of the changes that were occurring in British English spread to the colonies, while others did not. And, of course, the colonies themselves were developing dialectal differences that helped to distinguish their speech from that of the "mother country."

How regional differences developed between the dialects of the colonies and between those colonies and Britain may be illustrated in the changes that took place in the pronunciation of words with an *r*. The British in southern England were already dropping their *r*'s before consonants and at the ends of words as early as the eighteenth century. Words such as *farm, farther*, and *father* were pronounced as [fa:m], [fa:ðə], and [fa:ðə], respectively. By the end of the eighteenth century, this practice was a general rule among the early settlers in New England and the southern Atlantic seaboard. Close commercial ties were maintained between the New England colonies and London, and Southerners sent their children to England to be educated, which reinforced the "*r*-dropping" rule. The "*r*-less" dialect still spoken today in Boston, New York, and Savannah maintained this characteristic. Later settlers, however, came from northern England, where the *r* had been retained; as the frontier moved westward and northward, so did the *r*. The *r*-less dialect was not, of course, found among the Irish and Scots of Newfoundland and Nova Scotia.

Before the American Revolution, English settlement outside the Thirteen Colonies was largely confined to the Maritimes, for there were few, if any, English settlements in what are now Quebec and Ontario. At the outbreak of war, the population of the Thirteen Colonies was some 2.5 million people, of which a little more than 19 percent (500,000) remained loyal to the Crown, and, as the memoirs of those involved reveal, the conflict between onetime neighbours, friends, and relatives was often brutal, leaving harsh memories for the Loyalist and the Patriot alike. Following the war, many who had remained loyal to the Crown had lands and possessions confiscated, especially if they had been vocal in their opposition to independence or militarily active in the struggle. As many as 100,000 of the Loyalists left or were expelled from the new United States, and of this number between 45,000 and 50,000 migrated to what are now the provinces of Nova Scotia, New Brunswick, Quebec, and Ontario (see Figure 12.1), the remainder returning to Britain or emigrating to the West Indies or to Florida, which at that time was not part of the United States (Stewart, 1985).

Although the American Revolution altered the political map of North America, it had, at the outset at least, little effect on the language spoken by Patriot and Loyalist alike. The dialects that the Loyalists carried northward with them did not differ from those of their former neighbours.

Following the Revolutionary War, citizens of the United States continued to spread westward, and over time their dialects began to change as intermingling "levelled" or "submerged" many of their dialectal differences. This process of levelling is one reason the English used in large sections of the Midwest and the West of the United States is similar, making up what is sometimes called General American English. A similar levelling occurred among Loyalists in Quebec and

FIGURE 12.1

Loyalist settlement in Nova Scotia, Lower Canada, and Upper Canada.

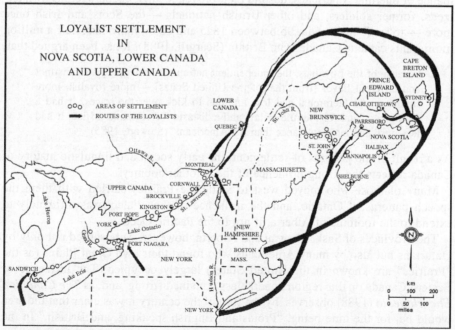

Joan Magee, *Loyalist Mosaic: A Multi-Ethnic Heritage.* Toronto: Dundurn Press, 1984. Reprinted with permission.

Ontario, the majority of whom came from the Midland dialect area. On the other hand, farther east large numbers of Northern dialect speakers moved into Nova Scotia, New Brunswick, and Newfoundland.

In addition to the English settlers, waves of immigration brought speakers of other dialects and other languages to the United States and to British North America, and each group left its linguistic imprint. The Scots and Irish brought their dialects with them into the Maritimes and Ontario, as well as into the Midland dialect area of Pennsylvania; Gaelic Scots came into Cape Breton Island, Nova Scotia, Prince Edward Island, Quebec, and Ontario; and, in the last half of the eighteenth century, Germans settled in the southeastern section of Pennsylvania, from which some subsequently moved into Ontario and still later onto the Canadian Prairies. The place names on a map of North America testify to the many peoples and their languages found on this continent.

The Loyalists who established themselves in British North America were soon joined by other migrants from the United States who were motivated less by politics than by the lure of available land. They came in such numbers, especially to the Ontario peninsula and to Quebec, that by the outbreak of war in 1812 large proportions of those areas were populated by former Americans. Governments on both sides of the border worried over these "Late Loyalists," but the question of their allegiance was quickly resolved when the majority rose in defence of their new homeland. Nevertheless, following the peace, London, wary of this predominance of onetime Americans, despite their proven loyalty, encouraged its own citizens, former soldiers, and other British nationals — the Scots and Irish once more — to settle in Canada. So between 1825 and 1846, more than half a million immigrants came to Canada from Britain (Scargill, 1988). It has been argued that,

> because of the Loyalists, the independent nation that emerged had a distinct
> and different flavor [from that of the United States] — more royalist, more
> British, more hierarchal and less inclined to kick over the traces. It had a
> strong penchant for the rule of law and a distaste for vigilante justice. It had
> less push and more tolerance than the Americans. (Stewart, 1985)

As a result of the patterns of settlement, the early social and linguistic history of Canada reflects the strong influence of the "mother country."

Many of those who moved west to settle the Prairies carried with them the speech patterns of Ontario, and the influence of that dialect was ultimately to extend to the foothills of Alberta, if not to the Pacific Ocean.[1]

The provinces of Saskatchewan and Alberta, however, were settled not only by Ontarians but also by many Americans who found their own Great Plains (as the "Prairies" are known in the United States) largely occupied. The influence of Eastern Canada on this region nonetheless remained strong, and, as *The Canadian Encyclopedia* (1988) observes, by the turn of the century it was clear that the area would be, for the time being, "Protestant, English speaking, and British." In the twentieth century, Prairie society began to change because of widespread immigration, and it now reflects a multiculturalism similar to that of other parts of the nation.

The settlement of British Columbia differs from that of the Prairies; because of the landscape, the area had little appeal for farmers from Central Canada. Instead, it attracted a sizable British population, so much so that it has been called the most British region in Canada (Scargill, 1988). This influence has been tempered, however, by the strong north–south axis of the Pacific area and by the influence of East Asia. During the 1980s and 1990s, immigration from Hong Kong and other nations of the Pacific Rim, as well as from Central Canada, modified the earlier "Englishness" of the area, especially in Vancouver and surrounding cities.

Increased immigration during the last half of the twentieth century has brought people from Africa, Asia, Europe, and Central and South America to North America, some fleeing war and persecution, others seeking, like those who came before them, a better life. As a result, the English language in North America — American and Canadian alike — continues to be enriched by the languages spoken by large numbers of new residents from the Pacific Rim countries of Japan, China, Korea, Malaysia, Vietnam, and Thailand. Eastern Europeans (Russians, Ukrainians, and Armenians), Bermudians, Jamaicans, Portuguese, and Central and South Americans have all added to the richness of the vocabulary of North American English. This cultural diversity is reflected in the various "mother tongues" — a mother tongue is the language first learned as a child and that continues to be understood — of Canadians as recorded in the 2006 census (see Table 12.1). The "Caribana" celebrations of Toronto, once a bastion of "Anglo-Saxon" Canada, the Italian neighbourhoods of Vancouver, the Portuguese clubs scattered across the land, the mosques and the Sikh temples — all have contributed to the "mosaic" of Canadian society. While the designation of "New Canadians" was created by older immigrants for these recent immigrants, both "new" and "old" have found a place in Canadian society. The English spoken in regions where new immigrants settle may ultimately be affected by the mother tongues of the settlers, further adding to the variety of the English language. But, despite the variations of Canadian speech, the language of middle-class, urban Canadians remains amazingly homogeneous.

English is the most widely spoken language in the world if one counts all those who use it as a native language or as a second or third language. It is the official national language of a number of countries, such as Australia, the British Isles, Canada, New Zealand, South Africa, and the United States. For many years, it was the official language in countries that were once colonies of Britain, including India, Nigeria, Ghana, Kenya, and the other "Anglophone" countries of Africa. One result of this contact between English and the languages of the onetime colonies has been an enrichment of English through the development of further dialects, each with its own grace and beauty.

TABLE 12.1
Selected Mother Tongues in Canada, 2006

Language	Numbers of Speakers	Percentage of Population
English	17,882,775	57.8
French	6,817,655	22
Chinese	1,012,065	3.3
Italian	455,040	1.48
German	450,570	1.46
Punjabi	367,505	1.2
Spanish	345,345	1.1
Arabic	261,640	0.85
Tagalog (Pilipino)	235,615	0.76
Portuguese	219,275	0.71
Polish	211,175	0.68
Vietnamese	141,630	0.46
Ukrainian	134,500	0.44
Dutch	128,900	0.42
Greek	117,285	0.38
Cree	78,855	0.26
Inuktitut	32,380	0.10

These figures do not include 392,760 people who indicated multiple mother tongues. According to Statistics Canada, 98,625 of this number listed both English and French as their mother tongues; 240,005 indicated English and a nonofficial language; 43,335 indicated French and a nonofficial language; and 10,790 indicated English, French, and a third language.

Adapted from "Population by Mother Tongue, by province and territory (2006 Census)", Statistics Canada http://www.statcan.ca/101/cst01/demolla.htm.

Canadian and American English

Wallace Stegner, the son of an American settler in Saskatchewan, was aware of the importance of the border separating the United States and Canada. Despite the apparent similarities between the two countries, that border "exerted uncomprehended pressures upon affiliation and belief, custom and costume. It offered us subtle choices even in language (we stooked our wheat; across the Line they shocked it)" (Stegner, 1962). "Subtle choices" continue to characterize the differences between American and Canadian dialects. Walter Avis (1956), one of the pioneering students of Canadian English, defined it as "neither American nor British, but a complex different in many respects from both in vocabulary, grammar and syntax, and pronunciation." With American English, it shares a language that developed out of the Early Modern English dialects of British settlers, joined with borrowings from North American Aboriginal languages and the influences of other immigrants from around the world. Indeed, it is often difficult to decide which borrowed specific words from North American Aboriginal languages first, Canadian or American English. Canadian English, however, also reflects the effects of continued political, social, and linguistic affiliation with Great Britain. Finally, of course, unique features have, over the centuries, grown up in the country itself. The morphology, phonology, and syntax that Canadians use may not, on the whole, be unique to Canada, but the blending of these elements has produced a distinctive dialect of North American English, even though it may not be immediately recognizable to others. As one account noted,

> Canadian English is difficult to distinguish from some other North American varieties without the tools of the phonetician, yet it is instantly recognisable to other Canadians, if not to the rest of the English-speaking world. In a crowd, where the Englishman or the Australian could not, the Canadian with a good ear will easily spot the other Canadian among the North Americans. (McCrum, Cran, & MacNeil, 1992, p. 245)

Phonological Differences

> I have noticed in traveling about the country a good many differences in the pronunciation of common words. . . . Now what I want to know is whether there is any right or wrong about this matter. . . . If one way is right, why don't we all pronounce that way and compel the other fellow to do the same? If there isn't any right or wrong, why do some persons make so much fuss about it?
>
> Letter quoted in "The Standard American," in J.V. Williamson
> and V.M. Burke, eds., *A Various Language* (1971)

A comparison between the *r*-less dialect and other dialects with *r* was used earlier to illustrate phonological differences between dialects. Similarly, some people in the United States pronounce *caught* as /kɔt/ with the vowel /ɔ/ and *cot* as /kat/, whereas other Americans and most Canadians pronounce them identically. Some Americans pronounce *Mary, marry*, and *merry* identically; others pronounce all three words differently as /meri/, /mæri/, and /mɛri/; and still others pronounce two of them the same. Canadians share this indecision; while few have three distinct pronunciations, a substantial number — especially older speakers — differentiate between /æ/ in *marry* and /ɛ/ in *Mary/merry*. In the southern areas of the United States, *creek* is pronounced with a tense /i/ as /krik/, and in the north Midlands it is pronounced with a lax /ɪ/ as /krɪk/. Both forms are found in Canadian English, but, according to a survey of high school students and their parents, /krɪk/ predominates (Scargill, 1974).[2]

   The sound structure of Canadian English, like its vocabulary, further reflects "subtle choices" that distinguish it from American English. The centred and raised diphthongs [ʌj] and [ʌw] (allophones of the phonemes /aj/ and /aw/ appearing before voiceless consonants) have been considered by many to be characteristic of Canadian English. These diphthongs are heard in words such as *light* [lʌjt] and *type* [tʌjp], *house* [hʌws] and *out* [ʌwt], where most Americans — and some

Canadians — use a low back diphthong, as in [lajt], [tajp], [haws], and [awt]. This "raising" is triggered by a following voiceless consonant, as is evident in the contrast between words such as *writer* and *rider*. The medial consonant of *writer* may be produced as a voiced flap allophone [ɾ] of /t/ that sounds to many people much like the [d] of *rider*. But speakers of Canadian English make a distinction in the diphthongs, for *writer* is pronounced with the raised vowel [rʌjɾər], while *rider* has the lower back vowel [rajdər]. Clearly, speakers are responding to the "voicelessness" of the medial consonant in the first word. Similarly, the initial vowel of the diphthong is raised in words such as *clout* [klʌwt] in contrast with *cloud* [klawd] under the same conditions. However characteristic of Canadian English this raised and centred diphthong may be, a feature much like it has been detected in some dialects of American English (Vance, 1987). The appearance of something like **Canadian raising** is apparently a recent development in parts of the northern United States (Thomas, 1991), and, curiously, at the same time, it has been seen to be disappearing in the speech of Toronto (Leon, 1979).

As the example of *writer* shows, Canadians, like Americans, employ a voiced allophone of /t/ between vowels. Hence, the capital city of Canada, *Ottawa*, is pronounced [ɑɾəwə]. British influence may be responsible for the use of voiceless /t/ in the careful speech of some British Columbians, but many of the same speakers employ the voiced allophone in casual speech. Similarly, many Canadians and Americans employ a voiced sound, [ǰ], instead of /č/ in words such as *congratulate* [kəngræǰəlet]. Some Canadians pronounce words such as *tune, duke, news*, and *student* with a /j/ glide between the alveolar consonant and /u/ (called yoddizing), as in British English, thus /tjun/, /djuk/, /njuz/, /stjudənt/, but most pronounce them without /j/ (yod dropping), as /tun/, et cetera. Forms with /j/ seem to have more prestige, presumably because they seem more British. In Ontario, hypercorrection to /ju/ in *moon, noon*, and so on, has been reported along the "middle border" from Thunder Bay to Saskatchewan. Yod coalescence to an affricate, as in *tune* /čjun/, also occurs (Wells, 1982).

As this suggests, there is a good deal of variation in Canadian English, even, at times, within the speech of the same person. Some Canadians, for example, use /ajl/ in words such as *hostile* or *futile*, while others employ syllabic [l̩] or [əl]. Many who say /ajl/ in *futile* also use syllabic /l̩/ in *missile* ([mɪsl̩]), perhaps because of American news broadcasts over the past fifty years. Some critics have likewise seen the use of [sk] instead of [š] in a word such as *schedule* as the result of American influence. In reality, both forms are evident in the Early Modern English of the settlers of North America. The apparent increase in the use of [əl] and [sk] may, nonetheless, be due to the influence of American films, radio, and television.

Many but not all Canadians use [šɑn] as the past tense of *shine* instead of American [šon], and they may use a high tense vowel in *been*, [bin], instead of the usual lax vowel, [bɪn], of American English. The same vowel may appear in *lever* [livər], though others use [lɛvər]. Similarly, *tomato* is [təmerə] or [təmeɾo] rather than [təmɑto]. It is a mistake to see these examples as an opposition of British versus

American forms, for both existed in earlier varieties of English brought to North America.

Stress may follow the British pattern in *coróllary, capíllary*, and *labóratory*, especially in Eastern Canada. But words ending in *-ary* and *-ery* will usually have secondary stress as in American English.

As noted in Chapter 5, the pronunciation of British English differs in systematic ways from that of Central Canadian or General American English. Britain has many regional dialects, and the British vowels described in the phonetics chapter are the ones used by speakers of the most prestigious dialect, often referred to as **RP, Received Pronunciation**, because it was once considered to be the dialect used in court and "received by" the king and queen. In this dialect, /h/ is pronounced at the beginning of both *head* and *herb* (though /r/ in *herb* is not), whereas in the English of North America it is not generally pronounced in the second word (though /r/ is). In some British dialects, the /h/ is regularly dropped from most words in which it is pronounced in both Canadian and American English, such as *house*, pronounced [aws], and *hero*, pronounced [iro]. A similar deletion of [h] occurs in broad Newfoundland English, in which the first word of *Harbour Grace* loses its initial [h]. On the other hand, [h] may be inserted in Newfoundland dialects before initial vowels of stressed syllables, as in *anchor* [hæŋkə]. Both words, *harbour* and *anchor*, illustrate yet another "dropping" in their omission of final *r*. In this dialect, *r*-dropping also occurs between a vowel and a consonant, as one hears in a word such as *scarce*. These are but a few examples of the many regular phonological differences found in the many dialects of English used around the world.

Lexical Differences

People hearing Americans, Britons, and Canadians speaking together probably observe in the Canadian that curious blend of British and "American" elements in Canadian speech that we have been discussing. And it is probably the vocabulary that is first noticed. Americans will hear what they consider to be "Britishisms," while the British will hear "Americanisms." In fact, many "Canadianisms" are of British origin, and those words that perplex the British may be those that are shared with Americans or, indeed, are of American origin. The resulting combination and the way these words are used, however, are uniquely Canadian.

Dialects, national and regional, may differ in the words people use for the same object, as well as in phonology. Hans Kurath (1971), an eminent American dialectologist, asked in an essay entitled "What Do You Call It?"

> Do you call it a *pail* or a *bucket*? Do you draw water from a *faucet* or from a *spigot*? Do you pull down the *blinds*, the *shades*, or the *curtains* when it gets dark? Do you *wheel* the baby, or do you *ride* it or *roll* it? In a *baby carriage*, a *buggy*, a *coach*, or a *cab*?

Some speakers of Canadian English might insist that they use none of Kurath's alternatives; others would suggest that they use some but with differences in meaning. In other instances, they use the word that is commonly attributed to "American" English, and in still other cases they use the "British" form. Canadians pull down the *blinds* to cover a window, as do many Americans. (*Curtains*, on the other hand, are made of cloth and may hang in front of the *blinds*.) Canadians and Americans do not take a *lift* to the *first floor* but an *elevator* to the *second floor*; Canadians, like Americans, get *gas* for their cars (not *petrol*, as in Britain); unlike the *gallons* (differing in size, however) of the British and Americans, it is measured in litres. Unlike in North America, a *public school* in Britain is private (you have to pay), and, if a student showed up there wearing *pants* ("underpants") instead of *trousers* ("pants"), he would be sent home to get dressed.

On the other hand, the differences between Canadian and American English are also apparent, and many of these differences reflect British influence. Canadians turn on a *tap* to obtain water, a word that some Americans consider "English." They may *queue up* ("line up") for tickets or the bus, a word that puzzles Americans — and a behaviour that amuses them as "so Canadian." H.B. Allen in his survey of the Upper Midwest of the United States (1976) found *chesterfield* to be "uniquely Canadian" even though he noted that it is also used in the San Francisco area.

Reprinted with permission from The Globe and Mail

Americans living close to the Canadian border know that the word refers to "a long upholstered seat or couch having back and arms" (Avis et al., 1967), but they consider it strictly a Canadianism (Allen, 1976). As we might expect, the word is originally English, but in the United Kingdom nowadays it refers primarily to a kind of overcoat. In Canada, *chesterfield* has produced a blend — one that is uniquely Canadian — in *chesterbed*, a "couch" that converts into a bed. It is also an element in compound words such as *chesterfield chair, chesterfield suite*, and even *chesterfield table* (the "coffee table") according to the *Dictionary of Canadianisms*.

Another word, British in origin, but used in a different sense in Canada is *riding* to designate a parliamentary constituency rather than an administrative district (e.g., the "West Riding of Yorkshire") as it does in British English. Originally Scandinavian (a "third"), it is one of the many remains of the Viking occupation of England. Similarly, Canadians speak of electing politicians by *acclamation*, a word defined in both American and English dictionaries as "loud approval" or "cheers" but that in Canada indicates election of a person "without opposition."

Like *chesterfield* and *riding*, the word *serviette* (a "table-napkin" according to the *Concise Oxford Dictionary* to contrast it with "napkin" = "diaper") was originally British. It is widely used in Canada, especially for the paper variety, but *napkin* seems to be gradually replacing it. *Zed* for the last letter of the alphabet is the preferred word in Canadian schools, but every child, influenced by American television, knows that it is called *zee* in the United States.

Many people around the world wear thick-soled canvas shoes for informal or athletic use, but Canadians apparently are singular in calling them *running shoes* or *runners*. Americans refer to them as *sneakers, sneaks,* or *tennis shoes* and Britons as *trainers* or *plimsolls*. In American English, *running shoes*, as Webster attests, are shoes with spikes for track-and-field athletes.

A common belief — it may even be true — is that Customs and Immigration officers on both sides of the 49th parallel distinguish Americans from Canadians by the use of *eh?* in sentences such as "I went over to visit my cousin, eh?" Certainly, parodies of Canadian English such as Mark Orkin's *Canajan, Eh?* (1973) exploit this "tic," as it has been called, as typical of Canadian speech. As with other words and expressions, *eh?* is not, in fact, exclusively Canadian, for it appears in both American and British English as well (Avis, 1972). If not uniquely Canadian, *eh?* is used to such an extent by speakers of Canadian English that few question the value of this expression to separate Americans from Canadians.

Lexical Variation Across Canada

The North American Regional Vocabulary Survey, carried out at McGill University, describes ways in which vocabulary use differs across Canada. For example, while Western Canadians tend to use *cabin* for the weekend country house, Eastern Canadians are more likely to refer to their *cottage*. The French word *chalet* is common in Quebec English, while in Northwestern Ontario and New Brunswick *camp* is largely used. The survey also revealed that a book of lined paper that children use to do school work is commonly called an *exercise book* in Newfoundland and Quebec, while in the Maritimes, *scribbler* is more common. Elsewhere in Canada, *notebook*, the most common American term, is used. Still in the domain of school items, the object used to carry books is called a *backpack* in the United States and in most of Canada. However, some Torontonians use the term *knapsack*, while *schoolbag* is commonly used in Prince Edward Island and by some Montrealers. *Bookbag* was found to be the most common term in New Brunswick and Newfoundland.

Newfoundland is particularly rich in regionalisms. The *Dictionary of Newfoundland English* points out, for instance, that the words *bank*, *berth*, *ground*, *fouly*, *ledge*, and *shoal* are all items referring to various aspects of fishing waters, an occupation that has long been vitally important to the local economy. Similarly, different aspects of ice are referred to by the following items: *ballicatter*, *clumper*, *quarr*, *sish*, and *slob*.

Dialect Atlases

Dialect atlases and **dialect maps** of various regions have been produced. For instance, in Figure 12.2A, black dots mark communities whose speakers use *settee*, and black squares identify places where the word *chesterfield* occurs. Concentrations of these markings help to define *dialect areas* and, in this case, to mark the border between

FIGURE 12.2A
Dialect map of Upper Midwest United States.

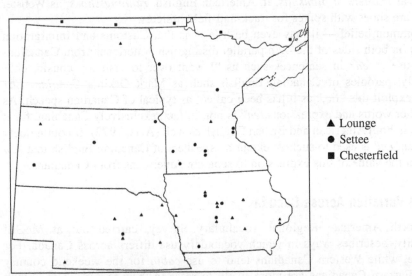

From Allen, Harold.Linguistic Atlas of the Upper Midwest Vol 3, 1E.(c) 1982 Gale, a part of Cengage Learning, Inc. Reproduced by permission. www.cengage.com/permissions.

FIGURE 12.2B
Dialect map of Nova Scotia.

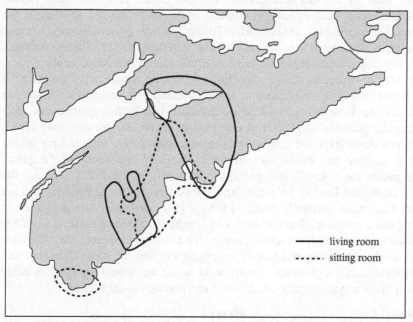

living room
sitting room

H. Rex Wilson, "The Dialect of Lunenburg County, Nova Scotia." Diss., University of Michigan, 1958, p. 72.

Canadian and American English. A line drawn on the map (as in Figure 12.2B) separating the areas is called an **isogloss**. When you "cross" an isogloss, you are passing from one dialect area to another. Sometimes several isoglosses will coincide, often at a political boundary or at a natural boundary such as a river or mountain range. Linguists call these groupings a bundle of isoglosses. Such a bundle will define a particular regional dialect.

The first four volumes of the *Dictionary of Regional English* by Frederick G. Cassidy have been published. This work represents years of research and scholarship by Cassidy and other American dialectologists and promises to be a major resource for those interested in American English dialectal differences. Unfortunately, there is at present no work of the same magnitude for Canadian English.

Syntactic Differences

The "standard" dialects of American, British, and Canadian English do not exhibit many syntactic differences. British English, it is true, can delete the verb in a sentence such as *I could have called* and replace it with *done* to form *I could have done*, which is not permitted in North American grammar, where speakers say instead *I could have*. Canadians may be more familiar than Americans with the British construction, but it is seldom used by any but immigrants from the United Kingdom. Like British speakers, Canadians speak of being *in hospital*, while Americans add an article to the expression: *in the/a hospital*. In Canada and Britain, students *go to university*, whereas in the United States they *go to college* as the generic designation. In all three countries, however, criminals end up *in jail*, although in Britain it may be spelled *gaol*.

The syntactic structures of Canadian English, like its vocabulary, thus reflect a unique blend of North American and British elements. A resident of Michigan will ask *Do you have any tea?* while an Ontarian, like British questioners, may well form the question as *Have you any tea?* or *Have you got any tea?* (Avis, 1955). Some Americans use *gotten* in a sentence such as *He should have gotten to school on time* and distinguish between *gotten* in the sense of "acquire" ("We've gotten the tickets") and *got* in the sense of "possess" ("We've got the tickets"); in British English only the form *got* occurs. As the question about tea suggests, Canadians generally prefer *got* as a past participle, though *gotten* is becoming more common. Some speakers of Northern American dialects say *They are to home*, while Canadians seldom use such a construction, preferring *They are at home*, as do most other dialects of American English. In some Canadian and American dialects, the pronoun *I* may occur when *me* would be used in other dialects. This is a syntactically conditioned morphological difference.

Dialect 1	**Dialect 2**
between you and I	between you and me
Won't he let you and I swim?	Won't he let you and me swim?

Although often irritated by those who mistake them for "Americans" — a designation that most of the world takes to refer to a resident of the United States — speakers of Canadian English may not stand out from their northern "American" cousins until they are heard to refer to a [lɛftɛnənt], *lieutenant*, ask *Have you got a [hʌws] house in the country?* or speak of a friend *in hospital*. It is this complex of sounds and forms that distinguishes a speaker of Canadian English from a speaker of American or British English.

Even though regional dialects differ as to pronunciation, vocabulary, and syntactic rules, they are minor differences when compared with the totality of the grammar. The largest part of the vocabulary, the sound–meaning relations of words and the syntactic rules, is shared, which is why dialects of one language are mutually intelligible.

The "Standard"

We don't talk fancy grammar and eat anchovy toast. But to live under the kitchen doesn't say we aren't educated.

Mary Norton, *The Borrowers* (1952)

> Standard English is the customary use of a community when it is recognized
> and accepted as the customary use of the community. Beyond this is the larger
> field of good English, any English that justifies itself by accomplishing its
> end, by hitting the mark.
>
> George Philip Krapp, *Modern English: Its Growth and Present Use* (1909)

Even though every language is a composite of dialects, many people talk and think
about a language as if it were a well-defined fixed system with various dialects
diverging from this norm. This is false, although it is a falsehood that is widespread. Such was the view of Mario Pei, the author of a number of books on language that were quite popular at one time. He accused the editors of *Webster's
Third New International Dictionary*, published in 1961, of confusing "to the point
of obliteration the older distinction between standard, substandard, colloquial,
vulgar, and slang," erroneously attributing to them the view that "good and bad,
right and wrong, correct and incorrect no longer exist" (Pei, 1964). In the next
section, we argue that such criticisms are ill founded.

Language Purists

> A woman who utters such depressing and disgusting sounds has no right to
> be anywhere — no right to live. Remember that you are a human being with
> a soul and the divine gift of articulate speech: that your native language is the
> language of Shakespeare and Milton and The Bible; and don't sit there
> crooning like a bilious pigeon.
>
> George Bernard Shaw, *Pygmalion* (1913)

Prescriptive grammarians, or language "purists," usually consider the dialect used
by political leaders, the upper socioeconomic classes, and the educated classes,
the dialect used for literature or printed documents, and the dialect taught in the
schools as the correct form of the language.

Otto Jespersen (1925/1964), the great Danish linguist, ridiculed the view that a
particular dialect is better than any other: "We set up as the best language that
which is found in the best writers, and count as the best writers those that best
write the language. We are therefore not further advanced than before."

The dominant or prestige dialect is often called the **standard** dialect. There is
not so much a single standard English as several varieties of national standards
throughout the world. The chief division is between British English and North
American English, the latter including the standard varieties spoken by educated
speakers in Canada and the United States. British English includes the standard
varieties spoken in England, Scotland, Ireland, and Wales.

Standard British English (SBrE), **Standard American English (SAE)**, and
Standard Canadian English (SCE) are dialects of English that many English
and North Americans *almost* speak; divergences from this "norm" are labelled
"Liverpudlian," "Yorkshire," "Chicago dialect," "African American English," and

"Newfie." The standard — whether it be SBrE, SAE, or SCE — is an idealization. Nobody speaks this dialect, and, if somebody did, we would not know it, because these dialects are not defined precisely. It used to be the case that the language used by national news broadcasters in Britain (called "Received Pronunciation" [RP]), Canada, and the United States (called "network standard") represented the standard, but today many of these people speak a regional dialect. Several years ago, conferences were held in both the United States and Canada to discuss what Standard American or Standard Canadian might be or, indeed, if there were such a thing as a standard. Neither meeting succeeded in satisfying even its participants. One linguist attending the Kingston, Ontario, conference argued, moreover, that in Canada, a country with two official languages, a country in which a vast number of citizens have neither French nor English as a first language and in which diversity is encouraged, a country strongly influenced by both British and American models, imposition of one standard of correctness is impossible and undesirable (Chambers, 1986).

Deviations from "standards" that remain undefined even in the minds of those who are most exasperated by the "errors" they detect on everyone's lips have been seen to reflect a "language crisis." The "Letters to the Editor" in American and Canadian newspapers reflect anxiety over the perilous state of the English language. Edwin Newman (1974), in his bestseller *Strictly Speaking*, asks "Will Americans be the death of English?" and answers "My mature, considered opinion is that they will." All this fuss is reminiscent of Mark Twain's cable to the Associated Press after reading his obituary: "The reports of my death are greatly exaggerated."

The idea that language change equals corruption goes back at least as far as the Greek grammarians at Alexandria of around 200–100 B.C.E. They were concerned that the Greek spoken in their time was different from the Greek of Homer, and they believed that the earlier forms were purer. They also tried to "correct" the imperfections but failed as miserably as do any modern counterparts. Similarly, the Arabic grammarians working at Basra in the eighth and ninth centuries C.E. attempted to purify Arabic to restore it to the perfection of Arabic in the Koran.

During the nineteenth and early twentieth centuries, commentators — both foreign and native — were critical of the English spoken in North America. Often their criticism had a political origin; thus, for many years after the American Revolution, British writers and journalists railed against American English. The *London Review* chastised Thomas Jefferson for his *Notes on the State of Virginia*:

> For shame, Mr. Jefferson! Why, after trampling upon the honour of the country, and representing it as little better than a land of barbarism — why, we say, perpetually trample also upon the very grammar of our language.... Freely, good sir, we will forgive all your attacks, impotent as they are illiberal, upon our *national character*; but for the future spare — O spare, we beseech you, our mother-tongue!

But equally sharp were the self-criticisms of one critic who worried that "Canadian English" was "a corrupt dialect growing up amongst our population ... until it threatens to produce a language as unlike our noble mother tongue as the negro patua, or the Chinese pidgeon English" (Geike, 1857), a comment that reveals the speaker's lack of knowledge about the grammatical complexities of African American English and the social circumstances that led to the development of a pidgin. But the fears of British journalists in 1787 and of Canadian commentators in 1857 have proven to be unfounded, and so will the fears of Edwin Newman and the anxious contributors to Letters to the Editor.

No academy and no guardians of language purity can stem language change, nor should anyone attempt to do so, since change does not mean corruption. The fact that for the great majority of English speakers *criteria* and *data* are now mass nouns, like *information*, is no cause for concern. Information can include one fact or many facts, but one would still say *The information is*. For some speakers, it is equally correct to say *The criteria is* or *The criteria are*. Those who say *The data are* would or could say *The datum* (singular) *is*.

A standard dialect (or prestige dialect) of a particular language may serve a social function — for example, to bind people together or to provide a common written form for multidialectal speakers. The primary function of standard varieties is public (including international) rather than personal and private. The standard or prestige dialect is appropriate to relatively formal styles and genres, for media addressing large numbers of people, and for utterances intended to have permanence (Crystal, 1997). It is not, however, more expressive, more logical, more complex, or more regular than any other dialect or language. Any judgments, therefore, as to the superiority or inferiority of a particular dialect or language are social judgments, not linguistic or scientific judgments. It is a matter more of manners than of morals. As Dwight Bolinger (1980) says,

> There will be a prestige variety so long as speakers and writers must take account of needs and desires as hearers and readers. And if producing messages and receiving and decoding them are psychologically opposed operations ... then that accountability will always be with us. Speakers naturally prefer to sing their half of the duet with no more effort than necessary — to use words and constructions that come first to mind, to speak at low volume, to slur the sounds. Hearers just as naturally want comprehension to require no more effort than necessary — to be favored with background information, unambiguous sentences, and reasonably crisp articulation. The speaker or writer of course is the one who has to make most of the concessions, especially if he has an audience of more than one and most especially if the audience is remote in space or time. This explains why a prestige variety is so needed in writing.

Banned Languages

Language purists wish to stem change in language or dialect differentiation because of their false belief that some languages are better than others or that change leads to corruption. Languages and dialects have also been banned as a means of political control. Russian was the only legal language permitted by the Russian tsars, who banned the use of Ukrainian, Lithuanian, Georgian, Armenian, Azerbaijani, and all the other languages spoken by national groups under the rule of Russia.

For many years, the languages of the First Nations were banned in religious and government schools on the reserves both in Canada and in the United States. Cajun French was banned in southern Louisiana by practice if not by law until about thirty years ago. Individuals over the age of fifty-five report that they were often punished in school if they spoke in French even though many of them had never heard English before attending school. Japanese movies and songs were once banned in Korea, and Færoese was banned in the Færoe Islands.

In France, a notion of the "standard" as the only correct form of the language is propagated by an official academy that determines which usages constitute the "official French language." A number of years ago, this academy enacted a law forbidding the use of "Franglais" words in advertising (words of English origin such as *le parking, le weekend*, and *le hotdog*), but the French continue to use them. Many of the hundreds of local village dialects (called *patois* [pætwɑ] by the academy) are actually separate languages, derived from Latin (as are French, Spanish, and Italian). There were political as well as misguided linguistic motivations behind the efforts to maintain only one official language.

In the past (and to some extent in the present), anyone from the provinces who wished to succeed in French society had to learn Parisian French and be bidialectal. In recent years in France, the regional "nationalist" movements have made a major demand for the right to use their own languages in their schools and for official business. In the section of France known as l'Occitanie, the popular singers sing in the regional language, Languedoc, both as a protest against the official "standard language" policy and as part of the cultural revival movement. Here is the final chorus of a popular song sung in Languedoc (shown below with its French and English translations):

Languedoc	French	English
Mas perqué, perqué	Mais pourquoi, pourquoi	But why, why
M'an pas dit à l'escóla	Ne m'a-t-on pas dit à l'école	Did they not speak to me at school
La lega de mon pais?	La langue de mon pays?	The language of my country?

In the province of Brittany in France, there has also been a strong movement for the use of Breton in the schools, as opposed to the "standard" French. Breton is not even in the same language family as French, which is a Romance language; Breton is a Celtic language in the same family as Irish, Gaelic, and Welsh. It is not, however, the structure of the language or the genetic family grouping that has led to the Breton movement. It is rather the pride of a people who speak a language or a dialect not considered as good as the "standard" and their efforts to change this political view of language use.

These efforts have proved successful. In 1982, the newly elected French government decreed that the languages and cultures of Brittany (Breton), the southern Languedoc region, and other areas would be promoted through schooling, exhibitions, and festivals. No longer would schoolchildren who spoke Breton be humiliated by having to wear a wooden shoe tied around their necks, as had been the custom.

In recent decades in the United States, a movement arose in the attempt to establish English as an official language by amending the Constitution. An "Official English" initiative was passed by the electorate in California in 1986, in Colorado, Florida, and Arizona in 1988, and in Alabama in 1990. Such measures have also been adopted by over twenty state legislatures. This kind of linguistic chauvinism is opposed by minority group advocates who point out that such measures prevent large numbers of non-English speakers from participating in the electoral process if ballots and other educational material are printed only in English. Leading educators also oppose such moves, since they could halt programs in bilingual education that are proving to be effective as means both to educate nonnative speakers and to aid their acquisition of English.

The Preservation and Revival of Languages

The attempts to ban certain languages and dialects should not be equated with the efforts by certain peoples to preserve their own languages and cultures. This attempt to slow down or reverse the dying out of a language is evident in the concern of Quebec to preserve and promote the province's French language and heritage. Francophones of Quebec, Acadians of New Brunswick, Franco-Ontarians, and Francophones in scattered communities across Western Canada (where they make up less than 3 percent of the population [Yalden, 1984] — islands of French in a sea of English) feel pressure upon their language and culture. The dominance of English, even in an officially bilingual Canada, imposes itself upon the consciousness of Francophones in a way unimaginable to Anglophones.

"Bill 101" of the Quebec National Assembly, which established French as the official language of the province, was designed to defend Francophones — within "la belle province" at least — from assimilation into the "English community" by insisting on French in all official acts, from the laws of the province and agencies down to the use of French on signs and menus. It also directs that all children be educated in French unless one of their parents was educated in English in Quebec. It further mandates the "francization" of businesses with more than fifty employees, and a bureau has been established "to keep a watch on language developments in Quebec with respect to the status and quality of the French language" and to "apprise the Minister of the questions pertaining to language that in its opinion require attention or action by the Government" (*Préfixe du recueil des lois de 1977*, 1977).

As one historian of Canadian English has observed, "the relationship between the two languages [French and English] dominates the linguistic and often the political scene throughout the country" (Fee, 1992). It is not easy to establish a bilingual and multicultural country, and there are those who might prefer the establishment of two distinct language areas (if not two countries). But, despite the shrillness of some opponents, most Canadians are supportive of bilingualism and, on the whole, believe that the existence of the two official languages adds to the quality of the nation, as a 1991 report discovered (*Annual Report of the Commissioner of Official Languages 1991*, 1992).

Efforts have been made in the past half-century not only to secure threatened languages, such as French in Quebec, but also to resurrect languages long dead. A dramatic example of this restoration of a language occurred in Israel. An Academy of the Hebrew Language in Israel was established to accomplish a task never before done in the history of humanity — to revive an ancient written language to serve the daily colloquial needs of the people. Twenty-three lexicologists work with the Bible and the Talmud in order to add new words to the language. While there is some attempt to keep the language "pure," the academy has given way to popular pressure. Thus, a bank cheque is called a *check* /ček/ in the singular and is pluralized by adding the Hebrew suffix to form *check-im*, although the Hebrew word *hamcha* was proposed. Similarly, *lipstick* has triumphed over *faton* and *pajama* over *chalifatsheina*.

African American English

> The language, only the language. . . . It is the thing that black people love so
> much — the saying of words, holding them on the tongue, experimenting
> with them, playing with them. It's a love, a passion. Its function is like a
> preacher's: to make you stand up out of your seat, make you lose yourself and
> hear yourself. The worst of all possible things that could happen would be to
> lose that language.
>
>   Toni Morrison, interview in *The New Republic* (March 21, 1981)

Most of the regional dialects of North America are, to a great extent, free from stigma even though they may be parodied — often quite inexactly — by members of other dialect groups. In the United States, the *r*-less Brooklynese or the "drawl" of Southerners is singled out for "humorous" treatment, as is the Ottawa Valley dialect or the rural speech of Maritimers in Canada. One dialect in the United States, however, has been a victim of prejudice. This dialect, **African American English (AAE)**,[3] is spoken by a large number of Americans of African descent. African American English is actually a group of closely related dialects also called African American Vernacular English, Black English (BE), Inner City English, and Ebonics.

What most Canadians know about African American English — or what passes for this dialect of English — has probably come to them through films in which it is carefully modified to prevent misunderstanding and confusion. The true dialect is found primarily in the large inner cities of the United States.

The distinguishing features of the dialect persist for social, educational, and economic reasons. Discrimination has created ghetto living and segregated schools, and where social isolation exists dialect differences are intensified. In recent years, many African Americans no longer think of their dialect as inferior, and for them it has become a means of positive identification. Similarly, in England, Jamaican "patois," differing considerably from AAE, has been used by younger people (most of whom also use Received Pronunciation or one of the dialects of British English) as a social and psychological protest against their treatment by society (Edwards, 1989).

Some critics attempt to equate the use of AAE with inferior genetic intelligence and cultural deprivation, justifying these notions by stating that AAE is a "deficient, illogical, and incomplete" language. Such epithets cannot be applied to any language, and they are as unscientific in reference to AAE as they would be to Russian, Chinese, Standard American English, or Canadian English.

Some people, of every race, have thought that they could identify race by hearing an unseen person talk, believing that different races inherently speak differently. This assumption is equally false; a Black child raised in an upper-class British neighbourhood will speak that dialect of English, as many British citizens of West Indian background prove daily. A white child raised in an environment where African American English is spoken will speak African American English. Children construct grammar based on the language they hear.

As with any dialect, there are systematic differences between AAE and other forms of English, just as there are systematic differences between Australian and Canadian English or Canadian and American English. AAE is discussed here at some length because it provides an informative illustration of the regularities of a dialect as well as of that dialect's systematic differences from the standard language. A vast body of research shows that there are the same kinds of linguistic differences between AAE and SAE or SCE as occur between many of the world's major dialects.

Phonology of African American English

A few of the differences and similarities between AAE and dialects of Canadian English are as follows:

1. Like a number of dialects of British and American English, AAE includes a rule that deletes /r/ everywhere except before a vowel. Pairs of words such as *guard* and *god, nor* and *gnaw, sore* and *saw, poor* and *pa, fort* and *fought*, and *court* and *caught* are pronounced identically in AAE because of this phonological rule in the grammar.

2. There is also an *l-deletion rule* for some speakers of AAE that creates homophones such as *toll* and *toe, all* and *awe*, and *help* and *hep*. AAE is not unique in this rule, for deletion rules of one form or another are common in English dialects; Torontonians refer to their city as [trʌnə] or [trɑnə] rather than

[tʰəɹɑnto]. They are, in fact, applying a medial cluster simplification rule, one that commonly deletes /t/ after /n/. Moreover, many speakers of Canadian and American English (CE and AE) normally delete nasals before final voiceless stops.

3. A regular *consonant cluster simplification rule* in AAE reduces a sequence of two or more consonants, particularly those occurring at the ends of words and when one of the two consonants is an alveolar (/t/, /d/, /s/, /z/). The application of this rule may delete the past-tense morpheme so that *meant* and *mend* are both pronounced as *men* and *past* and *passed* may both be pronounced as *pass*.

This deletion rule does not always apply, and studies have shown that it is more likely to apply when the final [t] or [d] does not represent the past-tense morpheme, as in nouns such as *paste* [pes] as opposed to verbs such as *chased* [čest], where the final past tense [t] will not always be deleted. This has also been found true with final [s] or [z], which will be retained by speakers of AAE more in words such as *seats* /sit + s/ where the /s/ represents "plural" than in words such as *Keats* /kit/ where it is more likely to be deleted.

Again, some Newfoundland speakers also simplify final consonant clusters ending in /t/ or /d/ in words such as *loft, sound,* and *field.* As this indicates, deletion and cluster simplification rules of one form or another are not uncommon in English dialects.

4. AAE shares with many regional dialects the lack of any distinction between /ɪ/ and /ɛ/ before nasal consonants, producing identical pronunciations of *pin* and *pen, bin* and *Ben, tin* and *ten,* and so on. The vowel used in these words is roughly between the [ɪ] of *pit* and the [ɛ] of *pet.*

5. In AAE the phonemic distinction between /aj/ and /aw/ has been lost, both having become /a/. Thus, *why* and *wow* are pronounced [wa].

6. Another change has reduced the /ɔj/ (particularly before /l/) to the simple vowel [ɔ] without the glide, so that *boil* and *boy* are pronounced [bɔ].

7. A regular feature is the change of a /θ/ to /f/ and /ð/ to /v/, so that *Ruth* is pronounced [ruf] and *brother* is pronounced [brʌvər]. This [θ]–[f] correspondence is also true of some dialects of British English, in which /θ/ is not even a phoneme in the language. *Think* is regularly [fiŋk] in Cockney English.

All these differences are systematic and rule governed and similar to sound changes that have taken place in languages all over the world, including Standard English.

Syntactic Differences between AAE, AE, and CE

Syntactic differences, as noted above, also exist between dialects. It is the syntactic differences that have often been used to illustrate the "illogic" of AAE, yet just such differences point to the fact that AAE is as syntactically complex and as "logical" as AE or CE.

Double Negatives

Following the lead of early prescriptive grammarians, some linguists have concluded that it is illogical to say *he don't know nothing* because two negatives make a positive despite the obvious disagreement of those who use the double negative. Indeed, there are few speakers of English, no matter of what dialect, who would think that the above sentence means *He knows something*. Multiple negation was the standard in an earlier stage of English, and Shakespeare for one was certainly not reluctant to use double negatives. It remains a regular rule for speakers of French and many other languages.

Deletion of the Verb Be

In most cases, if in Standard English the verb can be contracted, in African American English sentences it is deleted, as in the following sentences from Labov (1969):

AE and CE	AAE
He is nice/He's nice.	He nice.
They are mine/They're mine.	They mine.
I am going to do it/I'm gonna do it.	I gonna do it.

Habitual Be

In both AAE and some Newfoundland dialects, a form of the verb *be* is used when a speaker is referring to habitual action. In a sentence such as

> Aidan is happy.

a speaker of Standard Canadian English recognizes at least two possible meanings. It might mean that Aidan is happy at the present moment, or it could mean that he is generally happy. To disambiguate the sentence, a speaker of Standard English would have to employ lexical means, adding a word or two:

> Aidan is generally happy.
> Aidan is happy today.

But both AAE and some Newfoundland dialects can accomplish this disambiguation syntactically by using the verb *be*:

AAE	Newfoundland	
Aidan be happy.	Aidan bees happy.	("Aidan is always happy.")
Aidan happy.	Aidan's happy. / Aidan is happy now.	("At this moment, Aidan is happy.")

In this Newfoundland dialect, there is no provision for deleting the verb when it refers to an event at the present moment; instead, it employs the standard forms *am, is*, and *are*. But *-s* appears in all persons of the verb *be* — *I bes/bees, she bes/bees,* *they bes/bees* — used for "habitual or continuous action," and consequently it is not, as in Standard English, a marker of the third person, present tense.

This syntactic distinction between habitual and nonhabitual aspect occurs in other languages but not in Standard English. It has been suggested that the uninflected *be* in AAE is the result of a convergence of similar rules in African, Creole, and Irish-English sources (Holm, 1988–1989). African and Creole sources could not explain the similar use of *be* in Maritime Canada; on the other hand, "habitual *be*" may reflect an important strain in Newfoundland English and point to a common influence in AAE and Newfoundland English, dialects of two otherwise different cultures: the influence of the English of southeastern Ireland. Students of Irish-English, Hiberno-English, or Anglo-Irish, as it is variously called, record a similar "habitual present" tense in that dialect (Adams, 1985), and Alan Bliss (1984) notes the common use of *I be, you be*, and *he bees* in this manner, though he reports that *I do be, you do be*, and *he does be* are in more general use. William Kirwin (1993) finds that the "habitual *be*" is "of great frequency" in Newfoundland and that "a variant, *do be*, has been reported very frequently in the negative, for example, 'Don't be talking!' " Perhaps, then, one connection between African American speech (though certainly influenced strongly by the languages of Africa) and the dialects of Newfoundland is found in the speech of immigrants from the Emerald Isle.

There are, of course, other differences and similarities between the dialects we have been discussing, but those listed are enough to show the regularity of AAE (and of the other dialects) and to dispel the notion that there is anything "illogical" or "primitive" about any one of them.

The structure and history of any dialect reveals important information about language change in general, a subject that we discuss in the next chapter. In addition, the history of AAE reveals how social prejudices can distort our perceptions of language. There would be fewer communication breakdowns between teachers and their students if certain dialects were not considered inferior versions of the standard. Children who read *your mother* as *you muvver* or who say *I ain't got no . . .* would be more likely to respond positively to statements such as "In the dialect we are using, the *th* sound is pronounced [ð], not [v], as it is in yours" or that double negatives, though once common in English, are no longer used in the dialect they are learning in school than to a teacher who expresses contempt toward them and their speech.

History of African American English

It is simple to date the beginning of African American English — the first African Americans arrived in Virginia in 1619, and the history of slavery in what is now Canada goes back to these early years as well. Ten years after the arrival of African Americans in Virginia, Oliver Le Jeune, one of the first slaves for whom there is a name, was sold into slavery in New France. Many Loyalists were slave holders and brought slaves with them into British North America. But in addition to slaves, a large number of African Americans who earned their freedom through loyalty to the Crown immigrated to Nova Scotia and New Brunswick after the American Revolution. In 1833, Parliament in London abolished slavery in British North America, though the practice had been under severe restrictions in many parts of the country before that date. Upper Canada restricted slavery in 1793, with the intention of abolishing it. Because of such laws, escaping slaves sought refuge in Canada before and during the American Civil War, though many — if not most — returned to their homes in the United States afterward.

With changes in discriminatory immigration laws, the last half of the twentieth century brought increased immigration from the Caribbean and Africa. Most of these new Canadians continue to speak the English of their former homes, or they — and certainly their children — will have adopted Canadian English after settling in their new country. While AAE in the United States has been subjected to intense study in the past few decades, investigation of the English of Black Canadians has been slight. In part this is due to the smaller size of the Black community (approximately 2 percent of the population), in part to the perception that Black citizens have completely assimilated themselves into the general language community and speak the English of their white neighbours. Like many facets of Canadian English, however, this is an area that remains largely unexplored.

Nonetheless, there are communities, settled by Loyalist Blacks and those fleeing from slavery, that have been largely segregated from the surrounding white neighbourhoods and that may reflect earlier forms of AAE. Linguists have begun to explore the nature of the English spoken in these areas in an effort to determine exactly how these dialects relate to the AAE of the United States (Poplack & Tagliamonte, 1993) and to better understand the dialects of Canadian English.

The history and structure of AAE, then, are almost entirely based on a dialect that has been studied in the United States, where at least two views of the origin of that dialect are evident. One view suggests that AAE in North America originated when the African slaves learned English from their colonial masters as a second language. Although the basic grammar was learned, many surface differences persisted, which were reflected in the grammars constructed by the children of the slaves, who heard English primarily from their parents. Had the children been exposed to the English spoken by the whites, their grammars would have been similar if not identical to the general Southern dialect. The dialect differences persisted and grew because African Americans were isolated by social and racial barriers. The proponents of this theory point to the fact that the grammars of African American English and Standard American English are basically identical except for a few syntactic and phonological rules, which produce surface differences.

Another view that is receiving increasing support is that many of the unique features of African American English are traceable to influences of the African languages spoken by the slaves. During the seventeenth and eighteenth centuries, Africans who spoke different languages were purposely grouped together to discourage communication and to prevent slave revolts. In order to communicate, the slaves were forced to use the one common language all had access to, namely English. They invented a simplified form — called a pidgin — that incorporated many features from West African languages. According to this view, the differences between AAE and other dialects are due more to deep syntactic differences than to surface distinctions.

It is apparent that African American English of the United States is closer to the Southern dialect of American English than to other dialects. The theory that suggests that the slaves learned the English of white Southerners as a second language explains these similarities. They might also be explained by the fact that for many decades a large number of Southern white children were raised by African American women and played with their children. It is not unlikely that many of the distinguishing features of Southern dialects were acquired from African American English in this way. A publication of the American Dialect Society in 1908–09 makes this point clearly:

> For my part, after a somewhat careful study of east Alabama dialect, I am convinced that the speech of the white people, the dialect I have spoken all my life and the one I tried to record here, is more largely colored by the language of the negroes [sic] than by any other single influence. (Payne, 1909)

English, both inside and outside the borders of the United States, has been and continues to be enriched by the words, phrases, and usages originating in AAE. Disseminated through the power of film and television, it affects English throughout the world.

Lingua Francas

Language is a steed that carries one into a far country.
Arab proverb

In medieval times, a trade language came into use in Mediterranean ports based largely on the medieval languages that became modern Italian and Provençal. This language came to be called **lingua franca**, "Frankish language," and was used by common agreement for social or commercial communication between people speaking divergent languages. Subsequently, the term has been generalized to mean any language similarly used. English has been called "the lingua franca of diplomacy," and Latin and Greek were the lingua francas of Christianity in the West and East, respectively, for a millennium. Among Jews, Yiddish has long served as a lingua franca.

More frequently, lingua francas serve as "trade languages." East Africa is populated by hundreds of groups, each speaking its own language, but most Africans of this area learn at least some Swahili as a second language, and this lingua franca is used and understood in nearly every marketplace. A similar situation exists in West Africa, where Hausa is the lingua franca.

Hindi and Urdu are the lingua francas of India and Pakistan, respectively. The linguistic situation of this area of the world is so complex that there are often regional lingua francas — usually the popular dialects near commercial centres. The same situation existed in Imperial China.

In modern China, the Chinese language as a whole is often referred to as *Zhongwen*, which technically refers to the written language, whereas *Zhongguo hua* refers to the spoken language. Ninety-four percent of the people living in the People's Republic of China are said to speak Han languages, which can be divided into eight major dialects (or language groups) that for the most part are mutually unintelligible. Within each group, there are hundreds of dialects. In addition to these Han languages, there are more than fifty "national minority" languages, including the five principal ones: Mongolian, Uighur, Tibetan, Zhuang, and Korean. The situation is clearly complex, and for this reason an extensive language reform policy was inaugurated to spread a standard language, called *Putonghua*, that embodies the pronunciation of the Beijing dialect, the grammar of Northern Chinese dialects, and the vocabulary of modern colloquial Chinese. The native languages and dialects are not considered inferior; rather, the approach is to spread the "common speech" (the literal meaning of *Putonghua*) so that all may communicate with each other in this lingua franca.

Certain lingua francas arise naturally; others are developed by government policy and intervention. In many places of the world, however, people still cannot speak with neighbours only a few kilometres away.

Pidgins and Creoles

Padi dɛm; kɔntri; una ɔl we de na Rom.
Mɛk una ɔl kak una yes. A Kam bɛr siza,
a nɔ kam prez am.
William Shakespeare, *Julius Caesar*, III.ii, translated to Krio by Thomas Decker

I include "pidgin-English" . . . even though I am referred to in that splendid language as "Fella belong Mrs. Queen."
Prince Philip, husband of Queen Elizabeth II

Pidgins

A lingua franca is typically a language with a broad base of native speakers, likely to be used and learned by persons whose native language is in the same language family. Often in history, however, traders and missionaries from one part of the world have visited and attempted to communicate with peoples residing in another area. In such cases, the contact is too specialized and the cultures are too widely separated for the usual kind of lingua franca to arise. Instead, the two (or possibly more) groups use their native languages as a basis for a rudimentary language of few lexical items and less complex grammatical rules. Such a "marginal language" is called a **pidgin**.

There are a number of such languages in the world, including a large number of English-based pidgins. One such pidgin, called Tok Pisin, was originally called

Melanesian Pidgin English. It is widely used in Papua New Guinea. Like most pidgins, many of its lexical items and much of its structure are based on only one language of the two or more contact languages, in this case English. The variety of Tok Pisin used as a primary language in urban centres is more highly developed and more complex than the Tok Pisin used as a lingua franca in remote areas. Papers in Tok Pisin have been presented at linguistics conferences in Papua New Guinea, and it is commonly used for debates in the parliament of the country.

Although pidgins are in some sense rudimentary, they are not devoid of grammar. The phonological system is rule governed, as in any human language. The inventory of phonemes is generally small, and each phoneme may have many allophonic pronunciations. In Tok Pisin, for example, [č], [š], and [s] are all possible pronunciations of the phoneme /s/; [masin], [mašin], and [mačin] all mean "machine."

Tok Pisin has its own writing system, its own literature, and its own newspapers and radio programs, and it has even been used to address a United Nations meeting.

With their small vocabularies, however, pidgins are not good at expressing fine distinctions of meaning. Many lexical items bear a heavy semantic burden, with context being relied upon to remove ambiguity. Much circumlocution and metaphorical extension is necessary. All of these factors combine to give pidgins a unique flavour. What could be a friendlier definition of "friend" than the Australian Aborigine's *him brother belong me* or more poetic than this description of the sun: *lamp belong Jesus*? A policeman is *gubmint catchum-fella*, whiskers are *grass belong face*, and when a man is thirsty *him belly allatime burn*.

Pidgin has come to have negative connotations, perhaps because the best-known pidgins are all associated with European colonial empires. The *Encyclopedia Britannica* once described Pidgin English as "an unruly bastard jargon, filled with nursery imbecilities, vulgarisms and corruptions." It no longer uses such a definition. In recent times, there is greater recognition of the fact that pidgins reflect human creative linguistic ability, as is beautifully revealed by the Chinese servant who asked whether his master's prize sow had given birth to a litter: *Him cow pig have kittens*? as well as the description of Prince Philip quoted in the epigraph to this section.

Some people would like to eradicate pidgins. A pidgin spoken in New Zealand by the Maoris was replaced, through massive education, by Standard English, and the use of Chinese Pidgin English was forbidden by the government of China. Its use had died out by the end of the nineteenth century because the Chinese gained access to learning Standard English, which proved to be more useful in communicating with non-Chinese speakers.

Pidgins have been unjustly maligned; they may serve a useful function (Hall, 1955). For example, a New Guinean can learn Tok Pisin well enough in six months to begin many kinds of semiprofessional training. To learn English for the same purpose might require ten times as long. In an area with more than 800 mutually unintelligible languages, Tok Pisin plays a vital role in unifying similar cultures.

From the seventeenth through the nineteenth centuries, many pidgins sprang up along the coasts of China, Africa, and the New World to accommodate the Europeans. Chinook Jargon is a pidginized North American Native language used by various tribes of the Pacific Northwest to carry on trade. Some linguists have suggested that Proto-Germanic (the earliest form of the Germanic languages) was originally a pidgin, arguing that ordinary linguistic change cannot account for certain striking differences between the Germanic tongues and other Indo-European languages. They theorized that in the first millennium B.C.E. the primitive Germanic tribes that resided along the Baltic Sea traded with the more sophisticated, seagoing cultures. The two peoples communicated by means of a pidgin, which either grossly affected Proto-Germanic or actually became Proto-Germanic. If this is true, then English, German, Dutch, and Yiddish had humble beginnings as a pidgin.

Case, tense, mood, and voice are generally absent from pidgins. One cannot, however, speak an English pidgin by merely using English without inflecting verbs or declining pronouns. Pidgins are not "baby talk" or Hollywood's version of North American Natives talking English. *Me Tarzan, you Jane* may be understood, but it is not pidgin as it is used in West Africa.

Pidgins are simple but nonetheless rule governed. In Tok Pisin, most verbs that take a direct object must have the suffix *-m* or *-im*, even if the direct object is absent; here are some examples of the results of the application of this "rule" of the language:

Tok Pisin: Mi driman long kilim wanpela snek.
English: I dreamed that I killed a snake.

Tok Pisin: Bandarap em i kukim.
English: Bandarap cooked (it).

Other rules determine word order, which, as in English, is usually quite strict in pidgins because of the lack of case endings on nouns.

The set of pronouns may, in some cases, be simpler in pidgins than in English. In Cameroonian Pidgin (CP), which is also an English-based pidgin, the pronoun system does not show gender or all the case differences that exist in Standard English (data from Todd, 1984):

CP			SE		
a	mi	ma	I	me	my
yu	yu	yu	you	you	your
i	i/am	i	he	him	his
i	i/am	i	she	her	her
wi	wi	wi	we	us	our
wuna	wuna	wuna	you	you	your
dɛm	dɛm/am	dɛm	they	them	their

Pidgins may also have fewer prepositions than the languages on which they are based. In CP, for example, *fɔ* means "to," "at," "in," "for," "on," and "from," as shown in the following examples:

Gif di buk fɔ mi.   "Give the book to me."
I dei fɔ fam.   "She is at the farm."
Dɛm dei fɔ chɔs.   "They are in the church."

Du dis wan fɔ mi, a bɛg.	"Do this for me, please."
Di-mɔni dei fɔ tebul.	"The money is on the table."
You fit muf tɛn frangk fɔ ma kwa.	"You can take ten francs from my bag."

Characteristics of pidgins differ in detail from one pidgin to another and often vary depending on the native language of the pidgin speaker. Thus, the verb generally comes at the end of a sentence for a Japanese speaker of Hawaiian Pidgin English (as in *The poor people all potato eat*), whereas a Filipino speaker of this pidgin puts it before the subject (*Work hard these people*).

Creoles

One distinguishing characteristic of pidgin languages is that no one learns them as native speakers. When a pidgin comes to be adopted by a community as its native tongue, and children learn it as a first language, that language is called a **creole**; the pidgin has become creolized.

> Some creoles, such as Haitian (Haiti), Papiamentu (Curacao, Aruba, and Bonaire), Mauritian (Mauritius), and Tok Pisin (Papua New Guinea), have become national languages.

The term *creole* comes originally from the Portuguese word meaning "a white man of European descent born and raised in a tropical or semitropical colony.... The term was ... subsequently applied to certain languages spoken ... in and around the Caribbean and in West Africa, and then more generally to other similar languages" (Romaine, 1988, p. 38).

Creoles often arose on slave plantations in certain areas where Africans speaking different languages could communicate only via the plantation pidgin. Haitian Creole, based on French, developed this way, as did the "English" spoken in parts of Jamaica. Gullah is an English-based creole spoken by the descendants of African slaves on islands off the coasts of Georgia and South Carolina. Louisiana Creole, related to Haitian Creole, is spoken by large numbers of African Americans and whites in Louisiana. Krio, the language spoken by as many as 200,000 Sierra Leoneans, developed, at least in part, from an English-based pidgin.

Creoles become fully developed languages, having more lexical items and a broader array of grammatical distinctions than pidgins. In time, they become languages as complete in every way as other languages.

The study of pidgins and creoles has contributed a great deal to our understanding of the nature of human language and the genetically determined constraints on grammar.

Styles, Code Switching, Slang, and Jargon

Styles

Most speakers of a language know many dialects. They use one dialect when out with friends, another when in a job interview or presenting a report, and yet another when talking with family. These "situational dialects" — that is, those varieties of language one uses in specific social settings — are called **styles** or **registers**.

Nearly everyone has at least an informal and a formal style. Informal styles, although permitting certain abbreviations and deletions not permitted in formal speech, are also rule governed. The informal style employs the rules of contraction more often than the formal styles does, the syntactic rules of negation and agreement may be altered, and many words are used that do not occur in the formal style. Questions are often shortened with the *you* subject and the auxiliary deleted. One can ask *Running the marathon?* or *You running the marathon?* instead of the more formal *Are you running the marathon?*, but one cannot shorten the question to **Are running the marathon?* Everything doesn't go in informal talk, but the rules permit greater deletion than do the rules in the grammar of the formal language.

Many speakers can use a number of different styles, ranging between the two extremes of formal and informal. Speakers of minority dialects sometimes display virtuosic ability to slide back and forth along a continuum of styles from informal to "formal standard." When William Labov was studying the language of Black Harlem youths, he encountered difficulties because the youths (subconsciously) adopted a different style when in the presence of white strangers. It took time and effort to gain their confidence to the point where they would "forget" that their conversations were being recorded and thus use their less formal style.

Many cultures have rules of social behaviour that strictly govern style. In some European languages, there is the distinction between "you (familiar)" and "you (polite)." German *du* and French *tu* are to be used only with "intimates" and children, or the words may be construed as insulting; *Sie* and *vous* are more formal and used with nonintimates. French even has the verb *tutoyer*, which means "to use the *tu* form," and German uses the verb *duzen* to express the informal or less honorific style of speaking.

Other languages have much more elaborate codes of style usage. Speakers of Thai use *kin* "eat" informally with their intimates, but *thaan* is used informally with strangers, *rabprathaan* on formal occasions or when conversing with dignitaries or esteemed persons (such as parents), and *chan* when referring to Buddhist monks. Japanese and Javanese are also languages with elaborate styles that must be adhered to in certain social situations.

Code Switching

Speakers are not confined to one variety of speech, formal or informal, but often move from one variety of English to another or even from one language to another and sometimes do so within the same discourse. This movement between varieties or languages is called **code switching** and may occur in the midst of a sentence. Take, for example, the following sentences:

> Jim asked me to go to the pub with him tonight. He's a nice enough chap, and I like him — but, like, no way!

> The government claims that this bill will easily pass, but I wish to inform my honourable friends across the aisle — it ain't gonna happen!

In both instances, the switch from a more formal variety to "substandard" English serves to underline the speakers' negative responses.

Switching also occurs between languages; a young child, for example, was overheard on a Kitchener, Ontario, bus excitedly exclaiming, "Guck, Mutti, da fahrt ein police car" ("Look, Mummy, there goes a police car"), moving easily from colloquial German to English in the same sentence.

Among the many German-speaking people of the Kitchener–Waterloo area are a large number who employ as their mother tongue a low-German dialect similar to that known as "Pennsylvania Dutch" in the United States. This is not surprising, for their ancestors came to Ontario in the early nineteenth century from Pennsylvania seeking good farming land and freedom to practise their religion. The "Old Order" of Mennonites reject modern ways and modern devices, and their German dialect is the everyday speech of young and old alike. Most also have a working knowledge of English, which they reserve for use in the English-speaking world of town and business. When people employ different varieties of the same language or two distinct languages for different purposes in this fashion, they are said to be *diglossic*. Another instance of diglossia are the Francophones outside Quebec who live among largely English-speaking people; these people will probably restrict their use of their mother tongue, employing French in the home and among French-speaking friends, while using English for business and for the non-Francophone world around them.

Slang

> Slang is language which takes off its coat, spits on its hands — and goes to work.
>
> Carl Sandburg (1878–1967), American Poet

> In Canada we have enough to do keeping up with two spoken languages without trying to invent slang, so we just go right ahead and use English for literature, Scotch for sermons, and American for conversation.
>
> Stephen Leacock (1869–1944)

One mark of an informal style is the frequent occurrence of **slang**. Almost everyone uses slang on some occasions, but it is not easy to define the word. Slang has been defined as "one of those things that everybody can recognize and nobody can define" (Roberts, 1958, p. 342). The use of slang, or colloquial language, introduces many new words into the language by recombining old words into new meanings. *Spaced out, right on, hangup*, and *rip-off* have all gained a degree of acceptance. Slang may also introduce an entirely new word, such as *barf, flub*, and *pooped*. Finally, slang often consists of ascribing totally new meanings to old words. *Grass* and *pot* widened their meaning to "marijuana"; *pig* and *fuzz* are derogatory terms for "police officer"; *rap, cool, dig, stoned, bread, split*, and *gay* have all extended their semantic domain.

The words we have cited sound "slangy" because they have not gained total acceptability. Words such as *dwindle, freshman, glib*, and *mob* are former slang words that in time overcame their "unsavoury" origin. It is not always easy to know where to draw the line between "slang" words and "regular" words. This confusion seems always to have been around. In 1890, Farmer and Henley in *Slang and Its Analogues* (1965), remarked that "the borderland between slang and the 'Queen's English' is an ill-defined territory, the limits of which have never been clearly mapped out."

One generation's slang is another generation's standard vocabulary. *Fan* (as in "Leafs fan"[4]) was once a slang term, short for *fanatic*. *Phone*, too, was once a slangy, clipped version of *telephone*, as *TV* was of *television*. In Shakespeare's time, *fretful* and *dwindle* were slang, and more recently *blimp* and *hotdog* were both "hard-core" slang.

The use of slang varies from region to region, so slang in New York and slang in Vancouver differ. The word *slang* itself is slang in British English for "scold."

Slang words and phrases are often "invented" in keeping with new ideas and customs. They may represent "in" attitudes better than the more conservative items of the vocabulary. Their importance is shown by the fact that it was thought necessary to give the returning American prisoners of war from Vietnam a glossary of eighty-six new slang words and phrases, from *acid* to *zonked*. The words on this list — prepared by the U.S. Air Force — had come into use during only five years. Furthermore, by the time this book was published, many of the terms had passed out of the language, and many new ones have been added.

A number of slang words have entered English from the "underworld," such as *crack* for a special form of cocaine, *payola, C-note, Horseman, to hang paper* ("to write 'bum' cheques"), *sawbuck*, and so forth.

The now ordinary French word meaning "head," *tête*, was once a slang word derived from the Latin *testa*, which meant "earthen pot." Some slang words seem to hang on and on in the language, though, never changing their status from slang to "respectable." Shakespeare used the expression *beat it* to mean "scram" (or more politely, "leave!"), and *beat it* would be considered by most English speakers still to be a slang expression. Similarly, use of the word *pig* for "police officer" goes back at least as far as 1785, when a writer of the time called a Bow Street police officer a "China Street pig."

Jargon and Argot

> Police are notorious for creating new words by shortening existing ones, such as *perp* for *perpetrator, ped* for *pedestrian* and *wit* for *witness*. More baffling to court reporters is the gang member who ... might testify that he was in his *hoopty* around *dimday* when some *mud duck* with a *tray-eight* tried to *take him out of the box*. Translation: The man was in his car about dusk when a woman armed with a .38 caliber gun tried to kill him.
>
> *Los Angeles Times* (August 11, 1986)

Practically every science, profession, trade, and occupation has its own set of words, some of which are considered to be "slang" and others "technical," depending on the status of the people using these "in" words. Such words are sometimes called **jargon** or **argot**. Linguistic jargon, some of which is used in this book, consists of terms such as *phoneme, morpheme, case, lexicon, phrase structure rule*, and so on.

The existence of argots or jargons is illustrated by the story of a seaman witness being cross-examined at a trial who was asked if he knew the plaintiff. Indicating that he did not know what *plaintiff* meant brought a chide from the attorney: "You mean you came into this court as a witness and don't know what 'plaintiff' means?" Later the sailor was asked where he was standing when the boat lurched. "Abaft the binnacle" was the reply, and to the attorney's questioning stare he responded "You mean you came into this court and don't know where 'abaft the binnacle' is?"

The computer age not only ushered in a technological revolution, but also introduced a huge jargon of "computerese," including the words *modem* (a blend of *modulator* and *demodulator*), *bit* (a contraction of *binary digit*), *byte* (a collection of some number of *bits*), *floppy* (a noun or adjective referring to a flexible *disk*), *ROM* (an acronym for *read only memory*), *RAM* (an acronym for *random access memory*), *morf* (an abbreviation for the question *male or female?*), and *OOPS* (an acronym for *object oriented program systems*).

Many jargon terms pass into the standard language. Jargon, like slang, spreads from a narrow group until it is used and understood by a large segment of the population. In fact, it is not always possible to distinguish between what is jargon and what is slang, as illustrated in the book *Slang U: The Official Dictionary of College Slang* (Munro, 1990), a collection of slang used on the campus of the University of California, Los Angeles, by Professor Munro and the students in her seminar. One cannot tell from the hundreds of entries in this collection which are used solely by UCLA students, which by the definitions above would make it a UCLA student jargon. It is highly probable that the word *fossil*, meaning a "person who has been a college student for more than four years," is used in this way only on this one campus or on college campuses in general, but certainly the term *prick*, referring to a "mean, offensive, inconsiderate, rude person (usually, a male)," is used as a general slang term on and off university campuses.

Texting

txt commndmnts

1. u shall luv ur mobil fone with all ur hart
2. u & ur fone shall neva b apart
3. u shall nt lust aftr ur neibrs fone nor thiev
4. u shall b prepared @ all times 2 tXt & 2 recv
5. u shall use LOL & othr acronyms in conversatns
6. u shall b zappy with ur ast*r*sks & exc!matns!!
7. u shall abbrevi8 & rite words like theyr sed

8. u shall nt speak 2 sum1 face2face if u cn msg em insted

9. u shall nt shout with capitls XEPT IN DIRE EMERGNCY+

10. u shall nt consult a ninglish dictnry

Norman Silver

One indication of the adaptability of language is *texting*, or *Textspeak*, the language variety used with electronic communication technology such as mobile phones or in online chat sessions. One of its most common features is the use of abbreviations: *b* for *be*, *u* for *you*, and numerals, such as *8* as in *l8* for *late*.

The renowned linguist David Crystal published a glossary of texting abbreviations, *A Glossary of Textspeak and Netspeak* (2004), which includes over 500 Textspeak abbreviations. As Crystal (2008) points out, many of the abbreviations are not in common use and individuals are not consistent in their use of items. He reports as many as eight variants for *talk to you later*: *TTUL, TTUL8R, TTYL, TTYL8R, T2UL, T2UL8R, T2YL,* and *T2YL8R*.

While some people may object to the effect such abbreviated forms might have on standard language varieties, Crystal argues that texting is an excellent example of the ongoing adaptability of human language.

**"...and I'm proficient in two languages
— English and text messaging."**

Taboo or Not Taboo?

Sex is a four-letter word.

Bumper sticker slogan

An item in a newspaper once included the following paragraph:

"This is not a Sunday school, but it is a school of law," the judge said in warning the defendants he would not tolerate the "use of expletives during jury selection." "I'm not going to have my fellow citizens and prospective jurors subjected to filthy language," the judge added.

How can language be filthy? In fact, how can it be clean? The filth or beauty of language must be in the ear of the listener or in the collective ear of society.

There cannot be anything about a particular string of sounds that makes it intrinsically clean or dirty, ugly or beautiful. If you say that you *pricked* your finger when sewing, no one would raise an eyebrow; if you refer to your professor as a *prick*, the judge quoted above would undoubtedly censure this "dirty" word.

Words that are unacceptable in the United States are acceptable in Britain and vice versa. In the 1830s, when Fanny Trollope visited North America, she remarked:

Hardly a day passed in which I did not discover something or other which I had been taught to consider as natural as eating, was held in abhorrence by those around me; many words to which I had never heard an objectionable meaning attached, were totally interdicted, and the strangest paraphrastic phrases substituted.

Some of the words that were taboo at the time in the United States but not in England were *corset, shirt, leg,* and *woman.* She remarked that the word *woman* was thought to refer "only to the lower or less-refined classes of female humankind."

Certain words in all societies are considered **taboo** — they are not to be used, at least not in "polite company." The word *taboo* was borrowed from Tongan, a Polynesian language, in which it refers to acts that are forbidden or to be avoided. When an act is taboo, reference to this act may also become taboo. That is, first you are forbidden to do something; then you are forbidden to talk about it.

Which acts or words are forbidden reflect the particular customs and views of the society. Some words may be used in certain circumstances and not in others; for example, among the Zuni Natives of New Mexico, it is improper to use the word *takka,* meaning "frogs," during a religious ceremony; a complex compound word must be used instead, and literally translated it would be "several-are-sitting-in-a-shallow-basin-where-they-are-in-liquid" (Farb, 1975).

In certain societies, words that have religious connotations are considered profane if used outside formal or religious ceremonies. Christians are forbidden to "take the Lord's name in vain," and this prohibition has been extended to the use of curses, which are believed to have magical powers. Thus, *hell* and *damn* are changed to *heck* and *darn*, perhaps with the belief or hope that this change will fool the "powers that be."

In England, the word *bloody* has long been and continues to be a taboo word. The 1989 edition of the *Oxford English Dictionary*, quoting from its earlier editions (published as late as 1933), states that it has been in general colloquial use from the Restoration to about 1750; "now [it is] constantly in the mouths of the lowest classes, but by respectable people considered 'a horrid word,' on par with obscene or profane language, and usually printed in the newspapers (in police reports, etc.) 'b—y.'" While some assume that the word may originally have referred to the blood of Christ and others associate it with menstruation, the editors of the *OED* argue that

> it was at first a reference to the habits of the "bloods" or aristocratic rowdies
> of the end of the 17th and beginning of the 18th C. The phrase "bloody drunk"
> was apparently = "as drunk as a blood" (cf. "as drunk as a lord"), thence it
> was extended to kindred expressions, and at length to oaths.

And finally, "in later times, its association with bloodshed and murder (cf. a bloody battle, a bloody butcher) . . . have recommended it to the rough classes as a word that appeals to their imagination." But as the editors admit at the outset, "the origin is not quite certain." No matter what its origins, when George Bernard Shaw had Liza reject Freddie's offer of a walk across the park with "Walk! Not bloody likely. I am going in a taxi," he caused an uproar among *Pygmalion*'s 1910 audiences, and we are told that "much of the interest in the play was due to the heroine's utterance of this banned word. It was waited for with trembling, heard shudderingly" (Partridge, as cited in Johnson, 1950).

The uncertainty associated with words such as *bloody* gives us a clue about "dirty" words: people who use them often do not know why they are taboo, only that they are, and to some extent this is why they remain in the language — to give vent to strong emotions.

Words relating to sex, sex organs, and natural bodily functions make up a large part of the set of taboo words in many societies. Some languages have no native words to mean "sexual intercourse" but do borrow such words from neighbouring peoples. Other languages have many words for this common and universal act, most of which are considered taboo.

Two or more words or expressions can have the same linguistic meaning, with one being acceptable and the others causing embarrassment or horror. In English, words borrowed from Latin sound "scientific" and therefore appear to be technical and "clean," whereas native Anglo-Saxon counterparts are taboo. This fact reflects the opinion that the vocabulary used by the upper classes was superior to that used by the lower classes, a distinction going back at least to the Norman Conquest in 1066, when, as Farb (1975) puts it, "a duchess perspired and expectorated and menstruated — while a kitchen maid sweated and spat and bled."

There is no linguistic reason why the word *vagina* is "clean" whereas *cunt* is "dirty," or why *prick* or *cock* is taboo but *penis* is acknowledged as referring to part of the male anatomy, or why everyone *defecates* but only vulgar people *shit*. Many people even avoid words such as *breasts, intercourse*, and *testicles* as much as words such as *tits, fuck*, and *balls*. There is no linguistic basis for such views, but pointing out this fact does not imply advocating the use or non-use of any such words.

Euphemisms

> In our time, political speech and writing are largely the defense of the inde-
> fensible. . . . political language has to consist largely of euphemism, question-
> begging and sheer cloudy vagueness. Defenceless villages are bombarded
> from the air, the inhabitants driven out into the countryside, the cattle machine-
> gunned, the huts set on fire with incendiary bullets: this is called *pacifica-*
> *tion*. . . . Millions of peasants are robbed of their farms and sent trudging along
> the roads with no more than they can carry: this is called *transfer of popula-*
> *tion* or *rectification of frontiers*. . . . Such phraseology is needed if one wants
> to name things without calling up mental pictures of them.

George Orwell (1946)

The existence of taboo words or taboo ideas stimulates the creation of **euphemisms**. A euphemism is a word or phrase that replaces a taboo word or serves to avoid frightening or unpleasant subjects. In many societies, because death is feared, there are a number of euphemisms related to it. People are less apt to *die* and more apt to *pass on* or *pass away*. Those who take care of your *loved ones* who have passed away are more likely to be *funeral directors* than *morticians* or *undertakers*.

The use of euphemisms is not new. It is reported that the Greek historian Plutarch in the first century C.E. wrote that "the ancient Athenians . . . used to cover up the ugliness of things with auspicious and kindly terms, giving them polite and endearing names. Thus they called harlots *companions,* taxes *contributions,* and prison a *chamber.*"

NON SEQUITUR © Wiley Miller. Dist. by UNIVERSAL PRESS SYNDICATE. Reprinted with permission. All rights reserved.

While the use of euphemisms is a common occurrence, problems arise when important meanings become obscured through their use. Orwell's citation at the beginning of this section is a vivid description of the use of language to downplay the horrors of war. Recent history abounds with examples of similar attempts to cover up the destructive consequences of warfare through the sanitizing effects of euphemisms. The past few decades have contributed:

Euphemism	Meaning
collateral damage	dead civilians
soft targets	bombing of civilian targets
surgical strikes	bombing and shelling
friendly fire	killing people on your own side
shock and awe	sudden and bewildering assault by overwhelming force
military assets	bombs and missiles
service a target	bomb a target
bunker blaster	a powerfully destructive bomb that can blast through solid concrete structures
liquidate	kill
neutralize	kill
body count	the number of people killed
non-operative personnel	dead soldiers
security contractors	mercenaries
soften up	use torture to get information
permanent pre-hostility	peace

These euphemisms, as well as the difference between the accepted Latinate "genteel" terms and the "dirty" Anglo-Saxon terms, show that a word or phrase has not only a linguistic **denotative meaning** but also a **connotative meaning**, reflecting attitudes, emotions, value judgments, and so on. In learning a language, children learn which words are "taboo," and these taboo words differ from one child to another, depending on the value system accepted in the family or group in which the child grows up.

Racial and National Epithets

The use of epithets for people of a different religion, nationality, or colour tells us something about the users of these words. The word *boy* is not a taboo word when used generally, but when a twenty-year-old white man calls a forty-year-old African American man *boy*, the word takes on an additional meaning; it reflects the racist attitude of the speaker. So also words such as *frog, kike, wop, nigger*, and so forth, which express racist and chauvinist views of society. The use of verbs *to jew* or *to gyp/jip* also reflect the stereotypical views of Jews and the Romany people (the term "Gypsy" is considered derogatory). Most people do not even realize that *gyp*, which is used to mean cheat, comes from the view that the Romany people are duplicitous charlatans. In time, these words would either disappear or lose their racist connotations if bigotry and oppression ceased to exist, but they show no signs of doing so, and the continued use of such words perpetuates stereotypes, separates one people from another, and reflects racism.

Language, however, is creative, malleable, and ever changing. The very epithets used by a majority to demean a minority may be reclaimed as terms of bonding and friendship among members of the minority. Thus for some — we emphasize *some* — African Americans, the word *nigger* is used to show affection. Similarly, the ordinarily degrading word *queer* is used among *some* gay individuals as a term of endearment, as is *cripple* among *some* individuals who share a disability.

Language, Sex, and Gender

doctor, n. . . . a man of great learning
The American College Dictionary (1947)

A businessman is aggressive; a businesswoman is pushy. A businessman is good on details; she's picky. . . . He follows through; she doesn't know when to quit. He stands firm; she's hard. . . . His judgments are her prejudices. He is a man of the world; she's been around. He isn't afraid to say what is on his mind; she's mouthy. He exercises authority diligently; she's power mad. He's closemouthed; she's secretive. He climbed the ladder of success; she slept her way to the top.
From "How to Tell a Businessman from a Businesswoman," *The Balloon*,
Graduate School of Management, UCLA

The discussion of obscenities, blasphemies, taboo words, and euphemisms showed that words of a language cannot be intrinsically good or bad but may reflect individual or societal values. In addition, one speaker may use a word with positive connotations, while another may select a different word with negative connotations, to refer to the same person. For example, the same individual may be referred to as a *terrorist* by one group and as a *freedom fighter* by another. A woman may be called a *castrating female* (or *ballsy women's libber*) or may be referred to as a *courageous feminist advocate*. The words we use to refer to certain individuals or groups reflect our individual nonlinguistic attitudes and may also reflect the culture and views of society.

Language reflects sexism in society. Language itself is not sexist, just as it is not obscene, but it can connote sexist attitudes as well as attitudes about social taboos or racism.

Dictionaries often give clues to social attitudes. In the 1969 edition of the *American Heritage Dictionary*, examples used to illustrate the meanings of words include "manly courage" and "masculine charm." Women do not fare as well, as exemplified by "womanish tears" and "feminine wiles." In *Webster's New World Dictionary of the American Language* (1961), *honorarium* is defined as "a payment to a professional man for services on which no fee is set or legally obtainable."

Sections in history textbooks still in use are headed "Pioneers and Their Wives"; children read that "courageous pioneers crossed the country in covered wagons with their wives, children, and cattle." Presumably, wives are not considered to be as courageous as their husbands.

As late as the 1965–68 eleventh edition, Bowker Company (New York) was still publishing *American Men of Science: A Biographical Dictionary*. The editors were much in advance of Columbia University. Until 1972, the women's faculty toilet doors were labelled "Women," whereas the men's doors were labelled "Officers of Instruction."

Language also reflects sexism in society by the way we interpret neutral (non–gender-specific) terms. Most people, hearing *My cousin is a professor* (or *a doctor* or *the chancellor of the university* or *a steel worker*) still assume the cousin is a man. This assumption has nothing to do with the English language but a great deal to do with the fact that, historically, women have not been prominent in these positions. Similarly, if you heard someone say *My cousin is a nurse* (or *elementary school teacher* or *clerk-typist* or *housekeeper*), you would probably conclude that the speaker's cousin is a woman. It is less evident why the sentence *My neighbour is a blonde* is understood as referring to a woman; perhaps because the physical characteristics of women in our society assume greater importance than those of men.

Studies analyzing the language used by men in reference to women, which often has derogatory or sexual connotations, indicate that such terms go far back in history and sometimes enter the language with no pejorative implications but gradually gain them. Thus, from Old English *huswif*, "housewife," the word *hussy* was derived. In their original employment, "a laundress made beds, a needlewoman came to sew, a spinster tended the spinning wheel, and a nurse cared for the sick. But all apparently acquired secondary duties in some households, because all became euphemisms for a mistress or a prostitute at some time during their existence" (Schulz, 1975, pp. 66–67).

Words for women — all with abusive or sexual overtones — abound: *dish, tomato, piece, piece of ass, chick, piece of tail, bunny, pussy, pussycat, bitch, doll, slut, cow*, to name just a few. Far fewer such pejorative terms exist for men.

Marked and Unmarked Forms

Long afterward, Oedipus, old and blinded, walked the roads. He smelled a familiar smell. It was the Sphinx. Oedipus said, "I want to ask one question. Why didn't I recognize my mother?" "You gave the wrong answer," said the Sphinx. "But that was what made everything possible," said Oedipus. "No," she said. "When I asked, 'What walks on four legs in the morning, two at noon, and three in the evening,' you answered, 'Man.' You didn't say anything about woman." "When you say Man," said Oedipus, "you include women too. Everyone knows that." She said, "That's what you think."

Muriel Rukeyser, *Myth* (1978)

One striking fact about the asymmetry between male and female terms in many languages is that, when there are male–female pairs, the male form for the most part is unmarked and the female term is created by adding a bound morpheme or by compounding. We have many such examples in English:

Male	Female
prince	princess
author	authoress
count	countess
actor	actress
host	hostess
poet	poetess
heir	heiress
hero	heroine
Paul	Pauline

Since the advent of the feminist movement, many of the marked female forms have been replaced by the male forms, which are now used to refer to either sex. Thus, women, as well as men, are authors and actors and poets and heroes and heirs. Women, however, remain countesses if they are among a small group of female aristocrats in England.

Given these asymmetries, folk etymologies arise that misinterpret a number of nonsexist words. **Folk etymology** is the process, normally unconscious, whereby words or their origins are changed through nonscientific speculations or false analogies with other words. When English speakers borrowed the French word *crevisse*, for example, it became *crayfish*. The borrowers did not know that *-isse* was a feminine suffix.

Female is not the feminine form of *male* but came into English from the Latin word *femina*, with the same morpheme *fe* that occurs in the Latin *fecundas*, meaning "fertile" (originally derived from an Indo-European word meaning "to give suck to"). It entered English through the Old French word *femme* and its diminutive form *femelle*, meaning "little woman."

Other male–female gender pairs have interesting differences in meaning. Although a *governor* governs a state, a *governess* takes care of children; a *mistress*, in its most widely used meaning, is not a female master, nor is a *majorette* a female major. We talk of *unwed mothers* but not *unwed fathers*, of *career women* but not *career men*, because historically no stigma was attached to a bachelor who fathered a child, and men were supposed to have careers. It is only recently that the term *househusband* has come into being, again reflecting changes in social customs.

Possibly as a protest against the reference to new and important ideas as being *seminal* (from *semen*), Clare Booth Luce updated Ibsen's drama *A Doll's House* by having Nora tell her husband that she is pregnant "in the way only men are supposed to get pregnant." When he asks, "Men pregnant?" she replies, "With ideas. Pregnancies there (she taps her head) are masculine. And a very superior form of labor. Pregnancies here (she taps her stomach) are feminine — a very inferior form of labor."

Neutral nongender words often become compounds when the base form is associated with either sex. Thus, people talk of a *male nurse* because it is expected that a nurse will be female, and for parallel reasons we have the compound words *lady doctor, career woman*, and *woman athlete*, though these compounds now appear less frequently since women have begun to take more prominent places in formerly male-dominated fields such as medicine, business, and sports.

Other linguistic asymmetries exist, such as the fact that in North America, as well as in many other parts of the world, many wives continue to adopt their husbands' names in marriage. (Note, however, that in Quebec, provincial law stipulates that women retain their names on marriage.) This name change can be traced back to early (and, to a great extent, current) legal practices. Thus, we often refer to a woman as Mrs. Jack Fromkin, but seldom do we refer to a man as Mr. Vicki Fromkin, except in an insulting sense. We talk of Professor and Mrs. John Smith but seldom, if ever, of Mr. and Dr. Mary Jones.

It is insulting to a woman to be called a *spinster* or an *old maid*, but it is not insulting to a man to be called a *bachelor*. There is nothing inherently pejorative about the word *spinster*. The connotations reflect the different views society has about an unmarried woman as opposed to an unmarried man. It is not language that is sexist; it is society.

The Generic *He*

When Thomas Jefferson wrote in the Declaration of Independence that "all *men* are created equal" and that "governments are instituted among *men* deriving their just powers from the consent of the governed," he was not using *men* as a general term to include women. His use of the word *men* was precise at a time when women could not vote. In the sixteenth and seventeenth centuries, masculine pronouns were not used as the *generic* terms; the various forms of *he* were used when referring to males and of *she* when referring to females. The pronoun *they* was used to refer to people of either sex even if the referent was a singular noun, as shown by Lord Chesterfield's statement in 1759: "If a person is born of a gloomy temper . . . they cannot help it."

By the eighteenth century, grammarians (men to be sure) created the rule designating the male pronouns as the general term, and it wasn't until the nineteenth century that the rule was applied widely, after an act of Parliament in Britain in 1850 sanctioned its use. But this generic use of *he* was ignored. In 1879, female doctors were barred from membership in the all-male Massachusetts Medical Society on the basis that the bylaws of the organization referred to members by the pronoun *he*. The unmarked, or male, nouns also serve as general terms, as do the male pronouns. The *brotherhood of man* includes women, but *sisterhood* does not include men.

Changes in English reflect the feminist movement and the growing awareness by both men and women that language may reflect attitudes of society and reinforce stereotypes and bias. More and more the word *people* is replacing *mankind, personnel* is used instead of *manpower, nurturing* instead of *mothering*, and *to operate* instead of *to man*. *Chair* or *moderator* is used instead of *chairman* (particularly by those who do not like the "clumsiness" of *chairperson*), and terms such as *postal worker* and *firefighter* are replacing *mailman* and *fireman*.

Language and Gender

An increasing number of scholars have been conducting research on language and gender and language and sexism since 1973, when the first article specifically concerned with women and language was published in a major linguistics journal (Lakoff, 1973). Lakoff's study suggested that women's insecurity due to sexism in society resulted in more "proper" use of the rules of standard grammar than was found in the speech of men. Differences between male and female speech were also investigated.

Variations in the dialects of men and women occur in many countries around the world. In Japanese, women may choose to speak a distinct dialect even though they are fully aware of the standard dialect used by both men and women. It has been said that "seeing-eye" guide dogs in Japan are trained in English because the sex of the owner is not known in advance and because it is easier for a blind person to use English than to train the dog in both language styles.

In the Muskogean language Koasati, spoken in Louisiana, words that end in an /s/ when spoken by men end in /l/ or /n/ when used by women; for example, the word meaning "lift it" is *lakawhol* for women and *lakawhos* for men. Early explorers reported that the men and women of the Carib Aboriginals used different dialects. In Chiquita, a Bolivian language, the grammar of male language includes a noun-class gender distinction, with names for males and supernatural beings morphologically marked in one way and nouns referring to females marked in another.

Women in the Chinese province of Hunan (Jiangyong county) developed their own script called *nüshu* (or "women's writing") as early as the Tang Dynasty (618–907), according to some researchers' estimates. *Nüshu* also had a spoken form that was closely related to local dialects, but in its written form, used exclusively by women, it evolved into a distinct system of characters based on highly simplified Chinese characters. *Nüshu* material was largely written in verse and allowed women to exchange messages despite their restricted circumstances.

There is nothing inherently wrong in the development of different styles, which may include intonation, phonology, syntax, and lexicon. It is wrong, however, to continue stereotypes regarding female speech, which are more myths than truths. For example, a common stereotype is that women talk a lot, yet controlled studies show that just the opposite is true when men and women are together. That is, in mixed groups, women seem to talk less than men.

One characteristic of female speech is the higher pitch used by women, due, to a great extent, to the shorter vocal tracts of women. But research has revealed that the difference in pitch between male and female British voices was, on the average, greater than could be accounted for by physiology alone, suggesting that some social factor must be involved during the acquisition period.

This chapter has stressed the fact that language is neither good nor evil, but its use may be one or the other. If one views women or African Americans, for example, as inferior, then special speech characteristics will be viewed as inferior. Furthermore, when society itself institutionalizes such attitudes, the language reflects them. If everyone in society were truly equal, and treated as such, then there would be little concern for the asymmetries that exist in language.

Summary

Every person has an individual way of speaking called an **idiolect**. The language used by a group of speakers may also show systematic differences called a **dialect**. The dialects of a language are the mutually intelligible forms of that language that differ in systematic ways from each other. Dialects develop and are reinforced because languages change, and the changes that occur in one group or area may differ from those that occur in another. **Regional dialects** and **social dialects** develop for this reason. Some of the differences in the regional dialects of American and Canadian English may be traced to the different dialects spoken by the settlers from various parts of Britain; those from southern England who arrived first spoke one dialect, those from the north another, and of course those from Ireland and Scotland still others. In addition, the colonists who maintained close contacts with England reflected the changes occurring in British English, while earlier forms were preserved among Americans who spread westward as well as among those Loyalists who, at the conclusion of the American Revolution, moved north and, later, onto the Canadian Prairies. The study of regional dialects has produced **dialect atlases** with **dialect maps** showing the areas where specific dialectal characteristics occur in the speech of the region. Each area is delineated by a boundary line called an **isogloss**.

Dialect differences include phonological or pronunciation differences (often called **accents**), vocabulary distinctions, and syntactic rule differences. The grammar differences between dialects are not as great as their similarities, thus permitting speakers of different dialects to communicate with each other.

In many countries, one dialect or dialect group is viewed as the **standard**, such as **Received Pronunciation (RP)** in England or **Standard American English (SAE)** or **Standard Canadian English (SCE)**. While these particular dialects are not linguistically superior, they may be considered by some language "purists" to be the only "correct" form of the language. Such a view has led to the idea that some nonstandard dialects are "deficient," as is erroneously suggested regarding African American English (AAE), a dialect used by some African Americans. A study of African American English shows it to be as logical, complete, rule governed, and expressive as any other dialect and reveals that many of its features are to be found in English dialects from places as distant as Newfoundland.

Attempts to legislate the use of a particular dialect or language have been made throughout history and exist today, even extending to the banning of the use of languages other than the "accepted" one. In Quebec, concern for the preservation of French language and culture has led to strict legal enforcement of the use of French in many spheres of life.

In areas where many languages are spoken, one language may become a **lingua franca** to ease communication among the people. In other cases, where traders or missionaries or travellers need to communicate with people who speak a language unknown to them, a **pidgin** may develop, based on one language that is simplified lexically, phonologically, and syntactically. When a pidgin is widely used and is learned by children as their first language, it is creolized. The grammars of **creole** languages are similar to those of other languages, and languages of creole origin now exist in many parts of the world.

Besides regional and social dialects, speakers may use different **styles** or **registers** of their dialect depending on the context. **Slang** is not often used in formal situations or in writing but is widely used in speech; **argot** and **jargon** refer to the unique vocabulary used by professional or trade groups not shared "outside." **Texting** is an example of a recent language variety characterized by heavy recourse to abbreviations. Speakers may shift from one style to another in the course of a conversation or a sentence, a process called **code switching**.

In all societies, certain acts or behaviours are frowned on, forbidden, or considered taboo. The words or expressions referring to these **taboo** acts are then also avoided or considered "dirty." Language itself cannot be obscene or clean; the views toward specific words or linguistic expressions reflect the attitudes of a culture or society toward the behaviours and actions of the language users. At times, slang words may be taboo, whereas scientific or standard terms with the same meanings are acceptable in "polite society." Taboo words and acts give rise to **euphemisms**, words or phrases that replace the expressions to be avoided. Thus, *powder room* is a euphemism for *toilet*, which itself started as a euphemism for *lavatory*, which is now more acceptable than its replacement.

Just as the use of some words may reflect society's views toward sex, natural bodily functions, or religious beliefs, so also some words may reflect racist, chauvinist, and sexist attitudes in society. The language itself is not racist or sexist but reflects these views of various sectors of a society. Such terms, however, may perpetuate and reinforce biased views and be demeaning and insulting to those addressed. Popular movements and changes in the institutions of society may then be reflected in changes in the language.

Notes

1. Some studies of Canadian English identify six major dialect areas: Newfoundland, Maritimes, Eastern Ontario, Western Ontario, Prairies, and British Columbia. Others place Ontario and Prairies English in one grouping. Still others include British Columbia in the category, referring to the English spoken from Ontario to the Pacific coast as "General Canadian English."

2. This report is methodologically and statistically flawed, but it remains useful if handled critically.

3. *The Globe and Mail* for November 10, 1999, noted a parallel designation, "European American," as "an alternative to white." The paper cited the Knight-Ridder News Services' comment that "the language of race is constantly evolving, reflecting changing sensitivities and tastes. And in contemporary California, where the population is surging and shifting with breathtaking speed, people are once again grasping for new words to describe new racial realities."

4. Unlike tree leaves (/livz/), this hockey club is always the /lifs/.

Exercises

---

1. Each pair of words is pronounced as shown phonetically in at least one English dialect. Write in phonetic transcription your pronunciation of each word that you pronounce differently.

a.	horse	[hɔrs]	hoarse	[hors]
b.	morning	[mɔrnĩŋ]	mourning	[mornĩŋ]
c.	ice	[ʌjs]	eyes	[ajz]
d.	knife	[nʌjf]	knives	[najvz]
e.	mute	[mjut]	nude	[njud]
f.	din	[dĩn]	den	[dɛ̃n]
g.	marry	[mæri]	Mary	[meri]
h.	merry	[mɛri]	marry	[mæri]
i.	rot	[rɑt]	wrought	[rɔt]
j.	lease	[lis]	grease (v.)	[griz]
k.	what	[ʌat]	watt	[ʌɑt]
l.	ant	[ænt]	aunt	[ãnt]
m.	creek	[kʰrɪk]	creak	[kʰrik]

2. Below is a passage from *The Gospel According to St. Mark* in Cameroon English Pidgin. See how much you are able to understand before consulting the English translation given below. State some of the similarities and differences between CEP and CE.

   1. Di fos tok fo di gud nuus fo Jesus Christ God yi Pikin.
   2. I bi sem as i di tok fo di buk fo Isaiah, God yi nchinda (Prophet), "Lukam, mi a di sen man nchinda fo bifo yoa fes weh yi go fix yoa rud fan."
   3. Di vos fo som man di krai fo bush: "Fix di ples weh Papa God di go, mek yi rud tret."

Translation:

   1. The beginning of the gospel of Jesus Christ, the Son of God.
   2. As it is written in the book of Isaiah the prophet, "Behold, I send my messenger before thy face, which shall prepare thy way before thee."

3. The voice of one crying in the wilderness, "Prepare ye the way of the Lord, make his paths straight."

3. In the period from 1890 to 1904, *Slang and Its Analogues* by J.S. Farmer and W.E. Henley was published in seven volumes. The following entries are included in this dictionary. For each item, (1) state whether the word or phrase still exists; (2) if not, state what the modern slang term would be; and (3) if the word remains but its meaning has changed, provide the modern meaning.

all out: completely, as in "All out the best." (The expression goes back to as early as 1300.)

to have apartments to let: be an idiot; one who is empty-headed.

been there: in "Oh, yes, I've been there." Applied to a man who is shrewd and who has had many experiences.

belly-button: the navel.

berkeleys: a woman's breasts.

bitch: most offensive appellation that can be given to a woman, even more provoking than that of *whore*.

once in a blue moon: extremely seldom.

boss: master; one who directs.

bread: employment (1785 — "out of bread" = "out of work").

claim: to steal.

cut dirt: to escape.

dog cheap: of little worth. (Used in 1616 by Dekker: "Three things there are Dog-cheap, learning, poorman's sweat, and oathes.")

funeral: as in "It's not my funeral." "It's no business of mine."

to get over: to seduce, to fascinate.

groovy: settled in habit; limited in mind.

grub: food.

head: toilet (nautical use only).

hook: to marry.

hump: to spoil.

hush money: money paid for silence; blackmail.

itch: to be sexually excited.

jam: a sweetheart or a mistress.

to lie low: to keep quiet; to bide one's time.

to lift a leg on: to have sexual intercourse.

looby: a fool.

malady of France: syphilis (used by Shakespeare in 1599).

nix: nothing.

noddle: the head.

old: money. (1900 — "Perhaps it's somebody you owe a bit of the old to, Jack.")

to pill: talk platitudes.

pipe layer: a political intriguer; a schemer.

poky: cramped, stuffy, stupid.

pot: a quart; a large sum; a prize; a urinal; to excel.

puny: a freshman.

puss-gentleman: an effeminate.

4. Suppose someone asked you to help compile items for a new dictionary of slang. List ten "slang" words that you know, and provide a short definition for each.

5. Below are given some words used in British English for which different words are usually used in Canadian English. See if you can match the British and Canadian equivalents.

British				**Canadian**			
a.	clothes peg	i.	spanner	A.	candy	I.	elevator
b.	braces	j.	biscuits	B.	truck	J.	cop
c.	lift	k.	torch	C.	main street	K.	wake up
d.	waistcoat	l.	underground	D.	cookies	L.	trunk
e.	shop assistant	m.	high street	E.	suspenders	M.	vest
f.	sweets	n.	crisps	F.	wrench	N.	subway
g.	boot (of car)	o.	lorry	G.	flashlight	O.	clothes pin
h.	bobby	p.	knock up	H.	potato chips	P.	clerk

6. Below are sentences that might be spoken between two friends chatting informally. For each, state what the nonabbreviated full sentence in SCE would be. In addition, state in your own words (or formally if you wish) the rule or rules that derived the informal sentences from the formal ones.
   a.   Where've ya been today?
   b.   Watcha gonna do for fun?
   c.   Him go to church?
   d.   There's four books there.
   e.   Who ya wanna go with?

7. Compile a list of argot (or jargon) terms from some profession or trade (e.g., lawyer, musician, doctor, longshoreman, and so forth). Give a definition for each term in "nonjargon" language.

8. "Translate" the first paragraph of any well-known document or speech — such as Hamlet's famous soliloquy, "To be, or not to be" — into informal, colloquial language.

*9. In Column A are Cockney *rhyming* slang expressions. Match these to the items in Column B to which they refer.

A	**B**
a. drip dry	(1) balls (testicles)
b. in the mood	(2) bread
c. insects and ants	(3) ale
d. orchestra stalls	(4) cry

e. Oxford scholar   (5) food

f. strike me dead   (6) dollar

g. ship in full sail   (7) pants

Now construct your own version of Cockney rhyming slang for the following words:

h. chair

i. house

j. coat

k. eggs

l. pencil

*10. Column A lists euphemisms for words in Column B. Match each item in A with its appropriate B word.

A	**B**
a. Montezuma's revenge	(1) condom
b. joy stick	(2) genocide
c. friggin'	(3) fire employees
d. ethnic cleansing	(4) diarrhea
e. French letter (old)	(5) destroy
f. take out (military use)	(6) kill
g. holy of holies	(7) urinate
h. spend a penny (British)	(8) penis
i. ladies' cloak room	(9) die
j. knock off (from 1919)	(10) civilian deaths
k. vertically challenged	(11) vagina
l. hand in one's dinner pail	(12) women's toilet
m. sanitation engineer	(13) short
n. downsize	(14) fuckin'
o. collateral damage	(15) garbage collector

11. Find additional euphemisms in current newspaper articles or other publications and identify their meanings.

References

Adams, G.B. (1985). Linguistic cross-links in phonology and grammar. *Papers on Irish English*. Ed. P. Ó Baoill. N.p.: Irish Association for Applied Linguistics, 27–35.

Allen, H.B. (1976). *The linguistics atlas of the Upper Midwest* (Vol. 1.) Minneapolis: University of Minnesota Press.

Annual Report of the Commissioner of Official Languages 1991. (1992). Ottawa: Ministry of Supply and Services.

Avis, W.S. (1955). Speech differences along the Ontario–United States border, II. Grammar and syntax. *Journal of the Canadian Linguistic Association, 1*, 14–19.

Avis, W.S. (1956). Speech differences along the Ontario–United States border, III. Pronunciation. *Journal of the Canadian Linguistic Association, 2*, 41–59.

Avis, W.S. (1972). So eh? is Canadian, eh? *Canadian Journal of Linguistics, 17*, 89–104.

Avis, W., et al. (1967). *Dictionary of Canadianisms on historical principles.* Toronto: W.J. Gage.

Bliss, A. (1984). English in the south of Ireland. In Peter Trudgill (Ed.), *Language in the British Isles* (pp. 135–151). Cambridge, UK: Cambridge University Press.

Bolinger, D. (1980). *Language, the loaded weapon: The use and abuse of language today.* London: Longman.

Chambers, J.K. (1986). Three kinds of standard in Canadian English. In W.C. Lougheed (Ed.), *In search of the standard in Canadian English* (pp. 55–59). Kingston, ON: Queen's University, Strathy Language Unit.

Crystal, D. (1997). *The Cambridge encyclopedia of language* (2nd ed.). Cambridge, UK: Cambridge University Press.

Crystal, D. (2004). *A glossary of textspeak and netspeak.* Edinburgh: Edinburgh University Press.

Crystal, D. (2008). Texting. *ELT Journal, 62*, (1), 77–83.

Edwards, V. (1989). Patois and the politics of protest: Black English in British classrooms. In O. Garcia & R. Othegvy (Ed.), *English across cultures/cultures across English* (pp. 359–372). Berlin: Mouton de Gruyter.

Farb, P. (1975). *Word play.* New York: Bantam.

Farmer, J.S., & Henley, W.E. (1965). *Slang and its analogues.* (Reprinted. 7 vols. 1890–1904). New York: Krauss Reprints.

Fee, M. (1992). Canadian English. In T. McArthur & F. McArthur (Eds.), *The Oxford companion to the English language* (pp. 179–183). Oxford: Oxford University Press.

Geike, A.C. (1857). Canadian English. *The Canadian Journal of Industry, Science, and Art.*

Hall, R.A. (1955). *Hands off pidgin English.* New South Wales: Pacific Publications.

Holm, J. (1988–89). *Pidgins and creoles.* (Vols. 1 & 2). Cambridge, UK: Cambridge University Press.

Jespersen, O. (1964). *Mankind, nation, and individual.* Bloomington: University of Indiana Press. (Original work published 1925)

Johnson, F. (1950). The history of some "dirty words." *The American Mercury, 71*, 538–545.

Kirwin, W.J. (1993). The planting of Anglo-Irish in Newfoundland. In S. Clarke (Ed.), *Focus on Canada* (pp. 65–84). Amsterdam: John Benjamins.

Krapp, G.P. (1909). *Modern English: Its growth and present use.* New York: Charles Scribner's Sons.

Kurath, H. (1971). What do you call it? In J.V. Williamson & V.M. Burke (Eds.), *A various language: Perspective on American dialects* (pp. 245–254). New York: Holt, Rinehart and Winston.

Labov, W. (1969). *The logic of nonstandard English.* Georgetown University. 20th Annual Round Table, No. 22.

Lakoff, R. (1973). Language and woman's place. *Language in Society, 2*, 45–80.

Leon, P.R. (1979). Canadian English pronunciation: From the British to the American model. In P.R. Leon & P. Martin (Eds.), *Toronto English: Studies in Phonetics to Honour C.D. Rouillard* (pp. 1–9). Ottawa: Didier.

McCrum, R., Cran, W., & MacNeil, R. (1992). *The story of English*. London: Faber and Faber.

Munro, P. (1990). *Slang U: The official dictionary of college slang*. New York: Harmony Books.

Newman, E. (1974). *Strictly speaking: Will America be the death of English?* Indianapolis: Bobbs-Merrill.

Orkin, M. (1973). *Canajan, eh?* Don Mills, ON: General Publishing.

Orwell, G. (1946). *The politics of the English language*. London: Horizon.

Payne, L.W. (1909). A word-list from east Alabama. *Dialect News, 3*, 279–328, 343–391.

Pei, M. (1964, November 14). A loss for words. *Saturday Review*, 82–84.

Poplack, S., & Tagliamonte, S. (1993). African American English in the diaspora: Evidence from old-line Nova Scotians. In S. Clarke (Ed.), *Focus on Canada* (pp. 109–150). Amsterdam: John Benjamins.

Préfixe du recueil des lois de 1977. Lettres patentes/Prefix to the Statutes of 1977. Letters Patent. (1977). Quebec: Charles-Henri Dubé.

Roberts, P. (1958). *Understanding English*. New York: Harper & Row.

Romaine, S. (1988). *Pidgin and creole languages*. London: Longman.

Scargill, M.H. (1974). *Modern Canadian usage*. Toronto: McClelland & Stewart.

Scargill, M.H. (1988). Canadian English. *Canadian encyclopedia*. Edmonton: Hurtig.

Schulz, M.R. (1975). The semantic derogation of woman. In B. Thorne & N. Henley (Eds.), *Language and sex* (pp. 66–67). Rowley, MA: Newbury House.

Stegner, W. (1962). *Wolf willow*. Toronto: Macmillan Canada.

Stewart, W. (1985). *True blue: The Loyalist legend*. Toronto: Collins.

Thomas, E.R. (1991). The origin of Canadian raising in Ontario. *Canadian Journal of Linguistics, 36*, 147–170.

Todd, L. (1984). *Modern Englishes: Pidgins & creoles*. Oxford: Basil Blackwell.

Vance, T.J. (1987). "Canadian raising" in some dialects of the Northern United States. *American Speech, 62*, 195–210.

Wells, J.C. (1982). *Accents of English*. Vol. 3. Cambridge, UK: Cambridge University Press.

Williamson, J.V., & Burke, V.M. (1971). *A various language: Perspectives on American dialects*. New York: Holt, Rinehart and Winston.

Yalden, M. (1984). Some basic issues. *Language and Society, 14*, 6–8.

Further Reading

Alexander, K., & Glaze, A. (1996). *Towards freedom: The African-Canadian experience*. Toronto: Umbrella Press.

Allan, K., & Burridge, K. (1991). *Euphemism and dysphemism*. New York: Oxford University Press.

Andersson, L, & Trudgill, P. (1990). *Bad language*. Oxford: Basil Blackwell.

Ayto, J. (1993). *Euphemisms: Over 3000 ways to avoid being rude or giving offence*. London: Bloomsbury.

Baugh, J. (1983). *Black street speech*. Austin: University of Texas.

Bickerton, D. (1981). *Roots of language*. Ann Arbor, MI: Karoma.

Cameron, D. (1992). *Feminism and linguistic theory* (2nd ed.). London: Macmillan.

Coates, J. (1986). *Women, men, and language: A sociolinguistic account of sex differences in language.* London: Longman.

Crystal, D. (2008). *Txting: The Gr8 Db8.* Oxford: Oxford University Press.

Dillard, J.L. (1972). *Black English: Its history and usage in the United States.* New York: Random House.

Edwards, J. (Ed.). (1998). *Language in Canada.* Cambridge, UK: Cambridge University Press.

Fasold, R. (1990). *Sociolinguistics of language.* London: Blackwell.

Ferguson, C., & Brice Health, S. (Eds.). (1981). *Language in the USA.* Cambridge, UK: Cambridge University Press.

Folb, E. (1980). *Runnin' down some lines: The language and culture of black teenagers.* Cambridge, MA: Harvard University Press.

Frank, F., & Ashen, F. (1983). *Language and the sexes.* Albany: State University of New York Press.

Holm, J. (1988–1989). *Pidgins and creoles (Vols. 1 & 2).* Cambridge, UK: Cambridge University Press.

Holmes, J., & Meyerhoff, M. (Eds.). (2005). *The handbook of language and gender.* Malden, MA: Wiley-Blackwell.

Jay, T. (1992). *Cursing in America.* Philadelphia: John Benjamins.

King, R. (1991). *Talking gender: A guide to nonsexist communication.* Toronto: Copp Clark Pitman.

Kinlock, A.M., & Avis, W. (1989). Central Canadian and received standard English: A comparison of pronunciation. In O. García & R. Otheguy (Eds.), *English across cultures/cultures across English* (pp. 403–420). Berlin: Mouton de Gruyte.

Labov, W. (1969). *The logic of nonstandard English.* Georgetown University 20th Annual Round Table, Monograph Series on Languages and Linguistics, No. 22.

Lakoff, R. (1990). *Talking power: The politics of language.* New York: Basic Books.

Lakoff, R, & Bucholtz, M. (Eds.). (2004). *Language and women's place* (Rev. ed.). Oxford: Oxford University Press.

Meyerhoff, M. (2006). *Introducing sociolinguistics.* New York: Routledge.

Michaels, L., & Ricks, C. (Eds.). (1980). *The state of the language.* Berkeley: University of California Press.

Miller, C., & Swift, K. (1980). *The handbook of nonsexist writing.* New York: Barnes & Noble.

Mulhausler, P. (1986). *Pidgin and creole linguistics.* Oxford: Basil Blackwell.

Newmeyer, F.J. (Ed.). (1988). *Linguistics: The Cambridge survey, Vol. IV. Language: The socio-cultural context.* Cambridge, UK: Cambridge University Press.

Pringle, I.W.V. (1986). The complexity of the concept of standard. In W.C. Lougheed (Ed.), *Search of the standard in Canadian English* (pp. 20–38). Kingston: Queen's University Strathy Language Unit.

Reed, C.E. (1977). *Dialects of American English* (Rev. ed.). Amherst, MA: University of Massachusetts Press.

Romaine, S. (1988). *Pidgin and creole languages.* London/New York: Longman.

Romaine, S. (1994). *Language in society: An introduction to sociolinguistics.* Oxford: Oxford University Press.

Rudnýckyi, R.B. (1973). Immigrant language, language contact, and bilingualism in Canada. In T.A. Sebeok (Ed.), *Current trends in linguistics* (Vol. 10). The Hague: Mouton.

Shopen, T., & Williams, J.M. (Eds.). (1981). *Style and variables in English.* Cambridge, MA: Winthrop.

Smith, P.M. (1985). *Language, the sexes and society.* Oxford: Basil Blackwell.

Spears, R.A. (1981). *Slang and euphemism: A dictionary of oaths, curses, insults, sexual slang and metaphor, racial slurs, drug talk, homosexual lingo, and related matter.* New York: Jonathan David.

Talman, J.J. (1946). *Loyalist narratives from Upper Canada.* Toronto: The Champlain Society.

Tannen, D. (1990). *You just don't understand: Women and men in conversation.* New York: Ballantine.

Thorne, B., Kramarae, C., & Henley, N. (Eds.). (1983). *Language, gender, and society.* Rowley, MA: Newbury House.

Trahern, J.B. (Ed.). (1989). *Standardizing English: Essays in the history of language change.* Knoxville: University of Tennessee Press.

Trudgill, P. (2000). *Sociolinguistics: An introduction to language and society.* London: Penguin Books.

Trudgill, P. (2004). *New dialect formation.* Edinburgh: Edinburgh University Press.

Wardhaugh, R. (2005). *An introduction to sociolinguistics* (5th ed.). Malden, MA: Wiley-Blackwell.

Williams, G. (1992). *Sociolinguistics.* Middlesex, UK: Penguin Books.

Winks, R.W. (1971). *The Blacks in Canada: A history.* Montreal: McGill–Queen's University Press.

Websites

http://www.arts.mcgill.ca/linguistics/Faculty/boberg/research.htm A website by C. Boberg at McGill University describing the North American Regional Vocabulary Survey.

http://www.chass.utoronto.ca/~chambers/dialect_topography.html

http://dialect.topography.chass.utoronto.ca/ Websites at the University of Toronto on Canadian dialects which contain a number of interesting articles by J.K. Chambers.

http://www.heritage.nf.ca/dictionary/d2ction.html The website for the *Dictionary of Newfoundland English.*

http://privatewww.essex.ac.uk/~patrickp/Courses/CreolesIntro.html A website on pidgins and creoles created by Peter L. Patrick at the University of Essex, UK.

http://csumc.wisc.edu/AmericanLanguages/ A website on dialects spoken in the United States.

CHAPTER 13
Language Change: The Syllables of Time

Language change is inevitable, continuous, universal and multidirectional.
Languages do not get better or worse when they change. They just — change.

David Crystal, *How Language Works* (2006)

All living languages change with time, a fact that many have found so disturbing that they have sought to restrict the perceived changes. In 1712, Jonathan Swift insisted on "ascertaining and fixing our language forever. . . . I see no absolute necessity why any language should be perpetually changing." But the only language that does not change is a dead one. Fortunately, however, languages change slowly compared with the human life span, and we are scarcely aware of the changes. If we could turn on a radio and miraculously receive a broadcast in our "native language" from the year 3000, however, we would undoubtedly think we were hearing a foreign language, yet from year to year we hardly notice any change in our language.

We become most aware of linguistic change when we look at documents from the past, for many changes are revealed in those languages with written records. We know, for example, a great deal about the history of English because we have documents reaching back to the seventh and eighth centuries C.E. available to us. Old English (actually a group of related dialects spoken in England around the end of the first millennium and the foundation of modern English dialects) is, to a speaker of Modern English, largely unintelligible without special study. A few lines from *Beowulf*, an epic poem preserved in a manuscript of the tenth century C.E., may strike us as incomprehensible at first glance:

> Hordweard sōhte
> georne æfter grunde, wolde guman findan
> þone þe him on sweofote sāre getēode.
> (Note that the letter þ, called "thorn," is pronounced, in this instance, like the
> *th* in *think* — i.e., [θ].)

Clearly, most of us will need a translation to understand much of this text:

> The Guardian of the hoard [i.e., a dragon] sought
> eagerly along the ground, [he] wanted to find the man
> who sorely harmed him in [his] sleep.

If, at first glance, these lines do not seem to be English, further consideration reveals familiarity behind the surface strangeness: *him*, of course, and *on* are

Modern English words, but others — especially once we have looked at the translation — are also familiar if "distorted": so¯hte (sought), *findan* (find), *grunde* (ground), and perhaps even *sāre* (sorely). This may be English, but clearly it isn't our English.

Some 500 years after the epic of *Beowulf*, Chaucer wrote his *Canterbury Tales* in the London dialect of Middle English, spoken from around 1100 to 1500 (the dates are only approximate guides for us; no one woke on January 1, 1100, and began speaking Middle English). Chaucer's language is more easily understood by present-day readers, as we see from the opening of *The Canterbury Tales*:

> Whan that Aprille with his shoures soote
> The droughte of March hath pierced to the roote....

> When April with its sweet showers
> The drought of March has pierced to the root....

Chaucer's English is closer to our own than the language of many of his contemporaries who happened to speak other dialects of English. *Sir Gawain and the Green Knight*, a poem written in a Northwest Midlands dialect about the same time as *The Canterbury Tales*, is "inaccessible to the non-specialist because of the difficulty of its language, a language far more remote from the English of the present than that of Geoffrey Chaucer's London" (Boroff, 1967):

> Siþen þe sege and þe assaut watz sesed at Troye
> þe borȝ brittened and brent to brondez and askez
> þe tulk þat þe trammes of tresoun þer wroȝt
> Watz tried for his tricherie, þe trewest on erthe.

> Since the siege and the assault was ceased at Troy
> The city destroyed and burned to brands and ashes
> The knight who the trickery of treason there wrought
> Was tried for his treachery, the truest [greatest] on earth.

Despite the difficulties of this dialect, it is closer to Modern English than the language of the *Beowulf* text, especially if we compare it with many Modern English dialects, some of which are as difficult for us to grasp as the dialect of *Sir Gawain and the Green Knight* — if not more so.

A passage from *Everyman*, a play written about 1485, illustrates why (despite the use of *u* for *v* and *y* for *i* in early printing) it can be claimed that Early Modern English was being spoken by 1500:

> The Somonynge of Eueryman called it is,
> That of our lyues and endynge shewes
> How transytory we be all daye.
> The mater is wonders precyous,
> But the entent of it is more gracyous
> And swete to bere awaye.

We no longer need a translation to understand this passage, nor do we have much difficulty with Shakespeare, who, 200 years after Chaucer, has Hamlet say

> "A man may fish with the worme that hath eate of a king, and eate of the fish that hath fedde of that worme."

With these last two examples, we have clearly arrived at a recognizable form — if one with some oddities — of Modern English.

The division of English into Old English (449–1100 C.E.), Middle English (1100–1500), and Modern English (1500–present) is somewhat arbitrary, being marked by the dates of events in English history, such as the Norman Conquest of 1066 C.E. and the introduction of Caxton's printing press into England in 1476, that profoundly influenced the English language. Thus, the history of English and the changes that occurred in the language reflect, to some extent, nonlinguistic history, as suggested by the following dates:

449–1066	Old English	449	Saxons invade Britain
		6th century	Religious literature
		8th century	*Beowulf*
		1066	Norman Conquest
1066–1500	Middle English	1387	*Canterbury Tales*
		1476	Caxton's printing press
		1500	Great Vowel Shift
1500–	Modern English	1564	Birth of Shakespeare

Changes in a language are changes in the grammars of the speakers of the language and are perpetuated when new generations of children learn the language by acquiring the new grammar. An examination of the changes that have occurred in English during the past 1500 years shows changes in the phonology, morphology, syntax, lexicon, and semantics of the grammar. No part of the grammar remains the same over the course of history. Although most of the examples in this chapter are from English, the histories of all languages show similar changes.

The Regularity of Sound Change

> That's not a regular rule: you invented it just now.
> Lewis Carroll, *Alice's Adventures in Wonderland* (1871)

In the Ottawa Valley of Ontario, a dialect spoken by some older rural residents differs from Standard Canadian English in the use of a low front vowel [æ] before [r], where speakers of Standard Canadian English would normally use [ɑ]. Thus, words commonly pronounced as [kɑr] "car," [bɑrn] "barn," and [gɑrdən] "garden," appear in this dialect as [kær], [bærn], and [gærdən] (Chambers, 1975).

This [ɑ]–[æ] correspondence is an example of a **regular sound correspondence** that, in this case, is conditioned by the presence of the [r].

The different pronunciations of *far* and *barn* and so on did not always exist in English. This chapter will discuss how such dialect differences arose and why the sound differences are usually regular and not confined to just a few words.

Sound Correspondences

In Middle English, *mouse* [mʌws] was pronounced *mūs* [mu:s], *house* [hʌws] was *hūs* [hu:s], and *flower* [flawər] was [flu:r]. In general, where we now pronounce [ʌw] or [aw] (depending on the presence or absence of Canadian raising), Middle English speakers pronounced [u:]. This is a regular correspondence like the one between [ɑ] and [æ] before [r]. Thus, *out* [ʌwt] was pronounced *ūt* [u:t]. Many such regular correspondences can be found relating older and newer forms of English. Similarly, the North American languages Cree and Ojibwa show a *t–n* correspondence: Cree *atim*, Ojibwa *anim*, "dog"; Cree *nitim*, Ojibwa *ninim*, "my sister-in-law."

The regular sound correspondences we observe between older and modern forms of a language are due to phonological changes that affect certain sounds, or classes of sounds, rather than individual words. Centuries ago, English underwent a phonological change called a **sound shift** in which [u:] became [ʌw]/[aw]. We observe regularity precisely because *sounds* change, not words.

Phonological change can also account for dialect differences. The Ottawa Valley [æ] before [r] in place of the more common Canadian [ɑ] may have had its origin in the Irish dialects of the settlers who migrated into the area after the War of 1812 (Pringle & Padolsky, 1981). Because of the area's isolation during much of the nineteenth century, this change did not spread, and the dialect began to die out when outsiders moved into the valley. Its association with "country" and "old-fashioned" ways, joined with the impact of schooling and later the media, may also have restricted its use.

Ancestral Protolanguages

The Romance languages (French, Spanish, Italian, etc.) were once dialects of the Latin spoken in the Roman Empire. Regional dialect differences in pronunciation arose from sound changes that failed to spread. There is nothing degenerate about them. In fact, many of the world's modern languages were at first regional dialects that became widely spoken and highly differentiated, finally becoming separate languages. Because of their common ancestry, the Romance languages are said to be **genetically related**. Early forms of English and German, too, were once dialects of a common ancestor called **Proto-Germanic**. A **protolanguage** is the ancestral language from which related languages have developed. Both Latin and Proto-Germanic themselves were descendants of an older language called **Indo-European** or Proto–Indo-European. Thus, **Germanic** languages such as English and German are genetically related to the Romance languages such as French and Spanish. All these national languages were once regional dialects.

How do we know that the Germanic and Romance languages have a common ancestor? One clue is the large number of sound correspondences that exist between them. If you speak or have studied a Romance language, you may have noticed that, where an English word begins with *f*, the corresponding word in a Romance language often begins with *p*, as in the following examples:

English /f/	French /p/	Spanish /p/
father	père	padre
fish	poisson	pescado

This /f/–/p/ correspondence is another example of a regular sound correspondence. There are many correspondences between Germanic and Romance languages, and the prevalence cannot be explained by chance. What, then, accounts for them? A reasonable guess is that a common ancestor language used a /p/ in words for *fish, father*, and so on. A /p/ rather than an /f/ is posited here because more languages show a /p/ in these words. At some point, speakers of this language separated into two groups, retaining little contact. In one of the groups, a sound change of /p/ → /f/ took place. This group eventually became the ancestor of the Germanic languages. This ancient sound change left its trace in the /f/–/p/ sound correspondence that we observe today, as illustrated in the following diagram:

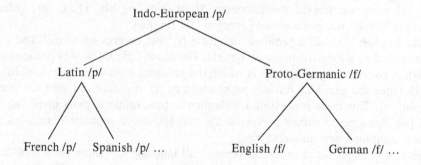

Phonological Change

Etymologists . . . for whom vowels did not matter and who cared not a jot for consonants.

Voltaire (1694–1778)

Regular sound correspondences illustrate changes in the phonological system. In earlier chapters, we discussed speakers' knowledge of their phonological system, including knowledge of the phonemes and phonological rules of the language. Any of these aspects of the phonology is subject to change.

The velar fricative /x/, once common, is no longer part of the phonemic inventory of most Modern English dialects. This phonological change — the loss of /x/ — took place between the times of Chaucer and Shakespeare, except in dialects such as Scottish, which has retained it in words such as *loch* [lɔx], a *lake*. In some cases, the /x/ disappeared altogether: *night* was once pronounced [nɪxt], *drought* was [druxt], and *saw* was [saux]. In other cases, the /x/ became a /k/, as in *elk* (Old English *eolh* [ɛɔlx]). In still other instances, it became a vowel, as in *hollow* (Old English *holh* [hɔlx]) and *sorrow* (Old English *sorh* [sɔrx]).

These examples show that the inventory of sounds can change by the loss of phonemes. The inventory can also change by the addition of new phonemes. Old English did not have the phoneme /ž/ of *leisure* [ližər] — [lɛžər] as some say it — or *confusion* [kõnfjužõn]. Through a process of **palatalization** — a change in the place of articulation to the palatal region — certain occurrences of /z/ were pronounced as [ž]. Eventually, the [ž] sound became a phoneme in its own right, reinforced by the fact that it is a common phoneme in French, a language that exerted a major influence on the English language after the Norman Conquest (note words such as *azure*).

An allophone of a phoneme may become phonemic. For example, Old English did not have the phoneme /v/, but it did have an allophone [v] of /f/. This phoneme was [f] when it occurred initially, finally, and between voiceless elements, but it was [v] when it came between vowels or vowels and voiced consonants. Just as [p] and [pʰ] are allophones of the same /p/ phoneme in Modern English, so too [f] and [v] were variants of the phoneme /f/ in Old English. Thus, *ofer* /ofer/, meaning "over," was pronounced [ɔvɛr] in Old English.

Old English also had a geminate phoneme /f:/ that contrasted with /f/ and was pronounced as a long [f:] between vowels. The name *Offa* /of:a/ was pronounced [ɔf:a]. A sound change occurred in which the pronunciation of /f:/ was simplified to [f]. Once the geminate /f:/ was pronounced as [f], it contrasted with the intervocalic [v]. This made it possible for English to have minimal pairs involving [f] and [v]. Speakers therefore perceived the two sounds as separate phonemes, in effect, creating a new phoneme /v/.

Similar changes occur in the histories of all languages. Neither /č/ nor /š/ was a phoneme of Latin, but /č/ is a phoneme of modern Italian and /š/ of modern French, both of which evolved from Latin. In an older stage of Russian, the phoneme /æ/ occurred, but in modern Russian [æ] is merely an allophone of /a/.

Phonemes may thus be lost (/x/) or added (/ž/) or result from a change in the status of allophones (the [v] allophone of /f/ becoming /v/).

Phonological Rules

An interaction of phonological rules may result in changes in the lexicon. The nouns *house* and *bath* were once differentiated from the verbs *house* and *bathe* by the fact that the verbs ended with a short vowel sound (still reflected in the spelling). Furthermore, the same rule that realized /f/ as [v] between vowels also realized /s/ and /θ/ as [z] and [ð] between vowels. This was a general rule that voiced intervocalic fricatives. Thus, the /s/, which was followed by a vowel in the verb *house*, was pronounced [z], and the /θ/ in the verb *bathe* was pronounced [ð] for the same reason.

Later, a rule was added to the grammar of English deleting unstressed short vowels at the ends of words. Once the unstressed final vowel was deleted, a contrast between voiced and voiceless fricatives resulted, and the new phonemes /z/ and /ð/ were added to the phonemic inventory. Prior to this change, they were simply the allophones of the phonemes /s/ and /θ/ between vowels. The verbs *house* and *bathe* were now represented in the mental lexicon with final voiced consonants.

Eventually, both the unstressed vowel deletion rule and the intervocalic-voicing rule were lost from the grammar of English. The set of phonological rules can change by both addition and loss of rules.

Changes in phonological rules often result in dialect differences. In Chapter 12, we discussed the addition of an "*r*-dropping" rule in English that did not spread throughout the language (/r/ is not pronounced unless followed by a vowel). Today we see the effect of that rule in the "*r*-less" pronunciation of British English and of American English dialects spoken in the Boston area and the southern United States.

From the standpoint of the language as a whole, phonological changes occur gradually over the course of many generations of speakers, although a given speaker's grammar may or may not reflect the changes. The changes are not planned any more than we are currently planning which changes will take place in English by the year 2300. Speakers are aware of the changes only through dialect differences.

The Great Vowel Shift

A major change in the history of English that resulted in new phonemic representations of words and morphemes took place approximately between 1400 and 1600. It is known as the **Great Vowel Shift**, and it affected the seven long or tense vowels. These vowels underwent the following changes:

	Shift			Example		
Middle English		Modern Canadian English	Middle English		Modern Canadian English	
[i:]	→ {	[ʌj]	[mi:s]	→	[mʌjs]	mice
		[aj]	[ri:d(ə)]	→	[rajd]	ride
[u:]	→ {	[ʌw]	[mu:s]	→	[mʌws]	mouse
		[aw]	[flu:r]	→	[flawər]	flower
[e:]	→	[i:]	[ge:s]	→	[gi:s]	geese
[o:]	→	[u:]	[go:s]	→	[gu:s]	goose
[ɛ:]	→	[e:]	[brɛ:ken]	→	[bre:k]	break
[ɔ:]	→	[o:]	[brɔ:ken]	→	[bro:k]	broke
[a:]	→	[e:]	[na:mə]	→	[ne:m]	name

FIGURE 13.1

The Great Vowel Shift.

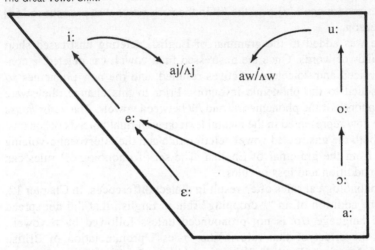

By diagramming the Great Vowel Shift on a vowel chart (see Figure 13.1), we can see that the highest vowels [i:] and [u:] "fell off" to become the diphthongs [aj]/[ʌj] and [aw]/[ʌw], while the long vowels underwent an increase in tongue height, as if to fill in the space left when the highest vowels became diphthongs. In addition, [a:] was "fronted" to become [e:].

These changes are among the most dramatic examples of regular sound shift. The phonemic representations of thousands of words changed. Today some reflection of this vowel shift is seen in the alternating forms of morphemes in English: *please, pleasant; serene, serenity; sane, sanity; crime, criminal; sign, signal;* and so on. At one time, the vowels in each pair were the same. In a sound change known as the **Early Middle English Vowel Shortening**, the vowels in the second word of each pair were then shortened, so those words were unaffected by the Great Vowel Shift, which occurred later. Thus, these morphologically related words are pronounced differently today (see Table 13.1).

TABLE 13.1

Effect of the Vowel Shift on Modern English

Middle English Vowel	Shifted Vowel	Short Counterpart	Word with Shifted Vowel	Word with Vowel
ī	aj	ɪ	divine	divinity
ū	aw	ʌ	profound	profundity
ē	i	ɛ	serene	serenity
ō	u	ɑ	fool	folly
ā	e	æ	sane	sanity

The Great Vowel Shift is a primary source of many of the spelling inconsistencies of English, because our spelling system still reflects the way words were spelled before the Great Vowel Shift took place.

Morphological Change

Of all the words of witch's doom
There's none so bad as which and whom.
The man who kills both which and whom
Will be enshrined in our Who's Whom.

Fletcher Knebel (1911–1993)

Like phonological rules, rules of morphology may be lost, added, or changed. We can observe some of these changes by comparing older and newer forms of the language or by looking at different dialects.

The suffix *-ize* — or, as many British writers and some Canadians prefer to spell it, *-ise* — that changes nouns and adjectives into verbs meaning "to make ____," as in *finalize* "to make final," is becoming more productive. Speakers are attaching this suffix to more words that previously did not take it. Words such as *privatize* "to make private" and, perhaps, *rigidize* "to make rigid" are achieving the status of *optimize, stabilize*, and *vitalize*. This change in the morphology of English is reflected in additions to the lexicon.

Extensive changes in rules of morphology have occurred in the history of the Indo-European languages. Latin inherited a complex system of **case endings** — suffixes added to the stem of the noun based on its grammatical relationship to the verb — from Indo-European. The different forms (the *declension*) of the noun *lupus* "wolf" in classical Latin are as follows:

Case	Noun Stem		Case Ending		
nominative	lup	+	us	lupus	The *wolf* runs. (subject of the verb)
genitive	lup	+	i	lupi	A sheep in *wolf's* clothing. (possession)
dative	lup	+	ō	lupō	Give food *to the wolf*. (indirect object)
accusative	lup	+	um	lupum	I love *the wolf*. (direct object)
ablative	lup	+	ō	lupō	Run *from the wolf*. (*by, with, from, on, in* + noun)
vocative	lup	+	e	lupe	*Wolf*, come here! (the thing/being addressed)

A seventh case, the "locative," referring to "the place where" something occurs, is not given here. These cases are no longer found in the Romance languages.

In *Alice's Adventures in Wonderland*, Lewis Carroll has Alice give us a brief lesson in grammatical case. Alice has become very small and is swimming around in a pool of her own tears with a mouse that she wishes to befriend:

"Would it be of any use, now," thought Alice, "to speak to this mouse? Everything is so out-of-the-way down here, that I should think very likely it can talk: at any rate, there's no harm in trying." So she began: "O Mouse, do you know the way out of this pool? I am very tired of swimming about here, O Mouse!" (Alice thought this must be the right way of speaking to a mouse: she had never done such a thing before, but she remembered having seen in her brother's Latin Grammar, "A mouse — of a mouse — to a mouse — a mouse — O mouse!")

Alice gives an English "translation" of the nominative, genitive, dative, accusative, and vocative cases.

Ancient Greek and Sanskrit also had extensive case systems expressed morphologically through noun suffixing, as did Old English, as illustrated in the following noun forms:

Case	OE Singular		OE Plural	
nominative	stān	"stone"	stānas	"stones"
genitive	stānes	"stone's"	stāna	"stones' "
dative	stāne	"stone"	stānum	"stones"
accusative	stān	"stone"	stānas	"stones"

The plural nominative and accusative cases of this declension became generalized to all the English regular nouns. In Middle English, a change lengthened the stem vowel and reduced the suffix vowel of certain word classes. Thus, Old English *nama* /nama/, "name," became Middle English /na:mə/. Another phonological rule change, mentioned earlier, resulted in the dropping out of certain short unstressed vowels, and this rule, together with the Great Vowel Shift, applied to the Middle English /na:mə/ gives Modern English /nem/ (with vowel length not indicated because it is not distinctive in Modern English). Similar changes occurred in the development of Old English *stānas* /stā:nas/, "stones," where the stem vowel was raised to /ɔ:/ in Middle English and to /o/ in Modern English and the suffix vowel was reduced and then lost:

OE /stā:nas/ → ME /stɔ:nəs/ → Mod. Eng. /stonz/

This change is representative of thousands of similar changes. When the "weak" syllables representing case endings in the forms of the singular, genitive plural, and dative plural were similarly dropped, only two distinct forms of the noun were left: *stone* and *stones*.

Modern English has preserved more of the case structure of pronouns, but even so the Old English pronoun was more complex, including a "dual" number along with the singular and plural numbers with which we are familiar:

Case	OE Singular		OE Dual		OE Plural	
nominative	ic	"I"	wit	"we two"	we	"we"
genitive	mīn	"my-mine"	uncer	"our two"	ūre	"our-ours"
dative	me	"me"	unc	"us two"	ūs	"us"
accusative	mec/me	"me"	uncit/unc	"us two"	ūsic/ūs	"us"

The dual number, as the translations show, can be expressed in Modern English only with a phrase such as *we two* or *of us two*. The short Old English lyric "Wulf and Eadwacer" illustrates this dual form:

> þæt mon ēaþe tōslīteð þætte næfrɛ gesomnad wæs
> uncer giedd geador.

> One can easily cut asunder that which was never joined together,
> The song of *us-two* together.

English has replaced its depleted case system with an equally expressive system of prepositions and with stricter constraints on word order — a tradeoff between morphological and syntactic rules. Where once a noun in the dative case could be used, Modern English often employs the preposition *to*, as in *She gave the letter to Mary*. English also retains something of the genitive case, which is written with an apostrophe + *s*, as in *Mary's letter*, but beyond this residual indicator there are no longer any morphological markers suffixed to the English noun to indicate case. Pronouns, as we have seen, retain a few more traces of the case system.

While a few languages, such as Lithuanian and Russian, retain much of the early Indo-European case system, changes have all but obliterated it in most modern Indo-European languages. English and most of the Indo-European languages, then, have undergone extensive morphological changes over time, many of them induced by changes that took place in the phonological rules of the language.

Syntactic Change

> Change alone is eternal, perpetual, immortal.
>
> Arthur Schopenhauer (1788–1860)

The loss of case endings in English occurred together with changes in the rules of syntax governing word order. In Old English, word order was freer because the case endings alone disclosed the thematic or meaning relations in a sentence. Thus, the following sentences were all grammatical in Old English, and all meant "The man slew the king":

> Sē man slōh þone kyning.
> þone kyning slōh sē man.
> Sē man þone kyning slōh.
> þone kyning sē man slōh.
> Slōh sē man þone kyning.
> Slōh þone kyning sē man.

(*Sē* was a definite article used only with the subject noun, and *þone* was the definite article used only with the object noun.)

In Modern English, only the first of the literal translations below means what the original meant, and four of the six are ungrammatical as sentences:

> The man slew the king.
> The king slew the man.
> *The man the king slew.
> *The king the man slew.
> *Slew the man the king.
> *Slew the king the man.

The syntactic rules of Modern English permit less variation in word order. Additionally, Modern English is an SVO (subject–verb–object) language, while Old English was both an SVO and an SOV language. (See the discussion of "Types of Languages" later in this chapter.) Consequently, SOV sentences such as *Sē man þone kyning slōh* (*The man the king slew*) were grammatical in Old English. The phrase structure rules that determine the word order of the basic sentences of the language changed in the history of English.

The syntactic rules relating to the English negative construction also underwent a number of changes from Old English to the present. In Modern English, negation is expressed by adding *not* or *do not*. We may also express negation by adding words such as *never* or *no*:

> I am going. → I am not going.
> I went. → I did not go.
> I go to school. → I never go to school.
> I want food. → I don't want any food; I want no food.

In Old English, the main negation element was *ne*. It usually occurred before the *auxiliary verb* or the verb, as illustrated by these examples (Traugott, 1972):

> þæt hē *nā*   siþþan geboren *ne* wurde
> that he never after   born   not would-be
> that he should never be born after that

> ac hīe *ne* dorston þǣr on cuman
> but they not dared   there on come
> but they dared not land there

In the first example, the word order is different from that of Modern English, and there are two negatives: *nā* (a contraction of *ne* + *ā*; "not" + "ever" = "never") and *ne*. Double negatives were, as the sentence shows, grammatical in Old English.

In addition to the contraction of *ne* + *ā* → *nā*, other negative contractions occurred in Old English: *ne* could be attached to *habb-* "have," *wes-* "be," *wit-* "know," and *will-* "will" to form *nabb-, nes-, nyt-,* and *nyll-,* respectively.

Similar negative contractions are common in Middle English; toward the end of the period, Chaucer writes:

> She sholde seye   she   *nyste* [i.e., *ne* + *wyste*]   where he was.
> She should say   she   knew not   where he was.

> But he *noot* [*ne* + *wot*]   which the righte wey is thider.
> But he knows not   which the right way is hence.

| And of this cry | they *nolde* [*ne + wolde*] | nevere stenten. |
| And of this lamentation | they wouldn't | never cease. |

Other equally common contractions are *nadde* (*ne + hadde*), *nam* (*ne + am*), *nas* (*ne + was*), and *nyl* (*ne + wyl*).

The negative force of *ne* before a verb or prefixed to a verb was increased by an additional negative such as *nought* or *not* following the verb, as in *He ne held it noght*. As these examples suggest, double negatives continue to be standard in Middle English. In fact, triple negatives are not unusual: the twelfth-century *Peterborough Chronicle* remarks that *Ne wæren nævre nan martyrs swa pined*, "No martyrs were not never so tortured" (Mossé, 1952). But then Chaucer uses four in *He nevere yet no vileynye ne sayde / In al his lif unto no maner wight*, "He never yet no rudeness not said in all his life unto no sort of person" ("He never spoke rudely to any person"). Shakespeare and his contemporaries had no worry about the "illogicality" of multiple negatives. Clearly, the more you say no, the more you mean no.

From around the middle of the fourteenth century, the *ne* appearing before the verb began to be dropped, leaving only the negative *not* following the verb: *cry not so* (Mustanoja, 1960). This method of negation was "the norm after any finite verb — I say not, I know not, a pattern which remained colloquial till the late 18c" (Strang, 1970).

Modern English also has contraction rules that change *do + not* into *don't*, *will + not* into *won't*, and so on. In these contractions, the phonetic form of the negation element always comes at the *end* of the word, because Modern English word order puts the *not* after the auxiliary verb. In Old English, the negative element occurred at the beginning of the contraction, because it typically preceded the auxiliary. The rules determining the placement of the negative morpheme have changed. Such syntactic changes may take centuries to be fully completed, and there are often intermediate stages.

Another syntactic change in English affected the rules of comparative and superlative constructions. Today we form the comparative by adding *-er* to the adjective or by inserting *more* before it; the superlative is formed by adding *-est* or by inserting *most*. In Malory's tales of King Arthur, written in 1470, double comparatives and double superlatives occur, which today are ungrammatical: *more gladder, more lower, moost royallest, moost shamefullest*.

When we study a language solely from written records, as we must with earlier periods, we encounter only those sentences that are grammatical — unless, of course, ungrammatical sentences are used deliberately. In fact, without native speakers to query, we can only infer what was ungrammatical. Such inference leads us to believe that expressions such as *the queen of England's crown* were ungrammatical in former versions of English. The title *The Wife's Tale of Bath* (rather than *The Wife of Bath's Tale*) in *The Canterbury Tales* supports this inference. Modern English, on the other hand, allows rather complex constructions that involve the possessive marker. An English speaker can use possessive constructions such as

The girl whose sister I'm dating's roommate is hilarious.
The man from Regina's hat fell off.

Older versions of English had to resort to an "*of* construction" to express the same thought (*The hat of the man from Regina fell off*). It is clear that a syntactic change took place that accounts for the extended use of the possessive morpheme *'s*.

Lexical Change

Changes in the lexicon also occur, including changes in the lexical category in which a word may function.

The word *menu* is ordinarily used only as a noun, but the waiter in the *New Yorker* cartoon uses it as a verb. If speakers adopt the usage, *menu* will take on the additional lexical category of verb in their mental lexicons. Such changes are common and are often put into effect in special usage situations. The noun *window* is used as a verb by carpenters as in, "Tomorrow we have to window the upper storey," where

"Have you folks been menued yet?"

to window means "put window frames in a house under construction." People can be said to be "to-ing and fro-ing" on a certain issue, to mean "wavering." This strange compound verb is derived from the adverb *to and fro*. In British English, *hoover* is a verb meaning "to vacuum up," derived from the proper noun *Hoover,* the name of a vacuum cleaner manufacturer. American police *Mirandize* arrested persons, meaning to read them their rights according to the Miranda rule. Since the judicial ruling was made in 1966, we have a complete history on how a proper name became a verb.

The word *telephone* was coined exclusively as a noun in 1844 and meant "acoustic apparatus." Alexander Graham Bell appropriated the word for his invention in 1876, and in 1877 the word was first used as a verb, meaning "to speak by telephone." In languages where verbs have a specific morphological form such as the *-er* ending in French (*parler* "to speak"), or the *-en* ending in German (*sprechen* "to speak"), such changes are less common than in English. Thus the French noun *téléphone* cannot be a verb, but becomes the different word *téléphoner* as a verb.

Other categorical changes may occur historically. The word *remote* was once only an adjective, but with the invention of control-at-a-distance devices, the compound *remote control* came into usage, which ultimately was shortened to *remote,* which now functions as a noun; witness the half dozen remotes every modern household loses track of.

A recent announcement at North Carolina State University invited "all faculty to sandwich in the Watauga Seminar." They were not invited to squeeze together, rather to bring their lunches. Although the verb *to sandwich* exists, the new verbal usage is derived from the noun *sandwich* rather than the verb.

Addition of New Words

> And to bring in a new word by the head and shoulders, they leave out the old one.
>
> Montaigne (1533–1592)

In Chapter 4 we discussed ways in which new words can enter the language. These included deriving words from names (*sandwich*), blends (*smog*), back-formations (*edit*), acronyms (*NATO*), and abbreviations or clippings (*ad*). We also saw that new words may be formed by derivational processes, as in *uglification, finalize,* and *finalization.*

Compounding is a particularly productive means of creating words. Thousands of common English words have entered the language by this process, including *afternoon, bigmouth, cyberspace, egghead, force feed, global warming, icecap, jet set, laptop, moreover, nursemaid, offshore, pothole, railroad, skybox, takeover, undergo, water cooler, X-ray,* and *zookeeper.*

Other methods for enlarging the vocabulary that were discussed include word coinage. Societies often require new words to describe changes in technology, sports, entertainment, and so on. Languages are accommodating and inventive in meeting these needs. The words may be entirely new, as *steganography,* the concealment of information in an electronic document, or *micropolitan,* a city of less than 10,000 people. Even new bound morphemes may enter the language. The prefix *e-* as in *e-commerce, e-mail, e-trade,* meaning "electronic," is barely two decades old. The suffix *-gate,* meaning "scandal," derived from the Watergate scandal of the 1970s, may now be suffixed to a word to convey that meaning. Thus *Irangate* meant a scandal involving Iran, and *Dianagate,* a British usage, referred to a scandal involving wiretapped conversations of the late Princess of Wales, Diana. A change currently underway is the use of *-peat* to mean "win a championship so many years in succession," as in *threepeat* and *fourpeat,* which we have observed in the newspaper.

A word so new that its spelling is still in doubt is *dot com,* also seen in magazines as *.com,* and *dot.com.* It means a company whose primary business is on the Internet. The expression written 24/7, and pronounced *twenty-four seven,* meaning "all the time," also appears to be a new entry not yet found in dictionaries, but seen in newspapers and heard during news broadcasts.

Borrowings or Loan Words

> By such innovations are languages enriched, when the words are adopted by the multitude, and naturalized by custom.
>
> Miguel de Cervantes (1547–1616)

> We don't just borrow words; on occasion, English has pursued other languages down alleyways to beat them unconscious and rifle their pockets for new vocabulary.
>
> Booker T. Washington (1856–1915)

Another important source of new words is **borrowing** from other languages. Borrowing occurs when one language takes a word or morpheme from another language and adds it to its lexicon, often altering the pronunciation to fit the phonological rules of the borrowing language. Most languages are borrowers, so the lexicon can be divided into native and nonnative words (often called **loan words**). A *native word* is one whose history (or **etymology**) can be traced back to the earliest known stages of the language.

A language may borrow a word *directly* or *indirectly.* A *direct* borrowing means that the borrowed item is a native word in the language from which it is borrowed. *Feast* was borrowed directly from French and can be traced back to Latin *festum.* On the other hand, the word *algebra* was borrowed from Spanish, which in turn had borrowed it from Arabic. Thus, *algebra* was indirectly borrowed from Arabic, with Spanish as an intermediary.

Some languages are heavy borrowers. Albanian has borrowed so heavily that few native words are retained. On the other hand, most Aboriginal North American languages borrowed little from their neighbours.

English has borrowed extensively. Of the 20,000 or so words in common use, about three-fifths are borrowed. Of the 500 most frequently used words, however, only two-sevenths are borrowed, and, since these words are used repeatedly in sentences, the frequency of appearance of native words is about 80 percent. Words such as *and, be, have, it, of, the, to, will, you, on, that,* and *is* are all native to English.

History through Loan Words

The history of the English-speaking peoples can be followed by studying the kinds of loan words in the language, their source, and when they were borrowed. Until the Norman Conquest in 1066, England was inhabited chiefly by the Angles, the Saxons, and the Jutes, peoples of Germanic origin who came to England in the fifth century C.E. and eventually became the English. (The word *England* is derived from *Anglaland* — i.e., "land of the Angles.") Originally, they spoke Germanic dialects, from which Old English developed directly. These dialects contained a number of Latin borrowings but were otherwise undiluted by foreign elements. These Germanic tribes had displaced the earlier Celtic inhabitants, whose influence on Old English was largely confined to a few Celtic place names. (The modern languages Welsh, Irish, and Scots Gaelic are descended from the Celtic dialects.)

For three centuries after the Norman Conquest, French was the language used for affairs of state and for most commercial, social, and cultural matters. The West Saxon literary language was abandoned, but regional varieties of English continued to be used in homes, churches, and markets. During these three centuries, vast numbers of French words entered English, of which the following are representative:

government	crown	prince	state	parliament
nation	jury	judge	crime	sue
attorney	property	miracle	charity	court
lechery	virgin	saint	pray	mercy
religion	value	royal	money	society

Until the Norman Conquest, when an Englishman slaughtered an ox for food, he ate *ox*. If it was a pig, he ate *pig*. If it was a sheep, he ate *sheep*. However, "ox" served at the Norman tables was *beef (boeuf)*, "pig" was *pork (porc)*, and "sheep" was *mutton (mouton)*. These words were borrowed from French into English, as were the food-preparing words *boil* and *fry*. This showed who prepared the food and who ate it.

Indeed, over the years French foods have given English a flood of borrowed words for menu preparers:

aspic	bisque	bouillon	brie	brioche
canapé	caviar	consommé	coq au vin	coupe
crêpe	croissant	croquette	crouton	escargot
fondue	mousse	pâté	quiche	ragout

English borrowed many "learned" words from foreign sources during the Renaissance. In 1476, the printing press was introduced in England by William Caxton, and, by 1640, 55,000 books had been printed in English. The authors of these books used many Greek and Latin words, and as a result many words of ancient Greek and Latin entered the language.

From Greek came *drama, comedy, tragedy, scene, botany, physics, zoology*, and *atomic*. Greek roots have also provided English with a means for coining new words, which have been called "neoclassical compounds." *Thermos* "hot" plus *metron* "measure" give us *thermometer*. From *akros* "topmost" and *phobia* "fear" we get *acrophobia* "dread of heights."

Latin loan words in English are numerous and range from obscure learned words to ordinary words that few nowadays think of as anything but native stock. They include

candle	street	school	cucumber
describe	noon	exit	bonus
scientific	cedar	supplicate	alumnus
cardiac	lapidary	quorum	orthography

Latin, like Greek, has also provided prefixes and suffixes that are used productively with both native and nonnative roots. The prefix *ex-*, as in *ex-student, ex-wife*, comes from Latin; the suffix *-able/-ible*, a borrowing from Latin through French, can be attached to almost any English verb:

readable	doable	movable	singable

During the ninth and tenth centuries, the Scandinavians, who first raided and then settled in the British Isles, left their traces on the English language. The pronouns *they, their*, and *them* are loan words from Scandinavian. This period is the only time that English ever borrowed pronouns. Such borrowing was possible only because of the closeness of English and Scandinavian. Over the course of time, Germanic [sk] was palatized to [š] in English but remained [sk] in Scandinavian. Thus *skirt*, a borrowing into English from the Vikings, and *shirt* are derived from the same words in Proto-Germanic.

Bin, flannel, clan, slogan, and *whisky* are all words of Celtic origin, borrowed at various times from Welsh, Scots Gaelic, or Irish.

Dutch was a source of borrowed words, too, many of which are related to shipping: *buoy, freight, leak, pump, yacht*.

From German came *quartz, cobalt, noodle*, and — as we might guess — *sauerkraut*.

From Italian, many musical terms, including words describing opera houses, have been borrowed: *opera, piano, virtuoso, balcony, mezzanine*.

Words having to do with mathematics and chemistry were borrowed — indirectly, for the most part — from Arabic because early Arab scholarship in these, as in other intellectual and scientific fields, was considerably in advance of that found in Europe. Many of the words were initially borrowed by Spanish speakers who had close — often violent — contact with the Arab world. *Alcohol, algebra, cipher*, and *zero* are a representative sample.

Spanish has loaned us (directly) *barbecue, cockroach, guitar*, and *ranch*, as well as *California*, literally "hot furnace."

The English-speaking colonists of North America borrowed from the languages they encountered. First Nations provided them with words such as *pony, hickory, moose, skunk, toboggan, hominy, caribou, squash*, and, of course, *tomahawk, wigwam, papoose*, and *totem*. It is in the realm of place names, however, that English borrowed most extensively from Aboriginal North American languages. The names of four provinces — Ontario, Quebec, Manitoba, and Saskatchewan — and the names of innumerable cities, towns, rivers, and natural divisions and formations can be traced to First Nations languages. A few of these names include

Antigonish (NS)	Maniwaki (QC)
Athabaska (AB)	Nanaimo (BC)
Avayalik (NL)	Niagara (ON)
Coquitlam (BC)	Nipawin (SK)
Inuvik (NT)	Oka (QC)
Kamloops (BC)	Ottawa (ON)
Kitimat (BC)	Saskatoon (SK)
Miminegash (PE)	Toronto (ON)
Miramichi (NB)	Wetaskiwin (AB)
Mississauga (ON)	Winnipeg (MB)

Canada itself has been traced (through French) to Iroquoian *kanata*, "village."

French place names are also found throughout the nation, often marking the paths of French explorers and settlers: Belle Isle (NL), Sault Ste. Marie (ON), Portage-la-Prairie (MB), Souris (MB), Qu'Appelle (SK), Lac La Biche (AB).

Loan Words in Quebec

Concern about the preservation of French in a largely English-speaking continent and worry over the inroads of anglicisms (e.g., *sandwich au poulet* and *un hot dog*) have led, as we have seen in Chapter 12, to stringent measures by the government of Quebec to restrict borrowing from English and to ensure that immigrants become French speaking. To offset the powerful influence of the English language, Quebec has established an Office de la langue française, which annually prepares a volume, the *Grand dictionnaire terminologique* (now also on the Internet at http://www.granddictionnaire.com and on CD-ROM), to provide the public with alternatives to borrowing from English. It provides words for a wide array of items ranging from office furniture to truck axles. It proposes, for example, *courriel*, a compound word formed from *courrier électronique*, literally "electronic mail," in place of "e-mail." But, on the whole, translations — or what appear to be translations — from English are frowned upon; thus, *binette* is recommended for the smiling emoticon employed by computer users, and they are further advised to avoid *souriant*, the equivalent of the English "smiley face." Instead of employing the word *fax*, the *Dictionnaire* suggests *télécopie*; however, as *The Globe and Mail* has observed, "the truth is that plenty of people in Quebec say *fax*, not *télécopie*" (Nolen, 1999), and the Office de la langue française is also aware of the fact that, if the public prefers a borrowed word to a "native" word, there is little it can do about it.

But if French shows the inroads of English, English in Quebec has likewise been affected by its contact with French. The vocabulary of "Quebec English" employs, as we might expect, French words and constructions; for example, English speakers may refer to a *depanneur* (a corner store) and discuss the policies of the *Parti Québécois* or the *Bloc Québécois*. More significant, however, is the use of "English" words that are familiar enough on the surface but that, as used in Quebec, seem odd or confusing to English speakers from elsewhere. Some Quebeckers speak, for example, of an *animator*, by which they mean not a creator of TV cartoons but an "organizer or group leader." They offer to *give a conference*, which, it turns out, is not a meeting or series of meetings but a lecture. Speakers of English both in Quebec and on the CBC speak of *sovereignists* instead of *sovereigntists*, reflecting the influence of French *souverainiste*. Other words used in senses different from their usual English meanings include

        collectivity — a community, people as a whole
        confessional schools — denominational schools
        inscription for a course — enrolment in a course
        permanence — permanent employment, tenure
        syndicate — trade union
        scolarity — schooling

(data from McArthur, 1989)

The meanings of these words reflect the meanings of the equivalent French words.

The Globe and Mail, Saturday, November 27, 1999. Reprinted with permission from The Globe and Mail.

Three other words, *Anglophone*, *Francophone*, and *allophone* (a speaker of a language other than French or English), have recently become part of general Canadian English, especially following the *Official Languages Act* of 1969 in which both French and English were declared official languages of the country.

Further Loan Words

A glance at a map provides an insight into the multicultural mosaic that is modern Canada. Edward McCourt noted that, "within a radius of twenty miles [of one small area of eastern Saskatchewan], we find Dubuc, Bangor, Stockholm, Esterhazy, Langenburg, Thingvilla, Churchbridge — in origin French, Welsh, Swedish, Hungarian, German, Icelandic, British — intermingled with American and eastern Canadian settlements whose centres bear no distinguishing ethnic labels" (as cited in McConnell, 1979).

In 1996, some 21,000 people (0.1 percent of the total population) spoke Yiddish as their mother tongue (*Canadian Global Almanac,* 1999), but many Yiddish words are known, if not used, by non-Jews as well as by non–Yiddish-speaking Jews, as is evident from *The Apprenticeship of Duddy Kravitz* by Mordecai Richler. *Lox* "smoked salmon," *bagel* "a hard roll resembling a doughnut," and *matzo* "unleavened cracker" belong to North American English, as do Yiddish expressions such as *chutzpah, schmaltz, schlemiel, schmuck, schmo,* and *kibitz.*

Other languages also borrow words, and many of them have borrowed from English. Twi speakers drank palm wine before Europeans arrived in Africa. Now they also drink [bia] "beer," [hwiski] "whisky," and [gɔrdɔn ǰin] "Gordon's gin."

Italian is filled with "strange" words such as *snack* (pronounced "znak"), *poster*, and *puzzle* ("pootsle"), and Italian girls use *blushes* and are warned by their mothers against *petting*.

Young Russians have incorporated into their language words such as *jazz, rock*, and the *twist*, which they dance in their *blue jeans* to *rock music*. When former president of the United States Richard Nixon was considered for impeachment by the Congress, the official Communist party newspaper *Pravda* used the word *impeech-mente* instead of the previously used Russian word *ustraneniye* "removal."

For thousands of years, Japanese borrowed heavily from Chinese (to which it is unrelated). Because Japanese uses Chinese characters in its writing system, many native Japanese words coexist with a Chinese loan word. Japanese even has two ways of counting, one using native Japanese words and the other using Chinese loan words for the numbers.

In the past 100 years, Japanese has borrowed heavily from European languages, especially English from which it has thousands of loan words, including technical vocabulary, sports terms, and the jargon used in advertising. The Japanese have a special "syllabary" (similar to our alphabet, but see Chapter 14 on writing systems), which is used primarily to transcribe loan words.

Loan translations are compound words or expressions whose parts are translated directly into the borrowing language. *Marriage of convenience* is a loan translation borrowed from French *mariage de convenance*. Spanish speakers eat *perros calientes*, a loan translation of *hot dogs* with an adjustment reversing the order of adjective and noun, as required by the rules of Spanish syntax. And the *Grand dictionnaire terminologique* urges computer users to say *j'ai sauvegardé* and not *j'ai sauvé*, which it deems a loan translation from English (Nolen, 1999).

Loss of Words

> Pease porridge hot
> Pease porridge cold
> Pease porridge in the pot nine days old
>
> Nursery Rhyme

Words can also be *lost* from a language, though an old word's departure is never as striking as a new word's arrival. When a new word comes into vogue, its unusual presence draws attention, but a word is lost through inattention — nobody thinks of it, nobody uses it, and it fades out of the language.

A reading of Shakespeare's work shows that English has lost many words, such as these taken from *Romeo and Juliet: beseem* "to be suitable," *mammet* "a doll or puppet," *wot* "to know," *gyve* "a fetter," *fain* "gladly," and *wherefore* "why."

Words describing rural objects, such as *stile*, meaning "steps crossing a fence or gate," are fading out of the language due to urbanization.

Pease, from which *pea* is a back formation, is gone, and *porridge*, meaning "boiled cereal grain," is falling out of usage, though it is sustained by a discussion of its ideal serving temperature in the children's story "Goldilocks and the Three Bears."

Technological change may also be the cause for the loss of words. Progress in transportation may eventually cause words like *hansom* and *buckboard* to become obsolete.

Semantic Change

> His talk was like a stream which runs
> with rapid change from rocks to roses.
> It slipped from politics to puns;
> It passed from Mahomet to Moses.
>
> Winthrop Mackworth Praed, "The Vicar" (1829)

We have seen that a language may gain or lose lexical items. Additionally, the meanings or semantic representations of words may change, shifting or becoming broader or narrower.

Broadening

When the meaning of a word becomes broader, that word means everything it used to mean and then some. The Middle English word *dogge* meant a specific breed of dog, but it was eventually **broadened** to encompass all members of the species *canis familiaris*. The word *holiday* originally meant "holy day," a day of religious significance. Today the word signifies any day on which we do not have to work. *Butcher* once meant "slaughterer of goats" (and earlier "of bucks"), but its modern usage is more general. Similarly, *picture* used to mean "painted representation," but today you can take a picture with a camera. A *companion* used to mean a person with whom you shared bread, but today it is a person who accompanies you. *Quarantine* once had the restricted meaning "forty days' isolation." More recent broadening, spurred by the computer age, are *computer* itself, *mouse, cookie, cache, virus,* and *bundle,* to name a few.

Narrowing

In the King James Version of the Bible (1611), God says of the herbs and trees, "to you they shall be for meat" (Genesis 1:29). To a speaker of seventeenth-century English, *meat* meant "food," and *flesh* meant "meat." Since that time, semantic change has **narrowed** the meaning of meat to what it is in Modern English. *Deer* once referred to any "beast" or "animal," as its German cognate *Tier* still does. The meaning of *deer* has been narrowed to a particular kind of animal. Similarly, the word *hound* used to be the general term for "dog," like the German *Hund*. Today *hound* means a special kind of dog. The Old English word that occurs as modern *starve* once meant "to die." Its meaning has narrowed to become "to die of hunger" and in colloquial language "to be very hungry," as in "I'm starved." *Token* used to have the broad meaning "sign," but long ago it was specialized to mean a physical object that is a sign, such as a *love token*. *Liquor* was once synonymous with *liquid, reek* used to mean "smoke" (as it still does in the Scottish dialect), and *girl* once meant "young person of either sex."

Meaning Shifts

The third kind of semantic change that a lexical item may undergo is a shift in meaning. The word *bead* originally meant "prayer." During the Middle Ages, the custom arose of repeating prayers (i.e., *beads*) and counting them by means of little wooden balls on a rosary. The meaning of *bead* shifted from "prayer" to the visible sign of a prayer. The word *knight* once meant "youth" but shifted to a "mounted man-at-arms" and latterly to a person holding a nonhereditary title (which he may have gained through playing in a rock band). *Lust* used to mean simply "pleasure," with no negative or sexual overtones. *Lewd* was merely "ignorant," and *immoral* meant "not customary." *Silly* used to mean "happy" in Old English. By the Middle English period, it had come to mean "naïve," and only in Modern English does it mean "foolish." The overworked Modern English word *nice* meant "ignorant" a thousand years ago. When Juliet tells Romeo "I am too *fond*," she is not claiming she likes Romeo too much. She means "I am too *foolish*."

Reconstructing "Dead" Languages

The branch of linguistics that deals with how languages change, what kinds of change occur, and why they occur is called **historical and comparative linguistics**.

It is *historical* because it deals with the history of particular languages; it is *comparative* because it deals with relationships between languages.

The Nineteenth-Century Comparativists

> When agreement is found in words in two languages, and so frequently that rules may be drawn up for the shift in letters from one to the other, then there is a fundamental relationship between the two languages.
>
> Rasmus Rask (1787–1832)

The nineteenth-century historical and comparative linguists based their theories on observations that there are regular sound correspondences among certain languages and that languages displaying systematic similarities and differences must have descended from a common source language — that is, they were genetically related.

The chief goal of these linguists was to develop and elucidate the genetic relationships that exist among the world's languages. They aimed to establish the major language families of the world and to define principles for the classification of languages. Their work grew out of earlier research.

In 1786, Sir William Jones (an English judge in India) delivered a paper in which he observed that Sanskrit bore to Greek and Latin "a stronger affinity . . . than could possibly have been produced by accident." Jones suggested that these three languages had "sprung from a common source" and that probably Germanic and Celtic had the same origin. The classical philologists of the time attempted to disprove the idea that there was any genetic relationship among Sanskrit, Latin, and Greek, because if such a relationship existed it would make their views on language and language development obsolete. Scottish philosopher Dugall Stewart, for example, put forth the hypothesis that Sanskrit and Sanskrit literature were inventions of Brahmans, who used Greek and Latin as models. He wrote on this issue without knowing a single Sanskrit character, whereas Jones was an eminent Sanskritist.

About thirty years after Jones delivered his important paper, German linguist Franz Bopp pointed out the relationships among Sanskrit, Latin, Greek, Persian, and Germanic. At the same time, a young Danish scholar named Rasmus Rask corroborated these results, bringing Lithuanian and Armenian into the relationship as well. Rask was the first scholar to describe formally the regularity of certain phonological differences between related languages.

Rask's investigation of these regularities was followed up by German linguist Jakob Grimm (of fairy-tale fame), who published a four-volume treatise (1819–1822) that specified the regular sound correspondences among Sanskrit, Greek, Latin, and the Germanic languages. It was not only the similarities that intrigued Grimm and the other linguists but also the systematic nature of the differences. Where Latin has a [p], English often has an [f]; where Latin has a [t], English often has a [θ]; where Latin has a [k], English often has an [h].

FIGURE 13.2

Grimm's Law (an early Germanic sound shift).

Earlier stage:	bh	dh	gh	b	d	g	p	t	k
	↓	↓	↓	↓	↓	↓	↓	↓	↓
Later stage:	b	d	g	p	t	k	f	θ	x (or h)

Grimm pointed out that certain phonological changes that did not take place in Sanskrit, Greek, or Latin must have occurred early in the history of the Germanic languages. Because the changes (illustrated in Figure 13.2) were so strikingly regular, they became known as **Grimm's Law**.

The "earlier stage" referred to in Figure 13.2 is the parent language of Sanskrit, Greek, the Romance and Germanic languages, as well as other languages — namely, Indo-European. The symbols *bh, dh,* and *gh* are breathy voiced stop phonemes, often called "voiced aspirates."

Grimm's Law can be expressed in terms of natural classes of speech sounds: voiced aspirates become unaspirated; voiced stops become voiceless; voiceless stops become fricatives.

Cognates

Cognates are words in related languages that developed from the same ancestral root, such as English *horn* and Latin *cornū*. Cognates often, but not always, have similar meanings in the different languages. From cognates, we can observe sound correspondences and from them deduce sound changes. Thus, from the cognates of Sanskrit, Latin, and English (representing Germanic) shown in Figure 13.3, the regular correspondence *p–p–f* indicates that the languages are genetically related. Indo-European *p is posited as the origin of the *p–p–f* correspondence.[1]

A more complete chart of correspondences is given in Figure 13.4, where a single representative example of each regular correspondence is presented. In most cases, many cognate sets exhibit the same correspondence, which leads to the **reconstruction** of the Indo-European sound shown in the first column.

FIGURE 13.3

Cognates of Indo-European ***p**.

Indo-European	Sanskrit	Latin	English
*p	**p**	**p**	**f**
	pitar-	pater	father
	pad-	pedis	foot
	No cognate	piscis	fish
	paśu	pecu	fee

FIGURE 13.4

Some Indo-European sound correspondences.

Indo-European	Sanskrit		Latin		English	
*p	p	pitar-	p	pater	f	father
*t	t	trayas	t	trēs	θ	three
*k	ś	śun	k	canis	h	hound
*b	b	No cognate	b	labium	p	lip
*d	d	dva-	d	duo	t	two
*g	j	ajras	g	ager	k	acre
*bh	bh	bhrātar-	f	frāter	b	brother
*dh	dh	dhā	f	fē-ci	d	do
*gh	h	vah-	h	veh-ō	g	wagon

Sanskrit underwent the fewest consonant changes, while Latin underwent somewhat more, and Germanic (under Grimm's Law) underwent almost a complete restructuring. Still, the fact that it was phonemes and phonological rules that changed, and not individual words, has resulted in the remarkably regular correspondences that allow us to reconstruct much of the sound system of Indo-European.

Exceptions can be found to these regular correspondences, as Grimm was aware: "The sound shift is a general tendency; it is not followed in every case." Karl Verner in 1875 explained some of the exceptions to Grimm's Law. He formulated **Verner's Law** to show why Indo-European *p*, *t*, and *k* failed to correspond to *f*, *θ*, and *x* in certain cases:

> Verner's Law: *When the preceding vowel was unstressed, f, θ, and x underwent a further change to b, d, and g.*

A group of young linguists known as the **neogrammarians** went beyond the idea that such sound shifts represented only a tendency and claimed that sound laws have no exception. They viewed linguistics as a natural science and therefore believed that laws of sound change were unexceptionable natural laws. The "laws" they put forth often had exceptions, however, that could not always be explained as dramatically as Verner's Law explained the exceptions to Grimm's Law. Still, the work of these linguists provided important data and insights into language change and why such changes occur.

The linguistic work of the early nineteenth century had some influence on Charles Darwin, and in turn Darwin's theory of evolution had a profound influence on linguistics and on all science. Some linguists thought that languages have a "life cycle" and develop according to evolutionary laws. In addition, it was believed that each language can be traced to a common ancestor. This theory of biological naturalism has an element of truth to it, but it is a vast oversimplification of the way languages change and evolve into other languages.

Comparative Reconstruction

> . . . Philologists who chase
> A panting syllable through time and space
> Start it at home, and hunt it in the dark,
> To Gaul, to Greece, and into Noah's Ark.
>
> William Cowper, "Retirement" (1782)

When languages resemble one another in ways not attributable to chance or borrowing, we may conclude that they are related. That is, they evolved via linguistic change from a single ancestral protolanguage. Even if the **parent language** no longer exists, by comparing the **daughter languages** we may deduce many facts about the parent language. The similarities of the basic vocabularies of languages such as English, German, Danish, Dutch, Norwegian, and Swedish are too pervasive for chance or borrowing. In addition to similar vocabularies, the Germanic languages share grammatical properties such as irregularity in the verb *to be* and similar irregular past-tense forms of verbs. We therefore conclude that these languages have a common parent, Proto-Germanic. Of course, there are no written records of Proto-Germanic and certainly no native speakers alive today. Proto-Germanic is a hypothetical language whose properties have been deduced based on its descendants.

Once we know — or suspect — that several languages are related, their protolanguage may be partially determined by **comparative reconstruction**. One proceeds by applying the **comparative method**, which we illustrate with a brief example.

Restricting ourselves to English, German, and Swedish, we find that the word for "man" is *man*, *Mann*, and *man*, respectively. This is one of many word sets in which we can observe the regular sound correspondence [m]–[m]–[m] and [n]–[n]–[n] in the three languages. Using this evidence, we reconstruct *mVn as the word for "man" in Proto-Germanic. The *V* indicates a vowel whose quality we are unsure of since, despite the similar spelling, the vowel is phonetically different in the various Germanic languages, and it is unclear how to reconstruct it without further evidence.

Although we are confident that we can reconstruct much of Proto-Germanic with accuracy, we may never know for sure, and many details remain obscured. To give us confidence in the comparative method, we can apply it to Romance languages such as French, Italian, Spanish, and Portuguese. Their protolanguage is similar to the well-known Latin, so we can verify the method. Consider the following data, focusing on the initial consonant of each word (Lehmann, 1973):

French	Italian	Spanish	Portuguese	
cher	caro	caro	caro	"dear"
champ	campo	campo	campo	"field"
chandelle	candela	candela	candeia	"candle"

In French, [š] corresponds to [k] in the three other languages. Note that in these examples *ch* = [š] and *c* = [k]. This regular sound correspondence, [š]–[k]–[k]–[k], along with other facts, supports the view that French, Italian, Spanish, and Portuguese descended from a common language. The comparative method leads to the reconstruction of [k] in "dear," "field," and "candle" of the parent language and shows that [k] underwent a change to [š] in French but not in Italian, Spanish, or Portuguese, which retained the original [k] of the parent language, Latin.

To use the comparative method, analysts identify regular sound correspondences (not always easy to do) in the cognates of potentially related languages. For each correspondence, they deduce the most likely sound in the parent language. In this way, much of the sound system of the parent may be reconstructed. The various phonological changes that occurred in the development of each daughter language as it descended and changed from the parent are then identified. Sometimes the sound that analysts choose in their reconstruction of the parent language will be the sound that appears most frequently in the correspondence. This approach was illustrated above with the four Romance languages.

Other considerations may outweigh the "majority rules" principle. The likelihood of certain phonological changes may persuade the analyst to reconstruct a "minority" sound or even a sound that does not occur in the correspondence. For example, consider data in these four hypothetical languages:

Language A	Language B	Language C	Language D
hono	hono	fono	vono
hari	hari	fari	veli
rahima	rahima	rafima	levima
hor	hor	for	vol

Wherever Languages A and B have an *h*, Language C has an *f*, and Language D has a *v*. Therefore, we have the sound correspondence *h–h–f–v*. We might be tempted by the comparative method to reconstruct *h* in the parent language, but from other data on historical change, and from phonetic research, we know that *h* seldom becomes *f* or *v*. Generally, the reverse is the case: /f/ and /v/ becoming [h] occurs both historically and as a phonological rule with an acoustic explanation. Therefore, linguists reconstruct an **f* in the parent and posit the sound change "*f* becomes *h*" in Languages A and B and "*f* becomes *v*" in Language D. The other correspondences are not problematic insofar as these data are concerned. They are

o–o–o–o   n–n–n–n   a–a–a–e   r–r–r–l   m–m–m–m

They lead to the reconstructed forms **o, *n, *a, *r,* and **m* for the parent language and to the sound changes "*a* becomes *e*" and "*r* becomes *l*" in Language D. They are "natural" sound changes often found in the world's languages.

It is now possible to reconstruct the words of the protolanguage. They are *fono, fari, rafima,* and *for*. Language D, in this example, is the most innovative, as it has undergone three sound changes. Language C is the most conservative, being identical to the protolanguage insofar as these data are concerned.

The sound changes seen in the previous illustrations are examples of **unconditioned sound change**. The changes occurred irrespective of phonetic context.

Below is an example of **conditioned sound change**, taken from three dialects of Italian:

Standard	Northern	Lombard	
fisso	fiso	fis	"fixed"
kassa	kasa	kasə	"cabinet"

The correspondence sets are

f–f–f   i–i–i   o–o–<loss of sound>   k–k–k   a–a–a   a–a–ə   s:–s–s

It is a straightforward task to reconstruct *f, *i, and *k. Knowing that a geminate such as s: commonly becomes s (recall that Old English f: became f), we reconstruct *s: for the s–s–s correspondence. A shortening change took place in the Northern and Lombard dialects.

There is evidence in these (very limited) data for a weakening of word-final vowels, a change we discussed earlier for English. We reconstruct *o and *a for o–o–*loss of sound>* and a–a–ə. In Lombard, conditioned sound changes took place. The sound o was deleted in word-final position but remained o elsewhere. The sound a became ə in word-final position and remained a elsewhere. The conditioning factor is word-final position as far as we can tell from the data presented. Vowels in other positions don't undergo change.

We reconstruct the protodialect as having had the words *fisso meaning "fixed" and *kassa meaning "cabinet."

It was by means of the comparative method that nineteenth-century linguists, beginning with August Schleicher in 1861, were able to initiate the reconstruction of the long-lost parent language so aptly conceived by Jones, Bopp, Rask, and Grimm. This is the language, which we believe flourished about 6,000 years ago, that we have been calling Indo-European.

Historical Evidence

> You know my method. It is founded upon the observance of trifles.
>
> Sir Arthur Conan Doyle, "The Boscombe Valley Mystery,"
> *The Memoirs of Sherlock Holmes* (1891)

How do we discover phonological changes? How do we know how Shakespeare or Chaucer or the author of *Beowulf* pronounced their versions of English? We have no phonograph records or tape recordings that give us direct knowledge.

For many languages, historical records go back more than 1,000 years. These records are studied to find out how languages were once pronounced. The spelling in early manuscripts tells us a great deal about the sound systems of older forms of modern languages. Two words, for example, spelled consistently in a different manner were probably pronounced differently. Once a number of orthographic contrasts are identified, good guesses can be made as to actual pronunciation. These guesses are supplemented by common words that show up in all stages of the language, allowing their pronunciation to be traced from the present, step by step, into the past.

Another clue to earlier pronunciation is provided by non-English words used in the manuscripts of English. Suppose a French word known to contain the vowel [o:] is borrowed into English. The way the borrowed word is spelled reveals a particular letter–sound correspondence.

Other documents can be examined for evidence. Private letters are an excellent source of data. Linguists prefer letters written by naïve spellers, who will misspell words according to the way they pronounce them. For instance, at one point in English history, all words spelled with -*er* in their stems were pronounced as if they were spelled with -*ar*, just as in Modern British English *clerk* and *derby* are pronounced "clark" and "darby." Some poor spellers kept writing *parfect* for *perfect*, which helped linguists to discover the older pronunciation.

Clues are also provided by the writings of the prescriptive grammarians of the period. Between 1550 and 1750, a group of prescriptivists in England known as **orthoepists** attempted to preserve the "purity" of English. In prescribing how people should speak, they told us how people actually spoke. An orthoepist alive today might write in a manual "It is incorrect to pronounce *Cuba* with a final *r*." Future scholars would know that there were speakers of English who pronounced it that way.

Some of the best clues to earlier pronunciation are provided by puns and rhymes in literature. Two words rhyme if the vowels and final consonants are the same. When a poet rhymes the verb *found* with the noun *wound*, it strongly suggests that the vowels of these two words were identical:

> Benvolio: ... 'tis in vaine to seeke him here
> That meanes not to be found.
> Romeo: He ieasts [jests] at Scarres that neuer felt a wound.

Shakespeare's rhymes are helpful in reconstructing the sound system of Elizabethan English. For example, the rhyming of *convert* with *depart* in Sonnet XI strengthens the conclusion that -*er* was pronounced as -*ar*. Such rhymes were still possible in the eighteenth century when Alexander Pope linked *clerk* with *dark* and *wound* with *bound*.

Dialect differences may provide clues as to what earlier stages of a language were like. There are many dialects of English spoken around the world, and by comparing the pronunciation of various words in several dialects we can arrive at some notion of earlier forms and see what changes took place in the inventory of sounds and in the phonological rules.

For example, since some speakers of English pronounce *Mary, merry,* and *marry* with three different vowels (i.e., [meri], [mɛri], and [mæri], respectively), we suspect that at one time all speakers of English did so. (The different spellings are also a clue.) For some dialects, however, only one of these sounds can occur before /r/ — namely, the sound [ɛ]. Those dialects underwent a sound shift in which both /e/ and /æ/ shifted to /e/ when followed immediately by /r/, another instance of a conditioned sound change.

Historical comparativists working with written records have a difficult job, but it is not nearly as difficult as that of scholars who are attempting to discover genetic relationships among languages with no written history. Linguists must first transcribe large amounts of language data from all the languages; analyze them phonologically, morphologically, and syntactically; and establish a basis for relatedness such as similarities in basic vocabulary and regular sound correspondences that could not be due to chance or borrowing. Only then can the comparative method be applied to reconstructing the extinct protolanguage.

The difficulty of this task can be appreciated when we realize the vast number of readily available texts for nearly all the Indo-European languages dating back thousands of years. Even so, Indo-European is far from being completely reconstructed or completely understood. And it is only one of many families of languages around the world. Linguists such as Franz Boas, Edward Sapir, and Mary Haas have discovered many relationships among Native American languages and have successfully reconstructed Native American protolanguages. Similarly, linguists have been able to group the large number of languages of Africa into four overarching families: Afro-Asiatic, Nilo-Saharan, Niger-Congo, and Khoisan.

Extinct and Endangered Languages

Any language is the supreme achievement of a uniquely human collective genius, as divine and unfathomable a mystery as a living organism.

Michael Krauss, American linguist

I am always sorry when any language is lost, because languages are the pedigree of nations.

Samuel Johnson (1709–1784)

Languages embody the intellectual wealth of the people that speak them. Losing any one of them is like dropping a bomb on the Louvre.

Kenneth Hale, American linguist (1934–2001)

A language becomes extinct when no children learn it.

Sudden language death occurs when all of the speakers of the language die or are killed. Such was the case with Tasmanian and Nicoleño, a Native American language once spoken in California.

Radical language death is similar to sudden language death in its abruptness. Rather than the speakers dying, however, they all stop speaking the language. Often, the reason for this is survival under the threat of political repression or even genocide. Indigenous languages embedded in other cultures suffer death this way. Speakers, to avoid being identified as "natives," simply stop speaking their native language. Children are unable to learn a language not spoken in their environment, and when the last speaker dies, the language dies.

Gradual language death is the most common way for a language to become extinct. It happens to minority languages that are in contact with a dominant language, much as Aboriginal languages are in contact with English. In each generation, fewer and fewer children learn the language until there are no new learners. The language is said to be dead when the last generation of speakers dies out. Cornish suffered this fate in Britain in the eighteenth century, as have many Aboriginal languages in both the North and South continents.

Bottom-to-top language death is the term that describes a language that survives only in specific contexts, such as a liturgical language. Latin, and at one time, Hebrew, are such languages. It contrasts with gradual language death, which in its dying throes is spoken casually and informally in homes and villages. People stopped speaking Latin in daily situations centuries ago, and its usage is confined to scholarly and religious contexts.

> According to a 2002 report by Indian and Northern Affairs Canada, more than a dozen Aboriginal languages spoken in Canada are near extinction. Languages already extinct include Huron (Iroquoian family), Beothuk (Salish family), and Tsetsaut (Athabaskan family).

It is estimated that two of the world's languages are lost every month. According to UNESCO's (2001) *Atlas of the World's Languages in Danger of Disappearing* (Wurm, 2001), a language is considered endangered if it is not learned by at least 30 percent of the children in the community. It is estimated that only 20 percent of the remaining Aboriginal languages in the United States are being learned by children. Already hundreds have been lost. Once widely spoken, languages such as Comanche, Apache, and Cherokee have fewer and fewer native speakers every generation. The same holds true in Canada. The 2001 Canadian Census (Statistics Canada, 2002) indicated that only 20 percent of Aboriginal children in Canada learn an Aboriginal mother tongue. UNESCO considers Canada's Aboriginal languages to be among the most endangered in the world. In the recent past, First Nation children were frequently sent to schools some distance from their home reserves, schools that actively discouraged the children's own languages.

Elsewhere in Canada, a recent study (Kennedy, 2002) found that Nova Scotia's Scottish Gaelic is rapidly disappearing on Cape Breton Island. While 100 years ago there were about 50,000 speakers of Gaelic in the province, today there are fewer than 500 native speakers left on the island.

Doomed languages have existed throughout time. The Indo-European languages Hittite and Tocharian no longer exist, Hittite having passed away 3,500 years ago and the two dialects of Tocharian during the first millennium C.E. Cornish, a Celtic language akin to Breton, expired in England in the late eighteenth century.

Linguists have placed many languages on an endangered languages list. They attempt to preserve these languages by documenting their grammars — that is, the phonetics, phonology, syntax, and morphology — and by recording for posterity the speech of the last few speakers. Through its grammar, each language provides new evidence about the nature of human cognition. And in its literature, poetry, ritual speech, and word structure, each language stores the collective intellectual achievements of a culture, offering unique perspectives on fundamental problems of the human condition. The disappearance of a language is tragic, for not only are these insights and perspectives lost, but the major medium through which a culture maintains and renews itself is gone as well.

Dialects, too, may become extinct. For example, the dialect spoken on Ocracoke Island off the coast of North Carolina is being studied extensively by dialectologist Walt Wolfram. One reason for the study is to preserve the dialect, which is in danger of extinction because so many young Ocracokers leave the island and raise their children elsewhere. The dialect-speaking population is also becoming diluted by vacationers and retirees, attracted to the island by its unique character, including, ironically, the quaint speech of the islanders.

Linguists are not alone in their preservation efforts. Under the sponsorship of language clubs, and occasionally even governments, many endangered languages, such as Irish, are learned by adults and children as a symbol of the culture. In Hawaii, a movement is under way to preserve and teach Hawaiian, the native language of the islands.

The United Nations, too, is concerned. In 1991, UNESCO passed a resolution stating that "as the disappearance of any one language constitutes an irretrievable loss to mankind, it is for UNESCO a task of great urgency to respond to this situation by promoting . . . the description — in the form of grammars, dictionaries, and texts — of endangered and dying languages." In 1996, UNESCO, along with several non-governmental organizations, signed the *Universal Declaration of Linguistic Rights*, a document supporting linguistic rights, especially those of endangered languages.

Occasionally, a language is resurrected from written records. For centuries, classical Hebrew was used only in religious ceremonies, but today, with some modernization, and through a great desire among Jews to speak the language of their forebears, it has become the national language of Israel.

The preservation of dying languages and dialects is essential to the study of Universal Grammar, an attempt to define linguistic properties shared by all languages. This in turn will help linguists to develop a comprehensive theory of language that will include a specific description of the innate human capacity for language.

The Genetic Classification of Languages

> The Sanskrit language, whatever be its antiquity, is of a wonderful structure, more perfect than the Greek, more copious than the Latin, and more exquisitely refined than either, yet bearing to both of them a stronger affinity, both in the roots of verbs and in the forms of grammar, than could possibly be produced by accident; so strong, indeed, that no philologer could examine all three, without believing that they have sprung from some common source, which, perhaps, no longer exists. . . .
>
> Sir William Jones (1786)

We have discussed how different languages evolve from one language and how historical and comparative linguists classify languages into families, such as

Germanic or Romance, and reconstruct earlier forms of the ancestral language. When we examine the languages of the world, we perceive that some are closely related, others more distantly related, and still others apparently unrelated.

Counting to five in English, German, and Vietnamese shows similarities between English and German not shared by Vietnamese:

English	German	Vietnamese
one	ein	mot
two	zwei	hai
three	drei	ba
four	vier	bon
five	funf	nam

This similarity between English and German is pervasive. Sometimes it is extremely obvious (*man/Mann*), at other times a little less obvious (*child/Kind*). No regular similarities or differences apart from those due to chance are found between them and Vietnamese.

Pursuing the metaphor of human genealogy, we say that English, German, Norwegian, Danish, Swedish, and Icelandic are sisters in that they descended from one parent and are more closely related to one another than any of them is to non-Germanic languages such as French or Russian.

If we carry the family metaphor further, we might describe the Germanic and Romance languages as cousins since their respective parents, Proto-Germanic and early forms of Latin, were siblings. The Romance languages of French, Spanish, Portuguese, Italian, and Romanian, then, are sister languages to each other and daughter languages of Latin. The numbers from one to three in English and two Romance languages, compared with the unrelated Japanese numbers, reveal something of this relationship:

Spanish	French	English	Japanese
uno	un	one	ichi
dos	deux	two	ni
tres	trois	three	san

As with human families, there are cousins, and then there are distant cousins. If the Germanic and Romance languages are truly cousins, then languages such as Greek, Armenian, Albanian, and even the extinct Hittite and Tocharian are distant cousins. So are Irish, Scots Gaelic, Welsh, and Breton, whose protolanguage, Celtic, was once widespread throughout Europe and the British Isles. Breton is spoken by the people living in the northwest coastal region of France called Brittany. It was brought there by Celts fleeing from Britain in the seventh century and has been preserved as the language of some Celtic descendants in Brittany ever since. Russian is also a distant cousin, as are its sisters, Bulgarian, Serbo-Croatian, Polish, Czech, and Slovak. The Baltic language Lithuanian is related to English, as is its sister language, Latvian. A neighbouring language, Estonian, however, is not a relative. Sanskrit, as was pointed out by Sir William Jones, though far removed geographically and temporally, is nonetheless a relative. Its daughters, Hindi and Bengali, spoken primarily in South Asia, are distantly related to English. Even the Persian spoken in modern Iran is a distant cousin of English.

All the languages mentioned in the previous paragraph, except for Estonian, are related, more or less distantly, because they descended from Indo-European.

Figure 13.5 is an abbreviated "family tree" of the Indo-European languages that gives a genealogical and historical classification of the languages shown. All the languages of the world may be similarly classified. The diagram is, of course, simplified. It may appear from it, for example, that all the Slavic languages emerged at once, when in fact the nine languages appearing here can be organized hierarchically, showing that some are more closely related than others. In other words, the various separations that resulted in the nine Slavic languages we see today occurred at different times over a long period.

Another simplification in the diagram is that the "dead ends" — languages that evolved and died leaving no offspring, such as Hittite and Tocharian — are not included.

The family tree also fails to show a number of intermediate stages that must have existed in the evolution of modern languages. Languages do not evolve abruptly, which is why comparisons with the genealogical trees of biology have limited usefulness.

Finally, the diagram fails to show a number of Indo-European languages because of lack of space.

Languages of the World

> And the whole earth was of one language, and of one speech.
>
> Genesis 11:1

> Let us go down, and there confound their language, that they may not understand one another's speech.
>
> Genesis 11:7

> There are no primitive languages. The great and abstract ideas of Christianity can be discussed even by the wretched Greenlanders.
>
> Johann Peter Suessmilch (1756)

The Northwest Territories recognize eleven official languages from several language families: English, French, Gwich'in, Cree, Dogrib, Chipewyan, Inuinnaqtun, Inuktitut, Inuvialuktun, North Slavey, and South Slavey.

Most of the world's languages do not belong to the Indo-European family, including many of the languages spoken among First Nations communities in Canada (see Figures 13.6 and 13.7). Linguists have also attempted to classify the non–Indo-European languages according to their genetic relationships. The task is to identify the languages that constitute a family and the relationships that exist among them.

Linguists are frequently asked about the number of languages in the world, but it is hard to ascertain that number because of disagreement over what constitutes a language as opposed to a dialect. How different must two dialects be

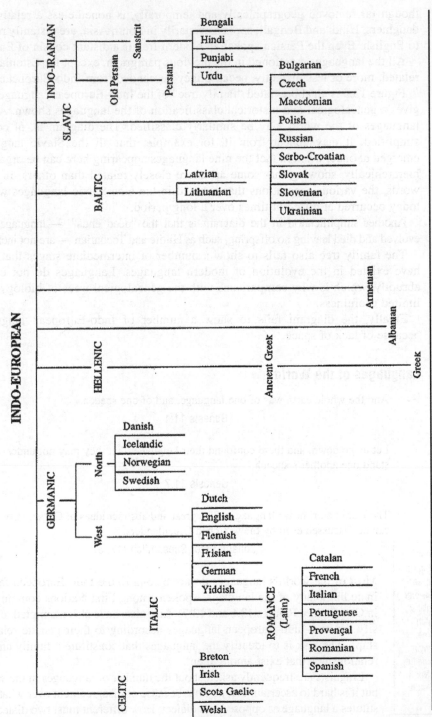

FIGURE 13.5

The Indo-European family of languages.

FIGURE 13.6

Major language families of the world.

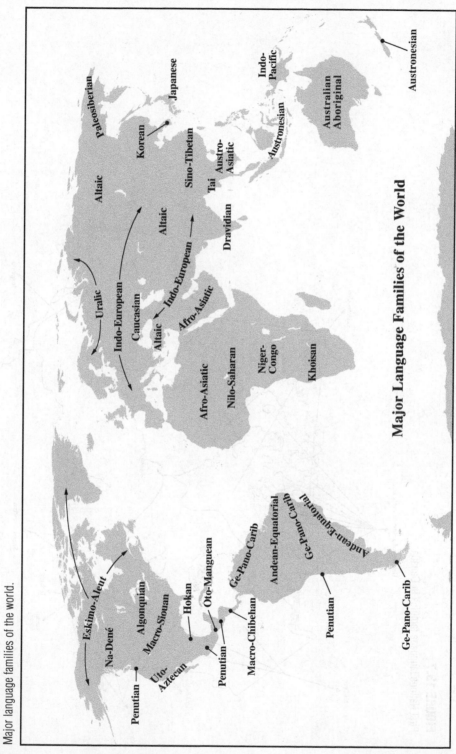

Major Language Families of the World

FIGURE 13.7

First Nations language families in Canada.

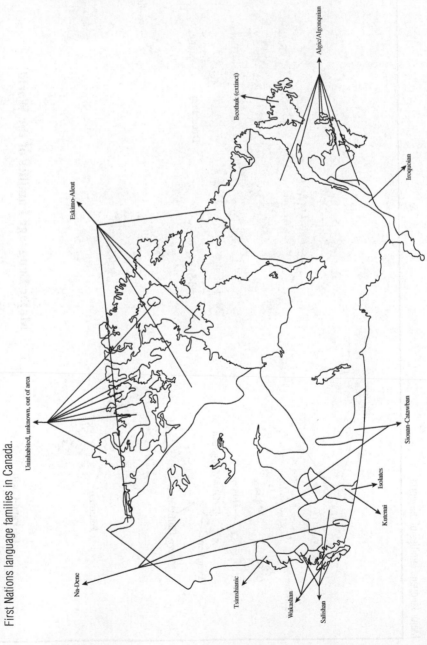

before they become separate languages? One criterion is that of mutual intelligibility. As long as two dialects remain mutually intelligible, it is generally believed that they cannot be considered separate languages. But mutual intelligibility itself lies on a sliding scale, as all of us know who have conversed with persons speaking dialects of our native language whom we do not understand completely.

The Indo-Iranian languages Hindi and Urdu are listed as separate languages in Figure 13.5, yet they are mutually intelligible in their spoken forms and are arguably dialects of one language. However, each uses a different writing system, and each is spoken in communities of differing religious beliefs and nationalities. Hindi, for the most part, is spoken in India by Hindus. Urdu is spoken in Pakistan by Muslims. So what constitutes a separate language is not always determined by linguistic factors alone.

On the other hand, mutually unintelligible languages spoken in China, because they share the same writing system and culture and are spoken within a single political boundary, are often thought of as dialects.

Estimates of the number of languages in the world vary widely: the minimum has been set at 4,000 and the maximum at 8,000. It is often surprising to discover which languages are genetically related and which ones aren't. Within the Indo-European family, we find that faraway Punjabi is an Indo-European language, whereas Hungarian, surrounded on all sides by Indo-European languages, is not.

It is not possible in an introductory text such as this to give an exhaustive table of families, subfamilies, and individual languages. Besides, a number of genetic relationships have not yet been firmly established. For example, linguists are divided as to whether Japanese and Turkish are related or not. We will simply mention several language families with a few of their member languages. These families are not thought to be related to one another or to Indo-European. This may be a result, however, of our inability to delve into the past far enough to see commonalities that time has since erased. We can never entirely eliminate the possibility that all the world's languages sprang ultimately from a single source, an "ur-language" that some have termed **Nostratic**, concealed in the depths of the past.

> Most of the indigenous languages of Europe belong to the Indo-European family; exceptions include Finnish, Saami, Estonian, Hungarian and Basque.

Uralic is the other major family of languages, besides Indo-European, spoken on the European continent. Hungarian, Finnish, and Estonian are the major representatives of the group.

Afro-Asiatic languages are a large family spoken in northern Africa and the Middle East. They include the modern Semitic languages of Hebrew and Arabic, as well as languages spoken in biblical times, such as Aramaic, Babylonian, Canaanite, and Moabite.

The *Sino-Tibetan* family includes Mandarin, the most populous language in the world, spoken by about one billion Chinese. It also includes all of the Chinese "dialects" plus Burmese and Tibetan.

Most of the languages of Africa belong to the *Niger-Congo* family. It includes more than 900 languages, such as Swahili, Kikuyu, and Zulu.

Equally numerous, the *Austronesian* family contains about 900 languages, spoken over a wide expanse of the globe, from Madagascar, off the coast of Africa, to Hawaii. Hawaiian itself, of course, is an Austronesian language, as is Maori, spoken in New Zealand; Tagalog, spoken in the Philippines; and Malay, spoken in Malaysia and Singapore, to mention only a few.

Dozens of language families include hundreds of languages that are, or were, spoken in North and South America. Knowledge of the genetic relationships among these families of languages is often tenuous, and, because so many of the languages are approaching extinction, there may be little hope for as complete an understanding of the Amerindian language families as linguists have achieved for Indo-European.

Types of Languages

All the Oriental nations jam tongue and words together in the throat, like the Hebrews and Syrians. All the Mediterranean peoples push their enunciation forward to the palate, like the Greeks and the Asians. All the Occidentals break their words on the teeth, like the Italians and Spaniards. . . .

Isidore of Seville (seventh century C.E.)

There are many ways to classify languages. One way discussed in this chapter is according to the language "family." This method would be like classifying people according to whether they were Johnsons, Singhs, Cohens, or Liangs. Another way is by certain linguistic traits, regardless of family. With people, this method would be like classifying them according to height and weight or hair and eye colour.

Every language has sentences that include a subject (for this section only, S will be an abbreviation of *subject* rather than of *sentence*), an object (O), and a verb (V), although some sentences do not have all three elements. Languages have been classified according to the basic or most common order in which these elements occur in the language.

There are six possible orders — SOV (subject, object, verb), SVO, VSO, VOS, OVS, OSV — permitting six possible language types. Examples of some of the languages in these classes are

SVO: English, French, Swahili, Hausa, Thai
VSO: Tagalog, Irish, (classical) Arabic, (biblical) Hebrew
SOV: Turkish, Japanese, Persian, Georgian, Inuit
OVS: Apalai (Brazil), Barasano (Colombia), Panare (Venezuela)
OSV: Apurina and Xavante (Brazil)
VOS: Cakchiquel (Guatemala), Huave (Mexico), Coeur d'Alene (Idaho)

(examples of VOS, OVS, OSV from Pullum, 1981)

The most frequent word orders found in languages of the world are SVO, VSO, and SOV. The basic VSO and SOV sentences may be illustrated as follows:

VSO (Tagalog): Sumagot siya sa propesor
answered he the professor
"He answered the professor."

SOV (Turkish): Romalilar barbarlari yendiler
Romans barbarians defeated
"The Romans defeated the barbarians."

Languages with OVS, OSV, and VOS basic word order are much rarer.

The order of other sentence components in a language is most frequently correlated with the language type. If a language is of a type in which the verb precedes the object — a VO language, which includes SVO, VSO, and VOS — then the auxiliary verb tends to precede the verb, adverbs tend to follow the verb, and the language utilizes prepositions, which precede the noun, among other such ordering relationships. English exhibits all these tendencies.

In OV languages, most of which are SOV, the opposite tendency occurs; auxiliary verbs tend to follow the verb, adverbs tend to precede the verb, and there are postpositions, which function similarly to prepositions but follow the noun. Japanese, an SOV language, has postpositions, as we saw in a previous section. Also in Japanese, the auxiliary verb follows the verb, as illustrated by the following sentence:

Akiko   wa   sakana   o   tabete   iru
Akiko   *topic marker*   fish   *object marker*   eating   is
"Akiko is eating fish."

We should emphasize that the correlations between language type and the word order of syntactic categories in sentences are "tendencies," not inviolable rules; different languages follow them to a greater or lesser degree.

The knowledge that speakers of the various languages have about word order is revealed in the particular phrase structure rules of the languages. In English, an SVO language, the verb precedes its NP object: VP → V NP. In Turkish and Japanese, SOV languages, the NP object precedes the verb in the corresponding phrase structure rules. Similarly, the rule PP → P NP (the preposition in a prepositional phrase precedes the noun phrase) occurs in SVO languages, whereas the rule PP → NP P is the correlate occurring in SOV languages.

If a language is, say, SVO, this does not mean that SVO is the only possible word order. Yoda, the Jedi Master from the motion picture *Return of the Jedi*, speaks a strange but perfectly understandable style of English that achieves its eccentricity by being OSV. Some of Yoda's utterances are

Sick I've become.
Strong with the Force you are.
Your father he is.
When 900 years you reach, look as good you will not.

For linguists, the many languages and language families provide essential data for the study of Universal Grammar. Although these languages are diverse in many ways, they are also remarkably similar. We find that the languages of the Maoris of New Zealand, the Zulus of Africa, and the Aboriginal peoples of North and South America all have similar sounds, similar phonological and syntactic rules, and similar semantic systems.

Why Do Languages Change?

Stability in language is synonymous with rigor mortis.
Ernest Weekley (1865–1954)

There is no single explanation for language change, nor can every change be fully explained. No one knows exactly how or why languages change. As we have shown, linguistic changes do not happen suddenly. Speakers of English did not wake up one morning and decide to use the word *beef* for "ox meat"; nor do all the children of one particular generation grow up to adopt a new word. Changes are more gradual, particularly changes in phonology and syntax.

Of course, certain changes may occur instantaneously for any one speaker. When a new word is acquired by a speaker, it is not gradually acquired, although full appreciation of its possible uses may come slowly. When a new rule is incorporated into a speaker's grammar, it is either in or not in the grammar. It may at first be an optional rule, so that sometimes it is used and sometimes it is not, possibly determined by social context or other external factors; however, the rule is either there or not there for use. What is gradual about language change is the spread of certain changes over an entire speech community.

A basic cause of change is the way children acquire the language. No one teaches a child the rules of the grammar; each child constructs a personal grammar alone, generalizing rules from the linguistic input received. The child's language develops in stages until it approximates the adult grammar. The child's grammar is never exactly like that of the adult community, because children receive diverse linguistic input. Certain rules may be simplified or overgeneralized, and vocabularies may show small differences that accumulate over several generations.

The older generation may be using certain rules optionally. For example, at certain times they may say *It's I* and at other times *It's me*. The less formal style is usually used with children, who as the next generation may use only the *me* form of the pronoun in this construction. In such cases, the grammar will have changed.

The reasons for some changes are relatively easy to understand. Before television, there was no such word as *television*. It soon became a common lexical item. Borrowed words, too, generally serve a useful purpose, and their entry into the language is not mysterious. Other changes are more difficult to explain, such as the Great Vowel Shift in English.

One plausible source of change is **assimilation**, a kind of **ease of articulation** process in which one sound influences the pronunciation of another adjacent or nearby sound. Due to assimilation, vowels are frequently nasalized before nasal consonants because it is easiest to lower the velum to produce nasality in advance of the actual consonant articulation. This results in the nasalization of the preceding vowel. Once the vowel is nasalized, the contrast that the nasal consonant provided can be equally well provided by the nasalized vowel alone, and the redundant consonant may be deleted. The contrast between oral and nasal vowels that exists in many languages of the world today results from such a historical sound change.

In French at one time, *bol* "basin," *botte* "high boot," *bog* "a card game," *bock* "Bock beer," and *bon* "good" were pronounced [bɔl], [bɔt], [bɔg], [bɔk], and [bɔ̃n], respectively. Notice that in *bon* there was a final nasal consonant, which *conditioned* the nasalization of the preceding vowel. Due to a conditioned sound change that deleted nasal consonants in word-final position, *bon* is pronounced [bɔ̃] in modern French; the nasal vowel alone maintains the contrast with the other words.

Another example from English illustrates how such assimilative processes can change a language. In Old English, word-initial [kʲ] (like the initial sound in *cute*), when followed by /i/, was further palatalized to become our modern palatal affricate /č/, as illustrated by the following words:

Old English (*c* = [kʲ])	Modern English (*ch* = [č])
ciese	cheese
cinn	chin
cild	child

The process of palatalization is found in many languages. In Twi, for example, the word meaning "to hate" was once pronounced [ki]. The [k] became first [kʲ] and then finally [č], so that today "to hate" is pronounced [či].

Ease-of-articulation processes, which make sounds more alike, are countered by the need to maintain contrast. Thus, sound change also occurs when two sounds are acoustically similar, with risk of confusion. We saw a sound change of /f/ to /h/ in an earlier example that can be explained by the acoustic similarity of [f] to other sounds.

Another kind of change that can be thought of as "economy of memory" results in a reduction of the number of exceptional or irregular morphemes. This kind of change has been called **analogic change**. It may be through analogy to *foe/foes* and *dog/dogs* that speakers started saying *cows* as the plural of *cow* instead of the earlier plural *kine*. By analogy to *reap/reaped, seem/seemed*, and *ignite/ignited*, children and adults are now saying *I sweeped the floor* (instead of *swept*), *I dreamed last night* (instead of *dreamt*), and *She lighted the bonfire* (instead of *lit*).

The same kind of analogic change is exemplified by our regularization of exceptional plural forms, which is a kind of morphological change. We have borrowed words such as *datum/data, agendum/agenda, curriculum/curricula, bandit/banditi, memorandum/memoranda, medium/media, criterion/criteria*, and *virtuoso/virtuosi*, to name just a few. The irregular plurals of these nouns have been replaced by regular plurals among many speakers: *agendas, curriculums, memorandums, criterias, virtuosos.* In some cases, the borrowed original plural forms were considered to be singular (as in *agenda* and *criteria*), and the new plural is therefore a "plural-plural." Also, many speakers now regard *data* and *media* as nouns that do not have plural forms, like *information.* All these changes lessen the number of irregular forms that must be remembered.

Some Additional Sound Changes

Old English words that have survived into Modern English provide examples of some additional systematic sound changes that have helped shape language. While some of these processes have been discussed previously, it may be useful to review them and a few others at this point.

The Old English words *ðridda* and *brid* became Modern English *third* and *bird* through a process of **metathesis**, that is, through an interchange and reordering of segments that effectively reverses the order of their sequence.

Epenthesis consists of the insertion of vowels in a word. This frequently serves to break up heavy **consonant clusters**, and a vowel intervening between consonants increases the ease of pronunciation. It has been suggested that the presence of an epenthic sound may be the result of incoordination in the movement from one sound segment to another. Thus, the Old English word *ofen* (our word *oven*) developed from Germanic *ofn* with an inserted vowel. We often hear an epenthic vowel [ə] between the consonants in modern words such as *elm* and *film*; similarly, *athletic* often becomes [æθəlɛtɪk].

Consonant clusters can also undergo simplification by the loss of a segment as in Old English *betst* and *godspell* (Modern English *best* and *gospel*). Initial consonant groupings such as *hl-, hn-, hr-, gn-,* and *kn-* (often spelled *cn-*) were also simplified; thus, Old English *hnappian, hring,* and *hlāf* become *nap, ring,* and *loaf.* In some instances modern spelling preserves older pronunciations as does the *gn-* of *gnæt* (*gnat*) and the *kn-* in *knight* (*cniht*). The rules of Modern English restrict the choice or location of consonant clusters available to speakers, and these initial groupings are no longer permitted, whatever their status might have been in Old and Middle English.

Loss of vowels in all positions in a word is a major process that has affected the grammatical structure of English. **Apocope**, the loss of a final vowel, is common in languages with a strong stress accent on the initial syllables of words such as English and German. This process eliminated final vowels, thereby affecting the markers for case and person. Thus, the past-tense, first-person singular of the Old English verb *temman* was *temede* /temədə/, which, as Winfred Lehmann (1973) points out, became the Modern English *tamed* with the loss of final -*e*. Apocope further affected nouns, reducing many to monosyllables as in Old English *nama* /namə/ (Modern English *name* /nem/). The medial vowel of *temede* was also lost, a process known as **syncope**. This process is apparent in our everyday pronunciation of words such as *business, Wednesday, family,* and *evening.*

Aphesis or **aphaeresis** — the loss of initial vowels — occurs in the pronunciation of *possum* for *opossum* and in the colloquial *cross* in a sentence such as "*I live cross the street*" or *bout* for *about,* "*It's bout time!*" In the thirteenth century, *estate* was borrowed from French and became the English word *state* by the process of aphesis while the French word subsequently lost *s* before *t,* leading to the modern form *état.*

A less common process in the history of English, **hapology**, the loss of repeated identical or nearly identical segments, is apparent in the name of *Engla land,* the land of the Angles, which was reduced to *England.* Hapology occurs among many speakers of modern British dialects who say /tɛmpərɪ/ for *temporary* and /sɛkətrɪ/ for *secretary.*

Many more changes, both conditioned and unconditioned, have taken place in English since the Germanic peoples settled in the British Isles. We have not, for example, discussed the development of excrescent sounds — the /t/ one sometimes hears at the end of *across,* or considered the loss of final nasal consonants in Old English. While these examples have been drawn largely from the history of English, they are by no means unique to English. Every language is historically rich and complex; the changes that mould a language over time can only be touched on in the few paragraphs available to us.

Simplification and regularization of grammars occur, but so does elaboration or complication. Old English rules of syntax became more complex, imposing a stricter word order on the language, at the same time that case endings were being simplified. A tendency toward simplification is counteracted by the need to limit potential ambiguity. Much of language change is a balance between the two.

Many factors contribute to linguistic change: simplification of grammars, elaboration to maintain intelligibility, borrowing, and lexical additions. Changes are actualized by children learning the language, who incorporate them into their grammars. While the exact reasons for linguistic change are still elusive, it is clear that the imperfect learning of the adult dialects by children is a contributing factor. Perhaps language changes for the same reason that all things change: it is the nature of things to change. As Heraclitus pointed out thousands of years ago, "All is flux, nothing stays still. Nothing endures but change."

Summary

Languages change. Linguistic change such as **sound shift** is found in the history of all languages, as evidenced by the **regular sound correspondences** that exist between different stages of the same language, different dialects of the same language, and different languages. Languages that evolve from a common source are **genetically related**. Genetically related languages were once dialects of the same language. For example, English, German, and Swedish were dialects of an earlier form of Germanic called **Proto-Germanic**, while earlier forms of Romance languages, such as Spanish, French, and Italians, were dialects of Latin. Going back even further in time, earlier forms of Proto-Germanic, Latin, and other languages were dialects of **Indo-European**.

All components of the grammar may change. Phonological, morphological, syntactic, lexical, and semantic changes occur. Words, morphemes, phonemes, and rules of all types may be added, lost, or altered. The meaning of words and morphemes may **broaden, narrow**, or shift. The lexicon may expand by **borrowing**, which results in **loan words** in the vocabulary. It also grows through word **coinage, blends, acronyms**, and other processes of word formation. On the other hand, the lexicon may shrink as certain words are no longer used and become obsolete.

No one knows all the causes of linguistic change. Change comes about through the restructuring of the grammar by children learning the language. Grammars may appear to change in the direction of simplicity and regularity, as in the loss of the Indo-European case morphology, but such simplifications may be compensated for by other complexities, such as stricter word order. A balance is always present between simplicity — languages must be learnable — and complexity — languages must be expressive and relatively unambiguous.

Some sound changes result from **assimilation**, a fundamentally physiological process of **ease of articulation**. Others, like the **Great Vowel Shift**, are more difficult to explain. Some grammatical changes are **analogic changes**, generalizations that lead to more regularity, such as *sweeped* instead of *swept*.

The study of linguistic change is called **historical and comparative linguistics**. Linguists use the **comparative method** to identify regular sound correspondences among the **cognates** of related languages and systematically reconstruct an earlier **protolanguage**. This **comparative reconstruction** allows linguists to peer backward in time and determine the linguistic history of a language family, which may then be represented in a tree diagram similar to Figure 13.5.

Linguists estimate that there are 4,000 to 8,000 languages spoken in the world today. These languages are grouped into families, subfamilies, and so on, based on their genetic relationships. A vast number of these languages are dying out because in each generation fewer children learn them. However, attempts are being made to preserve dying languages and dialects for the knowledge they bring to the study of Universal Grammar and the culture in which they are spoken.

Note

1. The **asterisk** before a letter indicates a "reconstructed" sound. It does not mean an unacceptable form. This use of the asterisk occurs only in this chapter.

Exercises

1. Many changes in the phonological system have occurred in English since 449 C.E. Below are some Old English words (given in their spelling and phonetic forms) and the same words as we pronounce them today. They are typical of regular sound changes that took place in English. What sound changes have occurred in each case?

> Example: OE hlud [xlu:d] → Mod E loud
> Changes: (1) The [x] was lost.
> (2) The long vowel [u:] became [aw].

	OE		Mod E
a.	crabbe [krabə]	→	crab
b.	fisc [fɪsk]	→	fish
c.	fūl [fu:l]	→	foul
d.	gāt [ga:t]	→	goat
e.	lǣfan [læ:van]	→	leave
f.	tēþ [te:θ]	→	teeth

2. The Early Middle English Vowel Shortening and the Great Vowel Shift in English left its traces on Modern English in meaning-related pairs such as

   a. serene/serenity [i]/[ɛ]
   b. divine/divinity [aj]/[ɪ]
   c. sane/sanity [e]/[æ]

   List five such meaning-related pairs that relate [i] and [ɛ] as in example a, [aj] and [ɪ] as in b, and [e] and [æ] as in c.

	[i]/[ɛ]	[aj]/[ɪ]	[e]/[æ]
(1)			
(2)			
(3)			
(4)			
(5)			

3. Below are some sentences taken from Old English, Middle English, and early Modern English texts, illustrating some changes that have occurred in the syntactic rules of English grammar. (*Note*: In the sentences, the earlier spelling forms and words have been changed to conform to Modern English. That is, the OE sentence *His suna twegen mon brohte to þæm cynige* would be written as *His sons two someone brought to that king*, which in Modern English would be *His two sons were brought to the king*.) Underline the parts

of each sentence that differ from Modern English. Rewrite the sentence in Modern English. State, if you can, what changes must have occurred.

> Example: It *not* belongs to you. (Shakespeare, *Henry IV*, Part II)
> Mod. Eng.: *It does not belong to you.*
> Change: At one time, a negative sentence could be formed by placing *not* before the main verb. Today the word *do*, in its proper morphological form, must appear before the *not*.

   a.   It nothing pleased his master.
   b.   He hath said that we would lift them whom that him please.
   c.   I have a brother is condemned to die.
   d.   I bade them take away you.
   e.   I wish you was still more a Tartar.
   f.   Christ slept and his apostles.
   g.   Me was told.

4.   It is not unusual to find a yearbook or almanac publishing a "new word list." In the past few decades, numerous new words have entered the English language, such as *Teflon, liposuction, and blog*. From the computer field, we have new or incipient words such as *byte* and *biochip*. Other words have been expanded in meaning, such as *memory* to refer to the storage part of a computer and *crack* to refer to a form of cocaine.

   a.   Think of five other words or compound words that have entered the language in the past ten years. Describe briefly the source of the word.
   b.   Think of three words that might be "on the way out." (*Hint:* Consider *flapper, groovy,* and *slay/slew*. Dictionary entries that say "archaic" are a good source.)

*5.   Here is a table showing, in phonemic form, the Latin ancestors of ten words in Modern French:

Latin	French	
kor	kœr	"heart"
kantāre	šāte	"to sing"
klārus	kler	"clear"
kervus	sɛrf	"hart" (deer)
karbō	šarbɔ̃	"coal"
kwandō	kã	"when"
kentum	sã	"hundred"
kawsa	šoz	"thing"
kinis	sãdrə	"ashes"
kawda koda	kø	"tail"

Note: œ and ø are mid-front, rounded vowels.

Are the following statements true or false?

a. The Modern French word for "thing" shows that a [k], which occurred before the vowel [o] in Latin, became a [š] in French.

b. The French word for "tail" probably derived from the Latin word [koda] rather than from [kawda].

c. One historical change illustrated by these data is that [s] became an allophone of the phoneme /k/ in French.

d. If there was a Latin word *kertus*, then the Modern French word would probably be [sɛr]. (Consider only the initial consonant.)

*6. Here is how to count to five in a dozen languages. Six of these languages are Indo-European, and six are not. Circle the Indo-European ones.

	L1	L2	L3	L4	L5	L6
1	en	jedyn	i	eka	ichi	echad
2	twene	dwaj	liang	dvau	ni	shnayim
3	thria	tři	san	trayas	san	shlosha
4	fiuwar	štyri	ssu	catur	shi	arbaʔa
5	fif	pjeć	wu	pañca	go	chamishsha

	L7	L8	L9	L10	L11	L12
1	mot	ün	hana	yaw	uno	nigen
2	hai	duos	tul	daw	dos	khoyar
3	ba	trais	set	dree	tres	ghorban
4	bon	quatter	net	tsaloor	cuatro	durben
5	nam	tschinch	tasŏt	pindze	cinco	tabon

7. More than 4,000 languages exist in the world today. State one reason this number might grow larger and one reason it might grow smaller. Do you think the number of languages will increase or decrease in the next 100 years? Justify your answer.

8. The vocabulary of English consists of "native" words as well as thousands of loan words. Look up the following words in a dictionary that provides the etymologies (histories) of words. Speculate how each word came to be borrowed from the particular language.

a.	size	h.	robot	o.	skunk	v.	pagoda
b.	royal	i.	check	p.	catfish	w.	khaki
c.	aquatic	j.	banana	q.	hoodlum	x.	shampoo
d.	heavenly	k.	keel	r.	filibuster	y.	kangaroo
e.	skill	l.	fact	s.	astronaut	z.	bulldoze
f.	ranch	m.	potato	t.	emerald		
g.	blouse	n.	muskrat	u.	sugar		

9. Analogic change refers to a tendency to generalize the rules of language, a major cause of language change. We mentioned two instances, the generalization of the plural rule (*cow/kine* becoming *cow/cows*) and the generalization of the past-tense formation rule (*light/lit* becoming *light/lighted*). Think of at least three other instances of "nonstandard" usage that are analogic; they are indicators of possible future changes in the language. (*Hint:* Consider fairly general rules, and see if you know of dialects or styles that overgeneralize them — e.g., comparative formation by adding *-er*.)

10. Below is a passage from Shakespeare's *Hamlet,* Act IV, scene iii.

> HAMLET: A man may fishe with the worme that hath eate of a king, and eate of the fish that hath fedde of that worme.
> KING: What doost thou meane by this?
> HAMLET: Nothing but to shew you how a king may goe a progresse through the guts of a beggar.
> KING: Where is Polonius?
> HAMLET: In heauen, send thither to see, If your messenger finde him not there, seeke him i'th' other place your selfe, but indeed, if you find him not within this month, you shall nose him as you goe up the stayres in the lobby.

Study these lines and identify every difference in expression between Elizabethan and Modern English that is evident (e.g., in line 3, *thou* is now *you*).

11. Here are some data from four Polynesian languages.

Maori	Hawaiian	Samoan	Fijian	Gloss	Proto-Polynesian (see part c)
pou	pou	pou	bou	"post"	
tapu	kapu	tapu	tabu	"forbidden"	
taŋi	kani	taŋi	taŋi	"cry"	
takere	kaʔele	taʔele	takele	"keel"	
hono	hono	fono	vono	"stay, sit"	
marama	malama	malama	malama	"light, moon"	
kaho	ʔaho	ʔaso	kaso	"thatch"	

a. Find the correspondence sets. (*Hint:* There are fourteen. For example: o–o–o–o, p–p–p–b.)

b. For each correspondence set, reconstruct a proto-sound. Mention any sound changes that you observe. For example:

o–o–o–o   *o

p–p–p–b   *p   p → b in Fijian.

c.   Complete the table by filling in the reconstructed words in Proto-Polynesian.

*12.   Consider these data from two North American Native languages:

Yerington Paviotso = YP	Northfolk Monachi = NM	Gloss
mupi	mupi	"nose"
tama	tawa	"tooth"
piwɨ	piwɨ	"heart"
sawaʔpono	sawaʔpono	"a feminine name"
nɨmɨ	nɨwɨ	"liver"
tamano	tawano	"springtime"
pahwa	pahwa	"aunt"
kuma	kuwa	"husband"
wowaʔa	wowaʔa	"Indians living to the west"
mɨhɨ	mɨhɨ	"porcupine"
noto	noto	"throat"
tapa	tape	"sun"
ʔatapɨ	ʔatapɨ	"jaw"
papiʔi	papiʔi	"older brother"
patɨ	petɨ	"daughter"
nana	nana	"man"
ʔatɨ	ʔetɨ	"bow," "gun"

A.   Identify each sound correspondence. (*Hint:* There are ten different correspondences of consonants and six different correspondences of vowels — e.g., *p–p, m–w, a–a,* and *a–e.*)

B.   a.   For each correspondence you identified in A not containing an *m* or *w*, reconstruct a proto-sound (e.g., for *h–h, *h; o–o, *o*).
   b.   If the proto-sound underwent a change, indicate what the change is and in which language it took place.

C.   a.   Whenever a *w* appears in YP, what appears in the corresponding position in NM?
   b.   Whenever an *m* occurs in YP, what two sounds may correspond to it in NM?
   c.   On the basis of the position of *m* in YP words, can you predict which sound it will correspond to in NM words? How?

D.   a.   For the three correspondences you discovered in A involving *m* and *w*, should you reconstruct two or three proto-sounds?
   b.   If you chose three proto-sounds, what are they, and what did they become in the two "daughter" languages, YP and NM?

c. If you chose two proto-sounds, what are they, and what did they become in the "daughter" languages? What further statement do you need to make about the sound changes? (*Hint:* One proto-sound will become two different pairs, depending on its phonetic environment. It is an example of a conditioned sound change.)

E. Based on the above, reconstruct all the words given in the common ancestor from which both YP and NM descended (e.g., "porcupine" is reconstructed as *mɨhɨ*).

References

Boroff, M. (1967). *Sir Gawain and the green knight: A new verse translation.* New York: W.W. Norton & Co.

Canadian Global Almanac. (1999). Toronto: Macmillan Canada.

Chambers, J.K. (1975). Ottawa Valley twang. *Canadian English: Origins and structures* (pp. 55–59). Toronto: Methuen.

Crystal, D. (2006). *How language works.* London: Penguin Group.

Kennedy, M. (2002). *Gaelic Nova Scotia: An economic, cultural, and social impact study.* Halifax: Nova Scotia Museum.

Lehmann, W.P. (1973). *Historical linguistics* (2nd ed.). New York: Holt, Rinehart and Winston.

McArthur, T. (1989). *The English language as used in Quebec.* No. 3. Kingston, ON: Queen's University, Strathy Language Unit.

McConnell, R.E. (1979). *Our own voice: Canadian English and how it is studied.* Toronto: Gage.

Mossé, F. (1952). *A handbook of Middle English* (J.A. Walker, Trans.). Baltimore: Johns Hopkins University Press.

Mustanoja, T.F. (1960). *A Middle English syntax: Part I. Parts of speech.* Helsinki: Société Néophilologique.

Nolen, S. (1999, November 15). You've got ... courriel? *The Globe and Mail,* C1–C2.

Pringle, I., & Padolsky, E. (1981). The Irish heritage of the English of the Ottawa Valley. *English Studies in Canada, 7,* 338–351.

Pullum, G.K. (1981). Languages with object before subject: A comment and a catalogue. *Linguistics, 19,* 147–155.

Statistics Canada. (2002). *2001 census of Canada.* Catalogue number 970007XCB01001.

Strang, B.M.H. (1970). *A history of English.* London: Methuen.

Traugott, E.C. (1972). *The history of English syntax.* New York: Holt, Rinehart and Winston.

Wurm, S. (2001). *Atlas of the world's languages in danger of disappearing* (2nd ed.). Paris: UNESCO Publishing.

Further Reading

Aitchison, J. (1985). *Language change: Progress or decay.* New York: Universe Books.

Anttila, R. (1989). *Historical and comparative linguistics* (2nd ed.). Amsterdam: John Benjamins.

Baugh, A.C., & Cable, T. (2002). *A history of the English language* (4th ed.). London: Routledge.

Campbell, L. (1999). *Historical linguistics: An introduction.* Cambridge, MA: MIT Press.

Cassidy, F.G. (Ed.). (1986). *Dictionary of American regional English.* Cambridge, MA: The Belknap Press of Harvard University Press.

Comrie, B. (Ed.). (1990). *The world's major languages.* New York: Oxford University Press.

Cook, E.-D. (2000). Amerindian languages of Canada. In W. O'Grady & J. Archibald (Eds.), *Contemporary linguistic analysis: An introduction* (4th ed., pp. 358–371). Toronto: Addison Wesley Longman.

Hale, M. (2007). *Historical linguistics: Theory and method.* Malden, MA: Wiley-Blackwell.

Hock, H.H. (1986). *Principles of historical linguistics.* New York: Mouton de Gruyter.

Hock, H.H., & Joseph, B.D. (1996). *Language history, language change, and language relationships: An introduction to historical and comparative linguistics.* New York: Mouton de Gruyter.

Hoenigswald, H.M. (1960). *Language change and linguistic reconstruction.* Chicago: University of Chicago Press.

Jeffers, R.J., & Lehiste, I. (1979). *Principles and methods for historical linguistics.* Cambridge, MA: MIT Press.

Katzner, K. (1986). *The languages of the world.* London: Routledge and Kegan Paul.

Labov, W. (1994). *Principles of language change: Internal factors.* Oxford: Blackwell.

Lehmann, W.P. (1973). *Historical linguistics: An introduction* (2nd ed.). New York: Holt, Rinehart and Winston.

Lyovin, A.V. (1997). *An introduction to languages of the world.* New York: Oxford University Press.

Millward, C.M. (1989). *A biography of the English language.* New York: Holt, Rinehart and Winston.

Nichols, J. (1992). *Linguistic diversity in space and time.* Chicago: University of Chicago Press.

Pedersen, H. (1962). *The discovery of language.* Bloomington: University of Indiana Press.

Pullum, G.K. (1981). Languages with object before subject: A comment and a catalogue. *Linguistics, 19,* 147–155.

Pyles, T. (1993). *The origins and development of the English language* (4th ed.). New York: Harcourt Brace.

Renfrew, C. (1989). The origins of the Indo-European languages. *Scientific American, 261*(4), 106–114.

Ruhlen, M. (1994). *On the origin of languages.* Stanford, CA: Stanford University Press.

Traugott, E.C. (1972). *A history of English syntax.* New York: Holt, Rinehart and Winston.

Voegelin, C.F., & Voegelin, F.M. (1977). *Classification and index of the world's languages.* New York: Elsevier.

Wolfram, W. (2002). Language death and dying. In J.K. Chambers, P. Trudgill, & N. Schilling-Estes (Eds.), *The handbook on language variation and change* (pp. 764–787). Oxford, UK: Blackwell.

Websites

http://alpha.furman.edu/~mmenzer/gvs/ M. Menzer's website on the Great Vowel Shift.

http://www.indo-european.nl/ The *Indo-European Etymological Dictionary* site.

http://www.utexas.edu/cola/centers/lrc/ A website on historical linguistics at the University of Texas.

http://www.pbs.org/wgbh/nova/transcripts/2120glang.html Provides a transcript of the *NOVA* program "In Search of the First Language."

CHAPTER 14
Writing: The ABCs of Language

The Moving Finger writes; and, having writ,
Moves on: nor all thy Piety nor Wit
    Shall lure it back to cancel half a Line,
Nor all thy Tears wash out a Word of it.
                    Omar Khayyám, *Rubáiyát* (1048–1131)

The palest ink is better than the sharpest memory.
                    Chinese proverb

Either write something worth reading or do something worth writing.
                    Benjamin Franklin (1706–1790)

Throughout this book, we have emphasized the *spoken* form of language. The grammar, which represents one's linguistic knowledge, was viewed as the system for relating the sounds and meanings of one's language. The ability to acquire and use language represents a dramatic evolutionary development. No single individual or people discovered or created language. The human language faculty appears to be biologically and genetically determined. This is not true of the written forms of human languages.

Children learn to speak naturally through exposure to language, without formal teaching. To become literate — to learn to read and write — one must make a conscious effort and receive instruction. A large number of languages spoken today throughout the world lack writing systems, and oral literature still abounds among them. In such societies, crucial lore is passed from older to newer generations orally. However, human memory is short lived and the brain's storage capacity limited.

Writing overcomes such problems and allows for communication across space and over time. Writing permits a society to record permanently its literature, history, science, and technology. The development of writing systems is indeed one of the greatest human achievements.

By writing, we mean any of the many visual (nongestural) systems for representing language, including handwriting, printing, and electronic displays of these written forms. It might be argued that writing has become obsolete through electronic means of recording sounds and images. But computers — at least as we now have them and as most people use them — require us to write perhaps even more than before. Moreover, if writing became extinct, there would be no knowledge of electronics for TV technicians to study; there would be, in fact, little technology in years to come. There would be no film or TV scripts, no literature, no books, no mail, no newspapers. There would be some advantages — no bad novels, junk mail, poison-pen letters, or "fine print" — but the losses would far outweigh the gains.

The History of Writing

> An Egyptian legend relates that when the god Thoth revealed his discovery of the art of writing to King Thamos, the good King denounced it as an enemy of civilization. "Children and young people," protested the monarch, "who had hitherto been forced to apply themselves diligently to learn and retain whatever was taught them, would cease to apply themselves, and would neglect to exercise their memories."
>
> Will Durant, *The Story of Civilization 1,* Vol. I (1935)

There are many legends and stories about the invention of writing. Greek legend has it that Cadmus, prince of Phoenicia and founder of the city of Thebes, invented the alphabet and brought it with him to Greece. (He was later banished to Illyria and changed into a snake.) In one Chinese fable, the four-eyed dragon-god Cang Jie invented writing, but in another fable, writing first appeared to humans in the form of markings on a turtle shell. In an Icelandic saga, Odin was the inventor of the runic script. In other myths, the Babylonian god Nebo and the Egyptian god Thoth gave humans writing as well as speech. The Talmudic scholar Rabbi Akiba believed that the alphabet existed before humans were created; and according to Islamic teaching, the alphabet was created by Allah himself, who presented it to humans but not to angels.

Although these are delightful stories, it is evident that, before a single word was written, uncountable billions were spoken; it is highly unlikely that a particularly gifted ancestor awoke one morning and decided, "Today I'll invent a writing system." In fact, the invention of writing systems comes relatively late in human history, and its development was gradual.

Pictograms and Ideograms

> One picture is worth a thousand words.
>
> Chinese proverb

The seeds out of which writing developed were probably the early drawings made by ancient humans. Cave drawings, called **petroglyphs**, such as those found in the Altamira cave in northern Spain, drawn by humans living more than 20,000 years ago, can be "read" today. They are literal portrayals of life at that time. We have

FIGURE 14.1
Canadian Road Signs

| fuel | food | accommodation | camping |
| carburant | restaurant | hébergement | camping |

no way of knowing why they were produced; they may be aesthetic expressions rather than pictorial communications. Later drawings, however, are clearly "picture writings" or **pictograms**. Unlike modern writing systems, each picture or pictogram is a direct image of the object it represents. There is a nonarbitrary relationship between the form and the meaning of the symbol. Comic strips minus captions are pictographic — literal representations of the ideas to be communicated. This early form of "writing" did not have any direct relation to the language spoken, because the pictures represented objects in the world rather than the linguistic names given to these objects; they did not represent the sounds of spoken language.

Pictographic "writing" has been found among peoples throughout the world, ancient and modern: among Africans, First Nations of North America, the Inuit, the Incas of Peru, the Yukagirians of Siberia, and the people of Oceania. Pictograms are used today in international road signs and in other places where the native language of the region might not be adequate. The advantage of such symbols is that they can be understood by anyone because they do not depend on the words of any language. To understand many of the signs on Canadian highways, for example, a visitor does not need to know English or French (see Figure 14.1).

Once a pictogram was accepted as the representation of an object, its meaning was extended to attributes of that object or concepts associated with it. Thus, a picture of the sun could represent "warmth," "heat," "light," "daytime," and so on. Pictograms thus began to represent *ideas* rather than objects. Such generalized, abstract pictograms are called **ideograms** ("idea pictures" or "idea writing").

The difference between pictograms and ideograms is not always clear. Ideograms tend to be a less direct representation, and one may have to learn what a particular ideogram means. Pictograms tend to be literal. For example, the "no parking" symbol consisting of a black circle with a slanting red line through it is an ideogram: it represents the idea of no parking abstractly. A "no parking" symbol showing an automobile being towed away is more literal, more like a pictogram.

Pictograms and ideograms became stylized, possibly because of the ambiguities that could result from "poor artists" or creative "abstractionists" of the time. The simplifying conventions that developed so distorted the literal representations that it was no longer easy to interpret symbols without learning the system.

The ideograms became *linguistic* symbols as they came to stand for the *sounds* that represented the ideas — that is, for the words of the language. This stage represented a revolutionary step in the development of writing systems.

Cuneiform Writing

Much of our information on the development of writing stems from the records left by the Sumerians, an ancient people of unknown origin who built a civilization in southern Mesopotamia (modern Iraq) more than 6,000 years ago. They left innumerable clay tablets containing, among other things, business documents, epics, prayers, poems, and proverbs. So copious are these written records that scholars studying the Sumerians are publishing a seventeen-volume dictionary of their written language. The first of these volumes appeared in 1984.

The writing system of the Sumerians is the oldest one known. They were a commercially oriented people, and, as their business deals became increasingly complex, the need for permanent records arose. An elaborate pictography was developed along with a system of "tallies." Some examples are shown here:

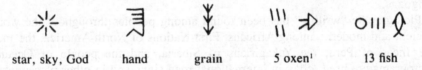

| star, sky, God | hand | grain | 5 oxen[1] | 13 fish |

Over the centuries, their pictography was simplified and conventionalized. The characters or symbols were produced by using a wedge-shaped stylus that was pressed into soft clay tablets. This form of writing is called **cuneiform** — literally, "wedge-shaped" (from Latin *cuneus* "wedge"). Here is an illustration of how Sumerian pictograms evolved to cuneiform:

became   became   star

became   hand

became   fish

The cuneiform "words" do little to remind us of the meanings represented. As cuneiform evolved, its users began to think of the symbols in terms more of the *name* of the thing represented than of the thing itself. Eventually, cuneiform script came to represent words of the language. Such a system is called **logographic** or **word writing**. In this type of writing, the symbol stands for both the word and the concept, which it may resemble however abstractly. Thus, **logograms**, the symbols of a word-writing system, are ideograms that represent, in addition to the concept, the word or morpheme in the language for that concept.

The cuneiform writing system was borrowed by the Babylonians, Assyrians, and Persians. In adopting cuneiform characters in their own languages, the borrowers used them to represent the *sounds* of the *syllables* in their words. In this way, cuneiform evolved into a **syllabic writing** system.

In a syllabic writing system, each syllable in the language is represented by its own symbol, and words are written syllable by syllable. Cuneiform writing was never purely syllabic; there was always a large residue of symbols that stood for whole words. The Assyrians retained a large number of word symbols, even though every word in their language could be written out syllabically if it were desired. Thus, they could write ⟨⟩ *mātu* "country" as

ma   +   a   +   tu

The Persians (ca. 600–400 B.C.E.) devised a greatly simplified syllabic alphabet for their language, which made little use of word symbols. By the reign of Darius I (522–468 B.C.E.), this writing system was in wide use. It is illustrated by the following characters:

da

di

fa

ma

tu

Emoticons are strings of text characters that, when viewed sideways, form a face expressing a particular emotion. They are used mostly in e-mail and newsgroup messages to express a feeling about the text. They are a modern, pictographic system similar to cuneiform in that the same symbols are combined in different manners to convey different concepts. Most everyone who uses e-mail recognizes the smiley face **:-)** to mean "not serious" or "just joking." Several less common emoticons, and their generally accepted meanings, are shown here.

:'-(	"crying"
:-S	"bizarre"
:^D	"love it!"
:-)~	"drooling"

The invention, use, and acceptance of emoticons reflect on a small scale how a writing system such as cuneiform might have spread throughout a country.

The Rebus Principle

When a graphic sign no longer has any visual relationship to the word it represents, it becomes a **phonographic symbol**, standing for the sounds that represent the word. A single sign can then be used to represent all words with the same sounds — the homophones of the language. If, for example, the symbol ⊙ stood for *sun* in English, it could then be used in a sentence such as *My ⊙ is a doctor.* This sentence is an example of the **rebus principle**.

A rebus is a representation of words or syllables by pictures of objects whose names *sound like* the intended word or syllable. Thus, ◉ might represent *eye* or the pronoun *I*. The sounds of the two words are identical, even though the meanings are not. In the same way, 🐝🍃 could represent *belief* (*be + lief = bee + leaf =* /bi/ + /lif/), and 🐝🍃🍃 could be the verb form, *believes*. Similarly, 2 👄 — /tu/ + /lɪp/ — could represent *tulip*.

Proper names can also be "written" in such a way. If the symbol ╎ is used to represent *rod* and the symbol ⚲ represents *man*, then ╎ ⚲ could represent *Rodman*, although nowadays the name is unrelated to either rods or men. Such combinations often become stylized or shortened so as to be more easily written. *Rodman*, for example, might be "written" in such a system as ╎ ⚲ or even ⋋.

This system is not an efficient one, because in many languages words cannot be subdivided into sequences of sounds that have meanings by themselves. It would be difficult, for example, to represent the word *English* (/ɪŋ/ + /glɪš/) in English according to the rebus principle. *Eng* by itself does not "mean" anything, nor does *glish*.

From Hieroglyphs to the Alphabet

At the time that Sumerian pictography was flourishing (ca. 4000 B.C.E.), a similar system was being used by the Egyptians, which the Greeks later called **hieroglyphics** (*hiero* "sacred" + *glyphikos* "carvings"). That the early "sacred carvings" were originally pictography is shown by the following hieroglyphics:

"eye"   "giraffe"   "to rule"[2]   "fresh" or "cool"[3]

Like the Sumerian pictograms, the hieroglyphs came to represent both the concept and the word for the concept. Once this happened, hieroglyphics became a bona fide logographic writing system. Through the rebus principle, hieroglyphics also became a syllabic writing system.

In this "syllabic" stage, hieroglyphics were borrowed by many people, including the Phoenicians, a Semitic people who lived on the eastern shores of the Mediterranean. By 1500 B.C.E., they developed a writing system of twenty-two syllabic characters, the West Semitic Syllabary. For the most part, the characters stood for consonants alone. The reader provided the vowels, and hence the rest of the syllable, through knowledge of the language. (Cn y rd ths?) Thus, the West Semitic Syllabary was both a **syllabary** and a **consonantal alphabet**.

The ancient Greeks tried to borrow the Phoenician writing system, but it was unsatisfactory as a syllabary because Greek has too complex a syllable structure. In Greek, unlike in Phoenician, vowels cannot be determined by grammatical context, so a writing system for Greek required that vowels have their own independent representations. Fortuitously, Phoenician had more consonants than Greek, so when the Greeks borrowed the system they used the extra symbols to represent vowel sounds. The result was **alphabetic writing**, a system in which both consonants and vowels are symbolized. (The word *alphabet* is derived from *alpha* and *beta*, the first two letters of the Greek alphabet.)

> Writing systems are characterized by a particular direction of writing, but the direction has been known to change throughout history. Early Sumerian writing shifted from right-to-left to left-to-right.

Alphabetic systems are those in which each symbol typically represents one sound unit. Such systems are primarily *phonemic* rather than *phonetic*, as is illustrated by the fact that the *p* in both *pit* and *spit* in the English alphabet is one rather than two "letters," even though the sounds are phonetically distinct.

A majority of alphabetic systems in use today derive from the Greek system. This alphabet became known to the pre-Latin people of Italy, the Etruscans, and through them to the Romans, who used it for Latin. Thus, the alphabet spread with Western civilization, and eventually most nations of the world were exposed to, and had the option of using, alphabetic writing.

According to one view, the alphabet was not invented; it was *discovered* (Ohman, 1969). If language did not include discrete individual sounds, then no one could have invented alphabetic letters to represent such sounds. When humans started to use one symbol for one phoneme, they had merely brought their intuitive knowledge of the language sound system to consciousness; they discovered what they already "knew." Furthermore, children (and adults) can learn an alphabetic system only if each separate sound has some psychological reality.

Modern Writing Systems

... but their manner of writing is very peculiar, being neither from the left to the right, like the Europeans; nor from the right to the left, like the Arabians; nor from up to down, like the Chinese; nor from down to up, like the Cascagians, but aslant from one corner of the paper to the other, like ladies in England.

Jonathan Swift, *Gulliver's Travels* (1726)

We have already mentioned the various types of writing systems used in the world: *word* or *logographic writing, syllabic writing, consonantal alphabet writing*, and *alphabetic writing*. Most of the world's written languages use alphabetic writing. Even Chinese and Japanese, whose native writing systems are not alphabetic, have adopted alphabetic transcription systems for special purposes, such as communicating with foreigners.

Word Writing

In a word writing or logographic system, the written character represents both the meaning and the pronunciation of a word or morpheme. The awkwardness of such a system is obvious. For example, the editors of *Webster's Third New International Dictionary* claim more than 450,000 entries. All these words are written using only twenty-six alphabetic symbols, a period, a hyphen, an apostrophe, and a space. It is understandable why, historically, word writing gave way to alphabetic systems in most places in the world.

The major exceptions are the writing systems used in China and Japan. The Chinese system has an uninterrupted history that goes back more than 3,500 years. For the most part, it is a word writing system, each character representing an individual word or morpheme. Longer words may be formed by combining two words or morphemes, as shown by the word meaning "business" *mǎimai*, which is formed by combining the words meaning "buy" and "sell." This system, which could create serious problems if used for English and other Indo-European languages, works for Chinese because *spoken* Chinese has little affixation of bound morphemes (e.g., the *un-* in *unhappy* or the *-fy* in *beautify*).

Chinese writing utilizes a system of **characters**, each of which represents a morpheme or word. Chinese dictionaries and rhyme books contain tens of thousands of these characters, but a person needs to know "only" about 5,000 to read a newspaper. In 1956, the Chinese government moved to simplify the characters. This process was first tried in 213 B.C.E., when Li Si published an official list of more than 3,000 characters whose written forms were simplified by omitting unneeded strokes. Since that time, successive generations have added new characters and modified old ones, creating redundancy and complexity. The character-simplification efforts that have been under way in the past decades are therefore of major importance. An example of the simplifications is given below (Lehmann, 1975):

The Chinese government has adopted a spelling system using the **Roman**

Original	Simplified	Pronunciation	Meaning
餐	歺	cān	"meal"
酒	氿	jiǔ	"wine"
漆	沏	qī	"paint"
稻	籾	dào	"rice crops"
副	付	fù	"deputy"
賽	宭	sài	"to compete"

alphabet, called **Pinyin**, which is now used for certain purposes along with the regular system of characters. Many city street signs are printed in both systems, which is helpful to foreigners. It is not the government's intent, however, to replace the traditional writing, which is viewed as an integral part of Chinese culture. To the Chinese, writing is an art — **calligraphy** — and thousands of years of poetry, literature, and history are preserved in the old system.

An additional reason for keeping the traditional system is that it permits all literate Chinese to communicate even though their spoken languages are mutually unintelligible. Thus, writing has served as a unifying factor throughout Chinese history, in an area where hundreds of languages and different dialects exist. A Chinese proverb states that "people separated by a blade of grass cannot understand each other," but the unified writing system cuts across linguistic differences and allows the people to communicate with each other.

This use of written Chinese characters is similar to the use of Arabic numerals, which mean the same in many different countries. The "character" 5, for example, stands for a different sequence of sounds in English, French, and Finnish. In English it is *five* /fajv/, in French it is *cinq* /sæŋk/, and in Finnish it is *viisi* /viːsi/, but in all these languages, 5, whatever its phonological form, means "five." Similarly, the spoken word for "rice" is different in the various Chinese languages, but the written character is the same. If the writing system in China were to become alphabetic, then each language would be as different in writing as in speaking, and written communication would no longer be possible among the various language communities.

Syllabic Writing

Syllabic writing systems are more efficient than word writing systems, and they are certainly less taxing on the memory. However, languages with a rich structure of syllables containing many consonant clusters (e.g., *tr* or *spl*) cannot be efficiently written with a **syllabary**. To see this difficulty, consider the syllable structures of English.

I	/aj/	V	an	/æn/	VC
key	/ki/	CV	ant	/ænt/	VCC
ski	/ski/	CCV	ants	/ænts/	VCCC
spree	/spri/	CCCV	pant	/pænt/	CVCC
seek	/sik/	CVC	pants	/pænts/	CVCCC
speak	/spik/	CCVC	stamp	/stæmp/	CCVCC
scram	/skræm/	CCCVC	splints	/splɪnts/	CCCVCC
striped	/strajpt/	CCCVCC			CCCVCCC

With more than thirty consonants and over twelve vowels, the number of different possible syllables is immense, which is why English, and Indo-European languages in general, are unsuitable for syllabic writing systems.

The Japanese language, on the other hand, is more suited for syllabic writing, because all words in Japanese can be phonologically represented by about 100 syllables, mostly of the consonant–vowel (CV) type, and there are no underlying consonant clusters. To write these syllables, the Japanese have two syllabaries, each containing forty-six characters, called *kana*. The entire Japanese language can be written using *kana*. One syllabary, *katakana*, is used for loan words and for special effects similar to italics in European writing. The other syllabary, *hiragana*, is used for native words and may occur with Chinese characters, which the Japanese call *kanji*. Thus, Japanese writing is part word writing, part syllable writing.

During the first millennium, the Japanese tried to use Chinese characters to write their language. However, spoken Japanese is totally unlike spoken Chinese (they are genetically unrelated languages). A word writing system alone was not suitable for Japanese, which is a highly inflected language in which verbs may occur in thirty or more different forms. Using modified Chinese characters, the syllabaries were devised to represent the inflectional endings and other grammatical morphemes. Thus, in Japanese writing, Chinese characters will commonly be used for the verb roots and *hiragana* symbols for the inflectional markings.

For example, 行 is the character meaning "go," pronounced [i]. The word for "went" in formal speech is *ikimashita*, written as 行きました, where the *hiragana* symbols きました represent the syllables *ki, ma, shi, ta*. Nouns, on the other hand, are not inflected in Japanese, and they can generally be written using Chinese characters alone.

In theory, all of Japanese could be written in *hiragana*. There are many homophones in Japanese, however, and the use of word characters disambiguates a word that would be ambiguous if written syllabically. Also, like Chinese, Japanese *kanji* writing is an integral part of Japanese culture, and it is unlikely to be abandoned.

Two North American Syllabics

While relatively few originators or developers of scripts around the world are known by name, the same is not true of systems that came to be used among Aboriginal North Americans. The majority of North American scripts were created in the nineteenth century by missionaries of European backgrounds who were concerned to make their religious texts available to the First Nations with whom they worked. One of the earliest to establish a workable script was, however, neither a missionary nor a European. Sikwayi was a most remarkable man who, though he himself could neither read nor write, perceived the advantages these abilities would accord his people and set out to devise a system for the Cherokee language.

In 1821, Sikwayi (or Sequoyah), often called the "Cherokee Cadmus," invented a syllabic writing system for his native language, Cherokee. Sequoyah's script, which survives today essentially unchanged, proved useful to the Cherokee people and is justifiably a point of great pride for them. The syllabary contains eighty-five symbols, many of them derived from Latin characters, which efficiently transcribe spoken Cherokee. A few symbols are shown here:

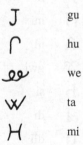

J	gu
ſ	hu
ℓℓ	we
W	ta
H	mi

An alphabetic character can be used to represent a syllable in some languages. In words such as *OK* and *bar-b-q*, the single letters represent syllables (*b* for [bi] or [bə], *q* for [kju]).

As Gaur (1984) has observed, creators of scripts have tended to follow similar lines: that is, "an idea script moved towards a word (picture) script and on to the introduction of phonetic elements, mostly on the basis of the rebus principle, to culminate finally in a syllabic script." Sikwayi, however, seems initially to have considered employing a logographic or word writing system but after a time came to the conclusion that such a method would be inappropriate for Cherokee and turned to a syllabic system as more suitable.

By 1824, Sikwayi had established a system of eighty-five symbols (six vowels, a symbol for /s/, and seventy-eight symbols for CV syllables). For a number of these "letters," he drew on his acquaintance with Roman script — which he nevertheless could not read — while other symbols were modifications of those Roman symbols, both of which he supplemented with his own creations. For this script, see Table 14.1.

Sikwayi's syllabic may not have been a perfect fit for Cherokee — a better system would require 114 symbols instead of 78 — but it was a remarkable achievement and was quickly put into use for books, newspapers, official and religious documents, and personal communication. By 1830, more than half of the adult male population of Cherokees could read and write in Sikwayi's script (Jensen, 1969), and while use of the script has subsequently declined there have been attempts to renew its use (DeFrancis, 1989).

TABLE 14.1
Sikwayi's System of 85 Symbols for the Cherokee Writing System

Sign	Value	Sign	Value	Sign	Value	Sign	Value	Sign	Value
D	a	R	e	T	i	Ꮼ	o	Oꞌ	u
f	ga	Ᏺ	ge	Y	gi	A	go	J	gu
Oᏺ	ha	?	he	Ꭿ	hi	Ᏺ	ho	Γ	hu
W	la	δ	le	Ᏼ	li	G	lo	M	lu
Ᏺ	ma	OI	me	H	mi	З	mo	Ᏺ	mu
θ	na	Ꭲ	ne	ƕ	ni	Z	no	q	nu
I	gwa	Ᏺ	gwe	Ᏺ	gwi	Ꮚ	gwo	Ꮚ	gwu
Ꮁ	sa	4	se	b	si	Φ	so	Ꮚ	su
b	da	Ꮎ	de	Ꮰ	di	Λ	do	S	du
Ꮚ	dla	L	dle	Ꮚ	dli	Ꮙ	dlo	Ꮚ	dlu
G	dza	Ꮙ	dze	Ᏺ	dzi	K	dzo	Ꮰ	dzu
Ꮚ	wa	Ꮚ	we	Ᏸ	wi	Ꮚ	wo	Ꮚ	wu
Ꮚ	ya	Ᏸ	ye	Ꮚ	yi	Ꮚ	yo	Ꮚ	yu
ι	ö	E	gö	Ꮚ	hö	Ꮚ	lö	Oꞌ	nö
Ᏻ	gwö	R	sö	Ꮚ	dö	P	dlö	Ꮚ	dzö
6	wö	B	yö	Ꮚ	ka	Ꮚ	hna	G	nah
Ꮚ	s	W	ta	Ꮚ	te	Ꭷ	ti	L	tla

Hans Jensen, *Sign, Symbol, and Script: An Account of Man's Efforts to Write*. Trans. George Unwin. New York: G.P. Putnam's Sons. 1969, p. 242.

The first European to devise a system of writing for a First Nations people was James Evans (Diringer, 1968). Evans, a young missionary to the Cree in Manitoba, employed his script in 1840 at Norway House on Lake Winnipeg. His script was also a syllabic, a system well suited to Cree, and consisted of forty-four geometric symbols in which vowel differences were signalled by the direction in which the symbol was drawn (see Table 14.2).

Evans's system — modified, of course — "spread beyond the Cree to other Algonquian languages in Canada. By 1880 it was even adapted for use in some Eskimo communities and in some Canadian Athapaskan languages" (Silver & Miller, 1997).

Some commentators have expressed surprise that American Aboriginal scripts did not "progress" to alphabetic systems, but we should keep in mind that,

TABLE 14.2
Evans's Syllabic Script for the Cree Language

a	e	i	o
ba pa	pe	pi	po
ta da	te	ti	to
ka	ke	ki	ko
tša	tše	tši	tšo
la	le	li	lo
ma	me	mi	mo
na	ne	ni	no
ra	re	ri	ro
sa	se	si	so
ya	ye	yi	yo

Hans Jensen, *Sign, Symbol, and Script: An Account of Man's Efforts to Write.* Trans. George Unwin. New York: G.P. Putnam's Sons. 1969, p. 242.

although a syllabary would not fit a language such as English, it functioned well in Cherokee and Cree. In fact, as Silver and Miller (1997) assure us, syllabics are more appropriate for Cree and Cherokee than the alphabetic system we have inherited for the English language.

Consonantal Alphabetic Writing

Semitic languages, such as Hebrew and Arabic, are written with alphabets that consist only of consonants. Such an alphabet works for these languages because consonants form the roots of most words. For example, the consonants *ktb* in Arabic forms the roots of words associated with "write." Thus, *katab* means "to write," *aktib* means "I write," and *kitab* means "a book." Inflectional and derivational processes can be expressed by different vowels inserted into the tri-consonantal roots.

Because of this structure, vowels can be figured out by a person knowing the spoken language, *jst lk y cn rd ths phrs, prvdng y knw nglsh*. English, however, is unrelated to the Semitic languages, and its structure is such that vowels are crucial for reading and writing much of the time. The English phrase *I like to eat out* would be incomprehensible without vowels: *lk t t t*.

Semitic alphabets, primarily to preserve the true pronunciations of religious writings, and secondarily out of deference to children and foreigners learning to read and write, provide a way to express vowels. These vowels come in the form of supplementary marks. In Hebrew, dots or other small figures are placed under, above, or even in the centre of the consonantal letter to indicate the accompanying vowel. For example, ל represents an *l* sound in Hebrew writing. Unadorned, the vowel that follows it would be determined by context. However, לֶ indicates that the vowel that follows is [e], so in effect לֶ represents the syllable [le].

These systems are called consonantal alphabets because only the consonants are fully developed symbols. Sometimes they are considered syllabaries because, once the vowel is perceived by the reader or writer, the consonantal letter appears to stand for a syllable. With a true syllabary, however, a person only needs to know the phonetic value of each symbol to pronounce it correctly and unambiguously. Once you learn a Japanese syllabary, you can read Japanese in a phonetically correct way without any idea of what you are saying. That would be impossible for Arabic or Hebrew.

Alphabetic Writing

Alphabetic writing systems are easy to learn, convenient to use, and maximally efficient for transcribing any human language.

The term **sound writing** is sometimes used in place of *alphabetic writing*, but it does not truly represent the principle involved in the use of alphabets. One sound–one letter is inefficient, because we do not need to represent the [pʰ] in *pit* and the [p] in *spit* by two different letters. It would also be confusing, because the nonphonemic differences between sounds are seldom perceptible to speakers. Except for the phonetic alphabets, whose function is to record the sounds of all languages for descriptive purposes, most, if not all, alphabets have been devised on the **phonemic principle**.

In the twelfth century, an Icelandic scholar developed an orthography derived from the Latin alphabet for the writing of the Icelandic language of his day. Other scholars in this period were also interested in orthographic reform, but the Icelander, who came to be known as "the First Grammarian" (because his anonymous paper was the first entry in a collection of grammatical essays), was the only one of the time who left a record of his principles. The orthography he developed was clearly based on the phonemic principle. He used minimal pairs to show the distinctive contrasts; he did not suggest different symbols for voiced and unvoiced [θ] and [ð], nor for [f] and [v], nor for velar [k] and palatal [č], because these pairs, according to him, represented allophones of the phonemes /θ/, /f/, and /k/, respectively. He did not use these modern technical terms, but the letters of this alphabet represent the distinctive phonemes of Icelandic of that century.

King Seijong of Korea (1417–1450) realized that the same principles held true for Korean when, with the assistance of scholars, he designed a phonemic alphabet. The king was an avid reader and realized that the more than 30,000 Chinese characters used to write Korean discouraged literacy. The fruit of the king's labour was the Korean alphabet called **Hangul**, which originally had seventeen consonants and eleven vowels.

The Hangul alphabet was designed on the phonemic principle. Although Korean has the sounds [l] and [r], Seijong represented them by a single letter because they are allophonic variants of the same phoneme.[4] The same is true for the sounds [s] and [š] and [ts] and [tš].

Seijong showed further ingenuity in the design of the characters themselves. The consonants are drawn so as to depict the place and manner of articulation. Thus, the letter for /g/ is ㄱ to suggest the raising of the back of the tongue to the velum; /m/ is the closed figure ㅁ to suggest the closing of the lips. Vowels in Hangul are easily distinguished from consonants, being drawn as long vertical or horizontal lines, sometimes with smaller marks attached to them. Thus, | represents /i/, – represents /u/, and ㅏ represents /a/.

In Korean writing, the Hangul characters are grouped into squarish blocks, each corresponding to a syllable. The syllabic blocks, though they consist of alphabetic characters, make Korean look as if it were written in a syllabary. If English were written that way, "Now is the winter of our discontent" would have this appearance:

No	i	th	wi	te	o	ou	di	co	te
w	s	e	n	r	f	r	s	n	nt

The space between letters is less than the space between syllables, which is less than the space between words.

These characteristics make Korean writing unique in the world, unlike that of the Europeans, the Arabians, the Chinese, or the Cascagians.

Many languages have their own alphabet, and each has developed certain conventions for converting strings of alphabetic characters into sequences of sounds (reading) and converting sequences of sounds into strings of alphabetic characters (writing). As we have illustrated with English, Icelandic, and Korean, the rules governing the sound system of the language play an important role in the relationship between sound and character.

Most European alphabets make use of Latin (Roman) letters, making minor adjustments to accommodate individual characteristics of a particular language. For example, Spanish uses ñ to represent the palatal nasal of *señor*, and German has added an "umlaut" for certain vowel sounds that did not exist in Latin (e.g., in *über*). Such "extra" marks are called diacritics. The forty-six *kana* of the Japanese syllabaries are supplemented by diacritics in order to represent the more than 100 syllables of the language. Diacritic marks are also used in writing systems of tone languages such as Thai to indicate the tone of a syllable.

Some languages use two letters together — called a **digraph** — to represent a single sound. English has many digraphs, such as *sh* /š/ as in *she* /ši/, *ch* /č/ as in *chop* /čap/, *ng* /ŋ/ as in *sing* /sɪŋ/, and *oa* /o/ as in *loaf* /lof/.

Besides the European languages, those such as Turkish, Indonesian, Swahili, and Vietnamese have adopted the Latin alphabet. Other languages that have more recently developed a writing system use some of the IPA phonetic symbols in their alphabets. Twi, a West African language, for example, uses ɔ, ɛ, and ŋ.

The Cyrillic alphabet, named for St. Cyril, who brought Christianity to the Slavs, is used by many Slavic languages, including Russian. It is derived directly from the Greek alphabet without Latin mediation.

Many contemporary alphabets, such as those used for Arabic, Farsi (spoken in Iran), Urdu (spoken in Pakistan), and many languages of the Indian subcontinent, including Hindi, are ultimately derived from the ancient Semitic syllabaries.

Figure 14.2 shows a coarse time line of the development of the Roman alphabet.

Reading, Writing, and Speech

... Ther is so great diversite
In English, and in wryting of oure tonge,
So prey I god that non myswrite thee ...
>   Geoffrey Chaucer, *Troilus and Cressida* (c. 1380–1387)

Literature is the immortality of speech
>   August Wilhelm von Schlegel (1767–1845)

The development of writing freed us from the limitations of time and geography, but spoken language still has primacy. Writing systems, however, are of interest for their own sake.

FIGURE 14.2

Time line of the development of the Roman alphabet.

15000 B.C.E. — Cave drawings as pictograms

.

.

.

4000 B.C.E. — Sumerian cuneiform

3000 B.C.E. — Hieroglyphics

1500 B.C.E. — West Semitic Syllabary of the Phoenicians

1000 B.C.E. — Ancient Greeks borrow the Phoenician consonantal alphabet
750 B.C.E. — Etruscans borrow the Greek alphabet
500 B.C.E. — Romans adapt the Etruscan/Greco alphabet to Latin

---

The written language reflects, to a certain extent, the elements and rules that together constitute the grammar of the language. The system of phonemes is represented by the letters of the alphabet, though not necessarily in a direct way. The independence of words is revealed by the spaces in the written string; but in languages in which words are composed of more than one morpheme, the writing usually does not show the individual morphemes, even though speakers know what they are. In fact, many languages, such as Japanese or Thai, do not put spaces between words, although speakers and writers are aware of the individual words. The sentences of some languages are indicated in the written form by capitals at the beginning and periods at the end. Other punctuation, such as question marks, italics, commas, and exclamation marks, is used to reveal syntactic structure and to some extent intonation, stress, and contrast; however, the written forms of many languages do not use such punctuation.

Consider the difference in meaning between restricted and unrestricted relative clauses illustrated by the following two sentences containing the relative clause *who were philosophers*:

(1) The Greeks, who were philosophers, loved to talk a lot.
(2) The Greeks who were philosophers loved to talk a lot.

Note that the unrestricted relative clause in (1) is set off by commas. This tells us that the sentence may be paraphrased as

(1) The Greeks were philosophers, and they loved to talk a lot.

The meaning of the second sentence, without the commas, can be paraphrased as

(2) Among the Greeks, it was the philosophers who loved to talk a lot.

Similarly, by using an exclamation point or a question mark, the writer can make his or her intention clearer:

(3) The children are going to bed at eight o'clock. (*simple statement*)
(4) The children are going to bed at eight o'clock! (*an order*)
(5) The children are going to bed at eight o'clock? (*a question*)

These punctuation marks reflect the pauses and the intonations that would be used in the spoken language.

In sentence (6), *he* can refer to either John or someone else, but in sentence (7) the pronoun must refer to someone other than John:

(6) John said he's going.
(7) John said, "He's going."

The apostrophe used in contractions and possessives also provides syntactic information not always available in the spoken utterance:

(8) my cousin's friends (*one cousin*)
(9) my cousins' friends (*two or more cousins*)

Writing, then, somewhat reflects the spoken language, and punctuation may even distinguish between two meanings not revealed in the spoken forms, as shown in examples (8) and (9).

In the normal written version of sentence (10),

(10) John whispered the message to Bill, and then he whispered it to Mary.

he can refer to either John or Bill. In the spoken sentence, if *he* receives extra stress (called **contrastive stress**), then it must refer to Bill; if *he* receives normal stress, then it refers to John.

A speaker can usually emphasize any word in a sentence by using contrastive stress. Writers sometimes attempt to show emphasis by using all capital letters, or italics, or by underlining the emphasized word:

(11) *John* kissed Bill's wife. (*Bill didn't*)
(12) John *kissed* Bill's wife. (*rather than hugging her*)
(13) John kissed *Bill's* wife. (*not Dick's or his own*)
(14) John kissed Bill's *wife*. (*not Bill's mother*)

Such devices may serve many functions in written language; for example, italics may indicate reference to the italicized word itself, as in *"The* is an article." Although such visual devices can help in English, it is not clear that they can be used in a language such as Chinese. In Japanese, however, this kind of emphasis can be achieved by writing a word in *katakana*.

Other differences between speech and writing appear lexically in the greater variety of vocabulary in writing, especially in selection of adjectives, longer versus shorter words, and Latin versus Anglo-Saxon words. Syntactically, speech is much less structured than writing, with incomplete sentences, little subordination, active declarative sentences rather than passive ones, or cleft sentences, such as "It was Sam that I saw at the films." Writing makes use of subordination rather than coordination and marks relationships between clauses explicitly with subordinating conjunctions such as *that* or *when/while* and logical connectors such as *moreover, however*, and *besides*, where speech uses coordinating conjunctions such as *and* and *but*. Speech is often much less explicit than writing.

Written language is also more conservative than spoken language. When we write something — particularly in formal writing — we are more apt to obey the "prescriptive rules" taught in school, or to use a more formal style, than when we speak. "Dangling participles" (e.g., *While studying in the library, the fire alarm rang*) and "sentences ending with a preposition" (e.g., *I know what to end a sentence with*) abound in spoken language but may be "corrected" by copy editors, diligent English teachers, and careful writers. A linguist wishing to describe the language that people regularly use cannot depend, therefore, on written records alone.

Reading

> A man can learn only two ways, one by reading, and the other by association with smarter people.
>
> Will Rogers (1879–1935)

Children learn to speak instinctively without being taught. Learning to read and write is not like learning to speak. What is sometimes referred to as the "Whole Language" approach to reading has suggested that children can generally learn to read just as they learn to talk, through constant interaction with family and friends, teachers and classmates. This view contrasts with the view that children be specifically taught to segment speech into individual sounds and relate these sounds to the letters of the alphabet, which is sometimes referred to as *teaching phonics.*

As we have seen in this chapter, most written languages are based on oral language. It is important to recognize that the ability to learn language is an innate, biologically determined aspect of the human brain, whereas reading and writing are not. Otherwise, one would not find so many people who speak so many languages that have no written form.

Many studies have shown that deaf children who have fully acquired a sign language have difficulty learning to read. This is understandable since the alphabetic principle in a system like English requires an understanding of sound–symbol regularities. Hearing children should therefore not be deprived of the advantage they would have if their unconscious knowledge of phonemes is made conscious.

In developing teaching methods for reading and writing, it is important to understand the interactions of speech, reading, and writing. Whatever methods are adopted, however, they should take advantage of the child's innate linguistic knowledge and include helping the child relate sounds to letters.

Spelling

"Do you spell it with a 'v' or a 'w'?" inquired the judge.
"That depends upon the taste and fancy of the speller, my Lord," replied Sam.

Charles Dickens, *The Pickwick Papers* (1836–1837)

If writing represented the spoken language perfectly, then spelling reformers would never have arisen. In Chapter 5, we discussed some of the problems in the English orthographic (spelling) system. These problems prompted George Bernard Shaw (1941) to write that

> it was as a reading and writing animal that Man achieved his human eminence above those who are called beasts. Well, it is I and my like who have to do the writing. I have done it professionally for the last sixty years as well as it can be done with a hopelessly inadequate alphabet devised centuries before the English language existed to record another and very different language. Even this alphabet is reduced to absurdity by a foolish orthography based on the notion that the business of spelling is to represent the origin and history of a word instead of its sound and meaning. Thus an intelligent child who is bidden to spell *debt*, and very properly spells it *d-e-t*, is caned for not spelling it with a *b* because Julius Caesar spelt the Latin word for it with a *b*.

The irregularities between **graphemes** (letters) and phonemes have been cited as one reason "why Johnny can't read." Homographs, such as *lead* /lid/ and *lead*

/lɛd/, have fuelled the flames of spelling reform movements. Different spellings for the same sound, silent letters, and missing letters are also cited as reasons English needs a new orthographic system. The examples below (and those given in Chapter 5) illustrate the discrepancies between spelling and sounds in English:

Same Sound, Different Spelling	Different Sound, Same Spelling		Silent Letters	Missing Letters
/aj/	thought	/θ/	listen	use /juz/
	though	/ð/	debt	fuse /fjuz/
	Thomas	/t/	gnome	
aye			know	
buy	ate	/e/	psychology	
by	at	/æ/	right	
die	father	/a/	mnemonic	
hi	many	/ɛ/	science	
Thai			talk	
height			honest	
guide			sword	
			bomb	
			clue	
			Wednesday	

The spelling of most of the words in English today is based on the Late Middle English pronunciation (that used by Chaucer) and on the early forms of Modern English (one of which was used by Shakespeare). The many changes in the sound system of English, such as the Great Vowel Shift, were not always reflected in the spellings of the words that were affected.

When the printing press was introduced in the fifteenth century, archaic and idiosyncratic spellings became widespread and more permanent. Words in print were frequently misspelled outright because many of the early printers were not native speakers of English. But even native spellers in earlier times saw no need to spell the same word consistently. Thus, the first-person singular pronoun appears in the texts of Shakespeare's plays as *I, ay,* and *aye.*

Spelling reformers during the Renaissance saw the need for consistent spelling that correctly reflected the pronunciation of words. To that extent, spelling reform was necessary. But many scholars became overzealous. Because of their reverence for classical Greek and Latin, they changed the spellings of English words to conform to their etymologies. Where the Latin had a *b*, they added a *b* even if it was not pronounced; where the original spelling had a *c* or *p* or *h*, these letters were added, as is shown by these few examples:

Middle English Spelling		"Reformed" Spelling
indite	→	indict
dette	→	debt
receit	→	receipt
oure	→	hour

© Dan Piraro. King Features Syndicate.

Such spelling habits inspired Robert N. Feinstein (1986) to compose the following poem, entitled "Gnormal Pspelling":

Gnus and gnomes and gnats and such —
Gnouns with just one G too much.
Pseudonym and psychedelic —
P becomes a psurplus relic.
Knit and knack and knife and knocked —
Kneedless Ks are overstocked.
Rhubarb, rhetoric and rhyme
Should lose an H from thyme to time.

Reprinted from National Forum: The Phi Kappa Phi Journal LXVI, 3 (Summer, 1986).
Copyright © by Robert Feinstein. By permission of the publisher.

Current English spellings are based primarily on earlier pronunciations of words. The many changes that have occurred in the sound system of English since then are not reflected in the current spelling system, which was frozen due to the widespread availability of printed material and to scholastic conservatism.

For these reasons, Modern English orthography does not always represent what we know about the phonology of the language. The disadvantage is partially offset by the fact that the writing system allows us to read and understand what people wrote hundreds of years ago without the need for translations. If there were a one-to-one correspondence between our spellings and the sounds of our language, then we would have difficulty reading even fairly recent works such as Catharine Parr Traill's *Backwoods of Canada* (1836).

We do not mean to say that certain reforms would not be helpful. Some "respelling" is already taking place; advertisers often spell *though* as *tho*, *through* as *thru*, and *night* as *nite*. For a time, the *Chicago Tribune* used such spellings, but it gave up the practice in 1975. Spelling habits are hard to change, and revised spelling is regarded as substandard by many.

Languages change. It is not possible to maintain a perfect correspondence between pronunciation and spelling, nor is it 100 percent desirable to try to do so. For instance, in the case of homophones, it is helpful at times to have different spellings for the same sounds, as in the following pair:

The book was red.   The book was read.

Lewis Carroll once more makes the point with humour:

"And how many hours a day did you do lessons?" said Alice.
"Ten hours the first day," said the Mock Turtle, "nine the next, and so on."
"What a curious plan!" exclaimed Alice.
"That's the reason they're called *lessons*," the Gryphon remarked, "because they *lessen* from day to day."

There are also reasons for using the same spelling for different pronunciations. A morpheme may be pronounced differently when it occurs in different contexts. The identical spelling reflects the fact that the different pronunciations represent the same morpheme. This is the case with the plural morpheme. It is always spelled with an *s* despite being pronounced [s] in *cats* and [z] in *dogs*. The sound of the morpheme is determined by rules in this case.

Similarly, the phonetic realizations of the vowels in the following forms follow a regular pattern:

aj/ɪ	i/ɛ	e/æ
divine/divinity	serene/serenity	sane/sanity
sublime/subliminal	obscene/obscenity	profane/profanity
sign/signature	hygiene/hygienic	humane/humanity

The spelling of such pairs thus reflects our knowledge of the sound pattern of the language and the semantic–morphological relationships between the words. These considerations have led some to suggest that English orthography is **morphophonemic** in addition to being phonemic. To read English with correct pronunciation, morphophonemic knowledge is required. English contrasts with a language such as Spanish, whose orthography is almost purely phonemic.

Other examples provide further motivation for spelling irregularities. The *b* in *debt* may remind us of the related word *debit*, in which the *b* is pronounced. The same principle is true of pairs such as *sign/signal, knowledge/acknowledge, bomb/bombardier,* and *gnosis/prognosis/agnostic*.

There are also different spellings that represent the different pronunciations of a morpheme when confusion would arise from using the same spelling. For example, there is a rule in English phonology that changes a /t/ to an /s/ in certain cases: *democrat → democracy*. The different spellings are due in part to the fact that this rule does not apply to all morphemes, so that *art + y* is *arty*, not *arcy. Regular phoneme-to-grapheme rules determine in many cases when a morpheme is to be spelled identically and when it is to be changed.

Other subregularities are apparent. A *c* always represents the /s/ sound when it is followed by a *y, i,* or *e,* as in *cynic, citizen,* and *censure*. Because it is always pronounced [k] when it is the final letter in a word or when it is followed by any other vowel (*coat, cat, cut,* and so on), no confusion results. The *th* spelling is usually voiced as [ð] between vowels (the result of a historical intervocalic voicing rule).

There is another important reason spelling should not always be tied to phonetic pronunciation. Different dialects of English have divergent pronunciations. Cockneys drop their "(h)aitches," and Bostonians and Southerners drop their "*r*'s"; *neither* is pronounced [niðər] and [niðə] by Americans, [najðə] by the British. Typically, Canadians — sometimes the same person — use alternatively [niðər] and [najðər]. Many Irish, and Canadians from the Maritimes, use still another vowel and say [neðər]. Some Scots pronounce *night* as [nɪxt]; people say *Chicago* and *Chicawgo, hog* and *hawg, bird* and *boyd; four* is pronounced [fɔ:] by the British, [fɔr] in Canada, and [foə] in the Southern United States; *orange* is pronounced in at least two ways in the United States: [arənǰ] and [ɔrənǰ].

While dialectal pronunciations differ, the common spellings indicate the intended word. It is necessary for the written language to transcend local dialects. With a uniform spelling system, a native of Sudbury and a native of Glasgow can communicate through writing. If each dialect were spelled according to its own pronunciation, then written communication among the English-speaking peoples of the world would suffer.

Spelling Pronunciations

> For pronunciation, the best general rule is to consider those as the most elegant speakers who deviate least from written words.
>
> Samuel Johnson (1755)

Despite the primacy of the spoken over the written language, the written word is often regarded with excessive reverence. The stability, permanence, and graphic nature of writing cause some people to favour it over ephemeral and elusive speech. Humpty Dumpty expressed a rather typical attitude: "I'd rather see that done on paper."

Writing has affected speech only marginally, however, most notably in the phenomenon of **spelling pronunciation**. Since the sixteenth century, to some extent spelling has influenced standard pronunciation. The most important of such changes stem from the eighteenth century under the influence of lexicographers and teachers. The struggle between those who demanded that words be pronounced according to spelling and those who demanded that words be spelled according to pronunciation generated great heat in that century. The preferred pronunciations were given in the many dictionaries printed in the eighteenth century, and the authority of the dictionaries influenced pronunciation in this way.

Spelling has also influenced pronunciation in words that are infrequently used in normal daily speech. Many words that were spelled with an initial *h* were not pronounced with any /h/ sound as late as the eighteenth century. Thus, at that time no /h/ was pronounced in *honest, hour, habit, heretic, hotel, hospital,* and *herb*. Frequently used words such as *honest* and *hour* continued to be pronounced without the /h/, despite the spelling, but all those other words were given a "spelling pronunciation." Because people did not hear them often, when they saw them written they concluded that they must begin with an /h/. *Herb* is currently undergoing this change; in Standard British English, the *h* is pronounced, whereas in Standard Canadian and American English it is not.

Similarly, many words now spelled with a *th* were once pronounced /t/, as in *Thomas*; later most of these words underwent a change in pronunciation from /t/ to /θ/, as in *anthem, author,* and *theatre*. "Nicknames" often reflect the earlier pronunciations: "Ka*t*e" for "Ca*th*erine," "Be*tt*y" for "Eliza*beth*," and "Ar*t*" for "Ar*th*ur." The words *often* and *soften*, which are usually pronounced without a /t/ sound, are pronounced with the /t/ by some people because of the spelling.

The clear influence of spelling on pronunciation is observable in the way place names are pronounced. *Berkeley* is pronounced [bərkli] in California, although it stems from the British [ba:kli]; *Worcester* is pronounced [wʊstər] or [wʊstə] in England as well as in large parts of Canada and the United States, but in Massachusetts it is often pronounced [wʊrčɛstər]; *Magdalen* is pronounced [mɔdlɪn] in England and [mægdələn] in North America. *Salmon* is pronounced [sæmən] in most parts of North America, but many Southern speakers in the United States pronounce the [l] and say [sælmən].

Although the written language has some influence on the spoken language, it does not change the basic system — the grammar — of the language. The writing system, conversely, reflects, in a more or less direct way, the grammar that every speaker knows.

Canadian Spelling

Most people who write in the English language employ a common spelling system. No matter how differently they may speak the language, they tend to spell it in the same way. The major difference in English spelling is between those who use "American" forms and those who employ what is called "British spelling," though the latter is used, in part or in whole, in many former British colonies. These two systems are distinguished by a few contrasting practices: the choice of *-our* (*favour*) instead of *-or* (*favor*) and *-ce* (*defence*) as opposed to *-se* (*defense*), the use of double or single consonants in various environments (*fulfil/fulfill; gravelled/graveled*), and the choice of long or short forms of a few words, such as *axe* or *ax* and *plough* or *plow*. Clearly such differences affect only a limited number of words and raise no real difficulties in comprehension. Some of these variations and the environments in which they occur are displayed in Table 14.3.

To many Americans, some spelling choices made by Canadians strike them as distinctly "British," while Britons point to "American" elements in the spelling. In fact, like Canadian English itself, Canadian spelling is a unique hybrid drawn from British and American forms. This blending of systems is apparent in the common Canadian spellings of the words in Table 14.4.

TABLE 14.3
Examples of British and American Spelling

British Spelling		American Spelling		
colour	neighbour	color	neighbor	-our/-or
harbour	mould	harbor	mold	-ou-/-o-
centre	theatre	center	theater	-re/-er
meagre	kilometre	meager	kilometer	
defence	offence	defense	offense	
practice (noun)		practise		-ce/-se
practise (verb)		practice		-se/-ce
distil	fulfil	distill	fulfill	single/double
omelette	programme	omelet	program	consonant
labelled	travelled	labeled	traveled	before
kidnapped	worshipped	kidnaped	worshiped	inflectional
jewellery	woollen	jewelry	woolen	before
marvellous	enrolment	marvelous	enrollment	derivational
analyse	criticise	analyze	criticize	-se/-ze
judgement	sizeable	judgment	sizable	silent e + suffix
co-operate		cooperate		hyphen
axe	catalogue	ax	catalog	terminal
cheque	plough	check	plow	variation
programme		program		

Adapted from "Canadian spelling: How much British? How much American?" Robert Ireland, 1979–80, *The English Quarterly*, 12 (4), 64–80.

Admittedly, the exact nature and extent of the blend varies regionally. Residents of Nova Scotia, Ontario, and British Columbia, for example, tend to value British over American forms, while the reverse is true for Alberta, Manitoba, and Prince Edward Island (Ireland, 1979–1980). An Ontarian is more likely to write *honour* and *labour* than an Albertan, who will likely choose *honor* and *labor*.

Despite regional differences, certain features are generally characteristic of Canadian spelling. Canadians are said to combine the American use of final double consonants (as in *distill*) with the British use of double consonants before inflectionals (as in *travelled*). The *Gage Canadian Dictionary* further suggests that Canadians employ double consonants before derivationals, as in *woollen* (Avis et al., 1983). Long forms such as *axe* (U.S. *ax*) are common, but Canadians

TABLE 14.4
Examples of Canadian Spelling

Canadian Spelling		
colour	neighbour	-our/-or
harbour	mould	-ou-/-o-
centre	theatre	-re/-er
meager/meagre		
defence/se	offence/se	-ce/-se
practice (noun)	practise (verb)[5]	
distill	fulfill	single/double consonants
omelette		
labelled	travelled	before inflectionals
kidnapped	worshipped	
jewelry	woolen	before derivationals
marvelous	enrollment[6]	
analyze	criticize	-se/-ze
judgement	sizeable	silent e + suffix
co-operate		hyphen
grey	pyjamas	miscellaneous words
gypsy		
axe	catalogue	terminal variation
cheque	plow	
program		

Adapted from L. Burton et al., 1987, *Editing Canadian English*, Vancouver and Toronto: Douglas & McIntyre, pp. 6–13.

seem to prefer the short form in *plow* (British *plough*), and many editors insist on *programme* except where computer programs are concerned (Burton et al., 1987).

It has been suggested that *maneuvre* is an example of a "Canadian compromise" in that it often takes a British final *-re* but rejects the British *-oeu-* in favour of *-eu*, which the *Collins English Dictionary* defines as "the usual U.S. spelling." But it is also an example of the complexity surrounding Canadian English; as long ago as his 1979–1980 survey, Robert Ireland found that among "double vowel" words — those that may be spelled with *-ae-* or *-oe-* (*mediaeval, encyclopaedia*) — *manoeuvre* was the most likely to occur, but even so more than half of his secondary school respondents chose *maneuver*, the "American" form.

Canadian newspapers and magazines frequently vacillate in their editorial practices, especially with respect to *-our/-or* and *-re/-er* forms. In 1962, a report prepared by the Canadian Linguistic Association and the Association of Canadian University Teachers of English predicted that, in such matters, "the tendency to adopt American spellings will spread." This report observed that "this process is already well underway in the newspapers of Canada though the accepted standard is still that of Britain" (*Some Arguments*, 1962). Thirty years later, the Canadian Press revealed that the process had not spread far, for it insisted that "we will use *-or* spellings come what may" (Buckley, 1992). But by the century's end, CP citations in various newspapers were employing *-our* forms. And in its *1999 Stylebook*, CP admitted that many daily newspapers had already "started switching to 'our' [from *-or* spellings] to reflect the preference of readers," and it bowed to widespread use, announcing that "in September 1998, The Canadian Press adopted 'our' spelling for words of more than one syllable in which the 'u' is not pronounced. This came after eighty years of writing with *color, ardor* and *rigor*" (Tasko, 1999). *The Globe and Mail*, which bills itself as "the National Newspaper," continues to ask for both *-our* and *-re* spellings (McFarlane & Clements, 1990).

-Re forms remain common in Canada; Burton, who inquired among editors, discovered a majority in favour of it, but Ireland found that high school students preferred *-er* forms. *-Re* forms have also been encouraged by bilingual designations such as "Interpretive Centre d'Interpretation" (McConnell, 1979; Pratt, 1993).

Style books and handbooks often suggest that bewildered writers consult "a good Canadian dictionary" for correct spelling, but this advice does not take into account either the conflicting practices of the major dictionaries or strong regional preferences. *The Nelson Canadian Dictionary of the English Language* (1997) (based, as are so many "Canadian" dictionaries, on an American text) lists the following words (from Table 14.4) as "equal variants" — that is, as forms that "occur with virtually equal frequency in edited sources": *jewellery/jewelry, marvellous/marvelous, centre/center, meagre/meager, woollen/woolen, fulfill/fulfil, labelled/labeled, travelled/traveled, worshipped/worshiped, enrolment/enrollment, plough/plow*. It is clear that this dictionary takes issue with the decisions of the editors surveyed by Burton. Moreover, dictionaries do not normally recognize that differing types of writing may require differing spelling forms. More formal genres, such as textbooks, favour British forms, while less formal types, such as newspapers, may follow American practices. The complexity of the situation often leads many style guides to insist only that writers be consistent. If, for example, they choose to use *-our* forms rather than *-or* forms, then they should do so consistently. On the other hand, choosing to mix *between* categories — that is, to use *-re* and at the same time *-or* spellings — "may well constitute the 'Canadian style'" (Burton et al., 1987). Perhaps as a result of regional differences and this tendency to mix categories, there is in general a greater tolerance for spelling diversity in Canada than in Britain or the United States.

Influence of Computer Spell Checkers

> Spel chekers, hoo needs em?
>
> Alan James Bean, American astronaut

Spell checkers — computer programs that check and replace "misspellings" — are too new for their influence to be fully appreciated. These systems may, in the end, enforce a regularity and consistency across regional boundaries. At present, however, the different word-processing systems themselves reflect those varying choices evident in the published dictionaries. The "Canadian" speller "bundled" with Corel WordPerfect accepts both *fulfil* and *fulfill, distil* and *distill*, but rejects *worshiped*. Microsoft Word's Canadian speller, on the other hand, accepts both *worshiped* and *worshipped* but rejects *fulfill* and *distill*. WordPerfect accepts both *woollen* and *woolen*, while Word rejects *woolen*. The effects of such programs across the various regions of the country are yet to be charted; however, as the number of people employing word-processing programs increases, these checkers may well influence Canadian spelling practices.

Summary

Writing is one of the basic tools of civilization. Without it, the world as we know it could not exist.

The precursor of writing was "picture writing," which used **pictograms** to represent objects directly and literally. Pictograms are called **ideograms** when the drawing becomes less literal and the meaning extends to concepts associated with the object originally pictured. When ideograms become associated with the words for the concepts they signify, they are called **logograms**. **Logographic** systems are true writing systems in the sense that the symbols stand for words of a language. The Sumerians first developed a pictographic writing system to keep track of commercial transactions. It was later expanded for other uses and eventually evolved into the highly stylized (and stylus-ized) **cuneiform** writing. Cuneiform was generalized to other writing systems by application of the **rebus principle**, which used the symbol of one word or syllable to represent another word or syllable pronounced the same.

The Egyptians also developed a pictographic system, which became known as **hieroglyphics**. This system influenced many peoples, including the Phoenicians, who developed the West Semitic Syllabary. The Greeks borrowed the Phoenician system, and in adapting it to their own language they used the symbols to represent both consonant and vowel sound segments, thus inventing the first alphabet.

There are four types of writing systems still being used in the world: **logographic** or **word writing**, in which every symbol or character represents a word or morpheme (as in Chinese); **syllabic writing**, in which each symbol represents a syllable (as in Japanese); **consonantal alphabetic**, in which each symbol represents a consonant and vowels may be represented by diacritical marks (as in Hebrew); and **alphabetic writing**, in which each symbol represents (for the most part) one phoneme (as in English).

The writing system may have some small effect on the spoken language. Languages change over time, but writing systems tend to be more conservative than spoken forms. Thus, spelling no longer accurately reflects pronunciation. Also, when the spoken and written forms of the language become divergent, some words may be pronounced as they are spelled, sometimes due to the efforts of pronunciation reformers.

There are advantages to a conservative spelling system. A common spelling permits speakers whose dialects have diverged to communicate through writing, as is best exemplified in China, where the "dialects" are mutually unintelligible. We are also able to read and understand the English language as it was written centuries ago. In addition, despite some gross lack of correspondences between sound and spelling, the spelling often reflects speakers' morphological and phonological knowledge.

Canadian spelling reflects both the influence of American spelling practices and the prestige still accorded to British customs. The extent of each influence varies from region to region. The result of these conflicting influences has been a tolerance for diversity in spelling.

Notes

1. The pictograph for "ox" evolved, much later, into our letter *A*.
2. The symbol portrays the Pharaoh's staff.
3. Water trickling out of a vase.
4. See Exercise 3 of Chapter 6 (p. 299).
5. "While variation is recognized for these words, the layman may be unsure of which form is which. Only for *practice* is the choice clearly for the *-ce* ending, especially when the word is used as a noun. Some spelling texts and usage handbooks teach the distinction between the *-ce* ending for the noun and *-se* for the verb. This may account for the higher use of *practise* as a verb" (Ireland, 1979–1980). Editors who responded to Burton (1987) preferred *defence, practice, pretence*, and *prophecy* as nouns and *practise* and *prophesy* as verbs. It is clear from this survey that Canadian editors and publishers have a strong inclination toward British forms.

6. The *Gage Canadian Dictionary* — like Burton's editors — disagrees with Ireland's findings, giving *jewellery, marvellous, woollen*, and *enrolment* as the first (and, in its eyes, the preferred) Canadian forms. It also prefers *judgment* and *sizable*, as well as *distil* and *fulfil*.

Exercises

1. A. "Write" the following words and phrases, using pictograms that you invent:

a.	eye	e.	tree	i.	ugly
b.	a boy	f.	forest	j.	run
c.	two boys	g.	war	k.	Scotch tape
d.	library	h.	honesty	l.	smoke

   B. Which words are most difficult to symbolize in this way? Why?

   C. How does the following sentence reveal the problems in pictographic writing? "A grammar represents the unconscious, internalized linguistic competence of a native speaker."

2. A *rebus* is a written representation of words or syllables using pictures of objects whose names resemble the sounds of the intended words or syllables. For example, might be the symbol for *eye* or *I* or the first syllable in *idea*.

   A. Using the rebus principle, "write" the following words:

a.	tearing	c.	bareback
b.	icicle	d.	cookies

   B. Why would such a system be a difficult system in which to represent all words in English? Illustrate your answer with an example.

3. A. Construct non-Roman alphabetic letters to replace the letters used to represent the following sounds in English:

   t r s k w č i æ f n

   B. Use these symbols plus the regular alphabet symbols for the other sounds to write the following words in your "new orthography."

a.	character	d.	photo	g.	psychotic
b.	guest	e.	cheat	h.	tree
c.	cough	f.	rang		

4. Suppose the English writing system were a *syllabic* system instead of an *alphabetic* system. Use capital letters to symbolize the necessary syllabic units for the words below, and list your "syllabary." Example: Given the words *mate, inmate, intake*, and *elfin*, you might use A = *mate*, B = *in*, C = *take*, and D = *elf*. In addition, write the words using your syllabary. Example: *inmate* — BA; *elfin* — DB; *intake* — BC; *mate* — A. (Do not use any more syllable symbols than you absolutely need.)

   a. childishness   e. likely   i. jealous
   b. childlike   f. zoo   j. witless
   c. Jesuit   g. witness   k. lesson
   d. lifelessness   h. lethal

*5. In the following pairs of English words, the boldfaced portions are pronounced the same but spelled differently. Can you think of any reason the spelling should remain distinct? (*Hint: reel* and *real* are pronounced the same, but *reality* shows the presence of a phonemic /æ/ in *real*.)

A		B	Reason
a.	I **am**	i**amb**	
b.	**goose**	pro**duce**	
c.	**fashion**	compli**cation**	
d.	New**ton**	or**gan**	
e.	**no**	k**now**	
f.	hy**mn**	**him**	

6. In the following pairs of words, the boldfaced portions are spelled the same but pronounced differently. State some reasons the spelling of the words in column B should not be changed.

A		B	Reason
a.	mi**ng**le	lo**ng**	The **g** is pronounced in *longer*.
b.	l**i**ne	ch**i**ldren	
c.	**s**onar	re**s**ound	
d.	**c**ent	my**s**tic	
e.	crum**b**le	bom**b**	
f.	cat**s**	dog**s**	
g.	sta**gn**ant	desi**gn**	
h.	ser**e**ne	obsc**e**nity	

7. Each of the following sentences is ambiguous in the written form. How can these sentences be made unambiguous when they are spoken?

   Example: John hugged Bill, and then he kissed him.

For the meaning "John hugged and kissed Bill," use normal stress (*kissed* receives stress). For the meaning "Bill kissed John," contrastive stress is needed on both *he* and *him*.

a. What are we having for dinner, Mother?
b. She's a German language teacher.
c. They formed a student grievance committee.
d. Antoine kissed his wife, and George kissed his wife too.

8. In the written form, the following sentences are not ambiguous, but they would be if spoken. State the devices used in writing that make the meanings explicit.

a. They're my brothers' keepers.
b. He said, "He will take the garbage out."
c. The red book was read.
d. The flower was on the table.

9. Below are ten samples of writing from the ten languages listed. Match the writing to the language. There are enough "hints" in this chapter to get most of them. (The source of these examples, and many others, is Kenneth Katzner, *Languages of the World.* New York: Funk & Wagnalls, 1975.)

a. _____ Cherokee
b. _____ Chinese
c. _____ German (Gothic style)
d. _____ Greek
e. _____ Hebrew
f. _____ Icelandic
g. _____ Japanese
h. _____ Korean
i. _____ Russian
j. _____ Twi

1. 仮に勝手に変えるようなことをすれば.

2. Κι ὁ νοῦς του ἀγκάλιασε πονετικὰ τὴν Κρήτη.

3. «Что это? я падаю? у меня ноги подкашиваются»,

4. וְהָיָה ׀ בְּאַחֲרִית הַיָּמִים נָכוֹן יִהְיֶה הַר

5. Saá sáre yi bɛ̃ŋ atɛkyé bí â mpɔtorɔ áhyɛ

6. 既然必须和新的群众的时代相结合.

7. ᎯᏳ ᎠᎠ ᏣᏈᎶ ᏣᏪ ᎤᏟ.

8. Þótt þú langförull legðir sérhvert land undir fót,

9. Pharao's Unblick war wunderbar.

10. 스위스는 독특한 체제

10. Compare the spelling guidelines of Canadian dictionaries and composition handbooks. What do the editors offer as rules for writers who wish to use a "Canadian style"?

11. The following appeared on the safety card of a Spanish airline. Identify each language. (You will probably have to spend some time in the library and/or visit various departments of foreign languages.)

a. **Para su seguridad**
b. **For your safety**
c. **Pour votre sécurité**
d. **Für ihre Sicherheit**
e. **Per la Vostra sicurezza**
f. **Para sua segurança**
g. **あなたの安全のために**
h. **Для Вашей безогіасности**
i. **Dla bezpieczeństwa
   pasażerów**
j. **Za vašu sigurnost**
k. **Γιά τήν ἀσφάλειά σας**
l. **Kendi emniyetiniz için**
m. **من اجـل سـلامتك**

12. Make up five or ten emoticons along with their meaning. Don't just look them up somewhere. Be creative! For example, **+id** to mean "good idea!"

References

Avis, W.S., et al. (Eds.). (1983). *Gage Canadian dictionary*. Toronto: Gage.

Buckley, P. (Ed.). (1992). *The Canadian Press stylebook*. Toronto: Canadian Press.

Burton, L., et al. (1987). *Editing Canadian English*. Vancouver and Toronto: Douglas & McIntyre.

Collins English dictionary (6th ed.). (2003). London: Collins.

DeFrancis, J. (1989). *Visible speech: The diverse oneness of writing systems*. Honolulu: University of Hawaii Press.

Diringer, D. (1968). *The alphabet: A key to the history of mankind*. London: Hutchinson.

Feinstein, R.N. (1986). Gnormal pspelling. *National Forum: The Phi Kappa Phi Journal*.

Gaur, A. (1984). *A history of writing*. London: British Library.

Ireland, R.J. (1979–1980). Canadian spelling: How much British? How much American? *The English Quarterly, 12*(4), 64–80.

Jensen, H. (1969). *Sign, symbol, and script: An account of man's efforts to write* (G. Unwin, Trans.). New York: Putnam.

Katzner, K. (1975). *Languages of the world*. New York: Funk & Wagnalls.

Lehmann, W.P. (Ed.). (1975). *Language and linguistics in the People's Republic of China*. Austin: University of Texas Press.

McConnell, R.E. (1979). *Our own voice: Canadian English and how it is studied*. Toronto: Gage.

McFarlane, J.A., & Clements, W. (1990). *The Globe and Mail style book*. Toronto: Globe and Mail.

The Nelson Canadian dictionary of the English language. (1997). Scarborough, ON: Nelson.

Ohman, S. (1969). Paper presented at the International Speech Symposium, Kyoto, Japan.

Pratt, T.K. (1993). The hobgoblin of Canadian English spelling. In S. Clarke (Ed.), *Focus on Canada* (pp. 45–64). Amsterdam: John Benjamins Publishing.

Shaw, G.B. (1941). Preface to R.A. Wilson, *The miraculous birth of language* (pp. 7–33) London: British Publishers Guild. (Reprinted 1946)

Silver, S., & Miller, W.R. (1997). *American Indian language: Cultural and social contexts.* Tucson: University of Arizona Press.

Some arguments for & against reforming English spelling. A report prepared for the Canadian conference on education by a committee representing the Canadian Linguistic Association and the Association of Canadian University Teachers of English. (1962). Kingston, Ontario.

Tasko, P. (Ed.). (1999). *The Canadian Press stylebook.* Toronto: Canadian Press.

Traill, C.P. (1836). *Backwoods of Canada.* London: C. Knight.

Further Reading

Adams, M.J. (1996). *Beginning to read.* Cambridge, MA: MIT Press.

Biber, D. (1988). *Variation across speech and writing.* Cambridge, UK: Cambridge University Press.

Coulmas, F. (1989). *The writing systems of the world.* Oxford: Oxford University Press.

Cummings, D.W. (1988). *American English spelling.* Baltimore: Johns Hopkins University Press.

Daniels, P.T., & Bright, W. (Eds.). (1996). *The world's writing systems.* New York: Oxford University Press.

DeFrancis, J. (1989). *Visible speech: The diverse oneness of writing systems.* Honolulu: University of Hawaii Press.

Diringer, D. (1962). *Writing.* New York: Holt, Rinehart and Winston.

Gaur, A. (1984). *A history of writing.* London: British Library.

Gelb, I.J. (1952). *A study of writing.* Chicago: University of Chicago Press.

Gnanadesikan, A.E. (2008). *The writing revolution.* Malden, MA: Wiley-Blackwell.

Jensen, H. (1970). *Sign, symbol, and script* (G. Unwin, Trans.). London: George Allen and Unwin.

Robertson, S., & Cassidy, F.G. (1954). *The development of modern English* (pp. 353–374). Englewood Cliffs, NJ: Prentice-Hall.

Robinson, A. (2007). *The story of writing: Alphabets, hieroglyphs, and pictograms* (2nd ed.). London: Thames & Hudson.

Rogers, H. (2004). *Writing systems: A linguistic approach.* Malden, MA: Wiley-Blackwell.

Sampson, G. (1985). *Writing systems: A linguistic introduction.* Stanford, CA: Stanford University Press.

Senner, W.M. (Ed.). (1989). *The origins of writing.* Lincoln: University of Nebraska Press.

Wang, W.S-Y. (1981). Language structure and optimal orthography. In O.J.L. Tzeng & H. Singer (Eds.), *Perception of print: Reading research in experimental psychology* (pp. 223–236). Hillsdale, NJ: Erlbaum.

Websites

http://www.omniglot.com/links/writing.htm Contains links to numerous sites on writing systems.

http://homepage.ntlworld.com/vivian.c/ A website on writing systems and English spelling by Vivian Cook at Newcastle University, UK.

PART FIVE
Animal Communication

We need to abandon the approach that sees "learning language" in a human sense as the only worthwhile goal, and use the communicative abilities that animals can acquire as a window into their cognitive processes more generally.

Steven R. Anderson, Doctor Dolittle's delusion: Animals and the uniqueness of human language (2004)

CHAPTER 15
Animal Communication

Animal "Languages"

No matter how eloquently a dog may bark, he cannot tell you that his parents were poor but honest.

Bertrand Russell (1872–1970)

Whether language is the exclusive property of the human species is an interesting question. The idea of talking animals probably is as old and as widespread among human societies as is language itself. No culture lacks a legend in which some animal plays a speaking role. All over West Africa, children listen to folk tales in which a "spider-man" is the hero. "Coyote" is a favourite figure in many Aboriginal North American tales, and there is hardly an animal who does not figure in Aesop's famous fables. Hugh Lofting's fictional Doctor Dolittle's major accomplishment is his ability to communicate with animals.

If language is viewed only as a system of communication, then many species communicate. Humans also use systems other than language to relate to each other and to send "messages." The question is whether the kinds of grammars that represent linguistic knowledge acquired by children with no external instruction, and that are used creatively rather than as responses to internal or external stimuli, are unique to the human animal.

"Talking" Parrots

Most humans who acquire language utilize speech sounds to express meanings, but such sounds are not a necessary aspect of language, as evidenced by sign language. The use of speech sounds is therefore not a basic part of what we have been calling language. The chirping of birds, the squeaking of dolphins, and the dancing of bees may potentially represent systems similar to human languages. If animal communication systems are not like human language, it is not due to a lack of speech.

Conversely, when animals vocally imitate human utterances, it does not mean they possess language. Language is a system that relates sounds (or gestures) to meanings. "Talking" birds such as parrots and mynah birds are capable of faithfully reproducing words and phrases of human language that they have heard; but when a parrot says "Polly wants a cracker," she may really want a ham sandwich or a drink of water or nothing at all. A bird that has learned to say "hello" or

© Dan Piraro. King Features Syndicate.

"goodbye" is as likely to use one as the other, regardless of whether people are arriving or departing. The bird's utterances carry no meaning. The birds are speaking neither English nor their own language when they sound like us.

Talking birds do not dissect the sounds of their imitations into discrete units. *Polly* and *Molly* do not rhyme for a parrot. They are as different as *hello* and *goodbye* (or as similar). One property of all human languages is the discreteness of the speech or gestural units, which are ordered and reordered, combined and split apart. Generally, a parrot says what it is taught, or what it hears, and no more. If Polly learns "Polly wants a cracker" and "Polly wants a doughnut" and learns to imitate the single words *whiskey* and *bagel*, she will not spontaneously produce, as children do, "Polly wants whiskey" or "Polly wants a bagel" or "Polly wants whiskey and a bagel." If she learns *cat* and *cats* and *dog* and *dogs* and then learns the word *parrot*, she will be unable to form the plural *parrots*, as children do by the age of three; nor can a parrot form an unlimited set of utterances from a finite set of units or understand utterances never heard before. Reports of an African grey parrot named Alex studied by Dr. Irene M. Pepperberg of the University of Arizona (Pepperberg, 1993; 2004) suggest that new methods of training may result in more learning than was previously believed possible. When the trainer uses words in context, Alex seems to relate some sounds with their meanings. This is more than simply imitation, but it is not in any way similar to the way children acquire the complexities of the grammar of any language. It is more like a dog learning to associate certain sounds with meanings, such as *heel, sit, and fetch*. Alex's ability may go somewhat beyond that. Therefore, the ability to produce sounds similar to those used in human language, even if meanings are related to these sounds, cannot be equated with the ability to acquire the complex grammar of a human language.

The Birds and the Bees

> The birds and animals are all friendly to each other, and there are no disputes about anything. They all talk, and they all talk to me, but it must be a foreign language for I cannot make out a word they say.
>
> Mark Twain, *Eve's Diary* (1906)

Most animals possess some kind of "signalling" communication system. Among spiders, there is a complex system for courtship. The male spider, before he approaches his lady love, goes through an elaborate series of gestures to inform her that he is indeed a spider and not a crumb or a fly to be eaten. These gestures are invariant. One never finds a creative spider changing or adding to the particular courtship ritual of his species.

A similar kind of gesture language is found among fiddler crabs. There are forty different varieties, and each variety uses its own particular claw-waving movement to signal to another member of its "clan." The timing, movement, and posture of the body never change from one time to another or from one crab to another within the particular variety. Whatever the signal means, it is fixed. Only one meaning can be conveyed. There is not an infinite set of fiddler crab sentences.

The imitative sounds of talking birds have little in common with human language, but the calls and songs of many species of birds do have a communicative function, and they resemble human languages in that there may be "dialects" within the same species. **Birdcalls** (consisting of one or more short notes) convey messages associated with the immediate environment, such as danger, feeding, nesting, and flocking. **Bird songs** (more complex patterns of notes) are used to stake out territory and to attract mates. There is no evidence of any internal structure to these songs, nor can they be segmented into independently meaningful parts as words of human language can be. In a study of the territorial song of the European robin, it was discovered that rival robins paid attention only to the alternation between high-pitched and low-pitched notes, and which came first did not matter (Busnel & Bremond, 1962). The message varies only to the extent of how strongly the robin feels about its possession and to what extent it is prepared to defend it and start a family in that territory. The different alternations therefore express intensity and nothing more. The robin is creative in its ability to sing the same thing in many different ways but not creative in its ability to use the same units of the system to express many different messages with different meanings.

Similarly, recent research (Templeton, Greene, & Davis, 2005) has revealed that black-capped chickadees vary acoustic features of their call with the degree of threat that a predator poses.

Despite certain superficial similarities to human language, bird calls and songs are fundamentally different kinds of communicative systems. The number of messages that can be conveyed is finite, and messages are stimulus controlled.

This distinction is also true of the system of communication used by honeybees. For a long time, it has been believed that a forager bee is able to return to the hive and tell other bees where a source of food is located. It does so by forming a dance on a wall of the hive that reveals the location and quality of the food source. For one species of Italian honeybee, the dancing behaviour may assume one of three possible patterns: round (which indicates locations near the hive, within six metres or so), sickle (which indicates locations at six to eighteen metres from the hive), and tail-wagging (for distances that exceed eighteen metres). The number of repetitions per minute of the basic pattern in the tail-wagging dance indicates the precise distance; the slower the rate of repetition, the longer the distance.

> **Bottlenose dolphins**
>
> Researchers have reported that dolphins appear to create a signature whistle for themselves, similar to a human name. Bottlenose dolphins were observed to react when they heard a synthesized version of a whistle delivered by a close relative.

The dance is an effective system of communication for bees. It is capable, in principle, of infinitely many different messages, like human language; but unlike human language, the system is confined to a single subject — distance from the hive. The inflexibility was shown by an experimenter who forced a bee to walk to the food source. When the bee returned to the hive, it indicated a distance 25 times farther away than the food source actually was. The bee had no way of communicating the special circumstances in its message. This absence of creativity makes the bees' dance qualitatively different from human language (Von Frisch, 1967).

In the seventeenth century, the philosopher and mathematician René Descartes pointed out that the communication systems of animals are qualitatively different from the languages used by humans:

> It is a very remarkable fact that there are none so depraved and stupid, without even excepting idiots, that they cannot arrange different words together, forming of them a statement by which they make known their thoughts; while, on the other hand, there is no other animal, however perfect and fortunately circumstanced it may be, which can do the same. (Descartes, 1637/1967)

Descartes goes on to state that one of the major differences between humans and animals is that human use of language is not just a response to external, or even internal, emotional stimuli, as are the sounds and gestures of animals. He warns against confusing human use of language with "natural movements which betray passions and may be . . . manifested by animals."

To hold that animals communicate by systems qualitatively different from human language systems is not to claim human superiority. Humans are not inferior to the one-celled amoeba because they cannot reproduce by splitting in two; they are just different sexually. All the studies of animal communication systems, including those of chimpanzees, provide evidence for Descartes' distinction between other animal communication systems and the linguistic creative ability possessed by the human animal.

Can Chimps Learn Human Language?

It is a great baboon, but so much like man in most things . . . I do believe it already understands much English; and I am of the mind it might be taught to speak or make signs.

Entry in Samuel Pepys's Diary, August 1661

What impresses one the most about chimpanzee signing is that fundamentally, deep down, chimps just don't "get it." They know that the trainers like them to sign and that signing often gets them what they want, but they never seem to feel in their bones what language is and how to use it.

Steven Pinker, *The Language Instinct* (1994)

Throughout this book, the discussion has centred on *human* language acquisition ability. In the past decades, much effort has been expended to determine whether non-human primates (chimpanzees, monkeys, gorillas, and so on) can learn human language. In their natural habitats, primates communicate with each other in systems that include visual, auditory, olfactory, and tactile signals. Many of these signals seem to have meaning associated with the animals' immediate environment or emotional state. They can signal danger and communicate aggressiveness and subordination. Females of some species emit a specific call indicating that they are anestrous (sexually quiescent), which inhibits attempts by males to copulate. However, the natural sounds and gestures produced by all nonhuman primates show their signals to be highly stereotyped and limited in the type and number of messages they convey. Their basic vocabularies occur primarily as emotional responses to particular situations. They have no way of expressing the anger they felt yesterday or the anticipation of tomorrow.

Despite their limited natural systems of communication, there has been an interest in whether these animals may have a capacity for acquiring more complex linguistic systems that are similar to human language.

Gua

In the 1930s, Winthrop and Luella Kellogg raised their infant son with an infant chimpanzee named Gua to determine whether a chimpanzee raised in a human environment and given language instruction could learn a human language. Gua understood about 100 words at sixteen months, more words than their son at that age, but she never went beyond that. Moreover, comprehension of language involves more than understanding the meanings of isolated words. When their son could understand the difference between *I say what I mean* and *I mean what I say*, Gua could not understand either sentence.

Viki

A chimpanzee named Viki was raised by Keith and Cathy Hayes, and she too learned a number of individual words, even learning to articulate with great difficulty the words *mama, papa, cup*, and *up*. That was the extent of her language production.

Washoe

Allen and Beatrice Gardner recognized that one disadvantage suffered by the primates was their physical inability to pronounce many different sounds. Without a sufficient number of phonemic contrasts, spoken human language is impossible. Many species of primates are manually dexterous, and this fact inspired the Gardners (Gardner & Gardner, 1969) to attempt to teach American Sign Language (ASL) to a chimpanzee whom they named Washoe, after the Nevada county in which they lived. Washoe was brought up in much the same way as a human child in a deaf community, constantly in the presence of people who used ASL. She was deliberately taught to sign, whereas children raised by deaf signers acquire sign language without explicit teaching, just as hearing children learn spoken language.

By the time Washoe was four years old (June 1969), she had acquired eighty-five signs with meanings such as "more," "eat," "listen," "gimme," "key," "dog," "you," "me," "Washoe," and "hurry." According to the Gardners, Washoe was also able to produce sign combinations such as "baby mine," "you drink," "hug hurry," "gimme flower," and "more fruit."

Sarah

At about the same time that Washoe was growing up, two researchers (Premack & Premack, 1972) attempted to teach a chimpanzee, named Sarah, an artificial language designed to resemble human languages in some aspects. The "words" of Sarah's "language" were differently shaped and coloured plastic chips that were metal backed. Sarah and her trainers "talked" to each other by arranging these symbols on a magnetic board. Sarah was taught to associate particular symbols with particular meanings. The form–meaning relationship of these "morphemes" or "words" was arbitrary; a small red square meant "banana," and a small blue rectangle meant "apricot," while the colour red was represented by a grey chip and the colour yellow by a black chip. Sarah learned a number of "nouns," "adjectives," and "verbs" and symbols for abstract concepts, such as "same as" and "different from," "negation," and "question."

There were drawbacks to the experiment. Sarah was not allowed to "talk" spontaneously, only in response to her trainers. There was also the possibility that her trainers unwittingly provided cues and that she responded to these cues rather than to the plastic chips.

Learning Yerkish

To avoid these and other problems, Duane Rumbaugh and Sue Savage-Rumbaugh and their associates at the Yerkes Regional Primate Research Center began in 1973 to teach a different kind of artificial language, called Yerkish, to three chimpanzees, Lana, Sherman, and Austin. Instead of plastic chips, the words, called lexigrams, are geometric symbols displayed on a computer keyboard. The computer records every button pressed; certain fixed orders of these lexigrams constitute grammatical sentences in Yerkish. The researchers were particularly interested in the ability of primates to communicate using functional symbols. The researchers admit that the chimps did not learn much.

Koko

Another experiment aimed at teaching sign language to primates involved a gorilla named Koko, who was taught by her trainer, Francine "Penny" Patterson. Patterson (Patterson, 1978; Patterson & Linden, 1981) claimed that Koko has learned several hundred signs, is able to put signs together to make "sentences," and is capable of making linguistic jokes and puns, composing rhymes such as BEAR HAIR (a rhyme in spoken language but not in ASL), and inventing metaphors such as FINGER BRACELET for ring.

Nim Chimpsky

In a project specifically designed to test the linguistic claims that emerged from these primate experiments, another chimpanzee, named Nim Chimpsky, who was taught ASL by an experienced teacher, was studied by H.S. Terrace and his associates (Terrace, 1979). Under carefully controlled experimental conditions that included thorough record keeping and many hours of videotaping, Nim's teachers hoped to show beyond a reasonable doubt that chimpanzees have a human-like linguistic capacity, in contradiction to the view put forth by Noam Chomsky (after whom Nim was ironically named) that human language is species specific. In the nearly four years of study, Nim learned about 125 signs, and during the last two years Nim's teachers recorded more than 20,000 utterances that incorporated two or more signs. Nim produced his first ASL sign (DRINK) after just four months, which greatly encouraged the research team at the start of the study. Their enthusiasm soon diminished when he never seemed to go much beyond the two-word stage. Terrace concluded that "his three-sign combinations do not . . . provide new information. . . . Nim's most frequent two- and three-sign combinations [were] . . . PLAY

ME and PLAY ME NIM. Adding NIM to PLAY ME is simply redundant." This kind of redundancy is illustrated by a sixteen-sign utterance of Nim's: GIVE ORANGE ME GIVE EAT ORANGE ME EAT ORANGE GIVE ME EAT ORANGE GIVE ME YOU. This utterance does not sound much like the early sentences of children cited earlier.

Nim rarely signed spontaneously as do children when they begin to use language (spoken or sign). Only 12 percent of his utterances were spontaneous. Most of Nim's signing occurred only in response to prompting by his trainers and was related to eating, drinking, and playing — that is, it was stimulus controlled. As much as 40 percent of his output was simply repetitions of signs made by the trainer. Children initiate conversations more and more frequently as they grow older, and their utterances repeat less and less of the adult's prior utterance. Some children hardly ever imitate in conversation. Children become increasingly more *creative* in their language use, but Nim showed almost no tendency toward such creativity. Furthermore, children's utterances increase in length and complexity as time progresses, finally mirroring the adult grammar, whereas Nim's "language" did not.

The lack of spontaneity and the excessive noncreative imitative nature of Nim's signing led to the conclusion that Nim's acquisition and use of language are qualitatively different from a child's. After examining the films of Washoe, Koko, and others, Terrace drew similar conclusions regarding the signing of the other primates.

Signing chimpanzees are also unlike humans in that when several of them are together they do not sign to each other as freely as humans would under similar circumstances. There is also no evidence to date that a signing chimp (or one communicating with plastic chips or computer symbols) will teach another chimp language or that its offspring will acquire language from the parent.

Clever Hans

Premack and the Rumbaughs, like Terrace, suggest that the sign language studies were too uncontrolled and that the reported results were thus too anecdotal to support the view that primates are capable of acquiring a human language. They also question whether each of the other studies, and all those attempting to teach sign language to primates, suffer from what has come to be called the Clever Hans phenomenon.

Clever Hans, a horse at the turn of the century, became famous because of his apparent ability to do arithmetic, read and spell, and even solve problems of musical harmony. He answered the questions posed by his interrogators by stamping out numbers with his hoof. It turned out, not surprisingly, that Hans did not know that $2 + 2 = 4$, but he was clever enough to pick up subtle cues conveyed unconsciously by his trainer as to when he should stop tapping his hoof.

Sarah, like Clever Hans, took prompts from her trainers and her environment to produce the plastic chip sentences. In responding to the string of chips standing for

SARAH INSERT APPLE PAIL BANANA DISH

all she had to figure out was to place certain fruits in certain containers, and she could decide which by merely seeing that the apple symbol was next to the pail symbol and that the banana symbol was next to the dish symbol. There is no conclusive evidence that Sarah actually grouped strings of words into constituents. There is also no indication that Sarah would understand a *new* compound sentence of this type; the creative ability so integral to human language is not demonstrated by this act.

Problems also exist in Lana's "acquisition" of Yerkish. The Lana project was studied by Thompson and Church (1980), who were able to simulate Lana's behaviour by a computer model. They concluded that the chimp's "linguistic" behaviour can be accounted for by her learning to associate lexigrams with objects, persons, or events and to produce one of several "stock sentences" depending on situational cues (like Clever Hans).

There is another difference between the way Sarah and Lana learned whatever they learned and the way children learn language. In the case of the chimpanzees, each new rule or sentence form was introduced in a deliberate, highly constrained way. As we noted earlier, when parents speak to children they do not confine themselves to a few words in a particular order for months, rewarding the child with a chocolate bar or a banana each time the child correctly responds to a command. Nor do they wait until the child has mastered one rule of grammar before going on to a different structure. Young children require no special training.

Kanzi

Research on the linguistic ability of nonhuman primates continues. Two investigators, Greenfield and Savage-Rumbaugh, studied a male pygmy chimpanzee, or "bonobo," named Kanzi, using the same plastic lexigrams and computer keyboard that were used with Lana. They concluded that Kanzi "has not only learned, but also invented grammatical rules that may well be as complex as those used by human 2-year-old children" (Greenfield & Savage-Rumbaugh, 1990; Savage-Rumbaugh, 1991). The grammatical rule referred to was the combination of a lexigram (e.g., that meaning "dog") with a gesture meaning "go." After combining them, Kanzi would go to an area where dogs were located to play with them. Greenfield and Savage-Rumbaugh suggest that this "ordering" rule was not an imitation of his caretakers' utterances, for his caretakers used an opposite ordering, in which "dogs" would follow "go." Needless to say, Kanzi could not use the same combination of "go" and "dog" to express the feeling of "going to the dogs."

The investigators do report that Kanzi's acquisition of "grammatical skills" was much slower than that of human children, taking about three years (he was five and a half years old when the study began).

Most of Kanzi's so-called sentences are fixed formulas with little if any internal structure. Kanzi has not yet exhibited linguistic knowledge of a complexity equivalent to a three- or four-year-old's knowledge of structure dependencies and hierarchical structure. Moreover, unlike Kanzi, who used a different word order from that of her caretakers, children rapidly set the word order parameters of UG to correspond to the input.

As often happens in science, the search for answers to one kind of question leads to answers to other questions not originally asked. The linguistic experiments with primates have led to many advances in our understanding of primate cognitive ability. Premack has gone on to investigate other capacities of the chimp mind, such as causality; the Rumbaughs and Greenfield continue to study the ability of chimpanzees to use symbols. These studies also point out how remarkable it is that human children, by the ages of three and four, without explicit teaching or overt reinforcement, create complex sentences never spoken and never heard before.

Summary

If language is defined merely as a system of communication, then language is not unique to humans. There are, however, certain characteristics of human language not found in the communication systems of any other species. A basic property of human language is its **creative aspect** — a speaker's ability to combine the basic linguistic units to form an infinite set of "well-formed" grammatical sentences, most of which are novel, never before produced or heard.

The ability to imitate the sounds of human language is not a sufficient basis for learning language. Talking birds imitate sounds but can neither segment these sounds into smaller units, nor understand what they are imitating, nor produce new utterances to convey their thoughts.

Birds make **birdcalls** and produce **bird songs**, bees, crabs, spiders, and most other creatures communicate in some way, but the information imparted is severely limited and stimulus bound, confined to a small set of messages. The system of language represented by intricate mental grammars, which are not stimulus-bound and that generate infinite messages, is unique to the human species.

Questions as to whether language is unique to the human species have led researchers to attempt to teach nonhuman primates systems of communication that purportedly resemble human language. Chimpanzees like Sarah and Lana have been taught to manipulate symbols to gain rewards, and other chimpanzees, like Washoe and Nim Chimpsky, have been taught a number of ASL signs. A careful examination of the utterances in ASL by these chimps shows that unlike children, their language exhibits little spontaneity, is highly imitative (echoic), and reveals little syntactic structure. It has been suggested that the pygmy chimp Kanzi shows grammatical ability greater than the other chimps studied, but he still does not have the ability of even a three-year-old child.

Exercises

*1. What do the barking of dogs, the meowing of cats, and the singing of birds have in common with human language? What are some of the basic differences?

2. A wolf is able to express subtle gradations of emotion by different positions of the ears, the lips, and the tail. There are eleven postures of the tail that express emotions, such as self-confidence, confident threat, lack of tension, uncertain threat, depression, defensiveness, active submission, and complete submission. This system seems to be complex. Suppose there were a thousand different emotions that the wolf could express in this way. Would you then say the wolf had a language similar to a human's? If not, why not?

3. Suppose you taught a dog to *heel, sit up, beg, roll over, play dead, stay, jump,* and *bark* on command, using the italicized words as cues. Would you be teaching it language? Why or why not?

References

Anderson, S.R. (2004). *Doctor Dolittle's delusion: Animals and the uniqueness of human language*. New Haven, CT: Yale University Press.

Busnel, R.G., & Bremond, J. (1962). *Recherche du support de l'information dans le signal acoustique de défense territoriale de rougegorge*. C.R Académie Scientifique Paris, 254, pp. 2236–2238.

Descartes, R. (1967). Discourse on method. In *The philosophical works of Descartes* (Vol. 1, E.S. Haldane & G.R. Ross, Trans.). Cambridge, UK: Cambridge University Press. (Original work published 1637)

Gardner, R.A., & Gardner, B.T. (1969). Teaching sign language to a chimpanzee. *Science, 165*, 664–672.

Greenfield, P.M., & Savage-Rumbaugh, E.S. (1990, September). Research notes. *The Chronicle of Higher Education, 36*.

Patterson, F.G. (1978). The gestures of a gorilla: Language acquisition in another pongid. *Brain and Language, 5*, 56–71.

Patterson, F., & Linden, E. (1981). *The education of Koko*. New York: Holt, Rinehart and Winston.

Pepperberg, I.M. (1993). Cognitive and communicative competence in an African Grey Parrot. In H. Roitblat, L. Herman, & P. Nachtigall (Eds.), *Language and communication: Comparative perspectives* (pp. 221–248). Hillsdale, NJ: Erlbaum.

Pepperberg, I.M. (2004). Cognitive and communicative abilities of Grey Parrots: Implications for the enrichment of many species. *Animal Welfare, 13*, S203–208.

Pinker, S. (1994). *The language instinct*. New York: William Morrow.

Premack, A.J., & Premack, D. (1972, October). Teaching language to an ape. *Scientific American*, 92–99.

Savage-Rumbaugh, E.S. (1991). Language learning in the bonobo: How and why they learn. In N.A. Krasnegor, D.M. Rumbaugh, R.L. Schiefelbusch, & M. Studdert-Kennedy (Eds.), *Biological and behavioral determinants of language development* (pp. 209–233). Hillsdale, NJ: Erlbaum.

Templeton, C.N., Greene, E., & Davis, K. (2005, June 23). Allometry of alarm calls: Black-capped chickadees encode information about predator size. *Science*, 1934–1937.

Terrace, H.S. (1979). *Nim: A chimpanzee who learned sign language*. New York: Knopf.

Thompson, C.R., & Church, R.M. (1980). An explanation of the language of a chimpanzee. *Science, 208*, 313–314.

Von Frisch, K. (1967). *The dance language and orientation of bees* (L.E. Chadvick, Trans.). Cambridge, MA: Belknap Press of Harvard University Press.

Further Reading

Anderson, S.R. (2004). *Doctor Dolittle's delusion: Animals and the uniqueness of human language.* New Haven, CT: Yale University Press.

Gould, J.L., & Gould, C.G. (1983). Can a bee behave intelligently? *New Scientist, 98*, 84–87.

Greenfield, P.M., & Savage-Rumbaugh, E.S. (1990). *Language and intelligence in monkeys and apes: Comparative developmental perspectives.* Cambridge, UK: Cambridge University Press.

Owings, D.H., & Morton, E.S. (1998). *Animal vocal communication: A new approach.* Cambridge, UK: Cambridge University Press.

Pinker, S. (1994). *The language instinct.* New York: William Morrow.

Rumbaugh, D.M. (1977). *Acquisition of linguistic skills by a chimpanzee.* New York: Academic Press.

Savage-Rumbaugh, S., & Lewin, R. (1996). *Kanzi: The ape at the brink of the human mind.* New York: Wiley.

Savage-Rumbaugh, S., Shanker, S.G., & Taylor, T.J. (2001). *Apes, language, and the human mind.* Oxford: Oxford University Press.

Searcy, W.A., & Nowicki, S. (2005). *Animal communication: Reliability and deception in signaling systems.* Princeton, NJ: Princeton University Press.

Sebeok, T.A. (Ed.). (1977). *How animals communicate.* Bloomington: Indiana University Press.

Sebeok, T.A., & Rosenthal, R. (Eds.). (1981). The Clever Hans phenomenon: Communication with horses, whales, apes and people. *Annals of the New York Academy of Sciences, Vol. 364.*

Websites

http://www.alphadictionary.com/articles/ling002.html   A website with an article discussing animal communication.

http://www.pbs.org/newshour/bb/science/chimp_5-6.html A PBS site with a transcript of a chimp study discussion.

http://www.geocities.com/RainForest/Vines/4451/KokoLiveChat.html Provides a transcript of a "conversation" with Koko the gorilla.

GLOSSARY

abbreviation Shortened form of a word (e.g., *prof* from *professor*). Cf. **clipping**.

accent (1) Prominence. Cf. **stressed syllable**; (2) the phonology or pronunciation of a specific regional dialect, e.g., Newfoundland or southern United States accent; (3) the pronunciation of a language by a nonnative speaker, e.g., French accent.

accidental gap Phonological or morphological form that constitutes possible but nonoccurring lexical items, e.g., *blick, unsad*.

acoustic phonetics The study of the physical characteristics of speech sounds.

acoustic signal The sound waves produced by any sound source, including speech.

acquired dyslexia Loss of ability to read correctly following brain damage in persons who were previously literate.

acronym Word composed of the initials of several words, e.g., *PET* scan from *positron-emission tomography* scan.

active sentence A sentence in which the noun phrase subject in deep structure is also the noun phrase subject in surface structure, e.g., *The dog chased the car*. Cf. **passive sentence**.

additive bilingualism L2 learning in a context in which both languages are well supported and maintained.

adjective (Adj) The syntactic category, also lexical category, of words that function as the head of an adjective phrase, and that have the semantic effect of qualifying or describing the referents of nouns, e.g., *tall, bright, intelligent*. Cf. **adjective phrase**.

adjective phrase (AP) A syntactic category, also phrasal category, whose head is an adjective possibly accompanied by modifiers, that occurs inside noun phrases and as complements of the verb *to be*, e.g., *worthy of praise, several miles high, green, more difficult*.

adverb (Adv) The syntactic category, also lexical category, of words that qualify the verb such as manner adverbs like *quickly* and time adverbs like *soon*. The position of the adverb in the sentence depends on its semantic type, e.g., *John will soon eat lunch, John eats lunch quickly*.

affix Bound morpheme attached to a stem or root. Cf. **prefix, suffix, infix, circumfix, stem, root**.

affricate A sound produced by a stop closure followed immediately by a slow release characteristic of a fricative; phonetically a sequence of stop + fricative, e.g., the *ch* in *chip*, which is [č] and like [š] + [t].

African American English (AAE) A dialect of English spoken by some African Americans, largely in the United States; formerly known as Black English.

agent The thematic role of the noun phrase whose referent does the action described by the verb, e.g., *George* in *George hugged Martha*.

agrammatism Language disorder usually resulting from damage to Broca's area in which the patient has difficulty with certain aspects of syntax, especially functional categories. Cf. **Broca's area**.

airstream mechanisms The various processes in which air from the lungs or mouth is moved to produce speech sounds, e.g., **pulmonic egressive**. Cf. **egressive airstream mechanism, ingressive airstream mechanism**.

allomorph Alternative phonetic form of a morpheme; e.g., the /-s/, /-z/, and /-əz/ forms of the plural morpheme in *cats, dogs,* and *kisses*.

allophone   A predictable phonetic realization of a phoneme, e.g., [p] and [pʰ] are allophones of the phoneme /p/ in English.

alphabetic writing   A writing system in which each symbol typically represents one sound segment.

alveolar   A sound produced by raising the tongue to the alveolar ridge, e.g., [s], [t], [n].

alveolar ridge   The part of the hard palate directly behind the top front teeth.

alveopalatal   A sound whose place of articulation is the hard palate immediately behind the alveolar ridge, e.g., [š] when it occurs before a front vowel.

ambiguous, ambiguity   The terms used to describe a word, phrase, or sentence with multiple meanings.

American Sign Language (ASL)   The sign language used by the deaf community in the United States. Cf. **sign languages**.

analogic change   A language change in which a rule spreads to previously unaffected forms, e.g., the plural of *cow* changed from the earlier *kine* to *cows* by the generalization of the plural formation rule or by analogy to regular plural forms. Also called internal borrowing.

analogy   The use of one form as an exemplar by which other forms can be similarly constructed, e.g., based on *bow/bows, sow/sows,* etc., English speakers began to say *cows* instead of the older *kine*. Analogy also leads speakers to say **brung* as a past tense of *bring* based on *sing/sang/sung, ring/rang/rung,* and so on.

analytic   Describes a sentence that is true by virtue of its meaning alone, irrespective of context, e.g., *Kings are male.* Cf. **contradictory**.

anaphora   The process of replacing a longer expression with a shorter one, especially with a pronoun, that is coreferential with the longer expression.

anomalous   Semantically ill formed, e.g., *Colourless green ideas sleep furiously.*

anomaly   A violation of semantic rules resulting in expressions that seem nonsensical, e.g., *The verb crumpled the milk.*

anomia   A form of **aphasia** in which patients have word-finding difficulties.

anterior   A phonetic feature of consonants whose place of articulation is in front of the palato-alveolar area, including **labials**, **interdentals**, and **alveolars**.

antonyms   Words that are opposite with respect to one of their semantic properties, e.g., *tall/short* are both alike in that they describe height, but opposite in regard to the extent of the height. Cf. **gradable pair**, **complementary pair**, **relational opposites**.

aphasia   Language loss or disorders following brain damage.

aphesis/aphaeresis   Loss of initial vowels as in the common pronunciation of *possum* for *opossum*.

apocope   Loss of final sounds in a word so that, for example, Old English *nama* /namə/ became *name* /nem/.

arbitrary   Describes the property of language, including sign language, whereby there is no natural or intrinsic relationship between the way a word is pronounced (or signed) and its meaning.

arc   Part of the graphical depiction of a transition network represented as an arrow labelled with syntactic category and connecting two nodes. Cf. **node, transition network**.

argot   The specialized words used by a particular group, such as pilots or linguists, e.g., *morphophonemics* in linguistics. Cf. **jargon**.

article (Art)   One of several subclasses of determiners, e.g., *the, a.*

articulators   The tongue, lips, and velum, which change the shape of the vocal tract to produce different speech sounds.

articulatory phonetics   The study of how the vocal tract produces speech sounds; the physiological characteristics of speech sounds.

aspirated   A term that refers to voiceless consonants in which the vocal cords remain open for a brief period after the release of the constriction, resulting in a puff of air (e.g., the [p^h] in *pit*). Cf. **unaspirated**.

assimilation rules/assimilation   A phonological process that changes feature values of segments to make them more similar, e.g., a vowel becomes [+nasal] when followed by a [+nasal] consonant. Also called feature-spreading rules.

asterisk   The symbol [*] used to indicate ungrammatical or anomalous examples (e.g., *cried the baby*, *sincerity dances*). Also used in historical and comparative linguistics to represent a reconstructed form.

audiolingual method (ALM)   Language teaching approach based on behaviourist and structuralist views in which there is a heavy reliance on language drills and repetitions.

auditory phonetics   The study of the perception of speech sounds.

automatic machine translation   The use of computers to translate from one language to another. Cf. **source language**, **target language**.

automatization, automatic processing   Cognitive processing that occurs rapidly with little or no need for attentional control.

aux   A syntactic category containing auxiliary verbs and abstract tense morphemes. It is also called **INFL** and functions as the **head** of a **sentence**.

auxiliary verb (Aux)   Verbal elements, traditionally called "helping verbs," that co-occur with, and qualify, the main verb in a verb phrase with regard to such properties as tense, e.g., *have, be, will.*

babbling   Sounds produced in the first few months after birth that gradually come to include only sounds that occur in the language of the household. Deaf children babble with hand gestures.

baby talk   A certain **style** of speech that many adults use when speaking to children that includes among other things exaggerated intonation. Cf. **child-directed speech (CDS)**.

back-formation   Creation of a new word by removing an affix from an old word, e.g., *donate* from *donation,* or by removing what is mistakenly considered an affix, e.g., *edit* from *editor.*

backtracking   The action in which a parser returns to a decision point where it went wrong and makes a different choice.

back vowels   Vowel sounds involving the back of the tongue.

basic interpersonal communicative skills (BICS)   Type of language skills found in interpersonal communicative settings in which contextual information is available (*context-embedded*) to interpret a message.

behaviourism   School of psychology that views learning as habit formation through establishing stimulus–response patterns; it emphasizes the role of environmental factors.

bilabial   A sound articulated by bringing both lips together.

bilingual acquisition   Acquisition of two languages simultaneously in childhood.

birdcall   One or more short notes that convey messages associated with the immediate environment, such as danger, feeding, nesting, and flocking.

bird song   Complex pattern of notes used to mark territory and to attract mates.

blend   A word composed of the parts of more than one word, e.g., *smog* from *smoke + fog.*

bootstrapping   See **syntactic bootstrapping**.

borrowing   The incorporation of a loan word from one language into another (e.g., English borrowed *buoy* from Dutch). Cf. **loan word**.

bottom-to-top language death The cessation of use of a language except in special circumstances, e.g., a liturgical language like Latin. Cf. **sudden language death, radical language death, gradual language death**.

bottom-up processing Data-driven analysis of linguistic input that begins with the small units like phones and proceeds stepwise to increasingly larger units like words and phrases until the entire input is processed, often ending in a complete sentence and semantic interpretation. Cf. **top-down processing**.

bound morpheme Morpheme that must be attached to other morphemes, e.g., *-ly, -ed, non-*. Bound morphemes are prefixes, suffixes, infixes, circumfixes, and some roots, such as *cran* in *cranberry*. Cf. **free morpheme**.

bound pronoun A pronoun (or more generally, a pro-form) whose antecedent is explicitly mentioned in the discourse. Cf. **unbound, free pronoun**.

broadening A semantic change in which the meaning of a word changes over time to become more encompassing, e.g., *dogge* once meant a particular breed of *dog*.

Broca, Paul A French neurologist of the nineteenth century who identified a particular area of the left side of the brain as a language centre.

Broca's aphasia See **agrammatism**.

Broca's area A front part of the left hemisphere of the brain, damage to which causes **agrammatism** or **Broca's aphasia**. Also called Broca's region.

calligraphy The art of writing or drawing Chinese characters.

Canadian raising An allophonic variation typical of many speakers of Canadian English (and some speakers of American English) whereby /aj/ and /aw/ become [ʌj] and [ʌw] before voiceless consonants. The centred and raised diphthongs are considered typical of Canadian English.

case A characteristic of nouns and pronouns, and in some languages articles and adjectives, determined by the function in the sentence, and generally indicated by the morphological form of the word, e.g., *I* is in the nominative case of the first-person singular pronoun in English and functions as a subject; *me* is in the accusative case and functions as an object.

case endings Suffixes on the noun based on its grammatical function, such as *'s* of the English genitive case indicating possession, e.g., Cathy*'s* dog.

case theory The study of thematic roles and grammatical case in languages of the world.

cause/causative The thematic role of the noun phrase whose referent is a natural force that is responsible for a change, e.g., *the wind* in *The wind damaged the roof.*

central vowels Vowel sounds in which the tongue is in a central position in the mouth.

cerebral hemispheres The left and right halves of the brain, joined by the **corpus callosum**.

characters (Chinese) The units of Chinese writing, each of which represents a morpheme or word. Cf. **ideogram, logogram**.

child-directed speech (CDS) The special intonationally exaggerated speech that some adults use to speak with small children, sometimes called **baby talk** or motherese.

circumfix Bound morpheme, parts of which occur in a word both before and after the root, e.g., *ge - - - t* in German *geliebt,* "loved," from the root *lieb*.

classifier A grammatical morpheme that marks the semantic class of a noun, e.g., in Swahili, nouns that refer to human artifacts such as beds and chairs are prefixed with the classifiers *ki* if singular and *vi* if plural; *kiti,* "chair" and *viti,* "chairs."

click   A speech sound with an **ingressive airstream mechanism** that produces sounds by sucking air into the mouth and forcing it between articulators to produce a sharp sound, e.g., the sound often spelled *tsk*.

clipping   The deletion of some part of a longer word to give a shorter word with the same meaning, e.g., *phone* from *telephone*. Cf. **abbreviation**.

closed class   A category, generally a **functional category**, that rarely has new words added to it, e.g., prepositions, conjunctions. Cf. **open class**.

coarticulation   The transfer of phonetic features to adjoining segments to make them more alike, e.g., vowels become [+nasal] when followed by consonants that are [+nasal].

coda   One or more phonological segments that follow the **nucleus** of a syllable, e.g., the /st/ in /prist/ *priest*.

code switching   The movement back and forth between two languages or dialects within the same sentence or discourse.

cognates   Words in related languages that developed from the same ancestral root, such as English *man* and German *Mann*.

cognitive/academic language proficiency (CALP)   Type of language skills such as those found in academic settings in which there is little available context (*context-reduced*) to allow one to interpret the message.

cognitive approach/cognitive theory   Theoretical approach that refers to internal mental representations that regulate and guide performance associated with learning.

cognitive strategy   Type of language learning strategy that involves direct operations on incoming information in order to increase learning.

cognitive style   Predisposition to process information in a characteristic manner.

coinage   The construction and/or invention of new words that then become part of the lexicon, e.g., *e-commerce*.

collocation analysis   Textual analysis that reveals the extent to which the presence of one word influences the occurrence of nearby words.

communicative competence   The learner's knowledge of how to use a language in pragmatically and socially appropriate ways.

communicative language teaching (CLT)   Language teaching approach in which there is an emphasis on the acquisition of overall communicative competence.

community language learning approach   Teaching approach that emphasizes interpersonal relationships and involves a "counsellor" who directs language instruction in small group settings.

comparative method   The technique linguists use to deduce forms in an ancestral language by examining corresponding forms in several of its descendant languages.

comparative reconstruction   The deducing of forms in an ancestral language of genetically related languages by application of the **comparative method**.

complement   The constituent(s) in a phrase other than the head that complete(s) the meaning of the phrase. In the verb phrase *found a puppy*, the noun phrase *a puppy* is a complement of the head verb *found*.

complementary distribution   The situation in which phones never occur in the same phonetic environment, e.g., [p] and [pʰ] in English. Cf. **allophone**.

complementary pair   Two **antonyms** related in such a way that the negation of one is the meaning of the other, e.g., *alive* means not *dead*. Cf. **gradable pair**, **relational opposites**.

complementizer (Comp)   A syntactic category, also functional category, of words, including *that, if, whether,* that introduce an embedded sentence, e.g., *his belief that sheepdogs can swim,* or, *I wonder if* sheepdogs can swim. The complementizer has the effect of turning a sentence into a complement.

compound   A word composed of two or more words, e.g., *washcloth, childproof cap.*

compound bilingualism   Type of bilingualism proposed by Weinreich in which a single concept underlies the two separate words expressing that concept in each language.

comprehensible input   In the **monitor model**, refers to exposure to the target language that is slightly beyond the learner's current level.

computational linguistics   A subfield of linguistics and computer science that is concerned with computer processing of human language.

computational morphology   The programming of computers to analyze the structure of words.

computational phonetics and phonology   The programming of computers to analyze the speech signal into phones and phonemes.

computational pragmatics   The programming of computers to take context and situation into account when determining the meaning of expressions.

computational semantics   The programming of computers to determine the meaning of words, phrases, sentences, and discourse.

computational syntax   The programming of computers to analyze the structure of sentences. Cf. **parse, bottom-up processing, top-down processing**.

concordance   An alphabetical index of the words in a text that gives the frequency of each word, its location in the text, and its surrounding context.

conditioned sound change   Historical phonological change that occurs in specific phonetic contexts, e.g., the voicing of /f/ to [v] when it occurs between vowels.

connectionism   Modelling grammars through the use of networks consisting of simple neuronlike units connected in complex ways so that different connections vary in strength, and can be strengthened or weakened through exposure to linguistic data. For example, in phonology there would be stronger connections among /p/, /t/, and /k/ (the voiceless stops and a natural class) than among /p/, /n/, and /i/. In morphology there would be stronger connections between *play/played,* and *dance/danced,* than between *play* and *danced.* Semantically, there would be stronger connections between *melody* and *music* than between *melody* and *sheepdog.* Syntactically there would be stronger connections between *John loves Mary* and *Mary is loved by John* than between *John loves Mary* and *Mary knows John.*

connotative meaning/connotation   The evocation or affective meaning associated with a word. Two words may have the same referential, denotative meaning but different connotations.

consonant   A speech sound produced with some constriction of the airstream. Cf. **vowel**.

consonantal   Phonetic feature distinguishing the class of obstruents, liquids, and nasals, which are [+ consonantal], from other sounds (vowels and glides), which are [– consonantal].

consonantal alphabet   The symbols of a **consonantal writing** system.

consonantal writing   A writing system of symbols that represent only consonants; vowels are inferred from context , e.g., Arabic.

consonant cluster   Two or more consonants in sequence (e.g., /str/ in the word *string*).

constituent   A syntactic unit in a **phrase structure tree**, e.g., *the girl* is a noun phrase constituent in the sentence *the boy loves the girl.*

constituent structure   The hierarchically arranged syntactic units such as noun phrase and verb phrase that underlie every sentence.

constituent structure tree   See **phrase structure tree**.

content words   The nouns, verbs, adjectives, and adverbs that constitute the major part of the vocabulary. Cf. **open class**.

continuant   A speech sound in which the airstream flows continually through the mouth; all speech sounds except stops and affricates.

contour tones   Tones in which the pitch glides from one level to another, e.g., from low to high as in a rising tone.

contradiction   Negative entailment: the truth of one sentence necessarily implies the falseness of another sentence, e.g., *He opened the door* and *The door is closed*. Cf. **entailment**.

contradictory   Describes a sentence that is false by virtue of its meaning alone, irrespective of context, e.g., *Kings are female*. Cf. **analytic**.

contralateral   Refers to stimuli that travel between one side of the body (left/right) and the opposite **cerebral hemisphere** (right/left).

contrast   Different sounds contrast when their presence alone distinguishes between otherwise identical forms, e.g., [f] and [v] in *fine* and *vine,* but not [p] and [pʰ] in [spik] and [spʰik] (two variant ways of saying *speak*). Cf. **minimal pair**.

contrasting tones   In tone languages, different tones that make different words, e.g., in Nupe, *bá* with a high tone, and *bà* with a low tone mean "be sour" and "count," respectively.

contrastive analysis (CA)   Comparison and contrast of the linguistic structures of two languages in order to identify similarities and differences.

contrastive analysis (CA) approach   Approach to L2 learning based in behaviourist notions stipulating that where there are differences in linguistic structures, difficulties would normally occur.

contrastive analysis hypothesis (CAH)   Prediction that differences between two languages will lead to learning difficulties.

contrastive stress   Additional stress placed on a word to highlight it or to clarify the referent of a pronoun, e.g., in *Joe hired Bill and he hired Sam,* with contrastive stress on *he,* it is usually understood that Bill rather than Joe hired Sam.

controlled processing   Cognitive processing that is under attentional control, requires more time, and takes up more processing capacity.

convention, conventional   The agreed-on, though generally arbitrary, relationship between the form and meaning of words.

conversion   The process in which an existing word becomes assigned to another syntactic category, e.g., *ink* (noun), to *ink* (verb).

cooperative principle   A broad principle within whose scope fall the various **maxims of conversation**. It states that in order to communicate effectively, speakers should agree to be informative and relevant.

coordinate bilingualism   Type of bilingualism proposed by Weinreich in which there are two distinct language systems such that separate concepts underlie equivalent words in each language.

coordinate structure   A syntactic structure in which two or more constituents of the same syntactic category are joined by a conjunction such as *and* and *or*, e.g., *bread and butter, the big dog or the small cat, huffing and puffing.*

coordinate structure constraint   A constraint of **Universal Grammar**, and therefore applicable to all languages, that prohibits the movement of constituents out of a coordinate structure.

copula A verb, usually a form of *to be*, that equates the expressions on either side of it (e.g., *is* in *Bob is the professor*).

coreferential Describes noun phrases (including pronouns) that refer to the same entity.

core instruction The typical language class in which specific language instruction is given.

coronals The class of sounds articulated by raising the tip or blade of the tongue, including **alveolars** and **palatals**, e.g., [t], [š].

corpus A collection of language data gathered from spoken or written sources used for linguistic research and analysis.

corpus callosum The nerve fibres connecting the right and left **cerebral hemispheres**.

cortex The approximately ten billion neurons that form the outside surface of the brain; also referred to as grey matter.

count nouns Nouns that can be enumerated, e.g., *one potato, two potatoes*. Cf. **mass nouns**.

creativity of language, creative aspect of linguistic knowledge Speakers' ability to combine the finite number of linguistic units of their language to produce and understand an infinite range of novel sentences.

creole A language that begins as a **pidgin** and eventually becomes the first language of a speech community through its being learned by children.

critical or sensitive period The time during which it is proposed that native-like language proficiency can be achieved. Researchers differ as to the age marking the end of such a period.

critical period hypothesis The hypothesis that there is a window of time (up to a certain age) for learning a language, but beyond that period native-like proficiency is rarely achieved. In L2 acquisition, the strongest evidence appears to be in regard to pronunciation.

cuneiform A form of writing in which the characters are produced using a wedge-shaped stylus.

data mining Complex methods of retrieving and using information from immense and varied sources of data through the use of advanced statistical tools.

daughter language A descendant of an earlier form of a language (e.g., French is a daughter language of Latin, which is the parent).

deep structure Any phrase structure tree generated by the phrase structure rules of a transformational grammar. The basic syntactic structures of the grammar.

definite Describes a noun phrase that refers to a unique object known to the speaker and listener.

deictic/deixis Refers to words or expressions whose reference relies entirely on context and the orientation of the speaker in space and time, e.g., *I, yesterday, there, this cat*.

deletion A process that removes phonemic segments in certain contexts (e.g., in contractions, such as *he is* becoming *he's* or *I will* becoming *I'll*).

demonstrative articles, demonstratives Words such as *this, that, those,* and *these* that function syntactically as articles but are semantically **deictic** because context is needed to determine the referent of the noun phrase in which they occur.

denotative meaning The referential meaning of a word or expression.

dental A place-of-articulation term for consonants articulated with the tongue against, or nearly against, the front teeth. Cf. **interdental**.

derivation The steps in the application of rules to an underlying form that results in a surface representation, e.g., in deriving a syntactic surface structure from a deep structure, or in deriving a phonetic form from a phonemic form.

derivational morpheme   Morpheme added to a stem or root to form a new stem or word, possibly, but not necessarily, resulting in a change in syntactic category, e.g., *-er* added to a verb like *kick* to give the noun *kicker.*

derived word   The form that results from the addition of a derivational morpheme, e.g., *firm* + *ly* = *firmly* is a derived word.

descriptive grammar   A linguist's description or model of the mental grammar, including the units, structures, and rules. An explicit statement of what speakers know about their language. Cf. **prescriptive grammar, teaching grammar**.

determiner (Det)   The syntactic category, also functional category, of words and expressions that when combined with a noun form a noun phrase. Includes the articles *the* and *a*, **demonstratives** such as *this* and *that*, quantifiers such as *each* and *every*, expressions such as *William's*, etc.

diacritics   Additional markings on written symbols to specify various phonetic properties such as **length, tone, stress, nasalization**; extra marks on a written character that change its usual value, e.g., the tilde [~] drawn over the letter *n* in Spanish represents a palatalized nasal rather than an alveolar nasal.

dialect   A variety of a language whose grammar differs in systematic ways from other varieties. Differences may be lexical, phonological, syntactic, and semantic. Cf. **regional dialect, social dialect, prestige dialect**.

dialect atlas   A book of **dialect maps** showing the areas where specific dialectal characteristics occur in the speech of the region.

dialect levelling   Movement toward greater uniformity or decrease in variations among dialects.

dialect map   A map showing the areas where specific dialectal characteristics occur in the speech of the region.

dichotic listening   Experimental method for testing brain lateralization in which subjects hear different auditory signals in the left and right ears.

digraph   Two letters used to represent a single sound, e.g., *gh* represents [f] in *enough*.

diphthong   Vowel + glide, e.g., [aj, aw, ɔj] as in *bite, bout, boy*. Cf. **monophthong**.

direct method   The learning of a second language by "total immersion." The native language is never (or rarely) used in the classroom, and the students supposedly acquire the second language in a way similar to the way they acquired their first language. Cf. **grammar translation, audiolingual method**.

direct object   The grammatical relation of a noun phrase when it appears immediately below the verb phrase (VP) and next to the verb in deep structure; the noun phrase complement of a transitive verb, e.g., *the puppy* in *the boy found the puppy.*

discontinuous dependency   The relationship of two words separated in surface structure that are linked, or dependent on each other, in deep structure, e.g., the verb *pull* and the verbal particle *over* in *the police pulled the speeder over* (from the deep structure *the police pulled over the speeder*).

discontinuous morpheme   A morpheme with multiple parts that occur in more than one place in a word or sentence, e.g., *ge* and *t* in German *geliebt,* "loved." Cf. **circumfix**.

discourse   A linguistic unit that comprises more than one sentence.

discourse analysis   The study of discourse.

discreteness   A fundamental property of human language in which larger linguistic units are perceived to be composed of smaller linguistic units, e.g., *cat* is perceived as the phonemes /k/, /æ/, /t/; *the cat* is perceived as *the* and *cat.*

dissimilation rules   Phonological rules that change feature values of segments to make them less similar, e.g., a fricative dissimilation rule: /θ/ is pronounced [t] following another fricative. In English dialects with this rule, *sixth* /sɪks + θ/ is pronounced [sɪkst].

distinctive   Describes linguistic elements that contrast, e.g., [f] and [v] are distinctive segments; voice is a distinctive phonetic feature of consonants.

distinctive features   Phonetic properties of phonemes that account for their ability to contrast meanings of words, e.g., *voice, tense.*

ditransitive verb   A verb that appears to take two noun-phrase objects (e.g., *give* in *He gave Sally the gift*). Ditransitive verb phrases often have an alternative form with a prepositional phrase in place of the first noun phrase, as in *He gave the gift to Sally.*

dominate   In a **phrase structure tree**, when a continuous downward path can be traced from a node labelled *A* to a node labelled *B*, *A* dominates *B*.

downdrift   The gradual lowering of the absolute pitch of tones during an utterance in a tone language. During downdrift, tones retain their *relative* values to one another.

Early Middle English Vowel Shortening   A sound change that shortened vowels such as the first *i* in *criminal*. As a result *criminal* was unaffected by the **Great Vowel Shift**, leading to word pairs such as *crime/criminal.*

ease of articulation   The tendency of speakers to adjust their pronunciation to make it easier, or more efficient, to move the articulators. Phonetic and phonological rules are often the result of ease of articulation, e.g., the rule of English that nasalizes vowels when they precede a nasal consonant.

egressive airstream mechanism   The articulation of speech sounds in which air is pushed out of the mouth.

egressive sound   Sound produced with an **egressive airstream mechanism**, including all the speech sounds of English.

ejective   A speech sound produced when air in the mouth is pressurized by an upward movement of the closed glottis, and then released suddenly.

embedded sentence   A sentence that occurs within a sentence in a phrase structure tree, e.g., *You know that **sheepdogs cannot read.***

emoticon   A string of text characters that, when viewed sideways, forms a face expressing a particular emotion, e.g., [8<\ to express "dismay." Frequently used in e-mail.

entailment   The relationship between two sentences where the truth of one necessarily implies the truth of the other (e.g., such a relationship holds between *Corday assassinated Marat* and *Marat is dead* since, if the first is true, the second must be true).

entails   One sentence entails another if the truth of the first necessarily implies the truth of the second, e.g., *The sun melted the ice* entails *The ice melted* since if the first is true, the second must be true.

epenthesis   The insertion of one or more phones in a word, e.g., the insertion of [ə] in *children* to produce [čɪlədrən] instead of [čɪldrən].

eponym   A word taken from a proper name, such as *john* for "toilet."

error analysis (EA)   An approach to L2 learning that considers errors as indicators of the learner's unfolding new linguistic system and emphasizes the creative contributions of the L2 learner.

etymeme   A bound base that has etymological relevance (e.g., *-ceive* in *receive*).

etymology   The history of words; the study of the history of words.

euphemism   A word or phrase that replaces a taboo word or is used to avoid reference to certain acts or subjects, e.g., *powder room* for *toilet.*

event/eventive A type of sentence that describes activities such as *John kissed Mary,* as opposed to describing states such as *John knows Mary*. Cf. **state/stative**.

event-related brain potentials (ERP) The electrical signals emitted from different areas of the brain in response to different kinds of stimuli.

experiencer The thematic role of the noun phrase whose referent perceives something, e.g., *Helen* in *Helen heard Robert playing the piano*.

extension The referential part of the meaning of an expression; the referent of a noun phrase. Cf. **reference**, **referent**.

extrinsic motivation Behaviours carried out for rewards coming from outside the self.

feature-changing rules Phonological rules that change feature values of segments, either to make them more similar (Cf. **assimilation rules**), or less similar (Cf. **dissimilation rules**).

feature matrix A representation of phonological segments in which the columns represent segments and the rows represent features, each cell being marked with a + or − to designate the value of the feature for that segment.

feature-spreading rules Cf. **assimilation rules**.

field dependence Type of cognitive style characterized by a holistic approach to processing information.

field independence Type of cognitive style characterized by an analytic approach to processing information.

finger spelling In signing, hand gestures that represent letters of the alphabet used to spell words for which there is no sign.

flap Sound in which the tongue quickly touches the alveolar ridge and withdraws. It is often an allophone of /t/ and /d/ in words such as *latter* and *ladder*. Also called **tap**.

folk etymology The process whereby the history of a word is derived from nonscientific speculation or false analogy with another word, e.g., *hooker* for "prostitute" is falsely believed to be derived from the name of the U.S. Civil War general Joseph Hooker.

form Phonological or gestural representation of a morpheme or word.

formant In the frequency analysis of speech, a band of frequencies of higher intensity than surrounding frequencies, which appears as a dark line on a **spectrogram**. Individual vowels display different formant patterns.

form-focused instruction (FFI) Any pedagogical effort used to draw the learner's attention to language form either implicitly or explicitly.

fossilization A characteristic of second language learning in which the learner reaches a plateau and seems unable to acquire some property of the L2 grammar.

free morpheme A single morpheme that constitutes a word.

free pronoun A pronoun that refers to some object not explicitly mentioned in the sentence, e.g., *it* in *Everyone saw it*. Also called **unbound**. Cf. **bound pronoun**.

free variation Alternative pronunciations of a word in which one sound is substituted for another without changing the word's meaning, e.g., pronunciation of *bottle* as [batəl] or [baʔəl].

fricative Consonant sound produced with so narrow a constriction in the vocal tract as to create sound through friction.

front vowels Vowel sounds in which the tongue is positioned forward in the mouth.

functional category One of the categories of function words, including **determiner**, **aux**, **complementizer**, and **preposition**. These categories are not lexical or phrasal categories. Cf. **lexical category**, **phrasal category**.

function word   A word that does not have clear lexical meaning but has a grammatical function; function words include conjunctions, **prepositions, articles, auxiliaries, complementizers,** and pronouns. Cf. **closed class**.

fundamental frequency   In speech, the rate at which the vocal cords vibrate, symbolized as F_0, called F-zero, perceived by the listener as **pitch**.

gapping   The syntactic process of deletion in which subsequent occurrences of a verb are omitted in similar contexts, e.g., *Bill washed the grapes and Mary the cherries.*

geminate   A sequence of two identical sounds; a long vowel or long consonant denoted either by writing the phonetic symbol twice as in [biiru], [sakki] or by use of a colon [bi:ru], [sak:i].

generic term   A word that applies to a whole class, such as *dog* in *the dog is found throughout the world*. A word that ordinarily has the semantic feature [+ male] when used to refer to both sexes, e.g., *mankind* meaning "the human race"; the masculine pronoun when used as a neutral form, as in *Everyone should do his duty.*

genetically related   Describes two or more languages that developed from a common, earlier language, e.g., French, Italian, and Spanish, which all developed from Latin.

Germanic   The family of languages that includes German, English, Dutch, the Scandinavian languages, and related dialects.

glide   A sound produced with little or no obstruction of the airstream that is always preceded or followed by a vowel, e.g., /w/ in *we*, /j/in *you.*

gloss   A word in one language given to express the meaning of a word in another language, e.g., "house" is the English gloss for the French word *maison.*

glottal/glottal stop   Sound produced with constriction at the glottis; when the air is stopped completely at the glottis by tightly closed vocal cords, a glottal stop is produced.

glottis   The opening between the vocal cords.

goal   The thematic role of the noun phrase toward whose referent the action of the verb is directed, e.g., *the theatre* in *The kids went to the theatre.*

gradable pair   Two antonyms related in such a way that more of one is less of the other, e.g., *warm* and *cool;* more warm is less cool, and vice versa. Cf. **complementary pair, relational opposites**.

gradual language death   The disappearance of a language over a period of several generations, each of which has fewer speakers of the language until finally no speakers remain. Cf. **sudden language death, radical language death, bottom-to-top language death**.

grammar   The mental representation of a speaker's linguistic competence; what a speaker knows about a language, including its phonology, morphology, syntax, semantics, and lexicon. A linguistic description of a speaker's mental grammar.

grammar translation   A method of second language teaching in which the student memorizes words and syntactic rules and translates them between the native language and target language. Cf. **direct method, audiolingual method**.

grammatical, grammaticality   Describes a well-formed sequence of words, one conforming to rules of syntax.

grammatical case   See **case**.

grammatical categories   Traditionally called "parts of speech"; also called syntactic categories; expressions of the same grammatical category can generally substitute for one another without loss of grammaticality, e.g., **noun phrase, verb phrase**.

grammatical morpheme   Function word or bound morpheme required by the syntactic rules, e.g., *to* and *s* in *he wants to go*. Cf. **inflectional morpheme**.

grammatical relation   Any of several structural positions that a noun phrase may assume in a sentence. Cf. **subject**, **direct object**.

graphemes   The symbols of an alphabetic writing system; the letters of an alphabet.

Great Vowel Shift   A sound change that took place in English sometime between 1400 and 1600 C.E. in which seven long vowel phonemes were changed.

Grimm's Law   The description of a phonological change in the sound system of an early ancestor of the Germanic languages formulated by Jakob Grimm.

Hangul   An alphabet based on the phonemic principle for writing the Korean language designed in the fifteenth century.

hapology   The loss of repeated identical or nearly identical segments (e.g., Old English *Engla land* became *England*).

head (of a compound)   The rightmost word, e.g., *house* in *doghouse*. It generally indicates the category and general meaning of the compound.

head (of a phrase)   The central word of a phrase whose lexical category defines the type of phrase, e.g., the noun *man* is the head of the noun phrase *the man who came to dinner;* the verb *wrote* is the head of the verb phrase *wrote a letter to his mother;* the adjective *red* is the head of the adjective phrase *very bright red.*

hemiplegic   An individual (child or adult) with acquired unilateral lesions of the brain who retains both hemispheres (one normal and one diseased).

heritage language programs   Language programs in which children from Aboriginal or ethnic minority communities receive instruction in their ancestral language in order to help teach or maintain that language.

heteronyms   Different words spelled the same (i.e., **homographs**) but pronounced differently, e.g., *bass,* meaning either "low tone" [bes] or "a kind of fish" [bæs].

hierarchical structure   The groupings and subgroupings of the parts of a sentence into syntactic categories, e.g., *the bird sang* [[[the] [bird]] [sang]]; the groupings and subgroupings of morphemes in a word, e.g., *unlockable* [[un] [[lock][able]]]. Hierarchical structure is generally depicted in a **tree diagram**.

hierarchy of difficulty   Within the **contrastive analysis approach**, a proposed ordering of learning difficulty based on degree of difference between the structures of two languages.

hieroglyphics   A pictographic writing system used by the Egyptians around 4000 B.C.E.

high (vowels)   Vowels formed with the tongue raised high in the mouth accompanied by raised jaw and closed mouth, as in *beat, bit, boot,* and *book.*

hiragana   A Japanese syllabary used to write native words of the language, most often together with ideographic characters. Cf. **kanji**.

historical and comparative linguistics   The branch of linguistics that deals with how languages change, what kinds of changes occur, and why they occur.

holophrastic   The stage of child language acquisition in which one word conveys a complex message similar to that of a phrase or sentence.

homographs   Words spelled identically, and possibly pronounced the same, e.g., *bear* meaning "to tolerate," and *bear* the animal; or *lead* the metal and *lead,* what leaders do.

homonyms/homophones   Words pronounced, and possibly spelled, the same, e.g., *to, too, two;* or *bat* the animal, *bat* the stick, and *bat* meaning "to flutter" as in "bat the eyelashes."

homorganic consonants   Two sounds produced at the same place of articulation, e.g., [m] and [p]; [t], [d], [n]. Cf. **assimilation rules**.

homorganic nasal rule   A phonological assimilation rule that changes the place of articulation feature of a nasal consonant to agree with that of a following consonant, e.g., /n/ becomes [m] when preceding /p/ as in *impossible.*

hyponyms   Words whose meanings are specific instances of a more general word, e.g., *red, green,* and *blue* are hyponyms of the word *colour; triangle* is a hyponym of *polygon.*

iconic, iconicity   A nonarbitrary relationship between form and meaning in which the form bears a resemblance to its meaning, e.g., the male and female symbols on (some) toilet doors.

ideogram, ideograph   A character of a word-writing system, often highly stylized, that represents a concept, or the pronunciation of the word representing that concept.

idiolect   An individual's way of speaking, reflecting that person's grammar.

idiom/idiomatic phrase   An expression whose meaning does not conform to the **principle of compositionality**, that is, may be unrelated to the meaning of its parts, e.g., *kick the bucket* meaning "to die."

ill formed   Describes an ungrammatical or anomalous sequence of words.

illocutionary force   The effect of a speech act, such as a warning, a promise, a threat, and a bet, e.g., the illocutionary force of *I resign!* is the act of resignation.

imitation   A proposed mechanism of child language acquisition according to which children learn their language by imitating adult speech.

immediately dominate   If a node labelled A is directly above a node labelled B in a phrase structure tree, then A immediately dominates B.

immersion education/immersion program   Education program that uses the target language as the language of instruction for school subjects.

implication   Some linguists describe presupposition in terms of implication. Thus *John wants more coffee* carries the implication or **entails** that John has already had some coffee. Cf. **entailment, presupposition**.

implosive   Sounds produced with an **ingressive airstream** that involves movement of the glottis.

impoverished data   Refers to the incomplete, noisy, and unstructured utterances that children hear, including slips of the tongue, false starts, and ungrammatical and incomplete sentences, together with a lack of concrete evidence about abstract grammatical rules and structure. Also referred to as poverty of the stimulus.

Indo-European   The descriptive name given to the ancestor language of many modern language families, including Germanic, Slavic, and Romance. Also called Proto–Indo-European.

infinitive   An uninflected form of a verb, e.g., (to) *swim.*

infix   A bound morpheme that is inserted in the middle of a word or stem.

INFL   Abbreviates "inflection," a term sometimes used in place of **Aux**; the head of a **sentence**. Also abbreviated as "I".

inflectional morpheme   Bound grammatical morpheme that is affixed to a word according to rules of syntax, e.g., third-person singular verbal suffix *-s.*

information-processing approach   View that complex behaviour is composed of simpler cognitive processes and that component processes can be isolated and studied independently of other processes.

information retrieval   The process of using a computer to search a database for items on a particular topic. Cf. **data mining**.

ingressive airstream mechanism   The method of producing speech sounds in which air is sucked into the vocal tract through the mouth.

innateness hypothesis   The theory that the human species is genetically equipped with a **Universal Grammar**, which provides the basic design for all human languages.

instrument   The thematic role of the noun phrase whose referent is the means by which an action is performed, e.g., *a paper clip* in *Houdini picked the lock with a paper clip.*

instrumental motivation   When a language is learned as a tool to reach other goals.

integrative motivation   When a language is learned in order to identify with the target language community.

intension   The inherent, nonreferential part of the meaning of an expression, also called **sense**. Cf. **sense**, **extension**.

intensity   The magnitude of an acoustic signal, which is perceived as loudness.

interdental   A sound produced by inserting the tip of the tongue between the upper and lower teeth, e.g., the initial sounds of *thought* and *those.*

interference   Use of L1 words or structures where they do not apply in the L2.

interlanguage/interlanguage grammars   The intermediate grammars that second language learners create on their way to acquiring the (more or less) complete grammar of the target language.

International Phonetic Alphabet (IPA)   The phonetic alphabet designed by the International Phonetic Association to be used to represent the sounds found in all human languages.

International Phonetic Association (IPA)   The organization founded in 1886 to further phonetic research and develop the **International Phonetic Alphabet**.

intonation   Pitch contour of a phrase or sentence.

intransitive verb   A verb that must not have a direct object complement, e.g., *sleep.*

intrinsic motivation   Behaviours carried out for one's own personal satisfaction.

IP   Inflection phrase. A term sometimes used in place of *Sentence*. A phrasal category whose head is **INFL**.

ipsilateral   Refers to the processing of auditory signals by the same side of the brain in which the signal is received. Cf. **contralateral**.

isogloss   A geographic boundary that separates areas with dialect differences, e.g., a line on a map on one side of which most people say *faucet* and on the other side of which most people say *spigot.*

jargon   Special words peculiar to the members of a profession or group, e.g., *airstream mechanism* for phoneticians. Cf. **argot**.

jargon aphasia   Form of aphasia in which phonemes are substituted, resulting in nonsense words; often produced by people who have **Wernicke's aphasia**.

kana   The characters of either of the two Japanese syllabaries, **katakana** and **hiragana**.

kanji   The Japanese term for the Chinese characters used in Japanese writing.

katakana   A Japanese syllabary generally used for writing loan words and to achieve the effect of italics.

labial   A sound articulated at the lips, e.g., [b], [f].

labiodental   A sound produced by touching the bottom lip to the upper teeth, e.g., [v].

labiovelar   A sound articulated by simultaneously raising the back of the tongue toward the velum and rounding the lips. The *w* of English is a labiovelar glide.

language faculty   That part of human biological and genetic makeup specifically designed for language acquisition and use.

language learning strategy   Particular behaviours that individuals use to help them comprehend, learn, or retain new second language material.

larynx   The structure of muscles and cartilage in the throat that contains the vocal cords and **glottis**; often called the "voice box."

late closure principle   A psycholinguistic principle of language comprehension that states: Attach incoming material to the phrase that was most recently processed, e.g., *he said that he slept yesterday* associates *yesterday* with *he slept* rather than with *he said*.

lateral   A sound produced with air flowing past one or both sides of the tongue, e.g., [l].

lateralization, lateralized   Term used to refer to cognitive functions localized to one or the other side of the brain.

lax vowel   Short vowel produced with little tension in the vocal cords, e.g., [ʊ] in *put*, [pʊt]. Cf. **tense/lax**.

learning style   Typical preference for approaching learning in general.

length   A prosodic feature referring to the duration of a segment. Two sounds may contrast in length, e.g., in Japanese the first vowel is [+long] in /biiru/ "beer" but [−long], therefore short, in /biru/ "building."

level tones   Relatively stable (nongliding) pitch on syllables of tone languages. Also called **register tones**.

lexical access   The process of searching the mental lexicon for a phonological string to determine if it is an actual word.

lexical category   A general term for the word-level syntactic categories of noun, verb, adjective, and adverb. These are the categories of content words like *man, run, large,* and *rapidly,* as opposed to functional category words such as *the* and *and*. Cf. **functional category, phrasal category, open class**.

lexical decision   Task of subjects in psycholinguistic experiments who on presentation of a spoken or printed stimulus must decide whether it is a word or not.

lexical gap   Possible but nonoccurring words; forms that obey the **phonotactic rules** of a language yet have no meaning, e.g., *blick* in English.

lexical paraphrases   Sentences that have the same meaning due to synonyms, e.g., *She lost her purse* and *She lost her handbag*.

lexical semantics   The subfield of semantics concerned with the meanings of words and the meaning relationships among words.

lexicographer   One who edits or works on a dictionary.

lexicography   The editing or making of a dictionary.

lexicon   The component of the grammar containing speakers' knowledge about morphemes and words; a speaker's mental dictionary.

lingua franca   A language common to speakers of diverse languages that can be used for communication and commerce, e.g., English is the lingua franca of international airline pilots.

linguistic competence   The knowledge of a language represented by the mental grammar that accounts for speakers' linguistic ability and creativity. For the most part, linguistic competence is unconscious knowledge.

linguistic context   The discourse that precedes a phrase or sentence and helps clarify meaning.

linguistic performance   The *use* of linguistic competence in the production and comprehension of language; behaviour as distinguished from linguistic knowledge.

linguistic theory   A theory of the principles that characterize all human languages; the "laws of human language"; **Universal Grammar**.

liquids   A class of consonants including /l/ and /r/ and their variants that share vowel-like acoustic properties and may function as syllabic nuclei.

loan translations   Compound words or expressions whose parts are translated literally into the borrowing language, e.g., *marriage of convenience* from French *mariage de convenance*. Also called *calque*.

loan word   Word in one language whose origins are in another language, e.g., in Japanese *besiboru*, "baseball," is a loan word from English. Cf. **borrowing**.

localization   The hypothesis that different areas of the brain are responsible for distinct cognitive systems. Cf. **lateralization**.

location   The thematic role of the noun phrase whose referent is the place where the action of the verb occurs, e.g., *Ottawa* in *It snows in Ottawa*.

logograms   The symbols of a **word writing** or logographic writing system.

logographic writing   See **word writing**.

low (vowels)   Vowels produced by lowering the tongue from a central position in the oral cavity accompanied by a lowered jaw and open mouth, such as the vowels in *bat* and *bother*.

machine translation   See **automatic machine translation**.

manner of articulation   The way the airstream is obstructed as it travels through the vocal tract. Stop, nasal, affricate, and fricative are some manners of articulation. Cf. **place of articulation**.

marked   In a gradable pair of antonyms, the word that is not used in questions of degree, e.g., *low* is the marked number of the pair *high/low* because we ordinarily ask *How high is the mountain?* not **How low is the mountain?*; in a masculine/feminine pair, the word that contains a derivational morpheme, usually the feminine word, e.g., *princess* is marked, whereas *prince* is unmarked. Cf. **unmarked**.

markedness   In some theoretical approaches, refers to the idea that some linguistic structures are less natural or less common (marked) than others (unmarked).

markedness differential hypothesis   Hypothesis that speakers of languages with a more marked structure than that which occurs in the target language will have less difficulty acquiring the equivalent unmarked target language feature.

mass nouns   Nouns that cannot ordinarily be enumerated, e.g., *milk, water; *two milks* is ungrammatical except when interpreted to mean "two kinds of milk," "two containers of milk," and so on. Cf. **count nouns**.

maxim of manner   A conversational convention that a speaker's discourse should be brief and orderly, and should avoid ambiguity and obscurity.

maxim of quality   A conversational convention that a speaker should not lie or make unsupported claims.

maxim of quantity   A conversational convention that a speaker's contribution to the discourse should be as informative as is required, neither more nor less.

maxim of relevance   A conversational convention that a speaker's contribution to a discourse should always have a bearing on, and a connection with, the matter under discussion.

maxims of conversation   Conversational conventions such as the **maxim of quantity** that people appear to obey to give coherence to discourse.

meaning   The conceptual or semantic aspect of a sign or utterance that permits us to comprehend the message being conveyed. Expressions in language generally have both form — pronunciation or gesture — and meaning. Cf. **extension, intension, sense, reference**.

mean length of utterances (MLU)   A measure applied to children's language to gauge syntactic development; the average length of utterances is calculated in morphemes.

mental grammar   The internalized grammar that a descriptive grammar attempts to model. Cf. **linguistic competence**.

meronym   A part-to-whole relationship in which the meronym is "part of" a larger entity.

metacognitive strategy   Higher-order language learning strategy that involves planning, monitoring, or evaluating the success of a learning task.

metalinguistic awareness   A speaker's conscious awareness *about* language and the use of language, as opposed to linguistic *knowledge*, which is largely unconscious. This book is very much about metalinguistic awareness.

metaphor   Nonliteral, suggestive meaning in which an expression that designates one thing is used implicitly to mean something else, e.g., *The night has a thousand eyes,* to mean "One may be unknowingly observed at night."

metathesis   A phonological rule that reorders segments, often by transposing two sequential sounds.

metonym, metonymy   A word substituted for another word or expression with which it is closely associated, e.g., *Ottawa* indicates the federal government.

mid (vowels)   Vowels produced by raising the tongue from a position midway between high and low vowels, as in *bait, bet, boat*, and *butt*.

mimetic   Similar to imitating, acting out, or miming.

minimal attachment principle   The principle that in comprehending language, listeners create the simplest structure consistent with the grammar, e.g., *the horse raced past the barn* is interpreted as a complete sentence rather than a noun phrase containing a relative clause, as if it were *the horse* (that was) *raced past the barn*.

minimal pair (or set)   Two (or more) words that are identical except for one phoneme that occurs in the same position in each word, e.g., *pain* /pen/, *bane* /ben/, *main* /men/.

modal   An auxiliary verb other than *be, have,* and *do,* such as *can, could, will, would,* and *must.*

modularity   The organization of the brain and mind into distinct, independent, and autonomous parts that interact with each other.

monitor   Part of the proposed **monitor model**, refers to language editor resulting from what has been "learned," which goes into effect under specific circumstances allowing utterances to be "monitored."

monitor model   A model of second language acquisition consisting of a series of hypotheses, one of which proposes a distinction between consciously acquired "learning" about a language and subconsciously acquired knowledge called "acquisition."

monogenetic theory of language origin   The belief that all languages originated from a single language. Cf. **Nostratic.**

monomorphemic word   A word that consists of one morpheme.

monophthong   Simple vowel, e.g., *ε* in *bed*. Cf. **diphthong.**

monosyllabic   Having one syllable, e.g., *boy, through.*

morpheme   Smallest unit of linguistic meaning or function, e.g., *sheepdogs* contains three morphemes, *sheep, dog*, and the function morpheme for plural, *s.*

morphological rules   Rules for combining morphemes to form stems and words.

morphology   The study of the structure of words; the component of the grammar that includes the rules of word formation.

morphophonemic orthography   A writing system, such as that for English, in which morphological knowledge is needed to read correctly, e.g., in *please/pleasant* the *ea* represents [i]/[ε].

morphophonemic rules   Rules that specify the pronunciation of morphemes; a morpheme may have more than one pronunciation determined by such rules, e.g., the plural morpheme in English is regularly pronounced /s/, /z/, or /əz/.

motherese   See **child-directed speech (CDS).**

motivation   In L2 learning, a variable proposed by Gardner as consisting of Effort + Desire to achieve a goal + Attitudes toward learning a language.

naming task   An experimental technique that measures the response time between seeing a printed word and saying that word aloud.

narrowing   A semantic change in which the meaning of a word changes in time to become less encompassing, e.g., *deer* once meant "animal."

nasal cavity   The passageways between the throat and the nose through which air passes during speech if the velum is open (lowered). Cf. **oral cavity**.

nasal (nasalized) sound   Speech sound produced with an open nasal passage (lowered velum) permitting air to pass through the nose as well as the mouth, e.g., /m/. Cf. **oral sound**.

natural class   A class of sounds characterized by a phonetic property or feature that pertains to all members of the set, e.g., the class of stops. A natural class may be defined with a smaller feature set than that of any individual member of the class.

neogrammarians   A group of nineteenth-century linguists who claimed that sound shifts (i.e., changes in phonological systems) took place without exceptions.

neurolinguistics   The branch of linguistics concerned with the brain mechanisms that underlie the acquisition and use of human language; the study of the neurobiology of language.

neutralization rules   Phonological rules that obliterate the contrast between two phonemes in certain environments, e.g., in some dialects of English /t/ and /d/ are both pronounced as voiced flaps between vowels as in *writer* and *rider*, thus neutralizing the voicing distinction so that the two words sound alike.

node   A labelled branch point in a phrase structure tree; part of the graphical depiction of a transition network represented as a circle, pairs of which are connected by arcs. Cf. **arc, phrase structure tree, transition network**.

noncontinuant   A sound in which air is blocked momentarily in the oral cavity as it passes through the vocal tract. Cf. **stops, affricates**.

noncount noun   See **mass nouns**.

nondistinctive features   Phonetic features of phones that are predictable by rule, e.g., aspiration in English.

nonredundant   A phonetic feature that is distinctive, e.g., *stop, voice*, but not *aspiration*.

nonsense word   A permissible phonological form without meaning, e.g., *slithy*.

Nostratic   A hypothetical language that is postulated as the first human language.

noun (N)   The syntactic category, also lexical category, of words that can function as the head of a noun phrase, such as *book, Jean, sincerity*. In many languages nouns have grammatical alternations for number, case, and gender and occur with determiners.

noun phrase (NP)   The syntactic category, also phrasal category, of expressions containing some form of a noun or pronoun as its head, and which functions as the subject or as various objects in a sentence.

nucleus   That part of a syllable that has the greatest acoustic energy; the vowel portion of a syllable, e.g., /i/ in /mit/ *meet*.

obstruents   The class of sounds consisting of nonnasal stops, fricatives, and affricates. Cf. **sonorants**.

onomatopoeia/onomatopoeic   Words whose pronunciations suggest their meaning, e.g., *meow, buzz*.

onset   One or more phonemes that precede the syllable **nucleus**, e.g., /pr/ in /prist/ *priest*.

open class   The class of lexical content words; a category of words that commonly adds new words, e.g., nouns, verbs.

oral cavity   The mouth area through which air passes during the production of speech. Cf. **nasal cavity**.

oral sound   Nonnasal speech sound produced by raising the velum to close the nasal passage so that air can escape only through the mouth. Cf. **nasal sound**.

orthoepists Prescriptivist grammarians in the sixteenth to eighteenth centuries who were concerned with the pronunciation of words and the spelling–pronunciation relationship.

orthography The written form of a language; spelling.

overgeneralization Children's treatment of irregular verbs and nouns as if they were regular, e.g., *bringed, goed, foots, mouses,* for *brought, went, feet, mice.* This shows that the child has acquired the regular rules but has not yet learned that there are exceptions. Also occurs in second-language learning.

palatal A sound produced by raising the front part of the tongue to the palate.

palatalization A change in the place of articulation to the palatal region.

paradigm A set of forms derived from a single root morpheme, e.g., *give, gives, given, gave, giving;* or *woman, women, woman's, women's.*

parallel processing The ability of a computer to carry out several tasks simultaneously due to the presence of multiple central processors.

parameters The small set of alternatives for a particular phenomenon made available by Universal Grammar. For example, Universal Grammar specifies that a phrase must have a head and possibly complements; a parameter states whether the complement(s) precedes or follows the head.

paraphrases Sentences with the same truth conditions; sentences with the same meaning, except possibly for minor differences in emphasis, e.g., *He ran up a big bill* and *He ran a big bill up.*

parent language An earlier form of a language (e.g., Latin is the parent language of French, which is the daughter).

parse The act of determining the grammaticality of sequences of words according to rules of syntax, and assigning a linguistic structure to the grammatical ones.

parser A computer program that determines the grammaticality of sequences of words according to whatever rules of grammar are stored in the computer's memory and assigns a linguistic structure to the grammatical ones.

passive sentence A sentence in which the verbal complex contains a form of *to be* followed by a verb in its participle form, e.g., *The girl was kissed by the boy; The robbers must not have been seen.* In a passive sentence, the direct object of a transitive verb in deep structure functions as the subject in surface structure. Cf. **active sentence**.

performative sentence A sentence containing a performative verb used to accomplish some act. Performative sentences are affirmative and declarative, and are in first-person, present tense, e.g., *I now pronounce you husband and wife,* when spoken by a justice of the peace in the appropriate situation, is an act of marrying.

performative verb A verb, certain usages of which constitute a **speech act**, e.g., *resign* when the sentence *I resign!* is interpreted as an act of resignation.

person deixis The use of terms to refer to persons whose reference relies entirely on context, e.g., pronouns such as *I, he, you* and expressions such as *this child.* Cf. **deictic, time deixis, place deixis, demonstrative articles**.

petroglyph A drawing on rock made by prehistoric people.

pharynx The tube or cavity in the vocal tract above the glottis through which the air passes during speech production.

phone A phonetic realization of a **phoneme**.

phoneme A contrastive phonological segment whose phonetic realizations are predictable by rule.

phonemic principle The principle that underlies alphabetic writing systems in which one symbol typically represents one phoneme.

phonemic representation   The phonological representation of words and sentences prior to the application of phonological rules.

phonemic transcription   The phonemic representation of speech sounds using phonetic symbols, ignoring phonetic details that are predictable by rule, usually given between slashes, e.g., /pæn/, /spæn/ for *pan, span* as opposed to the phonetic representation [pʰæn], [spæn].

phonetic alphabet   Alphabetic symbols used to represent the phonetic segments of speech in which there is a one-to-one relationship between each symbol and each speech sound.

phonetic features   Phonetic properties of segments (e.g., voice, nasal, alveolar) that distinguish one segment from another.

phonetics   The study of linguistic speech sounds, how they are produced (**articulatory phonetics**), how they are perceived (**auditory** or perceptual **phonetics**), and their physical aspects (**acoustic phonetics**).

phonetic similarity   Refers to sounds that share most phonetic features.

phonetic transcription   The representation of speech sounds using phonetic symbols between square brackets. They may reflect nondistinctive predictable features such as aspiration and nasality, e.g., [pʰat] for *pot* and [mæn] for *man*.

phonographic symbol   A symbol in a writing system that stands for the sounds of a word.

phonological rules   Rules that apply to phonemic representations to derive phonetic representations or pronunciation.

phonology   The sound system of a language; the component of a grammar that includes the inventory of sounds (phonetic and phonemic units) and rules for their combination and pronunciation; the study of the sound systems of all languages.

phonotactics/phonotactic constraints   Rules stating permissible strings of phonemes, e.g., a word-initial nasal consonant may be followed only by a vowel (in English). Cf. **possible word, nonsense word, accidental gap**.

phrasal category   The class of syntactic categories that occur on the left side of phrase structure rules, and are therefore composed of other categories, including other phrasal categories, e.g., noun phrase. Cf. **lexical category, functional category**.

phrasal semantics   See **sentential semantics**.

phrase structure rules   Principles of grammar that specify the constituency of syntactic categories, e.g., NP → (Det) (AP) N (PP).

phrase structure tree   A tree diagram with syntactic categories at each node that reveals both the linear and hierarchical structure of phrases and sentences.

phrenology   A pseudoscience, the practice of which is determining personality traits and intellectual ability by examination of the bumps on the skull. Its contribution to neurolinguistics is that its methods were highly suggestive of the modular theory of brain structure.

pictogram   A form of writing in which the symbols resemble the objects represented; a nonarbitrary form of writing.

pidgin   A simple but rule-governed language developed for communication among speakers of mutually unintelligible languages, often based on one of those languages.

Pinyin   An alphabetic writing system for Mandarin Chinese using a Western-style alphabet to represent individual sounds.

pitch   The **fundamental frequency** of sound perceived by the listener.

pitch contour   The "melody" or movement from one pitch to another in a speech utterance (e.g., the pattern of falling and rising pitch in an English expression).

place deixis   The use of terms to refer to places whose reference relies entirely on context, e.g., *here, there, behind, next door.* Cf. **deictic, time deixis, person deixis, demonstrative articles**.

place of articulation   The part of the vocal tract at which constriction occurs during the production of most consonants. Cf. **manner of articulation**.

plosives   Oral, or nonnasal, stop consonants, so called because the air that is stopped explodes with the release of the closure.

polysemous/polysemy   Describes a single word with several closely related but slightly different meanings, e.g., *face,* meaning "face of a person," "face of a clock," "face of a building."

possessor   The thematic role of the noun phrase to whose referent something belongs, e.g., *the dog* in *The dog's tail wagged furiously.*

possible word   A string of sounds that obeys the **phonotactic constraints** of the language but has no meaning, e.g., *gimble.* Also called a **nonsense word**.

poverty of the stimulus   See **impoverished data**.

pragmatics   The study of how context and situation affect meaning.

predictable feature   A nondistinctive, noncontrastive, redundant phonetic feature, e.g., aspiration in English voiceless stops, or nasalization in English vowels.

prefix   An **affix** that is attached to the beginning of a morpheme or stem, e.g., *in-* in *inoperable.*

preposition (P)   The syntactic category, also lexical category, that heads a prepositional phrase, e.g., *at, in, on, up.*

prepositional object   The grammatical relation of the noun phrase that occurs immediately below a **prepositional phrase (PP)** in deep structure.

prepositional phrase (PP)   The syntactic category, also phrasal category, consisting of a preposition and a noun phrase.

prescriptive grammar   Rules of grammar brought about by grammarians' attempts to legislate what speakers' grammatical rules should be, rather than what they are. Cf. **descriptive grammar, teaching grammar**.

prestige dialect   The dialect usually spoken by people in positions of power, and the one deemed correct by prescriptive grammarians, e.g., **RP (Received Pronunciation)** (British) English, the dialect spoken by the English royal family.

presupposition   Implicit assumptions about the world required to make an utterance meaningful or appropriate, e.g., "some tea has already been taken" is a presupposition of *Take some more tea!*

primes   The basic formal units of sign languages that correspond to phonological elements of spoken language.

priming   An experimental procedure that measures the response time from hearing to accessing a particular word as a function of whether the participant has heard a related word previously.

principle of compositionality   A principle of semantic interpretation that states that the meaning of a word, phrase, or sentence depends both on the meaning of its components (morphemes, words, phrases) and how they are combined structurally.

productive   Refers to morphological rules that can be used freely and apply to all forms to create new words, e.g., the addition to an adjective of *-ish* meaning "having somewhat of the quality," such as *newish, tallish, incredible-ish.*

proper name   A word that refers to a person, place, or other entity with a unique reference known to the speaker and listener. Usually capitalized in writing, e.g., Nelson Mandela, Montreal, Atlantic Ocean.

prosodic feature   Duration (**length**), **pitch**, or loudness of speech sounds.

Proto-Germanic   The name given by linguists to the language that was an ancestor of English, German, and other Germanic languages.

protolanguage   The first identifiable language from which genetically related languages developed.

protoword   Sequence of sounds produced by a child with a relatively consistent meaning, but not necessarily based on an adult word.

psycholinguistics   The branch of linguistics concerned with **linguistic performance**, language acquisition, and speech production and comprehension.

pulmonic egressive   Speech sounds produced by movement of air flowing out of the lungs through the vocal tract and out the mouth or nose. Cf. **ingressive airstream mechanism, ejective**.

radical language death   The disappearance of a language when all speakers of the language cease to speak the language. Cf. **sudden language death, gradual language death, bottom-to-top language death**.

raising   See **Canadian raising**.

rebus principle   In writing, the use of a **pictogram** for its phonetic value, e.g., using a picture of a bee to represent the verb *be* or the sound [b].

Received Pronunciation (RP)   A prestige dialect of southern British English supposedly "received" in court and thus approved by those in authority and by linguistic purists.

reconstruction   Using the comparative method to establish the forms of words in a parent language. Cf. **comparative method**.

reduced vowel   A vowel that is unstressed and generally pronounced as schwa [ə] in English.

redundancy rules   Principles in the lexicon stating generalizations between semantic features (e.g., a word that is [+human] is [+animate]).

redundant   Describes a nondistinctive, nonphonemic feature that is predictable from other feature values of the segment, e.g., [+voice] is redundant for any [+nasal] phoneme in English since all nasals are voiced.

reduplication   A morphological process that repeats or copies all or part of a word to produce a new word, e.g., *wishy-washy, teensy-weensy*.

reference   That part of the meaning of a noun phrase that associates it with some entity. That part of the meaning of a declarative sentence that associates it with a truth value, either true or false. Also called **extension**. Cf. **referent, sense**.

reference grammar, scholarly grammar   A description of a language that attempts to be as thorough and comprehensive as possible; it can serve as a reference for those interested in establishing grammatical facts.

referent   The entity designated by an expression, e.g., the referent of *John* in *John knows Sue* is the actual person named John; the referent of *Toronto is the capital of Canada* is the truth value *false*. Also called **extension**.

reflexive pronoun   A pronoun ending with *-self* that generally requires a noun-phrase antecedent within the same S, e.g., *myself, herself, ourselves, itself*.

regional dialect   A dialect spoken in a specific geographic area that may arise from, and is reinforced by, that area's integrity. For example, a Newfoundland dialect is maintained because large numbers of Newfoundlanders and their descendants remain in Newfoundland. Cf. **social dialect**.

register   A stylistic variant of a language appropriate to a particular social setting. Also called **style**.

register tones   Level tones; high, mid, or low tones.

regular sound correspondence   The occurrence of different sounds in the same position of the same word in different languages or dialects, with this parallel holding for a significant number of words, e.g., [aj] in non-Southern American English corresponds to [a:] in Southern American English. Also found between newer and older forms of the same language.

relational opposites   Pair of **antonyms** in which one describes a relationship between two objects and the other describes the same relationship when the two objects are reversed, e.g., *parent/child, teacher/pupil; John is the parent of Susie* describes the same relationship as *Susie is the child of John*. Cf. **gradable pair**, **complementary pair**.

response/reaction time (RT)   The measurement of the time it takes subjects to respond in psycholinguistic experiments (e.g., in making lexical decisions, naming objects). RT is assumed to reflect processing time.

restructuring   Term used in **information-processing approach** to second language acquisition to refer to changes or reorganization in the learner's interlanguage at various developmental stages.

retroflex sound   Sound produced by curling the tip of the tongue back behind the alveolar ridge, e.g., the pronunciation of /r/ by many speakers of English.

retronym   An expression that would once have been redundant, but which societal or technological changes have made nonredundant, e.g., *silent movie,* which was redundant before the advent of the "talkies."

rime   The **nucleus** + **coda** of a syllable (e.g., the /en/ of /ren/ *rain*).

Roman alphabet   The characters used in many of the alphabetic writing systems of the world (e.g., English, French).

root   The morpheme that remains when all affixes are stripped from a complex word, e.g., *system* from *un* + *system* + *atic* + *ally*.

rounded vowel   Vowel sound produced with pursed lips, e.g., [o].

rules of syntax   Principles of grammar that account for the grammaticality of sentences, their hierarchical structure, their word order, whether there is structural ambiguity, etc. Cf. **phrase structure rules**, **transformational rule**.

savant   Individual who shows special abilities in one cognitive area while being deficient in others. Linguistic savants have extraordinary language abilities but are deficient in general intelligence.

second language acquisition (SLA, L2 acquisition)   The acquisition of another language or languages after first language acquisition is under way or completed.

segment   (1) An individual sound that occurs in a language; (2) the act of dividing utterances into sounds, morphemes, words, and phrases.

selection   A specification in the lexical entry of a word that determines the constituents required or permitted as complements when that word is the head of a phrase. For example, in a verb phrase, a transitive verb such as *find* requires a direct object complement, whereas a verb such as *eat* permits a direct object complement.

semantic features   A notational device for expressing the presence or absence of semantic properties by pluses and minuses, e.g., *baby* is [+young], [+human], [–abstract], etc.

semantic network   A network of **arcs** and **nodes** used to represent semantic information about sentences.

semantic properties   The components of meaning of a word, e.g., "young" is a semantic property of *baby, colt, puppy*.

semantics   The study of the linguistic meaning of morphemes, words, phrases, and sentences.

sense   The inherent part of an expression's meaning that, together with context, determines its referent. Also called intension. For example, knowing the sense or intension of a noun phrase such as *the prime minister of Canada in 2009* allows one to determine that Stephen Harper is the referent. Cf. **intension, reference**.

sensitive period   See **critical period**.

sentence (S)   A syntactic category of expressions consisting minimally of a **noun phrase** (**NP**), followed by an **auxiliary (Aux)**, followed by a **verb phrase (VP)** in deep structure. Also called an inflection phrase (IP), whose head is inflection (**INFL**).

sentential semantics   The subfield of semantics concerned with the meaning of syntactic units larger than the word.

separate systems hypothesis   View that the bilingual child builds a distinct lexicon and grammar for each language being acquired.

shadowing task   An experiment in which subjects are asked to repeat what they hear as rapidly as possible as it is being spoken. During the task, subjects often unconsciously correct "errors" in the input.

sibilants   The class of sounds that includes affricates, and alveolar and palatal fricatives, characterized acoustically by an abundance of high frequencies perceived as "hissing," e.g., [s].

sign languages   The languages used by deaf people in which linguistic units such as morphemes and words as well as grammatical relations are formed by manual and other body movements.

simplification of consonant clusters   The reduction of two or more consonants in sequence, such as *best* from Old English *betst*.

sisters   In a phrase structure tree, two categories that are directly under the same node, e.g., V and the direct object NP are sisters inside the verb phrase.

situational context   Knowledge of who is speaking, who is listening, what objects are being discussed, and general facts about the world we live in, used to aid in the interpretation of meaning.

slang   Words and phrases used in casual speech, often invented and spread by close-knit social or age groups, and fast changing.

slip of the tongue   An involuntary deviation of an intended utterance. Cf. **spoonerism**. Also called **speech error**.

sluicing   The syntactic process in which material following a *wh-* word is deleted when it is identical to previous material, e.g., *John is talking with* is deleted from the second clause in *John is talking with someone but nobody knows whom _____*.

social dialect   A dialect spoken by a particular social class (e.g., Cockney English) that is perpetuated by the integrity of the social class. Cf. **regional dialect**.

socioaffective strategy   Type of **language learning strategy** that involves interaction with others or exercising control over affective aspects that hinder one's own learning.

sociocultural approach   Theoretical approach in second language acquisition in which the social nature of language is emphasized.

sociolinguistics   The study of the relationship between language and society.

sonorants   The class of sounds that includes vowels, glides, liquids, and nasals; nonobstruents. Cf. **obstruents**.

sound shift   Historical phonological change.

sound symbolism   The notion that certain sound combinations occur in semantically similar words, e.g., *gl* in *gleam, glisten, glitter,* which all relate to vision.

sound writing   A term sometimes used to mean a writing system in which one sound is represented by one letter. Sound-writing systems do not employ the phonemic principle and are similar to phonetic transcriptions.

source   The thematic role of the noun phrase whose referent is the place from which an action originates, e.g., *Winnipeg* in *They just arrived from Winnipeg*.

source language   In automatic machine translation, the language being translated. Cf. **target language**.

specific language impairment (SLI)   Difficulty in acquiring language faced by certain children with no other detectable cognitive deficits.

spectrogram   A visual representation of speech decomposed into component frequencies, with time on the *x* axis, frequency on the *y* axis, and intensity portrayed on a grey scale — the darker, the more intense. Also called **voiceprint**.

speech act   The action or intent that a speaker accomplishes when using language in context, the meaning of which is inferred by hearers, e.g., *There is a bear behind you* may be intended as a warning in certain contexts, or may in other contexts merely be a statement of fact. Cf. **illocutionary force**.

speech error   An inadvertent deviation from an intended utterance that often results in ungrammaticality, nonsense words, anomaly, etc. Cf. **slip of the tongue, spoonerism**.

speech recognition   In computer processing, the ability to analyze speech sounds into phones, phonemes, morphemes, and words.

speech synthesis   An electronic process that produces speech.

speech understanding   Computer processing for interpreting speech, one part of which is **speech recognition**.

spell checker   Computer program that checks for misspellings.

spelling pronunciation   Pronouncing a word as it is spelled, irrespective of its actual pronunciation by native speakers, e.g., pronouncing *Wednesday* as "wed-ness-day."

split brain   The result of an operation for epilepsy in which the **corpus callosum** is severed, thus separating the brain into its two hemispheres; split-brain patients are studied to determine the role of each hemisphere in cognitive and language processing.

spoonerism   A speech error in which phonemic segments are reversed or exchanged, e.g., *you have hissed my mystery lecture* for the intended *you have missed my history lecture*; named after the Reverend William Archibald Spooner, a nineteenth-century Oxford University professor.

standard   The dialect (regional or social) considered to be the norm.

Standard American English (SAE)   An idealized dialect of English that some prescriptive grammarians consider the proper form of American English.

Standard British English (SBrE)   A dialect of English spoken in the British Isles employed by those in authority and valued by linguistic purists.

Standard Canadian English (SCE)   An idealized dialect of English that some prescriptive grammarians consider the proper form of Canadian English.

state/stative   A type of sentence that describes states of being such as *Mary likes oysters,* as opposed to describing events such as *Mary ate oysters*. Cf. **event/eventive**.

stem   The base to which one or more affixes are attached to create a more complex form that may be another stem or a word. Cf. **root, affix**.

stops   [–continuant] sounds in which the airflow is briefly but completely stopped in the oral cavity, e.g., /p, n, g/.

stress, stressed syllable   A syllable with relatively greater length, greater loudness, and/or higher pitch than other syllables in a word, and therefore perceived as prominent. Also called **accent**.

structural ambiguity   The phenomenon in which the same sequence of words has two or more meanings based on different phrase structure analyses, e.g., *He saw a boy with a telescope.*

structuralism/structuralist   An approach that analyses language into a set of structural components.

structure dependent   (1) A principle of **Universal Grammar** that states that the application of **transformational rules** is determined by phrase structure properties, as opposed to structureless sequences of words or specific sentences; (2) the way children construct rules using their knowledge of syntactic structure irrespective of the specific words in the structure or their meaning.

style   Situation dialect, e.g., formal speech, casual speech; also called **register**.

subject   The grammatical relation of a noun phrase to a S(entence) when it appears immediately below that S in a phrase structure tree, e.g., *the zebra* in *The zebra has stripes.*

subordinate bilingualism   Type of bilingualism proposed by Weinreich in which an L2 word is interpreted via the L1 equivalent word in order to reach the underlying concept.

subtractive bilingualism   L2 learning in a context in which the L1 is not fully supported.

sudden language death   The disappearance of a language when all speakers of the language die or are killed in a short time period. Cf. **radical language death**, **gradual language death**, **bottom-to-top language death**.

suffix   An **affix** that is attached to the end of a morpheme or stem, e.g., *-er* in *Lew is taller than Bill.*

suggestopedia   Language learning method characterized by the promotion of a relaxed state of mind through exposure to classical music in a comfortable setting.

summarization   The computer scanning of a text and condensation to its most salient points.

suppletive forms   A term used to refer to inflected morphemes in which the regular rules do not apply, e.g., *went* as the past tense of *go.*

suprasegmentals   **Prosodic features**, e.g., length, tone.

surface structure   The structure that results from applying transformational rules to a deep structure. It is syntactically closest to actual utterances. Cf. **transformational rule**.

syllabary   The symbols of a syllabic writing system.

syllabic   A phonetic feature of those sounds that may constitute the nucleus of syllables; all vowels are syllabic, and liquids and nasals may be syllabic in such words as *towel, button, bottom.*

syllabic writing   A writing system in which each syllable in the language is represented by its own symbol, e.g., **hiragana** in Japanese.

syllable   A phonological unit composed of an **onset**, **nucleus**, and **coda**, e.g., *elevator* has four syllables: *el e va tor; man* has one syllable.

syncope   The loss of a medial vowel, as is exemplified in the everyday pronunciation of words such as *Wednesday* and *family.*

synonyms   Words with the same or nearly the same meaning, e.g., *pail* and *bucket.*

syntactic bootstrapping   Children's use of their knowledge of syntax to learn the meaning of words. Experiments have shown that knowing that a word is a verb or a noun informs them that it has a meaning referring to an action or to an object of some kind, respectively.

syntactic category/class   See **grammatical categories**.

syntax   The rules of sentence formation; the component of the mental grammar that represents speakers' knowledge of the structure of phrases and sentences.

synthetic sentences   Unlike analytic sentences, synthetic sentences require more than linguistic knowledge to determine their truth value; they depend on our knowing something of the events and conditions in the world.

taboo   Words or activities that are considered inappropriate for "polite society," e.g., *cunt, prick, fuck* for "vagina, penis, sexual intercourse."

tap   Sound in which the tongue quickly touches the alveolar ridge, as in some British pronunciations of /r/. Also called **flap**.

target language   In automatic machine translation, the language into which the source language is translated; in **second language acquisition**, refers to the language being learned.

teaching grammar   A set of language rules written to help speakers learn a second or foreign language or a different dialect of their language. Cf. **descriptive grammar, prescriptive grammar**.

telegraphic speech   Utterances of children that may omit **grammatical morphemes** and/or **function words**, e.g., *He go out* instead of *He is going out*.

tense/lax   Features that divide vowels into two classes. Tense vowels are generally longer in duration and higher in tongue position and pitch than the corresponding lax vowels, e.g., in English [i, e, u, o] are tense vowels and carry the feature [+ tense], whereas the corresponding [ɪ, ɛ, ʊ, ɔ] are their lax counterparts and carry the feature [− tense]. Cf. **lax vowel**.

thematic role   The semantic relationship between the verb and the noun phrases of a sentence, such as **agent, theme, location, instrument, goal, source**.

theme   The thematic role of the noun phrase whose referent undergoes the action of the verb, e.g., *Martha* in *George hugged Martha*.

theta assignment   The process of assigning thematic roles to the subject and complements of a verb.

theta-criterion   A proposed universal principle stating that a particular thematic role (e.g., agent) may occur only once in a sentence.

time deixis   The use of terms to refer to time whose reference relies entirely on context, e.g., *now, then, tomorrow, next month*. Cf. **deictic/deixis, demonstrative articles, person deixis, place deixis**.

tip-of-the-tongue (TOT) phenomenon   The difficulty encountered from time to time in retrieving a particular word or expression from the mental lexicon. Anomic aphasics suffer from an extreme form of this problem. Cf. **anomia**.

tone   Contrastive pitch of syllables in **tone languages** in which two words may be identical except for such differences in pitch, e.g., in Thai [naa] with a falling pitch means "face," but with a rising pitch means "thick." Cf. **register tones, contour tones**.

tone language   A language in which the tone or pitch on a syllable is phonemic, so that words with identical segments but different tones are different words, e.g., Mandarin Chinese, Thai. Cf. **tone**.

top-down processing   Expectation-driven analysis of linguistic input that begins with the assumption that a large syntactic unit such as a sentence is present, and then analyzes it into successively smaller constituents (phrases, words, morphemes, etc.), which are ultimately compared with the sensory or acoustic data to validate the analysis. If the analysis is not validated, the procedure backs up to the previously validated point and then resumes. Cf. **bottom-up processing, backtracking**.

topicalization   A transformation that moves a syntactic element to the front of a sentence, e.g., deriving *Dogs I love very much* from *I love dogs very much*.

transfer   In **second language acquisition** refers to the influences that result from similarities and differences between the target language and the L1. Positive transfer refers to the use of words or structures similar to those of the L1 in the L2; negative transfer refers to the use of L1 words or structures where they do not apply in the L2. Cf. **interference**.

transformational rule, transformation   A syntactic rule that applies to an underlying phrase structure tree of a sentence (either deep structure or an intermediate structure already affected by a transformation) and derives a new structure by moving or inserting elements, e.g., the transformational rules of *wh* movement and *do* insertion relate the deep structure sentence *John saw who* to the surface structure *Who did John see.*

transition network   A graphical representation that uses nodes connected by labelled arcs to depict syntactic and semantic relationships of grammar. Cf. **node, arc**.

transitive verb   A verb that selects an obligatory noun-phrase complement, e.g., *find*.

tree diagram   A graphical representation of the linear and hierarchical structure of a phrase or sentence. A **phrase structure tree**.

trill   Sound in which part of the tongue vibrates against some part of the roof of the mouth, e.g., the [r] in Spanish *perro* is articulated by vibrating the tongue tip behind the alveolar ridge; the [r] in French *rouge* is articulated by vibrations at the uvula.

truth condition   The circumstances that must be known to determine whether a sentence is true, and therefore part of the meaning, or **sense**, of declarative sentences.

turn-taking   A conversational principle involving our knowing when to speak and when to listen.

two-word stage   About the beginning of the second year, children produce sentences of two words with clear syntactic and semantic relations.

ultimate attainment   A term used in second language acquisition to refer to the ultimate degree of language learning achievement on the part of a given learner; particularly relevant in discussions on the effect of age in L2 acquisition.

unaspirated   Phonetically voiceless stops in which the vocal cords begin vibrating immediately upon release of the closure, e.g., [p] in *spot*. Cf. **aspirated**.

unbound   A pronoun or pro-form whose reference is determined from context rather than linguistic discourse. Cf. **free pronoun, bound pronoun**.

unconditioned sound change   Historical phonological change that occurs in all phonetic contexts, e.g., the **Great Vowel Shift** of English in which long vowels were modified wherever they occurred in a word.

ungrammatical   Structures that fail to conform to the rules of grammar.

uninterpretable   Describes an utterance whose meaning cannot be determined because of nonsense words, e.g., *All mimsy were the borogoves.*

unitary system hypothesis   View that a bilingual child initially constructs only one lexicon and one grammar for both (or all) languages being acquired.

Universal Grammar (UG)   The innate principles and properties that pertain to the grammars of all human languages.

unmarked   The term used to refer to that member of a gradable pair of antonyms used in questions of degree, e.g., *high* is the unmarked member of *high/low*; in a masculine/feminine pair, the word that does not contain a derivational morpheme, usually the masculine word, e.g., *prince* is unmarked, whereas *princess* is marked. Cf. **marked**.

Uralic   The family of languages including Hungarian, Finnish, and Estonian, all of which are spoken on the European continent.

uvula   The fleshy appendage hanging down from the end of the **velum**, or soft palate.

uvular   A sound produced by raising the back of the tongue to the uvula.

velar   A sound produced by raising the back of the tongue to the soft palate, or **velum**.

velum   The soft palate; the part of the roof of the mouth behind the hard palate.

verb (V)   The syntactic category, also lexical category, of words that can be the head of a verb phrase. Verbs denote actions, sensations, and states, e.g., *climb, hear, understand.*

verb phrase (VP)   The syntactic category of expressions that contains a verb as its head along with its complements such as noun phrases and prepositional phrases, e.g., *gave the book to the child.*

Verner's Law   The description of a conditioned phonological change in the sound system of certain Indo-European languages wherein voiceless fricatives were changed when the preceding vowel was unstressed. It was formulated by Karl Verner as an explanation to some of the exceptions to Grimm's Law. Cf. **Grimm's Law.**

vocalic   Phonetic feature that distinguishes vowels and liquids, which are [+vocalic], from other sounds (obstruents, glides, nasals) that are [–vocalic].

vocal tract   The oral and nasal cavities, together with the vocal cords, glottis, and pharynx, all of which may be involved in the production of speech sounds.

voiced sound   Speech sound produced with vibrating vocal cords.

voiceless sound   Speech sound produced with open, nonvibrating vocal cords.

voiceprint   A common term for a **spectrogram.**

vowel   A sound produced without significant constriction of the air flowing through the **oral cavity.**

wave form   Vibrations determined by the shape of the vocal tract when air is flowing through it.

well formed   Describes a grammatical sequence of words, one conforming to rules of syntax. Cf. **grammatical, ill formed.**

Wernicke, Carl   Neurologist who showed that damage to specific parts of the left cerebral hemisphere causes specific types of language disorders.

Wernicke's aphasia   The type of aphasia resulting from damage to Wernicke's area characterized by fluent, but semantically empty speech production.

Wernicke's area   The back (posterior) part of the left brain that if damaged causes a specific type of aphasia. Also called Wernicke's region.

word   A free sound–meaning lexical unit, which may be simple (monomorphemic) or complex (polymorphemic) (e.g., *boy, boys*).

word sets   Words related by virtue of including the same root morpheme or stem — that is, the same content morpheme (e.g., *phone, phonetic, phonetician, phonic, phoneme*).

word writing   A system of writing in which each character represents a word or morpheme of the language, e.g., Chinese. Cf. **ideograph.**

ANSWERS TO SELECTED EXERCISES

Chapter 1   What Is Language?

2. *Grammaticality judgments.* The following sentences are ungrammatical:

a. * *Robin forced the sheriff go.*
   The word *to* is missing in front of the verb *go*. The verb *force* requires a *to* infinitive in the embedded clause.

f. * *He came a large sum of money by.*
   Particles are preposition-like words that occur with verbs such as *look,* as in *look up the number* or *look over the data.* Particles can occur after their direct object: *look the number up; look the data over.* True prepositions do not behave this way. *He ran up the stairs* is correct, but *he ran the stairs up* is not. The *by* in *he came by a large sum of money* functions as a preposition and may not occur after the direct object.

g. * *Did in a corner little Jack Horner sit?*
   This question is formed from a sentence in which the prepositional phrase *in the corner* was moved to the front of the sentence for emphasis. *On the road I saw a dead possum.* (Such movement is called topicalization and is discussed in Chapter 3.) Once a sentence is topicalized, it may not be questioned. In terms of transformational grammar, the transformations that derive questions precede transformations such as topicalization in the rule order.

h. * *Elizabeth is resembled by Charles.*
   The verb *resemble* does not occur in passive sentences.

k. * *It is eager to love a kitten.*
   If the pronoun *it* refers to an animate (nonhuman) thing (e.g., a dog), the sentence is grammatical. If the word *it* is a "dummy subject," as in *It's a sin to tell a lie,* the sentence is ungrammatical because the adjective *eager* must have a referential subject.

l. * *That birds can fly amazes.*
   Amaze is a transitive verb; it requires a direct object. Compare *That birds can fly amazes John.*

n. ** Has the nurse slept the baby yet?*

The verb *sleep* is intransitive; it cannot take a direct object (in this case, *the baby*).

o. ** I was surprised for you to get married.*

The clause following the adjective *surprised* cannot be in the infinitive form, e.g., *to get*.

p. ** I wonder who and Mary went swimming.*

This "question" is derived from the more basic sentence *Someone and Mary went swimming*. The coordinate structure constraint (see Chapter 3 for mention, but not a complete description) requires coordinate structures to be treated as a whole, not in part. So it is ungrammatical in most, but not all dialects of English, to ask **Who and Mary went swimming* because there is an attempt to question one part, but not the other part, of the coordinate structure. This also explains the ungrammatical nature of **I wonder who and Mary went swimming* with similar caveats about dialectal and idiolectal variation.

q. ** Myself bit John.*

Reflexive pronouns like *myself, yourself, herself, themselves,* etc., do not occur as subjects of sentences but only as objects, e.g., *John hurt himself.*

Chapter 2   Morphology: The Words of Language

5. A. *Zulu morphology.*
   a.   The morpheme meaning "singular" is *um-*.
   b.   The morpheme meaning "plural" is *aba-*.
   c.   [Note: The analysis of some of the morphemes below depends on the information given in B; that is, without the further information about verb formation, one would conclude that *fundisi* is the morpheme meaning "teacher" rather than *fundis* being a stem, with *-i* being a nominal suffix.]

Zulu	English
-fazi	"married woman"
-fani	"boy"
-zali	"parent"
-fundis-	"teach"
-baz-	"carve"
-lim	"farm"
-dlal-	"play"
-fund-	"read"

   B. d.   The derivational suffix morpheme that specifies the category verb is *-a*.

e. The nominal suffix morpheme is *-i.*

f. A noun is formed in Zulu by adding the suffix morpheme *-i* to the stem (and adding a singular or plural prefix). Schematically, this is:

Noun = Number prefix + Verb stem + Nominal suffix

g. The morpheme meaning "read" is *-fund-.*

h. The morpheme meaning "carve" is *-baz-.*

8. *Swahili morphology.*

a. Indentification of morphemes

m-	noun prefix attached to singular nouns of Class I
wa-	noun prefix attached to plural nouns of Class I
a-	prefix attached to verbs when the subject is a singular noun of Class I
wa-	prefix attached to verbs when the subject is a plural noun of Class I
ki-	prefix attached to singular nouns of Class II
vi-	prefix attached to plural nouns of Class II
ki-	prefix attached to verbs when the subject is a singular noun of Class II
vi-	prefix attached to verbs when the subject is a plural noun of Class II
-toto	"child"
-tu	"person"
-su	"knife"
-kapu	"basket"
-fika	"arrive"
-lala	"sleep"
-anguka	"fall"
-me-	present perfect tense
-na-	present progressive tense
-ta-	future tense

b. The verb is constructed by stringing together from left to right (1) the verbal prefix indicating the noun class and the number of the subject, (2) the tense, (3) the verbal stem. Schematically, this is:

Verb = Class prefix + Tense prefix + Verbal stem

c. (1) "The child is falling."   = Mtoto anaanguka.
   (2) "The baskets have arrived." = Vikapu vimefika.
   (3) "The person will fall."   = Mtu ataanguka.

Chapter 3   Syntax: The Sentence Patterns of Language

4. *Representing structural ambiguity.*
The magician touched the child with the wand.

Meaning 1: The magician used the wand to touch the child.

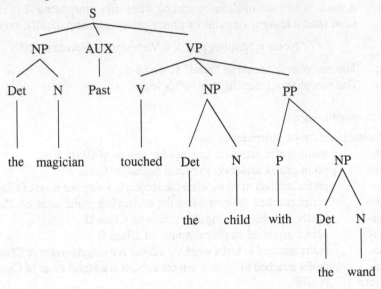

Meaning 2: The magician touched the child who had a wand.

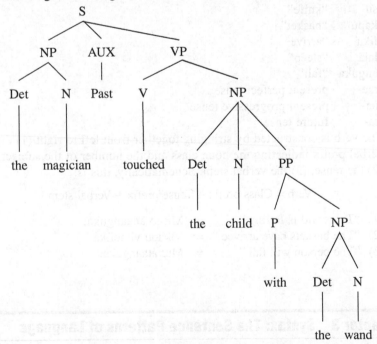

7. *Phrase structure trees.*

 a.   The puppy found the child.

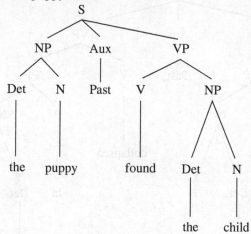

 b.   A frightened passenger landed the crippled airliner.

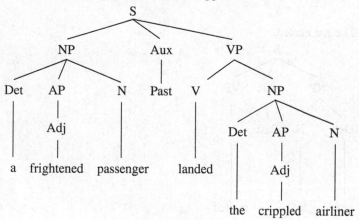

c.   The house on the hill collapsed in the wind.

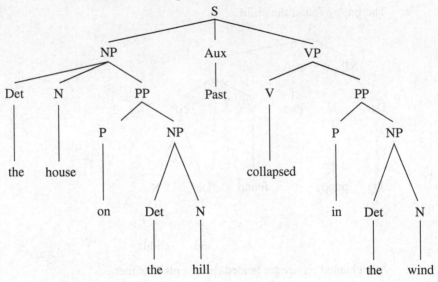

d.   The ice melted.

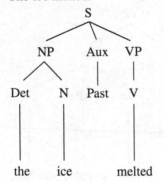

e. The hot sun melted the ice.

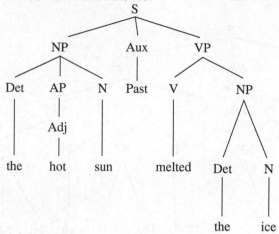

f. A fast car with twin cams sped by the children on the grassy lane.
    This sentence is structurally ambiguous:

    Meaning 1: A fast car with twin cams sped by the children who were on the
    grassy lane.

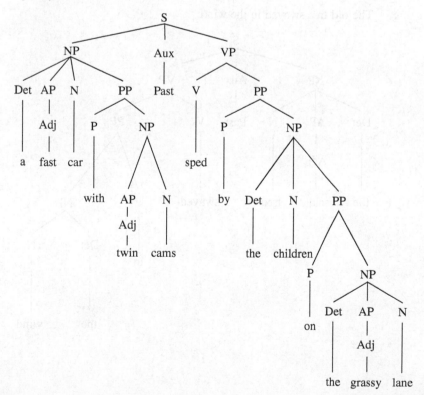

Meaning 2: A fast car with twin cams sped on the grassy lane by the children.

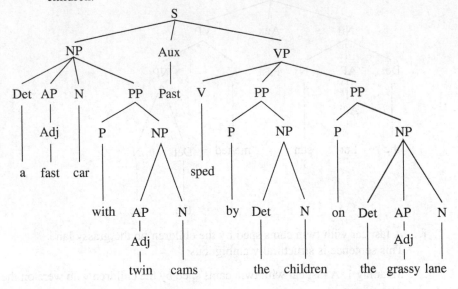

g. The old tree swayed in the wind.

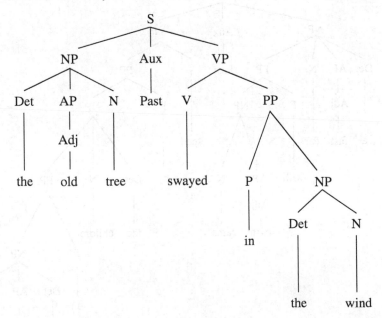

h.   The children put the toy in the box.

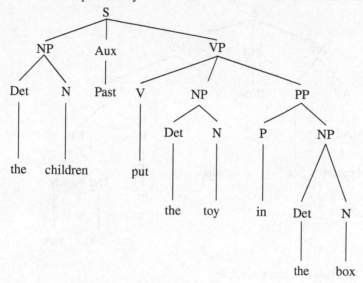

i.   The reporter realized that the MP lied.

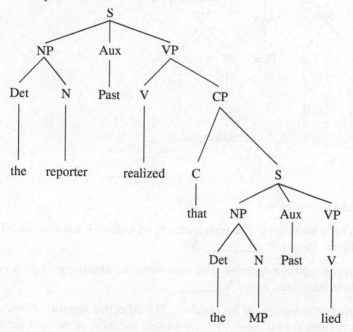

j. Broken ice melts in the sun.

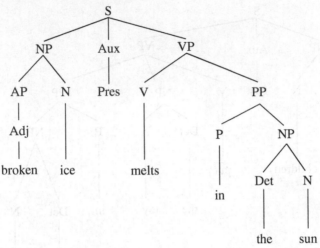

k. The guitarist practises daily.

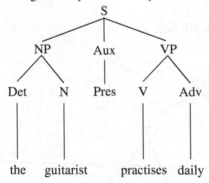

14. *Selectional restrictions.*

a. **The man located.* The verb *locate* is transitive: it requires an NP object. *locate*: V, _____ NP

b. **Jesus wept the apostles.* The verb *weep* is intransitive: it does not allow an object. *weep*: V, _____

c. **Robert is hopeful of his children.* The adjective *hopeful* allows an S complement (e.g., *that his children will succeed*) or no complement, but it cannot take a PP complement with *of*.
    hopeful: Adj, _____ (that S)

d. *Robert is fond that his children love animals.* The adjective *fond* allows a PP complement with *of*, but cannot take a sentential complement.
fond: Adj, _____ PP[of]

e. *The children laughed the man.* Like *weep*, the verb *laugh* is intransitive and may not take a direct object; however, unlike *weep*, *laugh* allows a PP with *at*.
laugh: V, _____ (PP)[at]

Chapter 4   Semantics: The Meanings of Language

4. *Complementary, gradable, and relational opposites.*

A	B	C
good	bad	g
expensive	cheap	g
parent	offspring	r
beautiful	ugly	g
false	true	c
lessor	lessee	r
pass	fail	c
hot	cold	g
legal	illegal	c
larger	smaller	r
poor	rich	g
fast	slow	g
asleep	awake	c
husband	wife	r
rude	polite	g

6. *Thematic relations.*

a.   a   t   l
    Natalie found a ball in the house.

b.   a   s   g
    The children ran from the playground to the wading pool.

c.   a   t   i
    One of the men unlocked all the doors with a paper clip.

d.   a   t   i
    Joshua melted the ice with a blowtorch.

e.   c   t
    The sun melted the ice.

f.   The ice melted.

           a   t   g

g.   The farmer loaded hay onto the truck.

        a   t   i

h.   The farmer loaded the hay with a pitchfork.

       t   g   a

i.   The hay was loaded on the truck by the farmer.

7. *Analytic vs. situational truth.*

   a.   Queens are monarchs. A

   b.   Queens are female. A

   c.   Queens are mothers. S

   d.   Dogs are four legged. S

   e.   Dogs are animals. A

   f.   Cats are felines. A

   g.   Dogs are stupid. S

   h.   Audrey McLaughlin is Audrey McLaughlin. A

   i.   Audrey McLaughlin was the first woman to lead a federal political party in Canada. S

   j.   Uncles are male. A

9. *Pronouns.* (B = bound; F = free; B/F = bound or free)

   a.   Louise said to herself(B) in the mirror: "I(B)'m having a bad hair day."

   b.   The fact that he(F) considers her(B/F) astute pleases Maria.

   c.   Whenever I(B) see you(B), I(B) think of her(F).

   d.   Avi discovered that a picture of himself(B) was hanging in the post office, and that fact bugged him(B/F), but it pleased her(F).

   e.   It(B) seems that she(F) and he(F) will never stop arguing with them(F). (*It* may be regarded as bound to the sentence *she and he will never stop arguing with them.* Some linguists regard it as a syntactic placeholder and not actually a pronoun or pro-sentence.)

   f.   Persons are prohibited from picking flowers from any but their(B) own graves. (The word *own* forces *their* to be bound to *persons.*)

12. *Presuppositions.*

   a.   Presupposition: You have taken me out to the ball game before.
   b.   Presupposition: Valerie did not receive a new T-bird for Labour Day.
   c.   Presupposition: Emily's pet turtle ran away.
   d.   Presupposition: The professors support the students.
   e.   Presupposition: Canada entered World War II in 1939.

f. Presupposition: Canada entered World War II in 1939.
g. Presupposition: Disa has had some popcorn already.
h. Presupposition: Pigs don't have wings.
i. Presupposition: Somebody arrived in America in 1492.

Chapter 5   Phonetics: The Sounds of Language

1. *Initial sound.*

a.	judge	[ǰ]	f.	thought	[θ]
b.	Thomas	[tʰ]	g.	contact	[kʰ]
c.	though	[ð]	h.	phone	[f]
d.	easy	[i]	i.	civic	[s]
e.	pneumonia	[n]	j.	usual	[j]

2. *Final sound.*

a.	fleece	[s]	f.	cow	[aw]
b.	neigh	[e]	g.	rough	[f]
c.	long	[ŋ] or [g]	h.	cheese	[z]
d.	health	[θ]	i.	bleached	[t]
e.	watch	[č]	j.	rags	[z] or [s]

3. *Phonetic transcription.* Note: Transcriptions will vary across dialects. For example, the *marry–merry–Mary* distinction is neutralized in many dialects.

a.	physics	[fɪzɪks]	f.	marry	[mæri]
b.	merry	[mɛri]	g.	tease	[tʰiz]
c.	weather	[wɛðər]	h.	heath	[hiθ]
d.	coat	[kʰot]	i.	[your name]
e.	yellow	[jɛlo]			

4. *Correcting major errors in transcription.*

	Error		**Correction**
a.	[cʌ̃m]	should be	[kʰʌ̃m]
b.	[sed]	should be	[sɛd]
c.	[tʰɑlk]	should be	[tʰɑk]
d.	[ãnd]	should be	[æ̃nd]
e.	[wæx]	should be	[wæks]
f.	[kʰæbəgəz]	should be	[kʰæbəǰəz]
g.	[ɪs]	should be	[ɪz]
h.	[wɛθər]	should be	[wɛðər]

8. *Phonetic properties.*

a. bath–bathe: The **th** in *bath* is voiceless; the **th** in *bathe* is voiced. Both are interdental fricatives.

b. reduce–reduction: The **c** in *reduce* is an alveolar fricative; the **c** in *reduction* is a velar stop. Both are voiceless obstruents.

c. cool–cold: The **oo** in *cool* is high; the **o** in *cold* is mid. Both are tense, back, and rounded.

d. wife–wives: The **f** in *wife* is voiceless; the **v** in *wives* is voiced. Both are labiodental fricatives.

e. cats–dogs: The **s** in *cats* is voiceless; the **s** in *dogs* is voiced. Both are alveolar fricatives (or both are sibilants).

f. impolite–indecent: The **m** in *impolite* is bilabial; the **n** in *indecent* is alveolar. Both are nasals.

9. *Transcriptions.*

Written word	Transcription
know	[no]
tough	[tʰʌf]
bough	[baw]
cough	[kʰaf]
dough	[do]
you	[ju]
hiccough	[hɪkəp]
thorough	[θʌro]
slough	[slu] ~ [slaw] ~ [slʌf]
through	[θru]
heard	[hərd]
word	[wərd]
beard	[bird]
bird	[bərd]
dead	[dɛd]
said	[sɛd]
bed	[bɛd]
bead	[bid]
deed	[did]
meat	[mit]
great	[gret]
threat	[θrɛt]
suite	[swit]
straight	[stret]
debt	[dɛt]
moth	[maθ] ~ [mɔθ]
mother	[mʌðər]
both	[boθ]
bother	[baðər]
broth	[braθ] ~ [brɔθ]
brother	[brʌðər]

10. *Shared features.*

    a. [g] [p] [t] [d] [k] [b] oral, stop, consonant
    b. [u] [ʊ] [o] [ɔ] back, round, nonlow, vowel
    c. [i] [ɪ] [e] [ɛ] [æ] front, vowel
    d. [t] [s] [š] [p] [k] [č] [f] [h] voiceless, oral, consonant[1]
    e. [v] [z] [ž] [ǰ] [ŋ] [g] [d] [b] [l] [r] [w] [j] voiced, consonant
    f. [t] [d] [s] [š] [n] [č] [ǰ] coronal, consonant

13. *Phonetic features distinguishing sounds in A from B.*

A	**B**
a. front	back
b. voiceless	voiced
c. labial	other places of articulation
d. high	nonhigh (mid and low)
e. continuant	not continuant
f. nonback (front and central)	back

Chapter 6   Phonology: The Sound Patterns of Language

3. *Korean [l]~[r].*

   [r] and [l] are allophones of one phoneme.

   a. No, they do not occur in any minimal pairs.
   b. Yes, [r] and [l] are in complementary distribution.
   c. [r] occurs word initially and before vowels. [l] occurs before consonants and word finally.
   d. The phoneme /l/ is realized phonetically as [r] when it occurs before a vowel, and as [l] in all other instances. This rule can be written as follows:

   $$/l/ \rightarrow [r] /\_\_\_V$$

   Note it is not necessary to include a rule that specifies where the allophone [l] occurs since /l/ will not be changed pre-consonantally or finally and will emerge phonetically as [l]. Note further that if the two allophones are derived from /r/ the rule would be more complex:

   $$/r/ \rightarrow [l] / \_ \begin{Bmatrix} C \\ \# \end{Bmatrix}$$

[1] Add obstruent if [h] is considered a fricative.

5. *Southern Kongo.*

    a.   Distributions:

        [t] – [č]: [t] occurs before the back vowels [o, a, u]; [č] occurs before [i].

        [s] – [š]: [s] occurs before [o], [u], and [e];   [š] occurs before [i].

        [z] – [ž]: [z] occurs before [u], [e], and [w];   [ž] occurs before [i].

    b.   In each pair, the nonpalatal segment should be used as the basic phoneme (e.g., [t] and [č] derived from /t/, [s] and [š] derived from /s/, and [z] and [ž] derived from /z/). Nonpalatal segments have a wider (less specific) distribution, so the phonemic rule will be simpler with the nonpalatal segment as the "elsewhere" (default) case.

    c.   One phonemic rule that will account for all of the above distributions is the following:

        Obstruent alveolar segments become palatalized before a high front vowel.

        This can be stated formally as:

$$\begin{bmatrix} -\text{sonorant} \\ +\text{alveolar} \end{bmatrix} \longrightarrow \begin{bmatrix} +\text{palatal} \\ -\text{alveolar} \end{bmatrix} \Big/ \underline{\quad} \begin{bmatrix} +\text{high} \\ -\text{back} \end{bmatrix}$$

9. *English stress.*

    a.   The following are essentially phonemic transcriptions, except for [ə], the symbol for all unstressed vowels.

A	B	C
/əstanɪš/	/kəlæps/	/əmez/
/ɛgzət/	/ɛgzɪst/	/ɪmpruv/
/ɪmæǰən/	/rəzɛnt/	/ikwet/
/kænsəl/	/rəvolt/	/kərin/
/əlɪsət/	/ədapt/	/rikal/ or /rəkal/
/præktəs/	/ɪnsɪst/	/əton/

    b.   The final syllable of the verb is stressed if it ends with a consonant cluster; otherwise the stress falls on the penultimate syllable.

    c.   All of the final vowels in column C are tense vowels. Thus the analysis in (b) must be modified to read: Stress the final syllable of a verb if its vowel is tense or followed by a consonant cluster; otherwise stress the penultimate syllable.

11. *Paku.*

    a.   Yes, stress is predictable. It falls on the penultimate (next to last) syllable.

    b.   No, nasalization is not a distinctive feature for vowels as it is predictable. A vowel is nasalized if it precedes a nasal consonant.

12. *Hebrew.*

    a.   [b] and [v] are allophones of one phoneme and are in complementary distribution. [b] occurs word-initially and after consonants while [v] occurs only after vowels.

$$/b/ \mapsto [v] \quad / V\_\_$$

    b.   Yes, [f] occurs only after vowels, [p] occurs word-initially and after consonants.

    c.   The correct statement is (1): [b] but not [v] could occur in the empty slot.

    d.   The correct statement is (2): [p] but not [f] could occur in the empty slot.

    e.   The correct statement is (1). These words would force you to revise conclusions reached on the basis of the first group of words since they show a distribution of sounds that differ from the first group, [b] occurring after a vowel, [v] occurring after a consonant, and [f] occurring word-initially. If we were doing a full analysis we would therefore have to look to additional data not supplied here, which would allow us to formulate more precise rules.

13. *Maninka.*

    a.   (1) -li

          (2) -ni

    b.   Yes, the phonetic variants are predictable. The form is *-ni* if the last consonant of the stem is a nasal and *-li* otherwise. Notice that the last consonant of the stem does not have to be the last segment of the stem for the nasalized variant to appear.

    c.

da	"lie down"	dali	"lying down"
men	"hear"	menni	"hearing"
famu	"understand"	famuni	"understanding"
sunogo	"sleep"	sunogoli	"sleeping"

14. *Luganda.*

    a.   No, nasal vowels are not phonemic in Luganda. Yes, they are predictable.

    b.   Yes, the phonemic representation of "garden" is /dimiro/.

    c.   The phonemic representation of "canoe" is /ato/.

    d.   [p] and [b] represent separate phonemes and not allophones of one phoneme because their occurrence is not predictable and they are not in complementary distribution. Both sounds occur in the same environment, a_i, that is, before [i] and after [a].

e. No, [ãmdãno] is not a possible phonetic form because [d] cannot follow [m] since sequences of nasal consonant followed by voiced oral consonants do not occur, and place of articulation does not agree.

f. Yes, there is a homorganic rule in Luganda.

g. Phonemic: /enpoobe/   Phonetic: [ẽmpoobe]

h. (1) /en/

i. [ẽntabi]

j. /akaugeni/

k. Rule 1: Vowel nasalization: a vowel is nasalized when it precedes a nasal consonant.
Rule 2: Homorganic nasal rule: /n/ assimilates to the place of articulation of a following consonant.
Rule 3: Voiced stop assimilation: A voiced stop becomes a nasal if preceded by a nasal consonant.

Chapter 7   First Language Acquisition

4. *"Two-word stage" grammar.*

A. (1) Mini-grammar (sample answer):

$S \rightarrow V_T$ NP	see boy, push it, see sock, move it, bye-bye melon
$S \rightarrow V_T$ ADJ	bye-bye hot
$S \rightarrow$ ADJ N	pretty boat, pretty fan, more taxi, more melon
$S \rightarrow N V_I$	mommy sleep
NP $\rightarrow$ N	
NP $\rightarrow$ PN	

LEXICON	
V_T:	see, push, move, bye-bye
V_I:	sleep
N:	boy, sock, melon, boat, mommy, fan, taxi
PN:	it
ADJ:	hot, pretty, more

Note: V_T = transitive verb
V_I = intransitive verb

(2) Phrase structure trees should correspond to the phrase structure rules in (1)
Sample answer:

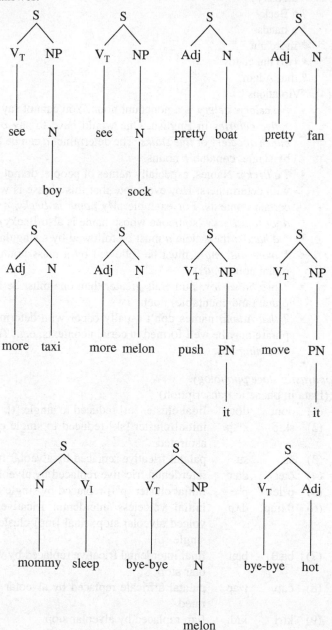

B. (3) "Ungrammatical" NPs:
* a celery
? a Becky
* a hands
* more nut
* two tinker-toy
? that Adam

(4) "Violations":

- * *a celery: celery* is a noncount noun. You cannot say * *one celery,* * *five celeries* in English. One would have to say *one stalk* or *a bunch of celery* or *five stalks.* The determiner *a* can be followed only by single, countable nouns.

- ? *a Becky:* Names, especially names of people, do not usually occur with determiners. However, note that this phrase is well formed in certain contexts. For example: *My name is Becky, and I live next door to a Becky* (someone whose name is also Becky).

- * *a hands:* the article *a* must be followed by a singular noun.

- * *more nut: more* must be followed by a mass noun (*coffee*) or a plural noun (*nuts*).

- * *two tinker-toy:* numerals greater than one must be followed by a plural (and countable) noun.

- ? *that Adam:* names don't usually occur with determiners, but the phrase may be well formed in certain contexts, e.g., *That Adam is a charming boy.*

5. *Holophrastic stage phonology.*
   A. (Data in phonetic transcription)

   (1) dont   dot   final cluster [nt] reduced to single [t].
   (2) skɪp   kʰɪp   initial cluster [sk] reduced to single consonant; [k] aspirated
   (3) šu   su   palatal fricative replaced by alveolar fricative
   (4) ðæt   dæt   interdental fricative replaced by alveolar stop
   (5) pʰle   pʰe   initial cluster [pʰl] replaced by single aspirated stop
   (6) θʌmp   dʌp   initial voiceless interdental fricative replaced by voiced alveolar stop; final [mp] cluster replaced by single [p]
   (7) bæθ   bæt   final interdental fricative replaced by voiceless alveolar stop
   (8) čap   tʰap   palatal affricate replaced by alveolar stop; [t] aspirated
   (9) kɪɾi   kɪdi   flap replaced by alveolar stop
   (10) lajt wajt   lateral liquid replaced by (labio)velar glide
   (11) dali dawi   lateral liquid replaced by (labio)velar glide
   (12) gro   go   initial cluster [gr] reduced to single consonant

B. General rules for children's pronunciation. Sample answer:
- In consonant clusters consisting of a stop and a fricative, liquid, or nasal, delete the fricative, liquid, or nasal.
- Replace interdental fricatives with alveolar stops. Voicing seems to be determined by the following rule: the stop is voiced word-initially and voiceless word-finally.
- Replace palatals with alveolars.
- Replace the lateral liquid with the (labio)velar glide.
- Replace the flap with the voiced alveolar stop.

Chapter 8   Second Language Acquisition

3. Match each teaching approach with the description that best characterizes it.
    a. Direct method   3
    b. Grammar translation approach   4
    c. Audiolingual method   1
    d. Communicative language teaching   7
    e. Suggestopedia   6
    f. Natural approach   5
    g. Community language learning   2

Chapter 9   Psycholinguistics: Language Processing

2. *Voiceprints.*

    Differences in speech signals of speakers. The following are some possible answers:

    Pitch: Some voices are higher than others. Male voices tend to be lower in pitch, but even within the same sex, pitch differences occur. These are due to physical differences in the larynx, vocal cords, vocal tract.

    Nasality: Some voices seem to be more nasal than others, even when not producing nasal sounds. This is due to physical differences in the nasal cavity and velum.

    Timbre or voice quality: Some voices are described as having a clear or bell-like quality, while others seem to have a rasping or creaky quality. This is due to physical differences in the larynx and oral/nasal cavities.

    Intonational patterns: Some voices tend to be more monotone than others; that is, there are fewer differences between high and low pitch. This is due to individual speech habits.

Tempo or speed: Some individuals speak more rapidly than others. This is due to individual speech habits. Also, the content of the speech affects speech rate.

Unstressed vowel deletion: Some speakers delete or slur over unstressed syllables. This may be due to speech rate or individual speech habits.

Dialect differences also show up in spectograms. These could be used to help identify a given speaker for as many reasons as there are dialect differences.

Chapter 10   Computational Linguistics:
Computer Language Processing

5. *Transition network.*

6. *Semantic networks.*

A.   Semantic network representations:

(i)   Birds fly.

(ii)   The student understands the question.

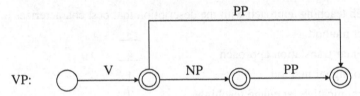

(iii) Penguins do not fly.

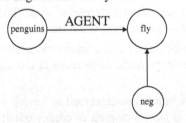

(iv) The wind is in the willows.

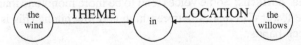

(v) Kathy loves her cat.

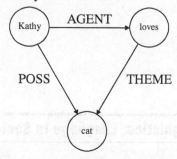

B. Predicate logic notations:
  (i)   Seals swim swiftly.
       SWIFTLY (SWIM (SEALS))
  (ii) The student doesn't understand the question.
       NOT (UNDERSTAND (THE STUDENT, THE QUESTION))
  (iii) The pen is on the table.
       ON (THE PEN, THE TABLE)
  (iv) My dog eats bones.
       EAT ([POSS (I, DOG)], BONES)
  (v)   Emily gives money to charity.
       GIVE (EMILY, MONEY, CHARITY)

Chapter 11   Neurolinguistics: Language and the Brain

3. *Rules relating spelling to pronunciation.* In the patient's system of spelling to pronunciation, the following are true:

Written *a* corresponds to /a/ or /æ/.
Written *e* corresponds to /ɛ/ or /i/.
Written *i* corresponds to /aj/.
Written *o* corresponds to /o/ or /ɔ/.
Written *c* corresponds to /s/.
Every letter is pronounced separately, and there is one vowel per syllable. There are no "silent" letters in this system.

In the patient's system of pronunciation to spelling, the same rules hold as itemized above. In addition, the sound [k] is always written K, and the third-person singular verb ending in *-s* (as in *goes*), when realized as [z], is written Z. This indicates that the patient is not doing lexical lookup or morphological analysis.

6. *Utterances of Broca's and Wernicke's aphasics.*

a. W

b. B

c. W

d. B

Chapter 12   Sociolinguistics: Language in Society

9. *Cockney rhyming slang.*

Slang		Word
a.	drip dry	4. cry
b.	in the mood	5. food
c.	insects and ants	7. pants
d.	orchestra stalls	1. balls
e.	Oxford scholar	6. dollar
f.	strike me dead	2. bread
g.	ship in full sail	3. ale

Constructed rhyming slang. Sample answers:

h.	chair	cut your hair
i.	house	dirty louse
j.	coat	around the moat
k.	eggs	eat the dregs
l.	pencil	window sill

10. *Euphemisms.*

Euphemism		Meaning
a.	Montezuma's revenge	4. diarrhea
b.	joy stick	8. penis
c.	friggin'	14. fuckin'
d.	ethnic cleansing	2. genocide
e.	French letter (old)	1. condom
f.	take out	5. destroy
g.	holy of holies	11. vagina
h.	spend a penny (British)	7. urinate
i.	ladies' cloak room	12. women's toilet

j. knock off (from 1919)   6. kill

k. vertically challenged   13. short

l. hand in one's dinner pail   9. die

m. sanitation engineer   15. garbage collector

n. downsize   3. fire employees

o. collateral damage   10. civilian deaths

Chapter 13   Language Change: The Syllables of Time

5. *Latin–French correspondences.*

   a. False.

   b. True.

   c. False.

   d. True.

6. *Indo-European.* The Indo-European languages are 1, 2, 4, 8, 10, and 11.

12. *Reconstruction of North American Native Languages.*

  A. **Consonants**   **Vowels**

     (1) m-m   1. u-u

     (2) p-p   2. i-i

     (3) t-t   3. a-a

     (4) m-w   4. ɨ-ɨ

     (5) w-w   5. o-o

     (6) s-s   6. a-e

     (7) ʔ-ʔ

     (8) n-n

     (9) h-h

    (10) k-k

  B. Proto-sounds.

    a. p-p   *p   u-u   *u

       t-t   *t   i-i   *i

       s-s   *s   a-a   *a

       ʔ-ʔ   *ʔ   ɨ-ɨ   *ɨ

       n-n   *n   o-o   *o

       h-h   *h   a-e   *e

       k-k   *k

    b. The only proto-sound listed above that underwent a change is *e,* which became *a* in Yerington Paviotso.

C. a. Whenever a *w* appears in Yerington Paviotso, the sound in the corresponding position in Northfork Monachi is also *w*.

b. Whenever an *m* occurs in Yerington Paviotso, the two sounds that may correspond to it in Northfork Monachi are *m* or *w*.

c. Yes, the correspondence is predictable. An *m* in Yerington Paviotso corresponds to an *m* in Northfork Monachi word-initially, and a *w* in Northfork Monachi between vowels.

D. a. Two proto-sounds should be reconstructed.

b. If you chose three, they would have to be *m,* *w*, and an abstract sound representing both of them, perhaps *b*. Then *m corresponds to *m* in both languages, *w corresponds to *w* in both languages, and *b corresponds to *m* word-initially and *w* between vowels in Northfork Monachi. But this solution is unmotivated; the simpler solution below is better.

c. The proto-sounds are *m and *w. Proto *m becomes *m* in Yerington Paviotso. In Northfork Monachi, proto *m becomes *m* word-initially and *w* between vowels. Proto *w becomes *w* in both Yerington Paviotso and Northfork Monachi.

E. The proto forms are the same as those in Yerington Paviotso except for the words with a proto *e sound.

"nose"	*mupi
"tooth"	*tama
"heart"	*piwɨ
"a feminine name"	*sawaʔpono
"liver"	*nɨmɨ
"springtime"	*tamano
"aunt"	*pahwa
"husband"	*kuma
"Indians living to the west"	*wowaʔa
"porcupine"	*mɨhɨ
"throat"	*noto
"sun"	*tape
"jaw"	*ʔatapɨ
"older brother"	*papiʔi
"daughter"	*peti
"man"	*nana
"bow," "gun"	*ʔetɨ

Chapter 14   Writing: The ABCs of Language

5. *Pronunciation and spelling.*

	A	B	Reason
a.	I am	iamb	The *b* is pronounced in *iambic.* By spelling *iamb* with a *b,* the morphological relationship is revealed. In addition, English phonological rules will predictably delete the */b/* in *iamb.*
b.	goose	produce	Although the *c* in *produce* is pronounced /s/, in *production* it is pronounced [k]. It is helpful to have morphemes that occur in different contexts spelled the same.
c.	fashion	complication	The *t* is pronounced [t] in *complicate,* a morpheme that occurs in *complication.* The spelling reveals this.
d.	Newton	organ	The *a* is pronounced [æ] in *organic;* the *o* is pronounced [o] in *Newtonian.* All vowels reduce to [ə] in unstressed position. Spelling them differently reflects their pronunciation under stress.
e.	no	know	The *k* is pronounced in words like *acknowledge.* Spelling *know* with a *k* reveals the morpheme and what it means.
f.	hymn	him	The *n* is pronounced in *hymnal,* and should thus be spelled the same wherever the morpheme occurs. English phonology predicts that the final *n* after an *m* will be deleted, that is, not pronounced.

Chapter 15   Animal Communication

1. *Human and animal communication.*

Similarities. Animal sounds and human language share physical characteristics: both are transmitted by sound waves produced in the vocal tract with air from the lungs. Some imitative bird sounds resemble human speech. Both are used as systems of communication.

Differences. Animals can communicate only a small set of messages, while human language is infinitely creative in the kinds of messages transmitted. Animal messages cannot be segmented into meaningful parts as sentences of all human languages can be. Animal messages are stimulus controlled, while human messages are more than a simple response to stimuli.

INDEX